THE
KENNEDY YEARS

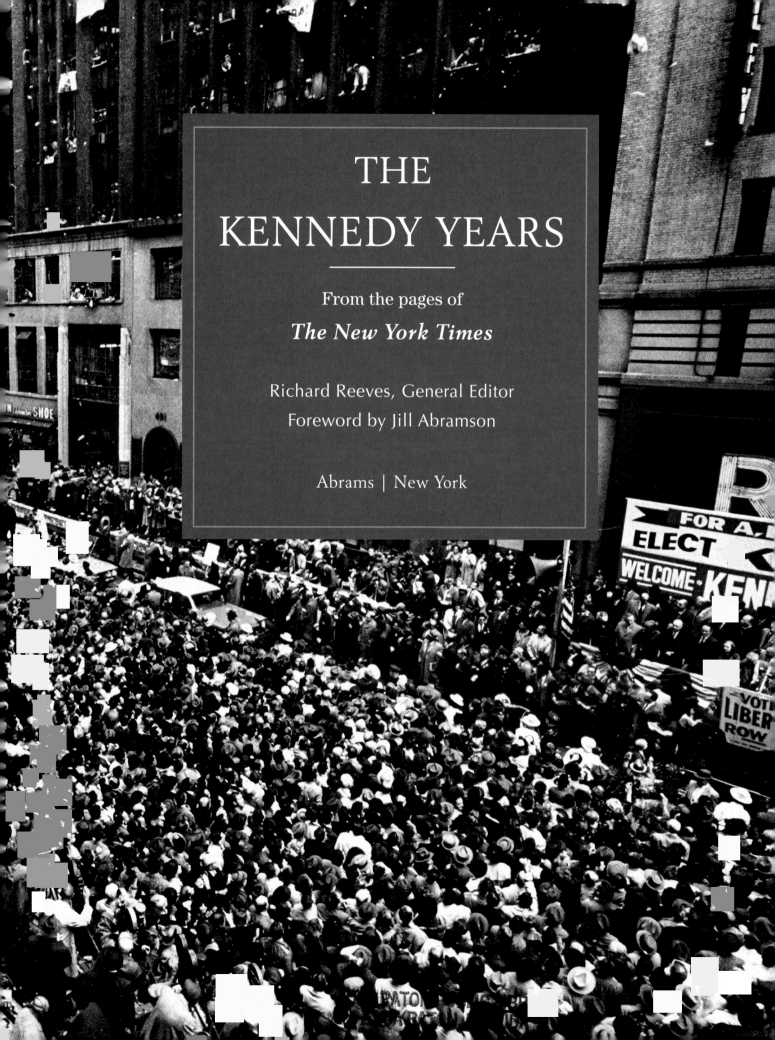

THE
KENNEDY YEARS

From the pages of
The New York Times

Richard Reeves, General Editor
Foreword by Jill Abramson

Abrams | New York

Editor: David Cashion
Production Manager: Anet Sirna-Bruder

Library of Congress Control Number: 2013935892

ISBN: 978-1-4197-0855-8

Printed and bound in China
10 9 8 7 6 5 4 3 2 1

Abrams books are available at special discounts when
purchased in quantity for premiums and promotions as well
as fundraising or educational use. Special editions can
also be created to specification. For details, contact
specialsales@abramsbooks.com or the address below.

ABRAMS
THE ART OF BOOKS SINCE 1949
115 West 18th Street
New York, NY 10011
www.abramsbooks.com

This book was assembled and edited by the staff of
Elizabeth Publishing:

General Editor: John W. Wright
Executive Editor: Philip Francis
Design and Layout: Virginia Norey

Copyediting and Proofreading: Ellen Chodosh
Proofreading: Jerold Kappes
Research: Lisette Cheresson
Photo Research: Philip Francis

For *The New York Times*:
Editors: Alex Ward and Mitchel Levitas
Photo editor: Phyllis Collazo

The New York Times would like to thank Jeff Roth,
William P. O'Donnell, Ryan Murphy and Heidi Giovine.

Note on the Text: All the dates on the Table of Contents are the
days the stories appeared in *The New York Times*. The dates on the
stories are the days the events occurred. We have edited most of
the stories for space considerations and we have preserved the
Times style for punctuation and capitalization as they appeared
in the paper at the time. —*The Editors*

Richard Reeves is a former *New York Times* reporter and the
author of *President Kennedy: Profile of Power*, which *Time* magazine
named its book of the year in 1993. He is Senior Lecturer at
the Annenberg School for Communication and Journalism at
the University of Southern California and has written 15 other
books, including studies of the presidencies of Richard Nixon
and Ronald Reagan.

Preceding spread: *A political rally in New York City for John F. Kennedy in October 1960.*
(Walter Sanders/Time & Life Pictures/Getty Images)

Table of Contents

Kennedy Confronts U.S. Steel

U.S. Resumes Nuclear Testing

Mississippi Rejects Integration

The Cuban Missile Crisis

Foreword

After the twin towers fell on 9/11, Todd Purdum, then one of the senior political reporters in the Washington bureau of the *Times*, began reciting, "America wept tonight, not alone for its dead young president, but for itself." The words belonged not to him but to James Reston, who wrote them on deadline late in the day on November 22, 1963. Reston, known as Scotty, had assembled some of the best talent ever known to journalism in the *Times'* Washington bureau: Tom Wicker, Anthony Lewis, Max Frankel, Russell Baker and others, all of whom had covered the presidency of John F. Kennedy, when Washington was the epicenter of everything.

All of them also covered his sudden death. That first day's paper included 250 columns of news, about 200,000 words, about the assassination. The *Times* team was writing at the exact moment when television came into its own as the primary way the nation got its news. Beginning at around 1 p.m. on November 22, the networks broadcast 72 straight hours of news about the assassination. While television became the vehicle for national mourning, *Times* correspondents were covering events with a kind of emotional vividness and detailed descriptiveness that would soon begin to fade, as everyone began seeing the news for themselves on the television screen.

The Kennedy presidency saw the *Times* at its zenith of influence. Arthur Krock, a former Washington bureau chief, had been unusually (perhaps uncomfortably) close to the Kennedy family, especially Joe Kennedy, the president's father. Punch Sulzberger, the publisher, lunched with Kennedy. Reston talked to him regularly. "No president paid more attention not only to the press but also reporters," Wicker wrote. "They became, however tenuously, part of his entourage."

Like most of the press, the *Times* did not investigate JFK's personal life, including his affairs and health problems. At the time there were rampant rumors about his Addison's disease, but the *Times* pronounced him to be in "superb physical condition." Later in life, Wicker recognized the down side to this coziness. "White House reporters, including me, were not skeptical enough, challenging enough, diligent enough, dedicated enough to the watchdog function of the press," he wrote much later.

During his prep school years at Choate, JFK became a subscriber to *The New York Times* and a lifelong reader. The *Times* helped fuel his political ascent, beginning with his career as a Navy lieutenant. KENNEDY'S SON IS HERO IN PACIFIC AS DESTROYER SPLITS HIS PT BOAT, was the *Times'* headline.

When JFK was first elected to Congress, the *Times* was among the East Coast papers that celebrated him as a young Galahad. But the relationship could sometimes be tempestuous. In the debate over whether Kennedy had authored his Pulitzer Prize–winning book, *Profiles in Courage*, he was annoyed that *Times* editor John Oakes was spreading gossip that he had a ghostwriter. But when Kennedy was angling to become Adlai Stevenson's running mate in 1956, the *Times* compared his appearance to that of a movie star "whose personality and good looks made him an instant celebrity."

Once he got to the White House the *Times* was both his tool and his conscience. He said the photos in the *Times* of Bull Connor's attack dogs biting students in Birmingham had made him sick to his stomach and strengthened his resolve to push for the civil rights bill in 1963.

In 1961, after the *Times* downplayed a news story on the impending Bay of Pigs invasion, a fiasco that badly bruised his young presidency, Kennedy told *Times* editor Turner Catledge, "Maybe if you had printed more about the operation you would have saved us from a colossal mistake." Still, he later asked the *Times* to hold off publishing emerging details about the danger of Soviet missiles in Cuba, some of his finest hours as president.

There was tension between the Kennedy White House and the *Times* over coverage of the American military presence in Vietnam. Kennedy felt pressured by David Halberstam's unrelenting coverage and he tried, unsuccessfully, to have Halberstam removed from Vietnam.

But the four days in November 1963 were the pinnacle, and the power of the words from those days is still haunting. It is hard for me to believe they were all written on incredible deadline pressure. Anthony Lewis began his story on Lyndon Johnson on November 22 this way, "Detachment, understatement, irony, sophistication, coolness—those were the qualities that were seen in the manner of John F. Kennedy. The trademarks of Lyndon Johnson are emotion, flamboyance, folksiness."

Wicker, who filed the main news story in Dallas, added his own emotion to the story he wrote the next day: "History, no doubt, will measure him unemotionally and impartially. But those who went with him almost all the way cannot."

Marjorie Hunter soulfully described every step as Jacqueline Kennedy, holding her children's hands, followed her husband's flag-draped coffin into the Capitol Rotunda. On the day of the funeral, Anthony Lewis described her face as looking "like that of a 34-year-old girl burdened with sorrow, instead of the president's wife."

On that sad day of history, Russell Baker wrote "It dawned cold, clear and quiet, this day when they buried the president. There was movement in the city, as there had been throughout the night, but it was crowd movement without the noise of crowds, and the silence was pervasive."

The golden era, when the press and the country had a leader who inspired them, was over.

—Jill Abramson
Executive editor of *The New York Times*

Introduction

Beginning in the mid-1980s, I spent eight years researching and writing *President Kennedy: Profile in Power*, supplementing information publicly available at the time with new interviews and fresh material.

Although the book remains in print, obviously new information about the 35th president has been released or revealed during the past two decades. Much of it is unflattering, including accounts of his careless sexual adventures, some drug use, an expansion of my reports of his persistent lying about the true state of his health, and a proliferation of conspiracy theories about his assassination, 50 years ago on November 22, 1963. Still, after half a century, John F. Kennedy is revered by hundreds of millions of people around the world. His martyrdom is classically the story of an athlete dying young, the young prince tragically struck down. Many Americans old enough to remember that hopeful time, which his widow later and memorably called "Camelot," rank him among our five greatest presidents. The question now is how he will be seen by new generations, young people whose parents were born after Kennedy died. Reputation, after all, is a mix of fact and legend, but also of memory, nostalgia and the word of people we trust.

Personally, I think his public persona will survive, because the story of his life and presidency is so compelling and accessible on film and videotape. Beyond that, the Kennedys—Jack and Jackie—were cultural icons, changing the way Americans thought about their country and its leaders, even how they dressed. Kennedy didn't wear hats and soon not many American men did either. Historians and political writers, by and large, consider him a "significant" president, not a transformative one in a class with George Washington, Abraham Lincoln, Franklin Delano Roosevelt, and perhaps Theodore Roosevelt and Ronald Reagan.

Kennedy, by the end of his days, did have at least three historic achievements: He prevented a possible nuclear World War III. He put Washington on the side of the minority in the black struggle for civil rights, no small thing in a democracy and an act of political courage in which his own Democratic Party controlled Southern states but whose representatives opposed him. He gambled confidently that the United States could overtake the Soviets' early lead in space, pledging that an American would walk on the moon before the end of the 1960s. He also experienced a couple of disasters, especially by approving an invasion of Cuba in 1961 at a place called the Bay of Pigs, and the military coup that toppled and killed President Ngo Dinh Diem of Vietnam in 1963, leaving in its wake a regime in Saigon distinguished by its corruption and incompetence, and a war that bitterly divided Americans.

Another factor in Kennedy's enduring popularity is that no presidency before his was covered as heavily by newspapers and the new medium of national television. The wealth of *New York Times* articles that follow in the pages below are an example of that.

It was no accident. Kennedy, a hungry political animal, wanted to center public attention on the administration in the White House. One of his first directives to federal agencies was that all good news and analyses be sent to the president's office and announced there. Reporters soon realized what was happening and more and more of them stopped covering agencies, applying instead for White House credentials. Kennedy was not only a good story, often he was the only story.

The president also organized his staff and Cabinet members in the same way. Forsaking the military and corporate organizational charts used by most of his predecessors in the Oval Office, Kennedy said soon after his election that he intended to manage by using what he called a "wheel with many spokes" with himself at the hub, "the vital center." "It was instinctive at first," he said, "I had different identities, and this was a useful way of expressing each without compromising the others." In other words, all his relationships were bilateral; his staff did not know what he was telling others.

He was an exceptional professional politician, charming and intelligent, detached and curious, candid if not always honest. He could be ruthless when he thought it was necessary. He was dangerously disorganized. He was addicted to excitement, living life as a race against boredom. Because he was sick most of his childhood and in pain most of his adult life, he always thought he would die young and was impatient and determined to make the most of it.

"No one ever knew John Kennedy, not all of him," said one of his closest friends, Charles Bartlett, a syndicated columnist. That too, was the way Kennedy wanted it. Only 44 men know what it is really like to be president of the United States. What it was like to be President Kennedy was dramatized by the events of just two days, June 10 and 11, 1963.

Bringing the president home from an address to the U.S. Conference of Mayors in Hawaii, Air Force One landed at San Francisco to pick up Theodore Sorensen, his confidant and speech writer, who had flown there after working alone in Washington on a draft of what the president called "The Peace Speech." At 10 a.m., June 10, at American University, Kennedy delivered what was probably his greatest speech. He said: "Let us re-examine our attitude toward the Soviet Union . . . We find communism profoundly repugnant . . . [But] we all breathe the same air. We all cherish our children's future. And we are all mortal."

Before noon he was back at the White House, where he was told that Governor George Wallace had appointed himself provost of the University of Alabama and was planning to stand in the doorway of its main building surrounded by state troopers. In the opening act of high political theater, Wallace was determined to block the first two black students admitted to the school. Good news also awaited Kennedy: *Izvestia*, the Soviet news service, was transmitting the full text of Kennedy's American University address and the Soviets had shut down their jamming equipment so that the Voice of America could broadcast it in Russian from Leningrad to Vladivostok. And there was awful news from Vietnam: a Buddhist monk had poured gasoline over himself and burned to death at Saigon's busiest intersection to protest the American-backed regime of Diem.

By the following night the turmoil in Alabama seemed to be calming down. Wallace saluted the just federalized National Guard troops and abruptly left the campus with his state troopers. Kennedy decided late in the day to go on television to push new civil rights legislation. He had only a couple of pages of text and some notes, but nonetheless delivered words that were memorable. "This is not a sectional issue . . . Nor is this a partisan issue . . . This is not even a legal or legislative issue alone. We are confronted primarily with a moral issue."

The presidency is often a reactive job, defined by events. No one remembers whether Lincoln balanced the budget. And no one knew during the 1960 campaign that the new president would be confronted by a racial crisis at home and Soviet missiles 90 miles from Florida.

"The Cuban Missile Crisis," as it came to be known, was President Kennedy's finest hour—or finest 13 days. For the president, who often worked in his bed during the morning, it began at 8:45 a.m. on October 16, 1962. His national security adviser, McGeorge Bundy, knocked on the bedroom door. He had aerial photographs under his arm. "Mr. President," said Bundy, "there is now hard photographic evidence, which you will see, that the Russians have offensive missiles in Cuba."

Kennedy was stunned. He had publicly dismissed Republican claims, based on information whispered to them by the Central Intelligence Agency, that medium-range missile bases had been built in Cuba. Kennedy said they were ordinary anti-aircraft weapons. He was wrong and initially thought that when the news became public, he would be defeated in the 1964 election. "We are probably going to have to bomb them," he said. But he quickly rejected that idea when members of the Joint Chiefs of Staff estimated that it would take hundreds of sorties to knock out the missiles—which turned out to number more than thirty—and could guarantee destroying only 90 percent of the installations.

Kennedy quickly came to realize that the crisis was political rather than military, an insight that served him and the world well. He was a decisive leader, but made decisions only when he had no choice and generally picked the most moderate options available. He assumed that the Soviet missiles had nuclear warheads and if the United States attacked Cuba, the Soviets would retaliate by taking West Berlin and perhaps invading West Germany. They had troops in place to do that—and it would probably trigger a world war. He decided to continue to keep the information secret and continue campaigning for Democratic candidates in the 1962 mid-term elections, as if nothing unusual was happening. He thought secrecy would buy time. Six days into the crisis, his most trusted advisers had been meeting almost around-the-clock.

By October 22, the president knew that he had to go on television to tell the American people why—and warn the Soviets that—troops were being called to report all along the east coast, which was in range of the Soviet missiles. He announced that the United States Navy was surrounding the island to quarantine and stop Soviet ships from reaching Cuba. It was a blockade, but he did not use that word because a blockade is an act of war. By October 24, after the Navy had stopped and boarded three ships, Soviet ships turned around or stopped short of the quarantine line.

By then, Kennedy and Soviet Premier Nikita Khrushchev were exchanging threatening messages. On October 25, in Moscow, a courier delivered to the American Embassy a long, rambling, sometimes incoherent letter from Khrushchev that hinted at a deal if the Americans would pledge not to invade Cuba and remove 15 missiles in Turkey along the Soviet border. Just 15 minutes after the so-called "night letter" was read by Kennedy, another letter arrived, much less conciliatory, which used Khrushchev's name but apparently was written by a committee. Kennedy chose to answer the first letter, saying: "You would agree to remove these weapons systems from Cuba . . . We on our part, would agree promptly to remove the quarantine measures now in effect . . . and give assurances against an invasion of Cuba."

Kennedy also agreed to remove "other armaments"—referring to already obsolete Jupiter missiles based in Turkey. The two politicians, men with the final say on the nuclear weapons, had an agreement they each could claim as a victory—Khrushchev saving Cuba, Kennedy, the world.

The president went to West Berlin on June 26, 1963, and was greeted by a roaring crowd of more than a million people. On August 28, as Martin Luther King Jr. gave his "I Have a Dream" speech, Kennedy signed off on the coup by South Vietnamese generals to depose President Diem.

After long negotiation, the United States, the Soviet Union and Great Britain signed, in August 1963, the Test Ban Treaty, a significant achievement, the first formal treaty of the atomic age. By then the "political animal" was thinking re-election and particularly about changing minds in Texas, where intra-party Democratic feuding could endanger his re-election chances in 1964. On Kennedy's itinerary of major cities were Houston and Austin, then Fort Worth and, of course, Dallas.

—By Richard Reeves

Prologue: The Early Years

John F. Kennedy Seen From the Hill of History

By Thomas Maier

Before his career in politics, John F. Kennedy was known simply as Jack. A smart but chronically ill youngster, he grew up the second son of Joseph P. Kennedy, a bold and sometime brazen Wall Street entrepreneur, and his wife Rose, the beautiful and deeply religious daughter of "Honey Fitz," former Boston Mayor John F. "Honey Fitz" Fitzgerald. Joe's father also had been a local politician, but his aim was much higher. He intended to see his oldest son, Joe Jr., become the first Catholic elected to the presidency. When Joe Jr. was killed in a plane explosion during World War II, Jack became the focus of his father's ambitions.

Until then, Jack had led a relatively carefree existence within a large family of nine children. He was full of charm, occasional mischief and an abiding curiosity about the world. As an avid reader, partly due to his repeated hospital stays, he learned a lot about history. Yet he was nearly expelled from Choate when the headmaster learned that young Jack and his pals had created a secret "Muckers Club" to mock the school's strict traditions. "After long experience in sizing up people, I definitely know you have the goods and you can go a long way," Joe Kennedy warned his son. "Now aren't you foolish not to get all there is out of what God has given you and what you can do with it yourself."

Jack, like his father and older brother, graduated from Harvard. But Kennedy's education as a public man began in earnest with his experiences in London, after his father was appointed in 1938 as U.S. Ambassador to the Court of St. James. Jack traveled widely in Europe and watched first-hand as the Nazi war machine threatened the world. His Harvard thesis about England's appeasement of Hitler was turned into a best-selling book, *Why England Slept*. When America entered the war, Jack joined the Navy and served in the Pacific, where one night a Japanese cruiser cut Lt. Kennedy's PT-109 boat in half. Despite the tragic loss of two men, Kennedy bravely helped his crew to safety. Once saved, Kennedy was hailed in the press at his father's urgings. When later asked how he became a hero, Jack offered a wry and more truthful response: "It was involuntary—they sank my boat."

After the war, Jack decided to run for Congress in 1946, and with the help of his father's money, "Honey Fitz's" political familiarity and, per-

The Kennedy children,
August 1928.
(John F. Kennedy Library)

(Left to right, back row) John F. Kennedy, Jean Kennedy, Joseph P. Kennedy, Rose Kennedy, Joseph P. Kennedy Jr., (left to right, bottom row) Robert F. Kennedy, Eunice Kennedy, Patricia Kennedy, Kathleen Kennedy, and Rosemary Kennedy posed for a family portrait sitting on the beach, 1931. (John F. Kennedy Library)

haps most importantly, his mother's well-attended tea parties to court fe-male voters, he won his first election. After a rocky start as a public speaker, Kennedy proved a natural. "Your Jack is worth a king's ransom," his father's political adviser told him. "He has poise, a fine Celtic map. A most engaging smile." Joe Kennedy, whose own political career blew up over his opposition to U.S. entry in World War II, was amazed by his son's affinity for shaking hands with voters. "I never thought Jack had it in him," he marveled. In Washington, Kennedy was considered a lackluster repre-sentative too often concerned with his active social life, but in Massachu-setts he remained very popular, gaining a U.S. Senate seat in 1952. His win over incumbent Republican Henry Cabot Lodge Jr. was seen as a victory for the rising fortunes of Irish Catholics who once faced bigotry from Boston's traditional Brahmins. The following year, Jack married Jac-queline Bouvier, a stunningly attractive Washington newspaper photogra-pher, in a grand Rhode Island wedding.

Behind the famous engaging smile there was constant pain. Jack's chronic ill health and a wartime back injury that required surgery kept him again in a hospital bed for seven months, during which time he wrote the 1956 book *Profiles in Courage*. This Pulitzer Prize–winning account recalled those in American politics who relied on principle rather than expediency in facing crucial questions of their time. Among this list of heroes, he lauded Senator George Norris, a Republican from Nebraska, for supporting Al Smith's 1928 bid for president and arguing that no Amer-ican should be discarded simply because of religion. It was an argument that Kennedy would soon make again in his own bid for the White House. During that 1960 presidential race, in which polls showed his religion was the number one issue, Kennedy made a carefully prepared speech embracing America's traditional separation of church and state. Kennedy's victory relied heavily on bloc voting among Catholics and other minority groups in urban areas, but he also won because this Harvard-educated son of a millionaire didn't look like the stereotype of a big-city pol like Smith, or even his own grandfather.

By examining Kennedy's private papers, we can see beyond the glossy photos orchestrated by his father and his political aides to gain public ap-proval. Though many have called his family "America's royalty," invoking Camelot imagery of British Knights of the Round Table, Kennedy's own story is very much rooted in American ascendancy, the idea that immigrant families who came to this nation like his own might one day reach the top of society. Both his brothers said this belief in open access to the ladder of success was among Jack's most cherished and deeply held convictions. Many of us are familiar with the extraordinary events that occurred during Kennedy's 1,000 days as president—the struggle for civil rights; the race to the moon; the Cold War struggles over Cuba, Berlin and Vietnam—but few remember his momentous decision to change America's laws about immigration, a decision rooted in his family's experience.

Kennedy's vision of the nation's future was described in his least known book, *A Nation of Immigrants*. A paean to the pulsing, flowing heart of America with photos of immigrants from around the world, it drew little attention when published in 1958. "There is no part of our nation that has not been touched by our immigrant background," he praised. "Everywhere immigrants have enriched and strengthened the fabric of American life." In looking back, his call for a fairer immigration system seemed remarkable for a presidential candidate who, two years later, would break a barrier as a Catholic elected president, the first from a minority background. Despite his Waspy all-American appearance, Kennedy was well aware of slights felt by his own Irish Catholic immigrant family in rising up the socioeconomic ladder. His grandfather, "Honey Fitz," apocryphally told of the "No Irish Need Apply" signs that once hung in Boston. "The Irish were in the vanguard of the great waves of immigration" during the 1800s, JFK recalled in his book. These new arrivals off the boat "were mostly country folk, small farmers, cottagers and farm laborers"—just like Patrick Kennedy, his great-grandfather, a migrant

The Kennedy family at Hyannis, Massachusetts, in the 1930s.
(Bachrach/Getty Images)

worker who came to the United States fleeing the Irish famine in County Wexford. His book reflected the Kennedys' own experience in America. Even JFK's millionaire father, Joseph Kennedy, felt the sting of discrimination and was hell-bent that his children not be held back. "I think that the Irish in me has not been completely assimilated," the Kennedy patriarch confided to a friend, "but all my ducks are swans."

Deeply rooted in his family's own experience, Jack Kennedy's little book became the blueprint for a law eliminating the racial discrimination inherent in the nation's immigration quota system and allowed for the reunification of families. Ultimately, JFK's idea became the Immigration and Nationality Act Amendments of 1965, pushed through Congress with little fanfare by his brothers, Ted and Robert. According to Ted, "He was very proud of his Irish heritage and while growing up came to realize how the Irish in Boston make great contributions to the life of the city. He came to see that immigrants from many other nations enhanced America and helped the nation move forward into the future . . . So he wrote that book to show how much immigration helped America . . ."

The great English writer, G. K. Chesterson, wrote that "History is a hill . . . from which alone men see the town in which they live or the age in which they are living." From that hill that history provides, we can see today how Kennedy's law created the new, far more diverse nation that our children live in today and will for generations to come. This is an important part of Kennedy's legacy that many historians of his time didn't recognize and only now can be fully understood.

We called him Mr. President for three years, until his life ended abruptly with an assassin's bullet, a national trauma jarring enough to obscure his true meaning. Only now, fifty years after his death, are we gaining the historical vantage to fully appreciate John F. Kennedy's legacy to America. With tragic irony, we stare at those family pictures of a young handsome president playing on the White House lawn or in a sailboat at Hyannis Port with his beautiful wife and two children, so full of life, so unaware of the cruel fate that awaits.

In the wake of his murder, former friends and colleagues recalled Kennedy's heroic life with a "Camelot" mythology suggested by his widow. Critics later disclosed his extramarital affairs, his reliance on heavy-duty drugs to control pain and illness, and administration plots to kill foreign leaders—the "dark side" of a personality with many compartments. Over time, the portrait of Kennedy became deeper, more complex, yet equally compelling. Americans still ranked him among their most admired leaders.

From the broadest vantage, his story reminds us of the glories and limits of America's melting pot and those histories that paint people from minority groups in familiar "just like us" tones. We better understand Ken-

Joseph P. Kennedy, former chairman of the S.E.C., with Mrs. Kennedy and their children at their home in Bronxville, New York, 1937.
(The New York Times)

nedy's appeal beyond Irish Catholics—to include countless immigrant and minority groups who want to share a common dream with all. By opening the door more fully, he changed the face of America and who we are, both demographically and spiritually, as a nation.

In this context, our understanding of Kennedy's legacy becomes richer and of far greater historical significance than singular incidents or individual achievements. Fifty years later, we're reminded of how far we've progressed since his 1960 election, and yet how many aspirations still remain today.

No one would understand better than Jack Kennedy.

Thomas Maier is an award-winning journalist and the author of several books, including *The Kennedys: America's Emerald Kings* (2003).

Kennedy's Son is Hero in Pacific As Destroyer Splits His PT Boat

By THE ASSOCIATED PRESS

A UNITED STATES TORPEDO BOAT BASE, New Georgia, Aug. 8, 1943 (Delayed)—Out of the darkness, a Japanese destroyer appeared suddenly. It sliced diagonally in two the PT boat skippered by Lieut. (j. g.) John F. Kennedy, son of the former American Ambassador in London, Joseph P. Kennedy.

Crews of two other PT boats, patrolling close by, saw flaming high octane gasoline spread over the water. They gave up "Skipper" Kennedy and all his crew as lost that morning of Aug. 2.

But Lieutenant Kennedy, 26, and ten of his men were rescued today from a small coral island deep inside Japanese-controlled Solomons Island territory and within range of enemy shore guns.

Two men of Lieutenant Kennedy's crew were lost when the enemy destroyer rammed the boat at a speed estimated at forty knots.

On three nights, Lieutenant Kennedy, once a backstroke man of the Harvard swimming team, swam out into Ferguson Passage hoping to flag down PT boats going through on patrol. Ensign Ross did the same one other night. But they made no contacts.

On the afternoon of the fourth day two natives found the survivors and carried to the PT boat base a message Lieutenant Kennedy crudely cut on a green coconut husk.

Chronologically, Lieutenant Kennedy, Ensign Thom and the crewmen told the story this way:

Four Japanese destroyers came down Blackett Strait around the south coast of Kolombangara Island about 2:30 A. M. on Aug. 2. In two phases of a confused engagement the PT's claimed three hits and three probable hits on one of the enemy ships.

It was while the destroyers were returning, probably after delivering supplies and reinforcements near Japan's base at Vila, on Kolombangara, that the enemy ship rammed the Kennedy boat. Ross and Kennedy saw the destroyer coming.

"The destroyer then turned straight for us," he said.

"It all happened so fast there wasn't a chance to do a thing. The destroyer hit our starboard forward gun station and sliced right through. I was in the cockpit. I looked up and saw a red glow and streamlined stacks. Our tanks were ripped open and gas was flaming on the water about twenty yards away."

Kennedy went out to get McMahon, who had been at the engine station and was knocked into the water in the midst of flaming gasoline.

"McMahon and I were about an hour getting back to the boat," Kennedy said. Watertight bulkheads had kept the bow afloat, the skipper explained. "There was a very strong current."

After getting McMahon aboard, Kennedy swam out again to get Harris.

Just before dawn the current changed to carry the survivors away from the Japanese-held coast. About 2 P.M. Kennedy decided to abandon the bow section and try to reach a small island.

Kennedy swam to the island, towing McMahon. The others clung to a plank and swam in a group. It took about three hours to make it. The men stayed on this island until Wednesday, when all coconuts on the island's two trees were eaten.

Late that afternoon they swam to a larger island, where there were plenty of coconuts.

At night, Kennedy put on a life-belt and swam into Ferguson Passage to try to signal an expected PT boat.

The two natives found the survivor group Thursday afternoon. That night, a little after midnight, a PT rescue boat, guided by a native pilot, went into the twisting passages to make contact with Kennedy on an outer island.

John F. Kennedy in a World War II photograph on the bridge of the famed PT-109 torpedo boat on which he served as commander. (Associated Press)

Notables Attend Senator's Wedding

Special to The New York Times

NEWPORT, R. I., Sept. 12, 1953—A crowd of 3,000 persons broke through police lines and nearly crushed the bride, Miss Jacqueline Lee Bouvier, when she arrived for her marriage here this morning to United States Senator John Fitzgerald Kennedy of Massachusetts. The throng had milled around St. Mary's Roman Catholic Church for more than an hour before the guests began to arrive.

The church was filled with some 800 guests, including most of the Newport summer colony, and many political notables.

The bride is the daughter of Mrs. Hugh D. Auchincloss of Hammersmith Farm, Newport, and Merrywood, McLean, Va., and John V. Bouvier 3d of New York. Senator Kennedy is the son of Joseph P. Kennedy, former Ambassador to the Court of St. James and Mrs. Kennedy of Hyannis Port, Mass., and Palm Beach, Fla.

The Most Rev. Richard J. Cushing, Archbishop of the Archdiocese of Boston, performed the ceremony and was the celebrant of the nuptial mass. He also read a special blessing from the Pope.

Luigi Vena of Boston was tenor soloist and sang "Ave Maria," "Panis Angelicus" and "Jesu Amor Mi" during the ceremony.

Escorted at the ceremony by Mr. Auchincloss because of the illness of her father, the bride wore a gown of ivory silk taffeta, made with a fitted bodice embellished with interwoven bands of tucking, finished with a portrait neckline, and a bouffant skirt. She wore an heirloom veil of rosepoint lace that had been worn by her grandmother. The veil was draped from a tiara of lace and orange blossoms and extended in a long train. She carried a bouquet of pink and white spray orchids and gardenias.

The bride, who was graduated from Miss Porter's School in Farmington, Conn., attended Vassar College and the Sorbonne in Paris. She was graduated in 1951 from George Washington University. Mrs. Kennedy is a granddaughter of James T. Lee of New York, the late Mrs. Lee and the late Mr. and Mrs. John Vernou Bouvier Jr. of New York.

Senator Kennedy was graduated in 1940 from Harvard College, where he was a member of the Hasty Pudding Institute of 1770 and the Spee Club. During World War II, he commanded a PT boat in the South Pacific.

He was elected to the House of Representatives in 1946 and elected to the Eighty-first and Eighty-second Congresses. In 1952, he was elected to the Senate on the Democratic ticket.

The bridegroom is a grandson of the late John F. Fitzgerald, former Mayor of Boston; the late Mrs. Fitzgerald, the late Patrick J. Kennedy, who was a former Massachusetts State Senator, and the late Mrs. Kennedy.

Senator and Mrs. John F. Kennedy at their wedding in Newport, Rhode Island, September 12, 1953. (Lisa Larsen/Time & Life Pictures/Getty Images)

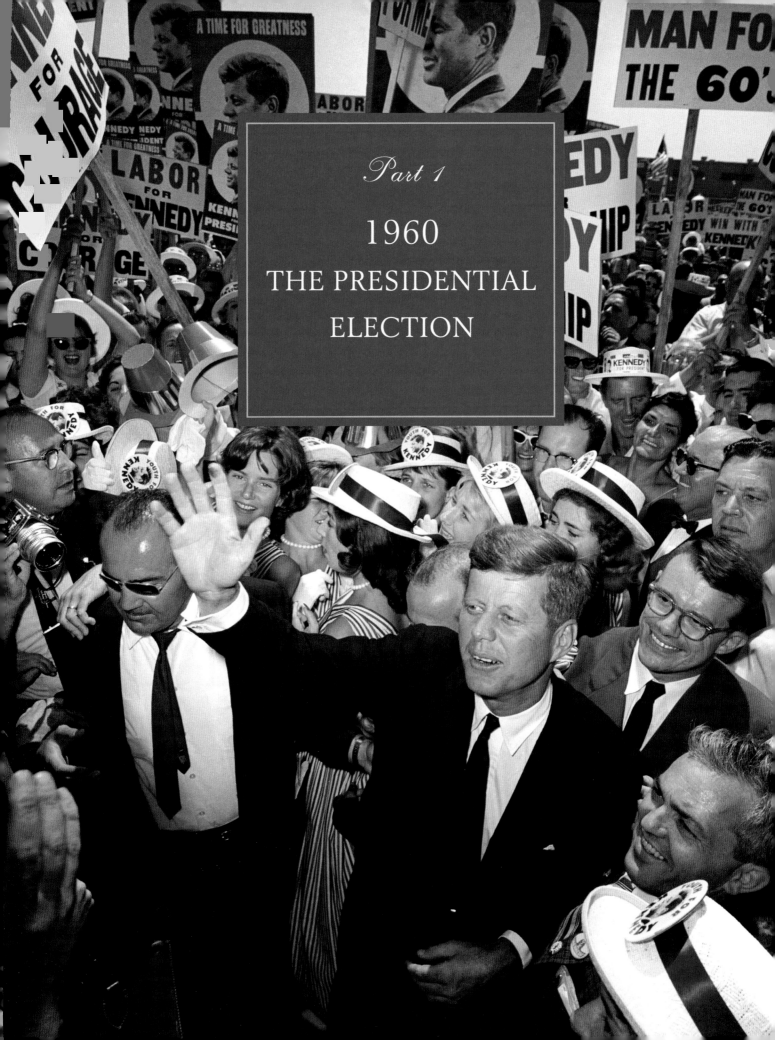

Part 1

1960
THE PRESIDENTIAL
ELECTION

(John F. Kennedy Library)

"In the past forty months, I have toured every state in the Union and I have talked to Democrats in all walks of life. My candidacy is therefore based on the conviction that I can win both the nomination and the election."

Preceding page: *Senator John F. Kennedy makes his way through a crowd of supporters and journalists as he arrives in Los Angeles for the Democratic National Convention, July 9, 1960.* (Associated Press)

A Young Man Changes the Rules

In 1960 John F. Kennedy reinvented the way in which candidates for president of the United States should secure the party nomination. He was not only the first of his generation to win the nation's highest office, but also the first self-selected nominee. He broke the rules and ran rings around the old system of selection by party leaders or "bosses," creating his own network of supporters around the country, mostly young fellow–World War II veterans and junior officers—16 million of them—and like many of them, he was impatient. "The New Generation Offers a Leader" was Kennedy's first political slogan.

The 43-year-old U.S. senator from Massachusetts campaigned vigorously for a year, particularly in states with early primary elections, and won in New Hampshire, Wisconsin and West Virginia, which weren't considered very important in those days. He courted the Washington press corps just as vigorously. Articulate and animated, he rode television, a relatively new medium penetrating American homes. Twenty years ago in *President Kennedy: Profile of Power,* I wrote:

> He did not wait his turn. He directly challenged the institution he wanted to control, the existing political system. After him, no one else wanted to wait either, and few institutions were rigid enough or flexible enough to survive impatient, ambition-driven challenges. He believed (and proved) that the only qualification for the most powerful job in the world was wanting it.

He got it, defeating Senator Hubert Humphrey of Minnesota in the primaries, and Lyndon Johnson, the majority leader of the Senate, and former Governor Adlai Stevenson of Illinois at the Democratic convention. Then he won the election against an equally ambitious Republican nominee—47-year-old Vice President Richard Nixon—like Kennedy a Navy lieutenant in the war. The campaign will be remembered for many things, most importantly the first television debates between presidential candidates, with Kennedy appearing at least as presidential as Nixon, and second, the religious issue: Kennedy was only the second Roman Catholic presidential candidate, following Governor Al Smith of New York in 1928, and the first to win. He showed his political skills most memorably in confronting skeptical, even hostile, conservative Protestant leaders and ministers by saying, more than once, "No one asked my religion in the South Pacific."

It was, in all, an extraordinary outcome. At first, Kennedy was repeatedly asked why he thought he should be president. "I look around me at the others in the race," he replied, "and I say to myself, well if they think they can do it, why not me? That's the answer. And I think it's enough."

—Richard Reeves

THE KENNEDY STATEMENT

WASHINGTON, Jan. 2—Following is the text of Senator John F. Kennedy's statement announcing his candidacy for the 1960 Democratic Presidential nomination:

I am announcing today my candidacy for the Presidency of the United States.

The Presidency is the most powerful office in the free world. Through its leadership can come a more vital life for our people. In it are centered the hopes of the globe around us for freedom and a more secure life. For it is in the Executive Branch that the most crucial decisions of this century must be made in the next four years:

How to end or alter the burdensome arms race, where Soviet gains already threaten our very existence.

How to maintain freedom and order in the newly emerging nations.

How to rebuild the stature of American science and education.

How to prevent the collapse of our farm economy and the decay of our cities.

How to achieve, without further inflation or unemployment, expanded economic growth benefiting all Americans.

And how to give direction to our traditional moral purpose, awakening every American to the dangers and opportunities that confront us.

These are among the real issues of 1960. And it is on the basis of these issues that the American people must make their fateful choice for their future.

In the past forty months, I have toured every state in the Union and I have talked to Democrats in all walks of life. My candidacy is therefore based on the conviction that I can win both the nomination and the election.

I believe that any Democratic aspirant to this important nomination should be willing to submit to the voters his views, record and competence in a series of primary contests. I am therefore announcing my intention of filing in the New Hampshire primary and I shall announce my plans with respect to the other primaries as their filing dates approach.

I believe that the Democratic party has a historic function to perform in the winning of the 1960 election, comparable to its role in 1932. I intend to do my utmost to see that that victory is won.

For eighteen years I have been in the service of the United States, first as a naval officer in the Pacific during World War II and for the past fourteen years as a member of the Congress. In the last twenty years, I have traveled in nearly every continent and country—from Leningrad to Saigon, from Bucharest to Lima. From all of this, I have developed an image of America as fulfilling a noble and historic role as the defender of freedom in a time of maximum peril and of the American people as confident, courageous and persevering.

It is with this image that I begin this campaign.

KENNEDY IN RACE

BARS SECOND SPOT IN ANY SITUATION

Formal Announcement Cites Confidence
He Will Win Election as President

CHALLENGES SYMINGTON

Insists All Aspirants
Should Be Willing to
Test Their Strength
in Primaries

By RUSSELL BAKER

WASHINGTON, Jan. 2—Senator John F. Kennedy made it official today.

He told a news conference that he was a candidate for the Democratic Presidential nomination and was convinced that he could win both the nomination and the election.

At the same time, Democratic leaders who believe that his following can be consolidated behind the Democratic ticket if Mr. Kennedy is given the Vice-Presidential nomination were given a sober warning.

If he is rejected for top place on the ticket, the Senator said, he will refuse to accept the Vice-Presidential nomination "under any condition."

'Not Subject to Change'

This decision, he added, "will not be subject to change under any condition."

The 42-year-old Massachusetts Democrat, the first serious Roman Catholic contender for the Presidency since Alfred E. Smith ran in 1928, delivered his long-expected announcement to a crowded news conference in the Senate Caucus Room.

Of the many Democratic contenders, Senator Hubert H. Humphrey of Minnesota is the only other who has announced his candidacy for the Presidential nomination.

Regarding religion, Mr. Kennedy said:

"I would think that there is really only one issue involved in the whole question of a candidate's religion—that is, does a candidate believe in the Constitution, does he believe in the First Amendment, does he believe in the separation of church and state. When the candidate gives his views on that question, and I think I have given my views fully, I think the subject is exhausted."

Audience Applauds

An audience of about 300 supporters and friends applauded various answers to the reporters, giving the session the flavor of a political rally. Mrs. Kennedy also attended the conference.

Mr. Kennedy has been openly campaigning for the Democratic nomination for months. Thus today's ceremonial announcement came as no surprise.

At present the Senator is the acknowledged front-runner in the crowded field of Democratic contenders. But the large number of serious candidates and favorite sons threatens to prevent him from building a strong lead.

Part of the Kennedy strategy is to break out of his political containing wall by showing strength in the Presidential primaries.

As expected, he announced that he would enter the New Hampshire primary of March 8. He will announce his intentions about other primaries—in Wisconsin, Oregon, Nebraska, Indiana, Maryland, Ohio, Florida and California—within the next six weeks, he said.

There is wide speculation within the party that no candidate will be able to win a clear majority of delegates before the July convention in Los Angeles and that, after a deadlock develops, the delegates will turn to a compromise nominee.

Kennedy Doubts Theory

Those most frequently mentioned as compromise choices are Senator Symington, Senator Lyndon B. Johnson of Texas and Adlai E. Stevenson, twice the standard bearer against General Eisenhower.

Senator Kennedy today took issue with this theory.

"My opinion is that by April or May we will have a pretty good idea of who is going to get nominated in July," he said. "I think when the primaries are through we are going to have a pretty clear idea as to who is going to be the nominee.

"I don't believe there is going to be a deadlocked convention. I don't agree with that concept at all. I would think that even before the convention the pattern will be quite clear."

The Primaries

Wisconsin Battle is Growing Rough

A Crucial Phase of Primary Facing Humphrey and Kennedy This Week

By AUSTIN C. WEHRWEIN

MADISON, Wis., Feb. 13—The bitter Wisconsin Presidential primary contest next week reaches a crucial phase of the test, the first in which two avowed candidates clash head-on.

The primary will take place on April 5. The election fight, which could knock Senator Hubert H. Humphrey of Minnesota out of the running for the Democratic nomination, or stall the bandwagon of Senator John F. Kennedy of Massachusetts, has become one of the roughest in recent Wisconsin political history.

There have been charges of "vote stealing." James R. Hoffa, president of the International Brotherhood of Teamsters, has injected himself into the campaign.

Returning to State

Name-calling has been rife—epithets such as "windbag" with reference to Senator Humphrey and "tough and amoral" and "soft on McCarthyism" with reference to Senator Kennedy have been exchanged in private conversation.

It is into this atmosphere that the two competitors will come back to Wisconsin for this crucial round, and when it is all over they will leave behind them a badly fractured Democratic party that is in power for the first time in Wisconsin in twenty-five years.

Senator Kennedy's Roman Catholic faith, one of the most widely discussed questions on the national scene, is constantly hashed over. But the general assumption is that his religion will help him more than it will hurt him in a state that is nearly one-third Roman Catholic.

Next week both Senators will take charge of campaign plans prepared by their organizations. Among other things Senator Kennedy will employ a variation of his Massachusetts "coffee with the Kennedys" formula that stresses his personal charm.

A Three-Day Visit

He will rely heavily on the help of women supporters and will travel with a party made up of members of his family. He will test his formula on the Wisconsin scene during a three-day sixteen-city swing starting Tuesday.

His organization also plans to sell at $1 each label insignia of a World War II PT boat, a reminder of the Senator's heroic war record. Senator Humphrey tried to get into uniform, but was turned down for physical reasons.

Polls show and many observers agree that Senator Kennedy is ahead and from now on the Humphrey camp's major effort will be to seize the initiative, largely by contending that Senator Humphrey is "more liberal" than his opponent on his voting record and by instinct and background.

Appeal by Humphrey

Senator Humphrey will make a strong appeal to Midwestern sectionalism, arguing that he represents a kind of agrarian liberalism that is foreign to the East Coast, according to his associates here.

What Senator Humphrey will be testing, in a sense, is whether the old Wisconsin tradition of regional liberalism is still an active force.

At stake in the Wisconsin primary are thirty-one convention votes. The "vote stealing" issue arose when the Humphrey-controlled Democratic State Central Committee allotted five instead of ten national convention votes to delegates elected at large.

The Kennedy forces contended that this had hurt their cause because they expected to win a majority of the popular vote.

Wisconsin has an open, or "crossover," primary. Unlike New York, a voter need not register in a party to vote in the primary. One imponderable, therefore, is the number of Republicans who, lacking a primary contest of their own, will vote in the Democratic primary. Conceivably, they could decide the outcome.

The Hoffa issue arose when the Teamster Union boss made a violent attack on Senator Kennedy in a speech last month and promised to come back for more.

Robert Kennedy, former counsel of the Senate labor rackets committee and an adversary of Mr. Hoffa, capitalized on this. Senator Kennedy later said, however, that neither he nor his brother was charging that Mr. Hoffa was helping Senator Humphrey.

Spokesmen for Senator Humphrey denied they were getting any money from Mr. Hoffa.

Senator John F. Kennedy getting a cheer from high school girls while on the campaign trail before the Wisconsin primary.
(Stan Wayman/Time & Life Pictures/Getty Images)

Stop-Kennedy Drive Fails; Nixon Loses Edge in Polls

Race Thus Far Helps Senator in North— Symington Gains as Johnson Slips—

Humphrey Still Trails

By JAMES RESTON

WASHINGTON, March 6—The first third of the 1960 pre-convention campaign for the Presidential nominations is now over and there seems to be general agreement here on these impressions:

The stop-Kennedy movement in the Democratic race has failed. The steady rise of the young Massachusetts Senator, particularly among the profes-sional politicians in the populous and decisive electoral states of the North, is perhaps the most noteworthy development of the first two months.

Vice President Nixon has cleared the field of opposition in his party, but has failed so far to win the enthusiastic support of Governor Rockefeller of New York, and has lost his New Year's Day lead over Mr. Kennedy in the public-opinion polls.

Adlai E. Stevenson, who went to South America early last month, appar-ently on the assumption that absence makes the heart grow fonder, seems to have lost ground and is now being discussed less as a compromise candidate than at the start of the year.

Senator Lyndon B. Johnson of Texas also seems to have lost support in the North despite his bold efforts, approved by Northern liberals, to get a more liberal civil rights bill through the Senate.

The explanation of this odd paradox is that the debate, accompanied by demonstrations against segregated restaurants in the South, has dramatized the race issue and evidently convinced the Democratic politicians in the large Northern cities that a Texan, even one responsible for putting over a good civil rights bill, would not be a popular candidate in the urban North.

Finally, Senator Hubert H. Humphrey of Minnesota, who has campaigned hard and well, remains about where he was, well back in the pack, pending the outcome of the Wisconsin primary election on April 5. His main hope is the test against Mr. Kennedy in the economically depressed areas of West Virginia in the primary there on May 10.

New Phase Beginning

Thus, as the campaign goes into the second, or primary election, third of the campaign with the first voting in New Hampshire on Tuesday, attention is focusing on Vice President Nixon and Senator Kennedy.

The estimate of Mr. Kennedy's chances among the professional politicians has clearly changed in these first two months of the year. When Mr. Kennedy announced his candidacy early in January, he was leading all other Democratic candidates in the public-opinion polls, but the pros were doubting that he could make it. Some of them were even scoffing.

The difference now is that they are now saying he probably will make it, and even his bitterest opponents are not scoffing.

There are several reasons for this change. Senator Kennedy has waged a shrewd, tough, energetic campaign. He has covered more ground than anybody else (he flew to Indianapolis to file in the Indiana primary Friday morning; flew on to Lincoln, Neb., to file in that primary the same afternoon; addressed a Democratic party rally in Hutchinson, Kan., that same night, and was back in New Hampshire campaigning early Saturday morning).

It is not only, however, that these quick flights in his private plane expose his personality and ideas over a wide area, or even that he makes more news than anybody else as a result. All this was true early in the year and even last year.

What is new is that the professionals in the big Northern cities, who were holding out against him at first, seem to be coming to the conclusion that he

will get out a big Democratic vote in their cities and thus strengthen their own personal political positions at home, and help the local and state Democratic candidates.

This is helping him in New York, where the pros are now saying he will get at least half of that state's 114 delegates (some say he will get as many as 100). It is helping him in Illinois, where Mayor Richard J. Daley needs a large vote in Chicago to overcome the latest police scandal, and it is helping him in Michigan where Gov. J. Mennen Williams has announced he will not seek reelection and is indicating that he will be available for the Vice-Presidential nomination on a ticket headed by Mr. Kennedy.

Mr. Kennedy has gone up in the estimation of the pros because he has demonstrated that he is tough enough to play the pros' game. He outmaneuvered the field to gain the upper hand in Ohio—his biggest coup so far.

He negotiated a compromise with Gov. Pat Brown of California under which he will get at least part of that state's large delegation. He has virtually assured himself of the Maryland delegation by timely power moves in that state, and he started the year with the assurance of all 114 of New England's delegates.

There has always been powerful opposition to Mr. Kennedy among the older liberal intellectuals of the party, but the passage of time has even worked with his opponents to the New Englander's favor. For there is an increasing realization—particularly among the Democratic intellectuals, regardless of whom they support— that one of their greatest problems is that no one has stood out above the rest. This has blurred the purposes of the party and led many Democrats to the conclusion that the quicker they decide on someone the better.

Time Helping His Cause

Thus in addition to his theatrical clamour, his intelligence that has im-

pressed many of the Democratic intellectuals and his new strength among the pros, he now finds time working on his side.

This does not mean that he is in. A defeat in Wisconsin, or in West Virginia, where he is more vulnerable to Senator Humphrey's more liberal arguments, could change the picture radically, but at this moment, instead of being "stopped"—as powerful Democrats such as Mrs. Franklin D. Roosevelt and Gov. David L. Lawrence of Pennsylvania hoped—he is running farther ahead than two months ago.

This, of course, creates an increasingly difficult problem for his opponents in the upper circles of the Democratic party. They have always known that, even if they wanted to drop him on grounds of age or experience or merely because they thought somebody else would make a better President, they could not do so while he was running well ahead without giving their numerous Roman Catholic supporters the impression that they were ditching him because he was a Catholic.

Meanwhile, Mr. Nixon is trying to deal with the consequences of his success in getting Governor Rockefeller out of the race. There is no doubt that the Governor resents the way he was treated on his exploratory trips into the West by party officials whom the Governor identifies with the Vice President.

Mr. Rockefeller's attitude when he withdrew was, "Okay, the Republican pros want Nixon and they can have him." He has talked to Mr. Nixon since then and got over some of his resentment, but other developments since then have kept some of the old feelings alive.

But Mr. Nixon's dilemma—and it is genuine—is that he cannot provide the leadership in a campaign for new policies for the future without seeming to criticize present programs that President Eisenhower regards as perfectly adequate.

Kennedy Victor By 106,000 Votes

Complete Wisconsin Returns Show a Record Turnout of 1.19 Million for Primary

By AUSTIN C. WEHRWEIN

MILWAUKEE, April 6—Senator John F. Kennedy flew back to Washington early this morning with 20½ convention-delegate votes in his pocket, the result of his comfortable victory in Wisconsin's Democratic Presidential primary.

His rival, Senator Hubert H. Humphrey of Minnesota, claimed a "great moral victory" at an early morning news conference. He had 10½ delegate votes.

With the unofficial returns in from yesterday's balloting, the Massachusetts Democrat had a total of 478,901 votes, compared with 372,034 for Senator Humphrey and 341,463 for Vice President Nixon. Mr. Nixon, unopposed in the Republican column, made no appearances in this contest.

As a result, the vote on the Democratic side was 71 per cent of the total. Primary results are inexact guides to general elections, but observers noted that President Eisenhower carried Wisconsin in 1956 with 61 per cent of the total vote.

Balloting Sets Record

Wisconsin voters, stirred by the primary campaign and the realization that their choice might determine the next Democratic Presidential nominee, turned out in a flood.

The 1,192,398 ballots they cast exceeded the previous record of 1,018,149 set in the 1952 Presidential primary.

Senator Kennedy won six of the state's ten Congressional districts, worth fifteen convention votes, or two and a half a district. He took five more by virtue of winning the statewide popular vote in the Democratic column, by a margin of 106,867 votes.

Mr. Humphrey won ten votes by carrying four Congressional districts.

Each candidate also received an additional half-vote. This is because one vote, the state's thirty-first, is split between the Democratic national committeeman and the national committeewoman. They are divided, one for each of the rivals.

The net result gave Senator Kennedy 56 per cent of the Democratic vote and 40 per cent of the total two-party vote.

Senator Humphrey got 44 per cent of the Democratic vote and 31 per cent of the total two party vote.

Mr. Nixon, who never campaigned and who ignored the contest, received 29 per cent of the total vote. He also won thirty Republican-convention votes.

Although Mr. Nixon ran third, it was not a "wobbly" third, as had been predicted by Senator Humphrey.

Mr. Nixon led Senator Humphrey in four Congressional districts in eastern Wisconsin and he led both Democrats in nine of seventy-one counties. His showing, while hardly spectacular, was better than Republican leaders had expected.

Wisconsin went Republican in the last two Presidential elections, but it is now under a Democratic state administration and it re-elected Senator William Proxmire in 1958 by a wide margin. Mr. Nixon's vote yesterday, achieved almost by default, must be measured against this Democratic trend.

Kennedy Victory Assessed

Senator Kennedy's victory was being interpreted here along these lines:

It was a triumph for moderate liberalism.

It indicated that he can poll farm votes, even though he is a Harvard-educated Bostonian.

It indicated that he has an "image" that appeals to voters as being more Presidential than Senator Humphrey's. This is especially true among middle-class voters, but the Bostonian can attract industrial workers too.

It indicated that his Roman Catholicism could be an advantage in some areas.

Senator Kennedy won handily, even in industrial areas, with a campaign pitched toward a gradual approach to social reform, offering a dispassionate promise to update rather than to innovate.

Senator Humphrey presented himself as the chief voice of authentic liberalism.

Senator Kennedy captured industrialized and unionized Congressional districts on the shores of Lake Michigan—the First, Fourth, Fifth and Sixth—even though Senator Humphrey had the backing of top union leaders.

Senator Humphrey's role as a prophet of liberalism was completely effective only in the Second District, which includes Madison, the egghead capital of Wisconsin.

Senator Humphrey also proved his theory that he would do well in his own backyard. But it turned out that he had title to a lot less Wisconsin real estate than he had imagined.

This damaged the Humphrey thesis that sectionalism, which he expressed as "Middle Western progressivism," is a powerful force.

Senator Humphrey's major campaign theme was that he was a "consistent friend of the farmer" and that a vote against Humphrey was a vote against the family farm.

In Wisconsin's western districts this approach, plus his Minnesota residence, enabled him to attract a crossover Republican farm vote.

Kennedy at Critical Point in Campaign

By JAMES RESTON

Apr. 7—Senator John F. Kennedy has reached a critical point in his quest for the Presidency. His personal charm, his money, his religion, and his dispassionate intelligence have carried him to a high plateau, still far below the summit; but, ironically, these very same factors are beginning to cause him trouble.

Having reached a height beyond any other candidate for the Democratic nomination, he would like to see the national debate turn now to the issues of the Sixties and the qualities necessary in a President of the future. But this is not happening.

Instead, he finds himself widely regarded as a young, rich, handsome, Catholic personality-boy, and while this is useful in the preliminary skirmishes for the nomination, it is too shallow and theatrical an image for the decisive phase of the campaign.

This, of course, has often been the fate of the handsome young men of every generation. They flutter the multitude, but after a while seem almost too attractive to be true.

If Kennedy were merely a well-heeled cover boy, benefiting from the natural resentments of the Catholic voters, there would be a certain rough justice in his present dilemma.

His money has given him advantages in this campaign. His father advanced him $270,000 to buy a plane.

Six members of his family put up $15,000 each to complete the deal, and while they have a contract to return it to the seller for $260,000, there is no doubt that this—plus a great deal more for paid assistants and television—has given him opportunities his competitors have not enjoyed.

His religion, to date, has also given him a political edge. He has benefited, most recently in Wisconsin, from the ancient feeling among Catholics that the Protestant majority in this country has willfully denied the Presidency to anyone of Catholic faith.

Kennedy's Edge

It is not too much to say that, if he were not the beneficiary of this feeling, if the other leaders of his party were not fearful of losing the support of the large Catholic constituency in the large Northern cities, he would probably not be leading the race today.

Kennedy with a group of nuns at Lady of Sorrows Convent in Wisconsin, March 1960. (Stan Wayman/Time & Life Pictures/Getty Images)

Also, he cannot complain if the religious issue is raised, because he was the first to raise it by circulating at the Democratic convention of 1956 a memorandum purporting to show that there was a "Catholic vote" that could help the Democrats win if a Catholic, and specifically Kennedy, were put on the ticket.

Nevertheless, there is a certain poignancy in his situation. For this is no mere handsome, shallow theatrical character. Good looks, money, and religion may have provided him with opportunities not available to other men, but he has had the other qualities of mind and spirit to take advantage of these opportunities.

This he demonstrated in Wisconsin. It is true that he exploited all the arts of the theatre and the television screen. It is also true that he was helped immensely there by his whole family, except his father, a controversial figure in the Democratic party, who has been banished to the opulence of Palm Beach. But that is not the whole story.

The candidate himself is a gifted and tough-minded young man, self assured, dispassionate, well informed and articulate. He took his chances in the rough and tumble of the political and journalistic scramble in Wisconsin and came out of it without once losing his composure or indulging in personal rancor or misleading argument.

His problem now is to elevate the debate above the superficial chatter of political tactics and personalities. He dare not leave the dialogue where it is after the evidence of mass religious voting in Wisconsin.

For the two major parties in this country have not come together over the last generation on questions of social security at home and collective security overseas in order to divide into a Catholic party and a Protestant party. We have seen what this kind of political division has done to the politics of Europe and Kennedy cannot desire this any more than anyone else. The question, therefore, is whether he will now broaden and deepen his appeal to the whole nation. Both good sense and politics point in this direction, for there is no "Catholic vote" in West Virginia, the next test, and no President can govern effectively in a nation divided along religious lines.

Kennedy, Backed By Humphrey, Hits Issue of Religion

Says He Is 'Not Catholic Candidate for President'—Symington Asks Unity

By WAYNE PHILLIPS

WASHINGTON, April 21—Senator John F. Kennedy, in a massive assault on the religious issue in politics, today told a convention of newspaper editors:

"I am not the Catholic candidate for President."

Senator Hubert H. Humphrey, his opponent in the Democratic primary in West Virginia on May 10, went before the same group a few hours later and declared:

"I would not want to receive the vote of any American because my opponent or opponents worship in a particular church whatever that church may be."

Symington Also Heard

Senator Stuart Symington of Missouri, the third candidate for the Democratic Presidential nomination to talk to the editors today, made no mention of the religious issue. But he spoke of the need for greater unity among all Americans.

Senator Kennedy, of Massachusetts, had been scheduled to talk of America's role in the under-developed world at the convention of the American Society of Newspaper Editors at the Statler-Hilton Hotel.

But he abandoned that subject entirely to discuss the way in which his religious beliefs had intruded into the campaign for the Democratic nomination for the Presidency.

The remarks of Senator Humphrey, of Minnesota, on the religious issue were in a preface he had prepared to a talk on disarmament policies.

Both men urged the 400 editors attending the convention to devote more space to other important issues in this year's campaigning.

Kennedy Changed Topic

The change in Senator Kennedy's topic became known two days ago, at about the same time that it appeared from his statements in West Virginia that he had decided the religious issue could no longer be disregarded, but had to be brought into the open and discussed.

". . . For my religion is hardly the dominant issue facing the United States in 1960."

His talk today appeared to be both a compendium of various views he had expressed previously on the subject of religion and politics, and a definitive statement of where he stood on every religious question that has been raised—for the benefit of the men who control what is printed in this country's newspapers.

"I know the press did not create this religious issue," he said "My religious affiliation is a fact—religious intolerance is fact. And the proper role of the press is to report matters of all public interest.

"But the press has a responsibility, I think you will agree, which goes far beyond the mere reporting of facts. It goes beyond lofty editorials deploring intolerance. For my religion is hardly the dominant issue facing the United States in 1960. It is hardly the most important criterion—or even a relevant criterion—on which the American people should make their choice for chief executive. And the press, while not creating the issue, will largely determine whether or not the issue becomes dominant—whether it is kept in perspective—whether it is considered objectively—and whether needless fears and suspicions are aroused."

Editors Taken To Task

The Senator went on to take the editors seriously to task for going beyond the religious beliefs of candidates into the religion of those who voted for them.

"Can we justify analyzing the voters and their religion as well as candidates?" he asked.

"I think the voters of Wisconsin objected to being categorized simply as either Catholics or Protestants or Jews. I think they objected to being accosted by reporters outside of meetings and asked one question only—not their occupation or education or philosophy or income—but only their religious affiliation."

Attempts to establish some correlation between the religious beliefs of voters and how they had voted in Wisconsin's primary election, where Senator Kennedy came out ahead of Senator Humphrey, had no statistical validity, he said.

"For voters are more than Catholics, Protestants and Jews," he continued. "They make up their minds for many reasons, good and bad. To submit the candidates to a religious test is bad enough—to apply it to the voters themselves is divisive, degrading and wholly unwarranted."

The Senator's talk held the editors and their guests in rapt attention. When he finished they applauded vigorously for nearly a full minute.

Kennedy chatting with miners as he campaigns in West Virginia during the primaries, April 1960.
(Hank Walker/Time & Life Pictures/ Getty Images)

Kennedy Winner Over Humphrey in West Virginia

Rival Quits Race

Minnesotan to Seek Re-election to Senate— He Lauds Victor

By W.H. LAWRENCE

CHARLESTON, W. Va., Wednesday, May 11—Senator John F. Kennedy of Massachusetts won a smashing upset victory in yesterday's West Virginia Presidential preferential primary.

The Senator promptly forecast that he would be nominated at the Democratic National Convention, which starts July 11.

His "significant and clear-cut" victory was conceded at 1 A. M. Eastern standard time by Senator Hubert H. Humphrey of Minnesota.

Senator Humphrey also announced that he would withdraw from the race for the Democratic Presidential nomination. For Senator Kennedy, a Roman Catholic, it was a surprising victory in a state where it had appeared that anti-Catholic sentiment had made Senator Humphrey the pre-primary favorite.

Turnout Is Heavy

The Associated Press, reporting on returns from 1,168 of 2,750 precincts, gave: Kennedy 93,341

Humphrey 60,889

Observers estimated that 400,000 of the 670,000 registered Democrats had turned out to vote on a raw, chilly day.

[In the Nebraska primary, Mr. Kennedy and Vice President Nixon received impressive popular support. Mr. Kennedy was the only Presidential candidate entered. Mr. Nixon was backed by write-in votes.]

Senator Kennedy flew here from Washington after the vote trend had established him as the probable winner. He told a television audience that the West Virginia vote had demonstrated that his religion was not a major issue with the nation's voters.

He said the results here should go far toward "quieting" the concern he said some Democratic leaders had felt about nominating a Catholic for the Presidency. The vote here, Senator Kennedy said, demonstrated that religion would not be a dominant issue if he were picked by the Democrats to run against Vice President Nixon, the expected Republican Presidential nominee.

Senator Kennedy said the West Virginia primary was "the key to all the primaries" and should be "extremely helpful on the road to Los Angeles."

"After our victory here, I think we are going to be nominated," Senator Kennedy told a television audience.

The Kennedy victory was built in every section of the state, but especially in the Southern coal fields where a combination of factors, including religion, had made Senator Humphrey appear the stronger candidate in advance of yesterday's balloting.

The Massachusetts Senator smashed the "stop-Kennedy" drive led by Senator Robert C. Byrd of West Virginia. He had urged all those who wanted any other Democratic nominee to vote for Senator Humphrey or they would lose their "last chance" to prevent Senator Kennedy's nomination.

Senator Byrd openly supported Lyndon B. Johnson of Texas, but his appeal for Humphrey votes also was aimed at those who preferred the nomination of Senator Stuart Symington of Missouri or Adlai E. Stevenson of Illinois, the Democratic nominee of 1952 and 1956.

This was a hard-fought, and often harsh, campaign between Senators Kennedy and Humphrey. Senator Kennedy abandoned the bland impersonal campaign he had followed to victory in Wisconsin over Senator Humphrey. Instead he struck directly at the Minnesotan as a front man for other candidates who had no hope of nomination himself.

Party Unity

But the work of restoring party unity and healing the wounds began as soon as the election here was decided.

Robert F. Kennedy, brother of the Senator, paid a quick call on Senator Humphrey at his hotel headquarters as soon as he had conceded defeat. Together they walked to the Humphrey campaign headquarters for a news conference.

In withdrawing from the Presidential race, Senator Humphrey said he would be a candidate for re-election to the Senate from Minnesota this year but would continue at the national level to seek nomination by the Democrats of "liberal candidates and a liberal platform." In conceding, he also congratulated Senator Kennedy and referred to him as his "friend and Senate colleague."

There were early reports of vote-buying and other election irregularities in the state and local races. But none of it was connected directly with campaign efforts for Senator Kennedy, who is wealthy, or Senator Humphrey, who has complained that he is in debt from his Presidential campaign efforts.

"There is a hell of a lot of vote-buying here," said Charles Hylton, managing editor of The Logan Banner. "It's the worst I've ever seen. But it is among the local, not Presidential candidates."

"One of my reporters said that the price fluctuated quite a bit right here in Logan," he said. "Some were selling their votes for $2 and a drink of whisky, while others were getting $6 and two pints of whisky."

The Democratic Convention

JOHNSON ENTERS RACE OFFICIALLY SEES 500 VOTES

Texan Says Kennedy Will Receive Fewer Than 600 on the First Ballot

HEALTH ISSUE IS BARRED

Majority Leader Criticizes New Englander Obliquely— Cheered by Backers

By JOHN D. MORRIS

WASHINGTON, July 5—Senator Lyndon B. Johnson announced today that he was a candidate for the Democratic Presidential nomination.

Senator Johnson said he expected to go to the convention with more than 500 first-ballot votes against fewer than 600 for Senator John F. Kennedy of Massachusetts. The nomination requires 761.

The 51-year-old Texan, majority leader of the Senate, had been campaigning for weeks. So his announcement was no surprise to anyone.

But he carried off the ritual of making a formal declaration before television cameras, now standard procedure for Presidential aspirants, in the approved manner.

Backers Cheer Him

Looking self-assured and dignified, he stood before a cluster of microphones and read a fifteen-minute prepared statement, then answered reporters' questions for fifteen minutes.

The performance was punctuated by cheers and applause from several hundred Johnson partisans who packed the spacious, coldly modern auditorium of the New Senate Office Building. House Speaker Sam Rayburn, the Senator's Texas colleague and campaign adviser, was among them.

The ceremony produced one surprise. It came during the question-and-answer period, when Senator Johnson passed up an opportunity to rule himself out as a possible nominee for Vice President.

"I have been prepared throughout my adult life to serve my country in any capacity where my country thought my services were essential," he declared.

"However," he went on, "I am a candidate for President and I expect to be nominated for President."

Associates later cautioned reporters against interpreting the remarks as meaning that the Senator might accept second place on the ticket if he failed to win the Presidential nomination. He has said privately that he would not, and the associates said he had not changed his mind.

The reason he did not say so today, it was explained, was that he did not want to place himself above the Vice-Presidency or to downgrade the job.

Senator Thruston B. Morton of Kentucky, the Republican National Chairman, has accused Senators Johnson and Kennedy of entering an arrangement for Senator Kennedy to head the Democratic ticket with Senator Johnson as the Vice-Presidential candidate.

Rules Out Health Issue

The charge has been widely discounted because of Mr. Johnson's known feeling that the majority leadership of the Senate is a more important post than the Vice-Presidency.

In replying to questions, Senator Johnson also disassociated himself from questions raised by campaign aides yesterday about the health of Senator Kennedy.

Mr. Johnson expressed confidence that he and Mr. Kennedy were both in good health. As evidence, he cited his recent attendance at all-night Senate sessions and Mr. Kennedy's vigorous campaigning throughout the country.

Senator Johnson expressed strong disagreement with a reported suggestion by Paul M. Butler, Democratic National Chairman, that Roman Catholic voters might turn away from the Democratic ticket if Senator Kennedy, a Catholic, was deprived of the Presidential nomination.

He called the suggestion "an insult to good Catholics" and said no candidate, obviously referring to Mr. Kennedy, would share such views.

Female supporters, called "Kennedy Cuties," form a conga line at the airport while awaiting their candidate's arrival for the Democratic National Convention in Los Angeles. (Hank Walker/Time & Life Pictures/Getty Images)

Avoids Direct Criticism

Refraining from directly criticizing Mr. Kennedy on any score, Senator Johnson told one questioner he had not implied that the Massachusetts Senator was using improper methods to line up convention delegates.

In addition, he volunteered a promise to support anyone nominated for President at the Los Angeles convention "with all the vigor and intelligence at my command." The convention opens next Monday.

There were passages in his prepared statement, however, that may be read by some as barbs aimed toward the Kennedy camp.

Senator Johnson said, for example, that he had delayed his announcement until the Congressional recess because "someone has to tend the store" while others engaged in active campaigns and missed hundreds of votes in the Senate.

At another point, he said he would never try to tell convention delegates to bind themselves in advance "to any choice except the choice of what is best for America."

"The next President," Mr. Johnson said, "is not going to be a talking President—or a traveling President. He's going to be and should be a working President."

In the question-and-answer period, there was a possible allusion to Mr. Kennedy's position in not taking a stand on the Senate's censure of Senator Joseph R. McCarthy, Republican of Wisconsin, in 1954.

Asked to classify himself on the liberal-conservative scale Senator Johnson said he was "progressive and prudent without being radical" and "conservative without being reactionary." He was called a liberal during the Administrations of Franklin D. Roosevelt and Harry S. Truman, he said, and went on:

"And I was a voting liberal when McCarthyism was an issue in the Senate of the United States."

Senator Johnson and a majority of the Senate voted to censure Senator McCarthy, who died in 1957. Senator Kennedy was in a hospital for a back operation and did not disclose his position. On his return to Washington in 1955 he declined to say how he would have voted; but in 1956 he said he would have supported the censure resolution.

Stevenson Edges Near Candidacy

Says He Would Do 'Utmost' to Win if Drafted —Plans 2 Appearances on Coast

By ANTHONY LEWIS

LOS ANGELES, July 8—Adlai E. Stevenson edged into the battle for the Democratic Presidential nomination today with his most explicit statement of availability thus far.

The nominee in 1952 and 1956 said he would accept a draft and "do my utmost to win." The statement cheered his supporters here, who until today had not had even a polite word of encouragement from their candidate.

Senator A. S. Mike Monroney, Democrat of Oklahoma, the head of the draft-Stevenson organization, expressed optimism. He told a news conference:

"We have the greatest growth potential of any of the candidates."

Mr. Stevenson arrives here tomorrow. He will take on a bit more of the candidate's air Sunday with two public performances—a brief talk to a Democratic fund-raising dinner and an appearance on a television interview program.

Analysts Skeptical

Nevertheless, no realistic political analyst here gives Mr. Stevenson more than a far-distant shot at a third nomination. A former supporter now backing Senator John F. Kennedy of Massachusetts, but personally sympathetic to Mr. Stevenson, predicted that his trip would be "a sad pilgrimage."

Today's statement that he would accept a draft was accompanied by more confusion and interpretation. The news was disclosed at a conference by Lieut. Gov. Glenn Anderson of California, who had announced for Mr. Stevenson. He described a telephone conversation he had with Mr. Stevenson last Wednesday as follows:

"Governor Stevenson said that under circumstances which were understandably difficult he headed the Democratic national ticket in two campaigns. He has, therefore, felt that it would be presumptuous and arrogant for him to claim squatter's rights or to seek actively a third nomination.

"He said, however, that if selected by the convention he would of course accept the draft and campaign with vigor and a sense of real purpose since the issues we face are of such great importance."

A short time later in Chicago, Mr. Stevenson said he was honored by Mr. Anderson's support, and added:

"His report of our conversation reflects no change in my position."

The last comment was somewhat mysterious, since Mr. Stevenson had hitherto carefully avoided an unequivocal statement that he was available for a draft. One of his backers here grumbled:

"Why can't he let well enough alone?"

The net of the two statements was to push Mr. Stevenson somewhat back into the nomination picture. But the fact remains that the campaign being made on his behalf here is a strange, amorphous affair that would need a miracle to succeed.

Kennedy and Adlai E. Stevenson enjoy a light moment at the Democratic convention.
(Paul Schutzer/Time & Life Pictures/Getty Images)

Caucuses Today Expected to Forecast Kennedy's Strength Among the Delegates

MOVE TO KENNEDY NEARS STAMPEDE; HIS RIVALS UNITE

Easterner Continues to Gain as Johnson and Symington Join to Prevent Bolts

By RUSSELL BAKER

LOS ANGELES, July 9—Senator John F. Kennedy of Massachusetts arrived today to find the Democratic National Convention on the verge of a stampede to his Presidential candidacy.

He arrived shortly behind Senator Stuart Symington of Missouri, whose backers were making common cause with Senator Lyndon B. Johnson of Texas in a desperate stand to stop a mass bolt to Mr. Kennedy.

Adlai E. Stevenson, whose chances for the nomination also rest with the "stop-Kennedy" forces, arrived today at International Airport and was cheered by the biggest reception of the day.

His arrival statement offered little succor, however, to the zealous band of nonprofessionals working to generate a draft movement in his behalf.

Stevenson Would Accept

Mr. Stevenson said he was "not here to promote my candidacy," but would "willingly accept" if he should be nominated.

In the swarming corridors and headquarters suites of the Biltmore Hotel, however, most of the breaks today were coming in Senator Kennedy's favor.

The importance of these breaks becomes evident in the light of a conservative poll compiled by The Associated Press. It indicates that Mr. Kennedy has 540 first-ballot votes without counting any support from the critical states now backing "favorite sons."

Conservative estimates are that Mr. Kennedy could add about 200 additional votes if the various "favorite sons" released their delegates early. This would put the Senator within easy distance of the 761 votes needed to nominate.

Backed by Carolinian

The move toward Mr. Kennedy opened this morning with an announcement by Terry Sanford, the Democratic nominee for Governor of North Carolina, that he would support the Senator and take a third of his state's thirty-seven votes with him into the Kennedy column.

Additional Southern defections may follow. If so, they can be attributed in part to favorable Southern reaction to reports of Senator Kennedy's position on lunch-counter sit-in demonstrations by Negroes seeking to break Southern segregation patterns.

Some Southern delegations reported that the Senator's brother, Robert F. Kennedy, had told them that Senator Kennedy was sympathetic to such tactics only where they were "peaceful and legal."

In other Southern delegations there were rumblings of restlessness as small bands of Kennedy backers began pressing the argument that Senator Kennedy was a certain winner and that their states should not be caught backing a loser.

Additional labor support for Mr. Kennedy came from Joseph A. Beirne, president of the Communication Workers of America. Mr. Beirne said Senator Kennedy was a preference of all but a minority of the labor leadership.

Another important break in the ranks of the "favorite sons" occurred this afternoon when Gov. George Docking of Kansas announced on a television broadcast that he was inclined toward Senator Kennedy and would probably release his twenty-one-vote delegation.

Johnson Claims Gain

Senator Johnson, who arrived yesterday, showed no signs of dismay about the apparent drift to Mr. Kennedy.

He picked up additional delegates within the last few days, Mr. Johnson insisted, but was "not buying any ads" to broadcast their identity because of the pressures now being exerted to stampede the convention.

> *Mr. Kennedy has 540 first-ballot votes without counting any support from the critical states now backing "favorite sons."*

At about the same time, however, Senator Johnson was losing another twenty-six first-ballot votes as Louisiana leaders announced they would support Gov. Jimmie H. Davis as a "favorite son."

The Arkansas delegation was also reported considering placing its twenty-seven votes behind Senator John L. McClellan as a "favorite son" if Senator Johnson showed signs of fading quickly.

The fact is that in both the Johnson and Symington camps, hopes for stopping a Kennedy nomination now rest with Gov. David L. Lawrence of

Pennsylvania, who remains inscrutable about his preference.

The Pennsylvania delegation, with eighty-one votes, will caucus Monday morning. The New Jersey delegation, with forty-one votes pledged to Gov. Robert B. Meyner, will also meet Monday morning. Though the New Jersey delegation contains a big bloc of Kennedy supporters, Governor Meyner is reportedly still determined to hold out against a swing to Senator Kennedy.

Three other big delegations will caucus tomorrow, and the Kennedy camp confidently expects a day filled with good news.

These caucuses are California with eighty-one votes, Illinois with sixty-nine, Minnesota with thirty-one and New Jersey with forty-one. Gov. Edmund G. Brown of California is expected to announce his support for Mr. Kennedy and swing between forty and fifty votes.

The floor at the Democratic convention in Los Angeles, where Kennedy supporters were confident of victory.
(Ralph Crane/Time & Life Pictures/Getty Images)

Illinois Majority Seen

Illinois is also expected to produce a large majority for Senator Kennedy. Informed estimates now give him as many as forty-nine of the state's sixty-nine votes.

The Minnesota delegation, pledged to Senator Hubert H. Humphrey, is one of the richest prizes still uncommitted and both the Johnson and Kennedy camps have been laboring to pluck it.

Senator Johnson and Senator Humphrey conferred early today and Mr. Humphrey was later sounded out by the Kennedy strategists.

Speculation at convention headquarters today was shifting from the question of whether Senator Kennedy could be stopped to the question of whether he would take the "northern route" or the "southern route" in his autumn campaign strategy.

KENNEDY NOMINATED ON THE FIRST BALLOT; OVERWHELMS JOHNSON BY 806 VOTES TO 409

LONG DRIVE WINS

Wyoming's Vote Puts Bostonian Over Top Before Acclamation

By W.H. LAWRENCE

LOS ANGELES, Thursday, July 14 —Senator John F. Kennedy smashed his way to a first-ballot Presidential nomination at the Democratic National Convention last night and won the right to oppose Vice President Nixon in November.

The 43-year-old Massachusetts Senator overwhelmed his opposition, piling up 806 votes to 409 ballots for his nearest rival, Senator Lyndon B. Johnson of Texas, the Senate majority leader. Senator Kennedy's victory came just before 11 o'clock last night [2 A.M. Thursday, New York time].

Then the convention made it unanimous on motion of Gov. James T. Blair Jr. of Missouri, who had placed Senator Stuart Symington of Missouri in nomination.

'We Shall Win'

Senator Kennedy, appearing before the shouting convention early today, pledged he would carry the fight to the country in the fall "and we shall win."

He thanked his defeated rivals for their generosity and appealed to all of their backers to keep the party strong and united in a tremendously important election. He spoke directly of Senators Johnson and Symington and the favorite sons, but made no reference to Adlai E. Stevenson.

The third session of the national convention adjourned after his speech. The next session will convene at 5 P. M. today.

Little Wyoming, well down the roll-call, provided the fifteen votes that gave victory to Senator Kennedy. Two favorite-son states, Minnesota and New Jersey, waited in vain to give the on-rushing Kennedy bandwagon the final shove.

When Wyoming came in with its vote, the Kennedy total had mounted to 765 votes, or four more than the 761 votes required for nomination.

It was a tremendous victory for Senator Kennedy. Mr. Johnson, the Senate majority leader, had fought desperately to reverse a Kennedy tide that had been running for months. But Senator Johnson quickly telephoned his congratulations to Senator Kennedy and forecast his election in November.

Senator Kennedy, who chose the tough preferential primary road to victory, had demonstrated to the party's big state leaders that he could win votes.

He reasoned that only through the primaries could he, as a Roman Catholic, remove the lingering fear of party leaders that he was destined for the same kind of defeat suffered by former Gov. Alfred E. Smith of New York, a Catholic, in 1928.

The convention will assemble today to ratify Senator Kennedy's choice of a Vice-Presidential running mate. Key names under consideration are those of Senator Symington, Gov. Orville L. Freeman of Minnesota and Senator Henry M. Jackson of Washington.

The Kennedy bandwagon could not be stopped despite the pressure of the combined Congressional leadership, including Speaker Sam Rayburn of Texas, and of former President Harry S. Truman. Mr. Truman had boycotted this meeting on a charge that the convention had been rigged for Senator Kennedy's nomination.

Efforts to breathe life in a "draft" movement for Mr. Stevenson, the 1952 and 1956 nominee, failed, despite a noisy, rowdy demonstration mostly by non-delegates who had infiltrated the hall by various devices.

At the end of the roll-call, Mr. Stevenson had only 79½ votes, slightly fewer than the 86 cast for Senator Symington.

Nine Put in Nomination

Senator Kennedy's victory was national in scope with the exception of the solid South, which gave nearly all its votes to Senator Johnson. Of the fifty-four delegations, including the District of Columbia, the Canal Zone, Puerto Rico and the Virgin Islands, Senator Kennedy ran ahead in thirty-two of them.

All but one of the big states—New York, Pennsylvania, Michigan, Illinois and Massachusetts—gave Senator Kennedy tremendous margins. California was the exception, where he narrowly topped Mr. Stevenson by a two and one-half vote plurality, picking up 33½, or well under a majority of the state's vote total.

As the balloting progressed alphabetically, Senator Kennedy was well over the 100 mark after Illinois, over the 200-vote mark with Iowa, over 300 with his own State of Massachusetts, just short of 500 after New York gave him 104½ votes, and over the 650 mark after Pennsylvania.

When West Virginia brought him to the 750 mark, the stage was set for Wyoming to move into the national limelight.

It was an orderly, swift roll-call without a challenge to any state and the resulting poll of the delegation to confirm the accuracy of the announced vote.

It had taken about six and a half hours to place the nine candidates in nomination and to allow their supporters to shout and parade around the hall in wild, but well-organized demonstrations. Only the Stevenson camp violated the convention rules limiting outside demonstrators to a maximum of 125 persons, including bands, for each candidate.

Charges Repeated

The Stevenson group passed entry badges back and forth until nearly 500 outsiders had come in, and then tried to crash through without any kind of passes, forcing a call for two-score more policemen to guard the gates.

Mr. Stevenson started out with the idea that he would not seek the nomination. But cheered by the enthusiasm of Southern Californians, he entered into the political in-fighting of the last few days.

He contributed to the faltering "stop-Kennedy" movement, which before his arrival had shown visible signs of pronounced political fatigue.

Even at the end, Senator Kennedy hoped that Mr. Stevenson would not seek a third nomination and would consent to place Senator Kennedy's name in nomination before the convention.

But finally Mr. Stevenson said that he could not reciprocate the favor Senator Kennedy had performed in 1956 when he placed Mr. Stevenson in nomination at Chicago.

The political in-fighting and maneuvering continued to the wire, with all the candidates, including Mr. Stevenson, working tirelessly to convince wavering or uncommitted delegates.

Senators Lyndon B. Johnson and John F. Kennedy, rivals for the nomination, at the Democratic National Convention.
(Frank Hurley/*New York Daily News Archive*/Getty Images)

Senator Johnson slashed harshly at Senator Kennedy in what many delegates interpreted as desperation maneuvers aimed at undermining the majority indicated for his young rival. He hit at the Senator's father, Joseph P. Kennedy, wartime Ambassador to Britain, as a friend of Prime Minister Neville Chamberlain and one who opposed American entry into the war against Hitler.

The Senate majority leader also attacked Senator Kennedy's failure to vote for censure of Senator Joseph R. McCarthy at a time when Senator Kennedy was critically ill in Florida.

The Johnson forces contended that a "revolt" of delegates "hogtied" to Kennedy already was under way and there was no doubt that the Texan would eventually win.

However, the Kennedy camp remained cool and confident, but watchful of any developing signs of weakness in the delegations.

As the serious business of nominating a candidate began, Governor Collins angrily demanded that the milling delegates take their seats and listen with more attentiveness than they had demonstrated at the first two sessions.

Alphabetical Switches

At the outset, Mr. Collins said he would permit orderly withdrawal of non-serious favorite-son candidates. He said the convention would proceed, in alphabetical order, to allow states to change their votes between the completion of the first roll-call of states and before tabulation of the final tally on any ballot. Opponents of Senator Kennedy at one stage had announced an effort to change the rules to prevent such vote switching, but this plan was abandoned.

Alabama, first on the list of states, yielded to Texas and the honor of being first placed in nomination went to Senator Johnson.

Speaker Rayburn in his nominating speech said it was the duty of Democrats to "choose the very best leader that we have," and that Senator Johnson had demonstrated "that he knows how to lead."

"This man is a winner," Speaker Ray-

Kennedy accepting his party's nomination at the 1960 Democratic National Convention in the Los Angeles Coliseum, July 15, 1960.
(Ed Clark/Time & Life Pictures/Getty Images)

burn declared. "He can bring together people of all walks of life, of every faith and persuasion. We must not be divided; we must be united. This man can unite us. He will lead us to reason and to work together, for over many years he has proven that he posseses the magic gift of being able to lead men in a common cause. There is no abler man in our party. "

"This man belongs to no class, no section, no faction. This is a man for all Americans—a leader matured by long experience, a soldier seasoned in many battles, a tall, sun-crowned man who stands ready now to lead America and lovers of freedom everywhere through our most fateful hours."

Pour Into the Aisles

Hoisting their placards and other paraphernalia of the traditional political demonstration high, Southern supporters of Senator Johnson poured into the aisles as Speaker Rayburn concluded his nominating speech.

While seconding speeches were being made for Senator Johnson, the big eighty-one vote California delegation was polled on the convention floor. Senator Kennedy took the lead from Mr. Stevenson with a one-vote margin. Mr. Stevenson had a one-vote edge yesterday.

Alaska yielded to Minnesota, and Senator Kennedy was the second candidate placed in nomination. The principal nominating speech was by Governor Freeman, who said his candidate was a "proven liberal" and a demonstrated leader who could win in November.

A new and unexpected favorite son developed during the long nominating process. He was Gov. Ross Barnett of Mississippi who chose Judge Tom Brady, author of "Black Monday," a book highly critical of the Supreme Courts' decision on racial segregation, to nominate him.

Mississippi leaders said the idea was to give Governor Barnett twenty-three complimentary votes on the first ballot

then swing into line with the rest of the South behind Senator Johnson.

Wires for Stevenson

Delegates reported an attempted telegraphic blitz for Mr. Stevenson, with thousands of telegrams urging his selection arriving while the nominating festivities were in progress. The clear signs also were that Stevenson fans had packed the galleries. He is perhaps stronger in Southern California than in any other place in the nation.

Governor Loveless withdrew as a candidate, after the demonstration in his favor, pointing out he already had seconded the nomination of Senator Kennedy.

"I am not running against John Kennedy, so I ask the chair to remove my name from nomination," Governor Loveless said.

This set off a demonstration by Kennedy supporters, as Governor Collins announced that no further consideration would be given to the Iowan's candidacy.

Mrs. Franklin D. Roosevelt touched off another wild demonstration as she entered the hall to take a balcony spectator's seat, interrupting the nominating speech for Governor Docking being made by Frank Theis, the Kansas Democratic chairman.

She was framed in a spotlight as she walked to her seat, and Governor Collins noted that the demonstration was in her honor.

"We hope you will come again, again and again," Governor Collins said.

The pro-Stevenson galleries roared with approval at Senator Eugene J. McCarthy's introduction of Mr. Stevenson.

The Minnesotan asked delegates to reconsider decisions taken earlier before "all the candidates" were in the race, and before the issues were clear.

"I say to all you candidates and spokesmen for candidates who say you are confident of your strength, let this go to a second ballot," Senator McCarthy said.

"Let it go to a second ballot when all of the delegates will be free of instructions," he added.

The cheers that went up were from the galleries and from the Stevenson demonstrators already lined up. The bulk of the delegates sat silent, or, occasionally, booed.

All-out Attack

The McCarthy speech was an all-out attack upon Senator Kennedy, using against him his own phrase about "a time for greatness."

"Power," the Minnesotan said, "is best exercised by those who are sought after.

"Do not reject this man who made us proud to be called Democrats."

"Do not reject this man who is not the favorite son of one state, but is the favorite son of fifty states and of every country on earth," Senator McCarthy said.

The big Stevenson demonstration that followed was dominated by outsiders who had infiltrated the convention hall. The great majority of delegates did not join the parading groups. It was the first major attempt of a gallery to blitz a convention since Wendell L. Willkie triumphed over other Republican hopefuls at Philadelphia in 1940.

Aided Movement

But once in the hall, Mr. Butler said, the Stevenson group sent the badges back out to others, until the police had counted as many as 450 outside demonstrators.

When the ten-minute time limit had expired, Governor Collins rapped repeatedly for order, and, in his anger, told the Stevenson demonstrators to keep on with their show "if you want the name of this convention associated with hoodlumism."

"We must stop this demonstration," Governor Collins exclaimed. "I am sure that if Governor Stevenson were here he would join me in telling you to end this demonstration."

Johnson is Nominated for Vice President; Kennedy Picks Him to Placate the South

CHOICE A SURPRISE

Senator Is Selected By Acclamation—Calls for Unity

By W.H. LAWRENCE

LOS ANGELES, July 14—Senator Lyndon B. Johnson of Texas was nominated for Vice President tonight by the Democratic National Convention as Senator John F. Kennedy's running mate.

Senator Johnson's was the only name placed in nomination. At 9:10 P.M. [12:10 A.M. Friday New York time] the convention suspended its rules and nominated him by acclamation. On a voice vote the roar of ayes far exceeded in volume the negative votes.

The Kennedy-Johnson ticket was ready to do battle with the Republican ticket, which will be headed by Vice President Nixon and will be chosen at the Republican National Convention opening July 25 in Chicago.

Kennedy's Choice

Senator Johnson was nominated on the recommendation of the Massachusetts Senator. Senator Kennedy overrode protests by labor and Northern liberals in the surprise move in naming the Senate majority leader for Vice President. The Texan's acceptance of second place was equally surprising.

Senator Kennedy, a Roman Catholic, moved boldly to win party unity

---

Opposite page:
Eleanor Roosevelt at the 1960 Democratic convention.

(Ed Clark/Time & Life Pictures/Getty Images)

and new strength below the Mason-Dixon Line by choosing the Texan, a Protestant, for his running mate.

The Presidential nominee is 43 years old, and his running mate is 51.

Until yesterday, they were bitter rivals for the Presidency. Senator Kennedy smashed to a first-ballot victory, polling 806 votes to 409 for Senator Johnson.

Convention Ends Today

Tomorrow, the two will accept their nominations formally at an open-air rally in the Coliseum, which seats more than 100,000 persons. That event formally ends the convention.

The Johnson choice was far from universally popular, but it satisfied the overwhelming majority of the delegates. As practical politicians, most leaders believed that Senator Johnson would add more strength to the Democratic ticket in the South than he would hurt it in the North. The choice was particularly offensive to leaders of Americans for Democratic Action. Negro leaders were divided, some favoring and some opposing Senator Johnson.

Gov. David L. Lawrence of Pennsylvania nominated Senator Johnson.

He hailed the Senator as the "strongest Democratic leader in the history of the United States Senate," and as one who had been, "the legislative ally of Franklin Roosevelt and Harry Truman." He noted that Senator Johnson had guided to passage the first "meaningful" civil rights bill in eighty years.

"Few men in this nation are as well informed on matters of national defense and world affairs as he is," Governor Lawrence said.

Senator Henry M. Jackson of Wash-

ington, who has been offered the post of Democratic National Chairman but has not yet accepted finally, and Representative William L. Dawson, of Illinois, a Negro leader in the Chicago area, made seconding speeches.

Senator Jackson said the Democrats were picking a strong ticket that would win in November. The Vice-Presidential choice, he said, had a great talent for legislative leadership and would be "Jack Kennedy's strong right arm" on Capitol Hill.

"Now is the time for the Democratic party to unite," he said.

Senator Johnson appeared before the convention after his nomination and said that the party must unite to win in November. Thanking the convention for his selection, he brought a cheer when he said, "And I congratulate you on your decision last night."

The Texan pledged warm and friendly cooperation with "the next President," Senator Kennedy. He said whatever capacities he might have were at Senator Kennedy's disposition.

Striking at the Republican Administration of President Eisenhower, Senator Johnson said the Kennedy Administration would offer bold new programs to bring the United States to "its only place—first place."

With the Senator were his wife, Lady Bird, and daughter, Lynda Byrd. They had been waiting in the wings just off the convention floor while the formalities of nomination were concluded.

Senator Johnson, runner-up to Senator Kennedy in yesterday's balloting for the Presidential candidacy, agreed to make the race for second place although he long had insisted that his powers and duties as Senate majority leader made that post more important than the Vice-Presidency.

The selection of Senator Johnson was urged upon Senator Kennedy by a coalition of powerful big state leaders, including New York, Pennsylvania, Illinois, Ohio, California and New Jersey.

Senator Kennedy said there had been "broad backing" for the Vice-

Presidential candidacies of Senator Stuart Symington of Missouri, Senator Jackson, Gov. Herschel C. Loveless of Iowa and Governor Freeman.

Gasps of surprise greeted the Johnson announcement at a news conference called by Senator Kennedy in the Biltmore Bowl just after 4 P. M.

The Massachusetts Senator emphasized that Senator Johnson was his personal choice and one that had been reviewed with "all elements" of the party leadership.

Senator Kennedy said the Texan had "earned the endorsement of all fifty states through his vigorous and positive leadership" in the Senate and in the House of Representatives before that.

"I have said many times that in these days of great challenge, Americans must have a Vice President capable of dealing with the grave problems confronting this nation and the free world," Senator Kennedy said. "We need men of strength if we are to be strong and if we are to prevail and lead the world on the road to freedom. Lyndon Johnson has demonstrated on many occasions his brilliant qualifications for the leadership we require today."

Also Sees Rayburn

A long series of huddles, including personal calls by Senator Kennedy upon Senator Johnson and his principal political ally, Speaker Sam Rayburn of Texas, preceded the selection of the Vice-Presidential nominee.

Many erroneously thought that Senator Kennedy's visits to Senator Johnson were simply courtesy moves after yesterday's Presidential balloting.

Senator Kennedy made it clear at once that he would like to have Senator Johnson for Vice President if the Texan would accept it.

Senator Johnson said he would. Then Senator Kennedy set out to survey party leadership opinion on the proposal. At one stage, the Johnson camp thought his selection had been vetoed by labor spokesmen, but Senator Kennedy insisted upon linking the Texan to his ticket.

But the big surprise was that Senator Johnson even would consider the Vice-Presidency, trading, as he had put it, a powerful position of leadership with voting power for the constitutionally limited task of presiding over the Senate with the right to vote only in cases of ties.

In the heat of the Presidential battle, Senator Johnson had struck desperate blows at Senator Kennedy, deploring his absenteeism in the Senate and his failure to vote to censure the late Senator Joseph R. McCarthy of Wisconsin. He also had aimed a heavy blow at Senator Kennedy's father, Joseph P. Kennedy. He implied that the latter had been friendly to the "appeasement" regimes of Prime Minister Neville Chamberlain, when Mr. Kennedy was Ambassador to Britain in the pre-World War II period, and that he had thought "Hitler was right."

Kennedy Calls for Sacrifices in U.S. to Help the World Meet Challenges of 'New Frontier'

NIXON IS ASSAILED

Johnson Joins Attack— Acceptance Talks Close Convention

By W.H. LAWRENCE

LOS ANGELES, July 15—Senator John F. Kennedy formally opened his Democratic Presidential campaign tonight with a warning that the national road to a "New Frontier" called for more sacrifices, not more luxuries.

He slashed at his probable Republican Presidential rival, as he joined with his surprise Vice-Presidential running mate, Senator Lyndon B. Johnson of Texas, in formally accepting nomination at the final session of the Democratic National Convention.

The 43-year-old Massachusetts Senator said that world and domestic challenges required new, positive answers to the unknown problems ahead. It is essential, he said, for Democrats to move beyond the New Deal and Fair Deal concepts.

'Challenges, Not Promises'

"Woodrow Wilson's New Freedom promised our nation a new political and economic framework," Senator Kennedy said. "Franklin Roosevelt's New Deal promised security and succor to those in need. But the New Frontier of which I speak is not a set of promises—it is a set of challenges.

"It sums up not what I intend to offer to the American people, but what I intend to ask of them. It appeals to their pride, it appeals to our pride, not our security—it holds out the promise of more sacrifice instead of more security "

"The New Frontier is here, whether we seek it or not.

"It would be easier to shrink from that frontier, to look to the safe mediocrity of the past, to be lulled with good and high rhetoric—and those who prefer that course should not vote for me or the Democratic party."

Senator Kennedy was interrupted by applause thirty-six times during his speech.

In accepting nomination, Senator Kennedy frankly raised the question of his Roman Catholic faith. He said that he recognized that many regarded this as a "new and hazardous risk" that Democrats had not taken since they last chose a Catholic, Alfred E. Smith, to head a ticket that lost in 1928. Mr. Kennedy denied that this was a risk. Then he said:

"But I look at it this way: The Democratic party has once again placed its confidence in the American people, and in their ability to render a free, fair judgment, and you have, at the same time, placed your confidence in me, and in my ability to render a free, fair judgment—to uphold the Constitution and my oath of office—and reject any kind of religious pressure or obligation that might directly or indirectly interfere with my conduct of the Presidency in the national interest. My record of fourteen years supporting public education—supporting complete separation of church and state—and resisting pressure from any source on any issue should be clear by now to everyone.

"I hope that no American, considering the really critical issues facing this country, will waste his franchise by voting either for me or against me solely on account of my religious affiliation."

Together, Senators Kennedy and Johnson proclaimed the need for party and national unity, and their own rapprochement from their fierce battle of this convention as a symbol of what they could do for the nation.

Vice President Nixon took the full brunt of the Democratic oratory.

Senator Kennedy said that the Nixon career was the direct antithesis of that of Abraham Lincoln in that Mr. Nixon often "seemed to show charity toward none and malice for all."

Senator Kennedy said that the millions of Americans who had voted for President Eisenhower well might conclude that Mr. Nixon "did not measure up to the footsteps of Dwight D. Eisenhower."

As a young Senator, the Democratic nominee insisted that the times called for young, new and vigorous leadership by men "who can cast off the old slogans and delusions and suspicions."

Likened to McKinley

"The Republican nominee-to-be, of course, is also a young man," he continued, "But his approach is as old as McKinley. His speeches are generalities from Poor Richard's Almanac."

But the Kennedy acceptance speech was much more than a partisan attack upon the Vice President and his Republican allies.

It was also a statement of the problems the Senator saw the nation and the world facing, a statement compressed by him into a description of the New Frontier.

It was a far sterner message than most of the political acceptance speeches of the past, which were designed largely to reflect partisan political appeals that would cheer the party's followers.

Senator Johnson, who had been Senator Kennedy's bitter foe for the Presidential nomination, emphasized the implications of his nomination for second place. He said that this action boded well for "a new day of hope and harmony for all Americans—regardless of religion, race or regions."

Senator Johnson provoked a roar of approval from the crowd of 50,000 when he moved that the nomination of Senator Kennedy be made unanimous. The crowd rose to its feet applauding.

★ ★ ★

"Woodrow Wilson's New Freedom promised our nation a new political and economic framework. Franklin Roosevelt's New Deal promised security and succor to those in need. But the New Frontier of which I speak is not a set of promises—it is a set of challenges. It sums up not what I intend to offer the American people, but what I intend to ask of them. It appeals to their pride, not to their pocketbook—it holds out the promise of more sacrifice instead of more security.

But I tell you the New Frontier is here, whether we seek it or not. Beyond that frontier are the uncharted areas of science and space, unsolved problems of peace and war, unconquered pockets of ignorance and prejudice, unanswered questions of poverty and surplus. It would be easier to shrink back from that frontier, to look to the safe mediocrity of the past, to be lulled by good intentions and high rhetoric—and those who prefer that course should not cast their votes for me, regardless of party."

Kennedy Versus Nixon

Southern Rebellion Hurts Senator Kennedy

By JAMES RESTON

WASHINGTON, Aug. 25—Anybody who doubts the depth and width of the split between the conservative Southern Democrats and their national leaders in the Presidential election need only study the Senate voting record in this recessed session of the Congress.

In vote after vote on both domestic and foreign policy issues, the objectives of Senator John F. Kennedy have been opposed by his Democratic colleagues from the South.

The key vote killing the "Social Security" approach to the problem of medical care for the nation's 16,000,000 old people was 51–44. Of the nineteen Democrats who voted with the Republicans against Kennedy on this measure, eighteen were from the South.

Similarly, the Southerners rejected his proposals on raising foreign aid appropriations, extending the coverage of higher minimum wages, approving a new aid program for Latin America, and ratifying the Antarctica treaty.

Sometimes, as in the old age medical assistance bill, the Southern opposition was enough to defeat the legislation supported by Senator Kennedy and the party's Senate majority leader and Vice-Presidential nominee, Senator Lyndon Johnson. Other times it was enough to weaken the force of the Kennedy-Johnson bills. And even the diluted or compromise bills which were finally passed could get the support of only a few Southern Democrats.

The Opposition Score

For example, of the nineteen Democrats who opposed the higher foreign aid appropriation, sixteen were Southerners. Of the sixteen Democrats who voted against passage of the watered-down minimum wage bill, thirteen came from the South. Meanwhile, by keeping "sentinels" on the Senate floor all the time to watch against parliamentary maneuvers for civil rights legislation, the Southern bloc imposed on the leadership a strategy of refusing to approve any civil rights legislation at this session.

In short, the opposition in the South toward the welfare state and foreign aid policies of the Democratic liberals has not been overcome by Kennedy's appeals for party unity in the campaign.

If anything, the split has widened since the party convention in Los Angeles. For the Southerners feel, with justification, that their views were ignored in the Democratic platform, and their attitude now is that since the liberals were not interested in party unity then, why expect party unity from the Southerners now?

Even if Senator Johnson had been nominated for the Presidency last month, the chances are that this same pattern of suspicious hostility toward big government, and big labor, and big foreign aid appropriations would have prevailed.

As the South's power over the party platform has waned, its regional patriotism has increased; as its industry has grown, its free trade spirit of the cotton and tobacco export days has dwindled.

The Southern Fears

There were many and diverse reasons for the Southern opposition to the Kennedy programs, some economic, some ideological, some personal.

Ever since Herman Talmadge demonstrated that the power of regional voters in Georgia could force the retirement of even so powerful a national figure as Senator Walter George, few Southern Senators have been willing to risk antagonizing the strong feelings of the voters back home.

They see larger and larger foreign aid bills producing new competition from overseas suppliers for the new industries of the South. They see the raising of the minimum wage as one more effort by the Northerners to prevent the shift of industry into the lower-wage areas of the South.

If this were the whole story, even Kennedy would not be too distressed. But the renewal of the religious issue and the determination and unity of the Southern opposition at this critical moment in Kennedy's campaign have raised the question whether the South is really prepared to help him win, or is willing to see him lose Virginia, North Carolina, Florida, Kentucky, Tennessee, Oklahoma and Texas, as Al Smith did in 1928.

Kennedy's aides do not think the outlook is that gloomy, but somehow they expected that the selection of Johnson as Vice-Presidential nominee would bring them through this session better than it has. Instead, regional loyalty has proved to be stronger than party loyalty, and the only surprising thing about that is that the Kennedy camp is surprised.

KENNEDY ASSURES TEXAS MINISTERS OF INDEPENDENCE

Says He'd Quit Presidency if Unable to Withstand Any Church Pressure

By W.H. LAWRENCE

HOUSTON, Tex., Sept. 12—Senator John F. Kennedy told Protestant ministers here tonight that he would resign as President if he could not make every decision in the national interest "without regard to outside religious pressures or dictates."

Senator Kennedy's address, to the Greater Houston Ministerial Association, was televised throughout Texas.

It constituted an affirmation of his belief in the separation of church and state. It was also his answer to critics who have sought to mobilize anti-Catholic sentiment against him by contending he would not resist church pressure on major issues.

"I do not speak for my church on public matters," Senator Kennedy declared, "and the church does not speak for me."

Would Ignore 'Pressures'

"Whatever issue may come before me as President—on birth control, divorce, censorship, gambling, or any other subject—I will make my decision in accordance with what my conscience tells me to be the national interest, and without regard to outside religious pressures or dictates."

Public officials, the Senator said, should not request or accept instruc-

Kennedy speaking to Protestant ministers in Houston. (Paul Schutzer/Time & Life Pictures/Getty Images)

tions on public policy directly or indirectly from the Pope, from the National Council of Churches, or from any other ecclesiastical source seeking to impose its will on the general public.

Mr. Kennedy said, "No power or threat of punishment could cause me" to deviate from the national interest.

No Conflict Seen

"But if the time should ever come—I do not concede any conflict to be even remotely possible—when my office would require me to either violate my conscience or violate the national interest," Senator Kennedy said, "then I would resign the office; and I hope any conscientious public servant would do the same."

Mr. Kennedy also struck at the group of Protestant clergymen, led by the Rev. Dr. Norman Vincent Peale, that has questioned his ability to withstand Roman Catholic pressures if he were President. Dr. Peale is minister of the Marble Collegiate Church in New York.

Such groups, Mr. Kennedy said, are working to "subvert" the declaration, in Article VI of the Constitution, that there shall be no religious test of office. They should be out openly working for repeal of Article VI, he said, rather than to change it by indirection.

The speech represented a major effort by Senator Kennedy to meet the religious issue head on. In it, he also continued to try to draw back into the Democratic party a segment of its membership, particularly in the South and the Midwest, that has made known its unwillingness to vote for a Catholic.

Asks Judging of Record

Mr. Kennedy asked voters to judge him on his public record from fourteen years of Congress. This record, he said, included his "declared stands against an Ambassador to the Vatican, against unconstitutional aid to parochial schools, and against any boycott of the public schools." He pointed out he had gone to public schools himself.

He said he believed that no Catholic

prelate should tell a President how to act and that no Protestant minister should tell his parishioners how to vote.

"This is the kind of America I believe in," he asserted, "and this is the kind of America I fought for in the South Pacific, and the kind my brother died for in Europe. No one suggested then that we might have a 'divided loyalty,' that we did 'not believe in liberty' or that we belonged to a disloyal group that threatened the 'freedoms for which our forefathers died.'"

The quotations Mr. Kennedy cited were from the manifesto of the Peale group, which calls itself the National Conference for Religious Freedom.

Controversy Recalled

One passage in Senator Kennedy's speech bore on a controversy with another clergyman, the Rev. Dr. Daniel Poling, a Baptist and former unsuccessful Republican candidate for Mayor of Philadelphia. It concerns his not participating in 1947 in the dedication of the Chapel of the Four Chaplains. The chapel is an interfaith memorial in the Temple Baptist Church in Philadelphia.

It honors four Protestant, Catholic and Jewish chaplains who perished together on a Navy ship during World War II, giving up their chances of survival in favor of others. One of the victims was Dr. Poling's son.

Dr. Poling has asserted that Mr. Kennedy was forced by pressure from the late Dennis Cardinal Dougherty to decline an invitation he originally had accepted.

Senator Kennedy explained before the National Press Club last January that he canceled his appearance when he learned that the chapel was in a Protestant church. Thus, he said, the Catholic altar could not be consecrated under the tenets of his church, which does not participate with other faiths in religious ceremonies.

★ ★ ★

"But because I am a Catholic, and no Catholic has ever been elected President, the real issues in this campaign have been obscured . . .

So it is apparently necessary for me to state once again—not what kind of church I believe in, for that should be important only to me—but what kind of America I believe in.

. . . I believe in an America where religious intolerance will someday end—where all men and all churches are treated as equal—where every man has the same right to attend or not attend the church of his choice—where there is no Catholic vote, no anti-Catholic vote . . . and where Catholics, Protestants and Jews . . . will refrain from those attitudes of disdain and division which have so often marred their works in the past, and promote instead the American ideal of brotherhood."

———

NIXON AND KENNEDY CLASH IN TV DEBATE ON SPENDING, FARMS AND SOCIAL ISSUES EXCHANGE IS CALM

Sharp Retorts Are Few as Candidates Meet Face to Face

By RUSSELL BAKER

CHICAGO, Sept. 26—Vice President Nixon and Senator John F. Kennedy argued genteelly tonight in history's first nationally televised debate between Presidential candidates.

The two men, confronting each other in a Chicago television studio, centered their argument on which candidate and which party offered the nation the best means for spurring United States growth in an era of international peril.

The candidates, without ever generating any real heat in their exchanges, clashed on the following points:

Mr. Nixon's farm program, which Senator Kennedy said was merely another version of policies that had been tried and had failed under Ezra Taft Benson, Secretary of Agriculture.

The Republican and Democratic performance records on efforts to increase the minimum wage of $1 an hour and broaden its coverage, school construction legislation and medical care for the aged. Mr. Kennedy charged that the Republican record on these measures showed the party gave only "lip service" to them.

The comparative records of the Truman and Eisenhower Administrations on fiscal security. Mr. Nixon asserted that in school and hospital construction the Republican years had seen an improvement over the previous seven Democratic years. Moreover, he said, wages had risen "five times as much" in the Eisenhower Administration as during the Truman Administration, while the rise in prices has been only one-fifth of that in the Truman years.

In one of the sharper exchanges of the hour-long encounter, Mr. Nixon charged that the Democratic domestic program advanced by Senator Kennedy would cost the taxpayer from $13,200,000,000 to $18,000,000,000.

This meant, Mr. Nixon contended, that "either he will have to raise taxes or you have to unbalance the budget."

Unbalancing the budget, he went on, would mean another period of inflation and a subsequent "blow" to the country's aged living on pension income.

"That," declared Senator Kennedy, in one of the evening's few shows of incipient heat, "is wholly wrong wholly in error." Mr. Nixon, he said, was attempting to create the impression that he was "in favor of unbalancing the budget."

In fact, Mr. Kennedy contended, many of his programs for such things as medical care for the aged, natural resources development, Federal assistance to school construction and teachers' salaries could be financed without undue burden on the taxpayer if his policies for increasing the rate of economic growth were adopted.

"I don't believe in big government, but I believe in effective government," Mr. Kennedy said. "I think we can do a better job. I think we are going to have to do a better job."

Continuing his portrayal of the Eisenhower years as a period of stagnation, he asserted that the United States last year had the lowest rate of economic growth of any industrial state in the world. Steel production, he noted, was only 50 percent of capacity. The Soviet Union, he said, is "turning out twice as many engineers as we are."

At the present rate of hydroelectric-power construction, he went on, the Soviet Union would be "producing more power than we are," by 1975.

"I think it's time America started moving again," he declared.

Nixon Disagrees

Mr. Nixon replied that he had no quarrel with Mr. Kennedy's goal of increasing the rate of national growth. But, he said, Mr. Kennedy's statistics showing a slow growth rate last year were misleading because they were based on activity in a recession year. This year, by contrast, the rate is 6.9 percent: "one of the highest in the world," he said.

In other areas of debate, these were the major points:

Mr. Nixon asserted that Senator Kennedy's failure to get any significant part of his program enacted at the August session of Congress was not due to President Eisenhower's threatened vetoes but to lack of national support for items in the program. It was "not because the President was against them," Mr. Nixon said. "It was because the people were against them. They were too extreme."

Mr. Kennedy answered Mr. Nixon's frequently repeated campaign assertion that he was too immature for the Presidency by asserting that Abraham Lincoln had come out of obscurity, as an inexperienced Congressman, to the White House. He and Mr. Nixon had "both come to Congress together" in the same year—1946, Mr. Kennedy noted.

"Our experience in government is comparable." And, he contended, "there is no certain road to the Presidency. There is no guarantee that if you choose one road or the other you will be a successful President."

Mr. Nixon, using the only language heard all evening that bordered on the colorful, contrasted the Republican program for national growth with Mr. Kennedy's in these terms. Mr. Kennedy's, he said, "seem to be simply retreads of programs of the Truman Administration."

For the most part, the exchanges were distinguished by a suavity, earnestness and courtesy that suggested that the two men were more concerned about "image projection" to their huge television audience than about scoring debating points.

Senator Kennedy, using no television makeup, rarely smiled during the hour and maintained an expression of gravity suitable for a candidate for the highest office in the land.

Mr. Nixon, wearing pancake makeup to cover his dark beard, smiled more frequently as he made his points and dabbed frequently at the perspiration that beaded out on his chin.

The debate was carried simultaneously by all three major television networks, the American Broadcasting Company, the National Broadcasting Company and the Columbia Broadcasting System. It was also carried by the radio networks of all three and that of the Mutual Broadcasting System.

The first debate, produced by C. B. S., took place in a big studio at the C. B. S. Chicago outlet, Station WBBM-TV. Studio One, in which they met, was sealed off from the hundreds who swarmed through its corridors and sat in adjoining studios to watch the show on station monitors.

When the debate was over, the two candidates were spirited out of the studio through a freight driveway.

Nixon Noncommittal

At his hotel later, Mr. Nixon was noncommittal about how well he thought he had done. "A debater," he said, "never knows who wins. That will be decided by the people Nov. 8."

Mr. Kennedy was not available for comment, but his advisers said they were elated over his performance.

The only persons permitted in the studio besides television crewmen were two wire service reporters, three photographers and one aide to each candidate.

When the show ended, each man was asked how he felt about the outcome.

"A good exchange of views," said Mr. Nixon.

"We had an exchange of views," Mr. Kennedy agreed.

Under the rules agreed upon by the candidates, each man opened with an eight-minute exposition of his general position on domestic affairs.

This was followed by about thirty-five minutes of question-and-answer with the questions being put by four television newsmen selected by each of the four networks. This was followed by three-minute closing statements by each candidate.

The television news representatives on the panel were Sander Vanocur of N.B.C., Robert Fleming of A.B.C., Charles Warren of Mutual and Stuart Novins of C.B.S. Howard K. Smith of the C.B.S. Washington staff acted as moderator, but except for introducing the two, had a quiet evening.

Senator Kennedy and Richard Nixon debating in a Chicago television studio on September 26, 1960. (Paul Schutzer/Time & Life Pictures/Getty Images)

Opposite page:
The first televised presidential debate drew 70 million viewers.

(Time & Life Pictures/Getty Images)

BOTH CANDIDATES RETAIN BACKERS

Most Viewers Call Kennedy the 'Winner'—Many Say Nixon Looked Unwell

Following is a special election campaign report by The New York Times.

Sept. 27—Neither Vice President Nixon or Senator John F. Kennedy seems to have captured an appreciable number of voters from the other as a result of their face-to-face debate on television Monday night.

A sampling of public opinion throughout the country yesterday by The New York Times brought the clear indication that members of the television audience still held to their previous convictions.

Those who had been for Senator Kennedy before the debate were still for him, and the Vice President's adherents were also standing fast.

More than 360 persons—including Republican and Democratic voters, local leaders of both parties and "men in the street"—were interviewed in thirty widely scattered cities.

One Switch Disclosed

Of all these, only one said his allegiance had been changed through watching the debate. He was a janitor in Topeka, Kan., a regular Republican who was won over by the Democratic candidate's performance

Only two of the undecided voters said the show had made up their minds.

One was a Wisconsin farmer who supported President Eisenhower in the last two elections but was undecided about this election. After watching the two candidates on television, he decided to vote for the Democrat.

The other was an investigator for the District Attorney in Denver, who was also persuaded by Senator Kennedy.

Kennedy Called Winner

Although each candidate held the loyalty of his adherents, a majority of those canvassed indicated that Senator Kennedy had turned in a better performance. These included Republicans and a few of that party's leaders.

The Democratic leaders who were questioned were unanimous in their enthusiasm for their standard-bearer as a television star. A telegram to Senator Kennedy by Michael H. Prendergast, Democratic chairman of New York State, was typical. It said, in part:

"Congratulations upon a magnificent presentation of the views of the Democratic party. We are more certain

The fourth and final televised debate was in New York City on October 21, 1960. (Associated Press)

than ever that the people will show their appreciation of your courageous and sound position."

Many Republicans said the same of the Vice President. But the significant difference was that more than a few Republicans were willing to settle for a "draw" or a "stand-off."

Hope to Win Next One

Some conceded that Senator Kennedy had come off better, contenting themselves with the hope that Mr. Nixon would win the next debate.

For example, Patrick J. Hillings, Republican chairman of Los Angeles County, said:

"The general reaction from our party's leaders is surprise at Kennedy's able performance. We had a feeling that per-

haps the Vice President was not as aggressive in carrying the case to him. When Nixon can discuss foreign policy, it will put Kennedy more on the defensive."

Among individual voters, Walter R. Charles Jr., a salesman in Richmond, Va., and a Republican still for Mr. Nixon, said "Kennedy sold himself and got the better of it by a slim margin."

"He was definite, sure of himself and sharper," he said.

Nashville Reactions

In Nashville, Tenn., seven of eight voters who gave opinions on the debate thought Senator Kennedy had won the debate. This majority included Louis R. Farber, a sales manager who still intends to vote for Mr. Nixon, and Mrs.

Charles H. Lehning, a housewife and a Republican, who said: "Kennedy got the best of it; he came right back with his answers."

Republicans who commented concentrated on what they thought was the principal weakness in Senator Kennedy's argument—that he could finance a greater social welfare program without raising taxes or unbalancing the budget.

State Senator John H. Cooke, Republican chairman of Erie County (Buffalo), N. Y., said:

"The Vice President certainly presented a much more sensible program. Despite Kennedy's insistence to the contrary, his programs would lead to higher taxes, deficit financing, or both."

Looking Back

70 Million See First Televised Debate

By Alessandra Stanley

The candidates differed over taxes, the role of government and rather quaintly—given the current size and longevity of the federal deficit—the risks of "unbalancing" the budget.

Few people really remember what John F. Kennedy and Richard M. Nixon argued about in their first debate in 1960, but that encounter endures as one of those indelible milestones—like The Beatles on *The Ed Sullivan Show* or the first lunar landing—that, for better or for worse, changed the nation. Their hour-long debate in Chicago, in a drab, unadorned television studio that could pass for a bomb shelter, was the nation's first televised presidential debate. It forever shaped the way campaigns are run and the way people vote.

But not, as some would have it, for the worse.

That first debate—they held four—is often held up as the moment when electoral politics turned into a television reality show, a contest that favors looks, money and style over experience and ability. But actually, television was already turning out to be an essential and reductive tool of politics. John Kennedy may have perfected the art of courting the camera, but predecessors as far back as Franklin Delano Roosevelt had understood its potential—FDR was the first president to make a televised speech in 1939, at the New York City World's Fair. Harry S. Truman gave the first White House presidential address in 1947, asking Americans to support his relief plans for Europe after World War II.

In 1950, only one of ten households had a television; by 1960, nine out of ten did. By agreeing to a series of televised debates, Kennedy and Nixon set a precedent that was not mandated by law but that over time became ironclad.

Imagery can trump eloquence in television debates, but it can't mask blunders or personality. Especially now, when candidates are so hidden by political ads, scripted spontaneity and stump speech stagecraft, debates are a voter's last chance to watch a potential president perform without a net. And despite all the hindsight lore about five o'clock shadows and Camelot glamour, Kennedy and Nixon were evenly matched, and neither won hands down. Debates don't favor style over substance; they put style in the service of substance.

Jack Gould, then *The New York Times'* television critic, called the debate "a dignified and constructive innovation." (Though he couldn't resist a dig at the panel of journalists, saying that the questions of Sander Vanocur and others "contained the inevitable pear-shaped overtones of the electronic journalist.")

The first was an experiment so novel that it drew an estimated 70 million viewers out of a population of 179 million; more than 70 million tuned in for the second one, and that match still holds the record—more than 61 percent of television households watched it, a larger share of the American audience than for any other debate, including 1980, 2008 and 2012.

Audiences could be expected to grow more blasé, but they haven't. Nielsen estimated that 67.2 million households watched the first debate between President Barack Obama and Mitt Romney, and that figure doesn't include viewers who watched in offices, bars, on the Internet or even on their phones; the more likely figure is 70 million, less than the Super Bowl, but not by nearly as much as cynics could expect. In an age of balkanized viewing, when audiences are overwhelmed with niche choices, a few big spectacles still draw mass audiences. Debates, however, aren't a football game or a singing contest; there is prosaic civic duty beneath all the suspense and drama.

The innovation didn't become practice overnight. Presidential candidates didn't debate in the elections of 1964, 1968 or 1972 (though there were some notable primary matches, including one between Democratic candidates Robert F. Kennedy and Eugene McCarthy in 1968.)

It wasn't until 1976, when Jimmy Carter challenged President Gerald Ford, that a series of debates next pitted the nominees of the two parties against each other.

One reason that it took three election cycles to restore debates to the political process could be that they so often benefit the challenger. Nixon, who had been vice president for eight years under Dwight D. Eisenhower, should have had the advantage of familiarity and experience over Kennedy. Legend has it that those who followed the debate on radio felt Nixon won on points. But on camera that first time he looked shifty, pale and sweaty; he also sounded apologetic and oddly deferential to his opponent, as if already convinced in his mind that viewers favored the handsome, wealthy senator from Massachusetts.

Russell Baker, as a reporter for the *Times*, described the candidates' positions about the economy and the space race with Soviet Union and didn't get around to the glaring appearance gap until the end of his article.

"Senator Kennedy, using no television makeup, rarely smiled during the hour and maintained an expression of gravity suitable for a candidate for the highest office in the land," Baker wrote. "Mr. Nixon, wearing pancake makeup to cover his dark beard, smiled more frequently as he made his points and dabbed frequently at the perspiration that beaded out on his chin."

By the next debate, print journalists—like Mr. Nixon—caught up with the importance of camera-readiness. One entire *New York Times* story described how the two candidates' aides lobbied for adjustments in lighting and room temperature and evaluated the skill of "makeup artists and lighting experts."

James Reston deemed their performances equally persuasive, and used the term "Churchillian gloom" to describe Kennedy's warnings about the threat from Soviet Premier Nikita Khrushchev. (Nowadays, writers are more apt to cite Churchill's optimism and fortitude during World War II than the tone of his 1946 Iron Curtain speech, but this was the Cold War era.)

Presidential candidates debate less now—and with a lot more preparation and less substance and specificity. But they still do it because it's almost impossible to refuse, and those encounters can still spark the most revealing moments in a campaign.

Jack Gould called the debate a "public service," and his explanation still stands. "The main advantage in the home was the opportunity to match opposing views on the same issue at the same time."

Alessandra Stanley is the chief television critic of *The New York Times.*

NIXON AND KENNEDY CLASH ON TV OVER ISSUE OF QUEMOY'S DEFENSE; U–2 'REGRETS' AND RIGHTS ARGUED

EXCHANGES SHARP

Senator Is Accused of 'Woolly Thinking'—He, Too, Is Tough

By RUSSELL BAKER

WASHINGTON, Oct. 7—Vice President Nixon and Senator John F. Kennedy raised the campaign temperature tonight, clashing sharply on foreign policy and civil rights in the second of their nation-wide television debates.

The question of who won will have to await the surveys of voters, but the equally nagging question for Republicans—of how Mr. Nixon would "project" after his unhappy appearance in the first debate—was answered immediately. The Vice President did not have the thin, emaciated appearance that worried Republicans across the nation during the first debate.

One of the high points of tonight's debate was a direct conflict between the Presidential candidates over policy for dealing with the islands of Quemoy and Matsu off the Chinese mainland.

Criticizes Vagueness

Mr. Kennedy took the position that the islands were militarily worthless and, lying virtually in a harbor on the

Senator Kennedy and Vice President Nixon prior to their first televised debate. (Paul Schutzer/Time & Life Pictures/Getty Images)

Communist mainland, were indefensible.

Moreover, he said, Administration vagueness about whether the islands would be defended in case of Communist attack created a dangerous uncertainty for the Chinese about this country's intentions. While Taiwan (Formosa) should certainly be defended, he indicated, he favored a pullback from Quemoy and Matsu by the Chinese Nationalists.

Mr. Nixon denounced this as "the same kind of woolly thinking that led to disaster in Korea." He insisted that the islands should be held. "These two islands are in the area of freedom," he said. To give them up, he argued, would only encourage the Communists to press their drive on Taiwan.

The question was not of "two tiny pieces of real estate," he said, but a matter of principle.

Johnson Is Nixon Target

In a long-running exchange over civil rights, Mr. Nixon denounced the Democratic Vice-Presidential candidate, Senator Lyndon B. Johnson of Texas, as a man who had voted against most of the civil rights proposals in the Democratic platform and "who opposes them at the present time."

Although Mr. Johnson contends that, as Democratic Senate leader, he is responsible for the only two civil rights bills to be enacted since the Reconstruction period after the Civil War, Mr. Kennedy did not expand on this issue.

Instead, Mr. Kennedy charged that the Republican Administration had given no leadership to enforce the Supreme Court's school-desegregation decision of 1954. He also accused the Administration of lacking "vigor" in ending job discrimination.

The two men also clashed on the Administration's handling of the U-2 espionage flight over the Soviet Union on May 1. Mr. Kennedy charged that the Vice President had "distorted" his comment that this Government might have expressed "regrets" to Moscow if such

action could have saved the Paris summit meeting of May 16.

In fact, Mr. Kennedy said, diplomatic "regrets" were accepted practice on such occasions. They were routinely sent to Cuba last winter and to the Soviet Government after an American plane flew over Russian territory two years ago, he declared.

Mr. Nixon replied that Senator Kennedy was "wrong on three counts." He was wrong in suggesting that an expression of official "regrets" might have saved the summit, Mr. Nixon said. Mr. Khrushchev, he asserted, was determined to destroy the conference and merely used the U-2 case as a pretext to do so.

Calls Analogy Wrong

Second, he went on, Mr. Kennedy was "wrong in the analogy he makes." When this country did "something that is wrong, we can express regrets," he said. But the U-2 flight had been "right" because its purpose was to defend the country against surprise attack, and it should not apologize for doing what is "right," he said.

Third, he said, "we all remember Pearl Harbor." The lesson was that "we cannot afford an intelligence gap," Mr. Nixon said. Therefore, intelligence operations had to be continued without apology, he concluded.

The two candidates divided over the Eisenhower Administration's policies on Cuba. Mr. Nixon insisted that Cuba was not lost and that the Administration was following the proper course to see that the Cuban people "get a chance to realize their aspirations of progress through freedom."

He described Senator Kennedy's assertions that Cuba was lost as "defeatist talk." In fact, he said, if Mr. Kennedy wanted to compare the number of dictators bred under the Truman and Eisenhower Administrations in Latin America, he would find that eleven were ruling in Latin America under President Truman while only three remained today.

Senator Kennedy replied that he had "never suggested that Cuba was lost, except for the present." He criticized the Administration for not using "its great influence to persuade the Cuban Government to hold free elections." In 1957 and 1958, he said, he expressed the hope that Cuba would rise, but "I don't think it will rise if we continue the same policies toward Cuba that we did in recent years."

To what extent substantive points of debate affect a huge viewing audience like tonight's is a moot point among politicians, but all were intensely interested in the battle of "images."

The question as the show opened was how the two candidates would "project." That is, would television distort one man to the advantage of the other?

Mr. Nixon's advisers have argued for two weeks that the camera distorted his appearance during the first debate in Chicago Sept. 26. Great pains were taken to improve the "image" he would project tonight.

Nixon More Aggressive

In addition, Mr. Nixon, whose Chicago appearance was criticized by many Republicans as too agreeable toward Mr. Kennedy's policies, was consciously more aggressive tonight.

The result was a considerably different television "image" of the Vice President than was projected from Chicago. Mr. Kennedy, whose advisers regarded the Chicago show as a triumph of "image" projection, maintained the style he used so successfully there.

Neither man smiled at any time during the hour-long show. Each repeatedly accused the other of distorting the record and resorting to inaccuracies.

Both men were earnest. Mr. Kennedy seemed to start off with more assurance. Mr. Nixon appeared slightly tense at the start and stumbled on a few of his early sentences.

But as the debate progressed he seemed to gather assurance. Toward the close he went after Mr. Kennedy with gusto on the issue of Quemoy and Matsu.

Tonight's program consisted entirely of answers to questions from a panel of four newsmen. As in Chicago, the questions were rotated between the candidates. Each man had two-and-one-half minutes to answer and his opponent had a minute-and-a-half to rebut.

Thirteen questions were posed to the candidates. Eight dealt with foreign policy and five with domestic affairs or campaign tactics. Two of the domestic questions concerned civil rights.

Mr. Nixon listed three civil rights areas that he considered acute—jobs, school integration and the sit-in demonstrations to end discrimination at lunch counters in privately owned stores.

On jobs, he said, the President's Committee for Equality of Employment Under Government Contracts—now operating under Presidential appoint-ment—should be given statutory authority by Congress.

On schools, he said, Congress should provide Federal assistance for school districts desiring to make the transition from segregated to integrated facilities.

On sit-ins, he said, "we have to look to Presidential leadership." Lunch-counter discrimination in stores that sell Negroes other merchandise over the counter "is wrong, and we have to do something about it," he said.

"Mr. Nixon hasn't discussed the two basic questions," Mr. Kennedy countered.

Cites Court Decision

These, he said, were what the President would do to enforce the Supreme Court's decision of 1954 and how he would end job discrimination. President Eisenhower, he noted, had consistently refused to say whether he even thought the court decision was right.

And, he added, though Mr. Nixon now heads the President's Committee on Government Contracts, only two actions have been successfully brought in its lifetime to end discrimination by employers under Federal contract.

Mr. Nixon struck back hard with a personal blow at Senator Johnson, with a sarcastic reference to a Kennedy campaign song, "High Hopes."

"Senator Kennedy has expressed some high hopes in this field," he said. "But let's look at the performance. When he selected his Vice-Presidential running mate he selected a man who had voted against most of these proposals and a man who opposes them at the present time."

Following spread:
A political rally in New York City
for John F. Kennedy in October 1960.
(Walter Sanders/Time & Life Pictures/
Getty Images)

Huge crowds greet Kennedy's motorcade as it makes its way through the streets of New York. (The New York Times)

Kennedy Steps Up Attacks On Nixon

Senator Draws Big Crowds in Western Pennsylvania—Ridicules Opponent

By RUSSELL BAKER

JOHNSTOWN, Pa., Oct. 15—Senator John F. Kennedy bombarded Vice President Nixon today with his strongest attacks of the campaign so far.

Campaigning through Western Pennsylvania, the Democratic Presidential candidate suggested that his opponent's attitude on Quemoy and Matsu would take this country into war on the Chinese mainland.

In an area where unemployment is running high, he charged Mr. Nixon and the Republican party with following a policy of "indifference" toward the jobless and those "too young to retire, too young to die, too old to work."

He ridiculed Mr. Nixon as a man whose political philosophy seemed to shift from month to month, one who posed now as "a practical progressive," now as "an economic conservative."

"What is Mr. Nixon, anyhow?" he asked as a huge crowd in New Castle screamed its approval. It would be helpful to the electorate, he added, if Mr. Nixon "will make up his mind what he is."

Which Nixon would Republicans be voting for? he asked. "The practical progressive? the outspoken conservative? the old Nixon? the new Nixon? the modern Republican? the old-fashioned Republican?"

He also hit hard on the Cuban question. Mr. Nixon, he stated tonight in Johnstown, "talks about standing firm in the Far East, but he never mentions standing firm in Cuba."

"If you can't stand up to Castro, how can you be expected to stand up to Khrushchev?" he asked.

Even Mr. Nixon's use of television make-up was used as Mr. Kennedy poured on the scorn and ridicule. In Sharon this morning, the Senator recalled that he had debated labor policy in this area with Mr. Nixon in the late Nineteen Forties. "He did not wear make-up on that occasion," Mr. Kennedy said, "but regardless whether make-up is changed or lighting is changed, Mr. Nixon remains the same."

Working hard on the theme that the Republicans are adjusting their principles and pledges for political expediency, the Senator even got in a thrust at Henry Cabot Lodge, Mr. Nixon's running-mate.

A crowd in central Pennsylvania listening to Senator Kennedy speaking at a campaign event. (George Tames/The New York Times)

Enthusiastic young female supporters of Democratic presidential candidate John F. Kennedy. (Paul Schutzer/Time & Life Pictures/Getty Images)

"Mr. Lodge made a speech one day in the North pledging a Negro in the Cabinet," he said in Beaver Falls, "and the next day he said he had no right to make any pledges when he was down South." Mr. Nixon, he went on, sent Senator Barry Goldwater "down South to talk about civil rights and say he does not mean anything by it, and then he sent Senator [Hugh] Scott to the North to assure the Negroes he is with them all the way."

1948 Recalled

The vigor of Mr. Kennedy's assaults on the Vice President today was reminiscent of the fury of Harry S. Truman's successful campaign against former Gov. Thomas E. Dewey in 1948. In neither of the campaigns since has either candidate dealt such direct personal criticism at the other. The Kennedy barrage was laid down as he campaigned by motorcade with speeches in seven towns around Pittsburgh, and drives through dozens of small ones along the way.

The speeches were made at Sharon, New Castle, Beaver Falls, Butler, and Kittanning, with appearances tonight in Indiana and Johnstown. Crowds were big and enthusiastic at each stop and streets in towns along the route were so packed that the candidate's motor caravan was brought to a halt while people pressed around to shake hands or simply touch his. In New Brighton later, the Senator kissed his first baby of the campaign, 7-month-old Annette Luci of Beaver Falls. The Senator's car had stopped to take on a box of fruit offered by a woman in the street, and as he put it in the car, the child's mother offered her up for kissing.

Kisses Baby

Mr. Kennedy took the child, bussed her lightly on the cheek and moved on. The candidate arrived at Sharon at 3 o'clock this morning after a whistle-stop trip through Republican districts of Michigan that left his advisers highly encouraged about his chances of carrying that state.

Mr. Kennedy took up the Quemoy-Matsu issue immediately with his speech in New Castle. Mr. Nixon has said he would make it a major issue of the campaign, he noted. He would be "delighted" to deal with it as such, the Senator continued.

"If Mr. Nixon wants to engage the United States in military action four miles from the mainland of China," he said, "I will talk about it from now on."

"But I also want him to come here to New Castle to talk about Cuba, ninety miles off the coast of the United States. I want him to talk about what is happening to this country."

He went on:

"I am not so anxious that he take us into military action on the mainland of China as I am that we maintain our commitments; that we maintain our freedom." He referred to his own wartime record in combat with the Navy.

"I spent long enough in the Pacific Ocean to know the difficulties with which Mr. Nixon is now facing the United States if he has his way," he said.

"And I do not want any young man in this community involved in a military action on islands not worth the bones of a single American soldier."

Nixon Drives for Independent Vote; Kennedy Seeks to Remake F.D.R. Coalition

By W.H. LAWRENCE

SPRINGFIELD, Ill., Oct. 15—With little more than three weeks to go before the Nov. 8 election date, the Presidential campaign strategies of Republican Vice President Nixon and Democratic Senator John F. Kennedy still remain fluid and subject to change without notice.

Each candidate is saying the final election outcome will be close, and neither is entirely convinced that he has a surefire, demonstrable pattern of victory to make him the certain occupant of the White House after Jan. 20.

A George Washington statue wearing a John Kennedy hat. (Paul Schutzer/ Time & Life Pictures/Getty Images)

One thing is certain: the campaign is moving into a freewheeling, harder-hitting slugging-match, with an intensity and vigor far above the level that had prevailed from Labor Day until now. With the indicated close result, both candidates obviously felt that a big "break" for one or the other could determine the outcome.

Both thought they had met head-to-head this week on an issue that might provide the big advantage for one or the other Presidential candidate. The issue was the defense of the tiny islands of Quemoy and Matsu, held by the Chinese Nationalists a few miles off the mainland of Communist-ruled China.

Potent Medicine

Both thought it might be potent medicine in the states with the big prizes of electoral votes—New York (45), Pennsylvania (32), California (32), Illinois (27), Ohio (25), and Michigan (20)—on which both will concentrate most heavily in the immediate pre-election period on the obvious theory that these states must provide the key to victory for any candidate however well he may do elsewhere.

But where Mr. Nixon regards foreign policy as the No. 1 issue, these highly industrialized states, plus New England, also contain major pockets of unemployment—a domestic issue on which Senator Kennedy figures to capitalize heavily.

Aside from states that are both industrial and agricultural in an important sense—such as California, Ohio, Indiana and Illinois—both candidates have about completed their farm-belt tours, and their espousal of new Federal farm programs.

So far as the Midwest is concerned, most Republicans agree that Mr. Nixon's chances of victory depend on two factors: (1) how far he successfully has divorced himself from Secretary Benson by snubbing him politically outside of Utah and (2) the anti-Kennedy vote stirred up by anti-Catholic forces in an area where Protestants predominate.

The usually Democratic South—the solidarity of which was fractured by the Republicans in the 1928 campaign against Alfred E. Smith, a wet and a Catholic, and in two campaigns by President Eisenhower—presents campaign problems for both Senator Kennedy and Mr. Nixon this year.

The heart of the Nixon strategy is to be found in his persistent appeal for the votes of Democrats and independents because of his recognition that the Republican party, nationally, is in the minority and that he could not be elected with Republican votes alone. He has yet to demonstrate that he can cut across party lines with the success demonstrated by President Eisenhower in the last two elections. Every crowd, large and small, is exhorted to put country and individual ahead of party in choosing a President in 1960. His aides thought he added important ammunition for his bipartisan drive when he announced from Beverly Hills, Calif., Friday night that President Eisenhower had agreed, on leaving the White House, to continue as a close Nixon adviser and to continue his work for world peace.

Nixon's Problems

But while Mr. Nixon pushes these efforts, he is not without his problems with the Republican right-wing—a needed source of campaign funds and a bloc of votes that might stay home in pique on Election Day even if it did not

Senator John F. Kennedy waving from his car during his campaign in New York City, 1960. (Patrick Burns/*The New York Times*)

shift to the Democrats. Senator Barry Goldwater of Arizona is the foremost spokesman for this right-wing bloc, and he has been critical of some of Mr. Nixon's campaign positions. It was to appease this section of the Republican party that Mr. Nixon let it be known this week he had departed from the Eisenhower Administration recommendation for outright repeal of the Connally amendment to United States ratification of the World Court statute.

Yet the Vice President could not move greatly to the right without losing Republican liberal support, especially in key areas like New York. The electoral college arithmetic is such that no Republican can hope to win without New York. Democratic candidates, working from a substantial but not always solid Southern base, have won without New York.

Like F.D.R.

Senator Kennedy's strategy is basically that followed by the late Franklin D. Roosevelt when he wedded the Democratic liberals from the North with their big blocs of electoral votes to the conservatives of the South. This was part of his reasoning in selecting Senator Lyndon B. Johnson of Texas, the Senate majority leader, as his Vice-Presidential running mate but on a platform that met every "liberal" demand of the North. The Massachusetts Senator, a Roman Catholic, reasons that the religious issue of anti-Catholicism may cost him some Southern states and possibly some Midwestern states, but he also believes that the religious issue may work to his benefit in the big industrial states of the North. Certainly it should bring back to the Democratic party many Catholics who have been voting Republican since about 1940.

The Democratic aim is to revive the farmer-labor alliance fashioned by F. D. R. in the depression-ridden Nineteen Thirties, and there are more than a few signs that Senator Kennedy is making progress in this direction.

MASS DISTRIBUTION OF ANTI-CATHOLIC LITERATURE PLANNED IN LAST DAYS OF CAMPAIGN

Vast Anti-Catholic Drive Is Slated Before Election

By JOHN WICKLEIN

Oct. 16—Many conservative Protestant churchmen are planning mass distribution of anti-Catholic literature in the last ten days of the Presidential campaign in a bid to defeat Senator John F. Kennedy. The mailings and handouts will be spurred by sermons and rallies on Reformation Sunday, Oct. 30, when Protestant feeling is at its highest.

"Five days before the election," said Harvey H. Springer, the "cowboy evangelist" of the Rockies, "I'm releasing 1,500,000 volunteer workers to call on voters and give them our literature on Kennedy. I have a secret little letter that I think is going to defeat him."

His optimism is matched only by his enthusiasm for his goal: to keep any Roman Catholic from being elected President of the United States—ever.

Many Protestants Irked

Others in the religious mail campaign are more selective, but their object now is similar: to keep a specific Catholic, the Democratic nominee, from entering the White House next January.

The recent public retreat of the Rev. Dr. Norman Vincent Peale from the religious issue appeared to have turned the tide against those who wished to use Mr. Kennedy's Catholicism politically.

But the furor over Dr. Peale angered many militant Protestants. It turned them from public statements to a quietly determined drive to saturate the country with literature on the issue "before it is too late."

The distributions are being planned and carried out not by political but by religious organizations, both genuine and spurious, all of which have some basis in Protestantism.

The size and sponsorship of the literature drive became apparent in interviews in the last three weeks here and in Washington, Minneapolis, Dallas, Los Angeles and San Francisco, and telephone interviews reaching into other parts of the country.

144 Producers of Literature

Persons questioned, religious executives, "church and state" group leaders, politicians, mailers of "hate" literature and officials of the Department of Justice, disclosed a total of 144 producers of anti-Catholic literature in the campaign.

Estimates by the Fair Campaign Practices Committee and statements by the mailers themselves put the number of pieces in the tens of millions and the cost of distribution at hundreds of thousands of dollars.

The mailing lists for these distributions have been compiled chiefly from conservative Protestant church rolls and from church directories and other public sources. Not one of the literature sources questioned was willing to divulge the names of his chief financial backers.

To date not one piece of evidence has turned up to indicate that the Republican party, nationally or locally, has anything to do with the planning or direction of the religious drive against Mr. Kennedy.

Vice President Nixon has laid down this directive for guidance of the Republican National Committee:

"There should be no discussion of the religious issue in any literature prepared by any volunteer group or party organization supporting the Vice President, and no literature of this kind from any source should be made available at campaign headquarters or otherwise distributed."

No Formal Complaints

Neither the Democratic National Committee nor the bipartisan Fair Campaign Practices Committee has made any formal complaints that this directive has been violated.

The executive director of the Fair Campaign committee is Bruce L. Felknor, who believes strongly that religious prejudice has no place in politics.

Conservative laymen of wealth, Mr. Felknor said, are financing much of the religious literature drive by contributing to churches and tax-exempt Protestant organizations active in the campaign, and then deducting the contributions from their income taxes.

Charles Taft's Views

He pointed to this recent statement by Charles P. Taft, a Republican, the brother of the late Senator Robert A. Taft, and a Protestant Episcopalian who has served as chairman of the committee since 1956:

"The amounts involved in paying for millions of copies of a wide variety of leaflets are so great that they are clearly beyond the resources of the hate groups, or in the case of slightly more 'respectable' material, beyond the resources of organizations like churches and other nonprofit corporations.

"The religious garbage that is swamping us is clearly on the face, and often in so many words, aimed at the defeat of one of the candidates for President."

> *"How many Catholics came over on the Mayflower? Not one. I maintain that the Constitution is a Protestant Constitution and let's keep it that way."*

Largest Groups Named

Although no evidence of national political direction exists, there are indications of coordination of the literature campaigns among predominantly conservative church groups.

The largest and most influential grouping includes the National Association of Evangelicals, Protestants and Other Americans United for Separation of Church and State (popularly abbreviated to P.O.A.U.) and leading churchmen of the Southern Baptist Convention. Their effort is supported by Citizens for Religious Freedom, the ad hoc group from which Dr. Peale withdrew. They are united by a common cause, close communication, and interlocking directorates.

For its own members, the evangelical association has worked out a plan of campaign activity tied to Reformation Sunday.

Other, smaller church groups are also working together, but usually as regional federations, such as the Citizens United for a Free America in the Dallas-Fort Worth area.

These organizations concentrate on "church and state" arguments against a Catholic President. Their literature, for the most part, represents reasoned argument, although some of it slips over into emotional anti-Catholicism.

The more virulent mail comes from two other major sources: fundamentalists distributing anti-Catholic material from tract houses that have been in business for years, and the long-established professionals who support themselves by selling "hate" publications against minority groups.

Mr. Springer, who calls himself the "cowboy evangelist," is one of the more rabidly anti-Roman Catholic pamphleteers in the campaign. But he has had widespread collaboration and sponsorship from Southern Baptist, independent Baptist, Church of Christ and other conservative pastors.

"You'll know me," said the evangelist on the phone, agreeing to an interview during a stopover at the Denver airport. "I'm 6 foot 5."

He was, and he was also wearing a white cowboy hat and a black string tie.

Evangelist Explains

Towering over a cup of coffee and speaking with a drawl, the lanky evangelist said:

"I would oppose any Roman Catholic for President—the name doesn't make any difference. I ask: How many Catholics came over on the Mayflower? Not one. I maintain that the Constitution is a Protestant Constitution and let's keep it that way."

Mr. Springer said he had been ordained as a Southern Baptist minister. But for the last twenty-five years he has been pastor of an independent Baptist tabernacle in Englewood, Colo., and editor of The Western Voice, a weekly newspaper "from out of the Rockies."

During that time, his sermons have warned against the Jews and the Negroes as well as against the Catholics. He is now an executive officer of the ultra-fundamentalist International Council of Christian Churches.

"I'm perfectly willing to admit I'm a bigot," he said, quite seriously. "But I want 'em to say who else is a bigot—the Catholics are just as bigoted against the Baptists."

And having a Catholic in the Presidential campaign he said, is going to bring out thousands of Protestants who never voted before.

Through mailings and rallies—"I've delivered 270 speeches in twenty-five states in thirteen weeks"—he hopes to recruit enough volunteers to pass out enough literature to swing the election.

Expenses Are Listed

The evangelist said he had put out "millions" of pieces such as his "Kennedy Cannot Win—The Roman Octopus," spending $55,000 on printing and $10,000 on stamps in the last three weeks alone. Money to finance the mail campaign, he said, comes from "freewill offerings" at his rallies.

"For the drive at the end," said Mr. Springer, "I'm adding to my religious packet a special letter accusing Kennedy of getting ready to socialize the country. I think we're going to beat him."

An interesting thing about the anti-Catholic writings in this campaign is that the great percentage of the pieces are not in the realm of "hate literature."

And what vitrol is being thrown is not usually aimed at the person of Mr. Kennedy. There are exceptions.

One such is a piece by the Rev. Harrison Parker, a lone mailer in Washington, which refers to Senator Kennedy's father, Joseph P. Kennedy, an investment banker and former ambassador to Britain:

"Civil war is possible in the U.S.A.," this piece declares, "because of the un-American 'Catholic Party' being formed with Joe Kennedy, the Roman Catholic millionaire whisky merchant as boss."

Most of the actual hate mail—the bulk, if not the percentage, is sizeable—attacks the Democratic candidate inferentially through an attack on his church.

Kennedy Stresses Need for the Country to Move Ahead in Order to Recoup World Leadership

By RUSSELL BAKER

Oct. 23—Listen to Senator John F. Kennedy defining the central issue of the 1960 Presidential campaign to the voters of Mineola, L. I.:

"This is a contest between the contented and those who wish to move ahead, between those who are satisfied and those who want to do better, between those who look back and those who say, 'It is time America moved again.'"

From Miami to Saginaw to Yonkers, the words vary and the minor chords are interchanged to suit the locale, but the message is ever the same. Convinced that the temper of the country is ready to forego the comfortable placidity of the Eisenhower years and embark on stirring new adventures, Mr. Kennedy has deliberately chosen to cast himself as the Yankee Cato.

Presents a Choice

The choice, he argues, is to continue "standing still" or to "make this country move again." The election, he argues, will determine "whether our high noon has passed, whether our brightest days were in the past, and whether the future belongs perhaps to those who live in the Communist system."

For the Kennedy campaign, this is the paramount issue, the foundation on which the campaign is built. All the secondary issues are simply modulations on the basic theme.

Before audiences in the depressed

Candidate John F. Kennedy delivers a campaign speech in St. Charles, Illinois.

(Diamond Images/Getty Images)

industrial towns of Michigan, western Pennsylvania and Ohio, he blames Republican policies for keeping the lid on economic growth. "For the last eight years we have moved ahead each year growing at about 2.5 per cent each year," he said in Butler, Pa. "The Soviet Union grows at about 7.5 per cent each year."

Unemployment for 4,500,000 workers flows naturally from Republican policies, he contends. "And Mr. Nixon," he said in Beaver Falls, Pa., "runs on a slogan, 'You never had it so good.' I want him to run on that slogan in Pennsylvania. I want him to tell the people in this area, where there is 9 per cent of the people out of work, a quarter of them more than fifteen weeks, I want him to come on that slogan of peace and prosperity."

His favorite target is the famous portrait of Mr. Nixon poking a finger into Premier Khrushchev's chest. In Pittsburgh he talked about going to shake hands with Mr. Nixon after the second television debate:

"When I went over to shake hands and the photographers came, suddenly the finger came up in my nose. I thought, here it comes. He is going to tell me how wrong I am about the plight of America, and do you know what he said? 'Senator, I hear you have been getting better crowds than I have in Cleveland. I wonder when he put his finger in Mr. Khrushchev's nose whether he was saying, 'I know you are ahead of us in rockets, Mr. Khrushchev, but we are ahead of you in color television.'"

How does it all go down with the voters? Even following Mr. Kennedy for the last month, it has been difficult to determine the reason for his tumultu-

ous receptions, but a subjective guess would be that they are accountable more to some chemistry between his personality and the masses than to his exposition of the issues.

The fact is that in the last month he has flowered into a magnificent campaigner with a Pied Piper magic over the street crowds, and especially the ladies, and with a considerable talent for what is ingraciously called rabble-rousing.

Audiences Overwhelmed

His exciting, hypnotic speech cadences often seem to overwhelm his audiences, which usually seem far more stirred by his presence than by his message. This is the same sort of mastery that President Eisenhower exercised over his campaign audiences, which often seemed to have trouble staying awake during his speeches but inevitably lifted the roof with frenzy as he made his entrances and exits.

Mr. Kennedy's personal appeal seems more specialized. The female "jumpers" and "shriekers" are a well-known phenomenon, but the fact is inescapable that the jumping is highest and the shrieking loudest in the Northeastern tier of industrial states and that it is barely detectable in such enclaves as Kentucky and Tennessee.

Uncertain Factor

The crowds, then, remain an uncertain factor in this strange campaign, but at this point they must be reckoned a plus for Mr. Kennedy, as must his competent performances in the television debates and the rise in voter registration in the nation's Democratic strongholds.

A subjective guess would be that, should Mr. Kennedy win, the result will have less to do with his daring campaign arguments to the voters than to the impact of a remarkable new political personality which has been dramatized by the happenstance of Mr. Nixon's agreement to appear with him in the four television debates.

Foreign Policy Regarded As Primary Concern of Both Candidates and Voters

_____

By E.W. KENWORTHY

WASHINGTON, Oct. 31—On two things Vice President Nixon and Senator John F. Kennedy are fully agreed—that foreign policy is the paramount issue in the Presidential campaign and that leadership is the first essential in foreign policy.

On some of the fundamental questions—for example, the maintenance of Western rights in Berlin—the two candidates take identical positions. On others, such as a nuclear test ban, the difference is largely a matter of words rather than substance.

Therefore, the question that Mr. Nixon and Senator Kennedy are posing for the voters is this:

Which candidate can most effectively deal with the Communist challenge, marshal America's intellectual, moral and industrial potential, give "light and leading" to the Western alliance, handle with imagination and realism the problems of the emerging and neutralist nations, and get Congressional support for his policies?

Presumably the voter's judgment would be affected by the candidates' discussion of the overriding problems that will face the next administration. These are the stresses within the NATO alliance, aid to the under-developed nations, United States policy toward Algeria and the role of the United Nations in Africa.

Little Said On Problems

Unfortunately, the candidates have said little or nothing about these problems during the campaign.

Almost by accident—by a question asked of them in the television debates—they have allowed themselves to be diverted into the two emotion-soaked areas of Quemoy and Matsu, and Cuba.

The offshore islands were not in the news, and a decision was not pressing. Cuba is very much in the news, but the candidates have not been discussing policy, but battling in the realm of allegation and undefined intention.

QUEMOY AND MATSU

The uproar began in the second debate when Senator Kennedy said that the islands were "not strategically defensible." While he did not suggest "withdrawal at the point of a Communist gun," he said we should work with the Chiang Kai-shek Government "to work out a plan by which the [defense] line is drawn at the island of Taiwan.

Mr. Nixon promptly retorted that "principle" was involved, and that he would not surrender "one inch of free territory" to the Communists.

By the third debate both men had retreated to the cover of the President's policy, which is embodied in the "Formosa resolution" passed by Congress in January, 1955. This states that the President can take military action to defend Quemoy and Matsu if he decides an attack on them is directed at Taiwan and the Pescadores.

There the matter stands, though the issue does not rest.

CUBA

Before the campaign heated up, Mr. Nixon conceded that five years ago the Administration should have done something about the causes of the Castro revolution. For his part, Senator Kennedy found no quarrel with the Administration's easy-does-it policy toward Premier Fidel Castro.

What made the Cuban question ripe for campaign controversy was the quickening pace of Communist influence. When the Eisenhower Administration announced the export embargo on all goods except food and supplies, Senator Kennedy called this a "dramatic but almost empty gesture" that would "have virtually no effect by itself in removing Communist rule from Cuba."

"We must attempt," the Senator said, "to strengthen the non-Batista Democratic forces in exile, and in Cuba itself, who offer eventual hope of overthrowing Castro."

Treaty Violation Seen

Vice President Nixon asserted that such intervention would violate five treaties with Latin America, would lose us all our friends there, and "be an open invitation for Mr. Khrushchev to come in to Latin America and to engage us in what would be a civil war, and possibly even worse than that."

Mr. Nixon asked the voters to contrast this "irresponsible" counsel with the Administration's policy of "quarantining Mr. Castro" as it had quarantined the Communist Arbenz Government in Guatemala in 1954, with the result "that the Guatemalan people themselves rose up and they threw him out."

There is an air of unreality about this debate that, most diplomats agree, is no less dangerous for being unreal.

Mr. Kennedy did not say that the United States should arm anti-Castro democratic forces, and he may not have had that in mind, but his remarks were open to that interpretation.

Mr. Nixon, on the other hand, was aware that the United States had "quarantined" Arbenz by supplying arms clandestinely to his opponents.

NUCLEAR TEST BAN

Senator Kennedy would have the United States "make one last effort" to get Soviet agreement on an inspected test ban before resuming underground tests. He did not specify a time limit for this effort.

Mr. Nixon would give the Soviet Union until Feb. 1 "to bring an agreement in sight." If there were no progress by then, the United States would resume underground tests for peaceful uses, and if an agreement were not signed in "a reasonable period" after Feb. 1 the United States would resume underground weapons tests. Mr. Nixon has not said what, a "reasonable time" would be.

FOREIGN AID

The question here is not the policy of the candidates. Both have been consistent supporters of foreign aid, and economic assistance. The question is about their influence in Congress.

In the early years of the program, most Southern conservatives supported foreign aid, and many Republican conservatives opposed it. In the last four or five years, this situation was reversed as President Eisenhower managed to bring many of the Republican conservatives into line and many Southerners became disenchanted with the program.

The chances that the Southerners will return are regarded as slim, but the chances are obviously better if Senator Kennedy wins. On the other hand, the chances are that many Republican conservatives will withdraw their support no matter who is elected. But again, Mr. Nixon is more likely to prevent this defection than Senator Kennedy.

AFRICA

Long before the Congo crisis impelled President Eisenhower to propose a program for United Nations action, both candidates had made recommendations for greater American aid to the emerging nations south of the Sahara.

On his return from an African tour in 1957, Mr. Nixon submitted a report to the President. In it, he recommended United States support for sound loan applications to the World Bank, the strengthening of United States missions in Africa, the dispatch of more technicians there and the creation of a bureau of African affairs in the State Department under an Assistant Secretary of State.

In June, 1959, Mr. Kennedy called for an increase in the technical aid program for Africa on the ground that most of the new nations had primitive economies and should concentrate first on "increasing agricultural productivity and diversifying one-crop economies."

LATIN AMERICA

The Republicans contend that the Eisenhower Administration has done more for Latin America than did the Roosevelt and Truman Administrations combined. The Democrats argue that every move by President Eisenhower has been a tardy response to a crisis that could have been anticipated. There is some truth in both arguments.

Both candidates have been in advance of the Eisenhower Administration in recommending larger expenditures for development and technical assistance in Latin America. Mr. Kennedy has also advocated that the United States "act to stabilize the prices of the principal commodity exports of Latin America." But he does not say how this costly venture would be financed.

Finally, both men have warned against attributing Latin-American economic aspirations to Communist intrigue.

Issue Perhaps Not An Issue

A comparison of the candidates' positions on the great questions in foreign policy reveals a paradox. It is this:

That while they and the voters are agreed that foreign policy is the pre-eminent campaign issue, it is not strictly an issue at all, in the sense of there being a sharp division over objective and courses of action.

The similarity of the candidates' views reflects a national consensus that is itself a new phenomenon in American party history. It is hard to remember that only ten years ago, a great debate was waged over a real issue in foreign policy—whether United States troops should be sent to Europe or whether the nation should base its defense on the "Fortress America" concept. Such a debate would be inconceivable today.

Vandiver Criticizes Kennedy on Dr. King

ATLANTA, Oct. 31 (AP)—Gov. S. Ernest Vandiver criticized John F. Kennedy today for telephoning the wife of the Rev. Dr. Martin Luther King Jr. while the Negro integration leader was in jail last week.

However, the Governor said that barring unforeseen events, "I will support the Democratic party." He also predicted that Georgia would go Democratic.

"It is a sad commentary on the year 1960 and its political campaign when the Democratic nominee for the Presidency makes a phone call to the home of the foremost racial agitator in the country," Governor Vandiver said.

Senator Kennedy called Mrs. King to express sympathy over the jailing of her husband on a traffic charge. His brother, Robert F. Kennedy, telephoned Judge Oscar Mitchell of De Kalb Criminal Court about the same time to ask if Dr. King could constitutionally make bail.

Dr. King was later released on bond.

"Asked if he was ruling out independent elector action by the Democratic slate which he heads, if it defeats the Republican slate Nov. 8, Governor Vandiver said:

"I didn't say that."

Candidates' Remarks Show Difference In Views on Future of U.S. Defenses

By HANSON W. BALDWIN

Nov. 1—Vice President Nixon strongly opposes the merger of the four armed services into one service. He is against the replacement of the Joint Chiefs of Staff by a single Chief of Staff or any other immediate major reorganization of the services.

Senator John F. Kennedy favors extensive reorganization of what he has termed the "cumbersome, antique and creaking machinery of the Department of Defense." This difference is the sharpest and best defined point about the defense issue to be found among the published statements of the Presidential candidates.

Their general views also differ, though not so emphatically, on the present and future adequacy of our defense and space programs.

Senator Kennedy has promised expansion of the armed services more or less across the board. Mr. Nixon believes the present composition and manpower levels of the armed services are "roughly adequate" (about 877,000 Army; 624,000 Navy; 175,000 Marines; 814,000 Air Force). But he favors selective strengthening of specific areas.

Pattern Visible

A general pattern about defense emerges, though in some areas with little definition, from the candidates' statements and from the personalities, convictions and positions of their advisers.

Both candidates have agreed, after some verbal sparring, that the United States is still the world's strongest military power.

Senator Kennedy believes that Communist power is increasing faster than our own and he is concerned about the future. Mr. Nixon says that, "while we do have the power to destroy Russia or China if world war should start, I want to emphasize this doesn't mean we can rest on our laurels because they are moving ahead."

Both candidates have forecast increased expenditures for defense. The current annual expenditure of the Defense Department is about $41,000,000,000.

Mr. Nixon has declared that "there must be no dollar sign on defending America" and that "total spending will irresistibly rise."

Senator Kennedy has said that "we must provide whatever money is neces-

Kennedy checking over a speech during the 1960 presidential campaign, Baltimore, Maryland.
(Paul Schutzer/Time & Life Pictures/Getty Images)

sary to reverse the trend of what he calls "our declining relative strength."

Neither candidate has been specific about amounts.

Both have committed themselves to a comprehensive survey of our defense positions and needs and, inferentially, to a "new look."

Counter-force Deterrent

Mr. Nixon has specifically endorsed the strategic concept of a counter-force deterrent, a nuclear delivery capability powerful enough to destroy an enemy's air and missile forces. The Air Force is the principal exponent of this concept, as opposed to the Navy. Many naval officers have favored the so-called "finite" or limited deterrent, one capable of destroying an enemy's urban and industrial centers.

Mr. Nixon has also inferentially endorsed the Air Force concept of a "pre-emptive" strike, an attack "to destroy or blunt a large portion" of the enemy's nuclear force before that force could attack us. Mr. Nixon considers this "essential to our survival as a nation."

Expansion Promised

Senator Kennedy has promised, if elected, to urge Congress to expand, modernize, strengthen and accelerate the armed forces and their weapons programs almost across the board. He favors keeping about one-quarter of the Strategic Air Command bombers, now totaling about 2,000 heavy and medium bombers, on an air alert.

Mr. Nixon has said that "the concept of the anti-missile missile must be pursued with all deliberate speed." He has specifically mentioned the necessity for the continued "development of the manned bomber and fighter" and for the highest priorities for the Navy's Polaris and the Air Force's Minuteman programs. He considers the "missile programs in the present strategic force mix properly weighted" but would periodically re-examine them.

On defense organization, the differences between the two candidates are marked.

Senator Kennedy has said that he sees "no necessity for eliminating separate services at this time, but it may very well come in the Nineteen Sixties." He has, however, promised re-organization of the Defense Department, which he thinks is handicapped by committees.

> *Both candidates have agreed, after some verbal sparring, that the United States is still the world's strongest military power.*

Senator Kennedy has called for the creation of a Strategic Command, a Tactical Command, a Continental Defense Command, a Material Command and a Development Command, which would include in each command task forces of each service. Such a reorganization would apparently place the Navy's Polaris missile-firing submarines in the same Strategic Command with the Air Force's bombers, something the Navy has bitterly opposed.

Thus Senator Kennedy, declaring that "billions can be saved" by reorganization, has promised sweeping change, which would almost certainly imply, in time, at least a limited merger of the four armed services and a single Chief of Staff.

Criticized by Nixon

Mr. Nixon has specifically criticized this concept. He has scored "petty, interservice rivalry" and duplication and said some "heads will roll" if prejudiced partisans put their service first and the nation second.

But he has pointed out "competition between the services" can be constructive, and he has indicated that the Polaris missile probably would not have been developed if the Air Force had been "dominant in running all the services." He has specifically opposed, on the grounds of morale, tradition, efficiency and healthy competition, the establishment of "one single super-service."

He emphatically opposes the creation of a single Chief of Staff to replace the Joint Chiefs. And he opposes the creation of functional commands as "a multiplication of services instead of simplification." He has stated that "the present situation of the uniformed services may be imperfect but I find it to be generally preferable to any alternative which I have seen so far."

Advisers Important

Senator Kennedy's advisers have been chiefly, though not exclusively, associated with the Air Force, which has advocated the kind of sweeping reorganization the Senator has urged. Indeed, it would appear that the Air Force has hitched its fortunes to the hope and expectation of a Democratic victory.

The Army, too, judging by the magazine Army, seems to believe the Democratic platform offers more hope for the ground forces than the Republican. But the Navy, which is bitterly opposed to functional forces or a single service, frankly fears some of the statements made by Senator Kennedy and particularly his advisers.

Senator Kennedy, in other words, has tended to put himself on the side of the military "radicals." His election would seem to mean major changes and a larger defense budget.

Mr. Nixon, while he promises to maintain United States military primacy, is more conservative in his organizational and budgetary views. His experience rejects some of the "remedies" and "solutions" that Senator Kennedy advocates.

Proposals on Health Care for Aged Create Major Split Between Parties

By PETER BRAESTRUP

WASHINGTON, Nov. 4—What should the nation do to provide medical care for the aged?

After years of conflicting statistics, heavy lobbying and Congressional debate, this question has produced a major issue separating Vice President Nixon and Senator John F. Kennedy. Both candidates and President Eisenhower as well—have agreed that most of the 16,000,000 Americans over 65 years of age need some Federal assistance in meeting the mounting cost of medical care. But amid charges of "socialized medicine" and "inadequate protection," Republicans and Democrats disagreed as to ways and means.

In part, the problem arises from the fact that the nation's population of persons over 61 is growing rapidly. The total by 1975 is 20,000,000.

Hurt by Rising Costs

These Americans—and their younger relatives who may contribute to their support—have been hit hard by the cost of improved drugs and medical care.

Half of those over 65 have incomes of $1,000 a year or less. Almost 2,500,000 are "paupers"—as recipients of assistance. Perhaps 35 to 40 percent were insured for varying degrees of health coverage by private concerns in 1956, according to the Census Bureau.

So much for the medical economics. Politicians in both parties have been worried about the "rocking chair vote" since the Thirties, when the late Dr. Francis E. Townsend aroused a national following for his $200-a-month pension plan for everyone who retired at 60.

It was during those New Deal years that the Social Security Act of 1935 was passed, establishing a contributory pension system for the retired. Its provisions have been broadened in almost every post-war election year.

Potent Political Force

This year, with a majority of the aged hard put to pay medical bills, the "over 65" vote is considered a political force, extending far beyond such tranquil retirement centers as western Florida and Southern California.

Between the two candidates' approaches to the aged lie fairly clear-cut philosophical differences.

Senator Kennedy and the Democratic platform have urged medical care as "part of the time-tested Social Security insurance system."

"We reject any proposal which would require [the aged] to submit to the indignity of a means test—a 'pauper's oath'," the platform declares.

Vice President Nixon and the Republicans have evolved a more complicated "voluntary" plan tied in part to existing private insurance programs. The accent is on state participation and individual benefits based on income.

Republican Program

The Republican program, as the party platform puts it, would "provide the beneficiaries with the option of purchasing private health insurance, [encouraging] commercial carriers and voluntary insurance organizations to continue their efforts to develop sound plans for the [aged]."

Essentially, both plans were to supplement the compromise, conservative-backed program that was enacted during Congress' August session.

This plan was endorsed by the Republicans, although with some reported misgivings, and utterly attacked as "inadequate" by Senator Kennedy and liberal Democrats.

Complicated and dependent on the states for implementation, the compromise plan went into effect Oct. 1. Vice President Nixon urged the states to join with the "least possible delay."

Health benefits would go to some 1,000,000 persons in two classes—those already receiving old-age benefits and persons unable to carry the cost of health care. A "means test" would be required.

Partly because both parties are pledged to change it, the plan has been received with mixed feelings by the states.

Essentially, the Democratic "package" advocated by Senator Kennedy is an outgrowth of proposals put forth two years go by Representative Aime J. Forand of Rhode Island.

It would supplement the existing program of aid to the officially indigent by paying benefits, where needed, to those already eligible for Old Age and Survivors Insurance payments who are over 68 years of age. Some 8,500,000 such persons are now living, but not all are receiving such payments.

The Democratic program would impose an additional Social Security tax of one-fourth of 1 percent on employers and employees. This would build up a medical care fund that might involve as much as $1,000,000,000 a year in outlays.

The recipients would get benefits without a means test.

They would choose their own doctors, hospitals and nursing homes. Federal payments, through the Social Security Administration, would be made directly to those "vendors" of medical care, as is the case with private insurance programs.

Benefits Detailed

Benefits would exceed those of most Blue Cross-style private plans: 120 days of hospital care, 240 days of home nursing care, 360 home health visits and diagnostic and outpatient services.

The plan would be self-financing, without any drain on the Federal Treasury, or any dependence on state appropriations.

This package has powerful support from unions and academic and public health groups. Critics have contended that it excludes several million of the aged, burdens 70,000,000 Social Security taxpayers and exacts no contributions from those now on the old-age insurance rolls.

Moreover, the American Medical Association, the United States Chamber of Commerce and other conservative groups have attacked the Democrats' plan as "socialized medicine." President Eisenhower called it "compulsory medicine" and said it constituted a "very definite step" toward "socialized medicine."

G. O. P. Offers 3 Options

The Republican plan would give participants three options. One would provide benefits for preventive medicine and short-term illness, including the services of hospitals and physicians. The second would be a long-term-illness plan, including surgical and nursing home service. Beneficiaries would pay the first $250 in costs.

The third option would entail payments of 50 percent of the premium on an existing private insurance plan up to $60 a year.

In all cases, the individual would pay not less than 10 percent of costs, with the exact amount determined by his income. The state and Federal Government would participate only in the first $128 of such costs.

Senator Jacob K. Javits, a New York Republican who sponsored the proposals last August, put the Federal cost of the program at a maximum of $460,000,000, paid from Treasury funds. The states, if all participated, might contribute as much as $520,000,000.

Could Cover 11 Million

Up to 11,000,000 aged persons could be covered by the Nixon-Javits plan. Persons over 65 would be eligible, except those with annual incomes over $3,000 or $4,500 for couples, and except those covered under the current relief grant plan.

Thus, through the cloud of statistics, the differences protrude.

The total costs of both the Republican and the Democratic plans would be comparable. The contrast is that the Republican proposal would send Federal funds to the states, to be matched by state appropriations; the Democratic program would be financed outside the Treasury—through increased Social Security taxes—without requiring state action.

During the campaign, the Republicans have stressed "freedom" and the "voluntary" aspects of the Nixon-Javits proposals. The Democrats have emphasized their program's self-funding provisions and its lack of a "demeaning pauper's oath" requirement.

Most doctors, according to the A. M. A., are unhappy about both plans and indignant over the Kennedy proposals.

But their patients among the aged have more votes, and which of the two proposals the majority will prefer is anyone's guess.

★ ★ ★

"This year Social Security is twenty-five years old. And perhaps never, since its enactment, have the challenges to this program been as crucial and as far-reaching as they are today.

'The test of our progress,' said Franklin Roosevelt, 'is not whether we add more to the abundance of those who have too much; it is whether we provide enough for those who have too little.' It was in that spirit that our social security system was conceived. It was in that spirit that Franklin Roosevelt and Harry Truman fought to broaden its coverage and increase its benefits. And it is in that spirit that we battle today for a social security law which will truly provide our older citizens—under the present cost of living—with a decent and a dignified and a healthy way of life.

Today in America there are those who would shut the door of hope on our older citizens—who would deny them the medical care which they so desperately need. But there are others who will not let that door be closed—who intend to fight for the right of all men to live out their lives in dignity and in health."   —Senator Kennedy, April 1960

KENNEDY'S VICTORY WON BY CLOSE MARGIN; HE PROMISES FIGHT FOR WORLD FREEDOM; EISENHOWER OFFERS 'ORDERLY TRANSITION'

Results Delayed

Popular Vote Almost Even—300-185 Is Electoral Tally

By JAMES RESTON

Nov. 9—Senator John F. Kennedy of Massachusetts finally won the 1960 Presidential election from Vice President Nixon by the astonishing margin of less than two votes per voting precinct.

Senator Kennedy's electoral vote total stood yesterday at 300, just thirty-one more than the 269 needed for election. The Vice President's total was 185. Fifty-two additional electoral votes, including California's thirty-two, were still in doubt last night.

But the popular vote was a different story. The two candidates ran virtually even. Senator Kennedy's lead last night was little more than 300,000 in a total tabulated vote of about 66,000,000 cast in 165,826 precincts.

That was a plurality for the Senator of less than one-half of 1 per cent of the total vote—the smallest percentage difference between the popular vote of two Presidential candidates since 1880, when James A. Garfield outran Gen. Winfield Scott Hancock by 7,000 votes in a total of almost 9,000,000.

Opposite page:

Senator Kennedy's brothers and sister, Ted, Bobby, and Pat, watch results on election night. (Paul Schutzer/Time & Life Pictures/Getty Images)

End Divided Government

Nevertheless, yesterday's voting radically altered the political balance of power in America in favor of the Democrats and put them in a commanding position in the Federal and state capitals unknown since the heyday of Franklin D. Roosevelt.

They regained control of the White House for the first time since 1952 and thus ended divided government in Washington. They retained control of the Senate and the House of Representatives, although with slightly reduced margins. And they increased their hold on the state governorships by one, bringing the Democratic margin to 34-16.

The President-elect is the first Roman Catholic ever to win the nation's highest office. The only other member of his church nominated for President was Alfred E. Smith, who was defeated by Herbert Hoover in 1928.

Faces Difficult Questions

Despite his personal triumph, President-elect Kennedy is confronted by a number of hard questions:

In the face of such a narrow victory how can he get through the Congress the liberal program he proposed during the campaign?

Can so close an election produce any impetus for loosening the con-servative coalition of Republicans and Southern Democrats which has blocked most liberal legislation in the House?

Will the new President be able successfully to claim a mandate for legislation such as the $1.25 minimum wage, Federal school aid and a broader medical assistance to the aged which he advocated from the stump?

In the campaign Senator Kennedy promised a "first hundred days" equal to that great period of reform in the Administration of Franklin D. Roosevelt. But the result made it more than ever likely that he would have to reach an accommodation with the conservative South, which has opposed much of his program within the Democratic party.

Senator Lyndon B. Johnson of Texas, Senator Kennedy's Vice-Presidential running mate, contributed much to Mr. Kennedy's victory and more than justified the controversial last minute tactic of putting the Texan on the ticket over the loud protests of the Northern Democratic liberals.

Johnson's Contribution

Without much question, he was responsible for bringing Texas back to the Democratic fold for the first time since 1948, and for helping to hold North and South Carolina, which most of the experts gave to the Republicans a month ago. Meanwhile there was nothing to suggest that he had hurt the Democrats, as predicted, in the liberal areas of the urban North.

Not since President Harry S. Truman's surprising victory over Gov. Thomas E. Dewey of New York in the election of 1948—and perhaps not even since Woodrow Wilson's triumph in the photo-finish election of 1916—have there been so many dramatic swings and changes of political fortune as occurred all through the night Tuesday and even into yesterday afternoon.

It is worth recalling also that Mr. Truman's victory, dramatic as it was, came with a plurality of more than 2,000,000 votes—compared with Senator Kennedy's less than 400,000 so far.

Shortly before midnight Tuesday the signs had seemed to point to a substantial Kennedy victory.

Victory Projected Into West

The Senator's national plurality of the popular vote, which had been climbing steadily all evening, was about 2,000,000. The Chicago vote had given him a big lead in Illinois, and the analysts were projecting westward his smashing triumph in the Northeast.

But actually that was the peak of Senator Kennedy's momentum. Just about midnight a slow process of attrition set in that whittled away at his "sure" win until, in the dramatic hours of the early morning, it was clear that this was the closest election in generations.

The Kennedy popular vote margin melted to 800,000 by 5 A.M. yesterday, and the trend was still downward. The Senator's Illinois lead dropped from almost 200,000 to around 50,000 and state Democratic leaders began to sound brave when they forecast a final victory margin of "at least" 28,000.

And it became increasingly evident that the magic worked by Senator Kennedy in the East was less effective on the other side of the Mississippi.

The returns were so close in many Western states that it became impossible to get a clear picture. Leads of a few hundred or a few thousand votes changed hands again and again in Nevada, New Mexico, Montana, Washington, Hawaii and Alaska.

By 5 or 6 A.M. yesterday, the Kennedy margin seemed to be facing a real threat in Minnesota as well as Illinois.

Nixon Finally Concedes

It became clear that Senator Kennedy had to win one of the three big undecided states—Illinois, Minnesota or California—to get his needed 269 electoral votes.

At no time did Vice President Nixon have a chance to win 269 electoral votes on his own. Even if all three of the major doubtful states and every one of the smaller western states had fallen to him, he would have been four votes short.

But in such a situation Senator Kennedy would also have been denied a majority. The power to decide the winner would then have rested with fourteen unpledged electors from Alabama and Mississippi who bolted the regular Democratic ticket as a protest against Northern democratic views.

Throughout yesterday morning the result hung in the balance. Senator Kennedy's margin fell slowly in Illinois and Minnesota, and indeed at one point, Mr. Nixon pulled ahead in the former until a last batch of Chicago votes was produced for Mr. Kennedy.

Then at 12:33 o'clock Senator Kennedy clinched Minnesota and the election. Thirteen minutes later Mr. Nixon made his formal concession.

Strength Combined

Senators Kennedy and Johnson won by putting together their combined strength in the great cities of the North and the rural areas of the traditionally Democratic South; but they were remarkably weak elsewhere.

For example, they won eight of the nine so-called large decisive states, but in some of them their margins were tighter than a Pullman window: 6,000-6,500 in Illinois; 22,000 in New Jersey, 60,000 in Texas, 65,000 in Michigan, 131,000 in Pennsylvania.

Only in New York and Kennedy's home state of Massachusetts did the Democrats win by truly large majorities—404,000 in New York and 498,000 in Massachusetts. Each of these margins was larger than Mr. Kennedy's margin of victory in the nation as a whole.

The anomalies in the results were sometimes startling.

Why should Mr. Kennedy win by 131,000 in Pennsylvania and lose in neighboring Ohio, with much the same mixture of union and Catholic voters, by 263,000?

Senator Kennedy campaigned on a liberal program but could not have won without the support of conservative Catholics in the North and conservative Protestants in the South.

Contrasts in Jersey

In most areas populated by Catholics, Mr. Kennedy did well, but in some, Hudson County, N. J., for example, his showing was a great disappointment to his managers, while he did remarkably well in the more Republican territory of Essex County, N. J.

While the Senator was heavily supported in the cities of the North, Southern industrial areas such as Charlotte and Winston-Salem, N. C. went Republican. He did well in the Southern "Black Belts," as indeed did Smith in 1928, but he did poorly in the farm belts of the North, where he expected his attacks on Secretary of Agriculture Ezra Taft Benson might even swing some of the Plains States into the Democratic column.

Also, while Mr. Kennedy was regaining some of the Democratic party's lost strength in the South, he managed at the same time to pick up additional strength among Negroes, who have been complaining about the Democratic party's political associations with the South.

Senator Thruston B. Morton, the genial and relaxed chairman of the Republican National Committee, said yesterday that the main reason why Vice President Nixon had lost the election was that he had failed to hold the Northern Negro vote, which had gone so heavily to President Eisenhower in the two previous Presidential elections.

Chairman Morton's estimate was that the Vice President had got only between 10 to 12 per cent of the Negro vote, while President Eisenhower got about 26 per cent in 1952 and 1956.

Ironically, Senator Kennedy, whose political reputation rested primarily on his arresting and attractive personality, ran about 7 per cent behind the Democratic local candidates.

This was not true in the Northeast, where he was near his home base and where his sophisticated manner was quite popular, but it was definitely true in Illinois, Minnesota, Wisconsin, and Indiana, where he ran well behind the Democratic ticket.

Nevertheless, the most striking facts of all lay in the contrasts in the voting returns from the various regions of the country.

In New England, Senator Kennedy split the six states, three to three, but built up a plurality of 592,036 votes.

He swept all six Middle Atlantic States—Delaware, Maryland, New Jersey, New York, Pennsylvania and West Virginia with another huge plurality of 684,549. Then, as the voting moved westward, his power declined.

A Deficit in Midwest

He split the East Central States, winning Illinois by a whisker and Michigan, but lost Ohio and Indiana.

He lost six of the eight West Central States, Iowa, Kansas, Nebraska, North and South Dakota and Wisconsin and won only two, Minnesota and Missouri. Here again, Vice President Nixon piled up a plurality for the region of 526,235.

In the Mountain states, New Mexico swung to Kennedy last night, but Mr. Nixon took six of the others, and Senator Kennedy won only Nevada. The same trend prevailed here, with the Vice President getting a plurality of at least 160,000.

Even in the Pacific Coast states, Mr. Nixon's plurality was over 22,000, and while Mr. Kennedy had a plurality of 245,000 in the South, where he won everything except Florida, Oklahoma, Kentucky, Tennessee and Virginia, the Republicans piled up a comparatively large Southern vote, 5,300,000.

Members of the Kennedy family at their home in Hyannis Port, Massachusetts, celebrate on the night after John F. Kennedy won the presidential election, November 9, 1960. (Paul Schutzer/Time & Life Pictures/Getty Images)

"All the News That's Fit to Print"

The New York Times.

LATE CITY EDITION
U. S. Weather Bureau Report (Page 93) forecasts: Cloudy, periods of rain today. Partly cloudy, colder tomorrow. Temp. range: 55—41; yesterday: 53.8—40.4.

VOL. CX..No. 37,546. © 1960 by The New York Times Company, Times Square, New York 36, N. Y. NEW YORK, THURSDAY, NOVEMBER 10, 1960. 10 cents beyond 50-mile zone from New York City except on Long Island. Higher in air delivery cities. FIVE CENTS

KENNEDY'S VICTORY WON BY CLOSE MARGIN; HE PROMISES FIGHT FOR WORLD FREEDOM; EISENHOWER OFFERS 'ORDERLY TRANSITION'

DEMOCRATS HERE SPLIT IN VICTORY; LEHMAN ASSAILED

De Sapio Accepts Challenge for Party Control—Mayor Claims Leadership

Text of De Sapio statement appears on Page 43.

By LEO EGAN

Less than twenty-four hours after the polls closed, the political coalition that gave Senator John F. Kennedy New York's forty-five electoral votes began coming apart at the seams.

Its disintegration was signaled by Carmine G. De Sapio in a statement assailing former Gov. Herbert H. Lehman, key figure in the Democratic reform group, and Alex Rose, Liberal party master of strategy.

The statement accepted Mr. Lehman's election night challenge to a finish fight for control of the party organization in the city and state.

At the same time it appeared to rule out any chance of a Democratic-Liberal party coalition for next year's Mayoral election in New York City and for the Governorship election in the state in 1962 if Mr. De Sapio remains in control of the party machinery.

Kennedy's Delicate Problem

Mr. De Sapio, leader of Tammany and Democratic National Committeeman for New York, consulted Michael H. Prendergast, the Democratic State Chairman, and a number of party leaders in the city and upstate before issuing his statement.

The collapse of the coalition so soon after it achieved its goal gave President-elect Kennedy a delicate political problem before he takes office. At some stage soon he will have to decide whom in New York to consult about appointments for the new Administration.

Thus, in so far as New York is concerned, the election appeared to raise as many questions as it settled. Control of the Democratic party machinery is one of them. Among the others are: What is Mayor Wagner's political future? And what is Governor Rockefeller's?

When told of Mr. De Sapio's statement last night, Mayor Wagner commented that he in-

Continued on Page 43, Column 1

Registration Set-Up Called Faulty Here

By DOUGLAS DALES

Political leaders voiced dissatisfaction yesterday over the way permanent personal registration functioned here Tuesday in its first test in a Presidential election.

Charges were made that thousands of persons had been disfranchised because they were unable to convince election inspectors that they had registered and were eligible to vote.

How many voters may have been so affected was concededly a guess. But a check of the Supreme Courts in the five boroughs indicated that more than 1,300 persons had gone before the justices for orders directing the inspectors to permit them to vote.

"There was a minimum of 10,000 denied the right to vote," Abraham Gellinoff,

Continued on Page 43, Column 5

ASSEMBLY DELAYS U.N. CONGO DEBATE

Postpones It Indefinitely, 48-30, as Soviet Backs Step—U. S. Move Fails

By KATHLEEN TELTSCH
Special to The New York Times.

UNITED NATIONS, N. Y., Nov. 9—The General Assembly voted tonight to postpone the debate on the Congo indefinitely.

The 48-to-30 vote, with eighteen abstentions, was on a surprise move made by Ghana with the help of Guinea and Nigeria and the enthusiastic support of the Soviet bloc.

The United States tried to avoid the adjournment vote by asking for a suspension of the session until delegates could ponder the unexpected request.

Western sources said privately that Ghana's initiative appeared to have been prompted in part by the presence here of President Joseph Kasavubu of the Congo and the likelihood that the Assembly's Credentials Committee would agree to his request for the seating of a Congolese delegation of his supporters.

A Two-Hour Wrangle

Ghana, Guinea, India and five other states have joined in sponsoring a resolution that aims instead at having the Assembly seat a delegation designated by the deposed Congolese Premier, Patrice Lumumba.

The Assembly acted after a two-hour wrangle marked by two table-thumping demonstrations by the Soviet bloc and also by Ghana, both in protest against the efforts of Foreign Minister Pierre Wigny of Belgium to defend his country's position on the Congo issue.

The adjournment request was made by Alex Quaison-Sackey, Ghana's chief delegate. He appealed to the Assembly to hold off any further debate pending the efforts of a fifteen-member Asian-African commission to reconcile the clashing political factions in the Congo and restore some governmental stability.

He said that the commission probably would leave for the Congo in a week and that further acrimonious debate in the Assembly would only hamper the conciliation effort.

However, the adjournment as voted did not stipulate how long the debate should be suspended. United States sources said tonight that they understood this to mean that discussion could

Continued on Page 3, Column 1

WINNER'S PLEDGE

Family Is With Him as He Vows to Press Nation's Cause

Text of Kennedy's statement is printed on Page 36.

By HOMER BIGART
Special to The New York Times.

HYANNIS, Mass., Nov. 9—Senator John F. Kennedy accepted in solemn mood today his election as President.

He pledged all his energy to advancing "the long-range interests of the United States and the cause of freedom around the world."

He made this pledge inside the flag-decked Hyannis Armory at 1:45 P. M., an hour after Vice President Nixon, his Republican opponent, had conceded defeat.

His wife, Jacqueline, stood at his side as the 43-year-old President-elect faced 300 newsmen and massed batteries of TV cameras and gave his victory statement to the nation.

Behind him were arrayed the Kennedy family: his father, former Ambassador Joseph P. Kennedy; his mother, three sisters and three brothers.

No Sign of Jubilation

The Kennedys showed no evidence of jubilation. All wore expressions of solemnity. Mr. Kennedy's margin of victory was too slender to stir much elation. Some of his aides acknowledged disappointment over the startlingly narrow gap in the popular vote.

Mr. Kennedy, after responding to applause with a diffident bow and a smile, first read the telegram from Mr. Nixon conceding defeat and extending congratulations. The Senator had stayed up until 3:50 A. M. awaiting this concession and had gone to bed disappointed when the Vice President withheld it.

Replies to Nixon

Mr. Nixon wired the President-elect that all the nation would give him "united support" in the next four years.

Mr. Kennedy replied to Mr. Nixon:

"I know that the nation can continue to count on your unswerving loyalty in whatever effort you undertake, and that you and I can maintain our long-standing cordial relations in the years ahead."

Mr. Kennedy then read a congratulatory message from President Eisenhower.

In his message the President informed Mr. Kennedy that he would shortly receive suggestions from the President as to the change-over of responsibilities for national leadership.

To this Senator Kennedy had replied:

"I am grateful for your wire and good wishes. I look forward to working with you in the near future. The whole country is hopeful that your long ex-

Continued on Page 36, Column 7

United Press International Telephoto

THE MESSAGES WERE CONGRATULATORY: Senator John F. Kennedy displaying telegrams at Hyannis, Mass. With him are Mrs. Kennedy, his parents and Robert F. Kennedy, left, and R. Sargent Shriver, a brother-in-law.

KHRUSHCHEV NOTE SALUTES KENNEDY

Message of Congratulations Asks for Negotiations on Tensions in World

Text of Khrushchev message will be found on Page 42.

By The Associated Press.

MOSCOW, Nov. 9—Soviet Premier Khrushchev congratulated Senator John F. Kennedy today for his Presidential victory.

He expressed hope that Soviet-United States relations would "again follow the line along which they were developing in Franklin Roosevelt's time."

He urged negotiations aimed at easing the international situation.

[In Bonn, Chancellor Konrad Adenauer said he planned to go to Washington early next year for conferences with Mr. Kennedy.]

Mr. Khrushchev's statements in a congratulatory message to Mr. Kennedy coincided with Moscow's insistence that the policies of President Eisenhower had suffered a rebuff in the election.

The Soviet press contended that the election proved "the American people have blackballed the policy of the 'cold war' and the arms race, that they want changes and expect Washington to pursue a reasonable course in international affairs, a course dictated by life and the balance of forces now prevailing in the world." Mr.

Continued on Page 42, Column 4

Electoral Vote by States

	Rep.	Dem.		Rep.	Dem.		Rep.	Dem.
Alabama	..	5*	Louisiana	..	10	Ohio	25	..
Alaska	..	..	Maine	5	..	Oklahoma	8	..
Arizona	4	..	Maryland	..	9	Oregon	6	..
Arkansas	..	8	Mass.	..	16	Penna.	..	32
California	..	..	Michigan	..	20	Rhode Island	..	4
Colorado	6	..	Minnesota	..	11	So. Carolina	..	8
Conn.	..	8	Mississippi	**	**	So. Dakota	4	..
Delaware	..	3	Missouri	..	13	Tennessee	11	..
Florida	10	..	Montana	4	..	Texas	..	24
Georgia	..	12	Nebraska	6	..	Utah	4	..
Hawaii	..	..	Nevada	..	3	Vermont	3	..
Idaho	4	..	New Hamp.	4	..	Virginia	12	..
Illinois	..	27	New Jersey	..	16	Washington	9	..
Indiana	13	..	New Mexico	..	4	W. Virginia	..	8
Iowa	10	..	New York	..	45	Wisconsin	12	..
Kansas	8	..	No. Carolina	..	14	Wyoming	3	..
Kentucky	10	..	North Dakota	4	..	Total	185	300

*Five electors are pledged to Kennedy and six unpledged.
**Eight electors not pledged to vote for party candidates.

LIBERALS SUFFER SETBACK IN HOUSE

G. O. P. Picks Up 22 Seats to Aid Conservative Bloc

By JOHN D. MORRIS

The House of Representatives will have a more conservative tinge in the Eighty-seventh Congress.

Inroads into the present House Democratic majority of 283 to 154 scored by the Republicans in Tuesday's elections promised to strengthen their conservative coalition with Southern Democrats.

The liberal legislative program to be submitted early next year by the new Democratic President, John F. Kennedy, may consequently face handicaps in the new Congress, which convenes Jan. 3.

In the Senate, Republicans cut the Democratic margin by two seats, to 64 to 36. That chamber remains predominantly liberal in membership, although conservatives dominate key committee posts.

Gubernatorial Shifts

The Democrats achieved a net gain of one governorship and now control thirty-four of the fifty state houses. In twenty-seven gubernatorial contests the Democrats won fifteen and the Republicans twelve, with an exchange of party control in thirteen.

In the House races, nearly complete unofficial returns showed that the Democrats had elected 257 House candidates and the Republicans 175, with five contests still in doubt.

The Republicans captured twenty-nine seats held by Democrats and lost seven of their own, for a net gain of at least twenty-two. For a bare numerical majority of 219 they would have had to achieve a net gain of sixty-five.

Among the eleven states of the Old Confederacy the Republicans maintained their hold on seven seats of the Eighty-

Continued on Page 33, Column 4

NIXON WIRE GIVES HIS 'BEST WISHES'

Sends Kennedy a Message —500 in Capital Hail Him

By BILL BECKER
Special to The New York Times.

LOS ANGELES, Nov. 9—Vice President Nixon conceded today the Presidential election of his Democratic opponent, Senator John F. Kennedy.

About twelve hours after the polls had closed, the Vice President sent the following telegram to Senator Kennedy at Hyannis Port, Mass.:

"I want to repeat through this wire the congratulations and best wishes I extended to you on television last night. I know that you will have the united support of all Americans as you lead the nation in the cause of peace and freedom in the next four years."

Read by Aide

The telegram was read to newsmen by Mr. Nixon's press secretary, Herbert G. Klein, at 9:45 A. M., Pacific standard time (12:45 P. M., Eastern standard time).

The Vice President did not make a personal appearance. Mr. Klein said Mr. Nixon was resting with Mrs. Nixon and their two daughters in their suite at the Ambassador Hotel.

It was obvious that the Vice President had considered his remarks late on election night a virtual concession.

[A crowd of several hundred greeted Mr. Nixon as he arrived Wednesday night at Andrews Air Base, near Washington, after a flight of four and a half hours from Los Angeles.]

Mr. Nixon remained in seclusion most of the morning although Mr. Klein said he was up about 6 A. M. after little more than three hours of sleep. The secretary said Mr. Nixon

Continued on Page 42, Column 5

NEED less salt in your diet? Now, try Fleischmann's Sweet (Unsalted) Margarine, the first and only unsalted margarine made from 100% golden corn oil.—Advt.

PRESIDENT SENDS WIRE TO KENNEDY

He Felicitates Senator and Orders Agency Chiefs to Cooperate With Him

By FELIX BELAIR Jr.
Special to The New York Times.

AUGUSTA, Ga., Nov. 9—President Eisenhower congratulated President-elect John F. Kennedy today on his election and then invited him to designate representatives to participate in all Federal policy discussions to assure an "orderly transition" to the new Administration.

The text of the President's telegram was withheld here at the request of Mr. Kennedy. But President Eisenhower is understood to have told the President-elect that he had instructed all heads of Federal departments and agencies to "cooperate fully" with Mr. Kennedy's representatives.

President Eisenhower arrived here for his customary fall holiday in midafternoon after a two-hour flight from Washington.

The President's message of congratulation to Mr. Kennedy was sent from the White House just before he took off for his favorite vacation retreat here at Augusta National Golf Club.

He also sent messages to the defeated Republican candidate, Vice President Nixon, and his running mate, Henry Cabot Lodge, as well as Vice President-elect Lyndon B. Johnson.

In his telegram to Mr. Nixon

Continued on Page 42, Column 7

RESULTS DELAYED

Popular Vote Almost Even—300-185 Is Electoral Tally

By JAMES RESTON

Senator John F. Kennedy of Massachusetts finally won the 1960 Presidential election from Vice President Nixon by the astonishing margin of less than two votes per voting precinct.

Senator Kennedy's electoral vote total stood yesterday at 300, just thirty-one more than the 269 needed for election. The Vice President's total was 185. Fifty-two additional electoral votes, including California's thirty-two, were still in doubt last night.

But the popular vote was a different story. The two candidates ran virtually even. Senator Kennedy's lead last night was little more than 300,000 in a total tabulated vote of about 66,000,000 cast in 165,826 precincts.

That was a plurality for the Senator of less than one-half of 1 per cent of the total vote—the smallest percentage difference between the popular vote of two Presidential candidates since 1880, when James A. Garfield outran Gen. Winfield Scott Hancock by 7,000 votes in a total of almost 9,000,000.

End Divided Government

Nevertheless, yesterday's voting radically altered the political balance of power in America in favor of the Democrats and put them in a commanding position in the Federal and state capitals unknown since the heyday of Franklin D. Roosevelt.

They regained control of the White House for the first time since 1952 and thus ended divided government in Washington. They retained control of the Senate and the House of Representatives, although with slightly reduced margins. And they increased their hold on the state governorships by one, bringing the Democratic margin to 34—16.

The President-elect is the first Roman Catholic ever to win the nation's highest office. The only other member of his church nominated for President was Alfred E. Smith, who was defeated by Herbert Hoover in 1928.

Faces Difficult Questions

Despite his personal triumph, President-elect Kennedy is confronted by a number of hard questions:

¶In the face of such a narrow victory how can he get through the Congress the liberal program he proposed during the campaign?

¶Can so close an election produce any impetus for loosening the conservative coalition of Republicans and Southern Democrats which has blocked most liberal legislation in the House?

¶Will the new President be able successfully to claim a mandate for legislation such as the $1.25 minimum wage, Fed-

Continued on Page 35, Column 1

ATOM BILL BEATEN IN FRENCH SENATE

Debre to Push Compromise on Nuclear Force Plan

By W. GRANGER BLAIR
Special to The New York Times.

PARIS, Thursday, Nov. 10—The Senate early today rejected President de Gaulle's project for an independent French nuclear striking force.

By a vote of 186 to 83, with seventeen abstentions, this conservative Upper House approved a procedural motion to table the national nuclear deterrent bill that had been passed to it by the National Assembly Oct. 27.

Although the Senate's action was a stinging blow to President de Gaulle and a sharp indication of mounting parliamentary opposition, it did not mean that the Government's measure would not eventually become law.

It was announced after the vote that Premier Michel Debré would call for the creation of a mixed committee of Senators and Deputies to work out a compromise measure. Should this conference committee fail to find a compromise, the Government would resubmit its measure to the Assembly for a second reading, and virtually certain approval. The measure would then become law with or without Senate's approval.

The Senate motion to table

Continued on Page 8, Column 1

NEWS INDEX

10 Irish Soldiers Slain in Congo When U.N. Patrol Is Ambushed

By PAUL HOFMANN
Special to The New York Times.

LEOPOLDVILLE, the Congo, Nov. 9—A patrol of eleven Irish soldiers of the United Nations force in the Congo was ambushed in the northern part of Katanga Province yesterday. The bodies of four men were sighted.

[The United Nations Command said that ten soldiers had been slain in the ambush, Reuters reported. The Irish Army announced in Dublin that one private had survived the attack. Reports received by the United Nations in New York said the surviving soldier was "badly wounded," according to United Press International.]

The patrol belonged to the Irish Thirty-third Battalion, which has headquarters in the industrial city of Albertville. The battalion, with a strength of about 550 men, is responsible for maintaining order in a vast area of North Katanga. The region has been the scene of intertribal warfare and clashes between Baluba tribesmen and the gendarmerie controlled by Moise Tshombe, President of Katanga.

United Nations officials here were unable to say who had attacked the Irish patrol. The ambush occurred south of Niemba, a village between Albertville and Kabalo. The zone is described as "Baluba country," but it is not known whether Baluba tribesmen were responsible for the assault.

Announcing the loss, a United Nations spokesman said it brought the toll of dead in the international force in the Congo to about thirty since the world organization's troops arrived

Continued on Page 2, Column 3

Vatican Calls Kennedy Election Proof of American Democracy

By ARNALDO CORTESI
Special to The New York Times.

ROME, Nov. 9—The election of Senator John F. Kennedy, a Roman Catholic, to the Presidency was received with keen satisfaction in the Vatican today.

During the campaign the Vatican remained neutral. Its newspaper, L'Osservatore Romano, abstained from all comment lest it be accused of siding with one candidate against the other.

Today the editor of the newspaper, former Italian Deputy Raimondo Manzini, said:

"Kennedy's victory strengthens the appreciation for the high democratic principles of freedom that guide American public life and assure access to the highest office to every citizen regardless of social class, race, or religion.

"The effective support given by large numbers of Protestant citizens to a Catholic considered suitable for the Presidency has been significant in this respect. Catholics are, of course, satisfied at the solemn confirmation of the principle that the office of President is open to a son of the Catholic Church, which enjoys such large prestige in the United States. Catholics have, however, always admired Nixon's irreproachable attitude of deferential respect for the Catholic hierarchy."

Senator Kennedy's victory was announced under large headlines by the whole morning press in Italy today. In most newspapers it took precedence over the results of the provincial and municipal elections that were held in Italy over the week-end.

Government circles received the news without astonishment

Continued on Page 38, Column 7

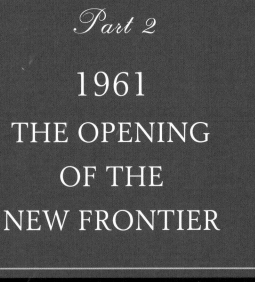

President Eisenhower and President-elect Kennedy meeting at the White House, December 7, 1960.
(George Tames/*The New York Times*)

*"Let the word go forth from this time and place
to friend and foe alike, that the torch has been passed to
a new generation of Americans. . . ."*

1961: Small Victories, Major Defeats

Although John F. Kennedy won the presidency by the narrowest plurality since James A. Garfield edged Winfield S. Hancock in 1880, he was greeted with the highest hopes of a new generation. The torch was passed from the 70-year-old former Supreme Commander of Allied Forces to a 43-year-old former Navy lieutenant. "The New Generation Offers a Leader" was Kennedy's first campaign slogan. Age wasn't the only reason that the two presidents were uneasy with each other. As they rode up Pennsylvania Avenue to the Capitol for the formal swearing in, Kennedy tried to make conversation by asking Eisenhower what he thought of Cornelius Ryan's book *The Longest Day*, the popular account of the D-Day Allied landing in 1944. Kennedy was surprised when Ike said he had not read it. After another awkward silence, Eisenhower said, "I didn't have to read it, I was there."

The nation was united, or so it seemed. Kennedy's Republican opponent, Vice President Richard Nixon, also had been a Navy lieutenant. But despite the many differences of a bruising campaign, they had the same perspective on the most ominous issue of the day: the Cold War struggle against Communism and the Soviet Union. The president's eloquent inaugural address ("Ask not what your country can do for you, ask what you can do for your country.") was a foreign policy speech, a war cry. Harris Wofford, an adviser on civil rights, begged him to say "and at home" when he talked about "freedom." Kennedy did, and although his words were aimed at Eastern Europe, they were heard clearly in places like Greensboro, North Carolina, where young Negro students, some of them war veterans, were ready to demand those same freedoms at voting booths and lunch counters.

The president said there could be no "100 days" of whirlwind achievement to match Franklin D. Roosevelt's in 1933 because the nation was facing too many problems. But he launched an equivalent burst of energy when he announced the creation of the innovative, imaginative Peace Corps, which was promptly deluged by applications from thousands of young American men and women from campuses, farms, offices, and the ranks of the unemployed.

I was a young engineer at the time, working on pumping systems for a company called Ingersoll-Rand. Work stopped when Kennedy spoke on television, especially for men like me, after Soviet engineers lifted Yuri Gagarin into space, orbiting the Earth three times in a capsule called *Vostok*. The sense of an urgent new era escalated further when Kennedy boldly pledged in a message to Congress in March that the United States would put a man on the moon before the decade's end.

But the Russian lead in space was just one of several embarrassing crises for the fledgling president in the months ahead.

He trusted the "experts," of the C.I.A., as Kennedy later bemoaned his naïveté by neglecting to seriously challenge the rosy scenario of an almost comically inept operation to topple Fidel Castro. In April, C.I.A.-trained rebels landed at Cuba's Bay of Pigs, but instead of inspiring a nationwide counter-revolution, they were soon routed by Castro's army—outgunned, killed or captured.

Waking up one morning in May, Kennedy was startled to see a front page photograph of a burning bus in Anniston, Alabama. Segregationists had ambushed and attacked white and Negro "Freedom Riders" with clubs; 400 U.S. marshals were sent to Montgomery, where more bus riots erupted, and Dixie seemed primed for civil war.

In June, again to his own chagrin, Kennedy conceded he had performed "like a schoolboy" at a Vienna summit with Soviet Premier, Nikita Khrushchev, whose East German henchmen proclaimed themselves a sovereign nation and exempt from the terms of postwar treaties.

In August, while resolving to preserve Allied access and the freedom of West Berlin, the president stood aside as East Germany built a concrete wall separating the Western-occupied sector of the divided capital from the rest of the country.

Throughout this rude awakening to international tensions and domestic violence, however, the president's popularity in his first 100 days remained remarkably high. Kennedy's approval rating was 83 percent *after* the Bay of Pigs debacle.

—Richard Reeves

The Inauguration

Crowds Flocking to Inauguration

Capital Braces for 'Largest' Throng Ever on Friday—Tickets Are at Premium

By DAVID HALBERSTAM

WASHINGTON, Jan. 14—Anyone familiar with the daily difficulties of traveling, eating and parking here winces at the prospect of the week ahead.

It is inauguration week, time for the changing of the guard.

In the cold, analytical words of Edward H. Foley, head of the inaugural proceedings, "the largest crowd ever in Washington" will converge here for the ceremonies Friday.

No hotel man, restaurant owner, hair dresser or tuxedo renter is about to dispute Mr. Foley's word.

While no figure of the expected inaugural crowd is available, Mr. Foley estimates that about 500,000 will watch or participate in the ceremonies.

There are no tickets left to the Inaugural Ball, no tickets to the inauguration, no tickets to the inaugural parade, no rooms at any of the leading hotels or motels.

"There's not even any room left at my house," said Mr. Foley. "We're putting up twelve people there."

Million Is Guaranteed

As far as the inaugural committee is concerned, the week is a stunning success. Mr. Foley said the committee was guaranteed a minimum of $1,214,413 in returns. This will take care of all costs and leave up to $50,000 for the next inaugural, and some proceeds for charities to be selected. Previous inaugurations have on occasion become deficit affairs to be made up by Washington businessmen.

But the surplus also will bring problems. "The one thing you've got to remember," one member of the inaugural committee said today, "is that all these people are going to want to eat at the same time, ride taxis in the same direction at the same time and go out on the town at the same time."

Thus, the city will swell with more than pride. But the pride is there too, as Washington begins to sport more bunting, more pictures of President-elect John F. Kennedy and more red, white and blue signs that rule out parking on certain side streets.

Gala Thursday Night

The inauguration includes a series of events. One of the most complex is the gala to be held Thursday night. Frank Sinatra, the singer and actor, is in charge of this. He reports booming ticket sales and no problems.

For the Inaugural Ball, things are still expanding. The demand for invitations has been so great that three sites have been selected. Mr. Foley announced today that an additional ballroom in the Sheraton-Park Hotel had been taken over.

The Sheraton-Park was already a part of the ball, but the addition of the Cotillion Room will accommodate several thousand more persons. About 15,000 are expected to attend the ball.

But the crowd at the ball is nothing to compare with what is expected for the inaugural parade earlier in the day.

30,000 to March in Parade

Thirty thousand service men and civilians will march in the parade, and hundreds of thousands will watch. Yet F. Joseph Donohue, parade chairman, is aiming for what he believes is the shortest inaugural parade in recent history—one of two hours and forty-six minutes. This would compare with the first Eisenhower inaugural parade of four hours and thirty-nine minutes.

Army Issues Booklet

To get the giant show on the road, the Army has issued an eighty-three-page book of orders. It closely resembles a battle plan (the closed television circuits for coordinating the parade are known as Blueberry 1-8 and Red Carpet 1-11). The booklet warns in capital letters that lagging units will be pulled out and placed at the end of the line.

"We intend to make this two hours and forty-six minutes," Mr. Donohue said, "not two hours and forty-seven minutes."

Mr. Foley said that every detail of the inauguration had been taken care of. "The only thing left is the weather," he said.

But even here they are ready. The inauguration takes place regardless of rain or snow.

According to the Army's plan for snow, which has yet to fall, from 0001 hours 18 January until 1000 hours 21 January the service will remove all snow—and can call on two front-loaders from Fort Meade, Md., and fourteen front-loaders, ninety dump trucks and six road-graders from Fort Belvoir, Va.

Kennedy Sworn In, Asks 'Global Alliance' Against Tyranny, Want, Disease, and War

Nation Exhorted

Inaugural Says U.S. Will 'Pay Any Price' to Keep Freedom

By W.H. LAWRENCE

WASHINGTON, Jan. 20—John Fitzgerald Kennedy assumed the presidency today with a call for a "grand and global alliance" to combat tyranny, poverty, disease and war.

In his Inaugural Address, he served notice on the world that the United States was ready to "pay any price, bear any burden, meet any hardship, support any friend, oppose any foe to ensure the survival and the success of liberty."

But the nation is also ready, he said, to resume negotiations with the Soviet Union to ease, and if possible, to remove world tensions.

"Let us begin anew," Mr. Kennedy declared. "Let us never negotiate out of fear. But let us never fear to negotiate."

Asks Aid of Countrymen

He called on his fellow-citizens to join his Administration's endeavor:

"Ask not what your country can do for you—ask what you can do for your country."

At 12:51 P.M., he was sworn in by Chief Justice Earl Warren as the nation's thirty-fifth President, the first Roman Catholic to hold the office.

Ten minutes earlier, Lyndon Baines Johnson of Texas took the oath as Vice President. It was administered by Sam Rayburn, Speaker of the House of Representatives.

At 43 years of age, the youngest man ever elected to the Presidency, Mr. Kennedy took over the power vested for eight years in Dwight D. Eisenhower, who, at 70, was the oldest.

President Kennedy alluded to the change of generation in his Inaugural.

'Torch Has Passed'

He said:

"Let the word go forth from this time and place to friend and foe alike, that the torch has been passed to a new generation of Americans—born in this century, tempered by war, disciplined by a hard and bitter peace, proud of our ancient heritage—and unwilling to witness or permit the slow undoing of those human rights to which this nation has always been committed, and to which we are committed today at home and around the world."

A blanket of 7.7 inches of newly fallen snow, bitter winds and a sub-freezing temperature of 22 degrees held down the crowds that watched the ceremony in front of the newly renovated East Front of the Capitol.

But the crowds swelled under a cheering, if not warming, sun from a cloudless sky as the new President and his wife Jacqueline led the Inaugural parade from the Capitol back to the White House shortly after 2 P.M. The police estimated that the crowds might have totaled 1,000,000, but this seemed excessive.

A crowd estimated at 20,000 persons saw the new President assume office.

From snow-mantled Capitol Hill, he led the big parade, with peaceful themes as well as displays of military might, down broad Constitution and Pennsylvania Avenues to the White House. With his wife he rode in the familiar "bubbletop" Presidential limousine.

"Let every nation know, whether it wishes us well or ill, that we shall pay any price, bear any burden . . . to assure the survival and the success of liberty."

Reviews Parade

At the White House, he mounted the canopied reviewing stand, where he stayed for the entire three-and-a-half-hour parade. Most of the time he was bareheaded and occasionally sipped soup and coffee.

The retiring Republican leaders—Mr. Eisenhower and Richard M. Nixon—joined in the applause as the new President outlined in sober terms and a deliberate manner the general course of his Administration.

Mr. Nixon, defeated for the Presidency by Mr. Kennedy last Nov. 8 in the

John and Jacqueline Kennedy and others leaving the White House, January 20, 1961. (Paul Schutzer/Time & Life Pictures/Getty Images)

closest election of modern times, was the first after Chief Justice Warren to shake hands with President Kennedy after the oath-taking.

The Kennedy Inaugural, which was both firm and conciliatory in its approach to the Soviet-led Communist bloc, was well received by both Republicans and Democrats on Capitol Hill.

President Kennedy called on the Soviet Union for a new beginning. He asked a renewed effort to negotiate problems that he said threatened destruction of the world, but, if settled, could afford hope that all forms of human poverty might be abolished.

Warning that civility should not be mistaken for weakness and that sincerity was always subject to proof, Mr. Kennedy asked "both sides" to explore what problems "unite us instead of belaboring those problems which divide us."

"Let both sides, for the first time, formulate serious and precise proposals for the inspection and control of arms—and bring the absolute power to destroy other nations under the absolute control of all nations," he continued.

"Let both sides seek to invoke the wonders of science instead of the terrors," he went on. "Together let us explore the stars, conquer the deserts, eradicate disease, tap the ocean depths and encourage the arts and commerce."

'New World of Law'

If a beachhead of cooperation could "push back the jungles of suspicion," Mr. Kennedy said, both sides could then join in a new endeavor, not simply for a new balance of power, but rather "a new world of law, where the strong are just and the weak secure and the peace preserves."

With Mr. Eisenhower sitting about a yard away, President Kennedy emphasized some of the stands he will take on foreign policy.

He told the newly emerging nations

of Africa he would not "always expect to find them supporting our view."

"But we shall always hope to find them strongly supporting their own freedom," he declared, "and to remember that, in the past, those who foolishly sought power riding the back of the tiger inevitably ended up inside."

He emphasized that he favored a stronger North Atlantic Treaty Organization, unqualified support for the United Nations, and helping under-developed nations "break the bonds of mass misery."

"If a free society cannot help the many who are poor, it cannot save the few who are rich," he asserted.

In an apparent allusion to the regime of Premier Fidel Castro of Cuba, with which the Eisenhower Administration broke diplomatic relations earlier this month, the new President sounded a warning to the Russians not to interfere in the Western Hemisphere.

"Let all our neighbors know that we shall join with them to oppose aggression or subversion anywhere in the Americas," he said. "And let every other power know that this hemisphere intends to remain the master of its own house."

To the Latin-American nations generally, he offered "a special pledge" that good words would be converted "into good deeds" in an effort "to assist free men and free governments in casting off the chains of poverty."

Uses Family Bible

During his induction, President Kennedy's hand rested on a family Bible—a Douay version, the English translation made for Roman Catholics in the sixteenth century. He chose not to have it open to any particular passage, as has been the custom in some past inaugurations.

He took office with the prayers of four major faiths to bolster him in his pledges. The invocation was delivered by Richard Cardinal Cushing of Boston, a close friend of the Kennedy family.

The ceremonies were presided over by Senator John J. Sparkman, Democrat of Alabama, chairman of the Joint Congressional Committee on Inaugural Arrangements.

They opened with "The Star-Spangled Banner," sung by Marian Anderson, the contralto.

Robert Frost, the New England poet, read his poem, "The Gift Outright," which President Kennedy had especially requested in inviting Mr. Frost to the Inaugural. He also sought to preface it with a verse he had written for the occasion to praise Mr. Kennedy for "summoning artists to participate." But the bright sun and wind combined to defeat him. He did not need to read "The Gift Outright."

Has 4 Hours of Sleep

In his day of triumph President Kennedy seemed unaffected and unfrightened as he approached the responsibilities of leadership.

With barely four hours' sleep after

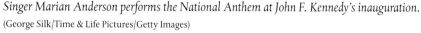

Singer Marian Anderson performs the National Anthem at John F. Kennedy's inauguration.
(George Silk/Time & Life Pictures/Getty Images)

President Kennedy giving his inaugural address; First row from left to right, Mamie Eisenhower, Lady Bird Johnson, Jacqueline Kennedy, Dwight Eisenhower, Justice Earl Warren, John F. Kennedy, Lyndon Johnson, Richard M. Nixon, Sen. John Sparkman, the Trumans, Sam Rayburn.

(Frank Scherschel/Time & Life Pictures/Getty Images)

last night's Inaugural Concert and gala and a victory celebration thereafter, he was up at 8 A. M. He attended a mass at Holy Trinity Roman Catholic Church at 9 A. M.

Bronzed by the Florida sun during his pre-inauguration holiday, with his brown hair neatly brushed, he looked the picture of health as he tackled the White House job.

He lost no time in getting to work. Minutes after he took the oath, he repaired to a Senate office to sign the of-ficial nominating papers for his ten Cabinet members and Adlai E. Stevenson as representative to the United Nations, a post with Cabinet status.

He also sent word to the White House staff to be on duty by 8:45 A. M. tomorrow, although tonight was a long night of celebration at five inaugural balls at the National Guard Armory and four Washington hotels.

He told the Inaugural crowd it could expect no swift miracles to solve the nation's problems or end the "cold war."

His Administration's aims, he said, could not be finished in "the first 100 days," the period for which the first Franklin D. Roosevelt Administration is remembered because of the speed with which Congress and the new Administration moved.

Indeed, Mr. Kennedy went on, the problems of this world would not be solved in the first 1,000 days, "nor even perhaps in our lifetime on this planet."

Inaugural Address, January 20, 1961

Vice President Johnson, Mr. Speaker, Mr. Chief Justice, President Eisenhower, Vice President Nixon, President Truman, Reverend Clergy, fellow citizens:

We observe today not a victory of party but a celebration of freedom—symbolizing an end as well as a beginning—signifying renewal as well as change. For I have sworn before you and Almighty God the same solemn oath our forbears prescribed nearly a century and three-quarters ago.

The world is very different now. For man holds in his mortal hands the power to abolish all forms of human poverty and all forms of human life. And yet the same revolutionary beliefs for which our forebears fought are still at issue around the globe—the belief that the rights of man come not from the generosity of the state but from the hand of God.

We dare not forget today that we are the heirs of that first revolution. Let the word go forth from this time and place, to friend and foe alike, that the torch has been passed to a new generation of Americans—born in this century, tempered by war, disciplined by a hard and bitter peace, proud of our ancient heritage—and unwilling to witness or permit the slow undoing of those human rights to which this nation has always been committed, and to which we are committed today at home and around the world.

Let every nation know, whether it wishes us well or ill, that we shall pay any price, bear any burden, meet any hardship, support any friend, oppose any foe to assure the survival and the success of liberty.

This much we pledge—and more.

... to those nations who would make themselves our adversary, we offer not a pledge but a request: that both sides begin anew the quest for peace, before the dark powers of destruction unleashed by science engulf all humanity in planned or accidental self-destruction.

We dare not tempt them with weakness. For only when our arms are sufficient beyond doubt can we be certain beyond doubt that they will never be employed.

But neither can two great and powerful groups of nations take comfort from our present course—both sides overburdened by the cost of modern weapons, both rightly alarmed by the steady spread of the deadly atom, yet both racing to alter that uncertain balance of terror that stays the hand of mankind's final war.

Kennedy delivers inaugural address while Jacqueline Kennedy and former president Dwight D. Eisenhower look on.

(*The Boston Globe*/Getty Images)

"And so, my fellow Americans: ask not what your country can do for you—ask what you can do for your country."

So let us begin anew—remembering on both sides that civility is not a sign of weakness, and sincerity is always subject to proof. Let us never negotiate out of fear. But let us never fear to negotiate.

Let both sides explore what problems unite us instead of belaboring those problems which divide us.

Let both sides, for the first time, formulate serious and precise proposals for the inspection and control of arms—and bring the absolute power to destroy other nations under the absolute control of all nations.

Let both sides seek to invoke the wonders of science instead of its terrors. Together let us explore the stars, conquer the deserts, eradicate disease, tap the ocean depths and encourage the arts and commerce.

Let both sides unite to heed in all corners of the earth the command of Isaiah—to "undo the heavy burdens . . . (and) let the oppressed go free."

And if a beachhead of cooperation may push back the jungle of suspicion, let both sides join in creating a new endeavor, not a new balance of power, but a new world of law, where the strong are just and the weak secure and the peace preserved.

All this will not be finished in the first one hundred days. Nor will it be finished in the first one thousand days, nor in the life of this Administration, nor even perhaps in our lifetime on this planet. But let us begin.

In your hands, my fellow citizens, more than mine, will rest the final success or failure of our course. Since this country was founded, each generation of Americans has been summoned to give testimony to its national loyalty. The graves of young Americans who answered the call to service surround the globe.

Now the trumpet summons us again—not as a call to bear arms, though arms we need—not as a call to battle, though embattled we are—but a call to bear the burden of a long twilight struggle, year in and year out, "rejoicing in hope, patient in tribulation"—a struggle against the common enemies of man: tyranny, poverty, disease and war itself.

Can we forge against these enemies a grand and global alliance, North and South, East and West, that can assure a more fruitful life for all mankind? Will you join in that historic effort?

In the long history of the world, only a few generations have been granted the role of defending freedom in its hour of maximum danger. I do not shrink from this responsibility—I welcome it. I do not believe that any of us would exchange places with any other people or any *other generation. The energy, the faith, the devotion which we bring to this endeavor will light our country and all who serve it—and the glow from that fire can truly light the world.*

And so, my fellow Americans: ask not what your country can do for you—ask what you can do for your country.

My fellow citizens of the world: ask not what America will do for you, but what together we can do for the freedom of man.

Finally, whether you are citizens of America or citizens of the world, ask of us here the same high standards of strength and sacrifice which we ask of you. With a good conscience our only sure reward, with history the final judge of our deeds, let us go forth to lead the land we love, asking His blessing and His help, but knowing that here on earth God's work must truly be our own.

Jacqueline Kennedy has a chuck under the chin for her husband moments after he became president, in the Capitol rotunda, January 20, 1961. (Henry Burroughs/Associated Press)

The Early Days

'Kennedy and Press' Seems a Hit; Star Shows Skill as Showman

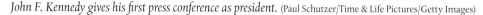

By RUSSELL BAKER

WASHINGTON, Jan 25—The new style Presidential news conference, which replaced "Popeye the Sailor Man" at kiddie time on the home screen tonight, looks like a hit.

It has a new star with tremendous national appeal and the skill of a consummate showman, the President of the United States. At one point he flabbergasted his supporting cast by giving a questioner the precise location of the seized cruise liner Santa Maria.

At 4:10 this afternoon, he told this man, she was 600 miles north of the Amazon River, at 10 Degrees 35 Minutes North, 45 Degrees 32 Minutes West, proceeding on a course of 117 degrees at a speed of fifteen knots.

In line with the trend of panoramic, all-day movies, the Kennedy news conference is bigger, longer, and compared with the intimate conferences that

President Dwight D. Eisenhower used to conduct, produced with a cast of thousands.

The setting is the auditorium of the New State Department Building, an amphitheatre done in the modern electronic mode and except for coral and black trim on the cushioned seats, about as warm as an execution chamber.

Under Mr. Eisenhower, the conferences were held in the Indian Treaty room of the Old State Department Building adjoining the White House. There, in a cubicle that heated up like the Black Hole of Calcutta when the floodlights went on, baroque brass cherubs looked down on the President and the newsmen, pressed together in indescribable misery, sat close enough to reach his pulse or feel the heat when his temper blew.

Not in the new production. Presi-

dent Kennedy stands behind a lectern on a stage, a deep spacious well separating him from his antagonists, who rise in tier upon tier before him like the audience in a theatre balcony.

There were 418 persons in the auditorium when Mr. Kennedy, a study in bronze skin and sandy hair, strode onto stage a moment after 6 P. M. wearing a blue pin-stripe suit and a white shirt.

From the beginning Mr. Kennedy clearly established himself as the star of the show. This was the result of a brilliant stroke executed Sunday by Pierre Salinger, Mr. Kennedy's press secretary.

Mr. Salinger simply announced that reporters questioning the President need not identify themselves and their organizations.

The requirement of identification had been in effect since the Truman Administration. Mr. Salinger's abandoning of it was a rending blow to the theatrical types in the press corps who, presented with their first opportunity to share billing with the President before a national audience, learned that they would appear anonymously.

John F. Kennedy gives his first press conference as president. (Paul Schutzer/Time & Life Pictures/Getty Images)

Nevertheless, at times there were as many as thirty persons on their feet shouting simultaneously for the President's attention.

Mr. Kennedy handled them, and some exceedingly delicate questions, with the controlled poise of a man who knew his brief. In his replies to difficult foreign policy questions, he was precise without permitting himself to say more than he wanted.

Replying to questions that he did not mean to answer, he avoided prolixity. The few questions that held a hook, he avoided. To one man whose premises seemed argumentative, he remarked that the question was a "statement," and finessed it graciously.

After thirty-eight minutes, Marvin Arrowsmith of The Associated Press called the traditional, "Thank you, Mr. President," and down in front there was some minor scuffling for the door.

In the old days, the world did not know what the President had said until the room was opened at the end. Tonight, however, it was all public knowledge before the first reporter hit the exit.

In the old days, one of the dramatic highlights of every conference was the thundering crash of bodies against the exit as newsmen fought to be first to the telephone. There was no need for that tonight.

Moscow Frees 2 RB-47 Survivors; Kennedy Calls Khrushchev Move a Step Toward Better Relations

---

Pair Flying Home

Soviet Released Men Without Conditions, President Says

By W.H. LAWRENCE

WASHINGTON, Jan. 25—President Kennedy announced tonight that the Soviet Union had released two United States airmen shot down in an RB-47 reconnaissance plane over the Barents Sea and held prisoner since July 1.

Conference Is Broadcast

At the conference, broadcast live by television and radio across the nation, President Kennedy also announced he had ordered a continuance of the ban on "overflights" of Soviet territory.

The President said at the meeting in the new State Department building that nothing had been promised the Soviet in return for the release of the fliers. No personal conferences were planned by him with Khrushchev.

Powers Still in Prison

President Kennedy was the first to announce the release of the fliers. Soviet authorities in Moscow followed with an announcement of their own about an hour after the President's statement.

A clear distinction was drawn by President Kennedy between the RB-47 fliers released today and Francis Gary Powers, the U-2 pilot who is still in prison.

It has been the contention of this Government that the RB-47 was shot down over international waters, whereas it was admitted that Mr. Powers was deep in Soviet territory.

The unarmed RB-47 was described officially as on a reconnaissance flight from its base in England to carry out an "electromagnetic survey" for making maps of the earth's magnetic field as a navigational aid. The Soviet contended, however, that the aircraft had entered Soviet territory and therefore the downing of the plane was justified.

He Meets Many Questions

Answering a broad range of questions in a thirty-eight-minute news conference President Kennedy also made these major points:

The United States had asked for a postponement of negotiations on a nuclear test ban, scheduled for Geneva in early February, until late March. This was to allow more time to develop a "clear" new United States position.

The Government would substantially increase its contributions to relieve famine in the Congo and would airlift 1,000 tons of food in a program which, United Nations authorities said, should be adequate to relieve the famine.

The United States is not considering a restoration of relations with Cuba. Though interested in movements throughout this hemisphere to provide "a better life for the people," it necessarily had to be concerned about movements that were "seized" by "aliens" in the hemisphere.

The United States was eager to have a "peaceful, independent" Government in Laos. It should be an "uncommitted country" that was "not dominated by either side."

Speaker Sam Rayburn's attempt to weaken the conservative coalition in the House Rules Committee was endorsed by the President "as an interested citizen" who thought every Congressman should have the chance to vote on his program and not be blocked from that opportunity by "a small group of men."

Sending food to Communist China seemed to have little point because of the probability that it would be refused and because despite the present shortage China was exporting food to Africa and Cuba.

Kennedy Confers With His Advisers on Policy in Asia

Receives Report on Vietnam—Relations With Soviet Believed Under Study

By WILLIAM J. JORDEN

WASHINGTON, Jan. 28—President Kennedy met at the White House for two and a half hours today with a group of his highest aides and advisers.

The White House press secretary, Pierre Salinger, said the discussion covered "over-all world problems." He said the ideas developed at the meeting would be reflected in Mr. Kennedy's State of the Union message Monday.

Those present at the meeting included Vice President Johnson, Secretary of State Dean Rusk, Defense Secretary Robert McNamara and Gen. Lyman L. Lemnitzer, chairman of the Joint Chiefs of Staff.

Also taking part were Paul H. Nitze, Assistant Secretary of Defense for International Security Affairs; McGeorge Bundy, the President's special assistant for national security affairs; Walt W. Rostow, deputy special assistant to the President, and Theodore C. Sorenson, White House special counsel.

Soviet Study Likely

It was assumed that prominent among the problems considered was the matter of relations with the Soviet Union.

One thing apparently not discussed was the charge by some Republicans that the Administration might be "compromising" in dealing with Moscow. Mr. Salinger said he was "sure that the subject never came up."

In addition to the broad discussion of world problems, President Kennedy received a detailed report on Vietnam. Secretary of State Rusk and others gave the President up-to-the-minute reports on developments in the divided country bordering on strife-torn Laos.

Sources here said they were sure that the special Vietnam study did not presage a new crisis or reflect any concern about developments there.

Third Meeting in Week

The special White House meeting, the third of its kind in a week, was part of what is shaping up as a systematic review of American policy in Asia. President Kennedy, Secretary Rusk and other top officials in the Administration have expressed a deep interest in and concern with Asian affairs and the search for steps to counter the many political and economic problems that face the United States there.

There were other clear indications that the Administration was taking a new look at some of the many problems confronting it in Asia.

A meeting with the Chinese Communists in Warsaw scheduled for Feb. 2 has been postponed until March 7. This is one of the many sessions between the United States and Chinese Ambassadors that have been held since 1957.

Officials insisted that the postponement did not mean that this Government planned to make any new or dramatic changes in its policy toward the Peiping Government. But it was felt the delay would permit the Administration to study the record of the past talks and make any new approaches it might desire.

It was also announced that Ambassador Winthrop G. Brown was returning from Vientiane to report on the situation in Laos. He is due to arrive in Washington Monday night. He will confer with State Department officials and possibly with the President.

The Administration has been taking a wary attitude toward all foreign policy issues. There is no disposition to change for the sake of change, sources here say, but the new men are taking the approach that policies of the past are not necessarily irreversible.

Officials and diplomats who follow these trends closely could discern no evidence of sweeping changes to come. What they expect is new approaches, new techniques, and new attitudes.

In Asia, it is considered likely that the future lines of action will follow those laid down in published and private statements by the President. This approach, in turn, reflects the feeling in high Administration circles that the United States has unnecessarily and unwisely dissipated much good-will and friendliness in Asian countries in recent years.

Among the more important changes that are widely expected here concern the following areas and problems:

Colonialism—The dominant view is that in its policy statements and its actions the Administration will come out with increasing vigor against colonialism. This may raise problems in relations with some of the allies who hold colonies and the Administration seems prepared to take that risk.

Economic Aid—The feeling is strong in the Kennedy Administration that there has been too much weight on military aid in the past and too little aimed at meeting what recipients consider their main problems. There is also a strong opinion in Administration circles that too much United States aid has been motivated negatively, by fear of or opposition to communism. They feel it should be directed positively at overcoming problems of poverty, disease and the like.

Neutralism—There is considerably more appreciation now than a few years ago of the forces that impel Asian and other peoples toward a neutral stance.

Kennedy Challenges Congress to Meet Grave Perils Abroad and Worsening Slump at Home

Action is Sought

State of Union Speech Calls for Drive to Step Up Defenses

By W.H. LAWRENCE

WASHINGTON, Jan. 30—President Kennedy challenged Congress and the nation today to face up to grave perils abroad and a worsening economic recession at home.

In his first State of the Union Message, given before a joint session of Congress, he called for executive and legislative actions to strengthen the national defenses to avert big and little wars and to spur the lagging economy.

Mr. Kennedy disclosed that he had already ordered a speed-up in the building of Polaris submarines, in missile development and in defense airlift capacity to meet the threat of Communist expansion.

Reports Troubled Economy

The President summarized the nation's economic condition, noting that bankruptcies were high, unemployment had increased and that profits were below what had been predicted. "In short," he said, "the American economy is in trouble."

The 43-year-old President emphasized the gravity of the threats facing the nation and his dissatisfaction with the tools he had for waging the struggles abroad and at home.

Mr. Kennedy declared:

"I speak today in an hour of national peril and national opportunity. Before my term has ended, we shall have to test anew whether a nation organized and governed such as ours can endure. The outcome is by no means certain. The answers are by no means clear. All of us together—this Administration, this Congress, this nation—must forge those answers."

The President said that he would make the nation ready to resist any effort by aggression or subversion to dominate the world. But he remains ready at all times, he indicated, to cooperate on peaceful projects such as the exploration of space or the planets. He also voiced hope that an enforceable arms control agreement could be negotiated in good faith.

Contrast With Eisenhower

The "state of the union" on which Mr. Kennedy reported today bore little resemblance to the "state of the union" on which President Eisenhower reported just before he left the White House.

What Mr. Eisenhower reported reflected his satisfaction over the results of his Administration; what Mr. Kennedy reported on was what seemed to him the harsh facts of life about the continuing struggle against the Communist powers abroad and an economic downturn at home.

President Kennedy's first State of the Union message focused on the economy and the struggle against Communism. (Paul Schutzer/Time Life Pictures/Getty Images)

He was interrupted by applause thirty-seven times in the forty-three minutes he spoke but most of the cheering came from Democrats. Looking on in addition to the members of the House and Senate were the Cabinet, the Supreme Court and nearly 100 members of the diplomatic corps.

Mrs. Kennedy, in a plum-colored suit, sat in the gallery with her mother and step-father, Mr. and Mrs. Hugh D. Auchincloss, and her sister-in-law, Mrs. Robert F. Kennedy, wife of the Attorney General.

President Kennedy received a fifty-eight-second standing ovation as he entered the House chamber. He took his place at the lectern directly below and in front of Vice President Johnson and Speaker Rayburn. He was introduced by the Speaker.

The President used gestures sparingly, but the familiar campaign sign—the chopping right hand—was noticeable from time to time.

Republicans cheered the loudest when the Democratic President pledged a firm defense of the value of the dollar against the outflow of gold without raising the gold price above $35 an ounce or without instituting exchange controls.

Both sides cheered his promise to keep the budget as close to balance as possible. He said his own planned program of expenditures for next year, barring development of urgent national defense needs or a worsening economy, would not "of and by themselves" unbalance the $80,900,000,000 budget submitted by President Eisenhower before he left office on Jan. 20.

Foresees Budget Deficit

But the loss of revenues due to the recession, Mr. Kennedy said, makes it almost certain that the current budget will show a deficit. This also makes precarious—he said, the hopes that balance can be achieved in the next fiscal year even if Congress provides the additional revenues recommended by Mr. Eisenhower.

Mr. Kennedy sketched his legislative program only in broad general terms.

He reminded his listeners he had been in office only ten days. Thus were he now to offer detailed legislative remedies for every national ill, he remarked, Congress would rightly wonder whether the desire for speed had replaced the duty of responsibility."

The President promised a special economic message within fourteen days. He said it would provide, among other things, for temporary extension in the duration of unemployment compensation benefits for millions now jobless, higher minimum wages, and "tax incentives for sound plant investment."

Not Despairing of Future

At the outset, Mr. Kennedy said his review of national problems was not intended "to despair the future nor indict the past." Many of the things he said, however, were subject to being interpreted as being critical of his predecessor, Mr. Eisenhower.

> *"Before my term has ended, we shall have to test anew whether a nation organized and governed such as ours can endure."*

The national economy, the President said, has been going through "seven months of recession, three and a half years of slack, seven years of diminished economic growth, and nine years of falling farm income."

The recovery from the recession in 1958, he said, has been "anemic and incomplete." As a result, he said, unemployment has never returned to normal levels and maximum use of industrial capacity has never been fully restored.

Amid applause by Democrats, Mr. Kennedy said that "this Administration does not intend to stand helplessly by."

Indirectly, he seemed critical of Mr. Eisenhower when he pledged that as President he would "withhold from neither the Congress nor the people any fact or report, past, present or future, which is necessary for an informed judgement of our conduct and hazards."

Mr. Eisenhower withheld several reports critical of his Administration that were demanded by Congress and the General Accounting Office.

On the military front, where President Eisenhower took pride in his own leadership, Mr. Kennedy said:

"Lack of a consistent, coherent military strategy, the absence of basic assumptions about our national requirements and the faulty estimate and duplication from inter-service rivalries have all made it difficult to assess accurately how adequate—or inadequate—our defenses really are."

For the most part, the new President was preoccupied with global concerns. In these he included the pressures of the Soviet Union and Communist China and his conviction, after only ten days in office, that "in each of the principal areas of crisis, the tide of events had been running out and time has not been our friend."

He paid special attention to Latin America and the need to develop "a new alliance for progress," which he also stated in the Spanish words, "Alianza para progreso." To this end he asked Congress to appropriate in full the $500,000,000 development fund pledged by the agreement at the Bogota conference.

Again Mr. Kennedy was critical of the Fidel Castro regime in Cuba, and its domination by Communists.

"Our objection with Cuba is not over the people's drive for a better life," he said. "Our objection is to their domination by foreign and domestic tyrannies. Cuban social and economic reform should be encouraged. Questions of economic and trade policy can always be negotiated. But Communist domination in this hemisphere can never be negotiated."

Kennedy Submits Aged Care Plan;
Stiff Fight Likely

Extension of Social Security Would Insure 14 Million Over 65 Against Illness

TAX RISE OF 1.5 BILLION

Republicans Openly Hostile—Some Key Democrats Are Cool to Program

By JOHN D. MORRIS

WASHINGTON, Feb. 9—President Kennedy laid before a divided Congress today a broad program of Federal insurance to provide medical care for the aged.

The message, read to the House and Senate by clerks, immediately drew manifestations of stiff opposition. Everett McKinley Dirksen, the Senate Republican leader, and Charles A. Halleck, House Republican leader, were among the first to record their opposition.

The health insurance part of the program faces especially strong resistance despite the backing of the Democratic leaders of Congress.

Aid to 14.2 Million

It calls for hospital, nursing home and other care for about 14,200,000 persons 65 years or more of age who are eligible for Social Security benefits under the Old Age, Survivors' and Disability Insurance System.

The new benefits would be financed by higher Social Security payroll deductions. Employers and employes would pay about $1,500,000,000 a year in additional taxes to finance the program.

The President's other recommendations supplement the health insurance keystone of his program. They are somewhat less controversial but are likely to meet considerable opposition from opponents of Federal spending for social-welfare projects.

They would be financed from general treasury revenues, presumably without a tax increase

They include:

Federal scholarships for medical and dental students.

Grants for construction, expansion and restoration of medical and dental schools.

Funds for construction of nursing homes and for improvement of nursing-home services.

Broader programs of research and rehabilitation, including increased appropriations for maternal and child health and welfare. A National Institute of Child Health and Human Development and a center for research in child health would be established.

To finance the new insurance system, President Kennedy recommended a two-part tax rise. Present Social Security rates are 3 per cent each for employes and 4½ per cent for the self-employed. They apply to the first $4,800 of a person's annual pay.

Under the Kennedy proposal, the first increase would take effect Jan. 1, 1962, when the tax would become applicable to the first $5,000 instead of $4,800 of earnings. Then, on Jan. 1, 1963, an additional levy of one-quarter of 1 per cent each would be imposed on employers and employes and an additional three-eighths of 1 per cent on the self-employed.

An employe who earns as much as $5,000 a year now pays $144 in Social Security taxes and his employer matches it. He would pay $150 in 1962 and $187.50 in 1963 as a combined result of the higher base, the proposed rate increase and the automatic rate increase already scheduled.

Benefits for all specified services except nursing home care would start July 1, 1962, with the nursing-home provisions taking effect six months later. The specified benefits are:

Up to ninety days of hospitalization in a single attack of illness. The patient would pay $10 of the daily costs for the first nine days. The insurance plan would pay the full costs after that.

Skilled nursing home services up to 180 days immediately after discharge from a hospital. Combined and nursing home care would be limited to 150 units, with each day of hospitalization counting as one unit.

Clinical diagnostic services for hospital outpatients, or those who visit hospitals for services without being admitted as inpatients. Costs in excess of $20 would be covered.

Community visiting nurse services and "related home health services" for a limited time. Officials said the limit would probably be 240 days.

Medical and surgical costs are not covered by the Administration plan. In his speech urging Congress to pass his health program, Mr. Kennedy said:

"As long as people are stricken by a disease which we have the ability to prevent, as long as people are chained by a disability which can be reversed, as long as needless death takes its toll, then American health will be unfinished business."

'Not Socialized Medicine'

Mr. Kennedy declared that his program was not "socialized medicine."

"It is a program of prepayment of health costs with absolute freedom of choice guaranteed," he said. "Every person will choose his own doctor and hospital."

Administration officials estimated the cost of benefits under the new insurance plan at about $1,100,000,000 in the first year of full operation.

Kennedy Sets Up Peace Corps To Work Abroad

Creates Pilot Plan and Asks Congress to Establish a Permanent Operation

Recruits To Get No Pay

President Aims to Have 500 on Job by the End of '61—Training Will Be Pushed

By PETER BRAESTRUP

WASHINGTON, March 1—President Kennedy issued an executive order today creating a Peace Corps. It will enlist American men and women for voluntary, unpaid service in the developing countries of the world.

The order set up the Peace Corps on a "temporary pilot basis." President Kennedy also sent Congress a message requesting legislation to make the corps permanent.

Announcing the move at his news conference, the President described the Peace Corps as a "pool of trained American men and women sent overseas by the United States Government or through private organizations and institutions to help foreign governments meet their urgent need for skilled manpower."

The President's expressed hope was to have 500 to 1,000 Peace Corps workers "in the field by the end of this year."

Shriver Heads Planners

The Administration's planning effort on the Peace Corps has been headed since late January by R. Sargent Shriver, a Chicago businessman and civic leader who is the President's brother-in-law. The President said today that a decision on who would head the agency would be made "in several days."

Life in the Peace Corps, the President stressed, "will not be easy." Members will work without pay but they will be given living allowances. They will live at the same level as the inhabitants of the countries to which they are sent.

The President emphasized that "we will send Americans abroad who are

President Kennedy greets the inaugural group of Peace Corps volunteers at a White House reception, August 28, 1961.

(Joseph Scherschel/Time & Life Pictures/Getty Images)

qualified to do a job," particularly those with technical skills in teaching, agriculture and health.

"There is little doubt," the President said in his subsequent message to Congress, "that the number of those who wish to serve will be far greater than our capacity to absorb them."

President Kennedy first broached his version of the Peace Corps idea in a campaign speech at San Francisco last Nov. 2. Previously, Senator Hubert H. Humphrey, Democrat of Minnesota, and Representative Henry S. Reuss, Democrat of Wisconsin, among others, had advocated such a plan.

In his San Francisco speech, Mr. Kennedy suggested that membership in the Peace Corps could be an alternative to the military draft.

Today President Kennedy said in his message that there would be no draft exemptions for members of the Peace Corps.

White House aides said that as a practical matter, draft boards would probably grant deferments to members of the Peace Corps.

White House spokesmen outlined the Peace Corps as follows: The initial cost for the fiscal year ending June 30 will be paid out of foreign aid funds that have already been appropriated.

For the following years, a special appropriation will be required from Congress. The cost for a worker a year is estimated at $5,000 to $12,000—including training, transportation, living allowances, medical care, and administrative overhead.

The State Department will be in charge of the program.

Personnel for the corps will also be made available through private universities, voluntary agencies, and United Nations bodies.

In the case of voluntary agencies, private institutions have the option of using their own recruitment system. Overseas, a small number of liaison officers from the Peace Corps or the International Cooperation Administra-tion will provide administrative support. Fifty to sixty persons will be employed at headquarters in Washington.

Screening will be rigorous, including security clearance by the Federal Bureau of Investigation.

Regional training centers will be set up by universities throughout the country to receive recruits after the school year ends. Each recruit will get three to six months training in language, culture, and work skills. In the pilot stage, in particular, applicants with language qualifications will be favored.

Negotiations are underway with foreign governments on service by the corps. Brazil, Colombia, Nigeria, Pakistan and the Philippines may become the first host nations.

The Administration will prohibit any use of the Peace Corps for religious missionary purposes. Nor will the Central Intelligence Agency be involved in any way.

Recruits Flocking to Join Corps

Rafer Johnson Asks to Serve—Work by Staff Is Heavy

By DAVID HALBERSTAM

WASHINGTON, March 1—Rafer Johnson, the Olympic decathlon champion, has volunteered to join the Peace Corps announced today by President Kennedy.

Forrest Evashevski, football coach at the University of Iowa and once a noted blocking back at the University of Michigan, will soon take a job at the headquarters of the corps in Washington.

Sally Bowles, daughter of Under Secretary of State Chester Bowles, and Nancy Gore, daughter of Senator Albert Gore of Tennessee, are already at work at corps headquarters.

Today, within an hour or two after President Kennedy had announced the establishment of the Peace Corps on a pilot basis, the switchboard at headquarters could not handle the calls from volunteers and inquirers.

The response to the idea of a voluntary organization in which American men and women could help the developing countries of the world has exceeded all expectations.

President Kennedy is reported to have received more letters about the Peace Corps than about any other issue—some 6,000 letters of suggestion, inquiry and open application. None mentions salary.

Ed Bayley, who is serving temporarily as public relations director for the corps, said that "not only do we get letters from young people who want to serve," but "I am amazed at the requests we have from people who want to work on the Washington staff—lawyers, newspaper men, business men.

"And for the young people—why this is a chance to participate directly in a Government which always seems so far away and distant."

Some of the headquarters staff members, such as Miss Gore, are not sure yet what they are being paid—and if they are being paid.

Miss Gore, 23 years old, said she chose the Peace Corps because:

"It's the first new idea of the New

Students at the University of Virginia discuss the Peace Corps in March 1961. (Joseph Scherschel/Time & Life Pictures/Getty Images)

Frontier. It's one of the few original things that's happened in a long time, and it's one that I can participate in, something that I can contribute to."

Miss Bowles, 22, said joining the staff of the Peace Corps "is exactly what I wanted to do—I feel very strongly about this and have ever since I was in India." She was there when her father was Ambassador to India. There, she said, she saw the potential for a group of dedicated young people.

Another young staff member, Miss Mitzi Mallina, 22, of Hastings-on-Hudson, N.Y., said the idea of the Peace

Corps had deeply touched today's college seniors.

"I know a lot of boys at Harvard and M. I. T. who have been waiting to hear the news about it—who have been hoping it would open up soon enough so that they could join when they got out of college," she said.

The letters are indicative too:

From Hartsville Ohio: "I could couple my knowledge of agriculture with a speaking knowledge of Spanish and work in Latin America."

From New York City: "I am willing to spend the rest of my life in work like

this because it can mean so much to our country."

From Cleveland: "Have you a place for me in your fight for peace?"

Mr. Johnson, who has volunteered for the corps, is serving as assistant track coach at the University of California at Los Angeles. The 25-year-old athlete was a track star at the university in 1956-58.

Mr. Evashevski, who is in his forties, is athletic director at the University of Iowa.

Kennedy Alerts Nation on Laos;
Warns Soviet Bloc, Asks Truce;
Stresses SEATO's Role in Crisis

Peril Emphasized

*President Voices U.S.
'Resolution'—Arms
Build-Up Pushed*

By W.H. LAWRENCE

WASHINGTON, March 23—President Kennedy told the people of the United States tonight of the dangers in the Laotian situation and warned the Communist world that "no one should doubt our resolution" to preserve an independent, neutral Laos.

In a nationally televised and broadcast news conference he said that hostilities must cease in Laos and negotiations for settlement of the country's problems must begin promptly.

The United States Government must consider with its allies, primarily those in the Southeast Asia Treaty Organization, what further military response from the non-Communist powers is necessary, he declared.

No Ultimatum Given

He delivered nothing like an ultimatum and did not fix a time limit for a halt to pro-Communist advances in Laos. But he said that the situation, critical to all Southeast Asia, was becoming "increasingly serious as the days go by."

Significantly, the President avoided a direct response to questions about whether United States military units had been alerted or already were on the move toward Laos. But as he spoke, the United States was reported to be sending its latest types of military equipment for use by the Southeast Asia Treaty Organization should the defense alliance find it necessary to take action in Laos.

Mr. Kennedy declared that "we strongly support the present British proposal of a prompt end of hostilities and prompt negotiation."

Moscow Gets Proposal

The British proposal, worked out in agreement with the United States, was given to the Soviet Government today. It calls for an immediate ceasefire, the

The President with Secretary of State Rusk and Secretary of Defense McNamara. (George Tames/The New York Times)

prompt recall of the International Control Commission for Laos to make sure that the cease-fire is effective and the calling of an international conference to work out a permanent settlement.

The President had a set of three maps of Laos, six by eight feet each, by his side and referred to them in the course of the news conference to show the advances made by pro-Communist forces.

Mr. Kennedy was unusually serious in manner as he began his news conference with a prepared statement on Laos. The conference, postponed from its normally scheduled Wednesday time, was broadcast and televised live to the nation.

"I want to make it clear to the American people and to all the world," Mr. Kennedy said, "that all we want in Laos is peace and not war, a truly neutral Government and not a cold war pawn, a settlement concluded at the conference table and not on the battlefield.

"Our response will be made in close cooperation with our allies and the wishes of the Laotian Government. We will not be provoked, trapped or drawn into this or any other situation but I know that every American will want his country to honor its obligations to the point that freedom and security of the free world and ourselves may be achieved."

The kind of response the United States Government receives on the Laotian question will help "to tell us what kind of a future this world will have," Mr. Kennedy declared.

Mr. Kennedy emphasized that the foreign ministers and other high officials of the Southeast Asia Treaty Organization, who meet Monday in Bangkok, Thailand, will have to consider their "necessary response" if the Communist-backed forces in Laos continue to advance.

"All members of SEATO have undertaken special treaty obligations toward an aggression in Laos," he said. "No one should doubt our resolutions on this point."

Secretary of State Dean Rusk, who was to depart tonight for the Bangkok conference, had a final twenty-minute talk with the President immediately after the news conference.

In a public statement before his departure, Secretary Rusk said that the treaty organization faced "a serious resurgence of danger to the independence of countries in the treaty area." He pledged continued United States adherence to the principle of collective security and said he was "confident" that our partners in SEATO fully subscribe to the same principle."

President Kennedy indicated that the Western response to continued aggression in Laos would depend on the will of all those concerned.

It is generally conceded among diplomats that any failure by the treaty group to respond would mean the demise of the treaty.

A sudden move by Moscow to accept the terms of a new Allied proposal for ending the fighting in Laos would relieve much of the pressure on the treaty group's ministers. But there was little expectation among United States and other Allied officials that the Soviet leadership would react so promptly.

The consensus here is that while the Communist-supported rebels are advancing in Laos, Moscow is not likely to halt their movement to accomodate the West. This is particularly true, it is believed, because the signs of Allied disunity on the whole problem were so apparent.

The President's statement on Laos at the beginning of the thirty-minute news conference consumed approximately one-third of the time allotted for the session, which was attended by a record number of 426 reporters.

The President called attention to the geographic position of Laos and its world implications in his answer to a question asking why the freedom of Laos was important to the security of the United States and to the individual American.

"It is quite obvious if the Commu-

nists were to move in and dominate this country, it would endanger the security of and the peace of all of Southeast Asia," the President said.

"And as a member of the United Nations and as a signatory of the SEATO pact, and as a country which is concerned with the strength of the cause of freedom around the world, that quite obviously affects the security of the United States," he added.

Mr. Kennedy stressed the obligations of the Southeast Asia Treaty Organization to the independence of Laos, even though that country was not a signatory to the pact.

The President's statement tonight seemed to confirm the view that has circulated here in recent days that the United States has no intention of becoming involved in the fighting in Laos alone or with only one or two of its allies.

Preliminary talks within the SEATO group have produced little enthusiasm among some of the members regarding military involvement in Laos. This has been particularly true of the French, British and New Zealanders. In fact, the only observable enthusiasm for strong action has come from Thailand and the Philippines, the countries with perhaps most to lose should Communist attacks succeed in the treaty area.

Security Issue Stressed

At each opportunity, he stressed his goal of awakening the American people to the problems this distant country posed for them and their security.

"My fellow Americans," he said, "Laos is far away from America but the world is small. Its 2,000,000 people live in a country three times the size of Austria. The security of all Southeast Asia will be endangered if Laos loses its neutral independence. Its own safety runs with the safety of us all, in real neutrality, observed by all."

The Bay of Pigs

Anti-Castro Units Trained To Fight At Florida Bases

Force There and in Central America Is Reported to Total 5,000 to 6,000

By TAD SZULC

MIAMI, Fla., April 6—For nearly nine months Cuban exile military forces dedicated to the overthrow of Premier Fidel Castro have been training in the United States as well as in Central America.

An army of 5,000 to 6,000 men constitutes the external fighting arm of the anti-Castro Revolutionary Council, which was formed in the United States last month. Its purpose is the liberation of Cuba from what it describes as the Communist rule of the Castro regime.

Many of those in the exile forces were companions of Dr. Castro in his revolution against the Batista regime.

Within Cuba, the Revolutionary Council counts on an ever-growing network engaged in organizing guerillas, carrying out sabotage and gathering intelligence.

Cuban leaders here expect that it will be possible to coordinate the activities of the external forces—those trained outside Cuba—and the internal forces when the time comes for a major move against the Castro fortress in Cuba.

Recruiting Ended

The recruiting of Cubans, which has been proceeding since last summer, is being discontinued as the anti-Castro leaders believe that their external forces have reached the stage of adequate preparation.

The external forces, many of them highly trained in landing, infiltration and sabotage operations, are now concentrated at two major camps in Guatemala and at a base in Louisiana, not far from New Orleans

This latest Cuban revolutionary army is reported by its leaders to include an air force, a navy and paratrooper units.

It is supported by commando type groups of infiltrators, saboteurs and guerrilla specialists who have been landing in Cuba for months from hidden bases in the Florida Keys in cooperation with the growing underground on the island.

Most of the instruction given to the anti-Castro forces was reported to have been centered in the Guatemalan camps where infantry and artillery units are being trained by United States experts.

But special instruction has been available in small camps in Florida.

Reports said that some of the air and paratroop units are in the Louisiana camps.

In the initial stages of the training that began last summer, groups were instructed in drill and the use of arms by individual Cuban organizations. Since last fall, the training has been centralized under the direction of a united Cuban political command.

This command was the Democratic Revolutionary Front, originally formed by five anti-Castro groups. It has enjoyed the tolerance and the active cooperation of United States officials

Opponents United

The front was organized in Miami late in the spring of 1960 as the principal anti-Castro organization. Last month it was absorbed into the Revolutionary Council formed to unite all the factions opposed to the Castro regime and to any resurgence of a Batista-type dictatorship.

Until the signing of the unity act last month and the establishment of the Revolutionary Council under Dr. Jose Miro Cardona, the military units of the Democratic Front operated separately from the groups of the Peoples' Revolutionary Movement headed by Manuel Ray, Dr. Castro's former Minister of Public Works.

The Ray movement is the foremost underground in Cuba, but it also has small military groups in the United States.

After the unity pact brought together the Democratic Front and the Peoples' Revolutionary Movement under the leadership of Dr. Miro Cardona, the Ray organization instructed its members to report to the training camps and staging areas in Guatemala where the Democratic Front officers remain in command.

This was done to maintain the unity of the exile groups although there are deep differences in political views between Senor Ray and the leaders of the Democratic Front.

Quick Action Opposed

Senor Ray, a soft-spoken engineer who studied in Utah, is opposed to any early military operation from abroad against Dr. Castro.

He thinks that it may open the United States to charges of collusion. He takes the view that it would be better to strike through an internal revolt aided from abroad.

Some of Senor Ray's military associates even question whether a force of 5,000 or 6,000 men, no matter how well trained and equipped, could actually succeed in establishing a substantial beachhead on Cuban territory against the powerful militia regiments armed with Soviet-bloc weapons.

Doctors Join Movement

Numerous Cuban doctors in exile in Florida have recently joined the revolutionary forces. Among them there were two of Cuba's most famous surgeons.

According to reports here, a hospital vessel—a converted yacht—has been equipped and is moored somewhere in the Florida keys. Surgical supply concerns here have reported that Cuban doctors have been making heavy purchases of blood plasma and other medical items.

The Cubans here—some of them with military training acquired in fighting with Dr. Castro—are being organized through a system of calls based on applications submitted by the volunteers.

A special intelligence unit of the Democratic Front investigates the volunteers to eliminate suspected Castro agents or persons connected with the former Batista regime.

The Castro agents—and hundreds of them are believed to be operating rather freely here—pose a more difficult problem. Although the Florida police and Federal authorities are aware of the presence of at least 100 of them little has been accomplished in efforts to deport them.

Occasionally, some are briefly detained on such charges as vagrancy and sometimes are brought into court on what a local police official describes as "selective law enforcement."

Officials here who read today of the charges made yesterday by Cuba's Foreign Minister, Raul Roa, in New York that an attack was being prepared here against the Castro regime are that most of his information came from these intelligence agents.

But, they said, many of the charges were completely inaccurate.

They said there appears to be no evidence to support Dr. Roa's accusation that the anti-Castro army is made up of "mercenaries and adventurers." It was declared that the vast majority of the Council's soldiers are Cubans and not what the Cuban Foreign Minister described as "Americans, Puerto Ricans, Spaniards, Nicaraguans, Guatemalans and former Nazis."

Flights to Guatemala

After the front's intelligence unit is satisfied that the volunteers are "clean" they are being advised to report to an assembly point in the Miami area where they are taken by trucks to one or more deactivated air bases. There they are issued khaki uniforms and board unmarked aircraft for flights to Guatemala.

In the strange atmosphere of Miami, bulging with refugees and revolutionaries, the preparations against Dr. Castro are an open secret. They are discussed in the streets, Cuban cafes and restaurants and almost everywhere that two or more Cubans congregate. Local newspapers openly refer to incidents in camps.

The families of the men in camp are reported to receive monthly checks from the Front. In the past, many of the Cubans were training at night or during week-ends while holding regular jobs here.

Even those commando specialists who engage in deliveries of weapons and sabotage material to the underground try to hold jobs.

Families receive letters from their husbands, sons and brothers who are in the army camps but the letters are often censored. It is impossible to determine from what precise spot they have been mailed.

The traffic of couriers between Florida and the island, serving the underground, goes on constantly, sometimes using the remaining passenger flights between Havana and Miami. More often the couriers travel by boats that run a virtual shuttle between the Florida coast and Cuba carrying instructions, weapons, and explosives

Some of the fast, patrol-type boats are built to specifications in the Miami area. Many of them are tied in the Miami River and navigate freely to and from the Caribbean on their missions.

Special boats equipped with powerful radio transmitters make daily runs to the Cuban coast and relay anti-Castro broadcasts originating here.

A few weeks ago a boat of the United States Fish and Wildlife Service captured a vessel carrying explosives for Senor Ray's underground. Subsequently the boat was released and the inspectors were told to be less observant next time.

Invasion Reported Near

The Columbia Broadcasting System issued a report last night saying that there were "unmistakable signs" that plans for an invasion of Cuba were in their final stages.

According to Stuart Novins, C. B. S. news correspondent now in Miami, mobilization orders have been issued by the anti-Castro command directing members of the invasion units to go to their previously assigned bases.

Bases in Florida were to have been cleared of Cuban exile troops. Mr. Novins said they had left by boat from secret ports and in planes from former United States air bases. Ships and planes loaded with uniforms and weapons were reported to be carrying special commando troops to final staging areas in the Caribbean and Central American areas.

The invasion force's first waves, according to the C. B. S. report, will probably have a strength of 4,000 to 5,000 men. They reportedly will be supported by some naval-based weapons and by air cover.

Several contingents of commando troops were said to be already at target areas inside Cuba, heavily armed with sabotage material. Some PT boats were reported to have been moving in and out of the Florida area for the past several days on transport missions to Central America.

ANTI-CASTRO UNITS LAND IN CUBA; REPORT FIGHTING AT BEACHHEAD; RUSK SAYS U.S. WON'T INTERVENE

PREMIER DEFIANT

Says His Troops Battle Heroically to Repel Attacking Force

By TAD SZULC

MIAMI, Tuesday, April 18—Rebel troops opposed to Premier Fidel Castro landed before dawn yesterday on the swampy southern coast of Cuba in Las Villas Province.

The attack, which was supported from the air, was announced by the rebels and confirmed by the Cuban Government.

After fourteen hours of silence on the progress of the assault, the Government radio in Havana broadcast early today a terse communiqué signed by Premier Castro announcing only that "our armed forces are continuing to fight the enemy heroically."

The announcement, made shortly before 1 A.M., said that within the next few hours details of "our successes" would be given.

The communiqué came amid a wave of rebel assertions of victories, new landings and internal uprisings. The rebel spokesmen were acclaiming important progress in new landings in Oriente and Pinar del Rio Provinces, but none of these reports could be confirmed.

Government Reports Battle

The Government communiqué said a battle had been fought in the southeastern part of Las Villas Province, where yesterday morning's landings occurred.

Although the communiqué was signed by Premier Castro, the Cuban leader has not spoken to his nation since the attack began. An earlier communiqué, issued yesterday, reported the rebel landings.

In a communiqué issued last night, the Revolutionary Council, the top command of the rebel forces, said merely that military supplies and equipment were landed successfully on the marshy beachhead. The communiqué added that "some armed resistance" by supporters of Premier Castro had been overcome.

Premier Castro was reported to have escaped injury in an early-morning air raid yesterday near the beachhead.

The Revolutionary Council's announcement spoke of action in Matanzas Province, indicating that the rebels might have crossed the provincial border from Las Villas. The border is about ten miles north of the presumed landing spot.

The communiqué also said that "substantial amounts of food and ammunition" had reached the underground units in that region.

The Government accused the United States of having organized the attack.

Late last night unconfirmed reports from rebel leaders asserted that the attacking force had penetrated deep into Matanzas Province, reaching the central highway near the town of Colon.

An insistent spate of reports said that numerous landings also had occurred in Oriente Province, in the eastern part of Cuba, in the vicinity of Santiago de Cuba. But a complete blackout of direct news from Cuba made it impossible to assess the situation accurately.

In New York, the Revolutionary Council announced that "much of the militia in the countryside has already defected from Castro." The council predicted that "the principal battle" of the revolt would be fought along with a coordinated wave of sabotage before dawn.

President Jose Miro Cardona of the council in an earlier statement had called for Western Hemisphere peoples to support the revolt "morally and materially." The council has announced its aim to set up a "government in arms" as soon as it can get territory in Cuba and then to ask for foreign recognition and help.

[A dispatch said that the Cuban naval station at Veradero had reported a fleet of eight strange ships off Cardenas, a north coast seaport about eighty-five miles east of Havana.]

National Alert Declared

The invaders, in undetermined numbers, are under the orders of the Revolutionary Council. In the words of its declaration, the Council seeks the overthrow of the Castro regime and the freeing of Cuba from "international communism's cruel oppression."

Premier Castro declared shortly before noon a state of national alert and

Cuban rebels before the Bay of Pigs invasion, April 1961. (Keystone/Getty Images)

called all his militia forces to their posts.

The Cuban official radio announced last night the arrest of Havana's Auxiliary Bishop, Msgr. Eduardo Roza Masvidal, on charges of hiding United States currency and medicine for anti-Castro rebels.

The Government-controlled radio stations offered their normal music programs and soap operas. There were no further references to the landings.

An occasional announcement spoke of foreign support for Cuba, including a mention of volunteers from Czechoslovakia seeking to enlist to fight in Cuba.

According to official statements by both sides, the rebel forces went ashore during the night near the Bay of Cochinos as paratroop units were dropped farther inland to link up with underground fighters.

It was believed that the rebels landed near Playa Larga, on the eastern bank of the Cochinos Bay, which means the Bay of Pigs. This bay is wedged into the vast swamp of the Cienega de Zapata.

Report of Capture Unconfirmed

Persistent reports in exile circles that Raul Castro, Fidel's brother and Minister of the Revolutionary armed forces, had been captured somewhere near Santiago could not be confirmed.

One Cuban in close touch with Democratic Revolutionary Front activities here said the report was given credence by the fact that Dr. Castro had assumed the military role that for recent months he had turned over to his brother.

Dr. Castro charged that the invaders were "mercenaries" in the service of United States "imperialism." He pledged the Cubans to fight until death for the preservation of their "democratic and Socialist revolution."

The Revolutionary Council members were standing by, ready to move into Cuba and proclaim a "government in arms" as soon as the beachhead is firmly secured.

It was not known early last night how many troops had participated in the Las Villas landing. Whether this was to be the principal thrust against the Castro forces or the first of several such attacks also was not known.

The total strength of forces available

to the rebels is estimated at somewhat over 5,000 men. Opposed to them is a military establishment of 400,000 of the regular army and the militia armed with the most modern Soviet bloc weapons.

The rebel command is known to believe that one or more major landings would set off internal uprisings and many desertions by soldiers and the militia.

Today it was too early to tell whether this optimism was justified.

The use by the rebels yesterday of planes and gunboats covering the landing indicated that it was an operation of major scope and not just another guerrilla foray of the type that has been occurring in the past.

It was believed here that the attacking forces came from the camps in Guatemala, where they have been trained for the last nine months. Some of the units may have come from a rebel camp in Louisiana.

Battle Area Strafed

It was believed however, that the rebel troops left their camps a day or so ago and were staged for the jump-off at Caribbean islands somewhere between Central America and the Cienaga de Zapata Peninsula of Las Villas Province.

A possible location of the staging area is the Swan Islands, where there is an anti-Castro radio station.

Capt. Manuel Artime a 29-year-old former Castro officer, is reported to be the field commander of the operation. He was appointed last week by the Revolutionary Council as its "delegate to the armed forces."

Rebel aircraft bombed and strafed the battle area that extends into Matanzas Province.

About 7 o'clock in the morning, Premier Castro, personally leading the defense operations, was reported to have found himself under an aerial bombardment in the small town of Boca de Laguna de Tesoro, about ten miles to the northeast of Cochinos Bay.

Cuban radio stations broadcast at 11:07 A.M. proclamations by Dr. Castro and President Osvaldo Doricos Torrado acknowledging that Cuba had been attacked and declaring a state of national alert.

Up to then, radio stations had kept up normal musical programs, which beginning at 8 A.M. were interrupted by constant "urgent" calls from the general staff of the army ordering militiamen to report immediately to their battle stations.

Opposed to them is a military establishment of 400,000 of the regular army and the militia armed with the most modern Soviet bloc weapons.

The only report issued during the day by the Castro regime on the progress of the fighting came in the Premier's proclamation. He declared that "our troops are advancing against the enemy in the certainty of victory."

Radio messages on the Government microwave network monitored here—which gave a dramatic minute-by-minute account of the first hours of the landing—included appeals for reinforcements from additional militia battalions and a request for ambulances for the "many wounded."

It was a frantic conversation between Government radio operators in the invasion area that provided the news that Premier Castro was in the town being bombed.

The network ceased transmitting at 7:20 A.M.—except for the sudden call for the ambulances that came at 11 A. M.

Varona's Visit Cited

There were many indications that the mechanism of the invasion was set finally into motion Sunday when Dr. Manuel Antonio De Varona, a member of the Revolutionary Council and Minister of Defense in the Provisional Government, made a quick flight and visit to Miami.

Simultaneously, a large number of exile leaders here, including military figures, vanished early Sunday. They have not been seen since.

The climate for the invasion—anticipated and promised by the Cuban rebels for many weeks—was created to a large extent by events of last week.

Since last Thursday a major wave of sabotage swept Cuba. Saturday three B-26 aircraft bombed three air bases on the island. Beginning in the middle of last week informants in Cuban groups made it known confidentially that "important events" were to be expected over the week-end.

Final preparations for the move against the Castro regime started in earnest about three weeks ago after the Revolutionary Council was formed and a secret mobilization order went out to rebel volunteers.

For the last three weeks hundreds of volunteers had been leaving the Miami and New York areas for the camps in the training grounds in Guatemala. Yesterday as word of the attack spread in Miami, additional hundreds of volunteers began appearing at the recruiting offices of several of the movements that make up the Revolutionary Council.

At least one sizable group of highly trained officers and men were still held back at a ranch on the outskirts of Miami.

In his proclamations, Dr. Castro appealed repeatedly for support by Latin-American nations. The Havana radio broadcast reports of Latin-American solidarity for the Cuban cause.

KENNEDY WARNS KHRUSHCHEV ON CUBA AFTER RUSSIAN VOWS HELP TO CASTRO; MIGS AND TANKS ATTACK BEACHHEAD

PRESIDENT IS FIRM

Tells Soviet U.S. Will Not Permit Meddling—Asks Laos Truce

By WALLACE CARROLL

WASHINGTON, April 18—President Kennedy warned the Soviet Union tonight that the United States would tolerate no outside military intervention in Cuba.

The President reacted in less than ten hours to a threat by Premier Khrushchev to give the Castro regime "all necessary assistance" in repelling attacks by forces.

In an icily worded message, the President rebuffed Mr. Khrushchev's request that the United States suppress the efforts of the anti-Castro exiles who are trying to maintain a beachhead in Cuba.

The President also took up the Soviet Premier's implied threat to stir up trouble in other parts of the world. If the Soviet Union sincerely wants to improve the international atmosphere, Mr. Kennedy said, it should accept a cease-fire in Laos, cooperate with the United Nations in the Congo and agree to reasonable proposals for a ban on tests of nuclear weapons.

Opposite page:

President Kennedy confers with former president Dwight D. Eisenhower at Camp David during the Bay of Pigs invasion.

(George Tames/*The New York Times*)

Communism Rejected

The President went beyond immediate issues to reject Soviet claims to the inevitable triumph of communism.

"The great revolution in the history of man, past, present and future, is the revolution of those determined to be free," Mr. Kennedy declared.

Secretary of State Dean Rusk handed the President's message to the Soviet Ambassador, Mikhail A. Menshikov, at 7 P. M. The message answered a communication from Premier Khrushchev that was given to the United States Embassy in Moscow this morning.

"You are under a serious misapprehension in regard to events in Cuba," Mr. Kennedy told the Premier.

The Castro dictatorship, he said, is "an alien-dominated regime." This was a restrained reiteration of the American contention that Dr. Castro's Government is under Soviet domination. Many Cubans, the President said, have found denial of liberties intolerable and have turned to resistance against Dr. Castro.

"Where the people are denied the right of choice," the President said, "recourse to such struggle is the only means of achieving their liberties."

The President then replied to Mr. Khrushchev's threat to aid Dr. Castro. Mr. Kennedy said:

"I have previously stated and I repeat now that the United States intends no military intervention in Cuba.

"In the event of any military intervention by outside forces we will immediately honor our obligations under the inter-American system to protect this hemisphere against external aggression."

This was an allusion to the pact of Rio De Janeiro of Aug. 15, 1947, that bound the republics of the hemisphere to consider "an armed attack by any state against an American state as an attack against all the American states." It also pledged the republics to "assist in meeting the attack."

The implication was that the United States would regard Soviet military intervention on the side of Dr. Castro as an attack on an American state and would answer in kind.

Although the United States is pledged not to intervene in Cuba, Mr. Kennedy said, "The United States admires the Cuban patriots who wish to establish a democratic system and will do nothing to curb them.

"The United States Government can take no action to stifle the spirit of liberty," Mr. Kennedy declared.

The President urged the Soviet leader not to use the situation in Cuba as a pretext to "inflame other areas of the world" and he warned him that such activity would be "dangerous to general peace."

The prevailing view among high officials, as well as in the embassies of allied nations, was that the Soviet Union would not risk an armed conflict with the United States over a country so far from its own borders.

The expectation was that the Russians would continue to give arms and military training to Dr. Castro's forces, but that they would stop short of anything that might draw them into a general war.

Despite this feeling, there was deep concern that arose mainly from two other circumstances.

U. S. Involvement Noted

The first was an uneasy awareness in the Government that the good name and prestige of the United States had become entangled in a small operation carried out by a few hundred Cuban exiles.

The second was a conviction that Premier Khrushchev, as well as Dr. Cas-

tro, had now determined to exploit the Cuban situation to the utmost—by Premier Khrushchev's personal skill in influencing world opinion, by maneuvers to pillory the United States in the United Nations, by mob attacks on American Embassies, and by all the other devices of propaganda.

All reliable sources here agree that the so-called "invasion" of Cuba by the exiles is only a limited operation. One high official said the landing forces might number 300 men. Another said there might be as many as 600, but certainly no more.

Both agreed that the objective was to carry supplies to the forces on the island already resisting the Castro Government.

This small-scale effort, however, was magnified from the beginning by exiles in their desire to encourage the Cubans to rise against Dr. Castro.

Both Dr. Castro and Premier Khrushchev have presumably been aware of the limited size of the landing forces. Thus, it is reasoned here, they are happy to go along with the exiles in exaggerating the scope of the landings, believing that the eventual propaganda effects of a disaster for the anti-Castro forces will be enhanced.

For the same reason, they are considered eager to heighten the appearance of United States involvement. A disaster for the anti-Castro exiles would then become a deadly blow to United States prestige.

The President discussed the Cuban situation at his weekly breakfast meeting with the Democratic leaders of Congress. News bulletins on Premier Khrushchev's message arrived while the meeting was going on, and the text came in a little later.

C.I.A. boss Allen W. Dulles, after a meeting of the National Security Council concerning the Cuban fiasco.
(Ed Clark/Time & Life Pictures/Getty Images)

CASTRO SAYS ATTACK IS CRUSHED; CUBA REBELS GIVE UP BEACHHEAD, REPORT NEW LANDINGS ON ISLAND

REAR GUARD IS HIT

But Foes of Regime Tell of a Link-Up With Guerrillas

By TAD SZULC

MIAMI, Thursday, April 20—The Government of Premier Fidel Castro claimed today that it had "completely defeated" the invasion force that landed Monday.

The announcement came amid insistent reports that two new rebel landings might be in progress on the northern coast of the island.

The rebel forces abandoned their beachhead on the southern coast and apparently merged with guerrillas in the near-by Escambray Mountains.

Premier Castro's claim of a victory came in a Government radio broadcast monitored here. The announcement said both sides had suffered heavy losses.

Rebels Reported Overrun

The Castro communiqué said that the last strongholds of the "mercenary troops" of the invasion force had been overrun at 5:30 P. M. yesterday. The attackers were said to have been on Cuban soil less than seventy-two hours.

Quantities of military equipment of North-American make were seized, including Sherman tanks, the broadcast said.

The Cuban radio said that part of the invasion force had attempted to evacuate their positions by boat, but that many boats had been sunk. The communiqué, which was signed by Premier Castro, said that the remnant of the liberation force had been trapped in a swampy area, apparently near their landing ground at Las Villas Province.

Early today, Radio Swan, an anti-Castro station on Swan Island off the coast of Honduras, reported that a rebel force had landed at, or near, Moron, a sugar port on the northern coast of Camaguey Province. The broadcast, which did not mention the scope of the operation, said that Capt. Nino Diaz, a one-time Castro lieutenant in the Sierra Maestra, had led the landing.

Yesterday a "terrific explosion" was reported in Moron by the Cuban Government communications network.

A communiqué of the Cuban Revolutionary Council declared last night that "the major portion" of the original landing party had reached the Escambray hills, despite "tragic losses among a small holding force."

The reported link up with the guerrillas, which earlier had been represented as a success, seemed to have been a defensive action under the impact of what the rebels described as an offensive by the Government's heavy tanks, MIG jet fighters and artillery.

As the military picture in strife-torn Cuba continued to present considerable confusion, indications appeared of a lack of coordination in the top rebel leadership.

These difficulties led to some doubts as to the future of joint operations involving the rebels. The force from the beach was reported to have broken through militia lines to move fifty miles to the Escambray area to join what is left of the guerrilla units there.

The area surrounding the Escambray Mountains is known to be heavily garrisoned by the troops of Premier Fidel Castro.

Yesterday Havana had announced that nine rebel aircraft had been shot down since Monday. Four of the planes had been downed early yesterday, the regime asserted. One of the planes was alleged to have been flown by a United States pilot.

'Invasion' Denied

Tuesday night a rebel plane bombed an air base near Havana.

The Cuban radio also announced last night that Maj. Raul Castro, the Premier's brother and Minister of Revolutionary Armed Forces, was in Santiago, capital of Oriente Province.

The Havana radio announced that "militias" from Ecuador were ready to travel to Cuba to fight "Yankee aggressors" and that a Soviet woman deputy now in Cuba, who is a doctor, had offered her services.

The communiqué of the Cuban Revolutionary Council announced that the landing Monday on the Bahia de Cochinos on the swampy coast of Las Villas Province had been "inaccurately" described as an invasion.

It was, the Council said, merely an operation designed to provide supplies

Cuban troops with Fidel Castro near Playa Giron, during the Bay of Pigs invasion. (Canadian Press Photo/Getty Images)

for the underground in Cuba. In its communiqué at dawn Monday, the Council had termed the landing the beginning of "the battle to liberate our homeland." Virtually the entire world took the landing to be a major military enterprise with equivalent political repercussions.

Last night, the Council said:

"We did not expect to topple Castro immediately or without setbacks. It certainly is true that we did not expect to face unscathed Soviet armaments directed by Communist advisers."

The anti-Castro rebels are reported to have about 5,000 more men at training camps outside Cuba.

Rally Is Called

A mass rally of support for the regime was called for this evening at Havana University. There were no indications, however, whether Premier Castro, who had dropped out of sight since the landings, would address the gathering.

Many observers here were skeptical about the rebel link-up. The view was taken because of reports that the Escambray guerrilla units had been virtually destroyed as a military force by the Government troops in recent months. A reported failure to supply the guerrillas properly from abroad was cited as the cause of their inability to hold out.

Another reason for skepticism was the report that in launching the landing in Las Villas Province Monday, the principal anti-Castro underground group, the People's Revolutionary Movement, as well as many other anti-Castro groups had been kept out of the operation.

This report, from sources close to some members of the rebel command, suggested that there might have been a considerable lack of coordination between the landing forces and the underground groups in Cuba.

Informants said that Manuel Ray, head of the Peoples' Movement, and a member of the Cuban Revolutionary Council, which is the rebels' top command, was not informed of the details of the landing. Along with the rest of the council, Ray left New York for an undisclosed site Sunday afternoon. At that time, it is said Senor Ray had no advance word of the landings.

The council members are somewhere in the Caribbean area awaiting a propitious time to land on the beachhead, if it can be firmly secured. The purpose is to proclaim a "government in arms" and request foreign recognition.

The landing in Cuba was carried out by what is believed to be a force of 300 to 400 men belonging to the Democratic Revolutionary Front. This organization is represented by three members on the seven-man Revolutionary Council.

One of the top underground leaders from Cuba, who went to New York last week to coordinate plans for a new campaign of sabotage, was in Miami when the Las Villas landings were reported. Although his task was to introduce a large shipment of explosives into Cuba and touch off a major wave of sabotage designed to soften up the Castro defenses in preparation for subsequent landings, the underground leader could not carry out his plans.

About 120 highly trained anti-Castro fighters, who are close to Senor Ray's movement, were also surprised by the landings.

These men were to have been sent from Miami to staging camps in Central America ten days ago. Their departure was inexplicably delayed. Some of them finally left Tuesday. The Central American camps were operated by the Democratic Front faction.

Another anti-Castro group here, made up of about 400 men, including some who had escaped in February from the Escambray area, are also held up in Miami.

Meanwhile, the picture of the silence-shrouded Cuban struggle was one of continuing in and around the marshy beachhead on the Bahia de Cochinos and reported infiltration landings throughout the night on the northern coast of Matanzas Province.

The communiqué of the Revolutionary Council reported that the break-through into the Escambray area, north of the port of Cienfuegos, was achieved "in spite of continuous attacks by Soviet MIG's, heavy tanks and artillery forces," completing successfully "the plan's first phase of the military operations in the south of Cuba."

Additional guerilla units, the communiqué said, had infiltrated central Matanzas Province, in what was presumed to be a thrust north toward the Central Highway that runs from the west to the east of Cuba.

The rebels apparently had been unable to capture their immediate objective, the town of Jaguey Grande, about twenty miles north of the original beachhead.

Pushing forward from the swamps of Cienaga de Zapata, they appeared to be operating between two sections of firm ground provided by the narrow gauge railroad that runs from La Criolla on the west shore of the Bahia de Cochinos north to Jaguey and a new highway somewhat to the east.

Yesterday, the Havana Revolutionary court at La Cabana Fortress began the trial of twenty-six persons accused of having plotted the murder of Dr. Castro.

The death sentence was given for seven persons, including Premier Castro's one-time Agricultural Minister, Dr. Humberto Sori Marin.

Castro's troops at Playa de Citron after successfully repelling the U.S.-backed invasion of the Bay of Pigs. (Graf/Getty Images)

Capital Views Rebel Defeat As Damaging Blow to U.S.

By WALLACE CARROLL

WASHINGTON, April 20—In the hours before daybreak last Monday, a force of about 500 exiles began to go ashore on the Cuban beaches. So tiny a force could hardly have been expected to play a weighty part in the course of world events.

Yet tonight, after four days of uncertainty, it is clear that the expedition has involved the United States in a disastrous loss of prestige and respect. Among high Administration officials there is recognition that a serious miscalculation was made. The nature of that miscalculation is now clear.

The strictly limited operation—a handful of exiles allowed by the United States to carry out the landings to take supplies to resistance forces already in Cuba—was so magnified by rumor, propaganda and international controversy that it seemed to the world to be a major military operation under United States sponsorship.

Appraisal of the Setback

The effects of the resulting setback were being appraised here in this way:

The regime of Premier Fidel Castro has presumably been strengthened. Dr. Castro himself could boast to his people, the hemisphere and the world that he had survived an invasion that had United States support.

Premier Khrushchev has been able to strike a pose as the protector of small nations. Because of his well-timed threat to aid the Castro regime, his diplomats and propagandists will be able to boast that the United States was deterred by fears of Soviet power.

The reviving confidence of the United States allies in its qualities of leadership has been shaken. In allied embassies here there was a feeling of shock at what had happened.

The momentum President Kennedy was gaining in foreign policy has been checked. The old feeling against "Yankee intervention" were stirred in the hemisphere and a division occurred among the delegations of the American republics at the United Nations. Prime Minister Jawaharlal Nehru, who was beginning to take a kindlier view of United States policy, condemned the supposed intervention. Mobs fanned anti-American sentiment in many parts of the world.

In short, the feeling here is that the repercussions could hardly have been worse if President Kennedy sent the Marines into Cuba.

How did all this come about?

A plan to help the anti-Castro exiles establish a sizable beachhead in Cuba was developed in the Central Intelligence Agency during the Eisenhower Administration.

The preparations went forward for months with official sanction under the general supervision of a deputy director, Richard M. Bissell Jr. The exiles were given training in landing operations, guerrilla tactics and communications, and their leaders were encouraged to believe the United States would enable them to get ashore under favorable conditions.

This project had become a considerable undertaking by the time Mr. Kennedy became President. Thus he was confronted with a difficult decision: Should he stop a project to which the United States Government had given encouragement, with all the damage to the morale of the anti-Castro forces that would result?

The question was hotly debated for weeks at the highest levels of government.

Arguments Pro and Con

Proponents argued that time was running out in Cuba. In six months more, Dr. Castro would have MIG fighters and other Soviet military equipment and it would be impossible for the anti-Castro forces at home and abroad to overthrow him.

His power to stir up mischief in the Caribbean would increase with each passing week, moreover, the argument ran. It would be impossible to sustain the morale of the exiles if they did not get into action.

Opponents contended that Cuba was not yet ripe for a counter-revolution. Though there were many signs of opposition to Dr. Castro, there could be no certainty that an uprising would be big enough to give the necessary support to a relatively feeble beachhead operation.

Besides, it was argued—and this was apparently the argument that carried the most weight with Mr. Kennedy—an American-supported landing in Cuba would have disastrous effects on foreign relations.

The new Administration, the argument ran, was beginning to turn world opinion in favor of the United States. The favorable trend would be reversed if it should do what it condemned the Soviet Union and Communist China for doing.

C. I. A. Also Divided

In this debate, the C. I. A. itself was divided. Some of its officers were reported to feel that the intelligence from Cuba did not encourage hopes of a successful uprising.

At the State Department, Adolf A. Berle Jr., the head of a Presidential task force on Latin America, was said to favor the project. But Secretary of State Dean Rusk and Under Secretary Chester Bowles were dead set against it.

On Capitol Hill, Senator George A. Smathers, a Florida Democrat and a friend of the President, argued publicly and privately for a move against the Castro regime. But Senator J. W. Fulbright of Arkansas, wrote privately to Mr. Kennedy to warn him against the dangers of the enterprise.

While this debate was running, magazines and newspapers began to print articles on and pictures of Cuban exiles preparing for invasion attempts at training camps in Florida.

Legal Aspects Raised

Attorney General Robert F. Kennedy and Abram J. Chayes, the State Department's legal adviser, checked on the laws covering such activities and raised questions about their legality.

Some of the Florida camps were being supported by private funds. Whether the C. I. A. ever contributed to their support could not be determined here, but high officials emphasized a few days ago that as of that time no Government money was being used to support training camps on United States soil.

The Kennedy Administration made a renewed effort to screen out of the exile forces anyone who had been identified with Fulgencio Batista, the Cuban dictator overthrown by Dr. Castro.

One prominent Batista supporter, Rolando Masferrer, was arrested and indicted in Florida.

He was charged with having directed an abortive invasion of Cuba by a small flotilla last October in violation of the Neutrality Act.

Meanwhile, President Kennedy and his advisers were dealing with the Congo, Laos, the gold drain, the deterioration of the North Atlantic Treaty Organization and other urgent problems, Prime Minister Macmillan spent four days in consultation at the White House. After him came Chancellor Adenauer.

All this time preparations for the beachhead operation were going forward, with several thousand exiles getting ready for the landings. Groups of Cubans moved out of Florida to staging areas somewhere in the Caribbean. Officials who opposed the project were becoming anxious about the President's decision.

It is not clear when Mr. Kennedy reached that decision. Apparently it was at the beginning of this month that he accepted the arguments against a large-scale beachhead operation. He agreed, however, to let the Cubans have ships, and other support for landings on a much smaller scale.

Supplies for Landing Parties

The purpose of these operations would be to supply the six landing parties that had gone ashore earlier and the resistance forces on the island.

Apparently the idea behind this bobtailed expedition was to forestall complete collapse of morale.

At his news conference April 12, the President tried to head off the impression that the United States would intervene.

"There will not be under any conditions," he said, "an intervention in Cuba by the United States armed forces." He added that the Government would do everything it could to prevent American citizens from becoming involved in Cuba.

Last Monday, with the landings already underway, Secretary Rusk repeated these assurances.

"There is not and will not be any intervention there by United States forces," he said. "What happens in Cuba is for the Cuban people themselves to decide."

By Monday night, according to the best information available to the officials, only 200 to 300 exiles had gone ashore.

The following day one high official said that the total might have risen to 600, and today the same official ventured an outside guess of 1,200. This seems, however, to be too high. It is improbable that the landing parties, made up entirely of volunteers, ever got up to a total of 1,000 men.

Yet some of the early press reports spoke of 5,000 men going ashore. Rumors—some of them spontaneous and others "planted" by the Cuban and United States groups involved—built up the impression of a large-scale invasion. Reports were circulated that Dr. Castro was preparing to flee to Mexico, that Maj. Ernesto Guevara, one of his two deputies, had been killed, and that the "invaders" had captured the Isles of Pines.

All this strengthened the impression in the world at large of an "invasion" that could only have been carried out with considerable United States support, if not outright intervention.

Even in allied embassies in Washington there was a general belief that a big operation was under way. With memories of the British and French failure at Suez in 1956, no one seemed to believe that the United States would become involved in an undertaking that aimed at anything less than decisive results.

It is doubtful however, that Dr. Castro and his Soviet supporters were fooled by the rumors and inflated reports. Yet they were happy to join in the propaganda build-up and to use all of their resources and the forum of the United Nations to drive home allegations of United States' intervention.

Castro Gain Foreseen

The purpose, as it was seen here, was to magnify Dr. Castro's eventual success in squelching the landing parties and to involve the United States in a disaster to its prestige.

Thus, on Tuesday morning, when the scale of the attack must have been quite clear and the fact of United States nonintervention well established, Premier Khrushchev apparently felt safe in sending President Kennedy a message containing a threat to aid the Castro regime.

The more immediate effects in Washington are still uncertain.

As for the political consequences, Republicans may find it hard to resist the temptation to exploit a miscalculation by the Kennedy Administration. They may be inhibited, however, by President Eisenhower's involvement in the beachhead project and his inaction while Dr. Castro was gaining power.

Cubans Say Rebels Will Get No Mercy

By TAD SZULC

MIAMI, Sunday, April 23—The Castro Government warned yesterday that there would be "no mercy" for those who attacked Cuba.

The Havana radio increased by 178 the number of rebels reported arrested in the landing last week on the southern coast of Cuba. This brought to 654 the total number of prisoners in the unsuccessful assault.

Threatening potential new invaders with "the rockets of the Soviet Union," the Cuban radio also broadcast in full the text of yesterday's note from Premier Khrushchev to President Kennedy charging direct United States intervention in the rebel attack last week. The radio emphasized that Mr. Khrushchev's declaration showed Soviet support for Cuba in her hour of crisis.

While the Cuban Government continued to shout its victory and threaten its enemies, the mystery surrounding Premier Fidel Castro was broken with a Havana announcement last night that he would speak to Cubans at noon today over television.

Reports had circulated earlier that the Premier might have been killed or injured in leading the fight against the rebel foes.

The "no mercy" statement was made over the Cuban radio network in the official news program "Vencermos" (We shall win). It may foreshadow executions for some or all of the prisoners captured last week after the ill-fated landings in Las Villas Province.

Interrogation Televised

The rebel prisoners were paraded Friday night and last night before television audiences in lengthy "interrogation" sessions by a panel of the regime's newsmen.

The line of questioning underlined that the entire production was designed principally to establish in painstaking detail that the United States had mounted, financed, directed and protected the assault and that the men themselves were duped into participation.

Last night, the moderator of the program announced that the latest batch of 178 prisoners included Jose Antonio de Varona, the son of the Defense Minister of the rebel exile government, Dr. Manuel Antonio de Varona.

Friday night it was announced that Jose Miro Torra, son of the president of the rebel front, Dr. Jose Miro Cardona, was among the prisoners. Young de Varona was a paratrooper in the rebel army.

Priest Among Captives

A Roman Catholic priest, who, according to Havana, refused to identify himself, was also said to be among the captives.

The answers brought out in the interrogation included statements that two United States Navy destroyers had escorted the invading force most of the way to Cuba and that United States Air Force planes had flown cover for the operation.

In what were quiet, low-key proceedings in which the prisoners seemed to tell all they knew without visible res-

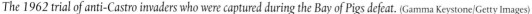

The 1962 trial of anti-Castro invaders who were captured during the Bay of Pigs defeat. (Gamma Keystone/Getty Images)

Cuban counter-revolutionaries, members of Assault Brigade 2506, after their capture. (AFP/Getty Images)

ervations, detailed descriptions were given of training of the rebels in Guatemalan camps and of the jump-off from Nicaragua for the landing operation Monday.

No clear indications were given of the fate that awaits the prisoners, but it was generally expected that they would be placed on trial in the most spectacular manner possible.

Two Executions Reported

As terror against actual and suspected "counter-revolutioners" went on unabated in Cuba, two more executions were reported by the Havana radio. This raised the total of executions for last week to thirty-one. The latest executions took place in Mantanzas Province.

Diplomatic reports from Havana spoke of the wave of arrests, steadily rolling across the country. One diplomat reported by telephone that "there are so many arrests that nobody has any idea of the numbers."

Hundreds of persons were said to be rounded up, held for a day or two, then released while new detentions were being made. Thousands of persons were believed to still be in prison.

Latin-American embassies in Havana were reported to be crowded with persons who have been granted asylum. One embassy said it was harboring forty persons.

None of the diplomats could estimate the number of United States citizens under arrest. The Swiss Embassy, which is in charge of United States interests in Cuba, reported that "the confusion is too great to tell who is free and who is in jail."

2 U. S. Newsmen Released

Several United States newsmen were among those under detention on unspecified charges. Two of them were released tonight and are in the Brazilian Embassy. Meanwhile, broadcasts from Cuba revealed a growing tendency of the Castro regime to identify itself openly with communism.

A special commentary was dedicated to the birth of Lenin, who was described as one of the greatest figures in history. It is fitting, the Havana commentator said, to remember that it was in Cuba that "the first Socialist revolution in the hemisphere took place, right under the noses of the imperialists."

Since the landings in Los Villas Monday, Cuban stations have been urging Cubans to rise to the defense of "our Socialist revolution."

Commentators read in full the text of Premier Khrushchev's latest message to President Kennedy on the Cuban question.

In what it called its "message" to counter-revolutionaries, the Havana radio said:

"Let them send us more mercenaries and this way we shall end once and for all with these worms.

"We shall have no mercy for anyone, no mercy for the Marine infantry of the United States.

"The courage of the Cubans is much weightier and the rockets of the Soviet Union are weightier."

Invasion Force Assessed

The questioning of the rebel prisoners reopened the question of how large the invading force was and what it hoped to achieve.

The Bay of Pigs: Anatomy of a Debacle

By Scott Shane

In early April 1961, an enterprising *New York Times* reporter, Tad Szulc, learned that the C.I.A. was training a small force of Cuban exiles to invade Cuba with the hope of touching off a revolt against Fidel Castro.

But the *Times'* publisher, Orvil E. Dryfoos, worried about being blamed for alerting Castro to the coming attack, ordered Szulc's article toned down. Partly because of the concerns of James Reston, the paper's revered chief Washington correspondent and columnist, the headline was shrunk from four columns to just one. The newspaper's top editor, Turner Catledge, directed that all references to the C.I.A. should be dropped and the assertion that the invasion was "imminent" excised.

The toning down infuriated Szulc, according to his son, Anthony Szulc. An oft-reported tale—that Dryfoos acted after a call from President Kennedy—appears to be a myth. But it turns out that another government official, Allen Dulles, the C.I.A. director, had made an appeal on national security grounds—to Szulc himself.

Anthony Szulc said his father described being summoned to the Georgetown house of his uncle, a retired ambassador, days before the story would run. At a discreet dinner with Dulles, the C.I.A. director asked Tad Szulc not to write about the invasion plans. Szulc replied that he believed it was his journalistic responsibility to do so. Dulles didn't press the matter: "I completely understand," the C.I.A. director said, Tad Szulc recalled to his son.

Just three weeks after the toned-down article ran, when the rebels had been slaughtered and captured at the Bay of Pigs and the invasion had become a catastrophe for the new administration, Kennedy himself offered a sarcastic quip about the fraught interaction of the press and the government. He had summoned a group of newspaper editors to the White House to urge them to exercise greater caution before running stories about national security. But in a whispered aside to Mr. Catledge, the president said: "Maybe if you had printed more about the operation, you would have saved us from a colossal mistake."

To read after half a century the *Times'* day-by-day account of the Bay of Pigs fiasco as it unfolded is to recognize a few permanent features of American operations overseas: the government's capacity for overreach, based on intelligence that is flat-out wrong; its entanglements with the press over semi-secret covert operations; the half-truths and outright lies it tells the public about its actions; and the inevitable finger-pointing of agencies and officials when plans backfire. Those who followed the saga of Iraq's nonexistent weapons of mass destruction will find themselves in similar terrain here.

The C.I.A., represented by Dulles, its director, and Richard M. Bissell Jr., its chief of covert operations, clearly misled the president about the rebels' prospects for success. But the agency itself seemed to believe that the rebels had a feasible escape route to the mountains, not realizing it passed through impenetrable swamps.

Suspicious of the agency and aware of the challenges facing the invaders, some advisers urged Kennedy to abandon the plan: Dean Acheson, Harry Truman's secretary of state; Dean Rusk, Kennedy's secretary of state; and J. William Fulbright, the Democratic chairman of the Senate Foreign Relations Committee, among others. Kennedy listened, but in the end he gave the green light for a plan that, after all, had first been approved by Eisenhower in March 1960.

Only later would it become clear that ranking C.I.A. and military officials confidently assumed that once the rebels established a beachhead on the Bay of Pigs, the president's hand would be forced: He would be compelled to commit American military power fully to the cause, ensuring Castro's overthrow.

In handwritten notes found after his death, Dulles admitted to the C.I.A. strategy of gaming the president: "We felt that when the chips were down, when the crisis arose in reality, any action required for success would be authorized rather than permit the enterprise to fail."

But from his first briefing, Kennedy insisted that the American military would not get involved. Taking the C.I.A.'s rosy prognostication at face value, he believed the rebels could succeed without American military support. He directed the C.I.A. to minimize even covert air support, first during preliminary bombing of Castro's warplanes and later when the bodies of dead and wounded rebels lay scattered on beach.

When Kennedy grasped the magnitude of the disaster, he was shattered. "All my life I have known better than to depend on the experts," he told his adviser Theodore Sorensen in a walk on the White House grounds: "How could I have been so stupid, to let them go ahead?'"

In retrospect, the greenhorn president's blunders were obvious. Because he never forced C.I.A. leaders to confront his skeptical advisers, he never got a realistic assessment of the odds against victory. By approving the mission but blocking crucial air support, he guaranteed that the rebels' rout, and his own humiliation, would be complete.

The articles included here—beginning with the toned-down Tad Szulc scoop—tell the story remarkably well, despite repeating some untruths handed out at the time by government officials.

Reston, for instance, reported that "no more than 200 or 300 men were involved in the weekend landings," attributing the claim—in the style of the time—to "reliable information reaching" Washington. The actual invasion force was about 1,500.

Later, Szulc reported a statement by the council of Cuban exiles nominally in charge, claiming that the operation had been "inaccurately described as an invasion" when it was merely a resupply mission for "patriots" who had been fighting in Cuba for months. The statement was a preposterous C.I.A. concoction.

Two weeks after editors had removed references to the C.I.A. from his initial article, Szulc accurately reported that, "as has been an open secret in Florida and Central America for months, the C.I.A. planned, coordinated and directed the operations." In his column the next day, Reston mused about the significance of "Kennedy's first defeat" and cautioned against a new invasion.

In an impressive retrospective just four days after the rebels hit the beach, Washington correspondent Wallace Carroll called the invasion "a disastrous loss of prestige and respect" for the United States based on a "serious miscalculation." He said Castro and his patron, Soviet leader Nikita Khrushchev, had both been strengthened. He correctly named the C.I.A.'s Bissell as the main organizer of the operation and gave a credible account of the internal debate over whether to go ahead with it.

Carroll suggested that the C.I.A.'s performance would renew demands for a Congressional watchdog committee over intelligence; that was true, though it would take more than a decade to create the Senate and House intelligence committees. The president would force the resignations of both Dulles and Bissell in September 1961.

Both before and after the Bay of Pigs, *Times* reporters assumed that the United States would not tolerate Castro's regime for much longer. "The self-interest of the nation," Reston wrote days before the invasion, "undoubtedly requires the overthrow of the Cuban Government of Fidel Castro, which is providing a political and, increasingly, a military base for communism in the Caribbean."

It might flabbergast Reston and his colleagues to learn that the regime would still be in place half a century later. But their reasoning was based in part on the notion that American officials could not tolerate a Soviet presence just 90 miles from Florida—an observation that presaged the second of Kennedy's momentous encounters with Cuba.

Scott Shane is a national security reporter in the Washington bureau of *The New York Times* and author of *Dismantling Utopia: How Information Ended the Soviet Union* (1994).

U.S. HURLS MAN 115 MILES INTO SPACE; SHEPARD WORKS CONTROLS IN CAPSULE, REPORTS BY RADIO IN 15-MINUTE FLIGHT IN FINE CONDITION

Astronaut Drops Into the Sea Four Miles From Carrier

By RICHARD WITKIN

CAPE CANAVERAL, Fla., May 5—A slim, cool Navy test pilot was rocketed 115 miles into space today.

Thirty-seven-year-old Comdr. Alan B. Shepard Jr. thus became the first American space explorer.

Commander Shepard landed safely 302 miles out at sea fifteen minutes after the launching. He was quickly lifted aboard a Marine Corps helicopter.

"Boy, what a ride!" he said, as he was flown to the aircraft carrier Lake Champlain four miles away.

Extensive physical examinations were begun immediately.

Tonight doctors reported Commander Shepard in "excellent" condition, suffering no ill effects.

Major U. S. Step

The near-perfect flight represented the United States' first major step in the race to explore space with manned space craft.

True, it was only a modest leap compared with the once-around-the-earth orbital flight of Maj. Yuri A. Gagarin of the Soviet Union.

The Russian's speed of more than 17,000 miles an hour was almost four times Commander Shepard's 4,500. The distance the Russian traveled was almost 100 times as great.

But Commander Shepard maneuvered his craft in space--something the Russians have not claimed for Major Gagarin.

All in all, the Shepard flight was welcomed almost rapturously here and in much of the non-Communist world as proof that the United States, though several years behind in the space race, had the potential to offer imposing competition.

Commander Shepard, a native of East Derry, N. H., was a long time starting his journey.

He lay on his contoured Fiberglass couch atop the Redstone missile—"the least nervous man of the bunch," the flight surgeon reported—for three and a half hours while the launching crew delayed the countdown because of weather and a few technical troubles.

Finally, at 10:34 A. M. Eastern daylight time, the count reached zero. A jet of yellow flame lifted the slender rocket off its pad as thousands watched anxiously from the Cape and along the public beaches south of here.

Hundreds of missiles had been launched here, but never before with a human being aboard. Only once before, so far as is known, had a human ridden a missile into space anywhere--and that was from the Soviet base at Tyura Tam, near the Aral Sea last month.

The rocket, and the pilot in the Project Mercury capsule on top, performed flawlessly.

Commander Shepard kept up a running commentary with the command center during the flight. He experienced six times the force of gravity during the rocket's climb, then there were five

minutes during which gravity seemed to have vanished. The abrupt re-entry into the atmosphere pressed him into his couch with a force of more than ten times gravity.

At 7,000 feet, his capsule descending by a red and white parachute, Commander Shepard radioed, as if returning from a routine flight by plane:

"Coming in for a landing."

Drops Gently to Water

The capsule, dropping then at a fairly gentle thirty feet a second, hit the water at 10:49 A. M. The commander, apparently as sound and healthy as when he had entered the capsule at 6:20 A. M., radioed that he would climb out immediately rather than ride it to the carrier.

A horse-collar-like sling was lowered from Marine helicopter 44 and he was pulled aboard, less than five minutes after hitting the gently rolling waves. His first words were:

"Thank you very much. It's a beautiful day."

A minute later, the capsule was hooked and flown, dangling below the helicopter, to a mattress-covered platform on the carrier. Moments later, as hundreds of sailors cheered, the astronaut, his silver space suit gleaming, debarked from the helicopter.

Instead of going directly to the admiral's quarters below, where he was to receive a thorough physical examination and pour out his fresh impressions

U.S. astronaut Alan Shepard is lifted up to the helicopter after he splashed down in the Atlantic Ocean aboard the Mercury capsule on May 5, 1961.
(AFP/Getty Images)

of his journey, he jogged to the capsule to retrieve his space helmet.

The formalities below were interrupted when a call came into the carrier bridge from the White House. It was President Kennedy.

'Very Thrilling Ride'

A naval officer who overheard the conversation quoted the astronaut as saying:

"Thank you very much, Mr. President. It was certainly a very thrilling ride. I'd like to thank everyone who made it possible."

While being checked by the doctors, Commander Shepard told one:

"I don't think there's much you'll have to do to me, doc."

In the twenty-four to forty-eight hours following the flight, Commander Shepard is to undergo the physical check-ups and interviews. All aboard the carrier, except for two physicians, were under strict orders not to speak to the astronaut unless he asked a question.

The precaution was taken so that the astronaut's reactions could be recorded with the meagerest possible distortion by intervening discussions.

The chief physician on the carrier, Comdr. Robert C. Laning, reported the astronaut in "excellent physical condition."

Commander Shepard's first refreshment was a glass of orange juice. He told the doctor that he was "thrilled and experienced a great sense of humility."

To Go to Washington

The astronaut spent two hours and twenty-five minutes on the carrier, then was flown to a special clinic on the Grand Bahama, where the examinations and questioning continued.

There, after an extensive examination, Col. William Douglas, personal physician for the seven astronauts, found Mr. Shepard in "excellent shape and health." He doubted that the further tests to be made would show any ill effects.

Plans are to fly Commander Shepard to Washington Monday for a hero's welcome and a meeting with President Kennedy.

What were the scientific contributions made by the fifteen-minute Mercury flight?

Chief among them, according to Dr.

Hugh A. Dryden, Deputy Administrator of the National Aeronautics and Space Administration, was information on the reactions of the astronaut under the stresses of space flight.

Commander Shepard was reported to have performed no differently during the actual rocket flight than he had in dozens of practice flights in ground simulators and whirling centrifuges.

He was able to click off moment-by-moment reports on the operations of the complex array of mechanisms, without missing a beat. His voice remained normal except during the exposure to the maximum gravity force. Then it became strained, as had the voices of all astronauts during training.

In addition, Shepard was able to control the attitude, or position, of the capsule in space by operation of a control stick that sent squirts of hydrogen peroxide rushing from sixteen strategically located jets.

In this way, Commander Shepard was able to change not the path of the capsule, which was determined by the ballistic trajectory established by the rocket, but the angle at which the capsule flew through space. Turning levers inside the capsule, he was able to con-

Astronaut Alan B. Shepard as he emerges from the Freedom 7 *capsule onto the flight deck of the recovery carrier USS* Lake Champlain *after his historic Mercury flight.* (CBS Photo Archive/Getty Images)

trol the pitch (nose up or down), yaw (right or left motion) and roll of the capsule.

The astronaut also regulated the attitude of the capsule for the firing of the retro or backward-firing rockets and fired the rockets as the capsule started descending toward earth. For the suborbital flight the firing of the three retro rockets on the blunt nose of the capsule was only practiced. But in orbital flight, the retro rockets are necessary to slow down the capsule and start it returning to earth.

Commander Shepard talked about his experiences "flying" the capsule to Capt. Ralph Weymouth, skipper of the Lake Champlain.

"He told me," the captain said, "that four or five years from now, we may look back at this as a pretty crude thing, but at this moment it seemed a tremendous event."

Dr. Stanley C. White of the Air Force said there had been very little change in the astronaut's pulse or respiration throughout the flight.

Temperatures both in the capsule and in the astronaut's air-tight air-conditioned double layer space suit rose only slightly during the friction-generating descent into the atmosphere.

According to Dr. White, the suit temperature rose from 75 to 78 Fahrenheit during re-entry and the cabin air temperature rose from 99 degrees to 102.

To indicate the decelerating impact of the atmosphere, it was calculated that the capsule, in one minute, slowed from a speed of 4,227 miles an hour at forty miles altitude to 341 miles an hour at twelve miles altitude.

The Mercury capsule was a compact, 2,300 pound steel and titanium craft shaped something like a television

tube. The astronaut, lying on his couch against the blunt "picture" end of the tube, had about as much space as he would in the cockpit of a jet fighter plane.

Before him were panels containing more than 100 switches, buttons, and levers for performing such functions as firing retro rockets; switching radio channels; turning on and off the manual control jets; blowing out the escape hatch at the side; and extending or retracting a periscope with which he could monitor operations of devices not visible to the direct-view porthole down through his legs.

The barrel-shaped capsule bore the name of "Freedom 7" painted in white letters on the black side of the capsule. The name was thought up by the seven Mercury astronauts.

Nation Exults Over Space Feat; City Plans to Honor Astronaut

By ROBERT CONLEY

May 6—The successful flight of America's first astronaut, Comdr. Alan B. Shepard Jr., roused the country yesterday to one of its highest peaks of exultation since the end of World War II.

The achievement brought relief from the strain of hearing about the Soviet Union's success in orbiting a man, feelings of new hope for the future from Maine to Hawaii and dancing in the streets at New York's Columbus Circle.

"Wonderful," "Tremendous," "The greatest thing that ever happened," thousands of persons said as the reaction took hold across the country.

Knots of people crowded sidewalks to watch television screens in store windows. Others jumped up to cheer, pounded friends on the back, ran into neighbor's houses or fell silent.

"He made it," a woman gasped in Chicago, then broke into tears. "He made it."

New York City laid plans for the "most fabulous" ticker tape welcome ever given—one that a city official said would be "even bigger than the one for Charles Lindbergh."

In Washington, Congressmen moved to bestow the nation's highest military award, the Medal of Honor, on the 37-year-old pilot.

President Kennedy, who watched the launching on television in the White House, called the fifteen-minute flight "a historic milestone in our own exploration of space."

At the moment the huge Redstone rocket was fired from the launching pad at Cape Canaveral, Fla., much of the country stopped in silence to watch or listen.

Mrs. Mary Lombardo of Newark touched a small crucifix at her neck.

"God bless him," she said, "my prayers were with him all the way."

Martin Goldie, a Los Angeles grocer in his sixties, did something else. After the flight he walked outside his store and quietly hoisted the American flag.

Taxi Drivers Skip Fares

Manhattan taxi drivers tried to avoid fares so they could listen to the crucial sequence at lift-off without interruption.

At City Hall Senora Felisa Rincon de Gautier, Mayor of San Juan, Puerto Rico, jumped with glee and shouted "hurray" on hearing the news as she paid a courtesy call on Mayor Wagner. Mr. Wagner emerged from a meeting and she embraced him. Outside a loudspeaker carried the flight to a crush in City Hall Park.

> *"A historic milestone in our own exploration of space."*

On the upper West Side, a transistor radio crackled on a Broadway newsstand

"He's coming down," the newsdealer shouted to a jumble of commuters descending from New Jersey buses.

Youngsters gamboled in a New Rochelle schoolyard amid the hustle of imaginary countdowns: "Five…four…three…two…one…Fire!"

Other persons clustered around a news ticker at Rockefeller Center and huddled beside radios in parked cars.

"I think its fantastic," said Keith Brushfield, a sheep and cattle rancher from Sydney, Australia, who was visiting the city. "It was thrilling—something the free world has been waiting for for several years."

'It's Terrific!'

Another visitor, Mrs. Tom Roche of Deland, Fla. beamed, "Gee, it's terrific! It's great!"

"All our safety precautions were justified," said Lawrence E. Gray, a stockbroker of suburban Rye.

The Government's decision to let the world see the space shot without secrecy or delay drew wide praise.

"This was entirely open and all aboveboard," commented Dr. Fred A. Hitchcock, Professor Emeritus of Physiology at Ohio State University, "so different than that of Russia. The whole thing is extremely encouraging."

Most Philadelphians experienced elation and relief.

"It was a horrible feeling watching the takeoff and not knowing what might happen," a housewife said. But some wondered how far the country had to go to "catch up with the Russians."

For the first time Philadelphians could remember, the strict decorum of the United States Court of Appeals was broken by a news event. A burst of applause ruffled the chamber after a clerk handed a note to Judge Herbert Goodrich, announcing the successful recovery.

"A definite first," one court officer said.

In Chicago, activity stopped in most offices in the downtown Loop so that workers could watch television. School children put aside books and classroom work to watch television screens or listen to commentary over loudspeakers.

"The flight certainly ought to revive the confidence of the American people in their scientists," said Mrs. Cecil Whalen, a secretary.

'Coming Up Fast'

"We're coming up fast on the outside," offered Leonard H. Lavin, a manufacturing executive.

Missourians in Kansas City were sterner in their views, with many taking the attitude that the shot was too little too late.

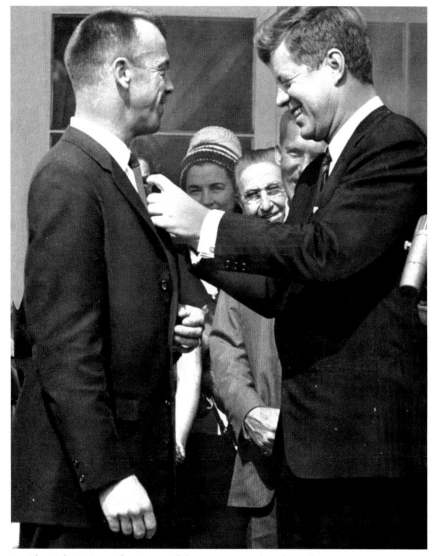

President John F. Kennedy pins a medal on astronaut Alan Shepard, May 9, 1961.

(Frank Hurley/New York Daily News Archive/Getty Images)

"They should have done it a month ago so we could have beat the Russians at something." Al Loomise said.

"We came up a very poor second," another man suggested, mindful of the orbit around the Earth made last month by Maj. Yuri Gagarin.

Flags flew over business concerns in suburban Mill Valley, Calif. to celebrate the successful space flight. San Franciscan newspapers, radio and television stations reported record numbers of inquiring telephone calls.

Bostonians greeted the news with exhilaration and pride.

"It was a tremendous accomplishment and a great boon to our national prestige," said Frank Neer Jr., an insurance executive.

"It was great for national morale," Calvin Shepard, a construction worker, agreed.

'So Very Proud'

"It makes me feel so very proud of my country and its scientists," was the reaction of Mrs. Dorothy Holt, a registered nurse.

In Pittsburgh Dean B.R. Tear at the Carnegie Institute of Technology made this statement:

"A tremendous triumph for Ameri-

can scientists. The most impressive thing was the way the test came off before millions of viewers and listeners."

R. L. Shepard, a Detroit investment consultant, saw something else.

"I had been wondering for years what justified all this expenditure for space exploration," he said, "but I'm beginning to be convinced. It was a wonderful achievement."

The Iowa Legislature ignored its pre-adjournment frenzy for a time as lawmakers in the House and Senate chambers, secretaries and committee members turned their attention to the flight. Bulletins were rushed into caucus rooms.

Free champagne flowed in a Fort Wayne, Ind., tavern.

The 3,400 men and women who made the Redstone rocket, which carried Commander Shepard to the edge of space, followed the flight reports with grim intentness at the Chrysler missile plant in Sterling Township, Ill.

When the shot was over, the workers gave little cheering or celebrating, only smiles and handshakes. About 500 workers expect to be laid off May 15.

On Los Angeles' sprawling freeways, traffic slowed just before launching time as motorists turned up their radios. Highway authorities said city-bound drivers were later than usual. Many stayed home to watch on television.

New York City's plans for a welcoming parade for the astronaut came after Mayor Wagner dispatched an invitation by telegram to Commander Shepard. The exact date would be at the pilot's convenience.

U.S. Will Give More Arms And Money to Vietnamese

By ROBERT TRUMBULL

MANILA, May 13—South Vietnam and the United States have agreed on an eight-point program for increased American military and economic assistance. Long-range measures to meet the Communist guerrilla threat and to improve social conditions in South Vietnam were announced in a communiqué issued following Vice President Johnson's visit to Saigon.

The agreement was made public after Mr. Johnson had arrived in Manila today from Saigon on the second leg of his Southeast Asian tour on behalf of President Kennedy.

[Mr. Johnson arrived in Taipei, Taiwan, Sunday and assured Chiang Kaishek's government the United States was determined to protect Taiwan from Communist aggression, The Associated Press reported.]

President Ngo Dinh Diem of South Vietnam and Mr. Johnson, on behalf of their Governments, declared that assistance from free nations in South Vietnam's fight against Communist forces "would be welcome," the communiqué said.

Army to Be Increased

"It was agreed by the two Governments to extend and build upon existing programs of military and economic aid and to infuse into their joint actions a sense of urgency and dedication," it added.

It was agreed that South Vietnam's armed forces should be increased and that the United States would extend its assistance programs to support the extra troops, the document continued.

This was understood to envisage the addition of 20,000 men to South Vietnam's army of 150,000. The Communist guerrilla force, the Viet Cong, is believed to number 12,000, while an army of about 300,000 exists in the Communist-held northern part of Vietnam.

President Ngo is known to believe that his forces are sufficient to cope with the Communists, if properly trained. A Military Assistance Advisory Group of about 650 officers and enlisted men is assisting in their training.

The communiqué said the United States had agreed to provide support for the Vietnamese civil guard force. The civil guard, equivalent to the National Guard in the United States, now numbers about 40,000. About 32,000 more men are in training.

The two Governments agreed to "collaborate in the use of military specialists to assist and work with the Vietnamese armed force in health, welfare and public works activities."

To achieve the best use of resources in the effort against the Communists, it was agreed that a group of highly qualified economic and fiscal experts would meet in Vietnam to work out a financial plan on which joint efforts should be based, the communiqué said.

The expected cost of the plan to the United States has been estimated at $40,000,000.

The United States and South Vietnam will also discuss new economic and social measures to be undertaken in rural areas, the joint statement said.

It was agreed finally that in addition to measures to deal with the immediate guerrilla threat, the two Governments would work to devise a long-range economic development program.

The communiqué said this program would include further progress in agriculture, health, education, fisheries, highways, public administration and industrial development. The goal would be a Vietnam capable of a self-sustained economic growth, the document said.

The steps agreed upon for immediate implementation may be followed by more far-reaching measures if necessary, the communiqué stated. It was assumed that such measures could include direct participation by the United States and its allies in the Vietnam fighting.

The Freedom Riders

BI-RACIAL BUSES ATTACKED, RIDERS BEATEN IN ALABAMA

By THE ASSOCIATED PRESS

ANNISTON, Ala., May 15—A group of white persons ambushed today two buses carrying Negroes and whites who are seeking to knock down bus station racial barriers. A little later, sixty miles to the west, one of the buses ran into another angry crowd of white men at a Birmingham bus station.

The integrated group took a brief but bloody beating, and fled. No serious injuries were reported.

Both buses were carrying members of the Congress of Racial Equality on a swing through the Deep South, testing facilities in bus stations. They call themselves "Freedom Riders."

State Investigator Ell M. Cowling, acting on a tip, was aboard a Greyhound bus attacked near Anniston. He barred the bus door with his body when the crowd of white men tried to board the bus. Two highway patrolmen fired their pistols into the air to quiet the crowd of about 200 that had followed the bus from Anniston.

Somebody threw a fire bomb through a bus window. Twelve persons were hospitalized, most of them for smoke inhalation. Ten of them later were released.

The bus, stalled about six miles out of Anniston by a flat tire, was destroyed by the blaze.

Those who were not hospitalized were taken back to Anniston and placed on another bus. They completed their ride to Birmingham and arrived at Birmingham's Greyhound station without incident.

The C. O. R. E. members left Washington ten days ago with six white and seven Negro Freedom Riders. The number has fluctuated at various stops. On the Anniston bus the C. O. R. E. group included five Negroes and four white persons. The number on the Trailways bus that reached Birmingham was not known.

They split into two groups in Atlanta and took separate buses into Alabama. The trouble started when the Greyhound, carrying the nine Freedom Riders and five other passengers, reached this city of about 30,000.

The Trailways bus that later ran into difficulty at Birmingham had its first trouble at Anniston, also.

Dr. Walter Bergman, 61 years old, a former Michigan State University professor and a member of the C. O. R. E. group, said a fight broke out on the bus.

The Trailways station was closed but Mr. Bergman said he got off, got sandwiches and was getting back on the bus when a policeman came up.

"The driver said he wasn't going to move until the Negroes moved to the back of the bus," Mr. Bergman said.

"At that time, about ten men attacked Charles Person, a student at Morehouse University, Atlanta.

"And then James Peck stepped forward, then they turned on us. Peck was beaten about the face and got a deep cut on his scalp.

"They beat me and were kicking me. And then they threw the Negroes and others over me. There was no other violence until we got to Birmingham."

Mr. Bergman said three policemen stood outside the bus at Anniston while this took place.

Mr. Bergman explained the group as a coordinated organization of nonviolent action groups that believed in racial equality and in achieving it through nonviolent means.

The courts have outlawed enforced segregation among interstate bus passengers, but the two bus stations in Birmingham still maintain white and Negro waiting rooms.

A spokesman at Greyhound said its waiting room signs read "white Intrastate passengers" and "Negro Intrastate Passengers." A neon sign at the Trailways station says "Negro Waiting Room."

The bus continued to Birmingham where Mr. Peck was admitted to a hospital in fair condition. The hospital said later that Mr. Peck, of New York, would be discharged tonight.

When the bus arrived at Birmingham it met more trouble.

Several white men attacked the group inside the Birmingham station, beating a Negro youth and a white man who was apparently accompanying the group.

The white men obviously were waiting for the bus, and covered telephone booths and exits.

The fighting broke out in several areas around the station in downtown Birmingham. No police were in evidence until several minutes after the outbreak.

A white man left the bus and shook hands with one of the Negro passengers at the Birmingham station.

The Negroes hesitated momentarily, then walked into a passageway leading to the waiting rooms.

To the left was a sign that designated

Passengers of the smoking Greyhound bus and Freedom Riders after the bus was set afire by a mob of white men who followed them from the station in Anniston, Alabama. (Bettmann/Corbis)

the Negro waiting room. The group hesitated, then a young Negro walked ahead.

He walked about ten feet into the white waiting room. The other Negroes followed, a few feet behind.

Several white men stopped the young Negro, and one of them told him:

"The Negro waiting room is back that way."

They turned him around forcefully, and pushed him. The group turned back into the passageway, but were met by another group of white men entering from the opposite end of the hall.

The Negro man tried to walk through, but a husky white man knocked him against the wall.

Several white men entered the passageway from the white waiting room. They stood behind the young Negro.

"Hit him," one of them said.

A man slammed his fist into the young Negro's face. He fell to the floor, bleeding from the nose.

As he got up, the white man hit him again. This time, the Negro fell backward into the arms of the white men. They pushed him up again. The white man struck him again.

A white man who had been riding the bus with the Negroes attempted to interfere. He was beaten in the face and fell on his back, blood streaming from his nose.

The injured Negro youth and the white man staggered outside to the bus parking area, with the white attackers behind them.

It was all over in three minutes.

There was no way to determine the number of attackers. Some apparently had been waiting in the bus station before the incident.

An aged Negro woman who was on the bus cried:

"It started on the bus. It started on the bus."

Two newsmen were attacked by the crowd outside the bus station. One, Tom Langston of The Birmingham

Post-Herald, was hurt painfully, but was not hospitalized.

Clancy Lake, a radio newsmen, was attacked as he sat in his closed automobile broadcasting an account of the violence. He escaped serious injury.

In an alley behind the bus station, a group of photographers had leaped into their automobile, but were blocked by another crowd of white men who seized several cameras. They smashed some and made off with the others.

Those hospitalized at Anniston were Genevieve Hughes, 28 years old, a white woman of Chevy Chase, Md., and Edward Blackenheim, 28, a white man of Tucson, Ariz., members of C. O. R. E.

They were reported in good condition.

Other members of C. O. R. E. who were treated and released were listed at the hospital as:

Henry Thomas, 19, a white man, of Washington; Albert Bigelow, 55, white, of Cos Cob, Conn.; James McDonald, a

Negro, New York City, and Mae Frances Moultrie, a Negro, of Sumter, S.C.

Also treated were two reporters accompanying the Freedom Riders. They were Moses J. Newson, 34, a Negro, of The Baltimore Afro-American, and Charlotte Devree, 50, a white woman, of New York City.

These passengers aboard the bus also were treated and released:

Roberta Holmes, a Negro, of Birmingham; Roy J. Powers, 39, white, Clinchport, Va., and Larry A. Harper, 22. a Negro, of Margaret, Ala., and Mr. Cowling, an Alabama state investigator.

Thomas J. Jenkins of Birmingham, an official of the Federal Bureau of Investigation, said his agents were making an inquiry into the bus-burning to determine whether there had been any violation of Federal law.

He declined to comment further.

EYEWITNESS ACCOUNT

Smith of C.B.S. Says 'Toughs' Used Pipes on Victims

An eyewitness account of the beatings at the Birmingham bus terminal yesterday was broadcast last night by Howard K. Smith, Columbia Broadcasting System commentator.

Mr. Smith said between thirty and forty heavy-set men had been waiting at the terminal all day.

"When the bus arrived," he related, "the toughs grabbed the passengers into alleys and corridors, pounding them with pipes, with key rings and with fists.

"One passenger was knocked down at my feet by twelve of the hoodlums and his face was beaten and kicked until it was a bloody pulp."

The scene was close to Police Headquarters, Mr. Smith said "but police did not appear until around ten minutes later, when the hoodlums had got into waiting cars and moved down the street a ways, where I watched some of them discussing their achievements of the day. That took place just under Police Commissioner [Eugene] Connors' window."

Telegram to President

Marvin Rich, the C. O. R. E. community relations director in New York, said last night that James Farmer, national director, had sent a telegram to Robert F. Kennedy, the United States Attorney General, "to protest the assaults and to ask for guarantees of freedom on the public highways."

Some of the nine Freedom Riders, who successfully integrated the Trailways bus station in Montgomery, Alabama, sit in the "white only" section of the waiting room, May 28, 1961. (Rolls Press/Popperfoto/Getty Images)

He said a similar telegram had been sent to President Kennedy.

There are now nineteen persons engaged in the Freedom Ride, he said, seeking to test segregation on bus company vehicles, restaurants and rest rooms during a trip to New Orleans scheduled to end Wednesday.

Before yesterday's incidents, Mr. Rich said, there had been three cases where violence broke out or where members of C. O. R. E. were arrested by local police.

On May 8, in Charlotte, N. C., Joseph B. Perkins Jr., 27 years old, was arrested on a charge of trespassing when he entered a barber shop inside the bus terminal. He was jailed for two days, and was acquitted of the charge on May 10. He later rejoined the group.

At Rock Hill, S. C., on May 9, John Lewis, a Negro, was punched by a group of whites when he tried to enter a segregated rest room. There were no arrests, Mr. Rich said.

The following day two of the group were arrested in Winnsboro, S. C. The police charged Henry Thomas, 23, a Negro, with trespassing when he attempted to enter a segregated restaurant. When James Peck tried to talk to the police officers, he was also arrested and charged with interfering with the police, Mr. Rich said.

The two men were questioned for nearly eight hours and then released without any charges being made against them. They rejoined the group the next day in Sumter, S. C.

Freedom Riders Attacked By Whites in Montgomery

By THE ASSOCIATED PRESS

MONTGOMERY, Ala., May 20— Street fighting that left at least twenty persons beaten with clubs and fists raged for two hours here today after a white mob had attacked a busload of Freedom Riders.

The fighting broke out and subsided three times before the police unable to restore order by other methods, tossed tear gas bombs into the crowds.

The mob, which at times numbered about 1,000, attacked the white and Negro bus riders within an instant after the Greyhound bus pulled into the downtown station from Birmingham at 10:15 A. M.

The violence engulfed some bystanders too. These included a representative of the United States Justice Department and of President Kennedy who had tried to rescue a white girl from the mob.

Slugged From Behind

John Seigenthaler, 32-years-old, also a representative of Attorney General Robert F. Kennedy, was taken to a hospital with a cut behind his ear. He was slugged from behind as he struggled to help the besieged girl, one of the Freedom Riders.

At least four out-of-town reporters and photographers were beaten as they attempted to film the rioting. Others had their cameras smashed.

Four white persons were arrested after the police arrived.

Tonight, Attorney General Mac-Donald Gallion said that a court judge had ordered the arrest of twenty-one Freedom Riders for contempt of an injunction he issued yesterday.

Mr. Gallion said that at his request Circuit Court Judge Walter B. Jones had "issued an order to show cause why twenty-one Freedom Riders should not be jailed for contempt and the judge has ordered their arrests."

Some of the Negroes beaten by the mobs had no apparent connection with the group of eighteen that came here from Birmingham on a trip into Alabama to challenge racial barriers at bus stations. The trip started at Nashville, Tenn.

Several young white boys waylaid four Negroes walking along a street near the bus station, poured a flammable liquid on one of the Negro's clothes and set it afire. The blaze burned out, but the man was left lying in the street. Another Negro with him suffered a broken leg when the white youths pounced on him.

An 18-year-old employe of The Montgomery Advertiser Journal, Paschal Pike, was attacked by the mob when he tried to enter the bus station to pick up a package. He said he was beaten when he identified himself as an employe of the newspaper.

The two white girls on the bus, Susan Wilbur, a student at Peabody College in Nashville, and Susan Hermann, a Fisk University exchange student who lives in Los Angeles, said they had escaped the pursuing crowd by running first into a church and then into an office building.

They were taken into protective custody by the police.

The rioting started at the bus station but spread quickly to adjoining streets. The police finally cleared the area for two blocks around.

Even after the police arrived, about ten minutes after the fighting had broken out, the battle raged, with white people chasing, catching, clubbing and stomping any targets of their anger.

Among other bystanders injured were Norman Ritter of Life Magazine and James Atkins of WBRC, Birmingham television station.

The identified injured Negroes included William Barbee and John Lewis, students from Nashville, believed to have been on the integrated bus.

Women shrieked their encouragement—"get those niggers."

And the white men, swinging metal pipes, sticks, and fists, clubbed and pummeled in all directions.

Several newsmen were beaten by the mobs today.

Cameramen Attacked

A Life magazine photographer, Don Uhrbrock, was among the cameramen beaten. He said "the roughs started attacking Moe Levy of N. B. C. News, and after they got his camera, they turned on me."

"There were about ten or twelve of them," Mr. Uhrbrock said, "but only three or four were doing the beating at first. Later some of the others got more courage and joined it."

A gang of women attacked two young white women who came in on the integrated Greyhound bus from Birmingham.

Men behind them shouted, "Hit 'em, hit 'em again."

The women flailed away with their purses and their hands.

A white man tried to protect the two women. The men attacked him, clubbed him to the ground, kicked him, and left him lying motionless and bloody on the ground.

2 Chased and Beaten

Horace Cort, an Associated Press photographer, said he had seen two members of the racially integrated group try to outrun a huge crowd of the roaring attackers.

The white men caught them, knocked them to the ground and jumped up and down on them, Mr. Cort said.

He said an ambulance had pulled into the area. Someone in the mob of white men shouted, and part of the mob started after the ambulance. The driver raced away.

The fighting came in waves. The first broke when a crowd of about 200, waiting at the station for the bus, jumped the riders and some newsmen standing alongside the bus with no police in evidence. The second developed

A bus station window in Jackson, Mississippi, May 1961.

(Paul Schutzer/Time & Life Pictures/Getty Images)

after a brief lull that came when the police arrived.

One Negro girl wept uncontrollably as the violence grew.

At one time, ten or fifteen white persons were beating one Negro as he struggled on the ground.

Police Commissioner L. P. Sullivan, sitting in a car on the other side of the station from the fighting during the first wave, was asked by a newsman if he had anticipated trouble. He said:

"We respond to calls here just like any place else. But we have no intention of standing guard for a bunch of troublemakers coming into our city and making trouble."

Highway patrol reinforcements arrived to help try to contain the rioters.

Floyd Mann, state public safety director, rescued one Negro who had been beaten to the ground. Mr. Mann pulled his pistol and ordered the crowd of white people back from the fallen Negro.

"We are going to keep law and order," he said.

Mr. Mann, pistol in hand, also forced some of the rioters to release a television newsman. An hour after the battle

started, at least 1,000 persons stood around the bus station. Apparently many were curious spectators.

The sheriff's mounted posse of deputies—formed for riot control—arrived at the scene an hour and 15 minutes after the first outbreak. The eleven officers on horseback were armed with billy sticks and pistols.

A few moments later ten more police cars arrived. Uniformed officers moved in and forced the crowd to leave the area.

The rioting broke out on the seventh straight day of mounting racial tension in Alabama—starting with the beating of a group of Freedom Riders at Anniston, Ala., and Birmingham last Sunday.

Bus drivers repeatedly refused to take the riders out of Birmingham—apparently fearing violence from white extremists.

But at 8:30 this morning, after almost eighteen hours in the white waiting room at the Greyhound station, the eighteen Negroes and three white persons unexpectedly got on board a bus and headed for Montgomery.

400 U.S. MARSHALS SENT TO ALABAMA AS MONTGOMERY BUS RIOTS HURT 20; PRESIDENT BIDS STATE KEEP ORDER

Force Due Today

Agents to Bear Arms—Injunction Sought Against the Klan

By ANTHONY LEWIS

WASHINGTON, May 20—The Federal Government dispatched 400 marshals and other armed officers to Alabama tonight to restore order in areas that were torn by racial violence.

The Government acted after a mob of white persons attacked a racially mixed group of bus riders in Montgomery, Ala. The disorders lasted two hours. At least twenty of the riders were beaten.

Attorney General Robert F. Kennedy announced the Federal action in a telegram to Alabama officials. He said it was necessary to "guarantee safe passage in interstate commerce."

Marshals Due by Noon

The 400 Federal marshals will be in Montgomery by noon tomorrow, a Justice Department spokesman said. He said they would have arm bands for identification and would carry sidearms as well as tear-gas bombs and riot clubs or night sticks.

Mr. Kennedy disclosed also that he would ask the Federal Court in Montgomery "to enjoin the Ku Klux Klan, the National States Rights Party, certain individuals and all persons acting in concert with them from interfering with peaceful interstate travel by buses."

A Justice Department spokesman said that there were reports of Ku Klux Klan and Negro groups converging on Montgomery County and that he was afraid of larger scale problems than had already developed.

Attacks Deplored

The Attorney General acted immediately after President Kennedy issued a statement deploring the mob attacks.

The President said the situation in Alabama was "a source of the deepest concern to me as it must be to the vast majority of the citizens of Alabama and all Americans."

"I have instructed the Justice Department to take all necessary steps," the President added.

He called on Gov. John Patterson of Alabama and other state and local officials "to exercise their lawful authority to prevent any further outbreaks of violence."

"I hope that state and local officials in Alabama will meet their responsibilities," the President said. "The United States Government intends to meet its."

The President said he hoped that all persons, whether citizens of Alabama or visitors, "would refrain from any action which would in any way tend to provoke further outbreaks." His brother, the Attorney General, said that this was not intended as a suggestion to the bus riders that they give up their trip, but was a general appeal for restraint.

The Justice Department said that it was sending marshals and specially deputized marshals to Montgomery from nearby areas and from the District of Columbia.

They are already on the way by air and automobile, a spokesman for the Justice Department said.

Byron R. White, the Deputy Attorney General, went to Montgomery to take charge of the operation there.

Justice Department officials emphasized that no members of the armed forces were being sent.

This was in contrast to the action of President Eisenhower in 1957. Paratroopers were sent then to end violence over school desegregation in Little Rock, Ark.

The marshals were dispatched to Alabama under authority of an 1871 statute which also had been the legal basis for the sending of troops to Little Rock.

The statute says that the President may use "the militia or the armed forces—or any other means—to suppress in a state any insurrection, domestic violence, unlawful combination or conspiracy" under certain specified conditions.

These conditions are that a class of citizens is deprived of a constitutional right "and the constituted authorities of that state are unable, fail, or refuse to protect that right."

Telegram Dispatched

Robert Kennedy announced his ac-

Freedom Riders Julia Aaron and David Dennis on board an interstate bus bound for Jackson, Mississippi, as they and 25 others are escorted by two National Guardsmen. (Paul Schutzer/Time & Life Pictures/Getty Images)

tion in a telegram sent to the Alabama public safety director, Floyd Mann, and the Mayors of Birmingham and Montgomery, besides Governor Patterson.

In the telegram Mr. Kennedy reviewed discussions that he and other Justice Department officials had had with the Governor and his aides since Monday about "this very explosive situation."

He noted that just last night his own administrative assistant, John Seigenthaler, had met with the Governor and had been given the assurance that the state government had "The will, the force, the men and the equipment to fully protect everyone in Alabama."

He added that the Governor had suggested the Justice Department notify the Greyhound Bus Company that a guarantee of safety had been given by the state.

"It was based on his assurance of safe conduct," the Attorney General telegraphed Governor Patterson, "that the students boarded the bus in Birmingham on their trip to Montgomery. These students boarded the bus this morning. They arrived and were attacked and beaten by a mob."

The suit that Mr. Kennedy said was being brought to enjoin interference with interstate travel was a most unusual legal step.

Ordinarily the Justice Department cannot bring an injunction suit unless there is a specific statute authorizing it to do so, and there is none here.

However, in 1895, in the landmark case of In re Debs, the Supreme Court held that the Federal Government had inherent authority to go to the courts to break up any violence interfering with interstate commerce.

ALABAMA ASKS U.S. HELP AS NEW VIOLENCE ERUPTS

By ANTHONY LEWIS

WASHINGTON, Monday, May 22—The State of Alabama called on the Federal Government last night to help put down a new eruption of racial violence in Montgomery. State officials changed their previous attitude of criticism of Federal intervention in the tense situation as a mob built up around a rally in the Negro First Baptist Church in Montgomery.

The State Director of Public Safety, Floyd Mann, asked the Justice Department to send any men it had, because "this is an ugly situation."

Justice Department officials had no immediate plans to send additional men to Montgomery.

The United States District Judge in Montgomery, Frank M. Johnson Jr., asked the Justice Department to protect him and his home from possible attack by the mobs. Marshals were placed around the house.

Judge Johnson had granted a Justice Department request for an injunction against the Ku Klux Klan, barring them from interfering with the freedom of travel in interstate commerce.

Attorney General Robert F. Kennedy disclosed details of the fast-breaking situation at his office here.

Earlier yesterday he had guarded optimistic reports from the Deputy Attorney General, Byron R. White, who was in Montgomery in charge of a force of more than 500 Federal marshals dispatched by Mr. Kennedy Saturday night.

Then, just after 10 P.M., Mr. White reported by telephone that the mob was gathering. Mr. Kennedy immediately called his brother, the President, who was at his country home in Middleburg, Va.

With the approval of the President, the Attorney General immediately telephoned Gov. John Patterson of Alabama in Montgomery and told him more men were needed to control the gathering mob. Governor Patterson assured Mr. Kennedy that everything was under control, but said he would do what he could.

At just about that moment, the Attorney General was telephoned by the Rev. Dr. Martin Luther King Jr., the Negro leader, who was leading the rally in the besieged church. Mr. King told the Attorney General, "They're moving in on the church."

Mr. Kennedy said he told Dr. King, "The marshals will stop them."

He said Dr. King left the phone for a moment, then returned and said, "You're right."

Within the next few minutes the Alabama Director of Public Safety, Mr. Mann, telephoned the Federal command post, at Maxwell Air Force Base, near Montgomery. He asked Deputy Attorney General White to "commit any reserves."

"We've committed all we have," Mr. White replied. "They are at your disposal."

No Plan to Add Men

At the Justice Department there were discussions of the possibility of sending additional men. But there were no immediate plans to do so, and it remained the officials' hope that no further Federal action would be necessary.

However, Federal officials in Montgomery said they planned to keep their men on duty through the night.

Earlier, the Attorney General said in a brief statement:

"Reports from Montgomery this evening indicate that there is increasing tension and a possibility of more mob action."

"I urge all citizens of Alabama and all travelers in Alabama to refrain from doing anything which will cause increased tension or provoke violence and result in further damage to our country."

At 1:30 this morning, Attorney General Kennedy expressed concern about the safety of 1,500 Negroes who were in the church.

Officials at the Justice Department indicated that the Montgomery situation might have reached a stalemate, with those inside the church safe for the moment, but not able to return to their homes in safety.

A spokesman said Mr. Kennedy had talked with Dr. King again to discuss the problem and had also talked it over with a Federal officer on the scene. The still undecided question was whether to attempt to get the Negroes home.

Mr. Kennedy told reporters here that the marshals were working together with the local police to disperse the mob. He said they were using tear gas.

The marshals carried side arms, tear gas bombs and riot sticks when they were sent to Montgomery. The Attorney General said they had only the general order to maintain the peace by whatever means necessary.

Late tonight Mr. Kennedy sent the following telegram to Mr. Mann:

"From the beginning of the problems and difficulties in your state you have been most helpful. Reports which I have received this evening indicate that you have handled yourself and those serving under you with great vigor and skill. We wish to extend all cooperation in your task, and the deputy United States marshals are at your disposal."

As late as 4 P.M. yesterday Governor Patterson had sent a lengthy telegram to Attorney General Kennedy saying that Alabama did not need assistance from any Federal marshals to maintain order.

'Do Not Send Help'

"We do not need their help, we do not want their help, and in fact we don't want them here in Alabama," the Governor said.

"Federal marshals do not have a legal or constitutional right to be here. Their presence is unwarranted and will only further complicate and aggravate the situation. I consider the presence of these Federal marshals a trampling upon and encroachment on the rights of the State of Alabama and our citizens as well."

The Attorney General sent back this curt reply, before the explosion of violence late last night:

"The United States Government needs assurance by action—not words—that its citizens will be safe in the State of Alabama."

Mr. Kennedy ordered in the marshals after a new incident. A biracial group of bus riders was severely beaten by a mob in Montgomery on Saturday. Although Governor Patterson had promised the night before to provide protection, no policemen were on hand.

The Attorney General had stayed in his office all Saturday night in case any new incident developed. Yesterday he met with several Justice aides to discuss the situation.

Few of those sent to Alabama were regular or deputy marshals. Most were men from other Federal law enforcement branches who had been specially deputized as marshals.

Three hundred were agents of the Treasury Department's alcohol and tobacco tax unit. All came from the southeastern region. One hundred and twenty were Federal prison guards, eighty from the penitentiary in Atlanta and the rest from the reformatory at Chillicothe, Ohio.

Some marshals were flown from the District of Columbia and other distant points. Others, stationed closer to Montgomery, were instructed to leave at once for the Alabama city.

There were twenty regular marshals from the District of Columbia and 100 from southeastern states. Many had attended a special school in which they received riot training. These were the same category of law enforcement officers sent to Little Rock, Ark., following the withdrawal of troops.

Later, 100 of the men assigned to Montgomery who were required back on their regular jobs were being replaced by 100 members of the Border Patrol of the Immigration and Naturalization Service.

A spokesman for the Federal officials said that one United States marshal, John Holt, had been hospitalized after being hit in the head by a stone during the melee outside the church.

The underlying legal question in the trip by the biracial group of "freedom riders" was whether a state could enforce segregation in transportation. The Supreme Court had ruled "no."

Under the court's rulings, it makes no difference what kind of transportation is used—bus, plane or train. Nor does it matter whether the journey is intrastate—wholly within a state—or interstate—crossing from one state to another.

The Supreme Court dealt with segregation in interstate travel in 1946. It held that segregation was an unconstitutional burden on interstate commerce.

As for intrastate travel, it first upheld the constitutionality of separate accommodations. That was the decision in the landmark case of *Plessy v. Ferguson* in 1896.

In the 1954 school segregation cases, however, the court overruled the "separate-but-equal" doctrine of the Plessy case. It held segregated schools unconstitutional.

Shortly afterward the court extended the new rule to intrastate transportation. That decision ended the Negro boycott of segregated street cars.

The court also settled that interstate waiting rooms in terminals could not be segregated. Just this term it held that a private restaurant in an interstate terminal, designed to serve interstate passengers, could not segregate.

Segregation in private restaurants or other facilities connected with an intrastate terminal presents more difficult questions.

It is clear that a state may not order such facilities segregated. But if there is no state law and a private restaurant, for example, decides not to serve Negroes, the restaurant presumably may take such a course.

The Fourteenth Amendment, which prohibits racial discrimination, applies only to state action, not private discrimination.

No Alternative Seen

Republican and Democratic leaders declared that President Kennedy and the Justice Department had had no choice but to send the marshals.

Senator Sam J. Ervin Jr., Democrat of North Carolina, said that sending marshals when local officials could not stem violence was in accordance with the law.

It was forecast that the riots might give new impetus to the rights bills recently introduced in Congress.

However, Mike Mansfield of Montana, Senate Democratic leader, said it remained to be seen whether the riots would cause new demands for rights action.

The Republican leader, Everett McKinley Dirksen of Illinois, suggested that the incidents would inspire such demands. So did Paul H. Douglas, Democrat of Illinois.

Mr. Dirksen said the trouble might have an impact on the school-aid bill nearing passage in the Senate. But Mr. Mansfield did not think so.

Hubert H. Humphrey, assistant Senate Democratic leader, said the trouble would embarrass the United States in the "cold war" because some uncommitted nations would regard Americans as "crude and immoral."

KENNEDY ASKS $1.8 BILLION THIS YEAR TO ACCELERATE SPACE EXPLORATION, ADD FOREIGN AID, BOLSTER DEFENSE

MOON TRIP URGED

He Assures Congress Nation Is Ready to Take On Burden

By W.H. LAWRENCE

WASHINGTON, May 25—President Kennedy proposed to Congress today bold and expensive new measures to rocket a man to the moon, to expand non-nuclear military strength and to increase foreign aid spending.

These actions, he said, are needed to promote a "freedom doctrine" around the globe.

For the first year, the cost of the new program exceeded $1,800,000,000 in appropriations including $679,000,000 for space projects. But the President made it clear that the new space program alone would cost $7,000,000,000 to $9,000,000,000 over the next five years, and that the costs of other projects would also increase sharply.

To emphasize the urgency of his proposals, Mr. Kennedy appeared personally before a joint session of Congress. His speech was televised and broadcast nationally by all networks.

Applauded 18 Times

The President called his forty-seven-minute talk a second State of the Union Message, departing from the tradition that such messages are usually delivered by Presidents once a year, in January.

Legislators, diplomats, Cabinet members and the packed public galleries interrupted the President eighteen times with applause.

The loudest and most sustained hand-clapping greeted his promise that he would make it clear to Premier Khrushchev at their meeting in Vienna next month that "America's enduring concern is for both peace and freedom."

Major Increases Listed

The major categories of governmental activity for which increased funds were asked for the fiscal year beginning next July 1 included the following:

For accelerated space exploration, including the manned moon shot, nuclear rocket development and communications and weather satellites—$679,000,000.

For increased foreign economic and military aid—$535,000,000.

For strengthening the Army and Marine Corps—$160,000,000.

For the Small Business Administration—$130,000,000.

For expanded retraining of unemployed workers—$75,000,000.

For the United States Information Agency, largely for new radio and television broadcasts to Latin America and Southeast Asia—$2,400,000.

The President also announced an Administration decision for Federal participation in the construction of civilian fall-out shelters to ward off nuclear attack. This program, he said, would "more than triple" current budget requests of $104,000,000 for civil defense.

He exercised his authority for governmental reorganization to shift civil defense activities from the Office of Civil and Defense Mobilization to the Secretary of Defense. He said new, increased budget estimates for civil defense would be submitted later.

David E. Bell, director of the Budget Bureau, estimated that actual spending in the fiscal year under the new programs, excluding civil defense, would total about $724,000,000.

This would mean a total Federal budget of $84,893,000,000 and an unexpected deficit of at least $3,500,000,000. The final budget submitted by President Eisenhower as he left office was $80,865,000,000, with an expected surplus of $1,500,000,000.

Calls for Sacrifices

Although he did not ask for new or increased taxes now to finance the new programs, Mr. Kennedy said sacrifices would be required of the American people in the battle for freedom.

The nation's greatest asset, he said, is the willingness of its people to pay the price for these programs, to accept a long struggle and to share their resources with less fortunate people. He expressed confidence that the nation would also exercise self-restraint against increasing wages or prices or over-producing certain crops.

He answered in some detail a question often asked of him since his Inaugural posed the challenge to Americans to "ask not what your country can do for you—ask what you can do for your country."

Self-restraint, he said, would also stop people from "spreading military secrets, or urging unessential expenditures or improper monopolies or harmful work stoppages."

This spirit, he continued, would lead them to serve in the Peace Corps, or the armed forces, or Congress and to strive for excellence in their schools, their cities and their physical fitness. It would also cause them to take part in civil defense, to pay higher postal rates, higher payroll taxes and higher teachers' salaries, he declared.

The President said the problems of survival for some of the nation's allies were complicated where conditions of social injustice and chaos were allowed to fester and to invite Communist subversion. It would be the nation's aim, he said, to help them solve such economic problems as well as to provide them with military assistance.

Of his forthcoming trip abroad, Mr. Kennedy told Congress he welcomed the opportunity to see President de Gaulle, whom he described as "the great captain of the Western world."

He conceded policy differences with General de Gaulle, saying the serious conversations they would have "do not require a pale unanimity—they are rather the instruments of trust and understanding over a long road."

As for the Soviet Union, the President expressed renewed hopes that an effective treaty banning nuclear weapons tests could be negotiated. Despite response from the Russians until now, he said, "we intend to go the last mile in patience."

He said amid applause, that the problem of general disarmament remained high on the Administration's agenda of hopes, and that he would soon ask Congress to establish a strengthened and enlarged disarmament agency.

The President's major emphasis was on the necessity of sending a man to the moon, and of getting him there first if possible. He told Congress a firm national decision was essential now on whether this nation would go all the way on a big space program that "will last for many years and carry very heavy costs."

"If we were to go only half way, or reduce our sights in the face of difficulty, it would be better not to go at all," he said.

The President conceded that Congress might not hold the same views he did. But "I believe we should go to the moon." he declared. It was time, he said, for the United States "to take a clearly leading role in space achievement," which may "hold the key to our future on earth."

★ ★ ★

"If we are to win the battle that is now going on around the world between freedom and tyranny, the dramatic achievements in space which occurred in recent weeks should have made clear to us all, as did the Sputnik in 1957, the impact of this adventure on the minds of men everywhere, who are attempting to make a determination of which road they should take. Since early in my term, our efforts in space have been under review . . . Now it is time to take longer strides—time for a great new American enterprise—time for this nation to take a clearly leading role in space achievement, which in many ways may hold the key to our future on earth.

I believe that this nation should commit itself to achieving the goal, before this decade is out, of landing a man on the moon and returning him safely to the earth. No single space project in this period will be more impressive to mankind, or more important for the long-range exploration of space; and none will be so difficult or expensive to accomplish. We propose to accelerate the development of the appropriate lunar space craft."

European Diplomacy

Kennedy and De Gaulle Agree to Defend Berlin; Discuss Asia and Africa Presidents Meet

Stand Firm on Soviet Threat—Parisians Hail Kennedys

By ROBERT C. DOTY

PARIS, May 31—President Kennedy and President de Gaulle proclaimed today their "complete identity of view" on Western action to counter any threat to Berlin by the Soviet Union.

In view of the position on Berlin authoritatively attributed to General de Gaulle on the question, this meant that the two leaders apparently had reached agreement to go to war if necessary to maintain Western rights in the divided city.

Pierre Salinger, White House press secretary, and Pierre Baraduc, spokesman for the French Foreign Ministry, reported agreement on Berlin as a result of the thirty-seven-minute conversation between the two leaders just before they lunched together today.

In an hour-and-fifty-minute conversation after lunch, Mr. Kennedy and General de Gaulle began discussions of problems in Southeast Asia, notably Laos, and in Africa.

Welcome Is Colorful

The state visit by President and Mrs. Kennedy got off to a colorful start.

After their arrival at Orly Airport at 10:20 A. M. (5:20 A. M. Eastern Daylight Time) they rode in a motorcade through flag-decked streets.

The morning was bright and sunny and 500,000 or 1,500,000 cheering Parisians—depending on whether skeptical professional estimates or enthusiastic official figures were followed—lined the streets.

The two Presidents had three occasions to exchange complimentary words in public —at the airport, in luncheon toasts, and in a final exchange at a state dinner at the Elysee palace tonight.

At the dinner, Mr. Kennedy made a strong statement on the interdependence of France and the United States and pledged that "American forces will remain in Europe as long as they are required, ready to meet any threat with whatever response is needed."

Taken in the context of the earlier talks on Berlin, this seemed to be a commitment to go all the way—including apparently, the threat of major nuclear war—in defense of that city.

But the real core and purpose of the visit was expressed in the private conversation the two leaders had today. This will be continued in five hours more of scheduled interviews.

The speed with which they dealt with the Berlin question indicated that Mr. Kennedy and General de Gaulle had confined themselves to broad principles—a reiteration of the "firm stand" first proclaimed by the West in 1958.

Full Praise for Kennedy

In his welcome to the Kennedys at the airport, General de Gaulle was whole-hearted in his praise of the President and noted "the fact that at your side is the gracious Mrs. Kennedy."

He declared:

"Monsieur le President, on your arrival on French soil, which has never known Americans other than as friends and allies, it is with joy that I address to you and to the United States, the very cordial salute of France."

Responding, Mr. Kennedy quoted from his host's past declarations calling America "the daughter of Europe" and graciously acknowledging the West's debt of civilization to France.

He used another phrase calculated to please French ears when he spoke of "the grandeur of France's present mission, the productivity of her workers, the brilliance of her universities, the vigor of her leaders."

"Grandeur" for France has been General de Gaulle's constant mission.

"You have been a captain in the field in defense of the West for more than twenty years," Mr. Kennedy said." Your vigour, your leadership, your long sense of history are needed now more than ever in the past."

"France and the United States have been associated in the past in many great causes, but I can think of no more happy cause than to be associated together in the climactic moment in the defense of freedom," he added.

Less resounding words were exchanged at the end of a small luncheon at the Elysee Palace after the morning meeting, and Mr. Kennedy hazarded a joke to make a point.

To General de Gaulle's remark that he could add nothing in the way of welcome to what the people in the streets had offered Mr. Kennedy replied with thanks and added:

President Kennedy and President de Gaulle by the Tomb of the Unknown Soldier at the Arc de Triomphe in Paris, June 1, 1961.
(Reporters Associes/Gamma-Rapho/Getty Images)

"A few years ago it was said that the optimists learned Russian and the pessimists learned Chinese. I prefer to think that those with vision study French and English."

Following the afternoon meeting with General de Gaulle Mr. Kennedy returned to the Foreign Ministry and received the Paris diplomatic corps. He then joined General de Gaulle in the latter's big open car for a rain-drenched ride up the Champs Elysees to the Arch of Triumph.

After a brief pause the President and Mrs. Kennedy returned to the Elysee Palace for the big formal dinner and reception.

They dined with 140 guests and received 1,500 afterward. The visitors struggled through monumental traffic jams to catch a glimpse of General de Gaulle, in military full dress, Mr. Kennedy in white tie and tails, and Mrs. Kennedy in a sophisticated sheath dress, moving through the mirrored salons.

French Urge Preparedness

The French view on the defense of Berlin, according to authoritative sources, is that the West must be prepared to go to war rather than accept Soviet arrangements with East Germany that would jeopardize Western access to Berlin.

Advance indications that Mr. Kennedy shared this preference for the most uncompromising stand on Berlin found confirmation in the speed with which the two leaders reached agreement.

It is likely, however, that when they reach a discussion of the actual physical means for enforcing the Western position they will touch on areas where their accord is less complete.

It should open up discussion of a whole range of differences on the broad topic of defense. These include General de Gaulle's insistence on French-British-United States planning and control of the use of strategic nuclear weapons and on similar tripartite political consultations on world-wide questions.

The list continues with his opposition to the integration of national forces under international command in the North Atlantic Treaty Organization and persistence in testing and developing France's nuclear weapons when his major allies are trying to negotiate a test ban treaty with the Soviet Union.

The Kennedys arrive at Elysee Palace in Paris to meet French president General de Gaulle on June 2, 1961.

(Reporters Associes/Gamma-Keystone/Getty Images)

Jackie Kennedy speaking with French president Charles de Gaulle during an official state visit. (Hank Walker/Time & Life Pictures/Getty Images)

Just an Escort, Kennedy Jokes As Wife's Charm Enchants Paris

First Lady Wins Bouquets From Press—

By W. GRANGER BLAIR

PARIS, June 2 —"I do not think it altogether inappropriate to introduce myself to this audience. I am the man who accompanied Jacqueline Kennedy to Paris, and I have enjoyed it."

This was how President Kennedy presented himself today to 400 journalists at a press luncheon. The remark was humorous and appreciated as such but it reflected the extraordinary impression that the President's wife has made on Paris.

Not since Queen Elizabeth II of Britain was here in 1957 have Paris' newspapers packed their pages with so many bouquets.

One of these was a cartoon in the newspaper Liberation. Mrs. Kennedy was so delighted with it that she asked for and received the original drawing.

The cartoon, drawn by an artist named Escaro, who harbors no warm feelings for President de Gaulle, depicts a great canopied double bed.

In the bed is General de Gaulle, the covers pulled up to his nose and his eyes tightly closed. Over his head is a cartoonist's balloon, which frames a photograph of Mrs. Kennedy.

Mme. de Gaulle is shown sitting bolt upright next to her husband with her mouth open and her eyes fixed on the dream.

The caption under the drawing simply says: "Charles!"

Today, after two days of almost uninterrupted state functions, Mrs. Kennedy was able to do a few things more in keeping with her interests than standing in reception lines and rushing from one official function to another.

Quick Trip to Museum

This morning, after it was hurriedly arranged yesterday, she visited the Jeu de Paume Museum, which houses France's finest collection of Impressionist paintings. She was escorted through the museum by Andre Malraux, the French Minister of Culture.

She was wearing a tailored gray suit. Her jewelry was pearls and a half-bow gold diamond shoulder pin. She also wore a back-of-the-head beret in a glazed straw fabric with a black border, and half-length white gloves.

When she emerged from the museum, which is in the Tuileries Gardens on the Place de la Concorde side, she brushed past the police cordon to pose for the tourists with cameras and to chat for a moment with journalists. She said that she had been most impressed by Manet's "Olympia," a painting of a nude reclining on a couch.

This evening, after saying their official farewells to President and Mme de Gaulle late in the afternoon, President and Mrs. Kennedy dined quietly at the United States Embassy residence. Originally scheduled to spend the night at the residence, they returned to their suite at the French Foreign Ministry for their final night in Paris.

KENNEDY AND KHRUSHCHEV STRESS PROBLEM OF LAOS IN 4-HOUR TALK; DISCUSSION 'FRANK AND COURTEOUS'

Parley Is Lively

By JAMES RESTON

VIENNA, June 3 —President Kennedy and Premier Khrushchev held today what was described as a "frank and courteous" four-hour discussion of the troubled world relationships between the United States and the Soviet Union.

A statement issued by the official spokesmen of the two countries at a joint news conference said special attention had been paid to the Southeast Asian country of Laos, whose Government is facing a Communist-backed rebellion.

It is understood that this produced some lively discussion of the recent Soviet insistence on a veto over the control of the present "cease-fire" in that country, but no agreement.

In fact, while the atmosphere of the conversations was apparently more cordial than had been expected after the rising controversies of the last few months, no agreements were expected.

Randolph Churchill 'Bored'

The leaders' discussions will be continued tomorrow.

At the end of the mammoth news conference this evening—broken up by Randolph Churchill, son of the former British Prime Minister, who forced his way out of the closed conference room because he was "bored"—it was not possible for the official spokesmen to agree on how to characterize the results of the day's talks.

Mikhail A. Kharlamov, chief of the

Soviet premier Nikita S. Khrushchev meeting President Kennedy in Vienna. (Paul Schutzer/Time & Life Pictures/Getty Images)

Khrushchev and Kennedy talked for about four hours in Vienna on June 3, 1961. (Paul Schutzer/Time & Life Pictures/Getty Images)

press department of the Soviet Foreign Office, described the conversations as "fruitful" as Pierre Salinger, White House press secretary, said he preferred to stand on his previous description of the meeting as "frank and courteous."

Fruitful or not, the meetings at least avoided both the false optimism of the first summit meeting of 1955 and the angry Soviet denunciations of the ill-fated U-2 summit meeting in Paris last year.

The unexpectedly small Soviet delegation arrived here by slow train yesterday complaining that the United States seemed determined to turn the Vienna meeting into a propaganda circus, but the President insisted personally today on precisely the opposite approach.

He greeted Mr. Khrushchev warmly at the beginning of the session at 12:45 P. M., running down the steps of the United States Embassy residence to meet him.

The President took the Premier into the building for a working session with their aides until 2 o'clock, entered into some good-natured bantering at lunch and then proposed that the afternoon sessions be held in private with only interpreters present.

President Kennedy started the afternoon talks during a ten-minute stroll through the garden with Mr. Khrushchev and they went on until 6:45 P. M., when the President, still pleasant, saw Mr. Khrushchev to his car to end what amounted to about four hours of tediously interpreted conversations.

Rusk and Gromyko Talk

The complex and sensitive topics of Germany and Berlin and the control of nuclear testing were not explored by the two leaders, though these topics will be on the agenda for the final meetings tomorrow.

It is understood, however, that they were discussed, without noticeable change in the positions of either side, by Secretary of State Dean Rusk and Andrei A. Gromyko, Soviet Foreign Minister, who conferred with their aides in another part of the embassy during the Kennedy-Khrushchev afternoon session.

On the basis of the limited information available tonight, it appeared that the only topic explored at length by the President and the Premier was Laos.

Recently, efforts to establish a commission to maintain the cease-fire in that country have led to Soviet insistence that all decisions involving inspection of violations of the cease-fire be taken by "unanimous agreement."

The United States is strongly opposed to this, not only in the specific case of Laos, but in principle. Ever since the United Nations intervened successfully to get the Soviet technicians and representatives out of the Congo, Moscow has been demanding that international action by the United Nations, or any other international group, be taken only when representatives of the Western world, the Communist world and the neutral world agree unanimously.

In the United States' view this not only would give the Communists a veto over international control of delicate disputes but would virtually paralyze the post-war movement toward the peaceful settlement and supervision of disputes by international organizations.

Doctrine Troubles U. S.

One of the President's reasons for coming to Vienna was to try to get some clarification of a Khrushchev doctrine that has troubled Washington ever since it was delivered in a report by the Soviet Premier to representatives of Communist and workers parties in Moscow last Jan. 6.

In this report Mr. Khrushchev defined what has been called the "doctrine of three wars." He ruled out atomic and hydrogen "world wars" and also "limited" or local wars on the ground that both might lead to the death of hundreds of millions of people.

"Wars of national liberation," however, he said, were not only permissible but necessary and would have the support of the Communist peoples. He gave as examples of these the war in Algeria and Fidel Castro's war against Fulgencio Batista in Cuba.

"These are revolutionary wars," he said. "Such wars are not only admissible but inevitable. In these uprisings these people are fighting for the implementation of their right of self-determination, for independent social and national development. These are uprisings against rotten reactionary regimes, against the colonizers. The Communists fully support such just wars."

This has raised a number of fundamental questions among the President's advisers on Soviet affairs, who were discussing them before today's meeting between the President and the Premier.

According to this doctrine, which has become the basis of Communist activity all over the world, Dr. Castro's war against President Batista was a "just war." which would justify Communist support as a "war of liberation," but the recent uprising against Dr. Castro would be regarded as a counter-revolutionary war by a "rotten reactionary" regime backed by the American "colonizers."

Similarly, under this doctrine Communist aid to the rebels in Laos and Vietnam is "just," but United States aid to the legitimate Government of Laos is "imperialism."

Need for Clarification

The point being made to Premier Khrushchev and his aides here by the United States is that this is a fallacious and highly dangerous argument. The United States is insisting that, as "limited" or "local" might lead to the big nuclear war, so this attempt to back whatever the Communists think is a "just' uprising might also lead to the intervention of other states that have a different notion of justice.

In short, the "wars of liberation," like the limited wars, could also lead to a major nuclear war and President Kennedy's point was that persistence in such a doctrine would inevitably produce precisely the kind of world tensions that Mr. Khrushchev says he wants to avoid.

No one on the American side expected Mr. Khrushchev to abandon the "just war" doctrine, or even to debate it at any length in the limited time available here, but nevertheless the point was being raised for a fundamental reason.

> *"These are revolutionary wars, . . . Such wars are not only admissible but inevitable. In these uprisings these people are fighting for the implementation of their right of self-determination."*
> —*Nikita Khrushchev*

If the Russians merely mean to provide limited aid to those engaged on their side in such wars, Washington would feel that the situation, while awkward might be controlled.

If, however, the Soviet Union decides to maintain its people at their present low standard of living and devote the rising Soviet production to such wars, then United States officials would be extremely gloomy about the outlook for peace.

This is why Washington was hoping to deter Mr. Khrushchev from the latter course.

More than a thousand reporters attempted to question Mr. Salinger and Mr. Kharlamov, but succeeded mainly in confusing each other.

This conference was held in the new palace, a wing of the Imperial Palace, which formerly housed Archduke Franz Ferdinand, the unfortunate nephew and heir of Franz Joseph, who was assassinated at Sarajevo in 1914.

Mr. Salinger refused to say whether any agreement had been reached on Laos, what the advisers to the two leaders had discussed or who said what in the toasts at lunch.

Kennedy and Khrushchev Find Limited Laos Accord but Split on Berlin and Key Arms Issues

Vienna Talks End

Meeting Closes With Hard Controversy— Kennedy Solemn

By JAMES RESTON

VIENNA, June 4—President Kennedy and Premier Khrushchev ended their two-day conversation today with a limited agreement on Laos and a sharp three-hour disagreement on all questions concerning Germany and Berlin.

The conference, which started well yesterday, ended in hard controversy today. There were no ultimatums and few bitter or menacing exchanges. Indeed, Premier Khrushchev described the conference tonight as a "very good beginning," but the differences on Germany were nevertheless both wide and deep.

This was true as well of the two leaders' differences on the control of nuclear testing, on the Soviet demands for a veto over international control of other disputes, on the means of controlling disarmament and on Mr. Khrushchev's doctrine of what he regards as "just" wars of "national liberation."

Kennedy in Solemn Mood

Accordingly, President Kennedy flew off to London tonight in a solemn, although confident, mood. He had re-established high-level United States-Soviet diplomacy, which was broken off last year after the U-2 spy plane incident, and had agreed to maintain diplomatic contact at all levels, but on the big disputes between Washington and

Moscow he had found absolutely no new grounds for encouragement.

In the hope, on both sides, that today's sharp disagreements might be modified after further conversations, the official statement on the meeting was vaguely incomplete.

It said merely that the two leaders had completed their "useful" meetings, had discussed Germany, nuclear tests and disarmament, had reaffirmed their support for a neutral and independent Laos and had agreed to continue discussions on all questions of interest.

In line with this moderate and even hopeful Soviet approach, which has characterized the comments of Soviet officials and journalists ever since they reached this lovely city, Premier Khrushchev decided against holding a news conference tomorrow as he did in his tumultuous exit from the Paris summit meeting with President Eisenhower, President de Gaulle and Prime Minister Macmillan in May, 1960.

Indeed, the Communists scarcely mentioned the German part of the talks, though this was the main preoccupation of the day and was the point the Soviet Premier insisted upon discussing more than anything else.

One possible reason for the Soviet display of satisfaction may have been an ambiguity in the day's discussion about the critical question of the Allied rights and duties toward Berlin.

The former German capital, responsibility for which rests jointly with the victorious powers of World War II— the United States, the Soviet Union, Britain and France—lies 110 miles inside Communist East Germany.

The Russians have been threatening to ignore the joint responsibility of the four for Berlin, to turn over the control of East Germany to the German Communist government of that state and thus to leave to the East Germans the power to check on the shipment of essential supplies to the military and civilian population of West Berlin.

Kennedy Takes Firm Stand

President Kennedy argued this whole legal and moral question, point for point, with the Soviet Premier for more than an hour.

He concluded his argument by reminding the Soviet leader that the United States had twice gone to war to prevent Western Europe from being overwhelmed, and he added that the United States regarded the freedom of West Germany as essential to the freedom of Western Europe.

This was not said provocatively but simply as an objective fact. But in the discussion that followed, the ambiguity arose.

The President placed his emphasis in this discussion not on the legal question of whether the Soviet Union had any right to recognize Communist East Germany as a sovereign Government, but on the practical question of getting necessary supplies through the Communist territory to West Berlin.

He insisted that this was not only a right of the Western powers, as a result of their conquest of Germany, but a duty to the 2,200,000 people of West Berlin, assumed not only by the United States, Britain and France but also by the Soviet Union.

This was interpreted by Communists here as an indication that the President was concerned, not about recognition of East Germany by Moscow, but only about freedom of access to Berlin, regardless of who controlled the checkpoints on routes between West Germany and the former German capital.

It is true that the United States is more concerned about the freedom and the lives of the people of West Berlin than in the legal aspects of the question, but this does not mean that the United States has agreed to acquiesce in turning over sovereign power to the East Germans.

Envoy Sent to Bonn and Paris

President Kennedy came here with a careful understanding on the Berlin question with both President de Gaulle and Chancellor Adenauer. Accordingly, he sent Secretary of State Dean Rusk to Paris this evening to report on the Vienna talks to President de Gaulle and instructed Foy D. Kohler, Assistant Secretary of State for European Affairs, to go to Bonn to report to Chancellor Adenauer.

Mr. Rusk will also discuss the Vienna meetings with the members of the Council of the North Atlantic Treaty Organization in Paris tomorrow.

At no time during these long discussions, eventually made tedious by translation, did Premier Khrushchev depart from the past positions that have been rejected by the United States, Britain and France in two long foreign ministers' conferences in Geneva.

Finally, the President told the Soviet leader that the Soviet Government was asking the United States to accept Mr. Khrushchev's policy for Germany in detail or run the risk of war.

It was at this point that the President reminded the Premier that the United States had fought in two wars to defend Western Europe and that he regarded the freedom of West Germany as essential to the freedom of Western Europe today.

No Progress on Test Ban

The discussions on the possibility of reaching a controlled ban on nuclear testing were equally negative. As a matter of fact, Mr. Khrushchev indicated that he was not very interested in reaching a test ban agreement unless it was made part of a general disarmament agreement.

Accordingly, United States officials left here without much hope for the stalemated United States-British-Soviet discussion in Geneva on a nuclear test ban agreement, which had virtually stopped in the hope that President Kennedy and Premier Khrushchev could break the deadlock.

President Kennedy told the Soviet leader quite explicitly that he would not enter into any nuclear or disarmament agreement that involved a Soviet veto on the control of such an agreement.

Premier Khrushchev insisted in turn that the Soviet Union would not permit its interests to be determined by international bodies unless it agreed with the decisions of such international groups.

These discussions went on, with time out for a lavish lunch, for approximately six hours in the Soviet Embassy while crowds of curious Austrians stood outside. Mr. Rusk and Mr. Gromyko and their principal aides were present most of the time.

Cuba was mentioned only once during the discussions, when Mr. Khrushchev said that "Castro is no Communist."

This came up during a discussion of the Khrushchev doctrine of the "three wars."

This doctrine was laid down by the Soviet leader in a major report last Jan. 6.

In it he said that, while world wars must be ruled out and limited local wars should also be banned because they might lead to world war, "wars of national liberation," such as the nationalist rebellion in Algeria and Dr. Fidel Castro's struggle to overthrow the regime of Fulgencio Batista in Cuba not only were permissible but were "just" and should have the support of the Communist peoples.

President Kennedy said these wars of national liberation were also dangerous because, while limited wars such as that in Korea could conceivably get out of control, so also could conflicts such as that in Laos, which Mr. Khrushchev regarded as "just." The President warned of the danger of miscalculation.

Khrushchev Objects

Mr. Khrushchev not only did not accept this argument, but added that he did not like the word "miscalculation," which he said was a misleading "Western word."

Once when the going got a little difficult, Mr. Khrushchev attacked the United States for defending a lot of "unrepresentative" governments. To this, the President replied that a free vote in the Eastern European countries might not return an overwhelming majority for the parties now in power.

This, however, merely led to charges that the President was attacking governments with which the United States had normal diplomatic relations—governments that were, Mr. Khrushchev added, truly representative of the people.

Most of this took place during a long morning session that lasted from shortly after 10 o'clock until shortly after 2, when the discussions broke up for lunch. Earlier in the morning the President and Mrs. Kennedy went to church.

Despite the hard going during the talks, the atmosphere at lunch was jovial, with the usual toasts to peace, freedom and a safe journey home.

Now tonight, at the end, though there has been no change on any major problem, they profess to be not only satisfied but pleased.

Meanwhile, President Kennedy, if not pleased, has had his first major experience in "cold war" diplomacy and has come out of it very well. He did not expect much and he did not get much, but he went away from here more experienced and he now rates more highly in the estimation of the men who watched these exchanges than he has at any time since he entered the White House.

President's Physician Describes His Condition as a Common One

By EUGENE J. TAYLOR

June 14—President Kennedy's back condition, which has been widely publicized as a result of his use of crutches publicly, has been described by his physician, Dr. Janet G. Travell, as a lumbosacral strain.

This condition, often called "sacroiliac" sprain, involves the area between the fifth or lowest lumbar vertebra and the sacrum.

The sacrum, located just above the coccyx, is the lowest bone of the spine and is attached to the pelvis.

The condition from which the President suffers is a common one and may result from undue exertion such as may occur in sports or gardening, or from a simple twist. It is not necessarily related to the overall physical fitness of the sufferer.

In the President's case it is an occupational disability resulting from his over-vigorous use of a silver ceremonial shovel in a tree-planting ceremony at Government House, Ottawa, on May 16.

He has had difficulty with his back since he suffered an injury playing football in 1937, during his sophomore year at Harvard.

Rejected by the Army

He was rejected for military service by the Army in World War II, because of this injury, but was accepted by the Navy.

In August, 1943, while a lieutenant in charge of a Navy PT boat, his back was re-injured when a Japanese destroyer cut the PT boat in half. He was in the water fifteen hours following the attack.

He spent most of 1944 in a Naval hospital, when he had a lumbar-disc operation in an attempt to correct the back injury.

The procedure was not completely successful, and in October, 1954, he underwent a delicate spinal fusion to stabilize the spine. This procedure involved the insertion of a small metal plate in the lumbar region.

This, too, was unsuccessful and in February, 1955, he had a third operation in which the plate was removed. It was following this third operation that President Kennedy was referred to Dr. Travell.

The White House press secretary, Pierre Salinger, has emphasized that the President's current problem is not related to his prior back problems.

Inflammation of Tissue

The basic factor that causes lumbosacral strain is fibromyositis, or inflammation of the supportive tissues of the musculoskeletal system.

Fibromyositis occurs at any age and may involve any region of the body. It is more prevalent in adults, more frequent in the male, and most common in cold and inclement climates.

Many authorities believe fibromyositis is almost universal and that few persons go through life without at some time suffering from the condition to some degree.

Among the various causes of fibromyositis is trauma or injury. "Charley horse" is an example.

When President Kennedy energetically turned six to ten spades of dirt in Ottawa instead of the traditional one or two, he put some muscles in his back to a use to which they were not accustomed. They became strained.

In such cases subcutaneous nodules that constitute sensitive, localized "trigger points" of pain may occur. In other instances the pain may be diffuse.

A standard treatment which often brings dramatic relief is the injection of the "trigger point" areas with procaine or other cocaine derivatives, which provide local anesthesia but are less toxic than cocaine.

An authority on pain, Dr. Travell developed much of her professional reputation as an exponent of this type of treatment.

Yesterday, the White House announced that Dr. Preston Wade, a New York surgeon, had flown to Palm Beach Sunday to examine the President and consult with Dr. Travell.

Mr. Salinger reported also that President Kennedy's condition "has improved and continues to improve." Democratic Congressional leaders who had met with the President earlier also reported that he showed no signs of fatigue or pain, and that he had told them he felt "just fine."

Wears Supporting Brace

He wears a light corset-like brace for support and it is reported he still uses a bed-board to promote hyperextension of the spine.

Since she became his physician, Dr. Travell has been using measures such as the brace and a quarter-inch lift for the left shoe to relieve the strain on his sensitive back through improved body mechanics.

The main point, however, is that the present difficulty is minor in nature.

It has been highlighted by the precautionary measures that the President has taken in using crutches and the mechanical lift for embarking and disembarking from the plane when returning from his week-end vacation in Palm Beach.

Opposite page:
President Kennedy on crutches due to a back ailment, June 1961.
(Ed Clark/ Time & Life Pictures/ Getty Images)

KENNEDY ORDERS DEFENSE REVIEW IN BERLIN CRISIS

Calls for a Survey of Need to Increase Arms Spending in Face of Soviet Threat

RUSSIAN BUILD-UP NOTED

Pentagon Warns of Danger—President Moves After Session With Advisers

By JOHN W. FINNEY

WASHINGTON, July 10—President Kennedy ordered an urgent review to determine whether the United States should increase its military strength to meet Soviet threats on Berlin.

The re-examination of the nation's military strength and budget was decided on Saturday in a conference at Hyannis Port between President Kennedy and his principal military and diplomatic advisers it was announced today by Secretary of Defense Robert S. McNamara.

> "... nothing that has developed in the United States or the free world calls for increased militarism."

The President convened with Secretary of State Dean Rusk, Gen. Maxwell D. Taylor, the White House military adviser and Mr. McNamara.

While the review, which could lead to further increases in the defense budget, was dictated primarily by the Ber-

lin crisis, a contributing factor was Premier Khrushchev's announcement that the Soviet Union was postponing a planned reduction in military strength and was increasing military spending by 33 1/3 per cent.

In a statement issued by the Pentagon Mr. McNamara pointed to the Soviet Proposal to increase its military spending by 3,000,000,000 rubles (nominally $3,330,000,000)

"The simplest precaution calls for another examination of our defense posture," he said.

"Currently we are as strong, not stronger—than any potential aggressor." Mr. McNamara went on. "But in the face of the inescapable realities that confront us, such as threats to dispossess us of our rightful presence in Berlin, we can do no less than re-examine our needs. This we are doing."

Defense Called Strong

That the Administration's action was dictated primarily by Berlin was indicated by Deputy Defense Secretary Roswell L. Gilpatric in testimony before the Senate Appropriations subcommittee. Asked by Senator A. Willis Robertson, Democrat of Virginia, whether the United States had an adequate military force to fight "a brush-fire war" over Berlin, Mr. Gilpatric replied:

"I think our military establishment today is very strong. If it is not strong enough to meet the threat in Berlin, we are going to come back and ask for some more money."

Meanwhile, the display in Moscow

yesterday of several new combat aircraft, including a supersonic heavy bomber, resulted in increased pressure from Congress for the accelerated development and production of manned bombers by the United States.

Mr. Gilpatric took the position, however, that the Soviet air show only confirmed past appraisals of Soviet bomber-missile power and for the moment at least necessitated no change in plans for the Strategic Air Command's bomber force.

Defense Budget Revised

Since taking office in January, the Kennedy Administration has made two revisions that added nearly $3,000,000,000 to the defense budget originally proposed by President Eisenhower for the present fiscal year, which began July 1. The Kennedy budget proposes $43,412,345,000 in new military appropriations—a request that was cut $231,210,000 by the House. The budget is before the Senate Appropriations Committee.

These budgetary increases combined with a build-up in Western military power were cited by Premier Khrushchev as the reasons why the Soviet Union must increase its military strength, just as the Khrushchev announcement was cited today by Mr. McNamara in explaining why the United States must now review its military strength.

In his statement, however, Mr. McNamara sought to emphasize that the increases in the defense budget did not justify an increase in Soviet military

President John F. Kennedy sits in his favorite rocking chair in his office during a meeting with Secretary of Defense Robert McNamara and Vice President Lyndon B. Johnson, right, at the White House. (Henry Burroughs/Associated Press)

spending or an abandonment of the Soviet plan, announced in January, 1960, to reduce Soviet military manpower from 3,623,000 to 2,423,000 by next year.

The Defense Secretary said the early budgetary actions to increase both the nuclear and non-nuclear strength of the United States armed forces "were inescapable in the face of the aggressive atmosphere in the East and nearer at home."

He said, however, that "nothing that has developed in the United States or the free world calls for increased militarism."

"On the contrary," Mr. McNamara continued, "the United States has demonstrated at the Geneva disarmament talks its desire to lighten, not to add to

the burden of disarmament and to world tension."

As Mr. Gilpatric opened the defense of the Administration's military budget before the Senate, subcommittee members repeatedly expressed concern over whether the nation's strength was adequate for possible conflict over Berlin.

Senator Robertson, the acting subcommittee chairman, pointed out that the Administration had made "drastic cuts" in the money originally requested by the military services and was now proposing that only $78,564,000 of the House cut be restored by the Senate.

'Very Gravely' Regarded

Mr. Gilpatric opposed for the moment many steps proposed within the

armed forces and Congress for increasing ground and air strength.

Mr. Gilpatric also opposed suggestions by subcommittee members that in light of the Soviet air show the United States should buy more B-52 intercontinental jet bombers and should accelerate the development and production of the B-70 supersonic bomber.

As of the moment, he said, "we feel our Air Force, despite all the Soviet modernization, is adequate to meet our needs."

Administration plans, he said, call for maintaining during this decade a manned bomber fleet composed of more than 600 B-52's and 100 B-58 medium bombers.

U.S. Again Fires Man Into Space; Capsule Lost After Sea Landing, But Astronaut Swims to Safety

Hatch Blown Off

Mishap Not Explained— Grissom Reported in Good Condition

By RICHARD WITKIN

CAPE CANAVERAL, Fla., July 21—Virgil I. Grissom became the nation's second space explorer today.

The Air Force captain rocketed aboard a Mercury capsule on an arching flight that took him 118 miles into the sky and 303 miles out into the Atlantic.

But the flight was denied complete success. A mishap forced the 35-year-old astronaut to take an unplanned swim and resulted in the sinking of the $2,000,000 capsule with precious films aboard.

From the take-off at 8:20 A. M., Eastern daylight time, until the capsule landed in the ocean sixteen minutes later, the mission appeared as successful as the nearly perfect journey of the nation's first space traveler, Navy Comdr. Alan B. Shepard Jr., on May 5.

Capsule Ships Water

For reasons unknown, explosive bolts blew out the side hatch of the bobbing capsule before a Marine helicopter overhead could hook on and lift the capsule upright.

This hooking-on procedure was provided so that water would not pour into the open hatch when the seventy explosive bolts blew off the cover.

Captain Grissom said he had not pulled the plunger that controls the bolts. The cover blew off before the helicopter had had a chance to lift the capsule to its upright position.

Water rolled into the capsule immediately, and the captain floated out. Two to four minutes later he was hauled to safety by a second helicopter. He had swallowed more sea water than he would have liked. He was somewhat shaky. But he was essentially in excellent condition.

Captain Grissom swam about seventy-five feet to the point where he was raised to the helicopter.

The first helicopter made a determined effort to save the Liberty Bell 7 capsule, a product of the McDonnell Aircraft Corporation. It managed to hook the metal "eye" near the top of the capsule.

But the added weight of the water inside was too much. The aircraft, its engines heating dangerously, had to cut loose.

Evidence Is Lost

Lost with the capsule were films of the pilot's face and his hand actions, and of simultaneous readings of the instrument panel. Lost, too, was any solid evidence in the mechanisms themselves of what might have caused the hatch cover to blow out prematurely.

Officials of Project Mercury emphasized, however, that they had obtained most of the vital data they wanted through instruments that radioed moment-by-moment readings to tapes on the ground.

The capsule sank in 2,800 fathoms of water—some three miles—too deep for any salvage operation.

During the sixteen-minute flight, Captain Grissom performed a complex succession of assignments despite severe stresses.

He called instrument readings. He maneuvered the craft about all its axes. He reported on the deep black of the sky and the brilliance of the sun.

After he had dropped into the water, he was so composed that he told the helicopters not to move it until he had finished a few chores on his checklist.

The missile community generally agreed that Project Mercury had much cause for gratification.

It could now boast two successful space travelers to one for the Soviet Union. Although the short-range United States flights were modest feats compared with the orbital trip of Soviet Maj. Yuri A. Gagarin on April 12, both American astronauts had maneuvered their craft. The Soviet major had left the controls to automatic devices.

Setback Is Seen

Nevertheless, the consensus among experts here was that the loss of the capsule today might be a far-from-negligible setback to the Mercury program and its hopes of placing an astronaut in orbit by early next year.

The mishap raised questions about elements of the capsule design. It raised questions about recovery procedures and it posed the likelihood that at least one more suborbital flight would have to be made.

Mr. Williams said, however, that he did not believe the loss of the capsule would delay the over-all Mercury program.

After Captain Grissom was hoisted aboard the helicopter in a horse-collar sling, he was landed aboard the Navy carrier U.S.S. Randolph.

Dr. Robert Laning reported later, after an examination of the astronaut, that Captain Grissom had developed a slight sore throat, apparently as a result of swallowing considerable sea water.

The Navy physician said Captain Grissom had felt "a bit shaky" when he was first brought aboard but that he had soon relaxed over a meal of orange juice, two eggs "easy over" and bacon.

KENNEDY ARMS PLAN WINS SUPPORT IN BOTH HOUSES; AUGUST DRAFT INCREASED

Note To Congress

President Seeks Rise in Funds and Right to Call Reserves

By JACK RAYMOND

WASHINGTON, July 26—President Kennedy sent to Congress today his plans for the armed forces build-up that he announced in his address to the nation last night.

He won immediate bipartisan support in both houses. Mr. Kennedy, who spoke last night on the possibilities of wars resulting from Soviet pressure on Berlin and elsewhere, sent a brief note to Congress today on the proposed budget amendments.

He asked for $3,454,600,000 additional in defense appropriations for more troops and weapons. This included $207,600,000 for Civil Defense preparations for possible nuclear war.

Seeks Reserves Authority

He also asked Congress for stand-by authority until July 1, 1962, to call up to 250,000 reservists, including National Guardsmen, to active duty for no more than one year. There are 2,415,000 in the Ready Reserve.

The President requested additional authority to extend for one year the active-duty obligations of regulars and reservists. This group includes about 57,000 reservists now taking their six months of active duty training.

There was no indication, however, that the President planned to call upon the Reserves in substantial numbers in the near future.

Meantime, the Defense Department announced that it had raised the August draft call for the Army to 13,000 instead of the 8,000 announced last week.

Students Reassured

The draft calls, which dwindled to 1,500 in May, have been averaging about 8,000 a month. The last monthly call for 13,000 was in May, 1958. During the Korean War the draft calls rose to 80,000.

A Selective Service official said the increased draft calls would probably not be allowed to disrupt the college plans of most service eligibles.

"We feel that going to college is very important to the nation's future," he said, adding that the increases might force the present average age of draftees down from 23.

Secretary of Defense Robert S. McNamara told a Senate committee that the draft call for the Army for September would be at least 20,000.

The Secretary also restated the Administration's reasons for the accelerated defense effort. The Soviet leaders, he said, believe "that the Western world will be very reluctant to invoke the use of nuclear weapons in response to anything short of a direct threat to its survival."

Thus, Mr. McNamara went on, the Russians "hope to create divisive influences within the alliance by carefully measured threats in connection with the Berlin situation."

"In order to meet such threats with firmness and confidence and to provide us with a greater range of military alternatives, we will need more non-nuclear strength than we have today," he said. "That is the basic short-term objective of the measures we now propose."

He said, however, that although Berlin was now the focus of attention the defense measures were directed "at the larger problem of Communist threats and pressures all around the globe."

It appeared that the bulk of the military manpower increases ordered by the President, particularly the move to raise the size of the Army from an authorized strength of 870,000 to 1,000,000, would be sought in increased enlistments and the draft.

Certain specialized reserve units and individuals would be among the first to be called, especially in the Air National Guard and Air Force Reserve.

Congress reacted affirmatively and swiftly to the President's call for increased military preparedness. Senator Mike Mansfield of Montana, the majority leader, predicted that the expanded defense appropriations measure could be sent to the Senate floor in about ten days.

The President can now call up to 1,000,000 reservists to active duty, but only upon declaration of a national emergency.

The President's plans were praised by the chairmen of the Armed Services Committees. Representative Carl Vinson said. "I endorse every word he said."

Senator Richard Russell said:

"Perhaps it is an oxymoron to say that the President was both resolute and restrained, but the circumstances require that our national attitude reflect both resolution and restraint, and the President effectively outlined the need for both."

Berlin 1961

EAST GERMAN TROOPS SEAL BORDER WITH WEST BERLIN TO BLOCK REFUGEE ESCAPE

Commuting Ended

Warsaw Pact States Say Allies' Routes Remain Open

By REUTERS

BERLIN, Sunday, Aug. 13—East Germany closed the border early today between East and West Berlin.

East German troops stood guard at the Brandenburg Gate, the main crossing point between the Eastern and Western sectors.

The East Berlin City Government banned its citizens from holding jobs in the Western part of the divided city. This will affect tomorrow the thousands of East Berliners who daily commute to work in the Western sector.

The Communists' orders do not affect the Western Allies' access routes to Berlin along the 110-mile passage from West Germany. Especially they do not affect Allied military trains, which are under Soviet jurisdiction.

Action Comes in Night

The quietness of East Berlin's deserted streets was shattered in the early hours of the morning by the screaming of police sirens as police cars, motorcycles and truckloads of police sped through the city.

The action came shortly after publication of a declaration by the Communist Warsaw Pact states that effective controls must be put into force on the borders of West Berlin because of a "perfidious agitation campaign" by the West.

The declaration made it clear these measures were directed at stopping the flow of refugees from East to West through West Berlin. The flow of refugees has recently been reaching 1,700 daily. From 4 P.M. Friday, to 6 P.M. yesterday, 2,662 new arrivals registered in West Berlin's reception camp.

Subways Are Closed

The East Berlin order barring commuters from reaching their jobs in West Berlin said that no East German could cross into the western sector of the city unless he had "a special certificate."

The orders would stand "as long as West Berlin is not changed into a neutral demilitarized free city," the East Germans said.

"Naturally these measures will not affect the valid conditions for traffic and control on the connection routes between West Berlin and West Germany," it added.

The necessity for these "protective measures" would cease to exist as soon as a peace treaty with Germany was signed and "question of strike resolved on this basis," the statement added.

The Warsaw Pact states are the Soviet Union, East Germany, Poland, Czechoslovakia, Romania, Bulgaria, Hungary and Albania. A week ago, ending a meeting in Moscow they issued a call for a German peace treaty soon. Shortly after 3 A.M., a Reuters reporter who tried to drive through the Brandenburg Gate from East Berlin was told by a policeman: "You are not allowed to go through—we received instructions to this effect about an hour ago."

The closing of the border came after East Berliners had waited nervously for the Iron Curtain to ring down on refugees' escape routes to the West.

Warsaw Pact Statement

The Warsaw Pact powers declaration accused the Western Powers and West Germany of " using the present traffic position on the West Berlin border to disrupt the economy of the (East) German Democratic Republic."

"In view of the aggressive efforts of the reactionary force of the (West German) Federal Republic and its NATO allies, the declaration said, "the Warsaw Pact states cannot avoid taking the necessary measures themselves to guarantee their safety and above all the safety of the German Democratic Republic.

"The Governments of the Warsaw Pact states the appeal to the People's Chamber (Legislature) and Government of the German Democratic Republic to all workers of the G.D.R. with the proposal to introduce such an order on the West Berlin border that the way is stopped for the agitation campaign against the G.D.R."

American tanks and troops at Checkpoint Charlie, a crossing point in the Berlin Wall between the American and Soviet sectors of the city at the junction of Friedrichstrasse, Zimmerstrasse and Mauerstrasse. (Express Newspapers/Getty Images)

Allies Bid Soviet End 'Illegal' Ban on Berlin Travel

Moscow Blamed

West Terms Barriers 'Serious' Violation of East-West Pacts

By MAX FRANKEL

WASHINGTON, Aug. 17—The Western Allies protested to Moscow today against the Communist's closing of the frontier between East and West Berlin. They called on the Soviet Union "to put an end to these illegal measures."

The United States, Britain, and France held Moscow responsible for the barricades erected by East German Communists in Berlin last week-end. They termed the action "a flagrant and particularly serious" violation of Berlin's four-power status.

The allies delivered parallel notes to Moscow while their representatives and those of West Germany met again here to plan further moves.

Among other courses reported to have been considered was a proposal to send Vice President Johnson on a special mission to Berlin to assure the city's restive population that it would not be abandoned.

Kennedy Sees Top Aides

President Kennedy was reported to have received this suggestion from Secretary of State Dean Rusk this evening. They met at a long Administration conference on disarmament and other issues of the "cold war."

The Vice President, the Secretary of State and Attorney General Robert F. Kennedy, the President's brother, have all been mentioned as possible visitors to West Germany and Berlin. Thus far, however, the President has been reluctant to do anything that might inject the United States into the current West German election campaign.

Mayor Willy Brandt of West Berlin is running against Chancellor Adenauer in the election to be held Sept. 17.

A White House decision may be affected by Mayor Brandt's complaint, in a letter to the President, that the Allies

East German soldiers on the top of the newly built Berlin Wall. The concrete obstruction was being built by the Soviet Army to prevent refugees from escaping the Soviet sector in the East to West Berlin. (Popperfoto/Getty Images)

had not reacted strongly or quickly enough.

Mr. Adenauer, who plans to visit West Berlin next week, is expected to meet the Mayor in a bipartisan show of unity on the Berlin issue.

President Kennedy asked the State Department to prepare a prompt reply for Herr Brandt assuring him of United States support and citing the President's vow to fight, if necessary, to preserve West Berlin's freedom.

Garrison Increase Possible

There were unconfirmed reports, also, that the Allies were thinking of further strengthening the garrisons of West Berlin with symbolic additions to their infantry or tank units. Officials at the Pentagon and the State Department would not comment on these reports.

The new Allied notes to Moscow were an attempt to assuage West German feelings of disappointment as well as to record the West's position that Moscow was still responsible for actions of the East German Communist regime.

The Allies chose words that in normal diplomatic exchanges would be

considered "tough." Some officials here expressed disappointment that the notes contained no "warnings" or effective propaganda slogans.

The sealing of the Berlin frontier, the Allies told Moscow, had "the effect of limiting, to a degree approaching complete prohibition, passage from the Soviet sector to the Western sectors."

Motive Tied to Refugees

The notes suggested that the purpose of the Communist action was to stop the flow of East German refugees to the west.

"The reasons for this exodus are known," the Allies said. "They are simply the internal difficulties in East Germany."

In addition to the erection of barricades, the notes protested the use of East German armed forces in the Soviet sector of Berlin and the treatment of East Berlin as the capital of the "so-called 'German Democratic Republic.'"

The Allies also objected to the intervention of the Warsaw Pact nations "in a domain in which they have no competence."

Reds Erect Concrete Wall

BERLIN, Aug. 18 (AP)—The communists closed a part of the boundary between East and West Berlin today with a concrete-block wall five feet high and topped with barbed wire.

The new wall is almost completely in the northern and central districts of the twenty-five-mile border, winding from Reinickendorf southeast to Nuekoelin.

Over it peered Communist troops, their rifles sometimes hung with flowers from girls of the East German youth organization.

It was thrown up, evidently to create a No Man's Land between it and the barbed wire fencing installed Sunday, after three East German men had escaped to West Berlin by racing a heavy truck through the wire.

U.S. Sending 1,500 Troops to Bolster West Berlin; Johnson Is Flying There

Clay Also on Trip

New Force Will Use Autobahn to Reach City Tomorrow

By MAX FRANKEL

WASHINGTON, Aug. 18—President Kennedy today ordered a battle group of 1,500 men to West Berlin to reinforce the United States garrison there.

Meanwhile, Vice President Johnson was flying to West Berlin as President Kennedy's special envoy with assurances for the German people on the crisis over Berlin. He took off at 9:14 P.M.

'Recent Developments'

The White House announced the troop movement after a high-level conference had set up the Johnson mission. The President said "recent developments, including the movement of East German military forces into East Berlin" had dictated the United States move.

Vice President Johnson was accompanied by Gen. Lucius D. Clay, retired, who was military governor of Germany during the 1948-49 airlift that broke a Communist blockade of Berlin.

The Vice President will confer in Bonn tomorrow morning with Chancellor Adenauer. In the afternoon, he will fly 110 miles across Communist territory to West Berlin to deliver a personal message from President Kennedy to Mayor Willy Brandt of West Berlin.

Mr. Johnson's visit will be dramatized Sunday by the arrival of the United States troops from West Germany. They are to move overland from Helmstedt along the Autobahn used to supply the Western garrisons in West Berlin. Thus the move will emphasize the Allies' determination to defend those routes of access.

Allies Accused Moscow

The Western Allies accused Moscow yesterday of violating four-power agreements by permitting East German Communist troops to enter Berlin. They also said the Communists had taken "illegal" action in closing the border between East and West Berlin to halt the flow of East German refugees. The city is still technically under occupation.

The United States will increase its Berlin garrison to 6,500 men. Britain, with 4,000 troops, and France, with 3,100, are also expected to increase their garrisons.

The Vice President, just before leaving Andrews Air Force base in near-by Maryland, declared that it was his purpose "to assure the people of West Berlin of our firm determination to use whatever means may be necessary to fulfill our pledge to preserve their freedom and their ties with the free world."

General Clay was apparently selected for the trip because his performance during the 1948-49 Berlin airlift made him one of the best-liked Americans in Germany. Also in the Johnson party will be Charles E. Bohlen, assistant on Soviet Affairs to Secretary of State Dean Rusk, and specialist in German affairs.

In a statement Mr. Johnson said:

"We have already protested the brutal, cynical and illegal action taken last week-end by the East German regime with Soviet approval and support.

"This arbitrary splitting of the city of Berlin is a flagrant violation of solemn international agreements and obligations undertaken by the Soviet Government.

"Now I want to see at first hand the effects of this tragic situation as they are translated in human terms—the separated families, the refugees who have had to abandon home and friends, tearing up their roots in order to start life anew in freedom.

"The Soviet and East German rulers discovered in June, 1953 (when East Germans revolted), and I am sure they will discover it again in this situation, that the more the urge for freedom is suppressed, the more insistently the demand for it grows."

May Visit East Berlin

The Vice President will be the highest United States official to visit the former German capital since the end of World War II. To dramatize the West's refusal to recognize the barricades erected by East Germans across the heart of the city last week-end, he may attempt to tour the Communist sector as well as the areas policed by United States, British and French troops.

The special mission was organized in response to repeated demands from West Germany that "more than words" were needed to protest East Germany's sealing of the frontier between East and West Berlin. The Allies have accused the Soviet Union of responsibility for what they call a violation of the four-power status of Berlin. But they have found it difficult to find suitable, more dramatic counter-measures.

United States military leaders do not expect any interference with the troop movement. Troops have been moved over the same routes before in accordance with existing agreements.

The White House and State Department are seriously disturbed by continuing reports from West Berlin about the population's disappointment, bitterness and resentment over Western inaction. Leading East German Communists are described as jubilant at their successful and apparently surprising closing of the city frontier.

Nuclear Tests Resume

SOVIETS EXPLODE ATOMIC WEAPON OF INTERMEDIATE FORCE OVER ASIA

ATMOSPHERE TEST

Long-Range Devices of U.S. Detect and Identify Blast

By TOM WICKER

WASHINGTON, Sept. 1—The White House announced today that the Soviet Union resumed the testing of nuclear weapons early this morning by exploding a device over Soviet Central Asia.

The announcement said the explosion took place "in the atmosphere" at Semipalatinsk, about 350 miles south of Novosibirsk.

Andrew Hatcher, the assistant White House press secretary, said the explosion was detected "early this morning, Western time" by what he described as "long-range detecting equipment." It was apparently the first nuclear test by the Soviet Union since its announcement that it would resume testing.

Event Was Anticipated

Mr. Hatcher said that after the detection of the explosion was confirmed as a nuclear device, the news was given to President Kennedy at the White House at 3:15 P. M. He explained that the lag between detection and the report to the President was caused by the time required to check the information obtained by United States detection equipment.

"This has been anticipated," he said. "It didn't come as a surprise."

There was no precise estimate of the size of the nuclear device. The announcement said only that it had had "a substantial yield in the intermediate range." Mr. Hatcher said this yield meant that the Soviet device was larger than the "average atomic bomb" and larger than the bomb exploded over Hiroshima in 1945.

First Test Since Agreement

He further explained that the device was not in the range of a megaton, the equivalent explosive force of 1,000,000 tons of TNT. Rather, he described it as being in the kiloton range. This would mean an explosive force of hundreds of thousands of tons of TNT, perhaps between 100,000 and 500,000 tons. The Hiroshima bomb was twenty kilotons, or the equivalent of 20,000 tons of TNT.

The Soviet explosion was the first known nuclear test by one of the three nuclear powers—Britain, the Soviet Union and the United States—that agreed in the fall of 1958 to refrain from testing while trying to negotiate a test ban. France, however, has set off four nuclear devices since then, one of them this year.

Despite the moratorium on testing, the United States maintained its secret global system that has detected atomic explosions in the Soviet Union over the years.

Semipalatinsk is an industrial and transportation center near the Mongolian border, 560 miles northeast of Alma-Ata and 1,700 miles east of Moscow. The Russians are believed to have launched many of their missiles from there.

Its principal industries are meat-packing, flour milling, wool washing, and tanning.

The White House announcement came after the President conferred with Arthur H. Dean, the United States representative at the Geneva test ban conference, and John J. McCloy, the President's disarmament adviser. Shortly after the meeting the President left for a week-end with his family at Hyannis Port, Mass.

Earlier Mr. Dean had charged:

"The Soviet policy is the policy of overkill. But the Soviet Government underestimates the people of the world if it thinks they will capitulate to a strategy of blackmail and terror."

Speaking with the approval of the President, to whom he had reported this morning, Mr. Dean said the Soviet announcement that it would resume testing showed a "determined Soviet purpose to rest its future policy on the terrorization of humanity."

Mr. Dean thus amplified the vigorous effort the Kennedy Administration is making to exploit world-wide indignation at the Soviet nuclear testing plan. He spoke from a brief text prepared at a White House meeting this morning with the President, Secretary of State Rusk and Mr. McCloy.

Mr. Dean and Mr. McCloy made it plain, however, that diplomatic contact with the Soviets is still being maintained on the issue of a nuclear test ban treaty, and the larger question of general disarmament.

"Now they want to lump it all back together," Mr. McCloy said. "It's kind of a shell game."

Belief Undermined

He added that many persons, "I suppose including me" had believed there was an "element of sincerity" in the expressed desire of the Soviets for an end to nuclear weapons testing. "This certainly undermines that," he said.

The statement approved by the President and read by Mr. Dean contained a caustic reference to Mr. Khrushchev's "boasting about a 100-megaton bomb, a weapon far too large for military objectives."

This referred to the announced Soviet intention to test a bomb with an explosive force of 100,000,000 tons of TNT. The device exploded early today by the Soviet Union was far below that level.

Mr. Dean bitterly denounced the intention to test so huge a weapon. Such a bomb, he said, is "not a military weapon" but a "weapon of mass terror."

He said it was impossible to direct a 100-megaton bomb with any degree of accuracy and "the use of it would be wanton and cruel in relation to the loss of human life."

By comparison, he said, a twenty-megaton bomb, which is regarded as a usable weapon, could destroy a 100-square-mile area or roughly an area the size of the District of Columbia.

Mr. McCloy said that the "strategy of blackmail and terror" attributed to the Soviets in the statement approved by Mr. Kennedy appeared aimed primarily at the neutrals rather than at the Western Allies.

Thus, both men seemed to believe that Premier Khrushchev had hoped to frighten the neutrals into supporting him on the Berlin issue. If so, the immediate testing of a 100-megaton bomb might be calculated to heighten the effect.

The use for the second consecutive day in an official statement of the term "blackmail," and the Administration's insistent hammering on the "terrorization of humanity" theme, showed, however, that officials here hope that exactly the opposite reaction will result.

The almost unanimous opinion here is that the United States will resume its own nuclear tests, but will do so in a manner carefully timed not to reduce the shock value of the Soviet action or to precipitate a final breaking off of diplomatic contact at Geneva or in the disarmament talks between Mr. McCloy and Valerian A. Zorin, the Soviet representative, in New York Wednesday.

President Kennedy in the Oval Office. In 1963 he would say, "I am haunted by the feeling that by 1970 . . . there may be 10 nuclear powers instead of four." (George Tames/*The New York Times*)

U.S. AND BRITAIN CALL FOR BANNING OF NUCLEAR TESTS IN ATMOSPHERE; ASK KHRUSHCHEV TO AGREE AT ONCE

FALL-OUT IS CITED

Allies Urge a Meeting in Geneva Saturday to Register Pact

By TOM WICKER

HYANNIS PORT, Mass., Sept. 3—President Kennedy and Prime Minister Macmillan proposed to Premier Khrushchev today that their governments voluntarily refrain from nuclear weapons tests in the atmosphere that produce radioactive fall-out.

The President and the Prime Minister urged the Soviet leader to send his immediate acceptance by cablegram.

They emphasized that they were not calling for additional means of policing an agreement to suspend tests in the atmosphere. The Soviet Union conducted such a test in Central Asia two days ago.

In the event of Soviet acceptance, they said, they are prepared to rely on existing means of detection, which "they believe to be adequate."

They said representatives of the three Governments could meet in Geneva Saturday to record the agreement and transmit it to the United Nations.

Great Urgency Felt

The United States and Britain said their purpose in making the new approach was "to protect mankind from the increasing hazards from atmospheric pollution and to contribute to the reduction of international tensions."

High Administration sources disclosed that the proposal had been worked out with the British and relayed to the Russians "with great urgency" in an effort to head off a new series of Soviet nuclear weapons tests.

Treaty Urged Anew

The statement also reaffirmed the "serious desire" of the two Western leaders to conclude a treaty banning all forms of nuclear weapons testing.

Mr. Kennedy and Mr. Macmillan, the statement continued, "regret that the Soviet government has blocked such an agreement."

It was disclosed also that Mr. Kennedy and Mr. Macmillan intended their new offer to cover any tests of tactical nuclear weapons the Soviet Union might be planning for its scheduled exercises in the Barents Sea.

The proposal further appeared to be calculated to put the Russians on the defensive by linking the atmospheric test they conducted Friday with the possibility of radioactive fall-out. They announced Wednesday a decision to resume testing in violation of the three-year-old uncontrolled moratorium that has coincided with the Geneva talks on a treaty prohibiting all tests of nuclear weapons. The talks are deadlocked.

An Administration source said it was too early as yet to tell how much fall-out might have resulted from the Soviet test, which has not yet been announced by the Soviet Government.

The announcement also seemed to indicate the confidence that the United States reposes in the size and variety of its nuclear arsenal, since it volunteered a limitation upon the kinds of tests this country might conduct.

The net effect of the proposal, if Mr. Khrushchev should accept it, would be to leave all powers uncommitted on nuclear tests underground or in outer space. In neither case is radioactive fall-out considered a hazard.

U. S. Feels Free to Test

Mr. Kennedy announced Wednesday night, after the Soviet Union had declared it would resume testing, that the United States had been freed from the voluntary commitment not to test that it had maintained for three years.

One obvious question about the new proposal concerned the attitude of the French Government. France has conducted tests above ground since the United States, Britain and the Soviet Union entered upon their voluntary moratorium, and President de Gaulle has resisted attempts to bring the French into the agreement.

Mr. Hatcher said today that "other allies" had been consulted in the preparation of the testing proposal.

Mr. Hatcher said the proposal had been made by the United States and Britain because they were the two powers meeting with the Soviet Union at Geneva in an effort to work out a nuclear test ban treaty.

Mr. Khrushchev in the past has taken the attitude that if a test ban is to be worked out it must also include France.

U.S. WILL RESUME NUCLEAR TESTS UNDERGROUND WITH NO FALL-OUT; REVEALS THIRD SOVIET EXPLOSION

'NO OTHER CHOICE'

President Calls New Blasts Essential to Nation's Safety

By TOM WICKER

WASHINGTON, Sept. 5—President Kennedy ordered today the resumption of nuclear weapons tests by the United States. He specified that the tests should take place "in the laboratory and underground, with no fall-out."

The decision was taken soon after the Atomic Energy Commission announced that the Soviet Union had exploded a third nuclear device in five days.

The President said in a statement that the United States had "no other choice."

The statement was issued by Pierre Salinger, White House press secretary. He said that laboratory and underground tests would take place this month at unspecified locations.

President's Statement

The text of the statement follows:

"In view of the continued testing by the Soviet Government, I have today ordered the resumption of nuclear tests in the laboratory and underground with no fall-out.

"In our efforts to achieve an end to nuclear testing, we have taken every step that reasonable men could justify.

"In view of the acts of the Soviet Government, we must now take those steps which prudent men find essential. We have no other choice in fulfillment of the responsibilities of the United States Government to its own citizens and to the security of other free nations.

"Our offer to make an agreement to end all fall-out tests remains open until Sept. 9."

The President's statement signaled the end of a voluntary undertaking by the U.S. not to test nuclear weapons. It was announced on Aug. 22, 1958, and went into effect Nov. 1, 1958.

U. S. Detected Blasts

The Soviet Union announced last Wednesday that it was ending its own voluntary moratorium on testing. Soviet tests were detected and announced by the United States on Friday, yesterday and today.

High Administration sources were convinced that one of the principal reasons for the resumption of Soviet tests was development work on a Soviet defense system against inter-continental missiles.

President Kennedy's statement left open the offer he and Prime Minister Macmillan of Britain made to the Soviet Union Sunday. It was a proposal that the three powers agree to conduct no atmospheric tests that produce radioactive fall-out.

The statement said this offer remained open until Saturday as originally proposed. Mr. Salinger would not say whether that meant the United States would consider itself free to conduct atmosphere tests after Saturday.

From Congressional sources, it was learned that President Kennedy had hoped originally to be able to delay a resumption of the United States' tests until after the United Nations General Assembly meeting opens Sept. 19.

The President's decision to resume testing was a result of the third Soviet explosion, Mr. Salinger said.

He added that it was the accumulation of three Soviet tests, despite the United States' and Britain's offer, rather than any special fact about the third test that influenced the President. All the Soviet explosions took place in the atmosphere.

Defense Termed Adequate

"It became apparent with the third test that the Soviet Government was not interested in protecting mankind from fall-out," Mr. Salinger said.

He repeated the assurance that Mr. Kennedy gave in a statement last Thursday that the United States' nuclear arsenal and means of delivery were "wholly adequate" to defend the free nations.

Nevertheless, Mr. Salinger said, in explaining the decision to resume certain kinds of tests, "it is also true that important advances can be made by further scientific development."

He said there would be no "crash program" of nuclear tests. He added that he did not know if it would be possible to conduct a test or tests before the Saturday deadline given to the Soviet Union on a voluntary ban.

U. S. Said to Be Ready

It was understood, however, that Congressional leaders were told last week that the United States could conduct certain tests in a day or two, if it became necessary.

It was learned from another source that some of the tests would be a part of Project Vela, which is designed to help the United States learn to detect underground nuclear explosions registering less than 4.75 on the seismographic scale.

The Soviet Union was invited to join the United States and Britain in Project Vela but declined. The Kennedy Administration further invited the Soviet Union, subject to Congressional approval, to observe Project Vela tests.

Both the White House and officials of the Atomic Energy Commission declined, on security grounds, to amplify the reference "nuclear tests in the laboratory." But one commission spokesmen, professing "surprise" at the public reference to such experiments, suggested on the basis of data already on the public record at Congressional hearings and elsewhere, that the statement might mean a new program to test missile propulsion systems involving "controlled explosion" of nuclear material.

There was an implication in the President's statement that the moratorium had applied to testing "in the laboratory." However, Atomic Energy Commission and other officials could not comment on this or explain such testing.

The Congressional leaders of both parties were understood to have been consulted again today, before Mr. Kennedy's statement.

The President was said to have learned of the third Soviet test shortly after a morning conference with Glenn T. Seaborg, the chairman of the Atomic Energy Commission, and Roswell Gilpatric, Deputy Secretary of Defense.

His decision to resume testing apparently was taken shortly after he was informed of the new Soviet explosion. It was understood that he and members of his staff consulted extensively with other officials before making a public announcement.

Allies Informed

The Governments of Britain, France and West Germany also were notified, Mr. Salinger said.

The Atomic Energy Commission announced the Soviet blast early this afternoon in two terse sentences:

"The A. E. C. announced today that the Soviet Union detonated a third nuclear device early today. The yield of this latest detonation was in the low to intermediate range."

A spokesman later added that the explosion took place in the Semipalatinsk area of Central Asia, where the Friday and Monday tests were conducted. He said it was an atmospheric test, like the others.

The description of its yield as having been in "the low to intermediate range" meant that the device exploded had been somewhere near the same size as the first two.

All in Kiloton Range

All three were apparently in the kiloton rather than the megaton range. That is, they had the explosive force of thousands, rather than millions, of tons of TNT.

Many here regarded the third test, and the President's response to it, as having all but scuttled the possibility of any agreement with the Soviet Union on nuclear testing in the near future,

After the second Soviet test, Administration officials let it be known that they did not believe enough time had elapsed for the explosion to be regarded as a negative response to the offer extended Sunday to refrain from atmospheric testing.

After the third shot, however, there was little expectation here that the Soviet Union would enter such an

agreement until it suited its purposes to do so.

There was equally little belief that the conference on a nuclear test ban treaty, still nominally under way in Geneva, could have a fruitful result.

McCloy and Zorin to Talk

A third possibility may lie in the general disarmament talks that will be resumed in New York tomorrow by John J. McCloy, the President's disarmament adviser, and Valerian A. Zorin, the permanent Soviet delegate at the United Nations.

Mr. McCloy has said that the United States will resist any Soviet effort to "lump in" a nuclear test ban treaty with the disarmament talks.

The President's announcement was received on Capitol Hill with general approval. Both Democrats and Republicans applauded when the news was read to the House by Representative Chet Holifield, the California Democrat who is the Chairman of the Joint Atomic Energy Committee.

A melancholy footnote was added to the resumption of nuclear testing by the two leading nuclear powers in a statement issued today by Abraham Ribicoff, the Secretary of Health, Education and Welfare.

He said that radiation levels in milk, food, water and air declined "dramatically—in some instances below measurable levels" in the United States during the weapons testing moratorium.

Mr. Ribicoff said that milk sampled in 1957 had averaged a content of nine micromicrocuries per liter of the radionuclide Strontium-90. The figure rose to thirteen micromicrocuries in 1959, but fell back to nine in the first quarter of this year.

The United States has not conducted a nuclear test since Oct. 30, 1958, and its last atmospheric test was on Aug. 12, 1958, at Johnston Island in the Pacific Ocean.

4th Soviet Blast Set Off

A.E.C. NOTES TEST

*Says Device Exploded
in Atmosphere
East of
Stalingrad*

By TOM WICKER

WASHINGTON, Sept. 6—The Atomic Energy Commission announced tonight that the Soviet Union had detonated a fourth nuclear device in the atmosphere.

A brief announcement said the explosion took place early this morning east of Stalingrad.

The yield of the device was reported to have been in the range of low to intermediate. Thus it was indicated that the explosion might have been of about the same size as the two that were detected and announced by the Atomic Energy Commission on Monday and yesterday.

If so, its power would have been in the kiloton range, having an explosive force equivalent to thousands of tons of TNT.

The explosion was the fourth detected by the United States since the Soviet Union announced last Wednesday that it would resume the testing of nuclear weapons. The first test, with a force of more than 20,000 tons, was conducted Friday.

Only One Test Noted

There were early reports that the A. E. C. would announce the detection of two explosions today. However. a spokesman said the agency knew of no other detonation.

"This is the only shot the A. E. C. is announcing and the only one we know about," he said.

Today's nuclear test apparently took place at a site west of that of the other three. However, the commission did not say how far east of Stalingrad the fourth test was conducted.

Stalingrad in southeast European Russia, is about 1,500 miles due west of the site of the earlier explosions. Stalingrad is an industrial and agricultural area, but several hundred miles to the east there are areas of sparsely populated desert. Traces of radioactive fall-out from the Asian blasts were in Alaska yesterday, it was disclosed today.

Abraham A. Ribicoff, the Secretary of Health, Education, and Welfare, said a Public Health Service detection station at Anchorage had collected air samples and discovered that they contained radiation levels of 7 micromicrocuries per cubic meter.

That was thirty-five times the average daily level for August. Dr. Luther L. Terry, the Surgeon General, said there was no immediate health danger.

John A. McCone, a former chairman of the A. E. C., warned, however, that a more serious fall-out danger might result from Soviet tests of "superbombs." Mr. McCone said this possibility "ought to be studied very carefully."

He was referring to threats by Premier Khrushchev to test a l00-megaton bomb. Such a bomb would have force equal to that of 100,000,000 tons of TNT.

Despite the new Soviet tests, and the announcement yesterday that the United States would resume underground and laboratory testing this month, a high Administration source disclosed that the United States had no intention of abandoning the Geneva conference seeking a treaty to prohibit nuclear tests.

Rejection Is Expected

The Kennedy Administration, it was said, will seek to keep the Geneva conference alive as an alternate course to the Soviet insistence on entangling the test-ban question with the subject of general disarmament.

The latter course, this official said, would provide "a neat way for the Soviets to scuttle the whole thing" and obtain their prime objective of a test ban without controls or inspections on their territory.

The Administration now expects that when the conference reconvenes Saturday, it will receive a negative answer or no answer at all to the latest proposal of President Kennedy and Prime Minister Macmillan.

They had suggested an agreement to refrain from atmospheric tests that cause fall-out.

Following the Saturday meeting of the Geneva conference, the United States intends to lay the proposed test-ban treaty, plus the conference record, before the United Nations General Assembly. The Assembly opens Sept. 19.

The Administration will seek to keep the Geneva talks at least technically in session, however, because it prefers to continue sessions between the three principal nuclear powers to starting all over again in a new forum.

The intention to continue negotiations at Geneva and the decision to resume testing announced by the United States yesterday were both influenced by apprehension here that the Soviet strategy eventually would put the United States at a serious political disadvantage.

Informed sources believe that Moscow, primarily for military and technological reasons, needed to conduct nuclear tests. The sources expect Moscow to proceed with about fifteen to twenty explosions in the next three weeks.

KHRUSHCHEV REJECTS BAN ON TESTS IN ATMOSPHERE; INSISTS ON GERMAN PACT

Kennedy and Macmillan Express 'Deepest Regret'

But They Are Regarded as Keeping Open a Channel for Eventual Agreement on Barring Nuclear Explosions

---

Special to the New York Times

HYANNIS PORT, Mass., Sept. 9—President Kennedy and Prime Minister Macmillan expressed today "deepest regret" over Premier Khrushchev's rejection of their proposal to curb atomic tests.

Their statement followed ten days of sharp diplomatic exchanges and public statements on the testing of nuclear weapons.

They had proposed that the United States, Britain and the Soviet Union agree to refrain from all nuclear tests in the atmosphere, which produce radio-active fall-out.

All three nations would have been left free to conduct such tests underground or in space.

Premier Khrushchev's refusal to accept the offer, Mr. Kennedy and Mr. Macmillan said in a joint statement, "contrasts vividly with the Soviet Union's repeated expressions of concern as to the health hazards of such testing."

The statement affirmed the readiness of the United States and Britain "to negotiate a controlled nuclear test ban agreement of the widest scope."

The language used in the statement was regarded here as designed to keep open a channel, however narrow, for agreement on the subject of a test ban treaty. It was also considered as an indirect invitation for Soviet counter-proposals.

The three-paragraph statement was issued here by Pierre Salinger, the White House press secretary. It also was made public in London.

The statement was in response to notes handed to the United States and British embassies in Moscow today and transmitted first to Washington and then to Mr. Kennedy's summer home here.

The White House had prepared for a rejection of the offer by earlier comment in the Soviet press. As late as yesterday, officials also had expected that the Soviet Union might not answer the proposal at all but continue to reject it by its actions.

Mr. Khrushchev's response ranged broadly over several subjects at issue between the West and the Communist bloc, including Soviet proposals for a German peace treaty and full disarmament.

Attention also was being paid here to the assertion by Mr. Khrushchev that the Western proposal would deny the Soviet Union equality with the West in the number of nuclear tests conducted.

The Premier said that while the proposal would restrict Soviet tests in the atmosphere, it would permit the United States and Britain to improve their atomic weapons through tests underground and in space.

There was believed to be an implication in the Khrushchev note that the West no longer needed to conduct atmospheric tests but that the Soviet Union felt a military and scientific necessity for such experiments.

The Kennedy-Macmillan statement concluded by affirming the desire of the United States and Britain for a controlled test ban "of the widest possible scope."

The President was prepared to issue a statement today regardless of whether the Soviet Union replied officially to the proposal on atomic tests. He and Mr. Macmillan had set today as the deadline for Mr. Khrushchev's acceptance or rejection of the proposal.

Text of Statement

Following is the text of the statement by President Kennedy and Prime Minister Macmillan:

President Kennedy and Prime Minister Macmillan note with deepest regret that the Soviet Union has not accepted their proposal of Sept. 3 that tests in the earth's atmosphere producing fall-out be stopped without delay.

This action contrasts vividly with the Soviet Union's own repeated expressions of concern as to the health and hazards of such testing.

The President and the Prime Minister reaffirm the readiness of the United States and the United Kingdom to negotiate a controlled nuclear test ban agreement of the widest possible scope.

Ngo Says Struggle With Vietnam Reds Is Now a 'Real War'

By ROBERT TRUMBULL

SAIGON, Vietnam, Monday Oct. 2—South Vietnam's struggle against armed Communist insurgents has grown from guerrilla action to "real war" in the last year, President Ngo Dinh Diem said today.

"It is no longer a guerrilla war we have to face but a real war waged by an enemy who attacks us with regular units fully and heavily equipped and who seeks a strategic decision in Southeast Asia in conformity with the orders of the Communist international," President Ngo declared.

The President spoke at the opening of the budget session of the National Assembly.

The conflict here has taken on a new dimension in the last twelve months, Mr. Ngo said, after the Communists failed in a program of political subversion.

He declared that the Communists had mounted new attacks in the high plateaus of the central and northeastern provinces, where the terrain is difficult, to compensate for losses in the southwest that he said had given the initiative to Government forces.

President Ngo said that a report on South Vietnam's needs prepared by a United States committee headed by Dr. Eugene Staley had recommended an increase in aid both for military measures and for "economic and social development."

The Staley committee, he added, considered "measures which could restore security within eighteen months" in making its report, which is now under consideration by both Governments.

Mr. Ngo estimated his nation's budgetary needs for 1962 at 23,500,000,000 piasters (about $677,000,000), compared with 18,000,000,000 piasters (about $518,000,000) last year. He said direct revenue would provide 12,000,000,000 piasters, with the rest of the needed funds to come from special taxes and foreign aid. Most of the aid is expected to be provided by the United States.

Authoritative sources here have predicted that the war in Vietnam may be intensified in the next few months, producing disruption that may imperil President Ngo's Government.

A renewed offensive by the Viet Cong (Vietnamese Communist) forces is expected with the imminent onset of the dry season. Recent damaging attacks by Communist guerrilla bands of battalion strength (up to 1,000 men) are thought to be a prelude to more severe Communist offensives.

Viet Cong units are making heavily damaging use of a safe corridor through southern Laos for increasingly strong attacks into the heart of the strategic central highlands of South Vietnam, according to intelligence reports here.

The use of the so-called Laotian corridor for infiltration and invasion of South Vietnam is said to have begun last May.

Major forays by Viet Cong insurgents using the Laotian corridor have been extended recently over a wide area from Quangnam to Banmethuot, two key towns in South Vietnam. Banmethuot is an important provincial center on South Vietnam's high plateau, about 250 miles north of Saigon. Quangnam is near the seacoast, about 210 miles farther north.

As defined by South Vietnamese officers at the scene of the recent fighting, the term "Laotian corridor" applies to a strip of Laotian territory about sixty miles wide extending along the Vietnamese border from North Vietnam all the way to Cambodia.

The Viet Cong units are apparently able to operate also in Cambodian frontier areas without much molestation by forces of the neutralist Government in Phnom Penh. The Communists thus seem to have a secure supply line from Communist-governed North Vietnam to any entry point selected along South Vietnam's entire western border.

In the Laotian corridor the Viet Cong forces have the use of parts of the "Ho Chi Minh Trail," employed by Vietnamese nationalist forces under Ho Chi Minh, now President of North Vietnam, in the operations against the French prior to 1954. The so-called trail actually consists of a series of connecting jungle paths running north and south.

Possession of the corridor also permits the Communists to keep unremitting pressure on South Vietnamese communications throughout the central part of the country.

An even more serious consideration arising out of the Viet Cong operations in the Laotian corridor has been the Communist infiltration of tribes inhabiting central Vietnam.

For several months, the tribes have been known to be assisting the Viet Cong activity. It is they who are believed responsible for the wicked bamboo stakes that have been planted in jungle paths by the thousands. Under camouflage, such sharpened stakes have disabled countless Vietnamese soldiers operating in the mountain areas.

Domination of the central highlands by the Viet Cong would leave the Communists in a position for a strong sweep toward Saigon and the rich rice-growing region of the southern delta.

Following page:
President Kennedy in the Oval Office
March 8, 1961.

(George Tames/*The New York Times*)

Berlin 1961, II

9 American M.P.'s Cross Berlin Line To Free Official

Soldiers With Rifles Enforce Right of U.S. Diplomat to Enter City's East Zone

TANKS SUPPORT MOVE

Mission Aide Is Detained Twice by Reds' Guards in 3 Trips Over Border

By GERD WILCKE

BERLIN, Oct. 22—Nine armed United States soldiers moved into East Berlin twice tonight to enforce the right of an American diplomat to enter the Communist-held sector. The diplomat had been stopped by East German border guards.

It was the first time armed United States troops had crossed into the Communist sector of Berlin during the current crisis.

The soldiers, a military police patrol, advanced from West Berlin to provide an escort for E. Allan Lightner Jr., assistant chief of the United States mission here.

Later, Mr. Lightner drove into East Berlin unhindered.

Lieutenant Leads Group

The military police group consisted of a lieutenant and eight enlisted men carrying rifles with fixed bayonets.

In the meantime, four M-48 tanks and two M-59 armored personnel carriers moved into position 500 yards south of the Friedrichstrasse checkpoint. It is the only crossing point available for passage into East Berlin by Western officials.

According to an account by a United States spokesman, Mr. Lightner drove with his wife in a private automobile to the checkpoint at 7:15 P. M. When East German guards demanded his identification card, Mr. Lightner refused to present it. Instead he asked for a Soviet officer.

Drives Ahead Forty Yards

After waiting in vain for thirty-five minutes, Mr. Lightner decided to drive ahead. He got about forty yards inside Communist territory when a second East Berlin patrol stopped him. Still refusing to show his identification papers, Mr. Lightner sat in his car surrounded by Eastern guards.

At 9 P. M., Lieut. Col. Robert A. Sabolyk, United States Provost Marshal here, ordered the escort to cross into East German territory.

Lieut. Claude L. Stults of Livingston Tenn., and his eight men, armed with M-14 automatic rifles, stepped across the white line marking the border.

The escort went to Mr. Lightner's car and accompanied him a few yards farther into East Berlin and then back over the dividing line. The spokesman said the Communist guards just stepped back and stared.

Unhampered Third Time

Returning to West Berlin Mr. Lightner left his wife, turned his car around and drove back toward the Eastern sector. Again he was stopped.

This time, the American soldiers accompanied Mr. Lightner about 200 yards inside East Berlin to the Leipzigerstrasse street crossing. Again the official and his escort returned to West Berlin.

At 9:40 P. M. Colonel Sabolyk went into the Eastern sector to deliver what was termed a "strong protest" to the Soviet officer who had arrived at the scene.

Thirty minutes later, Mr. Lightner crossed the border a third time. The Eastern guards let his car pass unhampered. The diplomat drove to Leipzigerstrasse and back.

A number of other Allied vehicles carrying civilian license plates followed Mr. Lightner's car. They, too, were permitted to pass through. The spokesman was asked whether United States soldiers would move again if the Communists prevented American officials from entering East Berlin without showing papers. He replied:

"An American official was held up in the Soviet sector. We ordered the escort in to prove his right of passage. That is all."

The new incident at the intra-city border came at the end of a calm Sunday whose mild and sunny weather seemed to calm the city's tension for both East and West Berliners. Residents of both parts of the city strolled in parks and boulevards.

On the Wilhelmstrasse in East Berlin, only a few hundred yards' from the Brandenburg Gate on the border, a young father patiently helped his daughter to climb into a swing.

Nearby, on a little hill that marks the former site of Hitler's bunker, two people's policemen squatted on the grass, their sub-machine guns lying beside them.

Russians In Berlin Insist U.S. Accept Travel Curb; 'Urgent' Protest Planned

GERMAN REDS ACT

Demand All Foreigners Show Papers Before Crossing Border

By E.W. KENWORTHY

WASHINGTON, Oct. 25—The State Department announced tonight that the Soviet commander in Berlin had rejected a protest by the United States commander against an East German order requiring all foreigners to show their passports to enter East Berlin.

Lincoln White, State Department press officer, said: "We regard this as a serious development and are taking it up urgently with the governments concerned."

The United States, Mr. White said, will take up the issue primarily with the Soviet Union, which, with the United States, Britain and France, shares responsibility for the protection of Allied rights in Berlin.

Instructions Requested

The protest on the scene was made this morning to Col. Andrei I. Solovyev, the Soviet commander, by Maj. Gen. Albert Watson 2d. Commander of United States forces in Berlin.

Announcement that the United States would take up the Russian rejection of its protest with the other occupying powers followed a "most urgent request" by General Watson to Washington for instructions on how to deal with the new border crisis.

Mr. White's statement indicated that the United States would now make a much stronger protest through diplomatic channels—probably through a note delivered to the Soviet Foreign Ministry.

When General Watson made his protest this morning he had behind him the full authority of the United States Government.

Long-Standing Practice

Shortly after he had gone to see his Soviet counterpart, Mr. White said at a news conference that United States officials, whether in military or civilian dress, had the right to enter East Berlin and to move freely within it without any identification to the East German police.

Mr. White said that this had been long-standing practice, and "there is no change in our position that these officials have the right to move freely in Berlin."

General Watson's protest followed a series of incidents at the border involving demands by the East German police to see the identification cards of United States officials seeking to enter East Berlin.

The incidents began last Sunday when E. Allan Lightner Jr., assistant chief of the United States mission, and his wife were held up just beyond the border and not allowed to proceed until nine armed American soldiers moved into the Eastern sector to uphold their right of passage.

The latest incident came this morning when United States military police with fixed bayonets rode 400 yards into East Berlin to escort two Americans in civilian clothes whose car had been halted by the East German police.

The Soviet commander had sought to change the longstanding rules following the Lightner incident.

In order to demonstrate to Soviet officials that the United States would not accept any change in existing rights, a number of American officials have passed into East Berlin today after refusing to produce identification demanded by the East German police.

Mr. White said today that the only identification that had ever been required was an official license plate on the car. With such a license plate, the officials have never been required to show "ID" cards.

However, Mr. White added, the practice has been for non-official Americans, for example, tourists, to show identification when asked.

Officials emphasized that there were two issues involved in the United States refusal to abide by the new Soviet ruling.

First, they said, is the right of officials of the three Western occupying powers to travel freely throughout Berlin.

Second, there is the question of the authority of the East German police at the border points. The Western powers do not recognize the East German Government and therefore do not recognize the right of the East German police to demand identification of Western personnel.

RUSSIAN TANKS GO INTO EAST BERLIN; U.S. SHOWS FORCE; SOVIET ADVANCE

33 Vehicles Are Mile From Crossing Point Used by Americans

By SYDNEY GRUSON

BERLIN, Oct. 26—Thirty-three Soviet medium tanks, manned by Soviet troops, moved into the center of East Berlin tonight.

It was a show of military power clearly calculated to counter the force displayed by the United States to assert the right of free entry into the Communist sector of the city.

The tanks were manned by black-uniformed Soviet troops believed to be from the Twentieth Guards Division stationed near Berlin.

The tanks were tentatively identified as T-54's, the Soviet medium tank, which mounts a long-barreled 100-millimeter gun. They were accompanied by jeeps and personnel carriers with troops.

Near Brandenburg Gate

The tanks parked for the night in an enclosure off Unter den Linden, the broad tree-lined avenue leading out of the Brandenburg Gate into East Berlin.

[The British Army moved three anti-tank guns into position near the Brandenburg Gate and trained them on the area where the Soviet tanks were parked, said an Associated Press dispatch early Friday. British armored cars and munitions trucks were with the guns.]

Western reporters heard the men of the Soviet tank crews talking in Russian. They were about a mile from the Friedrichstrasse border-crossing point between East and West Berlin.

The United States Army displayed military force at that point today—the third time in five days—to assert the right of free entry into East Berlin.

The Soviet tanks carried no markings except numbers and their crews wore black uniforms. The crews of the jeeps and personnel carriers were in regular Soviet Army uniforms and their vehicles carried Russian military license plates.

When the East German Communists sealed off East Berlin Aug. 13, the Soviet Army made a show of force in virtually every East German town and ringed Berlin. But it did not enter Berlin itself.

Two officials of the United States Berlin command were escorted in and out of East Berlin by armed military police during the day while ten American forty-ton tanks and five armored personnel carriers stood at the ready on the intra-city border.

They were clearly prepared to go into the Communist sector if the officials or the military police got into serious trouble.

The East Germans made a half-hearted attempt to impose their new controls on the officials but backed off from a test of strength that might have brought the tanks into action.

Reliable sources indicated that the United States was determined to continue showing force, if necessary, until the issue was resolved with the Soviet Union.

Col. Andrei L. Solovyev, the Soviet commandant, told the American command yesterday that the East German decrees "are binding on access to East Berlin."

Drama Lasts an Hour

Today's drama on the Friedrichstrasse border-crossing point was played for just over an hour to an audience of several hundred Berliners kept well back from the boundary line by the police on both sides. The Berliners looked on as if it were a game, even if a deadly-serious game.

The Soviet Berlin command was given two hours' notice that an American in civilian clothes would drive into East Berlin in a car with the army license plates issued to non-military vehicles. The East Germans announced Monday night that such foreigners would have to "display" their passports or credentials.

The Americans, who told Col. Solovyev yesterday that this was "illegal and inacceptable" and asked for a Soviet officer to be sent to the border in case an identification check was necessary.

Just after 3 P. M., the tanks rumbled up to the border, three of them right to the line on the Friedrichstrasse. Their engines were kept running and their guns were pointed straight down the street into East Berlin. A few minutes later the test of strength began.

An unidentified American at the wheel of a small blue Taurus—the German Ford—started across the border. He went by one policeman in front of the maze-like barriers placed to slow down cars. But another policeman stopped him at the exit of the maze.

They went through what has now become a ritual. The policeman asked for the American's documents. The American refused and demanded that a Soviet officer be brought to the scene.

There was a stand-off until Col. Robert Sabolyk, the United States Provost Marshal, walked over from the

West Berlin side and, ignoring the policemen, got in the car. Let's get out of here, he told the driver, and they started back.

Near the border line Colonel Sabolyk asked the police again to summon a Soviet officer. As they sat waiting for the answer, a young East German policeman pointed to the tanks, saying, "I hope they are not going to start shooting." Colonel Sabolyk did not reply.

"That means no," Colonel Sabolyk replied. Pointing to the West Berlin checkpoint where the tanks stood, he added: "We are coming over. Tell that to your superiors."

Three jeep-loads of soldiers, wearing bullet-proof vests and with bayonets fixed to their rifles, escorted the car the second time it headed over the border, with Mr. Firestone accompanying the driver. One jeep was in front and two in back.

The East German police stepped aside and the convoy sped ahead for a block, where the jeeps swung aside and came back.

The two Americans cruised for about five minutes, then tried to get back. They were stopped by the police just before entering the maze. Mr. Firestone made no reply to the demand for their documents.

"This is the worst example of international impudence the world has known." a police captain shouted at him.

"You seem to have forgotten that we do not recognize you, and God forbid that we ever should," Mr. Firestone replied.

The car driver flashed his lights in a prearranged signal and the jeeps, standing by at the American checkpoint, roared into East Berlin again, formed up around the car and escorted it back.

While the Americans were stopped, an official British car with three officers and one civilian drove out of East Berlin after the civilian had shown identification to the East German police. A British military police truck followed it.

Just before the tanks pulled out, the East Germans sent about sixty armed policemen and one of their water cannons to the border area. They had apparently deliberately kept any force away from the border while the American car was in their sector.

Shortly afterward the Communists installed two high-powered searchlights on each of three twenty-foot wooden towers about thirty yards down the East Berlin side of the Friedrichstrasse. The searchlights were being switched on and off during the evening. When they were on, the crossing point was flooded with bright light.

A car rides across the famous border of the American sector in Berlin, Checkpoint Charlie, between U.S. tanks in October 1961.
(AFP/Getty Images)

U.S. TANKS FACE SOVIET'S AT BERLIN CROSSING POINT

By SYDNEY GRUSON

BERLIN, Oct. 27—United States and Soviet tanks confronted each other tonight for the first time. They were less than 100 yards apart on the narrow Friedrichstrasse crossing point on the border between West and East Berlin.

As they remained in position with their guns pointing at each other, the situation was described by a responsible American source as fraught with danger. Even so, the direct confrontation was welcomed by the Western Allies here.

The Russian-manned tanks rumbled up to the border after the United States Army had displayed military force for the third day running to escort officials in civilian clothes in and out of East Berlin in defiance of East German controls.

Clay Sees 'Fiction' Ended

Lieut. Gen. Lucius D. Clay, President Kennedy's personal representative in West Berlin, declared in a statement:

"The fact that the Soviet tanks appeared on the scene proves that the harassments which were taking place at Friedrichstrasse were not those of the self-styled East German government but ordered by its Soviet masters," the retired general said.

There were ten Soviet T-54 medium tanks, part of a force of thirty-three that moved into East Berlin last night, at the border.

They were drawn up in a three-two-two-three formation on the Friedrichstrasse between the Schuetzenstrasse and the Krausenstrasse. Their black-uniformed crews remained in the tanks, an unsmiling soldier behind the long barreled 100-millimeter gun on each tank.

Down the street, bathed in a garish light from six high-powered search-lights mounted by the East Germans on wooden towers yesterday, four United States M-48 Patton medium tanks had been posted, the first pair right on the line dividing the West and East Berlin.

Two American tanks were in a lot just off the Friedrichstrasse and four more were in reserve in the Mehring Platz, about a quarter of a mile away. A number of armored personnel carriers were also in the area.

Both the Soviet and American tanks came up to the border twice during the tense action-filled period between 4:20 and 6 P. M., when the confrontation was made.

Shortly after the Russian tanks appeared for the first time, the entire 6,500-man United States garrison in Berlin was placed on the alert. The alert lasted two and a half hours. An American spokesman said that "adequate forces" would be kept at the ready

The Americans were expected to continue sending their officials in civilian dress into East Berlin. If the Russians stop them—and this is the Americans' hope—no effort is likely to be made to get them through with force.

The point the Americans were seeking to establish was that the East Germans had no right to control Allied personnel in or out of uniform.

Shortly after 4 P. M. the West Berlin police began clearing civilians off the street between the border and the first intersection, the Kochstrasse. This had been the signal that another forced crossing was to be made.

Five jeeploads of armed United States military police, once again wearing bullet-proof vests and with bayonets fixed to rifles, drove up to the border at 4:20 P. M., followed quickly by ten tanks and five armored personnel carriers.

A few minutes later the test began.

Two American officials took off in an Army-licensed Volkswagen and were stopped, as expected, by the East German police in front of the three low cement barriers through which the cars must snake their way.

There was no argument when the Americans were stopped. The Volkswagen turned around, sped back to "Checkpoint Charlie," the Army post just behind the borderline, and got in position between the soldier-laden jeeps.

The East Germans stepped aside as the convoy came through. The Volkswagen was escorted through the barrier, then went a block on its own while the jeeps waited for it. The convoy formed up again and went back into West Berlin.

The whole exercise lasted only four minutes. A few minutes later the American tanks pulled out and it seemed that the test would pass off with no more effect than the others earlier in the week.

It was 4:50 P. M. when the last of the American tanks pulled away. At 4:55 the Soviet tanks, their markings covered with black tape, rumbled up to the border area.

The word went quickly to United States headquarters. The five jeeploads of military police raced back. But with no tanks on the other side, the Soviet armor withdrew. Five minutes later the American tanks were back and thirty minutes after that so were the Russian tanks.

Opposite page:
A column of American tanks
travelling down Friedrichstrasse,
West Berlin, to various border points
in the divided city, October 28, 1961.
(Keystone/Hulton Archive/Getty Images)

U.S. AND RUSSIANS PULL BACK TANKS FROM BERLIN LINE

Withdrawal From Crossing Point Cuts Tension After 16-Hour Confrontation

SOVIET UNITS GO FIRST

Now a Mile From Border—Americans Send a Plane Over Eastern Sector

By SYDNEY GRUSON

BERLIN, Oct. 28—United States and Soviet tanks pulled back from Berlin's dividing line today after facing each other for sixteen hours through a chilly, drizzly night.

They did not go far, but their withdrawal from the Friedrichstrasse crossing point on the border between West and East Berlin helped lower the tension caused by the confrontation of the war-time allies. The Russians left first.

The Soviet tanks bivouacked behind the walls of the Kronprinzen Palais on Unter den Linden, about a mile from the Friedrichstrasse crossing point.

Pullback of U. S. Tanks

The United States tanks pulled back to an empty lot off the intersection of the Friedrichstrasse and the Mehring Platz, about six hundred yards from the border. Some American armored personnel carriers were on the street, but well back from the crossing point.

For the first time in four days the United States command in Berlin made no effort to send officials in civilian clothes into East Berlin, with or without a show of force.

It was the display of force to defy attempted East German control over these Americans that presumably led the Soviet Army to enter East Berlin and to appear at the border yesterday.

It was not clear what the next move would be. The United States command asked American civilians in Berlin not to enter the Communist sector of the city and maintained the order barring its officials in civilian clothes from crossing.

Two Sides Cross Over

The command continued to send over military cars with uniformed soldiers, some of them to keep track of the Soviet tank movements. Soviet officers kept coming across to West Berlin to observe the American tanks.

No one thought that the maneuvering on both sides was over.

The East German decree demanding control over all "foreigners," including Allied personnel out of uniform, remained in effect, and so did the Americans' intentions to disregard it in asserting their rights of free access.

United States officials here considered the Soviet tanks' appearance at the border a step towards establishing Soviet responsibility for East Berlin. There was no intention of forcing passage through the Soviet forces.

But the tanks were gone before any decision was reached on whether another foray should be made today into East Berlin by armed military policemen escorting non-uniformed personnel of the United States Berlin command.

Reliable sources said the command was determined to maintain its right of entry and to use force if necessary against attempted East German con-

trols. The policy, it was understood, has the approval of the White House.

A flash of apprehension swept through a crowd of several hundred West Berliners near the Friedrichstrasse crossing point when the Soviet tank engines suddenly roared into life at 10:30 A. M.

About an hour after the last of the ten tanks had gone, the Americans began pulling out. All ten of the American tanks were "on the line" this morning, the four held in reserve at the Mehring Platz having been brought up to the border during the night.

Soviet Soldiers Protected

Twice during the day, the United States military police and the West Berlin police stepped in to safeguard Soviet soldiers from an angry crowd in West Berlin.

A crowd of about 500 surrounded a Russian car in the first incident and began to kick it. The second time the Russians were stopped briefly by the crowd at the intersection just behind the border point until the police cleared a way for them.

The mood of the crowd was ugly and it almost got out of control. The Russians were cursed and the West Berlin police whisked away an elderly man who threw himself at the car shouting "Swine!"

For part of this gray chilly day the United States command sent one of its transport planes flying over both sides of the border. The plane flew comparatively deep into East Berlin, apparently

Soviet tanks and troops at Checkpoint Charlie. (Daily Express/Hulton Archive/Getty Images)

to underline the American contention that the "Berlin control zone" is an "area of free flight for the aircraft of the four powers that occupied Germany after the war"—the United States, Britain, France and the Soviet Union.

Soviet Objects to Flights

Earlier, an American spokesman announced that Col. Andrei I. Solovyev, the Soviet commandant in Berlin, had sent a letter two days ago to Maj. Gen. Albert Watson 2d, the United States commandant, taking exception to

American helicopter flights over East Berlin.

The flights were "completely in accordance with long established usage and in accordance with the quadripartite regulations" for an "area of free flight" over Berlin, the American spokesman said.

He disclosed that Colonel Solovyev had also sent what was described as an "unsatisfactory" reply to General Watson's request for a Soviet officer at the Friedrichstrasse to assure "free passage of United States personnel entering the

Soviet sector there."

At a meeting of the two last Monday, Colonel Solovyev told General Watson that the East German decrees were "binding on access to East Berlin."

Although the Soviet tanks had been seen by thousands of East Berliners, not a word of their presence in the city or their night-long duty at the border had appeared in the East German press or in the service of the Communist press agency, A. D. N.

Looking Back

Berlin, 1961

By Andrew J. Bacevich

The conundrum that lies at the heart of diplomacy is how to signal flexibility without conveying weakness, in other words how to project resolve without communicating an outright refusal to negotiate. Although history is replete with cases that illustrate this phenomenon, few if any can match the Berlin crisis of 1961 in their instructive value. That the principal protagonists involved—U.S. President John F. Kennedy and Soviet Premier Nikita Khrushchev—did manage to avoid war over Berlin owes less to their perspicacity than to their willingness to back away from the abyss once it stared them in the face.

At the end of World War II, the victorious allies had occupied Hitler's Third Reich and the Reich's capital according to arrangements negotiated during the war itself. The onset of the Cold War and the division of Germany into two halves transformed Berlin—still under joint U.S., Soviet, British, and French occupation—into an enclave completely surrounded by the German Democratic Republic (GDR). In 1948, Stalin had attempted to force the Western allies out of Berlin, severing all ground transport links between the Federal Republic of Germany (FRG) and the city. The United States and Great Britain responded with the heroic Berlin Airlift, which succeeded in not only preserving their presence in the city but also in investing Berlin with huge symbolic significance. Here freedom and slavery, democracy and totalitarianism stood eyeball-to-eyeball.

Facts, not symbolism, mattered to Walter Ulbricht, the iron-willed Stalinist who ruled East Germany. The fact that mattered most was the rate of emigration from east to west through Berlin, which in the late 1950s was becoming a flood tide. In 1960, the year preceding Kennedy's inauguration as president, more than 150,000 East German citizens had crossed into West Berlin and from there entered the FRG. Departures since 1948 totaled 2.5 million, with those leaving disproportionately young, educated, and talented. For a country with a total population of only some 16 million, this represented an existential threat. If East Germany continued to lose citizens at such a rate, it would become a police state populated by pensioners.

For years, Ulbricht had hammered at Khrushchev to staunch the flow. The Soviet leader had offered rhe-

torical support—variously describing Berlin as a cancer, a knot, a thorn, and a bone in his throat—but offering little by way of action. Then in 1958, he had issued an ultimatum demanding that Western troops evacuate West Berlin within six months, thereby ceding to the GDR control of the entire city. President Dwight D. Eisenhower was unmoved and the deadline lapsed without incident, leaving Ulbricht outraged.

During the 1960 presidential election campaign, Berlin simmered on the front burner of American politics. In debating Republican presidential nominee Richard Nixon on October 7, 1960, Kennedy himself had cited Berlin as "a test of our nerve and will." He predicted that within a year the next president would find himself "face-to-face with the most serious Berlin crisis since 1949 or 1950." The statement proved to be remarkably prescient.

Once in office, however, Kennedy proved anything but keen to make Berlin a testing place. His priority was to find common ground with Khrushchev on reducing the threat of nuclear war. Here, he believed, was where U.S. and Soviet interests aligned. Here he and Khrushchev could cut a mutually beneficial deal.

Unfortunately, misread signals and botched decisions during Kennedy's first months in office undercut the prospects for any such deal. Each side interpreted the rhetoric coming out of the other's camp as indicative of gauntlets being thrown down. Two weeks before Kennedy's inauguration, Khrushchev captured the president-elect's attention by vowing to support "wars of national liberation" throughout the developing world. For his part, less than ten days into his presidency Kennedy was telling Congress that "Our problems are critical. The tide is unfavorable. The news will be worse before it is better"—even as he promised to expand an already dominant U.S. nuclear arsenal. If Khrushchev expected Kennedy to understand that his speech was aimed at rebutting Chinese complaints about Soviet leadership in the Communist world, he miscalculated. So too did the American president if he expected his Soviet counterpart to discount his own hyperbolic language as intended for domestic consumption.

Worse still was Kennedy's mishandling of the Bay of Pigs invasion of April 1961, the first real foreign policy crisis of his administration. Whether it was wise or not to try to overthrow Cuba's Fidel Castro, by allowing the operation to fail, Kennedy marked himself in Khrushchev's eyes as an amateur and a weakling.

Seven weeks later, when the two met for a highly publicized summit in Vienna, Kennedy's performance confirmed this impression. Refusing to be charmed, Khrushchev rejected Kennedy's proposal to curb the nuclear arms race. Instead, he threatened war, declaring that one way or another the situation in Berlin would be resolved to his liking by year's end. Wittingly or not, Kennedy then gave Khrushchev what he wanted, making it clear that he had no interest in starting World War III in order to maintain the free movement of East Germans in and out of West Berlin. As long as Khrushchev left West Berlin alone, he could do whatever he wanted with the Soviet-occupied sector of the city. "All wars start from stupidity," Kennedy told an aide immediately following the summit, "but it seems particularly stupid to risk killing a million Americans over an argument about access rights on an Autobahn in the Soviet zone of Germany." Although mischaracterizing the immediate issue, Kennedy's comment captured the essence of his position, that fighting for Berlin did not rank high on his agenda.

Neither in truth was Khrushchev courting an armed showdown. All the Soviet leader sought was to end Ulbricht's badgering along with the embarrassment of workers fleeing a worker's "paradise" in their joyful haste to become tools of capitalism. Yet Kennedy's unilateral concession gave Ulbricht the opening he was looking for. Congratulating Khrushchev on his brilliant diplomacy, Ulbricht now pressed for decisive action that would divide the city and fix the problem once and for all. At a June 15 press conference attended by Western reporters, Ulbricht famously declared *Niemand hat die Absicht, eine Mauer zu errichten!* ("No one has the intention of erecting a wall!") In fact, that was precisely his intention and by August 1 he had secured the Soviet leader's concurrence. The risks appeared slight, the potential gain great.

At midnight on August 13, East German (not Soviet) security forces began the process of erecting the barrier, at first a temporary obstacle consisting primarily of barbed wire (purchased in West Germany and Great Britain). Over the weeks and months that followed, the barbed wire gave way to something more permanent and imposing: a concrete wall, illuminated by searchlights, reinforced by wire, mines, watchtowers, and anti-vehicular trenches, and patrolled by dogs and by armed guards with orders to shoot anyone trying to escape.

From Allied leaders, the wall's erection elicited strong condemnation but little else. Kennedy had no stomach for using force and therefore neither did anyone else. Gestures ensued, the president reinforcing the small U.S. garrison in West Berlin with a single battalion of infantry and dispatching General Lucius Clay to the scene to serve as his personal representative. While military governor of the U.S. sector of occupied Germany during the crisis of 1948, Clay had won wide admiration among both Americans and West Germans.

Yet this was only damage control. Kennedy's purpose was to look like he was doing something while actually doing very little. Few were fooled, American passivity reinforcing Adenauer's suspicion that West Germans could not rely on Kennedy. In truth, the president privately greeted the wall's construction with undisguised relief, remarking to aides that "a wall is a hell of a lot better than a war."

Yet if Kennedy thought he had finished with Berlin, he was deluding himself. In fact, the most dangerous moment was still to come. The problem was General Clay, who believed that his president had committed the cardinal sin of appeasement by allowing Ulbricht to divide the city. Kennedy was prepared to accept that outcome, but Clay was not. Indeed, he was intent upon reversing it.

The opportunity to do so presented itself on October 22, 1961, when the senior U.S. diplomat in West Berlin, E. Allen Lightner, attempted to enter East Berlin at the crossing point known as Checkpoint Charlie. Lightner's motives were entirely innocent: He was taking his wife to the theater. East German police manning the checkpoint asked to see Lightner's diplomatic passport. To comply would, in effect, constitute acknowledgment by the United States that East Germany rather than the Soviet Union exercised controlling authority over East Berlin. So Lightner refused—and was refused entry by the East German border police.

Matters did not end there, however. Lightner summoned U.S. troops, including several tanks, to back him up. Eventually, the East Germans stepped aside, allowing the American diplomat to proceed.

There things might have ended, were it not for Clay, who saw the incident as an opportunity to make a statement. With Kennedy's casually granted permission, he proceeded to launch a series of provocative probes into East Berlin. U.S. civilian officials arrived at Checkpoint Charlie. East German border guards demanded to inspect their credentials. The Americans refused and then called on U.S. troops as armed escorts, with the East Germans giving way.

Then on October 25, Clay upped the ante, ordering 10 tanks to Checkpoint Charlie in an unprecedented display of firepower. The Soviets rose to the bait. Although the Red Army did not normally keep heavy armored vehicles in Berlin, on October 26 the Soviet high command responded in kind, sending a battalion of thirty-three Soviet tanks to Checkpoint Charlie, to face the Americans. Eyeball-to-eyeball took on new meaning. A corporal with an itchy trigger finger might have touched off Armageddon.

What Kennedy did not know—although East German and Soviet military intelligence almost certainly did—was that Clay, without authorization, had ordered U.S. Army units in West Berlin to create a mock-up of the wall and to rehearse methods for plowing through it. In other words, the Soviets interpreted Clay's probes not as assertions of diplomatic rights but as provocations with a larger purpose. In Soviet eyes, the Americans were seeking a pretext for a full-scale assault on the wall. (Not insignificantly, some of the American tanks arrayed at Checkpoint Charlie mounted dozer blades.)

Finally, Kennedy intervened to rein in his wayward general. He ordered the probes to stop. More importantly, through his brother, Attorney General Robert Kennedy, he activated a secret back channel to communicate directly with Premier Khrushchev. For once the signal was clear and unambiguous. The president proposed a straightforward deal: If the Soviets would withdraw their tanks, the Americans would do likewise within 24 hours. Khrushchev, who had already achieved his objectives in Berlin, agreed and complied. U.S. forces followed suit.

The American secretary of state, Dean Rusk, wasted no time in declaring victory. Yet this was nonsense. Granted, never again would Berlin become a flashpoint threatening nuclear holocaust. But to avoid an unnecessary war, the United States had affirmed its irrevocable acceptance of the Berlin Wall. Khrushchev and especially Ulbricht had gotten what they wanted.

Andrew Bacevich is Professor of History and International Relations at Boston University. He is the author of several books, including *The New American Militarism* (2005, 2013) and *Breach of Trust* (2013).

SOVIET EXPLODES BIGGEST A-BOMB, BUT 50-MEGATON FORCE IS DOUBTED; U.S. JOINS IN WORLD-WIDE PROTEST

TEST DENOUNCED

White House Asserts Purpose Is to Incite 'Fright and Panic'

By JOHN W. FINNEY

WASHINGTON, Oct. 30—The Soviet Union detonated the most powerful man-made explosion in history today by setting off a hydrogen bomb with a force of up to fifty megatons.

The White House, joining in worldwide indignation, denounced the test as a "political" act designed to incite "fright and panic in the cold war."

The explosion, which Premier Khrushchev had said would be the climax of an intensive series of Soviet atomic tests, took place at 3:30 A. M., E.S.T., in the vicinity of Novaya Zemlya Island, the Soviet proving ground above the Arctic Circle. It was confirmed by the White House about thirteen hours later.

Plan Might Have Failed

The White House announcement said preliminary evidence indicated that the magnitude of the explosion was "on the order of fifty megatons"— or the equivalent of 50,000,000 tons of TNT.

There were reliable indications, however, that the Soviet Union might have fallen short in its vaunted plan to test the fifty-megaton device as a trigger for a 100-megaton bomb.

The exact size of the explosion will not be known until there has been more opportunity to examine the detection information. Well-informed officials, however, reported that the explosion might have been as low as thirty-five megatons.

The Atomic Energy Commission revised downward today the size of the huge Soviet explosion a week ago from the original estimate of thirty to fifty megatons to twenty-five megatons.

A Bigger Test Possible

If the latest Soviet explosion reached only thirty-five megatons, it raises the possibility that the Soviet Union may explode a still bigger device before ending its test series. Premier Khrushchev told the Communist Party Congress on Oct. 17 that the Soviet Union would conclude the series at the end of October by "probably" exploding a bomb equal to 50,000,000 tons of TNT, and thus "test the device for triggering a 100-megaton bomb."

The explosion took place in the atmosphere at an altitude of about 12,000 feet. This is a relatively low altitude for so large an explosion. It raised the possibility that fairly heavy fall-out might descend on the Soviet Union downwind from Novaya Zemlya.

'Great Leap Backward'

The Soviet action was condemned as an act of terror against mankind and an immoral act of intimidation. It was in defiance of a "solemn appeal" passed only three days ago by the United Nations General Assembly for Russia not to test its fifty-megaton weapon.

'An Incitement to Fright'

The White House statement branded the Soviet action as "a political rather than a military act" and said the test had been conducted as "primarily an incitement to fright and panic in the cold war." The statement went on:

"Fear is the oldest weapon in history. Throughout the life of mankind, it has been the resort of those who could not hope to prevail by reason and persuasion. It will be repelled today, as it has been repelled in the past—not only the steadfastness of free men but by the power of the arms which men will use to defend their freedom."

The Soviet test, the statement said, "does not affect the basic balance of nuclear power."

From a technical standpoint, the statement said there was no need for such a test.

From a military standpoint, it continued, the Soviet's new bomb would be "primarily a mass killer of people in war" and would "not add in effectiveness against military targets to nuclear weapons now available both to the Soviet Union and the United States."

Since it resumed atomic tests on Sept. 1, the Soviet Union has conducted twenty-six explosions announced by the United States and a few more that have been detected but not announced. Of these explosions, thirteen have been a megaton or larger in yield.

The effects of the Soviet test series will be to more than double the amount of radioactive debris created by testing by all the nuclear powers.

U.S. Will Increase Help For Vietnam

Kennedy, in Reply to Diem Appeal, Promises More Arms and Flood Aid

Special to The New York Times

WASHINGTON, Friday, Dec. 15—President Kennedy has promised more military assistance to South Vietnam in its fight against the Communists.

The President also told President Ngo Dinh Diem of the Southeast Asian country that the United States would help in overcoming the damage of recent disastrous floods.

Mr. Kennedy's pledge was in the form of a letter to President Diem in response to a written appeal from the latter at Saigon. The documents were made public by the White House early today. The dates of the letters were not disclosed.

Confidence Voiced

To President Diem, Mr. Kennedy wrote:

"We shall promptly increase our assistance to your defense effort as well as help relieve the destruction of the floods which you describe. I have already given orders to get these programs under way."

President Diem had written that, "if we lose this war, our people will be swallowed by the Communist bloc." He acknowledged the previous "great assistance" from the United States.

President Kennedy in his reply remarked that the United States' efforts to aid South Vietnam's defense would no longer be necessary, "if the Communist authorities in North Vietnam will stop their effort to destroy the Republic of Vietnam."

"We shall seek to persuade the Communists to give up their attempts of force and subversion," Mr. Kennedy said.

In conclusion, Mr. Kennedy emphasized the confidence of the United States that the Vietnamese people will preserve their independence.

It has been reported that the military program follows the recommendations made by Gen. Maxwell D. Taylor, the President's military adviser, who returned more than a month ago from a three-week mission to Southeast Asia.

Some Aircraft at Hand

The program does not include the dispatch of United States combat units. It does call for the sending of several hundred specialists in guerrilla warfare, logistics, communications, and engineering to train the Vietnamese soldiers.

The program, it is understood, also means fairly large scale shipments of aircraft and other equipment. Apparently some of this is already at hand. Dispatches to The Times from Saigon early this week reported the arrival of planes and at least thirty-three large double-rotor helicopters.

The helicopters were said to be flown by United States crews for reconnaissance and transporting Vietnamese troops in operation against the Communist guerrillas.

It is understood that the Pacific Commander in Chief, Admiral Harry D. Felt, is moving to provide major aid for South Vietnam with food and disaster relief needed because of the floods that have hit the Mekong Delta region.

President Kennedy's letter was current and its publication was evidently timed to assure delivery first to President Diem.

Neither letter referred to a problem between the two countries. This involves what has seemed to be resistance by President Diem to urgent United States' suggestions for democratic reforms.

President Diem's government has been widely criticized both by his own countrymen and by foreign observers as autocratic and centralized under the direct control of President Diem and his family.

A U.S. Army Sergeant in an advisory capacity, provides marksmanship training to Vietnamese troops. (John Dominis/Time & Life Pictures/Getty Images)

Premier Ngo Dinh Diem reviewing military parade marking the 8th anniversary of his regime. (Charles Bonnay/Time & Life Pictures/Getty Images)

G.I.'s In War Zone In South Vietnam

Join Tactical Operations— To Shoot if Fired On

By JACK RAYMOND

WASHINGTON, Dec. 19—United States military men in South Vietnam were understood today to be operating in battle areas with South Vietnamese forces that are fighting Communist guerrillas.

Although the Americans, who are in uniform, are not engaged in actual combat operations, they are to shoot back if fired upon.

About 2,000 Americans in uniform are in South Vietnam, instead of the officially reported 685 members of the military advisory group.

These soldiers, under new arrangements with the South Vietnamese Government, are taking part in tactical operations in battle areas. Officials here are aware that the American soldiers may be subject to attack by Communist guerrillas, who are known as the Viet Cong.

For example, two American companies of helicopters have arrived in South Vietnam and are about to start airlifting supplies and combat equipment to strategic places.

The units include 400 soldiers and forty helicopters. Additional aircraft, ground vehicles and amphibious ships are being sent to South Vietnam.

American soldiers will be manning transport planes and some amphibious vessels. They will also be operating radio communications from strategic places.

All these activities are within the boundaries of South Vietnam, it was noted. But by being active in rebel areas, the Americans are as subject to ambush and terrorism as the South Vietnamese.

The risk of a shooting involvement must be accepted, officials here believe, to strengthen the defenses of President Ngo Dinh Diem against the continuing and growing Communist guerrilla attacks.

The Communist operations are supported by North Vietnam, with Soviet and Red Chinese equipment, it is stressed.

Plastic Boats Sent

Included in additional equipment for the South Vietnamese forces, particularly units operating in the delta area, are plastic boats that are smaller than the usual landing craft and can be propelled by small motors. These boats can be carried through jungles and over mountains.

Among the increased American military groups in South Vietnam are so-called mobile training teams of eight to twelve men.

Most American military men in South Vietnam are engaged in training and teaching how to maintain the sizable increase in equipment under the accelerated aid program.

The United States has delivered $500,000,000 worth of military equipment to South Vietnam over seven years, including $65,000,000 worth in the last year.

President Names Panel On Women

Group Will Press for an End to Discrimination of Sex

———

By ALVIN SHUSTER

WASHINGTON, Dec. 14—President Kennedy established today a commission headed by Mrs. Franklin D. Roosevelt to advance the cause of women's rights.

The President said the group, known as the President's Commission on the Status of Women, would make studies of "all barriers to the full partnership of women in our democracy."

He said he expected the commission to report by Oct. 1, 1963, on what remained to be done to "demolish prejudices and outmoded customs."

The emphasis in the President's statement was on setting up Federal employment practices as a showcase of the value of giving women equal job opportunities. And he set an example. There are fifteen women to eleven men on the commission.

Employment Practices

Specifically, he directed the Civil Service Commission to review all Federal personnel policies and practices affecting the employment of women. The object, he said, will be to assure that "selection of any career position is hereafter made solely on the basis of individual merit and fitness, without regard to sex."

Among other things, the new commission will also look into Federal employment policies and practices, as well as those of Federal contractors.

It also will study the effects of Federal insurance programs and tax laws on women's income, and will appraise Federal and state labor laws dealing with hours and wages.

The group will also presumably go into the advisability of the Administration's throwing its full support behind the constitutional amendment for "equal rights" for women. First proposed in 1920 and introduced at every session of Congress since then, the amendment has never succeeded in winning the approval of both Houses.

It is intended to eliminate "discrimination" against women in areas of employment and property rights and reads in part: "Equality of rights under the law shall not be denied or abridged by the United States or any state on account of sex."

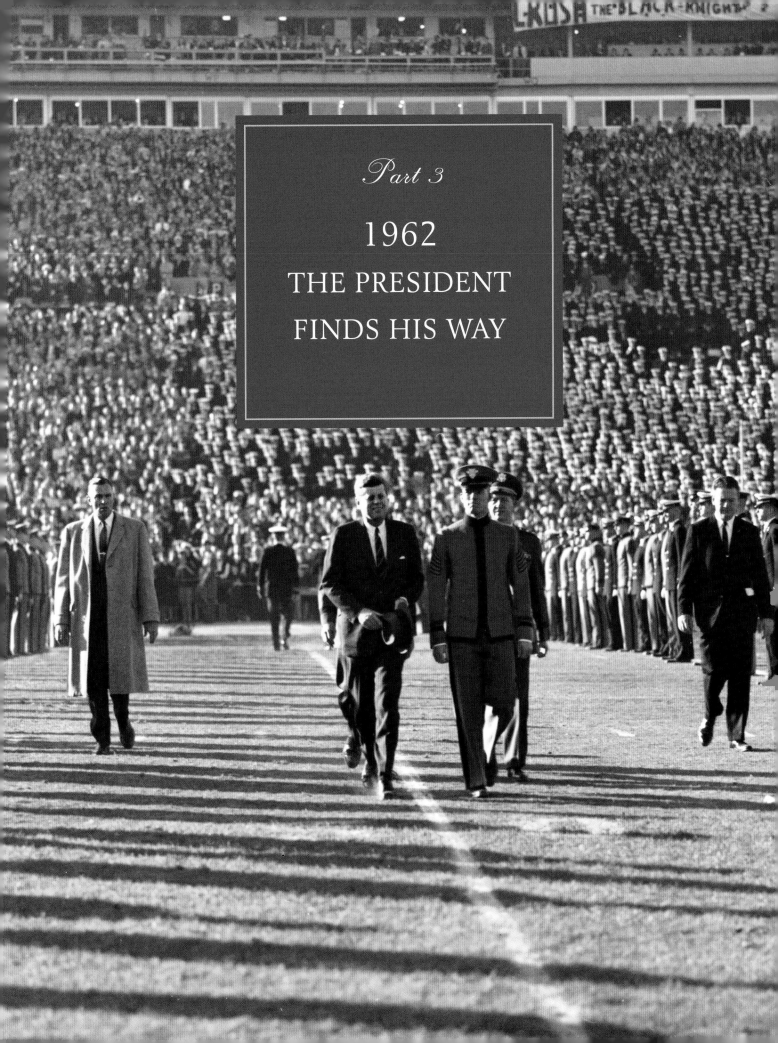

Part 3

1962
THE PRESIDENT
FINDS HIS WAY

President Kennedy aboard the Manitou *off the coast of Maine, August 12, 1962.*
(Robert Knudsen/John F. Kennedy Library)

"We set sail on this new sea because there is new knowledge to be gained, and new rights to be won, and they must be won and used for the progress of all people. For space science, like nuclear science and all technology, has no conscience of its own. Whether it will become a force for good or ill depends on man, and only if the United States occupies a position of pre-eminence can we help decide whether this new ocean will be a sea of peace or a new terrifying theater of war."

—*President Kennedy speaking at Rice University, September 12, 1962*

Preceding page: *President Kennedy is escorted across the field during halftime of the Army-Navy football game, Philadelphia Municipal Stadium, December 1, 1962.*

(Cecil Stoughton/John F. Kennedy Library)

A Year of Living Dangerously

An astonishing series of events punctuated the Kennedy years. In 1962 alone, John Glenn became the first American to orbit the earth, Jacqueline Kennedy became a beloved, style-setting public advocate of high culture, and a walled-off, fearful West Berlin was suddenly isolated from the American sector by a Communist regime in East Germany that could no longer face the international embarrassment of a rising river of fleeing refugees. Bloody violence was triggered by efforts to integrate public facilities in the South, ranging from transportation to lunch counters, while federal attempts to integrate state universities in Dixie were blocked by defiant governors—until they were faced with armed National Guardsmen. G.I.'s went overseas to turn back a drive to take over all of Vietnam by South Vietnamese Communist insurgents, called the Vietcong, reinforced by supplies and military cadres from North Vietnam.

The year of living dangerously began on January 18 when President Kennedy formally approved a secret war to protect governments in Southeast Asia. He signed a classified national security memorandum appointing a counter-insurgency special group "to insure proper recognition throughout the U.S. Government that subversive insurgency ("wars of liberation") is a major form of politico-military conflict equal in importance to conventional warfare." The group was to focus on Laos, South Vietnam and Thailand.

At his first press conference of the year, JFK was asked if any of the 1,000 or so American troops in South Vietnam were engaged in combat. "No," he answered. That was not true. Perhaps he didn't know. The military and intelligence agencies were lying not only to the public, but also the White House. One intelligence report that year stated there were more Vietcong killed and wounded than there were Vietcong insurgents. By September 1962, there were more than 3,000 American soldiers in Vietnam.

That same month, racial violence erupted at home. At the University of Mississippi, Governor Ross Barnett and angry mobs were trying to prevent the entry of the school's first African American student. Kennedy federalized the state's National Guard and dispatched troops. Three people were killed and six U.S. marshals wounded before order was restored and the student, James Meredith, was in a classroom.

Less than a month later, American spy flights confirmed hazy intelligence reports that the Soviets were constructing medium-range nuclear missile bases in Cuba. After reaching a compromise with Soviet Premier Nikita Khrushchev, Kennedy's approval rating jumped to almost 80 percent, but Khrushchev's hit rock bottom.

—Richard Reeves

Culture Makes a Hit At the White House

The flurry of cultural activities there reflects its occupants' interest in the arts.

By ARTHUR and BARBARA GELB

WASHINGTON, Jan. 28—The palpable love affair between the White House and a jade called Culture shows signs of reaching an impassioned peak this year. With Robert Frost's participation in the inaugural ceremony heralding the romance, and three command performances at the Executive Mansion cementing it in recent months, the extraordinary liaison between politics and art has been attracting comment abroad and speculation at home—particularly in the cultural wasteland of Washington itself. It is a notorious fact that the performing arts have few or inadequate facilities in the capital and have had, until very lately, even fewer. As a correspondent for The Sunday Times of London observed in hailing the new White House interest in culture, "Because Washington society prefers talk to listening, the performing arts suffer."

Unlike the great capitals of London, Paris and Moscow, Washington has little to offer artistically to native visitors from outlying communities or to diplomats from abroad; aside from its art galleries and chamber music concerts (admittedly among the finest) it has consistently lagged behind. It has only one experimental theatre—the Arena Stage—and one commercial playhouse—the National—where tryouts and road companies stop over; its National Symphony Orchestra is not in the first rank, its Opera Society, while enterprising, is limited in resources, and its homegrown ballet company performs only sporadically.

Indeed, among many politicians the arts are considered a laughing matter, if they are considered at all—as witness the recent comment by a Congressman from Virginia, who observed that poker playing was "an artful occupation" and that it was as logical to subsidize poker players as artists.

In the face of such well-established anti-estheticism in Washington, it now appears that President and Mrs. Kennedy are systematically planning to turn Washingtonians into better listeners and to expand their artistic "patronage" in the tradition of European heads of state. Not since Thomas Jefferson occupied what was then known as the President's Palace has culture had such good friends in the White House.

The flow of guests from the fields of the arts to the Executive Mansion has been unprecedented since Mr. Kennedy took office. Not only have Metropolitan Opera stars, a troupe of Shakespearean actors and Pablo Casals been issued formal invitations to perform in the East Room at state dinners, but the list of private and official guests invited to the White House over the past months forms a Who's Who of culture—everyone from Carl Sandburg, Gian Carlo Menotti and Leonard Bernstein to Igor Stravinsky, George Balanchine, Elia Kazan and Ralph Richardson have been welcomed there.

The President and his wife have attended the opening of both the Opera Society and the National Symphony Orchestra, and Mrs. Kennedy has attended the Washington Ballet and a performance at the Library of Congress of "The Importance of Being Oscar," Micheal MacLiammoir's one-man reading from the works of Oscar Wilde.

In addition, Mr. Kennedy has taken a public stand in favor of culture giving his support to the proposed National Cultural Center in Washington, a multi-million dollar project comparable in scope to New York City's Lincoln Center for the Performing Arts.

He has also gone out of his way to commend various groups for their artistic achievements, including the Theatre Guild American Repertory Company, which toured Europe, the Near East and Latin America under the auspices of the State Department; and he took the trouble to write personally to Jack Landau, who staged the command program of Shakespeare at the White House, congratulating him on "a very exciting performance" and expressing his and Mrs. Kennedy's pride in "our American theatre."

Perhaps none of these cultural pats on the back (as some snipers aver) add up to the start of a cultural renaissance in Washington. But those close to the President point out that command performances have set the machinery in motion. This is borne out by the fact that, for the first time in White House history, a permanent stage has been built that can be stored and put into place at almost a moment's notice; that future flirtations with all the lively arts—ballet, contemporary theatre, classical music and even jazz—are being planned on a bi-monthly basis at the White House; and that poetry seminars, sponsored by the Cabinet under the aegis of Mrs. Kennedy, are to be regularly scheduled events in the capital (Robert Frost has already presided over one and Carl Sandburg over another). Moreover, Presidential patronage of the arts in the form of annual contests, prizes, and an official cultural coordinator is promised.

The question being asked by some keepers of the flame of status quo is: will the arty atmosphere of the White House damage the President politically? They maintain that the majority of the voting public looks askance at the egghead and that things were much cozier with the Eisenhowers, who invited mainly popular television performers to entertain their guests. The Kennedys have endeared themselves to the country's intellectuals, say these lowbrows, but how many intellectuals are there among the registered voters, compared with the ranks of solid, stolid citizens to whom culture is a dirty word?

While no one denies that the President is aware of and pleased with the publicity value of his nod to culture, it is apparent that there is much more behind it, and the results have already proved a justification of his program. At any rate, he appears to discount the Neanderthal position and to take heart from the fact that there is considerable support, both at home and abroad, for his theory that a great nation may profit as much from the artistic achievement it fosters as from the wisdom of its political leadership.

The remarkable thing about the White House espousal of culture is that no one can justifiably bring a charge of bookwormism or arty insulation against a President who is as vigorous and physical-health-conscious as Mr. Kennedy, or his golfing, horseback-riding, water-skiing First Lady. Indeed, the public image of this handsome young couple, cheerfully endorsing the arts as part of a rich, full life, cannot fail to have an impact on the country in general, whatever the snipers may say.

"When Kennedy endorses ballet, painting and theatre, the average man is bound to change his mind about such things being effete," Dore Schary recently remarked.

Both Mr. and Mrs. Kennedy of course had more than a nodding acquaintance with the arts long before they moved into the White House. Their current program of patronage is a legitimate and natural extension of their accustomed way of life.

In the President's case, the extension may be a bit more strained than in Mrs. Kennedy's. He is, like most of us, not as well rounded culturally as he might wish—and his participation in cultural events is necessarily restricted by the pressures of more vital matters.

His tastes in classical music and painting range from middlebrow to noncommittal. He will sit happily through the portion of a concert that includes a well-known Tchaikovsky symphony, but after that he is apt to fidget. He admires the Cézannes his wife has hung in the Green Room of the White House, and will point them out proudly to visitors, but his admiration seems directed primarily toward his wife's expertise in this field.

In the theatre, his preference is for musicals and light comedy. Since his election, he has attended Broadway performances of "Do Re Mi" and "The Best Man." One of his favorite charac-

Famed cellist Pablo Casals gives a recital for American president John F. Kennedy and Jackie Kennedy at the White House, November 24, 1961. (Keystone/Hulton Archive/Getty Images)

French Minister of Culture André Malraux and his wife pose with President Kennedy, First Lady Jackie Kennedy, and Vice President Lyndon Johnson at the National Gallery opening for Leonardo Da Vinci's painting of the Mona Lisa, *which was on loan from France, January 8, 1963.*
(Walter Bennett/Time & Life Pictures/Getty Images)

terizations was Sam Levine's Nathan Detroit in "Guys and Dolls" and he can knowledgeably hold a discussion of Method acting with the actress, Shelley Winters—an ardent pre-election campaigner.

Mr. Kennedy is decidedly a movie fan—particularly of red-blooded films like "La Dolce Vita" and "Spartacus," which he watched at a theatre near the White House that has a wide screen. Private screenings are frequently given at the White House and when a film bores Mr. Kennedy, he either leaves his guests, or orders the final reel run so he can see how it turns out—as was the case with "L'Avventura," which he found slow-paced.

Again, all this does not add up to Culture; and the President is the first to admit that modern man, however willing to be culturally saturated, is confronted with certain difficulties. One of his close friends, and an occasional week-end guest at the White House, the playwright Gore Vidal has pointed out that the President is both aware of and regretful about the lack of comprehensive cultural training of modern man.

"We recently got onto the subject of the American Revolution," Mr. Vidal said, "and the President pointed out that while the eighteenth century produced, out of a little country of only 3,000,000 people, two all-around geniuses—Franklin and Jefferson—as well as an extraordinary number of slightly less gifted men, twentieth-century America had produced no equivalents. Where was today's equivalent for a man like Adams, he said, who could write and think and design a building and box a compass?

"The President observed rather wistfully that few Americans today even had a second language, or knew the classics intimately, and though we study, there are vast areas that were comprehended by our predecessors which are unfamiliar to us. We don't have long, leisurely winters at Monticello, the sort of atmosphere where you are forced onto your own mental resources."

Recognizing this lack, the President takes pains to express his support of highbrow art such as chamber music and ballet ("I think it is tremendously important that we regard music not just as part of our arsenal in the cold war, but as an integral part of a free society," he recently said) and he happily endorses Shakespeare.

Furthermore, he is pleased to follow the tastes of his wife, who happens to be well qualified for the role of unofficial Minister of Culture.

Culture has been an integral part of Jacqueline Kennedy's life since childhood, and she has been guiding her husband's participation in (if not always spontaneous enjoyment of) the esthetic since their marriage.

Mrs. Kennedy, an amateur painter herself, collects eighteenth and nineteenth century drawings, has several Renoirs on loan in her private rooms at the White House and owns a Boudin seascape and works by such contemporary painters as Goodenough, Walt Kuhn and William Walton. She is knowledgeable about antiques (her redecoration of the White House and restoration of historical objects d'art are well known by now).

She is a balletomane and a fond con-

certgoer, having a preference for the romantic music of the nineteenth century. She reads philosophy, one of her favorite playwrights is Oscar Wilde, and she regards among her best-liked authors Henry James, Henry Adams, Nathaniel Hawthorne, Ernest Hemingway, F. Scott Fitzgerald (whose daughter, Frances Lanahan, is a friend) and Edgar Allan Poe. She is partial to biographies of eighteenth-century figures.

Annual diplomatic reception at the White House. In the buffet throng, the president chatted with all hands, May 3, 1962.
(George Tames/*The New York Times*)

Attracted by the music at the diplomatic reception, 4-year-old Caroline Kennedy (at top right), and her guest, Mary Warner, slipped away from the nurse upstairs and got down as far as the landing. They had a small colloquy, exchanged some brief remarks with some of the guests, and then were called back upstairs, May 3, 1962. (George Tames/The New York Times)

First Lady Jackie Kennedy in the East Room with CBS correspondent Charles Collingwood during a televised guided tour of the White House.
(Paul Popper/Popperfoto/Getty Images)

Mrs. Kennedy TV Hostess to Nation

Tells of Restoration of Interior of the White House

By JACK GOULD

Feb. 15—Millions of television viewers went through the White House last night with Mrs. John F. Kennedy leading the way.

With verve and pleasure, the President's wife undertook to the restoration she has made in the interior of the Executive Mansion. She was to prove a virtuoso among guides.

In the hour-long program, recorded on tape last month, Mrs. Kennedy was a historian savoring the small facts and human story behind the evolution of White House decor. She was an art critic of subtlety and standard. She was an antiquarian relishing pursuit of the elusive treasure. She was a poised TV narrator.

Mrs. Kennedy, wearing a wool suit of simple line and three strings of pearls, animatedly strolled through rooms on the ground, first and second floors in what was described as the most extensive public view of the White House ever shown.

The hour was rich in detail and diversity. The viewer saw the magnificence of the State Dining Room, a battered old Lincoln chair plucked from a warehouse, many of the antiques and paintings recently donated to the White House in response to Mrs. Kennedy's pleas, the rich warmth of the Red Room and the unfinished Monroe Room that is to shield the President's visitors from the perils of a passing baby carriage.

But the First Lady's vivacious scholarship was fully as vital as the visual pageantry. With her soft and measured voice, she ranged in comment from warm appreciation of past First Ladies and Presidents to delicate but telling dismissal of the second-rate in the arts. Her effortless familiarity with dates and names attested to homework done for the occasion.

Carried on Two Networks

Mrs. Kennedy's companion on the tour was Charles Collingwood, a reporter for the Columbia Broadcasting System's news department, which conceived and produced the program. C. B. S. also made the presentation available to the National Broadcasting Company. Both networks carried the program simultaneously on a sustaining basis from 10 to 11 o'clock.

After Mrs. Kennedy completed the tour, the President appeared briefly to second his wife's efforts to impart a sense of living history to the White House.

But the First Lady's vivacious scholarship was fully as vital as the visual pageantry. With her soft and measured voice, she ranged in comment from warm appreciation of past First Ladies and Presidents to delicate but telling dismissal of the second-rate in the arts.

An awareness of history can be a source of strength in meeting the problems of the future, he said.

The President reported that more than 1,300,000 persons passed through the White House last year. Mrs. Kennedy's audience last night was expected to exceed that number by many-fold, but estimates of the program's rating were not expected to be available until today.

Competes With 'Naked City'

Mrs. Kennedy's competition in the ratings last night came from "Naked City," a police adventure series presented by the American Broadcasting Company. A.B.C. said that it could not afford to share in the total production costs of Mrs. Kennedy's program, estimated at more than $100,000, because of unforeseen expense in covering the delayed orbital flight of Lieut. Col. John H. Glenn Jr.

Mrs. Kennedy and her associates and a special C. B. S. staff, headed by Perry Wolff, the program's producer, and Franklin Schaffner, director, made careful preparations for the first televised tour of the White House since President Harry S. Truman inaugurated the format May 4, 1952.

Agreement on a final outline enabled Mrs. Kennedy to go through most of the program in a single day, Jan. 15, without retakes. Close-up shots of specific antiques were taken initially and were subsequently integrated into Mrs. Kennedy's running commentary, an editing procedure designed to spare the President's wife unnecessary delay. The President chose to record his part of the program a second time.

The program started with Mrs. Kennedy's own off-screen narration of the history of the White House. Then she and Mr. Collingwood met in the curator's office on the ground floor.

Visits Original Kitchen

Next was the Diplomatic Reception Room, and then came the original White House kitchen, later used by Franklin D. Roosevelt as a broadcast room. The kitchen is now Mrs. Kennedy's upholstery repair shop.

Mrs. Kennedy went up to the first floor and in succession through the East Room, the State Dining Room, where the table was fully set; the Red Room, Blue Room and Green Room. Then the First Lady went up the second floor, rarely visited by the public, and viewers were taken into the Lincoln and Monroe Rooms.

Mrs. Kennedy, whose restoration efforts have drawn Washington's bipartisan approval, had special praise for the past contributions of Theodore Roosevelt and James Monroe. Similarly, in admiring Gilbert Stuart's portrait of Washington, she deplored the fact that so many pictures of later Presidents had been done by inferior artists.

With delightful understatement, she recalled that Grant's renovation of the East Room had been called a unique mixture of two styles: ancient Greek and "Mississippi River Boat."

In terms of television viewing, "A Tour of the White House with Mrs. John F. Kennedy" will undoubtedly stand as a distinctive contribution of the electronic era: an unusual feminine personality imparting her own kind of excitement to national history and national taste.

Richard S. Salant, president of C.B.S. News, said last night that arrangements for the program had not included any conditions for a contribution to the Fine Arts Commission, which is assisting Mrs. Kennedy's restoration efforts.

"There is absolutely no truth to such a report," Mr. Salant said. "There was no suggestion from the White House for a quid pro quo. There has been no discussion of it."

May Make Contribution

C.B.S. might wish to make a contribution on its own initiative at a later date, Mr. Salant said.

If it were decided to aid the White House restoration efforts, he said, it had been suggested that any other network carrying Mrs. Kennedy's program might wish to join in. A.B.C., which did not carry the program, disapproved of the proposal, Mr. Salant said.

In Washington, however, it was understood that the White House had misgivings over the idea of any network contributions to aid Mrs. Kennedy's project.

Through the Federal Communications Commission, the Government exercises a degree of regulation over chain broadcasting and also licenses individual stations owned by the networks.

Looking Back

Jackie: Taste, Style, Culture

By Cathy Horyn

Despite Jacqueline Kennedy's premonition, buried in an article about her spending on clothes that ran in *The New York Times* on Sept. 15, 1960, that "a terrible, frightening decade is ahead," and despite the Russians and the Bomb and the civil rights sit-ins, 1960 exposed a terrible yearning for all things Kennedy. It is why people who were in kindergarten then can still remember the names of the Kennedy sisters, can still see them sitting around in their Bermudas and polo shirts in Hyannis Port. Flip the pages of a magazine—*Look*, *Life* or *Collier's*, it scarcely matters—and there is Jackie, in a pretty silk dress, playing with baby Caroline. The pictures are indelible. Historians have dwelled on these images and the intense fascination they aroused, invariably citing JFK's youthfulness and his wife's glamour ("Turn on the lights so they can see Jackie," the president-elect said as they rode through the snowy capital on the eve of the Inaugural), though it may well be that we were already a media-haunted nation.

Yet whether we knew it or not, the years between the 1960 campaign and the president's death were marked by energy and high purpose, in not only the areas of social progress but also aesthetics and the arts. With new kinds of painting and theater (the Happenings were taking place in New York and other cities around the world) and victories in major obscenity-law cases (*Tropic of Cancer* in 1964, *Lady Chatterley's Lover* in 1959), there was a remarkable sense of openness. Indeed, for all that President Kennedy and his wife did on behalf of the arts, for architecture and preservation, Jackie said later she regretted that more had not been done for experimental art. "Of course, the president and I talked of these things," she said. Of even greater impact was that *Mastering the Art of French Cooking* came out in 1961, followed two years later by Julia Child's television show. As millions of Americans were learning how to bundle asparagus or the tricks to making a good omelet, Jackie, ending three decades at the White House of grim chicken dinners and packaged desserts, was delighting guests with food prepared by her French chef, René Verdon. But while she surely raised fine-dining attitudes among the city's bureaucrats, just as she opened their minds to preserving its landmarks, many Americans had discovered this culinary experience on their own.

One reason that pictures of the Kennedys still hold so much power a half century on is that the couple wore their pleasure in beautiful things with unmatched confidence. American presidents often cloaked themselves in folksy virtue; Kennedy went to his inauguration in a patrician cutaway and a silk top hat, and then challenged a new generation. Jackie chose white for her inaugural gowns—"the most ceremonial color," she told the fashion editor Diana Vreeland. At 31, raised in a world of culture and manners, Jackie knew what she liked—in food and fashions, but also people. By today's populist standards, she comes off as catty on the oral history tapes she made in 1964 with Arthur M. Schlesinger, which were released in 2011. It's strange to hear the First Lady run down various world leaders with her impeccable diction. Charles de Gaulle was "an egomaniac," Indira Gandhi "a real prune."

Such spit seemed to intentionally spoil the soup, the idea that her taste was mainly a garnish. At one point she complained, "I was never any different once I was in the White House than I was before. But the press made you different." It cared about her clothes. Clearly, with the tapes she was seeking a wider, ultimately more truthful appraisal. Schlesinger provided a helpful clue in a 2001 essay about her White House years for an exhibition at the Metropolitan Museum of Art. He wrote that her social graces masked "ruthless judgment." As the president knew, Jackie's taste was a boon to his administration's altruistic message, just as it was good for the Seventh Avenue garment trade, department stores that sold copies of her dresses, and news media revenues. Americans had known uplifting presidents and reform-minded first ladies—few as worldly as Franklin and Eleanor Roosevelt—but their altruism had been directed at profound social needs rather than "the powers and pleasures of the mind," as writer and balletomane Lincoln Kirstein said, marveling at the presence of Robert Lowell, W.H. Auden, John Steinbeck, and 50 other writers and artists at JFK's inauguration.

Not all of the Kennedys' cultural ideas came across. Norman Mailer, after watching the CBS program *A Tour of the White House with Mrs. John F. Kennedy*, which aired in February 1962, wrote in *Esquire*, "I liked her, I like her still, but she was a phony..." It's entirely possible that the medium couldn't handle that much taste, or for that matter that much Jackie. On the other hand, 56 million Americans tuned in—only slightly fewer than the weekly audience for *The Beverly Hillbillies.*

We were still a long way from the need to dumb things down, and from women being cynical about the fashion industry. In 1960, when Jackie wrote to Vreeland for some advice, she, like her sister Lee Radziwill, was a connoisseur of couture. "Just remember I like terribly simple, covered up clothes," she told Vreeland, "the nearest to Balenciaga and Givenchy." In naming those two, along with Chanel, she had identified the pinnacle of fashion. Givenchy was then creating elegant clothes for a string of Audrey Hepburn movies, including *Breakfast at Tiffany's* (1961). Jackie was also used to New York stores that sold approved copies of Paris originals, like Saks and Chez Ninon, a couture salon that made her a number of interpretations of Givenchy suits and evening dresses during her White House years.

America had the greatest fashion oracles, like Vreeland and Eugenia Sheppard of the *New York Herald Tribune*, and some innovative designers, but, as the writer Kennedy Fraser noted about that period, while the nation was becoming a world power, Seventh Avenue dug in its chauvinistic heels. Press comments about Jackie's French wardrobe and its extravagant costs surfaced in the summer of 1960. When Nan Robertson of the *Times* asked her about the reports, Jackie replied, "I couldn't spend that much unless I wore sable underwear." In reality she probably spent much more than the amounts reported. Robertson wrote: "Mrs. Kennedy was also nettled by snide remarks about her bouffant hairdo. Some wrathful letter-writers have described it as a 'floor mop' and worse." With pressure from the Ladies' Garment Workers' Union—a supporter of her husband's election—and the milliners' union, which saw its own opportunity, Jackie made a greater effort to buy American fashion. Oleg Cassini designed many of her first lady garments, following her taste for crisp, unfitted lines with a single detail, like a flat bow. She also wore youthful styles by the American designers Joan Morse and Gus Tassell.

Is it a pity that she did not have free access to the best fashion, as she did in other aesthetical areas? Not really, suggested Hamish Bowles, the curator of the Met exhibit, who summed up her White House look as "a dashing synthesis of begloved propriety, discreet historicism, and reductive modernity." She determined her style. And she continued to wear French clothes, notably Givenchy.

JFK's wardrobe received scant attention, apart from his decision to go coatless at the inauguration and his casual attire in Hyannis Port and Palm Beach. Yet his indifference to certain conventions played into his sexual attractiveness. The writer Gloria Emerson, who met Kennedy in the early 50s when she was dating one of his Harvard classmates, recalled how he would walk around in front of guests wearing only a towel—"all bone, all rib, all shank." He had that much self-assurance, she told Seymour Hersh for his book *The Dark Side of Camelot*. Moreover, both Kennedys used an ironical manner to deflect interest from their appearance. ("Now as usual my hair is dripping wet 15 minutes before guests arrive," she wrote to Anne Morrow Lindbergh, inviting her to the White House to meet the couple's children.)

The Kennedys may have been "consummate performers," as the writer Kati Marton has said, but, like all great performers, they knew what the public needed at that moment. Again, the energy is concentrated in those four years from 1960 to 1963. Before then, Jackie's hair was a neat cap, her clothes a bit fussy. By the late 60s, she has disappeared into an everywoman uniform of pants and T-shirts.

"The Kennedys released a positive attitude toward culture, toward style," Vreeland wrote in 1984, "and, since then, we've never gone back." In fact, by the mid-70s, most women had adopted a passive attitude toward style as they discovered other ways to feel good and self-confident. And the industry that had once danced before its queen retrenched for a hatless, gloveless and largely taste-resistant world.

Cathy Horyn, the chief fashion critic of *The New York Times*, is working on a history of the *Times'* fashion coverage.

GLENN ORBITS EARTH 3 TIMES SAFELY; PICKED UP IN CAPSULE BY DESTROYER

81,000 Mile Trip

Flight Aides Feared for the Capsule as it Began its Re-Entry

By Richard Witkin

CAPE CANAVERAL, Fla., Feb. 20—John H. Glenn Jr. orbited three times around the earth today and landed safely to become the first American to make such a flight.

The 40-year-old Marine Corps lieutenant colonel traveled about 81,000 miles in 4 hours 56 minutes before splashing into the Atlantic at 2:43 P. M. Eastern Standard Time.

He had been launched from here at 9:47 A. M.

The astronaut's safe return was no less a relief than a thrill to the Project Mercury team, because there had been real concern that the Friendship 7 capsule might disintegrate as it rammed back into the atmosphere.

There had also been a serious question whether Colonel Glenn could complete three orbits as planned. But despite persistent control problems, he managed to complete the entire flight plan.

Lands in Bahamas Area

The astronaut's landing place was near Grand Turk Island in the Bahamas, about 700 miles southeast of here.

Still in his capsule, he was plucked from the water at 3:01 P. M. with a boom and block and tackle by the destroyer Noa. The capsule was deposited on deck at 3:04.

Colonel Glenn's first words as he stepped out onto the Noa's deck were: "It was hot in there."

He quickly obtained a glass of ice tea.

He was in fine condition except for two skinned knuckles hurt in the process of blowing out the side hatch of the capsule.

The colonel was transferred by helicopter to the carrier Randolph, whose recovery helicopters had raced the Noa for the honor of making the pick-up. After a meal and extensive "de-briefing" aboard the carrier, he was flown to Grand Turk by submarine patrol plane for two days of rest and interviews on technical, medical and other aspects of his flight.

The Noa, nearest ship to the capsule as it parachuted into the ocean, took just twenty-one minutes to close the six-mile gap, lift the capsule aboard with a boom-block-and-tackle rig and place it gently on the deck.

Colonel Glenn first was set to wriggle out of the narrow top. But when difficulty was encountered in getting one of the bulkheads loose, the explosive side hatch was blown off, and the man from space stepped out on deck, apparently in excellent shape. He was soon afterward transferred to the carrier Randolph.

In the course of his three orbits, Colonel Glenn reported frequently to tracking stations at various points on earth and to the control center here. Invariably, he said that his condition was fine.

Shortly after Colonel Glenn was picked up by the Noa, he received congratulations on his feat from President Kennedy by radio telephone.

A situation that seemed at the moment to pose the greatest danger developed near the end of the flight.

A signal radioed from the capsule indicated that the heat shield—the blunt forward end made of ceramic-like material that dispels the friction heat of re-entry and chars in the process might be torn away before it could do its job.

If it had, the flight would have had a tragic end.

Signal is Received

The signal, received as the capsule was traveling between Hawaii and the West Coast, indicated that the heat shield had become unlatched from the main capsule body. This action was not intended to happen until the final stage of the parachute descent.

At that point, it would fall a few feet, and deploy, between it and the capsule base, a cloth landing bag to cushion the impact on the water.

Colonel Glenn was asked by radio to flip a switch to check whether the shield had, in fact, become unlatched. When the light did not go on, it appeared that the "unlatch" signal had been spurious.

But the Mercury team was taking no chances. It changed the sequence of re-entry events to try to insure that, even if unlatched, the heat shield would not fall away prematurely.

Colonel Glenn, apparently sensing possible serious trouble, asked: "What are the reasons for this? Do you have any reasons?'

"Not at this time," came the reply from the control center.

Astronaut John Glenn training in a mock up of the planned space capsule. (Ralph Morse/Time & Life Pictures/Getty Images)

Normally, after the firing of the three braking rockets to bring the capsule out of orbit, the empty braking-rocket package is jettisoned.

Jettisoning was delayed today so that, in case the heat shield had become unlatched, the rocket-packet straps would hold the shield in place until this function was taken over by the force of re-entry into the atmosphere.

The package burned on re-entry. The heat shield did not drop away until it was supposed to. This indicated that the signal that had caused so much anxiety had, in fact, been a false one.

100,000 See Launching

The whole continent watched on television as Colonel Glenn's capsule was launched. The world listened by radio. And almost 100,000 persons had a direct view from here and the beaches around as the Atlas rocket booster bore the Project Mercury capsule upward with a thrust of 360,000 pounds.

The Friendship 7 was lofted into a trajectory that varied between a low point, or perigee, of about ninety-nine miles, and a high point, or apogee, of 162 miles.

It traveled at a speed of about 17,530 miles an hour and went from day to night three times before whirling east across the Pacific on the final leg of the flight.

Some 300 miles west of the California coast, three retro, or braking rockets slowed the capsule enough to bring it out of orbit.

The elated astronaut on board radioed, "Boy, that was a real fireball of a ride!" as the capsule rammed back into the atmosphere.

Besides generating heat that gave him a spectacular moment of fireworks outside his capsule window, the re-entry ended Colonel Glenn's long hours of weightlessness and shoved him forcefully back against his contoured couch.

At 2:43 P. M., a sixty-three foot red-and-white parachute deposited the Friendship 7 on gentle Caribbean waters.

After the capsule had been picked up by the Noa and safely placed on her deck, Colonel Glenn emerged triumphant in his gleaming silver space suit.

Sends Words of Trouble

It was on his first turn around the globe that Colonel Glenn sent word of erratic behavior by the attitude control system. This caused some concern almost to the end of the flight.

The system is designed to control the capsule's attitude in space.

This does not mean that it in any way alters the course of the capsule over the ground. The course is set once the Air Force Atlas booster has imparted to the capsule its speed and direction, and has been dropped away.

There were the usual cries of "Go! Go!" at take-off. Tears came to the eyes of some viewers . . .

The astronaut exercised control over the capsule attitude until after the Atlas booster rocket had finished burning and dropped away. During the climb to space, the Atlas provides the guidance and attitude control. Its engines swivel like a juggler's palm under a broom-stick.

The attitude system, rather, controls the orientation of the capsule— whether the forward end tilts up or down; whether the capsule rolls one way or the other.

If the capsule moves out of proper line on any of the three axes, it can be realigned by squirting hydrogen peroxide through tiny jets.

There are two completely independent systems for making these corrections. One is called automatic; the other manual. There are different ways to operate each system.

Used Automatic System

When the trouble developed, Colonel Glenn was flying by the completely automatic method. Gyroscopes were set to the desired attitudes. And when the capsule strayed too far, squirts of hydrogen peroxide were to be automatically ejected through the proper jets.

On this system, there are four jets for roll; four for pitch up and down; and four for yaw right and left. Two of the four jets in each set have a thrust of only one pound, while the other two have much larger thrusts.

Only the small jets are supposed to be brought into play during the main portion of the orbital journey. The large ones are mainly for more radical corrections necessary when attitude changes are likely to be most violent— coming back from orbit.

What happened to Colonel Glenn's capsule was that the small jets did not do their job. When the capsule drifted beyond the proper limits, and the small jets did not respond, the larger jets, with twenty-four pounds of thrust, automatically cut in.

Dangers Are Described

A similar malfunction occurred on the roll jets during the second orbit of the flight made by Enos the chimpanzee last year. Because there was no human aboard to analyze the trouble and make corrections, Enos's mission had to be ended one-orbit ahead of schedule.

The danger today was that the large jets would consume the hydrogen peroxide too fast and that, when it came time to perform the important return-from-orbit maneuver, there would be none left to orient the capsule properly for re-entry.

Colonel Glenn initially met the problem by switching to a technique called fly-by-wire. He controlled the vehicle by manually moving the control stick.

This was not the regular "manual" system. The stick was electronically connected to the same jets used in the completely automatic system. But it had the result of making very finely calculated corrections that did not waste hydrogen peroxide.

At later stages of the flight, Colonel Glenn switched to the completely independent "manual" system that used six different jets, two for each axis. The amount of squirt ejected through these jets was also determined by how far the control stick moved, and it wasted no hydrogen peroxide.

The original trouble seemed to have disappeared by the time the colonel was ready to return from orbit.

He successfully used the automatic system for the difficult re-entry maneu-ver, while keeping himself ready to switch immediately to manual controls if the trouble recurred. It did not.

10 Previous Attempts

Today's orbital flight had been scheduled for just before Christmas. There had been ten attempts to send Colonel Glenn on his trip, and ten frustrating postponements, either because of weather or technical problems.

Last night, the weather men talked about being "cautiously optimistic." But few observers agreed with them. It did not seem possible that the mess of weather bearing down on Florida could clear away in time, and that is the way it still looked when the swarm of official observers arrived here about 4 A. M.

Colonel Glenn had been awakened at 2:20 A. M. The countdown ritual was not much different from what had been witnessed on the suborbital 300-mile trips made last year by Comdr. Alan B. Shephard Jr., and on the attempt Jan. 27 to orbit Colonel Glenn.

A number of changes had been made in the mission plan since the short-range flights. The recovery system had been revised to minimize chances of another after-landing mishap that caused the loss of Capt. Virgil I. Grissom's capsule and almost cost that astronaut his life.

Colonel Glenn was given a special camera with which to try to take various types of pictures of cloud cover and other phenomena.

He had a "bungee" chord—a "king size rubberband"—on which he was to

President Kennedy and John Glenn inspect Friendship 7 *at Cape Canaveral on February 23, 1962.* (Universal History Archive/Getty Images)

Astronaut John Glenn with President Kennedy and Vice President Johnson after speaking at the joint session of Congress on February 28, 1962. (George Tames/The New York Times)

pull, like an oarsman pulling oars, to see how his blood pressure was affected by exercise when he was in a weightless state.

He had a medical kit of spring-loaded needles with which he could give himself various injections. One was to suppress nausea or other symptoms of motion sickness. (Colonel Glenn reported frequently that weightlessness bothered him not at all.)

He also had a pain-killer, morphine; a stimulant, benzadrine; and a drug to counter shock.

Under his flying suit Colonel Glenn wore a plastic tube and container for bladder relief.

As the sun rose, the low-hanging clouds disappeared, and left conditions here as ideal as anyone ever had seen them. The weather in key recovery areas at sea was equally perfect.

While waiting for the countdown to proceed, Colonel Glenn had a chance to talk by phone with wife Anna, his 16-year-old son David, and his 15-year-old daughter Lynn. They watched the proceedings on T.V. from their home in Arlington, Va.

Visually, there was nothing particularly memorable about take-off, at 9:47. Emotionally, the atmosphere was charged, because a man was going into orbit.

There were the usual cries of "Go! Go!" at take-off. Tears came to the eyes of some viewers, in the blockhouse, at the observer's stand two miles from the launching pad, and on the beaches. But, generally, the emotions were held in. Everyone waited.

Colonel Glenn apparently had a fine, exhilarating time, right from the start. He experienced some vibration along with acceleration force, as he climbed through the atmosphere.

Then it smoothed out; the rocket burning stopped; the acceleration switched abruptly to weightlessness; and the capsule automatically turned its blunt end forward for the almost five hours he was to be in orbit.

"Capsule is turning around," he radioed. "Oh, that view is tremendous."

He was the professional test pilot, and at the same time a human being experiencing pure joy. The tone was full of enthusiasm.

On the first orbit, over the Canary Islands, Colonel Glenn reported that "the horizon is a brilliant blue."

One after another of the stations in the eighteen-station world-wide tracking net locked its radar on the Friendship 7, and established communications with the astronaut on board.

Colonel Glenn received a special greeting from the citizens of Perth, Australia, who turned on the lights all over town.

"Thank everybody for turning them on," he radioed. About there, he tried the first of the special foods prepared for consumption in orbit, where there is no gravity to let liquids pour or meats stay on a dish. He ate tubes of food and meat, and malted milk tablets.

An odd phenomenon occurred

View down Broadway of the ticker tape parade that greeted astronaut John Glenn Jr.'s motorcade in honor of his Mercury-Atlas 6 space mission, New York, March 1, 1962. (PhotoQuest/Getty Images)

when he was within range of Guaymas, Mexico. He reported "luminous particles around the capsule—just thousands of them—right at sunrise over the Pacific."

Maj. Gen. Leighton Davis, a Project Mercury officer here, suggested later that they might have been dust particles, or chips of paint from the capsule.

Moment of Decision

Then started the troubles with the attitude controls system—troubles that were to occupy the pilot the rest of the flight.

The moment of decision came near the end of the second orbit. Colonel Glenn was reporting continued erratic behavior of the controls, apparently even with the manual system—the al-

ternative to the one that originally malfunctioned.

He also was reporting a warning light indicating that hydrogen peroxide fuel for at least one of the systems was getting low.

To many experts listening to these events unfold, there seemed no alternative to bringing Colonel Glenn back at the end of the second orbit rather than risking another circuit.

But the astronaut thought he could handle the situation without excessive trouble.

Greatest Day in Space

Today's flight gave the United States, by any standards, its greatest day in space.

The achievement, however, could

still not be considered quite up to what the Russians had done.

Colonel Glenn's flight was two orbits more than were flown by Maj. Yuri A. Gagarin, the Soviet space man, last April 12 but fourteen less than another Russian, Maj. Gherman S. Titov, flew on Aug. 6.

In addition, there were some technical respects in which both Soviet orbital flights appeared to observers here to have an advantage: the size of the capsule orbited (five tons as against a ton and a half); the reliability of automatic controls; and the cabin atmosphere in which the pilot had to work.

But Colonel Glenn's trip was considered by most observers here to have gone a long way toward erasing this nation's "second-best" look in space.

Kennedy Confronts U.S. Steel

U.S. Steel Raises Price $6 A Ton; Kennedy Angered, Sees Affront; Two Investigations Are Ordered

WIDE EFFECT SEEN

Kefauver and Justice Department Plan to Press Studies

By RICHARD E. MOONEY

WASHINGTON, April 10—President Kennedy was infuriated by tonight's news that the United States Steel Corporation was raising its prices.

The word from White House intimates was that he regarded the move as an unjustified and deliberate affront to his Administration. There was some feeling here that tonight's unexpected development would have a profound effect on the President's attitude toward the business community and possibly on his economic policies in general.

There was no immediate on-the-record comment from the White House on the increase. However, a spokesman for the Department of Justice said:

"Because of past price behavior in the steel industry the Department of Justice will take an immediate and close look at the current situation and any future developments."

The reference to "past behavior" was to the usual development of the other steel companies following the price policy of United States Steel.

Kefauver Vows Inquiry

Senator Estes Kefauver, Democrat of Tennessee, promised an investigation by his subcommittee.

President Kennedy has deliberately leashed some of his liberal instincts in an attempt to create good working relations with business. In the particular case of steel he applied intense pressure on labor to limit its wage demands this year. The breach of the steel price line will embarrass him with his supporters in the labor movement.

The President himself and his principal lieutenants have been working hard for almost a year to get this key industry and its workers to exercise restraint on prices and wages. With last week's signing of a new steel labor contract that the President hailed as "non-inflationary," the Administration thought its mission accomplished.

Roger M. Blough, chairman of United States Steel, went to the White House this evening and told the President of the price increase, after it had been announced in Pittsburgh.

The President's temper flared, it is said. There was no official on-the-record comment from the White House or any other part of the Administration, but one high official, hearing the news from a reporter, responded with an invective.

President Kennedy will have an opportunity to comment publicly himself at his news conference tomorrow. Whether he will show his temper then or will have adopted the Harvard approach that he often uses in public, was not known tonight.

The Administration has staked so much on steel because it believes that that industry's prices and wages are a major factor in price-wage developments throughout the economy. Directly, they contribute to the cost of the great many things that are made of steel. Indirectly, they set an example for non-steel industries and labor to follow.

The Administration has been particularly anxious to preserve price stability in the economy in order that this country remain competitive with industry abroad. An added embarrassment in tonight's announcement was the presence in Washington this week of Prof. Walter Hallstein, president of the Administrative Commission of Europe's six-nation Common Market.

There had been some rumor within the Administration in recent days that one of the smaller steel companies was preparing to announce a price increase, but the announcement from "Big Steel"—as United States Steel is known—came as a total surprise. There had been, however, some indication in public statements by the industry that it was indeed thinking of higher prices.

United States Steel announced its increase as three-tenths of one cent per pound, and termed it "modest." However, in the tonnage terms that are commonly used, it amounted to $6 per ton, and halfway between the biggest and smallest of the ten post-World War II steel price increases.

The company did not blame last week's contract settlement for tonight's action. Rather, it seemed to justify the increase on the basis of cost developments during the last four years, when there has been no important increase at all. In other words, the company is catching up with the cost increases it has experienced while holding the price line.

The Administration, clearly, does

President Kennedy meets with his cabinet June 4, 1962. (George Tames/*The New York Times*)

not believe the price increase is justified, either by the new contract or by the last four years' developments. The Administration started last spring to put pressure on the industry to hold the price line despite a wage increase that was scheduled to take effect in October.

Industry did hold the line, presumably as a result of the public pressure from the Administration, combined with such other factors as foreign competition, slack business and the President's open promise to help the industry resist excessive new wage demands when the union contract came up for renewal this year.

Industry is Surprised

The United States Steel Corporation price increase caught virtually every major steel company by surprise last night. Meanwhile, Wall Street analysts expressed disbelief when informed of the increase and then questioned whether the economy could make the price rise stick.

William A. Stele, president of Wheeling Steel Company, the country's eleventh largest producer and one of the first reached, said that the rise was "long overdue." However, he said that the situation would require some study before he could say what his company might do.

This attitude was echoed by other major producers reached by telephone. But one said he had "about given up hope" that a price increase would become a reality, revealing a yearning that is known to be general in the industry.

T.F. Patton, president of Republic Steel Corporation, the third largest American producer, was more direct. He indicated that his company would be likely to follow the United States Steel price increase.

"Republic certainly needs a price increase," Mr. Patton said. "We will review the reported action of United States Steel immediately."

Mr. Patton said that his company, since its last price increase in 1958, "has incurred substantial cost increases which have resulted in a severe squeeze on its profits, despite the fact it has invested tens of millions of dollars in capital improvements and conducted vigorous cost-reduction programs."

He said: "By reason of these facts, Republic's earnings have not been sufficient to pay a reasonable return to its stockholders and to contribute adequately to the cost of financing its capital improvement program which is so essential in keeping its plants and properties modern and competitive."

Steel Companies Give In, Rescind Price Increases Under Pressure From Kennedy

KENNEDY IS VICTOR

Uses His Full Powers for 72 Hours to Subdue Industry

By RICHARD E. MOONEY

WASHINGTON, April 13—President Kennedy triumphed today over the titans of the steel industry.

Almost precisely seventy-two hours after the United States Steel Corporation's abrupt announcement of a price increase, the corporation backed down and rescinded the increase late this afternoon.

The action by United States Steel, the nation's largest steel producer, followed announcements by the Inland Steel Company and the Kaiser Steel Corporation that they would not increase their prices, and a statement by Bethlehem Steel Corporation, the nation's second largest producer, that it was canceling its rises.

By early evening seven of the eight companies that had raised their prices in the last three days had canceled them. The eighth, Wheeling Steel Corporation, said it would announce its decision tomorrow.

Many Forms of Pressure

For three days the great forces at the command of the President of the United States had been brought to bear on the steel industry.

Some of the effort was exerted in the open—the President's open denunciation of the companies, calculated to arouse public opinion against them; the opening of grand jury proceedings leading to possible antitrust action, and the threat to divert orders to companies that had not raised prices.

But privately as well, the President and his advisers were bringing every form of persuasion to bear on the industry, trying to hold back the companies that had not yet raised prices and induce the others to roll back the price increase.

Kennedy's Statement

President Kennedy was informed of the actions by United States Steel and Bethlehem off Norfolk, Va., where he was aboard a cruiser observing naval maneuvers. He issued this statement:

"The people of the United States are most gratified by the announcements of Bethlehem and United States Steel Company that their proposed price increases are being rescinded.

"In taking the action at this time, they are serving the public interest and their actions will assist our common objective of strengthening our country and our economy."

Even during this dramatic day, as the steel industry started to weaken, the Administration pressed on with the actions that the price increase had started.

Secretary of Defense Robert S. McNamara announced that defense business would be channeled, if possible, to companies that had not raised steel prices. Grand jury subpoenas were served on some of the companies that had raised their prices. And the Labor Department issued a new set of statistics designed to prove the Administration's case that the price increase was not warranted.

Tonight it was evident that President Kennedy had scored a great personal success such as few Presidents had experienced in their relations with American industry.

He had strengthened his position for dealing with the business community. He had retained stature in the eyes of labor leaders. He had aroused a resounding chorus of popular support that would do his party no harm in next fall's elections.

The conflict between Government and the leading steel companies was set off Tuesday when United States Steel announced that it would raise the price of steel about $6 a ton.

White House Incensed

This announcement, which was quickly followed by similar announcements from seven other big companies, was received almost as a declaration of war at the White House.

Only a few weeks previously, the companies and the steel union had negotiated a new contract, to take effect July 1. The Administration had kept the two sides under pressure to match an agreement that would not set off a new wage-price spiral, and it hailed the agreement, which contained no wage increase but only fringe-benefit improvements, as noninflationary.

President Kennedy was furious at the price increase, regarding it as a "double cross" of the Administration. Immediately he and the highest officials of the Administration set to work to counter the steel companies' move.

The objective of the Administration was to prevent the nation's third largest industry—its sales are exceeded only by those in autos and petroleum—from setting off an upward spiral of prices and wages.

The strategy was to divide and conquer. If two big companies could be persuaded to hold the line, the rest would have to retreat.

The key target in the strategy was Inland Steel; eighth largest in the industry. A secondary target was Armco Steel Corporation, the sixth largest.

G.O.P. Denounces Kennedy Tactics In Steel Dispute

'Police State' Actions Used to Balk Price Rise, Chiefs in Congress Charge

NINE MOVES ARE CITED

Democratic Leaders Reply That Foes Are Silent on Issue of Increases

---

By RUSSELL BAKER

WASHINGTON, April 19—The Republican Congressional leadership charged today that President Kennedy, in dealing with the steel industry, had displayed "naked political power never seen before in this nation."

In his immediate reaction to United States Steel's $6-a-ton price rise, they charged the President had "directed or supported a series of governmental actions that imperiled basic American rights, went far beyond the law and were more characteristic of a police state than a free government."

Later the Democratic leadership of Congress issued a statement in response to the Republicans. This commended the President and chided the Republicans with being silent on the "central issue of price increases that would imperil the dollar and disadvantage our competitive position at home and abroad."

Leaders Sign It

It was issued by Mike Mansfield of Montana and Hubert H. Humphrey of Minnesota, the Senate Democratic leaders, and House Speaker John W. McCormick of Massachusetts and Representative Carl Albert of Oklahoma, the House majority leader.

Under White House pressure, the big steel companies that raised prices on April 10 and 11 rescinded their increases April 13. Many Democrats have hailed the success of the White House's tactics as a political triumph as well as a victory for the Administration's economic policy.

Until today the Republican party had avoided the issue, leaving it for individual members to take individual stands. Today's statement, issued under the imprimatur of the Joint Senate-House Republican Leadership, represented the stand of the men who direct the party in Congress.

The statement asserted that it was not a defense of the steel price increase. It concentrated on criticizing the President's tactics in forcing the companies to rescind the rise. It said:

"We, the members of the Joint Senate-House Republican Leadership, believe that a fundamental issue has been raised; should a President of the United States use the enormous powers of the Federal Government to blackjack any segment of our free society into line with his judgment without regard to law?"

The leaders cited nine events that, they said, were "punitive, heavy-handed and frightening" and that, taken cumulatively, constituted an unprecedented use of "naked political power."

Actions Listed

Following are the actions of which they complained:

1. The Federal Trade Commission publicly suggested the possibility of collusion, announced an immediate investigation and talked of $5,000-a day penalties.

2. The Justice Department spoke threateningly of antitrust violations and ordered an immediate investigation.

3. Treasury Department officials indicated they were at once reconsidering the planned increase in depreciation rates for steel.

4. The Internal Revenue Service was reported making a menacing move toward U. S. Steel's incentive benefits plan for its executives.

5. The Senate Antitrust and Monopoly subcommittee began subpoenaing records from twelve steel companies, returnable May 14.

6. The House Antitrust subcommittee announced an immediate investigation, with hearings opening May 2.

7. The Justice Department announced it was ordering a grand jury investigation.

8. The Department of Defense, seemingly ignoring laws requiring competitive bidding, publicly announced it was shifting steel purchases to companies that had not increased prices, and other Government agencies were directed to do likewise.

9. The F. B. I. began rousing newspapermen out of bed at 3:00 A. M. on Thursday, April 12, in line with President Kennedy's press conference assertion that 'we are investigating a statement attributed to a steel company official in the newspapers.

Regarding Point 3, the Treasury said that the department at no time considered taking retaliatory action involving depreciation allowances.

President Kennedy told his new conference April 11 that he had discussed this area with Secretary of the Treasury Douglas Dillon but the idea of taking action in the depreciation field had been rejected.

Regarding Point 4, the Internal Revenue Service said it never made "menacing moves" toward the benefits plan for United States Steel executives.

U.S. Resumes Nuclear Testing

U.S. OPENS A-TESTS IN AIR WITH BLAST OF MEDIUM YIELD; DAWN SHOT FIRED

Device is Dropped From a Plane Near Christmas Island

By JOHN W. FINNEY

WASHINGTON, April 25—The United States resumed nuclear testing in the atmosphere today by setting off an intermediate-size explosion near Christmas Island in the Pacific.

The explosion took place at about 10:45 A. M. (Eastern Standard Time), just as dawn was beginning to light the overcast skies above the equatorial atoll in the Central Pacific.

Rising through the overcast skies, the mushroom-shape cloud symbolized a new competitive phase in the atomic arms race and the frustration of more than three years of effort to reach an international agreement to prohibit atomic testing.

It was the first atmospheric explosion by the United States since Oct. 30, 1958, just before a voluntary moratorium went into effect. The moratorium came to an abrupt end last Sept. 1, when the Soviet Union resumed atmospheric testing, a step that led to today's action by the United States.

25 to 30 Tests Expected

The explosion today was the first in a series called Operation Dominic. The series is expected to consist of twenty-five to thirty explosions over the Pacific in the next two to three months.

In the first test, the nuclear device was dropped from a plane and deto-nated high over one of the coral atolls of the British-controlled island.

The explosion was described by the Atomic Energy Commission as in "the intermediate-yield range." This meant that its explosive force was more than twenty kilotons—the equivalent of the force of 20,000 tons of TNT—and less than one megaton, or 1,000,000 tons of TNT.

Christmas Island is just north of the Equator and 1,200 miles south of Hawaii.

Statement Is Terse

The test was announced in this terse, one-paragraph statement issued by the Atomic Energy Commission about three hours after the explosion:

"A nuclear test detonation took place at 10:45 A. M. E. S. T. today in the vicinity of Christmas Island. The detonation was in the intermediate-yield range. The device was dropped from an airplane. The test was the first detonation in Operation Dominic, now underway in the Pacific."

In line with its desire to hold to a minimum publicity about the experiments, the Administration supplied no statement explaining why the United States had resumed atmospheric testing. Rather, it rested its case on President Kennedy's speech March 2. In that speech, Mr. Kennedy declared that it would be militarily necessary to resume testing by the latter part of April if no agreement was reached by then on an effective test-ban treaty with international controls.

President Kennedy, who yesterday gave the order for the tests to resume, was informed of the initial explosion at about 1:20 P. M. He was cruising aboard the Presidential yacht Honey Fitz in Lake Worth near the vacation White House in Palm Beach, Fla.

The White House had said beforehand that there would be no statement from the President and that any announcement would come from the commission.

Notified by A.E.C. Head

Dr. Glenn T. Seaborg, commission chairman, called the president last night to notify him that the first test would be held today unless weather interfered. The Weather Bureau said that shortly before the test the weather had been cloudy with some showers and a northeast wind at ten miles an hour.

The commander of the task force for the tests is Maj. Gen. Alfred Dodd Starbird.

In Congress, the reaction was that the United States had no choice but to resume testing because of the significant advances made by the Soviet Union in some fifty explosions last fall.

A family-sized nuclear fallout shelter in McLean, Virginia. It combined two outer steel igloo shelters that could house up to six people and was recommended by the U.S. Office of Civil Defense. (Keystone/Getty Images)

"We have no choice in the matter," the Senate Democratic leader, Mike Mansfield, said. "The President has shown great forbearance. I fully concur in his decision."

The Senate Republican leader, Everett McKinley Dirksen, also supported the President's action. Noting that the Congressional Republican leadership had for the last year been urging a renewal of testing, he said. "We want it to be done and we applaud the decision."

At the same time, there were grumblings in Congress about the probably critical reaction of neutral countries.

Russell Decries Reaction

Richard B. Russell, chairman of the Senate Armed Services Committee, said such a reaction was "incomprehensible" because "their (the neutrals) safety and security is as much dependent upon our maintaining superiority in nuclear weapons as is our own."

Senator Kenneth B. Keating, Republican of New York, said, "The reaction to America's reluctant resumption of nuclear testing will provide one very interesting indication of who our friends really are in the world...and which one's just parrot Khrushchev's line."

Administration officials were braced for a wave of adverse reaction abroad, particularly in Africa and Europe. On the basis of some opinion polls in the last month, however, officials were hopeful that there would be some understanding of the United States' posi-

tion and that the reaction would not be so critical as when the Soviet Union resumed testing.

Senator Hubert H. Humphrey, the assistant Senate Democratic leader, touched on one problem that is causing considerable concern within the Administration. This is the fear that fallout from the last Soviet tests is likely to be attributed to the United States.

Soviet fall-out will reach a peak in the next two months, while the bulk of the fall-out from the American tests will not come down for another year, Senator Humphrey said. He predicted, "If world opinion reacts as it has in the past, we will get stuck with the blame for a double dose of radioactive fallout."

A. E. C. Cites Precautions

In an attempt to allay world fears about fall-out, the Atomic Energy Commission issued a supplementary statement reemphasizing that the United States tests "will be conducted under conditions which will restrict the radioactive fall-out to a minimum, far less than that from the Soviet Union's series of nuclear weapons tests in the fall of 1961."

Two principal measures are being taken to limit the amount of fall-out. One is to confine the tests to those deemed absolutely necessary. The other is to conduct the tests at relatively high altitudes, so that much of the radioactive debris goes into the stratosphere, where it will remain several years.

Depending upon the size and altitude of the explosions, some of the debris will remain in the troposphere—or lower atmosphere—and will be carried around the world by the prevailing winds. This debris will return to earth in a matter of months, probably in a 3,000 mile-wide band north of the Equator.

The commission statement said that the long-lived radioactive substances, such as strontium 90 and cesium 137, in fall-out this spring and summer "will be largely from the Soviet tests of 1961."

Debris to Be Short-Lived

The statement said that some short-lived radioactive debris, such as iodine 131, from the United States tests "will be detectable" shortly after the series. This material will come primarily from tropospheric fall-out, it said.

"However," the statement said, "since the nuclear yield [energy release] of the United States tests will be less than that of the Soviet 1961 tests, fall-out levels from the United States tests will be considerably lower."

The statement also said, as the President did in his speech March 2, that "the total [radiation] effects from the United States test series are expected to be roughly equal to only about 1 per cent of those due to natural radiation to which people always have been exposed."

This estimate, commission spokesmen said, was based on the average radiation a person would receive in his lifetime.

The commission did not rule out the possibility that there would be transient rises in fall-out, as there have been in past tests, in which the level of radioactivity would approach or exceed that received from natural radiation.

Energy Data Secret

The total energy expected to be released in the series was being kept secret by the Administration. However, officials indicated that the amount would be about one-half or one-third of that released in the Soviet tests last fall. The Soviet tests had a total force of about 120 megatons. Of this, some twenty-five megatons came from the fission process, which is primarily responsible for producing fall-out.

The American explosions are expected to range in yield from scores of kilotons to several megatons. None of the tests will approach in size the fifty-five-megaton explosion set off by the Soviet Union.

Highly placed officials said that the exact number of tests had not yet been fixed. The number will partly depend upon the results of the testing.

One purpose of the series will be to proof-test warheads and delivery vehicles that are entering the nation's atomic arsenal. For example, there will be a test firing of a Polaris missile from a submerged submarine as well as firings of warheads for such missiles as the Atlas, Titan and Minuteman.

Another objective will be to test new weapon designs and concepts.

The reference to a "nuclear device" in the test today might indicate that the explosion was a development shot rather than a proof test.

In the opinion of defense officials, the most important objective of the series will be to test the effects of nuclear explosions at high altitudes. Such explosions might be used to jam radar and radio communications or neutralize warheads of incoming missiles.

The explosions at altitudes of thirty miles or more will be set off primarily at Johnston Island, a small United States possession 900 miles southwest of Hawaii.

A rectangular danger area, 800 by 600 miles, has been declared around Christmas Island. Around Johnston Island, a danger zone resembling a cone has been declared, effective April 30. The circular zone has a radius of 470 nautical miles around the island at sea level and a radius of 700 nautical miles at 30,000 feet.

The Atomic Energy Commission issued today a regulation prohibiting United States citizens from the danger zones.

Airlines Get Briefing

Meanwhile, the Federal Aviation Agency said that United States and foreign airlines had been briefed in Honolulu today on effects that could be expected from the explosions at Johnston Island.

The agency said that communications and navigational aids in the high-frequency radio band were expected to be affected "through wide areas of the Pacific Ocean." It may become impossible for some aircraft to make scheduled position reports while flying, the agency said, and as a result "some interruptions" of airline schedules will be necessary.

The agency said, however, that "these detonations are expected to be few in number" and three or four days warning would be given before each detonation.

Submarine Fires Atomic Warhead In Pacific Tests

Polaris Missile Is Launched in Christmas Island Area—Force Not Disclosed

BLAST IS FIFTH IN SERIES

Device Is Nation's First to Be Carried Long Range— Details Are Lacking

By ROBERT F. WHITNEY

WASHINGTON, May 6—A nuclear warhead was exploded today after being carried aloft in a missile fired from the Polaris submarine Ethan Allen.

The explosion took place at 7:45 P. M., New York time, in the Christmas Island testing area of the Pacific. It was the fifth explosion in the current series of United States tests.

It was the first nuclear explosion by the United States of a warhead carried by a long-range missile. The announcement by the Atomic Energy Commission gave no details of the power of the warhead. However, it has been previously reported that a regular Polaris nuclear warhead has the explosive power of 500,000 tons of TNT.

Height of Blast Unknown

Nor were any details given by the commission spokesman of the altitude at which the warhead was detonated or the distance the missile traveled after being launched from the submarine.

The announcement did not explain either whether the missile was fired from a surfaced or a submerged vessel. The Polaris submarines can fire from either position.

The test undoubtedly was felt to be a major achievement by United States military authorities.

The Polaris submarines, with their capability of remaining unseen while they approach the range of enemy targets—the top range of the newer Polaris missiles is about 1,500 miles—are a main item in United States rocket armament.

Also, as Polaris submarines are nuclear-powered, their sailing range is very great. Thus they can remain at sea for long periods with their whereabouts a secret to enemy observers.

Can Remain Submerged

The atomic powered submarines can also sail long periods without surfacing and thus are not detectable by radar.

The United States now has six nuclear-powered Polaris submarines in operation. Thirty-five others are now either under construction or authorized.

Present Polaris missiles have a range of either 1,200 or 1,500 miles. Those that will be made for the newer submarines will be designed to go 2,500 nauti-

More than two years later, President Kennedy watched a Polaris missile launch from Cape Canaveral. (Bettmann/Corbis/Associated Press)

cal miles. A nautical mile is 1.15 land miles.

Some time during the current series the United States is also expected to test two types of Navy anti-submarine weapons. One of these is designed for use from destroyers and the other from submarines.

The four earlier tests at the Christmas Island testing area have been of devices dropped from planes. It is believed that the Polaris explosion and those to come of the anti-submarine devices will be the only tests of actual working weapons during the series.

About twenty-five explosions are expected to be set off in the current testing, which will last about two months. However, none are expected to approach the explosive power of the fifty-eight-megaton blast (68,000,000 tons of TNT) of the Soviet Union last fall in its series.

Included in the tests will be some high altitude explosions that will be carried out from another site—Johnston Island, also in the Pacific.

It is expected here that the United States' series will be followed by another group of tests by the Russians.

Polaris submarines will become important weapons for the North Atlantic Treaty Organization. Dispatches yesterday from the meeting of the NATO council at Athens said that the United States had committed five of the fully equipped vessels, when available, to the alliance.

The ships, although remaining part of the United States Navy, will be assigned and committed to NATO, Secretary of Defense Robert S. McNamara told the council. Control of warheads will remain with the President of the United States.

4th A-Blast Fired In New U.S. Series

Yield Is in Medium Range; Soviet Reported Ready for Massive Testing

By United Press International

WASHINGTON, May 4—The United States set off today the fourth nuclear explosion in its ten-day-old Pacific test series. The weapon was of "intermediate yield" and probably equaled the power of about 100,000 tons of TNT.

As in the previous tests, the device was dropped from an airplane and exploded in the atmosphere near British-controlled Christmas Island. It was the third Pacific shot with an explosive force of more than 20,000 tons of TNT but less than 1,000,000 tons.

The test was announced as Administration officials said evidence available to them indicated that the Soviet Union might begin a new series of massive tests within the next few days. They said all available intelligence showed that the new series was ready.

Apparently Warhead Tests

This could account for the relatively mild protests from Soviet officials against the United States tests. While some Communist publications have denounced the Pacific series in strong terms, official reaction from Moscow has been much calmer.

All the American tests to date appear to have involved attempts to pack more power into intercontinental missile warheads.

Last Wednesday the task force exploded a device believed equal to the power of one to five million tons of TNT. It could have been the actual warhead for the latest model ICBM's.

The three other shots have been in the range of 20,000 to 999,000 tons of TNT. The tests, known as Operation Dominic, started April 25.

The tests are expected to continue at the rate of several a week, when the weather permits, during the early summer months.

As for the expected Soviet series, American officials said evidence at hand indicated that the Russians were only waiting for what they considered the best time, from the weather and political standpoints.

Ban Proposals Weighed

Western sources in Geneva have suggested that the Soviet Union has been stalling the seventeen-nation disarmament conference because a new test series is imminent.

Officials declined to say how information on the Soviet preparations was obtained, but they said it was good.

Premier Khrushchev has said several times that the Soviet Union must hold another series of tests because the United States is testing. He has not given any specific idea as to when they would begin.

Government officials are discussing the wisdom of proposing an uninspected ban on atmospheric tests as soon as the current round of explosions ends.

Officials reported a ground swell of opinion that the United States should propose such a ban and rely on long-range detection to enforce it, since the Soviet Union has refused to allow on-site inspection.

United States scientists generally agree that present detection methods might not catch all atmospheric blasts. But the scientists and some political officials believe the risk would be small enough to warrant agreeing to a long-range inspection system.

Carpenter Orbits Earth Three Times Safely, But Overshoots The Landing Area By 250 Miles

ON OCEAN 3 HOURS

Capsule Picked Up—Nose of Craft Too High on Re-entry

By RICHARD WITKIN

CAPE CANAVERAL, Fla., May 24—M. Scott Carpenter became today the second American astronaut to orbit the earth.

His three-orbit trip ended, however, with a global audience suffering almost an hour's anxiety about his safe return.

It was three hours from the time his space capsule landed until he was plucked from a life raft by a rescue helicopter. And it was hours later before the capsule was picked up by the destroyer Pierce.

Tonight, on Grand Turk Island in the British West Indies, Commander Carpenter had an emotional reunion with two fellow astronauts, John H. Glenn, who made the first orbital flight, and Walter M. Schirra.

Carried Beyond Goal

Coming down from orbit, the 37-year-old Navy test pilot was carried 250 miles beyond the intended Caribbean landing point and the recovery ships waiting to pick him up.

The overshoot was said to have been caused by the fact that the nose of the Aurora VII capsule was pointed too high at the time the retro or braking rockets fired to slow its speed and bring it out of orbit.

Radio communication blacked out, as it was expected to, part way in the descent. But because the capsule was beyond its target point, voice communication did not resume, as it normally would, after a gap of four or five minutes.

Millions Await Word

Project Mercury officials had immediate indications from two seconds of radar reception as the capsule disappeared over the horizon, that it had survived the searing re-entry into the atmosphere, though the astronaut's fate was unknown.

The millions following the flight by television and radio did not even have this reed to lean on, since word of the radar reception was not relayed to them by Mercury officials.

It was only after thirty-five minutes of bleak silence following the initial blackout that the public had a reassuring word.

It was announced that an automatically transmitted signal had been picked up by a Navy search plane. But even this carried no clue, for the public or officials, as to whether the capsule's parachute had popped out properly and lowered Commander Carpenter safely.

It was not until about an hour after receipt of Lieutenant Commander Carpenter's last spoken message as he descended from space that the plane sighted the astronaut bobbing in the ocean in a bright orange life raft.

From Project Mercury's control center came this announcement by Lieut. Col. John A. Powers, project spokesman:

"An aircraft in the landing area has sighted the capsule and a life raft with a gentleman by the name of Carpenter riding in it."

It was a moment of profound relief for everyone from the astronaut's wife

The Mercury 7 astronauts: Front row (l to r), Walter M. Schirra Jr., Donald K. Slayton, John H. Glenn Jr., M. Scott Carpenter. Back row (l to r), Alan B. Shepard Jr., Virgil I. Grissom, and L. Gordon Cooper. (HO/AFP/Getty Images)

and four children to radio listeners at remote corners of the globe.

A few minutes later, three Air Force rescue men parachuted to the water. They fastened a large raft to the astronaut's small one and a flotation collar around the capsule to keep it from sinking.

At 4:38 P. M., a little less than eight hours after he had been rocketed into space, the astronaut was picked up by a twin-jet helicopter from the carrier Intrepid.

He Feels 'Fine'

He promptly dispatched a message: "I feel fine."

Thus ended a flight of high drama that produced more protracted anxiety for the world at large than the three-orbit flight of John H. Glenn Jr. Feb. 20 or the two short-range sub-orbital flights of Alan B. Shepard and Virgil I. Grissom.

It was a flight notable for an almost unbelievably smooth countdown and take-off; for nagging, though apparently not dangerous difficulties with space-suit cooling and the control-system's fuel; for new sightings of luminous particles; for concern whether the flight could continue for three orbits and, finally, for the agonizing search.

The flight drew the United States even with the Soviet Union in the number of manned orbital flights—two each. However, Maj. Gherman S. Titov of the Soviet Union has flown much the longest mission, a seventeen-orbit journey lasting about twenty-five hours.

Commander Carpenter was rocketed aloft atop an Atlas booster at 8:45 A. M., just forty-five minutes behind schedule. The delay was due purely to haze in the area.

He followed a trajectory that reached an apogee, or high point, of 167.4 miles and a perigee, or low point, of 99 miles.

The capsule came down at 1:41 P. M., having covered a distance of some 81,000 miles in about five hours.

It was at a news conference after the rescue that the 250-mile overshoot was attributed to the improper aim of the capsule at the time of retro rocket firing.

The flight had not completed half an orbit when it became apparent that the smooth sailing of the countdown and first minutes of the flight were definitely over.

The astronaut, approaching West Africa, reported that the attitude or position readings on his cockpit instruments did not quite agree with what he saw with his own eyes out the window.

But soon the astronaut had something else to worry about. His space suit began to heat up to excessive temperatures.

He had to cope with that problem for much of the flight. But it finally cleared up and became a secondary concern.

The attitude-control system turned up new aberrations early in the second orbit.

Commander Carpenter, communicating with the tracking station on the Canary Islands was told:

"We suggest you go to manual [control] at this point and conserve your auto [automatic] fuel, which are now pretty low at this point."

"'Roger, going to manual now," came the astronaut's reply. He is a man of few words, and proved it repeatedly throughout the flight.

A few moments later, he was told he would have to stay on the manual control system "for quite a spell now, or we will probably have to end [the flight after] this orbit."

"I will be sure and stay on manual," came the reply from the capsule, then overhead.

It was during the same sequences of messages that Commander Carpenter imparted the news that he could change the capsule's attitude slightly by simply moving his head and arms.

Path Is Fixed

In other words, he could make changes in the orientation about the three axes (nose up or down; nose side to side; or roll) just as did the control jets.

None of these changes—by jets or body—had any effect on the capsule's path through space. This was fixed by the speed and imparted by the Atlas booster. The capsule would follow a ballistic path, like a baseball released by a pitcher, until the retro rockets slowed it enough to bring it back to earth.

After the retro rockets had been fired and the capsule was over Texas, going into its steeper and steeper descent, the astronaut was advised to make the slightest possible attitude corrections in order to save fuel.

What Next?

Next came a message that held no reassurances. Fuel ran out on the manual system.

It was about this point that, as though in a bad script, the capsule ran into what is known as the "ionization blackout." This is a period—lasting a little more than four minutes on the Glenn flight—when radio messages cannot get through to or from the capsule because the atmosphere is heavily ionized by the shock of re-entry.

Observers waited tensely for the four-minute period to end, just as they had waited for word from Colonel Glenn that his heat shield had stayed in place.

But radio silence did not end when the capsule slipped below the ionization altitudes.

It was announced that the capsule was headed 200 miles beyond its target point. Could the silence from the capsule be explained by the fact that it had hurtled out of radio range of recovery ships? Or had the astronaut been incapacitated or killed in the final plunge to earth?

Actually, parachutes had deposited the capsule gently on the mild seas. And the lithe, 155-pound astronaut had wriggled out through the capsule's narrow neck, pulling his one-man life raft with him.

Stock Prices Dive In Sharpest Loss Since 1929 Break

$20,800,000,000 of Values Erased—1,212 Issues Drop, Only 74 Rise

---

VOLUME TOPS 9 MILLION

Turnover, the Fifth Biggest in History, Makes Ticker 141 Minutes Late

---

By BURTON CRANE

May 29—Shares on the New York Stock Exchange lost $20,800,000,000 of values yesterday in the widest one-day drop since 1929.

As trading mounted to 9,350,000 shares, reporting devices were swamped. It was not until 5:51 P. M.—141 minutes after the close of trading—that the final price limped across the ticker tape.

More issues—1,212—declined than had ever before done so in one day. Of the record total of 1,375 that were traded, only seventy-four rose.

Selling came from everywhere, predominantly from the issues with the most shares in the hands of the public. Thus, American Telephone slipped 11 points, General Motors 4 5/8, Standard Oil of New Jersey 5 points and du Pont 12 1/2 . But the individual trades were small because buyers were showing no eagerness. That is why the market was so late.

Market's Heaviest Days

The 9,350,000 shares traded made it the fifth greatest day for volume in the history of the New York Stock Exchange. The greatest was "Black Tuesday" Oct. 29, 1929—when 16,410,030 shares were traded. Second was Oct. 24, 1929, when 12,894,650 shares changed hands. Third was Oct. 30, 1929, when turnover was 10,727,320

shares. The fourth was the July 21, 1933 session, with 9,572,000 shares traded,

The only volume in recent years to approach yesterday's was the 7,716,650 shares traded on Sept. 26, 1955, the time of former President Eisenhower's heart attack.

There were 937 that sank to new lows for the year yesterday, while only five registered new highs.

Comment by Funston

Keith Funston, president of the New York Stock Exchange, said yesterday that the market drop "is not a calamity."

Interviewed in San Antonio, Tex., Mr. Funston said that people are selling to "protect profits they have already taken."

Western European stock markets, affected by last week's declines here, were sharply lower. Reports of margin calls there echoed here. Banks throughout the country were said to be forcing the sale of stocks deposited as collateral for "non-purpose" loans—that is, loans ostensibly made not for the purpose of carrying securities. Brokers were asking for cash from under-margined customers.

When a customer buys on margin he must pay a percentage of cash to his broker. The margin requirement on initial purchases is 70 per cent, as fixed by the Federal Reserve Board.

If a broker makes a margin call, the buyer of a security must restore his equity by putting up more money when the total value of the stock falls. Most brokerage houses make such demands when the investor's or trader's equity drops to about 30 per cent.

From Washington came word that

the Administration was not taking a gloomy view of the stock slump and that the day's setbacks should be interpreted as a return of the market to sanity.

The New York Times combined average of fifty stocks touched a low of 317.56—the bottom since Oct. 26, 1960—and closed at 319.34, down 17.87 points on the day and 47.17 on the month to date.

The rail average touched a low at 89.88—the bottom since Nov. 1, 1960—and closed at 90.57, off 4.53 points. The industrial average touched 545.25, its lowest level since Oct. 25, 1960, and closed at 548.11, off 31.21 points on the day.

The drop in The Times average was not as wide as that of 23.93 points on Sept. 26, 1955, which followed former President Eisenhower's heart attack. The loss, however, as measured by the Standard & Poor's Corporation index, which covers about 90 per cent of the market value of Big Board stocks, was greater. Standard & Poor's yesterday estimated that each point in its composite index accounted for $5,240,000,000 in paper values.

On Wall Street, brokers appeared sharply divided in their views of the market.

There were some optimists. One such analyst said, "This is the climax for which we have been waiting. There will be a tremendous rally Tuesday or Thursday."

There were the pessimists who brushed away thirty years of the semantics that have changed "slump" to "depression" to "recession" and revived the old word "panic."

"This is panic selling and we shall probably see more tomorrow," said one research partner. "We are in a full-fledged panic now," said a senior partner.

"One should buy at this point with the idea that, although he may take paper losses temporarily, he'll do well in the end and that if he doesn't buy here he may lose opportunities."

German Reds Kill Boy, 12, In Berlin

Shoot Youngster at Wall—Regime Fears Outbursts on Revolt Anniversary

Special to The New York Times

BERLIN, June 15—An East German border guard shot and killed a 12-year-old boy who was attempting to escape last Sunday, the West Berlin police reported today.

The report of the shooting came as a force of about 500 armed East German guards rushed work on new fortifications along the Berlin wall.

As the anniversary of the June 17, 1953, East German uprising approached, the Communists tightened security at the border. Apparently fearful of attempts at mass escapes, the East Germans erected more concrete shelters, dug trenches, made earthen breastworks and set up concrete posts for barbed wire.

The East German Government has protested to the United States, Britain and France against what it called the "provocative" plan of Chancellor Adenauer to visit West Berlin Sunday. The Chancellor is to attend ceremonies here marking the ninth anniversary of the East German uprising.

The latest victim of the East German guards was shot on a sports field in the East Berlin district of Treptow as he approached the border. The boy, identified as Wolfgang Gloede, was left lying on the field for an hour, then taken away to die.

The killing was reported by an East German policeman who fled to West Berlin last night. The boy's death raised to forty-one the number of persons killed in escape attempts.

West Berlin police officials likened the reinforced Communist wall to a "fortified national frontier." Firing slits in the new shelters permit the East German guards to shoot at fleeing East Germans without the danger of being hit by retaliating gunfire from West Berlin, the police said.

As tension rose on the border, 6,000 men of the United States garrison here went on a routine "readiness" exercise for four hours early this morning. Hundreds of jeeps, trucks and armored personnel carriers moved to strategic points in the city. Similar tests have been carried out before.

In another issue, the Soviet representative at the Four Power Air Safety Center here was understood to have protested flights by United States helicopters over East Berlin and East Germany.

An American spokesman declined to confirm the protest report. He said, however, that the United States would assert its right to operate flights freely over the Berlin area within a twenty-mile radius from the downtown Control Council building, in accordance with existing rules.

Sunday's anniversary marks a day on which East German workers fought Soviet tanks almost with their bare hands. On the evening of June 16, 1953, building employes in East Berlin struck against the Communists' control. The next morning a general strike flared into fighting. The Soviet force moved in and by 9 P. M. had crushed the revolt.

The Communists executed forty-two leaders; the number of workers killed in the streets was never fully reported.

A crowd of West Berliners gather at the Berlin Wall while an East German soldier patrols on the other side.
(Paul Schutzer/Time & Life Pictures/Getty Images)

Hydrogen Explosion Set Off
Underground in Nevada

By United Press International

NEVADA TEST SITE, July 6—The mightiest nuclear blast within the United States and the first known detonation of any hydrogen type of explosive in this country was set off underground today. It tore a great open-faced crater in the desert floor. The thermonuclear blast was the first in a concentrated series of atomic tests. It is scheduled to be followed tomorrow by the first atmospheric nuclear shots here in four years. Today's explosion created a crater about 300 feet deep and a third of a mile wide in rocky, sandy soil. A huge, dirty cloud also rose into the clear sky. The cloud—visible sixty-five miles to the southeast in Las Vegas—first had the shape of a stemless mushroom. Then it took the form of a stack of immense, inflated rubber tubes.

American scientists hailed today's test as an attempt to study peaceful utilization of nuclear force for a variety of purposes. The Atomic Energy Commission announced the explosion had a yield of 100 kilotons or more—equivalent to at least 100,000 tons of TNT. But the commission announced within two hours after the blast that 95 per cent of the radioactivity had been trapped in the ground, or brought back to earth by quickly falling debris.

The commission said the remainder of radioactive matter had fallen close to the test site.

Although the explosion at 10 A. M. Pacific daylight time (1 P. M. Eastern daylight time), came with a deep-throated rumble, witnesses on surrounding mountain tops said they had felt no concussion. However, the blast was recorded 300 miles away on seismographs of the California Institute of Technology at Pasadena, Calif., and the University of California at Berkeley.

A Flash of Light

A "flash of light" preceded the spray of dirt and rock that shot some 7,000 feet high, witnesses estimated. The Atomic Energy Commission placed the altitude of the cloud at 12,000 feet, although observers said it appeared twice that high.

Two low-yield atmospheric shots are scheduled for tomorrow. Both will be set off a few feet above ground. The commission said that one would be to allow the Defense Department "to conduct varied experiments to analyze the effects of nuclear explosions and the other will be a low-yield weapons effects test."

Test officials amplified preliminary reports on the outcome of today's explosion.

The Atomic Energy Commission disclosed that aerial surveys had confirmed that the diameter of the crater made by the blast was about 1,200 feet. The dust cloud moved almost due north from the test site, State Highway 25, which had been closed as a precaution by the Nevada State Police.

"To hold radiation to a minimum," the commission said, "ten people living at isolated ranches and a road maintenance station in the near vicinity of the test site to the north were moved temporarily to near-by communities."

They are expected to return in a day or so.

Highway Radiation

Tests made of radiation levels at Highway 25 were recorded at a maximum of eight-tenths of one roentgen an hour, well within a tolerance range, the commission said.

The thinning cloud was "losing identity as it dispersed," the commission said.

The shot, called Project Sedan, was fired 650 feet underground. It was another step in Project Plowshare, which is designed to determine whether atomic explosions can be used to dig harbors, canals and other excavations for peacetime uses.

The largest previous test here, on July 5, 1957, was a 74.3-kiloton shot suspended from a 1,500-foot high balloon. The last atmospheric detonation—also from a balloon—was a comparatively small one of 1.25 kilotons on Oct. 30, 1958. That was one day before this nation and other nuclear powers entered into a moratorium on nuclear tests.

Newsmen could not get on the test site for today's detonation. They viewed it from a hilltop a few miles away, at a radar installation.

After tomorrow's atmospheric shots, radiological monitoring will be conducted in a 300-mile surrounding area. The A. E. C. said that most of the fall-out was expected to come back down on the site. The commission sought to dispel undue concern over fall-out hazards.

Today's was the thirty-fifth in the current series of underground shots since the United States resumed nuclear testing on Sept. 15, 1961.

If weather conditions permit tomorrow's shots, they will be the first in the atmosphere at this test site since Oct. 31, 1958.

In its official release on today's shot, the Atomic Energy Commission said that after the explosion the "heavier components" fell back to earth immediately and trapped the bulk of radioactivity in the giant crater.

"Precautions were taken to fire only under weather conditions which would minimize offsite radiation exposure," the release said.

Careful studies will be made of the crater's measurements, shape and the pattern of earth thrown out by the explosion, the announcement said.

HYDROGEN BLAST FIRED 200 MILES
ABOVE THE PACIFIC

Night Sky Is Lighted From Hawaii to New Zealand by 2-Megaton U.S. Shot

SOVIET DENOUNCES TEST

Trial Believed Helpful in Weighing Effect on Radar and Missile Defenses

By JOHN W. FINNEY

WASHINGTON, July 9—The United States set off a thermonuclear explosion high over Johnston Island in the Pacific Ocean early today. It released a powerful flash of energy that lit up the night skies from Hawaii to New Zealand.

The explosion, the most powerful ever conducted on the fringes of outer space, produced probably the most spectacular, far-flung effects of any man-made event in history.

It was reliably reported to have had a force of "a couple of megatons." A megaton is equivalent to the force of 1,000,000 tons of TNT.

Although official announcements did not specify the altitude, it was understood that the blast took place at about 200 miles. That would place it in the upper layer of the ionosphere, the electrically charged region in the upper atmosphere.

The only official statement about the explosion was this terse announcement issued by Joint Task Force 8, which is conducting the Pacific test series in the atmosphere:

"A nuclear device carried aloft by a Thor booster was detonated at an altitude of hundreds of kilometers over Johnston Island at 11 P.M. tonight Hawaiian Standard Time. The detonation was in the megaton yield range. The test was part of Operation Dominic, now under way in the Pacific."

Under the tight secrecy policy laid down by the White House the Atomic Energy Commission and the Defense Department declined to elaborate on the announcement.

Night Turns to Day

In Hawaii, some 700 miles northeast of Johnston Island, people stood in awe as the overcast night sky was suddenly turned into day in a six-minute glare of light from the flash of the explosion.

At Auckland, New Zealand, 3,000 miles southwest of Johnston Island, an artificial aurora spread a luminous red band over the northern horizon, laced with quivering white shafts of light.

Radio communications across the Pacific were temporarily disrupted as the explosion upset the normal balance in the earth's ionosphere.

The explosion also set off political reverberations heard around the world. In Moscow, where the Communists were opening the World Congress on Disarmament and Peace, delegates denounced the explosion as a threat to peace. The Moscow radio set the theme by branding the explosion as a "crime" set off by "American atom-maniacs."

U. S. Makes No Reply

The United States made no attempt to answer the Communist denunciation. Rather it rested on a speech of March 2 in which President Kennedy announced that the United States had to conduct the high-altitude explosions to obtain information.

The purpose of the tests, the President explained, was to determine whether high-altitude, nuclear explosions might be useful in disrupting electronic warning systems or in defending against enemy missile attack.

In 1958 the United States set off two megaton explosions over Johnston Island, but they were at altitudes of fifty miles or less. In its test series last fall, the Soviet Union detonated a device at an altitude of more than 100 miles, but it was not believed to have reached the altitude or had the force of today's explosion.

In 1958 the United States also conducted three nuclear explosions at about a 300-mile altitude over the south Atlantic. But these Project Argus explosions were limited in force to a few kilotons, or thousands of tons of TNT.

Twice before, on June 3 and 19, Joint Task Force 8 had attempted to conduct high-altitude explosions, only to have them thwarted by malfunctions in the Air Force's Thor intermediate range ballistic missile.

For today's launching, the countdown was reported to have proceeded smoothly, and the device, after almost a fifteen minute ride upward, and then back towards earth, exploded on schedule. The preliminary reports were that the manifold experiments being conducted with the explosion had been successful.

Plans Subject to Change

The month-long delay in conducting the first high-altitude explosions, however, has become a matter of serious concern within the Administration. It may cause a change in plans for the test series in the Pacific.

Original plans had called for three and perhaps four explosions over Johnston Island. The question now arising is whether all these tests can be conducted within the two to three-month timetable set by the President for the series or whether it will be necessary to extend the deadline, which is near the end of July.

Highly placed officials said it was still undecided whether the United States would conduct all the planned high-altitude explosions. The matter, it was understood, is being carried up to the White House for a decision.

"The detonation was in the megaton yield range. The test was part of Operation Dominic . . ."

One of the planned tests is an explosion at less than 100 miles and another is a submegaton blast at about a 500-mile altitude.

The latter experiment has provoked an international scientific controversy. Some scientists have expressed fear that it could result in a long-term disruption of the Van Allen radiation belts.

Major Disruption Doubted

Because of the scientific objections, the Administration convened a panel of experts. They concluded that the explosion would produce only a transient, fairly minor perturbation in the radiation belts.

Today's explosion was so far beneath the Van Allen belts, which begin in that region at about 400 miles, that it was expected to have a negligible effect on the radiation zone.

Two satellites—the Injun and Traac,

carried piggyback into space in 1961 aboard Navy transit navigational satellites—will be in a position to measure any significant effects the explosion has upon the Van Allen belts. There is also a possibility that similar measurements can be made by some of the scientific satellites launched by the Soviet Union in recent months.

Today's experiment, along with the high-altitude explosions to follow, have two principal research objectives. Both are closely connected to the development of an anti-missile defense system.

One is to study the blast, heat and radiation effects of a nuclear explosion in the near vacuum of space. From this it will be possible to draw conclusions about whether a high-altitude nuclear explosion can destroy or neutralize an incoming ballistic missile warhead.

The other objective is to study the effects of high-altitude explosions in disrupting radio communications and jamming radar during an enemy attack.

Radio Signals Disrupted

High-altitude nuclear explosions can disrupt radio and radar signals by changing the electron density in the ionosphere.

The intense radiation from the explosion and its debris greatly increases the density of electrons in the ionosphere, particularly in the so-called D region, the lowest region in the ionosphere. The increased number of electrons tends to remove the energy from the radio signals, thus blacking out radio communications, and to reflect and bend the radar signals.

As was expected, the maximum disruptive effect for today's explosion was on the short-wave radio signals—in the high frequency band from 3 to 30 megacycles. These normally bounce between the D region and the Earth, thus traveling intercontinental distances.

The blackout effects, however, were apparently not so prolonged or severe as had been expected by officials. They had predicted that some trans-Pacific

short-wave radio communications would be disrupted for as long as sixteen to thirty hours after the explosion.

The Federal Aviation Agency reported that the explosion had "virtually no effects to speak of" on the high-frequency radio channels used by the airlines. There were "temporary outages," ranging from a few minutes to a half hour, on the circuits between Hawaii and Midway and Wake Island. Then, service was restored, the agency said.

The agency planned to ground flights in the Pacific Ocean area for several hours following the explosion. However, because the blackout was only transient, the agency said there had been no cancellations or any significant delays in commercial flights in the Pacific.

Widely Observed Test

The explosion was probably one of the most widely observed scientific experiments in history. To put foreign scientists on the alert, advance notice was sent out over the International World Day Service, established during the International Geophysical Year to warn scientists of events that should be observed.

Around the world, stations maintained by foreign scientists and those especially set up by the Defense Department made observations of the geomagnetic disturbances, radio noise and blackouts and artificial auroras caused by the explosion.

If the radio blackouts failed to live up to expectations, the auroral displays created by the explosion were far more spectacular than had been expected.

The artificial auroras were created by electrons from the explosion and its radioactive debris. These became trapped in the earth's magnetic field and spiraled at near the speed of light—186,000 miles a second—back and forth along the magnetic lines of force. As the electrons impinged upon the denser atmosphere, some gave off their energy, causing the displays similar to the northern lights.

VIETNAM VICTORY REMOTE DESPITE
U.S. AID TO DIEM

By HOMER BIGART

This article is by a correspondent of The Times *who has just ended a half-year assignment in South Vietnam.*

July 25—The United States, by massive and unqualified support of the regime of President Ngo Dinh Diem, has helped arrest the spread of Communist insurgency in South Vietnam. But victory is remote. The issue remains in doubt because the Vietnamese President seems incapable of winning the loyalty of his people.

From the strictly military point of view, the situation has improved. "We are now doing a little better than holding our own," was the cautious assessment made a few weeks ago by Maj. Gen. Charles J. Timmes, chief of the United States Army element of the Military Assistance and Advisory Group.

However, no decisive turn in the military struggle is expected this year. The combat effectiveness of the South Vietnamese has been temporarily weakened by robbing rifle companies of good officers and non-coms to provide cadres for two new divisions now being created.

These new divisions will increase the strength of the regular forces to more than 20,000 by the end of this year. In addition, the Civil Guard will be expanded to 72,000 and the Self-Defense Corps to 80,000.

Assuming that the Vietcong (Vietnamese Communist) guerrillas do not receive substantial outside aid, there would seem to be valid reason for optimism. For in 1963 the Republic of South Vietnam will put well equipped forces totaling more than 350,000 men against 25,000 guerrillas who have no artillery, no anti-aircraft guns, no air power, no trucks, no jeeps, no prime movers, and only basic infantry weapons.

Also by 1963 the Vietnamese armed forces should be adequately staffed with officers and noncoms and be somewhat better trained for fighting in jungles and swamps.

They will have more helicopters, armored personnel carriers and other gadgets to enhance mobility, more sentry dogs to sniff out guerrillas, more plastic boats for the delta region, more American advisers with fresh, new tactical doctrines.

Yet visions of ultimate victory are obscured by the image of a secretive, suspicious, dictatorial regime. American officers are frustrated and irritated by the constant whimsical meddling of the President and his brother, Ngo Dinh Nhu, in the military chain of command.

The President assumes direction of military operations. All major troop movements, all officer promotions, must have his approval. Acting on vague rumors of a coup, Ngo Dinh Nhu last February summoned elements of the Seventh Division to the outskirts of Saigon without notifying the Third Corps commander.

Failure to coordinate with area commanders has also marked the Presidential palace's use of general reserve troops. These have been dispatched on futile one-shot operations based on faulty intelligence and conducted with slipshod planning.

Tight Control Hampers Pursuit of Guerrillas

In situations demanding fast action or improvisation, the palace's tight control of the army has killed initiative. In June, guerrillas wiped out a convoy forty miles north of Saigon, killing two American officers. The only soldiers available for pursuit belonged to the general reserve.

Hours elapsed before Presidential consent could be obtained for the employment of these troops, and it was early evening when United States Marine helicopters put them down on the guerrillas' trail. The guerrillas got away easily despite their heavy booty in guns and ammunition.

This episode was a bitter revelation for Americans. The ambush took place on the outskirts of Bentre, a garrison town, and on a heavily traveled highway. Yet the guerrillas moved into position in daylight, prepared the ambuscade in full view of the road and waited for three hours for the convoy to appear. They must have been observed by scores of peasants. Yet no one informed the garrison in Bentre.

Could this have happened if peasants felt any real identification with the regime?

A family living at the scene said it was threatened with death if it informed. But the Vietcong probably would never have undertaken this action without full confidence that the peasants were with them, or at least indifferent.

There is no accurate gauge of sentiment in Vietnam. The press is rigidly controlled and there is no freedom of assembly. Even the election scheduled for this year was canceled when the rubber stamp National Assembly altered the Constitution to give itself another year of tenure.

In some areas the signs of disaffection are clear enough. Observers of sweeps by the Vietnamese army through the delta provinces are often struck by the phenomenon of deserted villages. As troops approach, all flee, except a few old men and children. No one offers information; no one hurries to put out flags. Most of the rural area is controlled by the Vietcong, whose agents will move back as soon as the troops have departed.

President Ngo Dinh Diem is well aware of the importance of securing the countryside. His brother has the vision of concentrating peasants into "strategic hamlets" ringed with mud walls, moats and barbed wire. The object is to isolate peasants from the Communists. Brother Ngo Dinh Nhu urged the creation of 8,000 hamlets by the end of this year.

But the American aid mission has advised the regime to come up with a less-expensive plan. While appalled by the dreary regimentation of life in these fortified villages, most Americans are convinced that the strategic hamlet is part of the answer to the pacification problem. They hope to persuade the President that forced labor on hamlet defenses is not the way to win the affection of the peasants.

There was urgency for action, for thousands of "montagnards," the primitive tribesmen of the central plateau, were streaming into the garrison towns. Some were fed up with Vietcong demands for food and services; others were lured by reports of medical attention and other amenities offered by the United States Special Forces. The Americans saw an opportune moment to win over tribesmen who had been ignored for years by the regime.

But the plan was coldly rejected by President Ngo Dinh Diem. He did not like the "political implications," an aide explained. The President evidently scented an American plot to undermine his control over local officials.

Rulers Are in No Mood To Relax Their Grip

Besides the President and brother Ngo Dinh Nhu, who has the title of "political adviser," there is Mme. Ngo Dinh Nhu, palace hostess and an influential member of the Assembly, whose "Family Bill," promulgated in 1959, prohibits divorce except under very unusual circumstances.

There are two other brothers, Ngo Dinh Can, who, like the President, is a bachelor, very strait-laced and aloof, and who runs the northern provinces from Hue, and Msgr. Ngo Dinh Thuc, Roman Catholic Archbishop of Hue.

All the Ngo family are Catholics. The population of South Vietnam is predominantly Buddhist.

At the time of the Taylor mission, American officials talked openly of "pressuring" the Saigon regime for administrative reforms that would oblige it to relinquish some power. This plan was hotly resented by Ngo Dinh Nhu. According to United States Embassy officials, he incited the controlled Saigon press to print bitterly anti-American tirades. The campaign was hushed after a protest by the United States Embassy.

But Washington decided it was risky to prod President Ngo Dinh Diem publicly. Efforts to obtain major political and social reforms were quietly dropped after a few major concessions had been obtained: higher pay, fringe benefits and merit promotions for the armed forces; creation of a National Economic Council, quite impotent, but useful as a forum; the establishment of provincial advisory councils and village councils and, at the top, the equivalent of a National Security Council.

These improvements failed to touch the main problem. The Vietnamese President, according to former intimates, has become more aloof, trusting only his family, refusing to delegate authority. American officials find that even routine matters affecting the aid program must now be referred to Ngo Dinh Diem.

"It's virtually impossible to get anything done without the Ambassador running to the palace like an errand boy," one official said.

Meanwhile, a complete reassessment of the aid program is desperately needed, American officials say. Economic aid must be more closely related to the counter-insurgency effort, they explain, and the Saigon regime must pump an increased flow of piasters into the countryside to pay local costs of the strategic hamlet program.

This tightening of aid policies by Washington should give Ambassador Frederick E. Nolting Jr., a little leverage in his bargaining with the Presidential Palace. The Ambassador has not enjoyed much leverage.

In the last fifteen months, a parade of VIP's, starting with Vice President Lyndon Johnson and ending with the recent visit by Secretary of Defense Robert McNamara, regaled President Ngo Dinh Diem with promises of "all the help you need." Hearing his leadership lauded as an "irreplaceable asset," the President presumably assumed he could reject any proposals he disliked and still get all the money and military equipment he wanted from his friends in Washington.

Americans Want Diem To Offer Amnesty

Now Ambassador Nolting may be able to force action on a number of issues the Americans regard as crucial. These include a determination, long overdue, of priorities for programs such as strategic hamlets and population identification—the photographing and fingerprinting of every Vietnamese who can be caught. Perhaps the Ambassador can also revive the plan, rejected by Ngo Dinh Diem, for a rapid, uninterrupted flow of piasters to the provinces.

Finally the Americans want the President to promulgate as soon as possible a general amnesty offer. They believe the Government's psychological warfare campaign will be more effective once guerrillas learn they stand a chance of pardon if they defect to the Government forces.

Americans hope that the amnesty offer will be launched with the fullest publicity, including a radio broadcast by President Ngo Dinh Diem stating the Government's policy on how the Vietcong are going to be treated, re-educated and integrated.

Apart from the purely propaganda

advantage, the national amnesty would inject a note of humanity in a struggle that has shocked American military observers with its senseless brutality. American advisers have seen Vietcong prisoners summarily shot. They have encountered the charred bodies of women and children in villages destroyed by napalm bombs.

This month a Defense Department spokesman in Washington said casualties were running at the rate of five Communists to every three for the South Vietnam Government forces. But casualty figures in South Vietnam are highly suspect, for they are often based on the estimates of air observers.

Guerillas Rarely Seen Wearing Uniforms

Moreover, one rarely sees a uniformed Vietcong guerrilla; generally the Communist rebels are indistinguishable from peasants. Thus, many of the "enemy" dead reported by the South Vietnam Government were ordinary peasants shot down because they had fled from villages as the troops entered. Some may have been Vietcong sympathizers, but others were running away because they did not want to be rounded up for military conscription or forced labor.

The presence of American observers has had an inhibiting effect on shooting. United States helicopters are now being used to evacuate prisoners to interrogation centers in the rear, where the prisoners are at least safe from the threat of execution. Later, at prison camps called "re-education centers," the prisoners are indoctrinated in "the rights and responsibilities of citizens," lectured on Vietcong crimes and told of the achievements of the Government.

Inadequate screening and identification has sometimes resulted in the unfortunate mixing of hard-core Vietcong and non-political prisoners. But the process is now being improved under the direction of Frank Walton, former deputy chief of the Los Angeles Police Department, now head of the Public Safety division of the United States aid mission.

Mr. Walton is sending Vietnamese to the United States to study prison administration. As for conditions at the forty-three "re-education centers," Walton says: "I've seen considerably worse prisons in the Southern United States." Some of the centers were well run, others overcrowded, he said. There was no follow-up rehabilitation, hence no insurance that the former Vietcong would not defect again after their release.

In the fighting areas, American advisers fresh from training camps in the United States are astonished to find that, despite all the talk back home about unconventional warfare, the tactics here remain quite orthodox.

The president meeting with Soviet minister Andrei Gromyko in March 1962. Tensions would soon rise over nuclear testing and Southeast Asia. (The New York Times)

Government forces attempt large-scale operations that seldom flush more than a handful of Vietcong. Americans have been preaching the necessity of sustained operations. But Vietnamese commanders persist in one-shot maneuvers.

"A one-shot deal is like pushing quicksilver," one adviser commented. "Communists disperse only to fill up the vacuum as soon as the troops leave."

Helicopters have made an important contribution to the tactical mobility of Government forces. They have enabled Government units to strike at former "safe havens" of the Vietcong deep in jungles and swamps, then return quickly to their posts to be available for other missions."

"Helicopters permit us to do in one day or two days what used to take two weeks," observed Col. Frank B. Clay, until recently American adviser to the Vietnamese Seventh Division.

Armored amphibious troop carriers were introduced in June. They were supposed to solve the problem of pursuit over rice paddies and swamps. It was evident that these vehicles cannot be used without careful reconnaissance of the terrain. They are easily balked by steep-banked canals and rivers. On one operation a whole company of vehicles was mired for hours.

On the political front Americans are less inventive. Washington insists there is no alternative to President Ngo Dinh Diem. United States official policy is tied to the status quo. This policy is doomed in the long run, some feel, because the Vietnamese President cannot give his country the inspired leadership needed to defeat the Vietcong.

In the last seven years, the United States has spent well over $2,000,000,000 to prevent a Communist take-over in South Vietnam. Holding the line in Southeast Asia was a major premise of the strategy for containing communism formulated by John Foster Dulles, President Eisenhower's Secretary of State, who felt the whole of Southeast Asia would go down the drain unless South Vietnam were saved.

U. S. Has Been Involved Since Indochina War

The United States has been deeply involved in South Vietnam ever since 1954 when, after the defeat of the French in the Indochina War, Vietnam was partitioned. The Communists took over North Vietnam. With American support, Ngo Dinh Diem, a strongly anti-Communist aristocrat, rose to power in the South.

Few Americans in Saigon during the first chaotic years of President Ngo Dinh Diem's leadership had much confidence in his ability to survive. In 1955, President Eisenhower's special representative in South Vietnam, Gen. J. Lawton Collins, recommended that the United States withhold support from the aloof and obstinate Vietnamese leader.

But General Collins' recommendation was countered by reports sent to Allen W. Dulles, then director of the Central Intelligence Agency, by Col. (now Brig. Gen.) Edward G. Lansdale, the chief United States intelligence agent in Saigon. Colonel Lansdale saw no alternative to Ngo Dinh Diem. Allen Dulles persuaded his brother, the Secretary of State, that Colonel Lansdale was right and General Collins was wrong.

Those who recall conditions in Saigon at the time may now agree that Colonel Lansdale was right. Ngo Dinh Diem's rivals were either notoriously corrupt, or tagged as collaborators in the former French colonial regime, or lacking in popular appeal. Ngo Dinh Diem had some following among the Catholic refugees from North Vietnam, and these were at least reliably anti-Communist.

The little President has shown a remarkable talent for coups and assassination attempts. He got rid of Emperor Bao Dai, established control over the army, won a small war against gangster elements of the Saigon police, eliminated the private armies of two powerful religious sects, the Cao Dai and Hoa Hao, and resettled a million refugees from the north.

In the relatively quiet years between 1955 and 1958, when the Communist insurrection supported by North Vietnam began, South Vietnam made some modest economic progress. Saigon looked relatively prosperous. But United States economic aid was slow to reach the villages. And Dinh Diem did little to generate enthusiasm for his regime.

By last year the Communists controlled most of the countryside. The Vietnamese President was forced to ask for greatly increased military aid. President Kennedy responded by rushing thousands of United States military personnel to South Vietnam to serve as advisers and instructors. A United States Military Assistance Command was established under Gen. Paul Donald Harkins.

Should the situation disintegrate further, Washington may face the alternative of ditching Ngo Dinh Diem for a military junta or sending combat troops to bolster the regime.

No one who has seen conditions of combat in South Vietnam would expect conventionally trained United States forces to fight any better against Communist guerrillas than did the French in their seven years of costly and futile warfare. For, despite all the training here of men for jungle fighting, of creating guerrillas who can exist in forests and swamps and hunt down the Vietcong, Americans may simply lack the endurance—and the motivation—to meet the unbelievably tough demands of jungle fighting.

German Reds Shoot Fleeing Youth, Let Him Die at Wall

By HARRY GILROY

BERLIN, Aug. 17—East German border guards shot down a young man fleeing to West Berlin today and allowed him to lie dying for an hour at the foot of the Communists wall dividing the city. A fellow refugee hurled himself over the barrier to safety. A crowd of West Berliners gathered at the wall shouting "Murderers!" at the East German guards. The guards then hurled tear-gas grenades at the crowd. The West Berlin police said the two fleeing men, both 18 years old, ran for the wall at 2:10 P.M. at a point where the Markgrafenstrasse runs into the barrier at the Zimmerstrasse.

This is two blocks east of the cross-ing point where foreigners are checked into and out of East Berlin.

The first the West Berlin police knew of the incident was when one of the young men was seen leaping over the wall while machine-gun fire broke out from two points.

The refugee who got across was cut by the barbed wire at the top of the six-foot barrier but was otherwise unhurt. His identity was not revealed.

From observation points the West Berlin police saw the second young man clinging to the wall. Then another shot struck him in the back and he fell.

He cried for help, but the West Berlin police could only throw bandages to him.

The rescue of the wounded man would have been possible only if the Communist guards had been fired on by the West Berlin police. But the police are under orders not to fire at the East German guards unless shots come into West Berlin and that did not happen.

The East German guards watched from two concrete blockhouses with their guns directed toward the dying man.

It was 3:40 P.M. before a group of the guards hurried through the barbed wire and took the limp figure back into East Berlin. He was apparently dead.

At Gera in East Germany a court sentenced a 20-year-old youth to death on the charge that he murdered a taxi driver Oct. 21, 1961, in order to take his vehicle and attempt to escape to West Germany. The young man was also accused of having been a spy for the United States.

Venus Probe Is Believed Succeeding

Craft on Its Course Despite a 'Wobble' in the Launching

By GLADWIN HILL

PASADENA, Calif., Aug. 27—Early fears that Mariner II might be woefully off course were dispelled today as the 447-pound spacecraft hurtled at 8,000 miles an hour toward the planet Venus.

The California Institute of Technology's Jet Propulsion Laboratory announced that a deviation reported in the spacecraft's direction after its launching could be easily corrected by radio impulses early in its flight.

Mariner II was launched from Cape Canaveral, Fla., at 2:53 A.M. Eastern daylight time, on a projected fifteen-week journey toward Venus, the earth's mysterious neighboring planet.

An early tentative computation estimated that the twelve-foot-high spacecraft was headed some 600,000 miles off from the planned point of intersection with Venus' orbit.

Later calculations, however, reduced the digression to about 250,000 miles—a tiny distance in terms of the vehicle's 180,200,000-mile trip.

A correction so that the Mariner would pass the planet close to the planned distance of 10,000 miles was said to be well within the capabilities of the craft's radio-activated rocket steering-motor.

The deviation was attributed to "normal dispersions" [aberration] in the launching rockets of the Mariner.

The launching was a pioneering step in a national program envisioning manned expeditions to Venus and also to Mars.

The program is a project of the National Aeronautics and Space Administration. The Cal Tech laboratory is the contract manager of the current phase of the program, and the post-launch control center on the Mariner flight. Robert J. Parks is director of the laboratory's "planetary program."

Venus was 68,500,000 miles from the earth today. If all goes well, the Mariner will travel on a long, curving, "overtaking" course of 180,200,000 miles, reaching Venus's vicinity in about 109 days, the second week in December.

All the $10,000,000 vehicle's complex navigation and communications equipment was reported working perfectly.

In the only previously known dispatch of a spacecraft toward Venus, undertaken by the Soviet Union in 1961, radio contact with the device was lost after eighteen days.

The United States' first effort of the sort, with the identical Mariner I, last July 21, failed when an erroneous guidance signal sent the launching rocket off course.

Correction Possible

Correction of the Mariner's deviation from the planned path mid-course, the Cal Tech laboratory said, could be effected by adding only 80 miles an hour to its velocity—well within the "mid-course motor's" capability of 120-mile-an-hour acceleration.

This impulse will be transmitted from the laboratory's Goldstone tracking station in the Mojave Desert near Barstow, 150 miles east of here, five days or more hence, depending on calculations yet to be made.

Scientists must wait until the spacecraft's position-sensing equipment is oriented to the sun rather than to the earth.

A fifty-pound "payload" of instruments aboard the Mariner, which looks rather like a big flying weathervane, is intended to transmit back observations in six scientific experiments.

Four of them involve spatial conditions encountered on the flight and two close-in observations of Venus itself. The close-in observations could not be made from a distance of more than 35,000 miles.

At the time of the projected close observations, Venus will be about 36,000,000 miles from the Earth. Venus revolves in an orbit some 67,000,000 miles from the sun, against the earth's distance of 93,000,000 miles.

On Nov. 17, Venus will be at its biennial closest point to the earth, a distance of only 26,000,000 miles. The "encounter" between the Mariner and Venus is set for some three weeks later to avoid interference by the sun in the desired observations. The "fly-by" plan is calculated to yield a longer span of data transmission than simply crashing the instrument package on the planet would produce.

Venus is about the same size as the earth, but little is known about its surface environment. Telescopic observations have indicated that it has carbon dioxide and nitrogen, but little of the oxygen and water necessary to support life like that on earth. Calculations of temperature close to its surface have ranged from 38 degrees below zero Fahrenheit to 615 degrees above.

The Mariner is carrying a microwave radiometer to determine the surface temperature of Venus and details of its atmosphere; an infrared radiometer to scrutinize its cloud structure; a device to measure magnetic fields; devices to measure electric particles in space and cosmic dust; and a solar plasma spectrometer to measure the intensity of low-energy protons emitted by the sun.

The launching was a pioneering step in a national program envisioning manned expeditions to Venus and also to Mars.

The spacecraft was built by the Cal Tech laboratory, with parts from the thirty-four subcontractors.

A collaborator in the charged-particle experiment is Dr. James A. Van Allen of the State University of Iowa, the foremost researcher on radiation belts near the earth. Other institutions concerned in the various experiments include Harvard University, the Massachusetts Institute of Technology, the University of California, and the University of Nevada.

At 3 P. M. today, twelve hours after the launching, the Mariner was estimated to be 113,294 miles from the earth.

It was lifted off the earth by a two-stage Atlas-Agena rocket combination.

The Atlas projected the load to an altitude of about 115 miles. Then an initial burst from the Agena projected it into a "parking orbit," in which it coasted to the best "escape" point, in terms of the earth's rotation, over the East Coast of Africa.

Here, about a half hour after launching, a second impulse from the Agena sent the craft to an "escape" speed of 25,551 miles an hour, in which it overcame the earth's gravitational attraction and took of into space.

Folded under a temporary hood in the nose of the launching rocket, the spacecraft measured five feet in diameter and 9 feet, 11 inches in length.

In "cruising" shape, with solar-power panels and instrument arms unfolded, it is 11 feet 11 inches high with a span of 16 feet 6 inches.

The spacecraft is being tracked by observation stations in Johannesburg, South Africa, and Woomera, Australia, as well as the Goldstone station near here. Each trains great "dish" antennas in turn on the spacecraft as the earth revolves. Signals from the craft received by the stations are funneled in over a round-the-world teleprinter circuit to computers in the laboratory here.

The big chart-paneled computer room, with clacking teleprinters and quietly spinning "electric brains," was a center of restrained jubilation today after weeks of successive disappointments.

A month of check-out work on Mariner II, after the near success of the Mariner I launching, ran into electrical malfunctions a week ago, causing a postponement. Again Saturday night the launching countdown got nearly to zero, only to run into another malfunction.

Throughout last night, suspense was high as computers closed in on the critical point of the degree of aberration in the spacecraft's course. Today, scientists and engineers, some bearded and most of them informally clad in sports shirts and slacks or shorts, moved about their duties with grins as the machines ground out encouraging numbers. With a few individuals, the joy reached the point of un-cosmic tears.

Moscow Agrees To Arm And Train Military In Cuba

Soviet Also Will Provide Economic and Industrial Aid Under New Pact

GUEVARA WINS ACCORD

Action Is Termed Response to Threats by 'Imperialists' Against Castro Regime

By SEYMOUR TOPPING

MOSCOW, Sept. 2—The Soviet Union announced tonight that it had agreed to supply arms to Cuba and to provide technical specialists to train Cuban forces.

Moscow said the agreement with the Cuban Government was made in response to Havana's request for aid to meet the "threats" of "aggressive imperialist quarters." This policy will be continued as long as the threat stands, the announcement said.

The United States was not cited by name, but the announcement made it clear that the Soviet Government was using the quarrel between Washington and Havana as justification for strengthening the Castro regime.

The Soviet statement was contained in a communiqué here on the talks conducted by Maj. Ernesto Guevara, Cuban Minister of Industry, with Premier Khrushchev and other Soviet leaders.

New Mill to Be Built

The communiqué did not disclose the quantity or type of armaments to be supplied to Cuba, nor did it say how many military instructors would be sent.

On other matters, the communiqué said that Moscow had agreed to help Cuba build an iron and steel mill, and to expand the capacity of three existing plants from 110,000 to 350,000 tons of steel annually.

Additional specialists in agriculture are to be sent to Cuba to help with irrigation projects, land reclamation and hydraulic engineering problems.

The statement was the most emphatic declaration of Soviet military involvement in the Caribbean since Premier Khrushchev on July 9, 1960, implied that Soviet rockets would defend Cuba against any armed invasion.

Remark Qualified

Khrushchev later qualified this remark as symbolic after there were signs in Moscow of public uneasiness at the extent of the commitment.

After the rebel landings in Cuba in April, 1961, Mr. Khrushchev warned President Kennedy that the Soviet Union would give Cuba all necessary assistance to beat back any armed attack.

The forces of Premier Fidel Castro crushed the rebels quickly, using military equipment from Soviet-bloc countries.

The Soviet public has not been told of the military aid already provided to Cuba. Several Cuban military missions have visited Moscow without announcement of the results of their negotiations.

This was the case with the earlier agreements but the Soviet public was informed tonight of the new military commitment to Cuba.

Western observers here viewed the announcement as an indication that Moscow now regards its strategic stake in Cuba to be worth the risks of a policy of open military aid.

Although the Soviet Union possesses long-range rocket power, it is believed to lack naval and air capabilities to protect a military supply line to Cuba, should the United States attempt to block such a route.

It was assumed here that the agreement signified an expansion of the Soviet military assistance program rather than a public ratification of an earlier understanding.

Threats to Cuba Cited

The communiqué said Major Guevara and Soviet leaders had exchanged views "in connection with the threats of aggressive imperialist quarters with regard to Cuba."

"In view of these threats," they said, "the Government of the Cuban Republic addressed the Soviet Government with a request for help by delivering armaments and sending technical specialists for training Cuban servicemen.

"The Soviet Government attentively considered this request of the Government of Cuba and agreement was reached on this question."

The Soviet-Cuban communiqué, with its omission of any reference to the United States, suggested to Western observers that Moscow was sensitive to the risks entailed in its new policy.

Public Preparation

The Soviet press apparently began to prepare public opinion for tonight's announcement immediately after Major Guevara met with Mr. Khrushchev Thursday at the Premier's vacation villa in the Crimea.

Prominent notice was also given to the shelling of Havana from the sea Aug. 24 by a group of Cuban exiles and to Havana's charges that the United States Government was involved in the attack.

While the Aug. 24 incident might be cited as a reason for the new aid agreement, it does not explain the reported increase since July of the number of Soviet shipments landed in Cuban ports.

Kennedy Pledges Any Steps To Bar Cuban Aggression

Says U.S. Would Protect Hemisphere From Threat Posed by Soviet Arms

CLOSE WATCH PROMISED

President Sees No Evidence of 'Significant' Increase in Castro's Military Power

By ARTHUR J. OLSEN

WASHINGTON, Sept. 4—President Kennedy said today that the United States would use "whatever means may be necessary" to prevent aggression by Cuba against any part of the Western Hemisphere.

In a statement issued after consultation with Congressional leaders, the President said that the military strength of the regime of Premier Fidel Castro had been bolstered by recent deliveries of Soviet equipment, including guided missiles.

However, there was no evidence of "significant offensive capability" in Cuban hands, President Kennedy said.

"Were it to be otherwise, the gravest issues would arise," he said.

"The Castro regime will not be allowed to export its aggressive purposes by force or the threat of force," he said. "It will be prevented by whatever means may be necessary from taking action against the Western Hemisphere."

Barrier to Communism

The President's statement thus announced a policy of close surveillance to insure that Communist influence in the hemisphere would be confined to Cuba. The phrase "whatever means may be necessary" indicated a determination to resist with force any aggressive actions by the Castro forces outside Cuba's territorial limits.

His statement, issued after an hour-long meeting with a bipartisan group of Congressional leaders, appeared to be intended to head off mounting Republican criticism of the Administration's go-slow response to the military build-up in Cuba.

It was also calculated to reassure the public that the United States would not allow the Castro Government to build up a serious threat to the security of the United States or of other American nations.

Republican leaders in Congress have indicated their intent to make Cuba an issue in the approaching election campaign. They have been sharply critical of the Administration, charging that it has failed to take counter-measures to stop the flow of Soviet military equipment and personnel to Cuba.

In his conference with Congressional leaders and in his statement, the President sought to make it clear that the Administration was watching developments closely in Cuba and was resolved not to let the Soviet-Cuban collaboration get out of hand.

"The Cuban question must be considered as a part of the world-wide challenge posed by Communist threats to peace," the President said. "It must be dealt with as a part of that larger issue as well as in the context of the special relationships which have long characterized the inter-American system."

Government sources said that the partners of the United States in the inter-American system might soon be asked to consider joint measures to contain the Cuban menace.

There was no doubt, they said, that inter-American consultations would soon take place. The undecided questions now are which organ of the O. A. S. to use and what concrete measures to propose.

President Kennedy's statement gave the most precise measure yet of the increase in Cuban military power brought about by Soviet deliveries in the last two months.

"Without doubt the Soviets have provided the Cuban Government with a number of anti-aircraft defense missiles with a slant range of twenty-five miles, which are similar to early models of our Nike," he said.

The early model of the Army's Nike rocket was designed to attach manned aircraft and short-range missiles with a non-nuclear warhead.

The President said several Soviet-made motor torpedo boats carrying ship-to-ship guided missiles with a fifteen-mile range were also in Cuban hands.

About 3,500 "Soviet military technicians" were known to be in Cuba or en route to the island, he said. The number was "consistent with assistance in setting up and learning to use this equipment," President Kennedy said.

The United States Naval Base at Guantanamo Bay in eastern Cuba has not been violated, the President said, nor is there evidence of "offensive ground-to-ground missiles" delivered to Cuba.

In its consideration of joint action through the inter-American system of collective security, the United States has several possible courses open to it.

It would be possible to ask the Inter-American Defense Board, a military body, to study the build-up in Cuba and recommend counter-action. A smaller group, the seven-nation Special Consultative Committee on Security, could also be set to work in similar fashion.

The council of the O.A.S., which sits in Washington, could be asked to consider joint measures to penalize Cuba for her military policy, including, perhaps, steps to stop further Soviet military deliveries.

Mississippi Rejects Integration

Mississippi Votes New Laws to Keep University White

By CLAUDE SITTON

JACKSON, Miss., Sept. 19—Gov. Ross R. Barnett, legislators and the state courts moved today to block the desegregation of the University of Mississippi.

The Barnett forces in the Legislature put through measures designed to thwart the orders of the Federal courts. A state court issued an injunction against implementing the desegregation rulings.

Meanwhile, attorneys for the Justice Department and the National Association for the Advancement of Colored People were preparing to go before Federal judges tomorrow in an effort to end the defiance.

Under directives from the Federal courts, James H. Meredith, 29-year-old Negro, is scheduled to enroll tomorrow at the university at Oxford, 170 miles north of here.

Authoritative sources here and in Washington said that Mr. Meredith, who served in the Air Force, would probably be driven to Oxford in the morning.

The Justice Department has said he will be accompanied by four unarmed deputy United States marshals.

Most of the state's moves have proved ineffectual when tried elsewhere in the South in attempts to halt desegregation. Nevertheless, many Mississippians seem convinced they will succeed.

The defiance was led by Governor Barnett, who has asserted that state officials should go to jail, if necessary, to prevent Mr. Meredith's admission. As a result, one of the most serious Federal-state conflicts in the South's racial troubles is threatened.

At the Governor's urging, the Legislature quickly shouted through two measures designed to prevent Mr. Meredith's enrollment or attendance at the school.

That action came after Mr. Barnett had added an amendment to his proclamation calling a special session to consider legislative reapportionment.

Governor Ross R. Barnett, who defied a federal court order to integrate the University of Mississippi. (Francis Miller/Time & Life Pictures/Getty Images)

The amendment enabled the lawmakers to take up the segregationist measures subsequently submitted by the Barnett forces.

Perjury Charge Foiled

One, effective on the Governor's signature, would bar from institutions of higher learning persons who have criminal records or criminal charges involving moral turpitude pending against them.

A perjury charge was filed here recently against Mr. Meredith. He was accused of having stated falsely that he resided in Hinds County (Jackson) when he registered to vote.

The United States Court of Appeals for the Fifth Circuit enjoined the prosecution of Mr. Meredith on the grounds that the charge was "frivolous" and had been filed to halt his admission to the university.

The bill provides a fine or a year's imprisonment, or both, for violators.

The second measure was a resolution to submit a constitutional amendment to the voters in November giving the Governor "sole and exclusive right, power and duty to determine the right of any person to registration" at an institution of higher learning.

The Senate passed the resolution unanimously in seven minutes. The House took only four minutes, but the vote was 130 to 3.

On the campus at Oxford the atmosphere was tense. Uniformed and plainclothes law officers—state, county and local—kept a close watch on the university and the surrounding area.

Fraternity members have received anonymous calls reporting the burning of crosses and effigies. Although several such incidents have taken place, The Mississippian, a student newspaper, contended that few students had been present.

"Students have almost overwhelmingly expressed a desire to continue their education without any interruption," the paper said.

Negro Rejected At Mississippi U.; U.S. Seeks Writs

---

3 Educators Face Contempt Action After Gov. Barnett Turns Away Applicant

---

By CLAUDE SITTON

Oxford, Miss., Sept. 20—Gov. Ross R. Barnett denied James H. Meredith, a 29-year-old Negro, admission to the University of Mississippi today. In so doing, the Governor defied orders of the Federal courts.

The Justice Department took steps immediately to obtain contempt of court citations against Dr. J. D. Williams, university chancellor; Dr. Robert B. Ellis, the registrar and Dean Arthur B. Lewis.

All three were named in Federal court desegregation orders directing the admission of Mr. Meredith to the all-white institution.

[In Meridian, Miss., Federal District Judge Sidney C. Mize ordered the three university officials to appear before him Friday and show cause why they should not be cited for contempt. He acted at the request of Justice Department lawyers.]

Critical Conflict

In rejecting the application of Mr. Meredith, an Air Force veteran, Mr. Barnett set the stage for one of the most critical conflicts between state and Federal authority yet seen in the South. The controversy poses grave problems of international significance for the Kennedy Administration.

Shortly before flying here from Jackson, the state capital, Governor Barnett persuaded the Board of Trustees of Institutions of Higher Learning to appoint him as special registrar to deal with the "registration or non-registration" of the Negro student.

The Governor, his aides and their supporters had waged a behind-the-scenes campaign for almost a week to force the 13 trustees to invest him with this authority.

One trustee, Tally Riddell of Quitman, suffered a heart seizure late last night as the board conferred in a conference room at the University of Mississippi Medical Center. His condition was reported to be not serious.

Governor Barnett, who has asserted his willingness to go to jail to prevent the desegregation of the university, confronted Mr. Meredith today in a dramatic, 20-minute meeting. It took place behind the curtained glass doors of the Mississippi Center for Continuation Studies on the campus.

Approximately 100 uniformed State Highway patrolmen and scores of sheriffs, deputies, plainclothesmen and policemen held back a crowd of 2,000 jeering students.

As the automobile carrying Mr. Meredith and Federal officials pulled away toward Memphis, the students swarmed across a grassy, tree-shaded mall in a futile attempt to stop them.

Mr. Meredith was accompanied by St. John Barrett, second assistant Attorney General in the Civil Rights division of the Justice Department; James McShane, chief United States marshal, and an unidentified deputy marshal.

Statement Is Brief

Following their departure, Governor Barnett emerged and told newsmen:

James Meredith walking to class accompanied by U.S. marshals. (Buyenlarge/Getty Images)

"The only statement I have to make is this: The application of James Meredith was refused."

During the meeting, the Federal officials served Dr. Ellis, the registrar, and Governor Barnett with copies of the injunctions directing Mr. Meredith's admission. They were issued by the Federal District Court and the United States Court of Appeals for the Fifth Circuit.

A law enforcement official who was present said Mr. Ellis had given way to Governor Barnett after reading the court order. Acting as a special registrar, the latter then denied the Negro student's application.

One of the Federal officials asked the Governor if he realized he was in contempt of court along with officials of the university and the trustees, according to the law enforcement officer.

The Governor was said to have replied by asking if the Federal official was telling him or whether this would be done by the court.

Officials found guilty of contempt are subject to heavy civil and criminal penalties and the possibility of a prison term limited only by the prisoner's willingness to purge himself by obeying the court.

There are no immediate indications as to the outcome of the dispute, which comes during the week of the 100th anniversary of the Emancipation Proclamation under which President Lincoln declared slaves in the Confederate States free.

Governor Barnett threw down the gauntlet of defiance in a television address a week ago tonight. He invoked the legally discredited doctrine of interposition.

By this act, he contended, he "interposed" the power of the state between the Federal Government and the university and thus nullified the desegregation order.

If the Governor's present strategy fails, his only apparent recourse is to close the university.

Mr. Barnett stepped into the situation today after attorneys for the Justice Department and N.A.A.C.P. Legal Defense and Educational Fund had blocked attempts by the Legislature, state courts and officials to halt Mr. Meredith's admission.

Only this morning, Homer Edge-worth, a Justice of the Peace in Jackson, found Mr. Meredith guilty of a charge of falsifying a voter-registration application. The student, who remained at the home of a Negro lawyer in Memphis until he was driven here, was not present for the proceedings.

Mr. Edgeworth sentenced the student to a year in jail and fined him $500.

Justice Department attorneys went before Federal District Judge Harold Cox and Sidney Mize at Meridian, Miss., and obtained an order striking down the conviction.

It was a clear, sparkling day in the high seventies here in Oxford, the home of the late William Faulkner. The novelist lies buried on a hill across town from the oak-shaded university campus.

Students gathered early this morning on the grassy mall in front of the Lyceum Building, where the Negro student was expected to pick up registration and fee cards.

At one point more than 500 students swarmed rowdily to the center of the mall and pulled the American flag halfway down its pole before student leaders stopped them.

Two coeds danced the twist with two youths on the asphalt drive before the Lyceum. Students responded to this performance with boos and cries of "Mickey Mouse."

Governor Barnett landed at the nearby Oxford Airport at 2:45 P. M., accompanied by Lieut. Gov. Paul B. Johnson. They were flown up from Jackson in a highway patrol plane.

Both officials went immediately to the Study Center, a one-story modernistic building of red brick on the edge of the campus.

Exactly at 4 P. M. a caravan of highway patrol cruisers began rolling across the railroad bridge that separates town and campus. Seventy-five husky troopers in Confederate gray and armed with revolvers cleared the lawn in front of the center and took up positions along the drive.

Students began to stream across the park in front of the building from the Lyceum Building and several climbed trees to get a better view.

The Meredith party, riding in a green and white sedan escorted by an automobile driven by deputy United States Marshals pulled up at 4:30 P. M.

A chorus of boos went up and one student shouted:

"Go home, nigger."

Mr. Meredith, dressed in a brown suit and white shirt, got out of the car and looked at the crowd. Then turning, with a furrowed brow, he walked with his escort into the building.

There was little tension among the students, who apparently believed that this was only an assault—not a breach—in the university's racial barrier.

Fifteen minutes later, the crowd set up a football chant:

"Hoddy toddy, gosh almighty, who in the hell are we. Hey, eh, flim flam, him bam, Ole Miss by damn."

This was followed by yells of "We want Ross!"

Federal officials, led by Mr. Barnett, walked out of the doorway at 4:51 P. M. Mr. Meredith followed them with a tightlipped smile on his face. They got into the car and drove away.

University of Mississippi students yell and scream insults as James Meredith was to arrive at the campus. (Rolls Press/Popperfoto/Getty Images)

BARNETT AIDE, IN SCUFFLES, BARS NEGRO FROM U. OF MISSISSIPPI; GOVERNOR REJECTS COURT NOTICE

U.S. DEFIED 3D TIME

Marshal Pushed Back During Attempt to Enroll Student

By CLAUDE SITTON

OXFORD, Miss., Sept. 26—Chief United States Marshal James P. McShane and Lieut. Gov. Paul B. Johnson scuffled repeatedly today near the main entrance to the University of Mississippi as state officials again prevented the registration of James H. Meredith, a Negro.

The incident came as the marshal sought to shoulder his way through 20 unarmed but resisting highway patrolmen to enroll Mr. Meredith.

It marked the third time that Gov. Ross R. Barnett and aides had flouted the desegregation orders of the Federal District Court, Court of Appeals for the Fifth Circuit and the Supreme Court.

[In Washington, Attorney General Robert F. Kennedy reiterated that the Federal Government was determined to execute Federal appeals court orders in Mississippi. He said that "the question of Federal troops is the same as it has been," adding: "We'll use whatever is necessary."]

The Governor, who had been cited twice for contempt of court, first denied Mr. Meredith admission last Thursday after having had himself appointed as a special registrar.

Blocked Way to Office

Yesterday, he blocked an office doorway at Jackson, the capital, and thus prevented the student and Federal officials from reaching Robert B. Ellis, the official university registrar.

Mr. Barnett, who has said he would go to jail to keep the university segregated, apparently had intended personally to turn the student away this morning. But low clouds forced him to cancel plans to fly here from Jackson. He arrived in his blue Cadillac 20 minutes after Mr. Meredith had left.

The 29-year-old student seemed undismayed as he climbed into a Border Patrol plane with Mr. McShane and John Doar, first assistant in the Justice Department's Civil Rights Division.

"At least, I'm getting in a lot of flying time," the Air Force veteran said.

The three were flown to Memphis to await the Kennedy Administration's next move in its efforts to resolve one of the most serious Federal-state conflicts ever faced by the nation.

> *"We have told you, you can't go in and we intend to use whatever force is necessary . . ."*

Despite Mr. Meredith's show of confidence, he and those who have assisted him were reported tonight to have become increasingly concerned for his safety. They were said to be reluctant to risk a trip here with only a handful of Federal officers to protect him.

Their concern likely will force cancellation of plans to make a fourth attempt tomorrow to enroll him at the university.

Governor Barnett has been ordered to appear Friday before the Appeals Court in New Orleans to answer contempt citations obtained by the Justice Department and the N. A. A. C. P. Legal Defense and Educational Fund.

Thus, no major step to put an end to the defiance of the courts decrees is expected until after that hearing.

It was reported today that Federal officials were prepared to use troops to force compliance if no other solution could be found. Many in this town of 6,400 persons in the hills of north-central Mississippi have expressed the belief that only military forces could accomplish the task.

Attorney General Robert F. Kennedy informed Governor Barnett yesterday by telephone that Mr. Meredith would seek to register this morning and begin classes.

Apparently at the Governor's order, highway patrolmen remained on duty throughout the night at entrances to the campus to bar the student's way should he appear.

The two-tone green Cessna carrying the Meredith party dropped out of the rolling gray clouds that hovered only 600 feet above the University-Oxford Airport at 10:20 A. M. Eastern standard time.

Confer With Patrolmen

Mr. McShane and Mr. Doar conferred briefly with state Highway Patrol officials, who confirmed that they would provide an escort to the campus. Fifteen minutes later Mr. Meredith entered a green sedan with Louisiana license plates.

The convoy was stopped at South Fifth Street and University Avenue, a block and a half from the main campus entrance by the 20 troopers under the command of Dave Gayden, chief of the Highway Patrol.

Fifteen or more sheriffs from surrounding counties formed a rank 100 feet behind the patrolmen and three patrol cars were parked across University Avenue to block the campus entrance.

Lieutenant Governor Johnson moved into the front rank of the troopers as the chief marshal and Mr. Doar, followed by Mr. Meredith, got out of the car.

Mr. McShane asked who was in charge and the Lieutenant introduced himself. "We want to take Mr. Meredith in under the direction of the Federal Court and have him registered," said the marshal.

"I'm going to have to refuse Mr. Meredith," replied the Lieutenant Governor, explaining that he was doing so on the grounds cited by Governor Barnett.

The Governor has contended that the state has "interposed" its power between the university and the courts, thus nullifying the desegregation orders.

Mr. Johnson said he was representing the Governor, "acting in his stead, by his direction and under his instructions."

Mr. Doar then stepped forward and introduced himself by name and as "an officer of the court." He called attention to the injunction prohibiting interference with Mr. Meredith's admission.

The Justice Department official then sought to give Mr. Johnson a copy of the contempt citation obtained by the department against Governor Barnett.

"I will not accept the papers," said the Lieutenant Governor.

Mr. Meredith, dressed in a neat gray suit, white shirt and red tie, stood between the Federal officials with his hands held stiffly by his sides, looking on but saying nothing.

Moving toward Mr. Johnson, the chief marshal said, "Governor, I think it's my duty to try to go through and get Mr. Meredith in there."

The troopers crowded in behind the Lieutenant Governor. "We are going to block you and if there is any violence it will be on your part," said Mr. Johnson.

"I'm only doing my duty as a United States Marshal," replied Mr. McShane. "I would like to go in."

The chief marshal then sought to shoulder his way past the Lieutenant Governor, who, with the troopers, pushed him back.

Mr. Johnson said he did not think the chief marshal should be "doing this for the television cameras" to be seen throughout the nation.

"You people understand that you're in violation of a court order," said Mr. Doar. And he began calling off names from the metal tags on the troopers shirts while the marshal took them down on a pad.

Mr. McShane then sought to go around the Lieutenant Governor's right side but Mr. Johnson and the troopers pushed him back again

"We have told you you can't go in and we intend to use whatever force is necessary," said Mr. Johnson.

"Governor, are these men acting under your authority, physically preventing us from going in?" asked the marshal.

"They are," was the reply.

Mr. Doar again warned the Lieutenant Governor and the troopers that they were defying the orders of the courts. And Mr. McShane made another futile attempt to clear a path for Mr. Meredith.

At one point, the chief marshal ordered the state officers to "stand aside

and let this man in." But they refused to budge.

"You're trying to make a big show," asserted Mr. Johnson. Mr. McShane denied this. He and the Lieutenant Governor then shook hands and the two Federal officials and the student got back into the car. The troopers and the sheriff cheered and applauded the Lieutenant Governor as the Meredith party, accompanied by a state patrol escort and six unidentified Federal officials, drove away.

Mr. Johnson told newsmen he would remain on the scene to turn back Mr. Meredith if he appeared again. Asked what further plans he had, he replied, "We're just taking it as it comes."

The state official, who was not named in the various injunctions, was asked if he would appear before the Federal Court if cited for contempt.

"I don't know," he replied. "At this time, it would be hard for me to say."

Then with a smile, he remarked: "They'll probably put me away for a long time."

One of the first to congratulate Mr. Johnson was William J. Simmons, national coordinator of the Citizens' Councils of America and a top adviser to Governor Barnett. He attended a conference of highway patrol officials and county and city law enforcement officers here Tuesday night at which the strategy executed this morning was planned.

"It's all in a day's work," commented Mr. Simmons with a smile. "Feeling all over the state is just as cocky and confident as it can be."

Mr. Simmons and his militantly segregationist organization possibly have more at stake in the controversy than others. Desegregation in Mississippi, the one state in which the councils wield considerable political influence, undoubtedly would weaken their campaign for support elsewhere in the South.

Troops patrolling streets during riots over the enrollment of James H. Meredith at the University of Mississippi.

(Lynn Pelham/Time & Life Pictures/Getty Images)

Robert Kennedy Vows to Back Court With Troops If Necessary

Showdown Expected Tomorrow

By ANTHONY LEWIS

WASHINGTON, Sept. 26—Attorney General Robert F. Kennedy reiterated tonight that the Federal Government would do "whatever is necessary" to carry out court orders in Mississippi.

"The situation is serious," he told reporters. "The question of Federal troops is the same as it has been. That is, we'll use whatever is necessary to do the job."

Officials made clear yesterday that they were prepared to use troops in Mississippi if needed and that this might be soon. The question of what will be needed is now expected to become clear after a hearing of the United States Court of Appeals for the Fifth Circuit in New Orleans Friday.

The court has ordered Gov. Ross R. Barnett of Mississippi to show cause then why he should not be held in contempt. The Governor has openly defied the Appeals Court's orders that James H. Meredith be admitted as the University of Mississippi's first Negro student.

The general expectation at the Justice Department is that Governor Barnett will refuse to attend the hearing or in some other way deny the court's authority. And then, the belief is, the court will assert that authority by a direct order to bring the Governor before it or take some other action against him.

Use of Marshals Seen

The Justice Department, in accordance with its policy of trying regular methods of law enforcement as long as possible, would probably first attempt to use marshals to enforce any such order against the Governor.

But Federal marshals in Mississippi have been vastly outmanned by state police, and marshals were physically turned back today when they tried to force their way into the university with Mr. Meredith.

If Governor Barnett and other Mississippi officials stick to this policy, something stronger than marshals will presumably have to be used to deal with the Governor. Officials reluctantly envisaged no alternative to troops.

"There are only two ways to make a man appear before a court in response to its order," a high Justice Department official remarked tonight. "One is to get him to do it voluntarily, and the other is to use force—whatever force is necessary in the circumstances."

In any case, there was clearly no weakening in the Justice Department's determination to prevail in what is regarded as the gravest clash of Federal and state power in many years.

Officials were confident they were in a good position legally for the test with Governor Barnett. They said they had answers in the law and precedents to various questions involved in the contempt action against the Governor.

U.S., TO AVERT VIOLENCE, CALLS OFF NEW EFFORT TO ENROLL MEREDITH; SENDS HUNDREDS MORE MARSHALS

200 Policemen With Clubs Ring Campus to Bar Negro

By CLAUDE SITTON

OXFORD, Miss., Sept. 27—A fourth attempt to enroll James H. Meredith in the University of Mississippi was canceled late today when it became evident that his life would be endangered. The 29-year-old Negro student and his escort of 25 deputy Federal marshals turned back to Memphis, Tenn., before reaching the campus in Oxford. Defiant state officials and a crowd of 2,500 had awaited them here. Two hundred policemen carrying clubs surrounded the university grounds.

With several hundred more deputy marshals having been dispatched to Memphis, 60 miles away, another attempt will be made tomorrow, under Chief Marshall James P. McShane, to carry out the desegregation orders of the Federal courts.

Clash is Feared

A serious clash is expected if the escort tries to force its way onto the campus past state, county and city law-enforcement units deployed here by Gov. Ross R. Barnett.

The Governor has been ordered to appear tomorrow in New Orleans before the United States Court of Appeals for the Fifth Circuit to answer contempt charges stemming from his flagrant defiance of the courts' directives. He has refused service of subpoenas. An aide indicated he would not appear.

[In Jackson, the Mississippi Legislature passed a bill designed to protect the assets of Governor Barnett and Lieut. Gov. Paul B. Johnson Jr. from seizure to satisfy any contempt penalty.]

After making an appearance here, Mr. Barnett and the state highway patrolmen left tonight, apparently to return to Jackson, 170 miles away.

Tension gripped this town of 6,400 in the North Mississippi hills. Some persons feared it might become the scene of an armed insurrection against Federal authority.

The crowd of students and adults waited impatiently for almost two hours at the university's main entrance for Mr. Meredith's arrival.

Roughly dressed whites sat in parked cars and trucks along Highway 6 East, the route that Mr. Meredith and his guards would have taken in approaching the school.

Governor Barnett, Mr. Johnson and the big force of patrolmen, sheriffs, deputies and policemen stood ready to block the student's admission.

Yesterday Mr. Johnson scuffled with Mr. McShane as the latter sought to shoulder his way through 20 patrolmen barring the campus.

The troopers guarding University Avenue, at the intersection of South Fifth Street, wore steel combat helmets. They carried riot sticks and gas masks, but no sidearms.

Sheriffs, and policemen from other cities were massed near the Hilgard railroad bridge, which separates the campus from the town. Police dogs brought in from Jackson and Vicksburg were in the rear of patrol cars.

Lieutenant Governor Johnson, Chief Burns Tatum of the university police and Richard Wilson, president of the student body, made several futile efforts to break up the crowd. But two dozen troopers merely looked on.

Mr. Johnson issued repeated warnings over a loudspeaker mounted on a patrol car that cruised on University Avenue near the main entrance to the campus.

"I plead with you, return, return to the campus," he said. "We have a tense situation. It is dangerous for you to be here.

"Someone could easily be killed and it might be an innocent party. If you would like to have this nigger in Ole Miss, just stay where you are."

Making a second round a few minutes later, Mr. Johnson said:

"I beg of you to get back out of this line of fire."

Governor Barnett arrived in his light blue Cadillac from the university's Alumni House, his field headquarters.

On leaving Alumni House, he told a crowd:

"I am glad to see you here today. The people of Mississippi have a wonderful reputation for keeping the peace and law and order."

"Let's let the world know that we can still control our citizens, so that we can have the admiration and confidence of all the people of the world."

KENNEDY FEDERALIZES MISSISSIPPI'S GUARD; MOBILIZES TROOPS, ORDERS STATE TO YIELD; ADDRESSES NATION TODAY ON RACIAL CRISIS

ACTS AT MIDNIGHT

President Holds Talks With Gov. Barnett but to No Avail

By ANTHONY LEWIS

WASHINGTON, Sept. 30—President Kennedy committed the full weight of the Federal Government at midnight last night to end Mississippi's defiance of the Union.

He called the state's National Guard into Federal service.

He sent troops of the United States Army to Memphis, Tenn., to stand in reserve if more force were needed.

And he issued a proclamation calling on the Government and people of Mississippi to abandon what had become the most serious challenge to Federal authority since the Civil War.

Addresses Nation Tonight

Tonight, the President goes on the air to explain the situation to the American people. He will speak over all national television and radio networks at 7:30 New York time.

The President took what one official called his "irrevocable steps" after three telephone conversations yesterday with Governor Ross R. Barnett of Mississippi.

In a statement issued at minutes before midnight, the acting White House press secretary, Andrew T. Hatcher, said that in the conversations "the President was unable to receive from Governor Barnett satisfactory assurances that law and order could, or would, be maintained in Oxford, Miss., during the coming week."

Mr. Hatcher said the action was being taken at that late hour—and telegrams dispatched to the guard commanders—so that the units "will be available for service Monday." Most Guardsmen are one-day-a-week soldiers, and it will take time to mobilize them.

The regular Army troops sent to Memphis comprised 900 military policemen, especially trained in riot control tactics, and one battle group.

The plan is to hold these forces back at first, leaving the job of restoring and maintaining order to Mississippians—the Guardsmen.

At 12:01 this morning, President Kennedy signed an executive order authorizing the Secretary of Defense, Robert S. McNamara, to use the Mississippi Guard for enforcement of the Federal court orders.

And he signed a historic proclamation commanding the people of Mississippi to end their defiance of Federal law. After citing the statutes and the history of the last week's events in a series of "whereas" paragraphs, the proclamation concluded:

Kennedy's Proclamation

"Now, therefore, I, John F. Kennedy, President of the United States, do command all persons engaged in such obstruction of justice to cease and desist therefrom and to disperse and retire peaceably forthwith."

The language was similar to that of a proclamation issued by President Eisenhower on Sept. 23, 1957, the day before he called up the Arkansas National Guard and sent Federal troops to end rioting over school desegregation in Little Rock.

But the Mississippi crisis was in every respect a much more serious threat to the Union than the Little Rock episode.

Governor Orval E. Faubus of Arkansas, though he tried to prevent school desegregation, stopped short of defying Federal Court orders. Governor Barnett and other officials and state police under his command have done precisely that.

United States Court of Appeals for the Fifth Circuit has found Governor Barnett in contempt of court and ordered him imprisoned and fined $10,000 a day unless he purges himself of contempt by Tuesday.

There is no sign that he will do so.

It was a last, desperate hope of finding any sign of a change of heart on Governor Barnett's part that the President's action was delayed until so late an hour.

Officials said that in the telephone

talks with the President, Governor Barnett repeated that he would not allow Mr. Meredith to enter the university. And he added he could not assure the physical safety of Mr. Meredith if another attempt were made to enroll him.

Three previous attempts to register Mr. Meredith were blocked by state troopers, and a fourth called off because of the possibility of violence. Observers in Oxford have expressed fear that state troopers could not control the gathering mobs now, even if they wanted to.

Present plans are to get the National Guard units to Oxford as soon as possible and to restore order there. That will be by tomorrow, if all works out as planned here. Then a fresh effort to bring Mr. Meredith into the university will be made.

The next day, Tuesday, the Government will face the task of arresting Governor Barnett as ordered by the court. Unless the state police guarding him abandon their resistance to Federal law, force again would be required.

Use of the guard will present the ironic picture of Mississippians requiring other Mississippians to obey Federal law. Or there could be a problem of Guardsmen obeying the authority of their commander in chief, the President.

Some 700 Federal marshals and other civilian Federal officers now gathered at the Naval Air Station in Memphis will undoubtedly play a part as well as the soldiers. They will serve the court orders and make any necessary arrests. The Federalizing of the Guard, and dispatch of regular Army forces, were both done under the authority of two statutes dating back to 1792.

President's Authority

These laws authorized the President to call out troops whenever he "considers that unlawful obstructions, combinations or assemblages, or rebellion against the authority of the United States, makes it impracticable to enforce the laws of the United States in any state or territory by the ordinary course of judicial proceedings."

The statutes were finally invoked, and most reluctantly on the Administration's part, after a long day of strategic backing and filing.

Some of the 2,500 National Guard troops that converged on the University of Mississippi, October 1, 1962.

(Donald Uhrbrock/Time & Life Pictures/Getty Images)

NEGRO AT MISSISSIPPI U. AS BARNETT YIELDS; 3 DEAD IN CAMPUS RIOT, 6 MARSHALS SHOT; GUARDSMEN MOVE IN

KENNEDY MAKES PLEA; TEAR GAS IS USED

Mob Attacks Officers—2,500 Troops Are Sent to Oxford

By CLAUDE SITTON

OXFORD, Miss., Monday, Oct. 1— James H. Meredith, a 29 year-old Negro, was admitted last night to the University of Mississippi campus and was scheduled to enroll today in the all-white institution.

A riot broke out shortly after his arrival, and marauding bands of students and adults, many of whom were from other states, were still ranging through the campus and the town early today.

At least three men were killed, one of them unidentified. Fifty persons were being treated for various injuries in the university. Six United States marshals were shot, one was critically wounded.

Although the riot started at about 7:30 P. M., Central standard time, Army troops did not arrive until five and a half hours later. About 200 military policemen arrived from Memphis shortly after 1 A.M. (3 A.M., E.D.T.)

[Army headquarters received word early today that about 200 more persons had joined the rioting mob and that the situation on the campus was "very bad," the Associated Press reported. About 2,500 regular Army military policemen and infantrymen were converging on Oxford. Army observers in Mississippi reported to headquarters that automatic weapons fire was being aimed at the registration building.]

Marshals Besieged

A small detachment of Mississippi National Guardsmen went to the aid of a besieged force of 300 deputy marshals in the university administration building. The marshals were under the command of top Justice Department officials, including Nicholas deB. Katzenbach, deputy attorney general.

For a time, it appeared that the marshals would not be able to hold the building, which is called the Lyceum. But barrage after barrage of tear gas discouraged the rioters, and they began to break up.

A number of other Mississippi National Guardsmen had arrived early today at the armory on the eastern outskirts of town. But there was considerable delay before they began a drive to the campus.

Automobiles loaded with roughly dressed whites, some of whom were from Alabama, began pulling into the campus shortly after the state patrol withdrew from the campus entrances early last night.

Clouds of tear gas billowed around the administration building.

The tree-dotted mall in front of the building had the appearance of a battlefield as students massed behind Confederate battle flags and repeatedly charged toward the marshals.

Travel to and from the campus was extremely dangerous. Roving bands of students halted cars and questioned their occupants to determine if they were friend or foe.

At one point, a second mob began forming at Baxter Hall, a dormitory where Mr. Meredith reportedly was housed. Word passed through the mob at the administration building that an attempt to burn the dormitory would be made. But it did not materialize.

The troops were bombarded with bricks and sticks, and obscenities were shouted at the men.

Five minutes later students brought a bulldozer up from a construction site. A yell went up from a nucleus of about 200 students among a milling throng of more than 1,000. Students and others moved in behind the bulldozer, which aimed straight for the main door of the administration building.

The plan seemed to be to abandon the machine at full throttle and let it plow wildly into the troops. But the dozer stalled and was quickly swallowed up in the clouds of tear gas.

Later, however, the students and their adult reinforcements retrieved the bulldozer and sent it crashing against the steps at the entrance of the building.

Others in the mob stole a fire truck and drove it around and around through the trees. At one point its driver sent it careening down the drive in front of the building, drawing a barrage of tear gas grenades.

Newsman Is Victim

Aside from the marshals, the chief targets of the rioters were newsmen. One of the dead was Paul Guihard, who carried press cards identifying him as a correspondent for Agence France Presse and The Daily Sketch of London.

The other man killed was Ray Gunter, 23 years old, of Abbeville, Miss., a small town north of here.

A spokesman at Oxford Hospital said Mr. Gunter had died of a gunshot wound in the forehead. The cause of Mr. Guihard's death was not determined definitely.

William Crider, an Associated Press reporter from Memphis, was wounded slightly by birdshot. A number of other newsmen were beaten.

State highway patrolmen, who had made a half-hearted attempt to hold the students back, climbed into their patrol cars and left the campus at 9:10 P. M.

Three students were taken prisoner in one clash with the deputy marshals. The Federal men, although carrying side-arms, depended chiefly on barrage after barrage of tear gas to hold back their assailants.

One newsman said a man wearing a policeman's uniform was throwing bottles and rocks at the marshals.

One of the mob's charges on the Lyceum, the administration building, followed a harangue by former Maj. Gen. Edwin A. Walker from the pedestal of a Confederate monument across the mall from the Greek-revival structure of white columns and brick masonry.

"Protest! Protest! Keep it up!" Mr. Walker shouted.

He did not advocate violence. But he told the students that help was coming from out of the state. He accused Mississippi officials of a "sellout" and named T. B. Birdsong, Commissioner of Public Safety.

The Rev. Duncan M. Gray, rector of St. Peter's Episcopal Church, stepped up on the pedestal and called on the students to end the violence. Some grabbed him and roughed him up.

He was led through the mob by an unidentified law-enforcement officer.

Mr. Walker then told the students he would give them his "moral support." He turned and, strode up a walkway toward the Lyceum with 100 students following behind.

"Sic 'em, John Birch," a student shouted from across the street.

A Volley of Tear Gas

The former general and his followers were greeted with a volley of tear gas after some among them had begun throwing rocks and bottles at the marshals.

The riot indicated that if Mr. Meredith went ahead with plans to enroll as a student, his future would be hazardous. He is scheduled for registration this morning, under an agreement between Attorney General Robert F. Kennedy and Gov. Ross R. Barnett.

State troopers, university officials and the campus police made no attempt to break up the mob, which began massing at the Lyceum even before Mr. Meredith's arrival.

The 300 or more deputy marshals who ringed the building fired a barrage of tear gas to force the mob back as it surged toward them.

A flaming missile was hurled atop a big Army truck used to transport the marshals. Its canvas cover began to burn.

A soldier climbed up and put the fire out. Members of the mob aimed squirts from a fire extinguisher at him.

The students then turned on the station wagon, which was loaded with equipment. They smashed its windows, ripped off its license plates and kicked dents in its sides.

Students let air out of the tires of three Army trucks in front of the Lyceum Building and tossed lighted matches at them.

Several state troopers looked on and laughed. Others walked away as the students charged in toward the deputy marshals, who were forced to fire the tear gas to protect themselves.

Governor Barnett's retreat followed the action of the United States Court of Appeals for the Fifth Circuit in finding him guilty of contempt for his defiance of orders to desegregate the university. He had been given until tomorrow to purge himself or face a $10,000-a-day fine and likely imprisonment.

Mr. Meredith was flown here yesterday in a two-engine Border Patrol plane from the United States Naval Air Station near Memphis. Besides the pilot, he was accompanied by John Doar, first assistant in the Justice Department's Civil Rights Division. They were met at the University-Oxford Airport on the outskirts of Oxford by Nicholas deB. Katzenbach, deputy attorney general, and Edwin O. Guthman, the Justice Department's public information chief.

Mr. Meredith climbed into a green Plymouth sedan with New York license plates. The car moved into a convoy of other automobiles and Army trucks.

Mr. Meredith, wearing a gray suit, white shirt and dark tie, appeared calm. He carried a small, tan case and a newspaper.

The deputy marshals arrived here by plane in two groups yesterday. There were 165 in the first contingent and 140 in the second.

The Federal officials wore white helmet liners. Some wore riot vests, bristling with tear gas canisters.

Students gathered in "The Grove," a tree-shaded grassy mall in front of the Lyceum Building, a neo-Greek revival building, as the marshals arrived.

They began to heckle the marshals. Some jeered and shouted such taunts as "nigger lover" and "We don't want Bobby Kennedy."

A campus source said the university's chancellor, John Davis Williams, had warned students against hooliganism. He told them there was agreement between the marshals and the highway patrolmen and that any students who interfered would incur the wrath of both groups.

As the marshals rolled onto the campus in the big Army trucks, Walker opened a news conference in the parking lot of the Ole Miss Motel.

He said he had been in touch with state and local officials. He said a "quite spontaneous movement" of thousands of men sympathetic to Governor Barnett's stand were heading for Oxford from all over the nation.

Troops To Stay Until Peril Ends

Marshals Will Guard Negro After Soldiers Withdraw

By ANTHONY LEWIS

WASHINGTON, Oct. 2—Federal officials said today that they hoped to withdraw troops from Oxford, Miss., soon.

However, they made clear that they would take no chances on allowing violence to erupt again. They said that whatever Federal force was required to maintain order would remain as long as necessary.

A particular concern is the safety of James H. Meredith, the Negro student at the University of Mississippi. The general feeling is that he will have to remain under the watchful eye of at least Federal marshals.

Attorney General Robert F. Kennedy and his aides feel that the removal of troops will help to restore a more normal atmosphere in Oxford. It would also be in accord with the Government policy of putting back on to Mississippi's shoulders the responsibility of maintaining order.

Pressure on Barnett

The feeling is that this postponement will keep the pressure on Governor Barnett to assume the duty of keeping the peace. A failure to do so might be construed by the court as contempt and lead to a heavy fine.

Justice Department officials expressed satisfaction that Governor Barnett had sent counsel to New Orleans to argue for him today. Previously he had ignored the court's hearings and had refused to appear personally or by counsel.

The court ordered him jailed and fined $10,000 a day for obstructing its orders, but gave him until today to purge himself. It was felt that the prospect of these penalties had hastened Governor Barnett's decision to abandon his position of total defiance.

Democratic Congressional leaders gave President Kennedy their support today for his actions in Mississippi.

Stennis Joins Inquiry

Senator James O. Eastland, meanwhile, went ahead with his plans to have the Senate Judiciary Committee investigate the conduct of the marshals in Oxford. The Mississippi Democrat, who is chairman of the committee, has charged that the marshals provoked the riot by 2,500 persons Sunday night.

Today Senator Eastland invited his Democratic colleague from Mississippi, John Stennis, to join the inquiry. Senator Stennis is not a member of the Judiciary Committee. But he accepted the invitation, saying, "The people of Mississippi and the nation are entitled to the full facts."

Astronaut Feeling 'Fine' After 9-Hour Space Trip

By JOHN W. FINNEY

ABOARD THE U.S.S. KEARSARGE AT SEA, Oct. 3—Comdr. Walter M. Schirra Jr., after orbiting the earth six times in his one-ton capsule, returned safely to earth today with pin-point accuracy and was picked up by this 41,000-ton aircraft carrier.

The 39-year-old astronaut, a broad smile wreathing his face, reported that he felt "fine" after his space trip of more than nine hours.

Awaiting the astronaut as he stepped aboard the carrier was a telephone call of congratulations from President Kennedy, who was at the White House.

Four Miles From Carrier

The Canaveral-to-Kearsarge trip by way of six orbits of the earth was performed with accuracy that brought the capsule down just four miles in front of the carrier. Commander Schirra stepped aboard the carrier, some 330 miles northeast of Midway Island in the central Pacific, almost exactly 10 hours after he was launched from Cape Canaveral.

Speaking of his spacecraft, he said, "This is a sweet little bird."

The astronaut landed so close to the carrier that he decided to bypass the usual recovery plan of climbing out of his Sigma 7 capsule and being lifted by a Marine helicopter to the vessel's flight deck.

Instead, he remained inside the capsule, which was lifted by a boom onto the elevator on the starboard side of the carrier. At 6:15 P. M., Eastern daylight time, he blew off the escape hatch on the side of the bell-shaped capsule.

Inspects Space Capsule

Sitting on the side of the capsule, the astronaut took off his white space helmet and looked over the capsule. Then he stood on the edge of the escape hatch so that he could see more closely how the cylindrical after-body of the capsule had been burned a brownish black in the searing heat of re-entering the earth's atmosphere.

After a quick check of the capsule, the astronaut turned around to acknowledge the cheers and whistles of the Kearsarge crew, peering over from the flight deck and crammed into every cranny on the starboard side of the ship.

The astronaut looked tired and hot from his long stay within the capsule, which included half an hour of bobbing in the sea before the capsule could be retrieved by the carrier. But on his face there was a triumphant smile.

As he walked away from the capsule to the ship's sick bay, reporters called out: "How do you feel, Wally?"

"Fine," he replied with a casual wave of his hand, as if to indicate there was really no reason for asking the question.

Leaves Vapor Trail

The return of the Sigma 7 capsule to earth was an extraordinary display of accuracy that elated space officials and brought cheers and whistles from the carrier crew.

The capsule, diving toward earth at about 270 miles an hour, was first sighted high in the sky, leaving a vapor trail.

The capsule was about five miles off the port beam of the carrier.

At about 21,000 feet the ribbon drogue parachute, designed to stabilize the capsule, could be seen fluttering behind the spacecraft. The capsule was a glistening speck, like a shooting star.

At 5:25 P. M. the 63-foot red landing parachute billowed out behind the capsule at about 10,000 feet and abruptly slowed the descent. The astronaut was safe. A cheer went up from the crew crowding the flight deck and the carrier's island superstructure.

Speed is Reduced

Suspended beneath the parachute, the capsule swung back and forth.

The Kearsarge turned to port and increased speed to about 25 knots to be as close as possible to the capsule. The capsule splashed into the water directly ahead of the carrier, about four miles away.

Had the landing been any closer, the carrier would probably have been forced to maneuver to avoid hitting the thin-skinned spacecraft.

At one point, the carrier's speed was deliberately reduced from 30 knots so that the ship would not bear down too closely on the bobbing capsule, barely visible in the waves.

From the moment the capsule landed in the water, staining the sea with its green dye, the recovery procedures moved with the same clocklike precision that characterized the flight.

Collar is Attached

Within three minutes after the capsule landed in the water at 5:29 P.M., four Marine HUS-1 helicopters had taken off from the flight deck and were circling over the capsule. By 5:37, three Navy frogmen had jumped into the water and attached a yellow flotation collar around the blunt base of the capsule to keep it from sinking.

At 5:08 P.M., the capsule was hoisted on board and placed on a special box in the starboard elevator. Seven minutes later, Commander Schirra pushed a plunger that blew off the side hatch with an explosive charge. Then the astronaut simply crawled head-first out of his cramped quarters, where he had sat since early morning.

The astronaut was greeted on the elevator by Capt. Thomas S. King, commander of the recovery task group.

Looking Back

The Challenge of Space

By John Noble Wilford

No new president wants to give the impression that he is not in control of events gusting about him. This was especially true of John F. Kennedy in the spring of 1961. He had won election projecting the vigor of youth. He had taken office speaking of new frontiers and the passing of the torch to a new generation. All the more reason that of Kennedy's first months in the White House, April was the cruelest.

On April 12, Yuri A. Gagarin became the first human to orbit Earth—one more space triumph for the Soviet Union. Since the stunning flight of Sputnik 1 in October 1957, Russians had set the pace in space exploration, boastfully. They had also sent a dog into orbit and a probe to the Moon. This tarnished the American self-image as world leaders in all things technological and raised doubts about the country's capacity to compete in the superpower struggle known as the Cold War. Though Gagarin's one complete orbit was not unexpected, it was nonetheless deflating, even humiliating. It would be a month before Alan B. Shepard Jr., one of the Mercury Seven astronauts selected in 1959, became the first American in space. His was to be only a 15-minute suborbital flight.

Kennedy and his advisers knew that all eyes, allied and adversarial, were fixed on how they responded to this first test of their leadership. Before they could recover from the first setback, though, a second staggering blow followed, on April 17. On that day, a force of anti-Castro exiles, trained by the C.I.A., invaded Communist Cuba at the Bay of Pigs—a fiasco within 36 hours.

The Cuba incident was not directly related to the Russian challenge in space flight, except in the minds of Kennedy and those around him. Something clearly had to be done soon to restore American self-confidence and affirm its world leadership. Something emphatic, galvanizing. Something on the new frontier in space.

Kennedy's close aide, Theodore Sorensen, described the president after this one-two punch as "anguished and fatigued" and "in the most emotional, self-critical state I had ever seen him." Nothing seemed to be going right. His brother Robert F. Kennedy told colleagues, "We've got to do something to show the Russians we are not paper tigers." At another time, the president pleaded: "If somebody can, just tell me how to catch up. Let's find somebody—anybody. I don't care if it's the janitor over there." Heading back to the Oval Office, Kennedy told Sorensen, "There's nothing more important."

Over the next five weeks, Vice President Lyndon B. Johnson oversaw secret meetings and the exchange of memorandums from high officials. As Senate majority leader in 1958, Johnson had pushed through NASA's founding legislation and was a forceful advocate for a strong space program. NASA officials just happened to have some drawing-board concepts in reserve, several of which had seemed too blue-sky before Gagarin. With a crash program on the order of the Manhattan Project to build the atomic bomb, it was now argued, men could probably fly to the Moon and back within the decade, ahead of the Russians.

So it was decided, and on May 25, 1961, President Kennedy addressed a joint session of Congress and a national television audience, declaring: "I believe that this nation should commit itself to achieving the goal, before this decade is out, of landing a man on the moon and returning him safely to Earth."

There it was, the challenge flung before an adversary and to a nation on edge in an unconventional war, the beginning of Project Apollo.

While the Apollo mobilization proceeded rapidly—nothing quite like it has been seen since—Americans first despaired of always being second to the Soviet cosmonauts. After Gagarin, Gherman S. Titov had spent 25 hours in orbit; Shepard and Virgil I. (Gus) Grissom each had 15-minute suborbital flights—only five minutes of weightlessness each time.

Then, on Feb. 20, 1962, an astronaut from small-town America stepped forward in response to the country's need. This was John Glenn, whom Tom Wolfe, author of *The Right Stuff*, has since called "the last true national hero America has ever had."

Squeezed into the cockpit of a Mercury spacecraft called *Friendship 7*, Glenn circled Earth three times, becoming the first American to orbit the planet. Perhaps no other space flight—all 4 hours, 55 minutes and 23 seconds of it—has been followed by so many with such paralyzing apprehension.

Although trouble with the autopilot forced Glenn to take manual control and a suspected loose heat shield had ground controllers bracing for a possibly catastrophic re-entry, the ending was a happy one. A collective sigh of relief was heard across the land. President Kennedy rushed to Cape Canaveral to hail the returning hero. Bands played, and people cried. As Wolfe later wrote, "John Glenn made us whole again!"

By 1963, after three more Mercury successes, the

Kennedy White House felt, as Sorensen said, that there was "a very real chance that we were even with the Soviets." But with rising criticism in Congress and the press of the Apollo costs, Kennedy began to waver but never backed away from the lunar commitment.

John M. Logsdon, a longtime space policy specialist who has studied memoirs and other documents relating to Kennedy and the Apollo decision, has pointed out that some White House advisers were eager to slip the end-of-the-decade goal to spread out the costs. There was even talk of pressing the Russians to cooperate in a venture to the Moon. As McGeorge Bundy, the national security adviser, said, either press for cooperation with the Russians or continue to use their space effort "as a spur to our own." In a memorandum, he said that "if we cooperate, the pressure comes off" regarding the decade goal, and "we can easily argue that it was our crash effort in '61 and '62 which made the Soviets ready to cooperate."

In a speech to the U.N. in September 1963, Kennedy invited the Soviet Union to join a cooperative lunar mission. He had proposed this informally to the Soviet leader, Nikita Khrushchev, at a meeting in Vienna shortly after his 1961 message to Congress. The invitation then was rejected out of hand. Russian accounts after the Cold War have linked the rejection to a fear of exposing the technological shortcomings of their country's space program.

Visiting Cape Canaveral on Nov. 16, 1963, Kennedy seemed to enjoy seeing preparations for the next astronaut flight. Days later, on Nov. 22, in the speech he never lived to deliver in Dallas, he intended to say "the United States has no intention of finishing second in space."

We all know the end of the story. On July 20, 1969, Neil Armstrong and Buzz Aldrin stepped out on the arid Sea of Tranquility. They were on the Moon, the goal of the decade, the Kennedy goal, now achieved. This was a finale to be proud of at the end of a decade that began with such promise and achieved heroic gains in civil rights only to descend into assassination and turmoil at home and an intractable war abroad.

On that climactic day it might have seemed the second coming of Jules Verne or perhaps a first step into a Ray Bradbury future. But since the last of six landings, in 1972, no one has been back to the Moon. It is not for us to know but, in a time to come, as some historians foresee, the 20th century may be remembered mainly for humanity's first ventures beyond its native planet. And those everywhere who heard and saw those things and told their children and grandchildren will have inspired a kind of Homeric oral history of the time people first took leave of Earth.

John Noble Wilford, who reported on every Apollo mission to the Moon, won a Pulitzer Prize in 1984 for his coverage of space flights. He shared a second one with his *New York Times* colleagues for their investigation into the *Challenger* shuttle disaster in 1986.

The Cuban Missile Crisis

U.S. IMPOSES ARMS BLOCKADE ON CUBA ON FINDING OFFENSIVE-MISSILE SITES; KENNEDY READY FOR SOVIET SHOWDOWN

PRESIDENT GRAVE

Asserts Russians Lied and Put Hemisphere in Great Danger

By ANTHONY LEWIS

WASHINGTON, Oct. 22—President Kennedy imposed a naval and air "quarantine" tonight on the shipment of offensive military equipment to Cuba.

In a speech of extraordinary gravity, he told the American people that the Soviet Union, contrary to promises, was building offensive missiles and bomber bases in Cuba. He said the bases could handle missiles carrying nuclear warheads up to 2,000 miles.

Thus a critical moment in the cold war was at hand tonight. The President had decided on a direct confrontation with—and challenge to—the power of the Soviet Union.

Direct Thrust at Soviet

Two aspects of the speech were notable. One was its direct thrust at the Soviet Union as the party responsible for the crisis. Mr. Kennedy treated Cuba and the Government of Premier Fidel Castro as a mere pawn in Moscow's hands and drew the issue as one with the Soviet Government.

The President, in language of unusual bluntness, accused the Soviet leaders of deliberately making "false statements about their intentions in Cuba."

The other aspect of the speech particularly noted by observers here was its flat commitment by the United States to act alone against the missile threat in Cuba.

Nation Ready to Act

The President made it clear that this country would not stop short of military action to end what he called a "clandestine, reckless and provocative threat to world peace."

Mr. Kennedy said the United States was asking for an emergency meeting of the United Nations Security Council to consider a resolution for "dismantling and withdrawal of all offensive weapons in Cuba."

He said the launching of a nuclear missile from Cuba against any nation in the Western Hemisphere would be regarded as an attack by the Soviet Union against the United States. It would be met, he said, by retaliation against the Soviet Union.

He called on Premier Khrushchev to withdraw the missiles from Cuba and so "move the world back from the abyss of destruction."

All this the President recited in an 18-minute radio and television address of a grimness unparalleled in recent times. He read the words rapidly, with little emotion, until he came to the peroration—a warning to Americans of the dangers ahead.

"Let no one doubt that this is a difficult and dangerous effort on which we have set out," the President said. "No one can foresee precisely what course it will take or what costs or casualties will be incurred."

"The path we have chosen for the present is full of hazards, as all paths are—but it is the one most consistent with our character and courage as a nation and our commitments around the world," he added.

"The cost of freedom is always high—but Americans have always paid it. And one path we shall never choose is the path of surrender or submission.

"Our goal is not the victory of might but the vindication of right—not peace at the expense of freedom, but both peace and freedom, here in this hemisphere and, we hope, around the world. God willing, that goal will be achieved."

The President's speech did not actually start the naval blockade tonight. To

A labeled aerial photograph showing trailers, trucks and medium-range missile equipment at a base in Cuba during the Cuban Missile Crisis.
(Rolls Press/Popperfoto/Getty Images)

meet the requirements of international law, the State Department will issue a formal proclamation late tomorrow, and that may delay the effectiveness of the action as long as another 24 hours.

Crisis Before Public

The speech laid before the American people a crisis that had gripped the highest officials here since last Tuesday, but had only begun to leak out to the public over the weekend. The President said that it was at 9 A. M. Tuesday that he got the first firm intelligence report about the missile sites in Cuba.

Last month, he said, the Soviet Government publicly stated that its military equipment for Cuba was "exclusively for defensive purposes" and that the Soviet did not need retaliatory missile bases outside its own territory.

"That statement was false," Mr. Kennedy said.

Just last Thursday, he continued, the Soviet foreign minister Andrei A. Gromyko, told him in a call at the White House that the Soviet Union "would never become involved" in building any offensive military capacity in Cuba.

"That statement was also false," the President said.

Appeal to Khrushchev

He made a direct appeal to premier Khrushchev to abandon the Communist "course of world domination." An hour before the President spoke, a personal letter from him to Mr. Khrushchev was delivered to the Soviet government in Moscow.

Mr. Kennedy disclosed that he was calling for an immediate meeting of the Organ of Consultation of the Organization of American States to consider the crisis.

The O. A. S. promptly scheduled an emergency session for 9 A. M. tomorrow. State Department officials said they were confident of receiving the necessary 14 votes out of the 20 nations represented.

The President said the United States was prepared also to discuss the situation "in any other meeting that could be useful." This was taken as an allusion to a possible summit conference with Mr. Khrushchev.

"All the News That's Fit to Print"

The New York Times.

LATE CITY EDITION
U. S. Weather Bureau Report (Page 94) forecasts:
Partly cloudy, breezy, cool today.
Fair and cool tonight and tomorrow.
Temp. range: 54—45; yesterday: 66—44.

VOL. CXII..No. 38,258.   © 1962 by The New York Times Company.
Times Square, New York 36, N. Y.   NEW YORK, TUESDAY, OCTOBER 23, 1962.   10 cents beyond 50-mile zone from New York City except on Long Island. Higher in air delivery cities.   FIVE CENTS

U.S. IMPOSES ARMS BLOCKADE ON CUBA ON FINDING OFFENSIVE-MISSILE SITES; KENNEDY READY FOR SOVIET SHOWDOWN

U. S. JUDGES GIVEN POWER TO REQUIRE VOTE FOR NEGROES

High Court Upholds Order Forcing the Registration of 54 in Alabama County

Special to The New York Times

WASHINGTON, Oct. 22 — The Supreme Court held today that Federal judges have the power to make state registrars put specific Negroes on the voting rolls.

Alabama had challenged an order by Federal District Judge Frank M. Johnson Jr. requiring the registration of 54 specific Negroes in Macon County, Ala. The order was upheld by the United States Court of Appeals for the Fifth Circuit.

Today the Supreme Court unanimously affirmed the disputed order. And it did so in a way that indicated once again its mood of impatience with Southern efforts to maintain denials of Negro rights.

One-Sentence Ruling

All that was before the court was an application for review of the Fifth Circuit decision. The usual alternatives would have been to deny the petition or to grant it and hear oral argument later.

Instead, the court granted review and then, unusually, affirmed the lower courts. It did so in a single sentence, with just one citation in the way of explanation.

The citation was to a decision in 1960 upholding a Federal Court order in a Louisiana voting case. There, a district judge had told Louisiana registrars to put back on the books 1,377 Negroes whose names had been removed in a purge by the segregationist Citizens Council.

Action by Congress

The Macon County case was one of the first brought by the Department of Justice under the Civil Rights Act of 1957. It is especially significant because the county is in the so-called Black Belt, with a predominantly Negro population.

In 1958, when the suit was started, virtually all of the 3,060 white persons of voting age in the county were registered. But only about 1,000 of the 12,000 potential Negro voters were actually eligible.

In a further move, the registrars resigned, and this was held to leave no defendants to be sued. Congress in 1960 handled this problem by providing

Continued on Page 24, Column 4

102 SAVED AT SEA AS PLANE DITCHES

Rescue Is Made off Alaska Minutes After Accident

By The Associated Press

SITKA, Alaska, Oct. 22—A military-charter airliner ditched in the ocean near here today, but all 102 persons aboard were saved in a quick rescue operation.

The plane, a DC-7C of Northwest Airlines, was going from McChord Air Force Base in Washington to Anchorage, Alaska. It carried 95 passengers and a crew of seven.

The rescue was reported by Northwest and the Alaska Coastal-Ellis Airline at Sitka, which also reported that there apparently were no serious injuries.

The plane went down shortly after the Federal Aviation Agency at Anchorage got word that it was being ditched because of propeller trouble.

A Coast Guard plane alighted on the water nearby. The Air Force sent two rescue planes and small boats from Sitka, about seven miles north of the

Continued on Page 8, Column 2

Chinese Open New Front; Use Tanks Against Indians

Nehru Warns of Peril to Independence —Reds Attack Near Burmese Border and Press Two Other Drives

Special to The New York Times

NEW DELHI, Oct. 22—Prime Minister Jawaharlal Nehru told the people of India tonight that the Chinese Communist attack was a threat to their liberty.

His grave warning followed word that the advancing Chinese had opened a third front in

Excerpts from Nehru's speech will be found on Page 2.

the Himalayas, near the Burmese border, and had used tanks for the first time. Five more Indian posts fell to the Chinese on the third day of savage fighting.

[A bid for negotiations for a peace accord was broadcast by the Chinese Communist radio early Tuesday. The Associated Press reported from Tokyo.]

In a broadcast, Mr. Nehru denounced the Peking regime as "a powerful and unscrupulous

opponent, not caring for peace or peaceful methods."

"The time has come," he said, "for us to realize fully this menace that threatens the freedom of our people and the independence of our country."

Prime Minister Nehru said India would not abandon her economic development program and policy of nonalignment with international blocs, but called on the nation to switch "from the slow-moving methods of peacetime to those which produce results quickly."

"We must build up our military strength by all means at our disposal," he said.

The third front in the Himalayan fighting was opened early today when the Chinese attacked an Indian post at Kibitoo, on the border between

Continued on Page 3, Column 1

U.S. Bids U.N. Bar China; Denounces Attack on India

BY SAM POPE BREWER

Special to The New York Times

UNITED NATIONS, N. Y., Oct. 22—Adlai E. Stevenson told the General Assembly today that Communist China's "naked aggression" against India was new proof that it was "unfit for membership in the United Nations.

The chief United States representative at the United Nations spoke as the Assembly took up the perennial question of admitting Peking.

Mr. Stevenson told the members that by their actions on the Indian frontier the Chinese Communists "again show their scorn for the Charter of this organization."

The Vice President of the Philippines, Emmanuel Pelaez, told the Assembly that there were more than 40,000,000 Chinese living outside China who would become "a Trojan horse" if the United Nations accepted the Communist Government.

Mr. Pelaez said that the Chinese abroad, 1,000,000 of them in the Philippines, would be used for subversion by the Peking Government. He said they could now be controlled because the Communist Government did not have the means to get at them.

On the fighting in India, Mr. Stevenson declared: "Should there be some among us who think that perhaps the whole point out that when a nation moves its troops with tanks and armor, it is no mistake. It is a premeditated act. It is naked aggression. And it has been going on with gathering momentum for some three years."

He quoted Prime Minister

Continued on Page 5, Column 3

U.S. SAID TO EASE KATANGA POLICY

Reported Willing to Put Off Any Economic Sanctions —Congolese Disturbed

By LLOYD GARRISON

Special to The New York Times

LEOPOLDVILLE, the Congo, Oct. 22 — Authoritative sources said today that the United States was no longer insisting that Katanga Province strictly meet the deadlines of the United Nations plan to end its secession from the Congo.

This has alarmed Congolese officials. They say that the United States shift is reflected in United Nations policy.

The United Nations plan, introduced Aug. 2 by U Thant, Acting Secretary General, was said to have been conceived largely by the United States.

As outlined by Mr. Thant, the plan's first stage called for the following timetable:

Within thirty days a program was to be decided on for the reintegration of Katanga's foreign currency reserves into the central Government, with 50 per cent of these reserves rebated to Katanga.

Unification of the Congo's currency was to have begun within 10 days.

Katanga was to have started immediately to share 50 per cent or her tax revenues with the central Government.

Not one of these conditions has been met.

Last week Cyrille Adoula, Premier of the central Government, declared that "the deadline for the first stage has passed." He said that it was now time for the United Nations to consider the second stage — economic sanctions.

A shift in United States policy became apparent over the weekend after the departure of George C. McGhee, Under Secretary of State for Political Af-

Continued on Page 3, Column 6

Stocks Plunge Early On Crisis, but Rally

By RICHARD RUTTER

An already badly battered stock market was hit by massive selling yesterday at talk of a new international crisis spread in Wall Street.

The selling was of dimensions reminiscent of late May when the market experienced its worst break in a generation. Yesterday, the tape ran as much as 19 minutes late before a half-hearted recovery set in that cut large losses.

Both tape lateness and volume were the greatest since July 10. Two million shares were traded in the first two hours. Stock markets in London, Frankfurt and Brussels, following Wall Street's lead, also took large losses.

The selling was directly ascribed to news in the morning about an air of crisis in Washington.

Continued on Page 49, Column 6

SHIPS MUST STOP

Other Action Planned If Big Rockets Are Not Dismantled

By JAMES RESTON

Special to The New York Times

WASHINGTON, Oct. 22 — President Kennedy drew the line tonight, not with Cuba, but with the Soviet Union. After almost a generation of trying to keep the "cold war" from reaching a direct confrontation between United States and Soviet power, a decision has been made to force Soviet missile bases from this hemisphere at the risk of war.

This is the official interpretation of President Kennedy's speech tonight, and the orders issued to the nation to carry it out. On the highest authority, it can be said that these orders include the following:

¶Ships carrying to Cuba weapons capable of striking the continental United States must either turn back or submit to search and seizure, or fight. If they try to run the blockade, a warning shot will be fired across their bows; if they still do not submit, they will be attacked.

¶This applies not only to ships but to any planes suspected of carrying additional offensive weapons to Cuba. There is no evidence that there are nuclear warheads in Cuba, but long-range aircraft suspected of carrying these or any other offensive weapons, will be intercepted, and instructions have been issued to check all Communist-bloc planes en route to Cuba via Newfoundland or Africa.

Prepared to Risk War

Even this will not satisfy the new policy announced by President Kennedy. Not only must new offensive weapons be stopped, under the President's orders, but those already in Cuba must be dismantled, or the United States will take whatever additional action is necessary, beginning with a much more rigorous blockade of such things as Cuba's essential oil supplies, to force compliance.

If this leads to Soviet retaliation, such as a counter-blockade of Berlin, the United States is prepared to risk a major war to defend its present position in the former German capital. Accordingly, American forces, not only in Berlin and West Germany but all over the world have been placed on emergency alert. The new policy has been defined in a private communi-

Continued on Page 19, Column 1

TRAFFIC DELAYED AT BERLIN BORDER

Reds Start Intensive Check of Civilian Trucks an Hour Before Kennedy Speech

By SYDNEY GRUSON

Special to The New York Times

BONN, Oct. 22—The East German police began to slow down civilian traffic between West Berlin and West Germany late tonight.

About an hour before President Kennedy announced the United States countermeasures against the Soviet build-up in Cuba, the police started intensive examination of the papers of trucks moving into East German territory.

The connection, if any, between the two actions was not immediately clear. Similar harassment of civilian traffic has occurred periodically over the years. The immediate reaction in West Berlin was to consider tonight's harassment as part of the regular order of things, rather than as an advance coun+termeasure to the American moves against Cuba.

Nevertheless, there was deep anxiety that the Soviet Union would retaliate by causing trouble on the West's access lines to the city.

The outcome of tomorrow's meetings between Andrei A. Gromyko, the Soviet Foreign Minister, and East German Communist leaders was awaited with concern. Mr. Gromyko

Continued on Page 17, Column 3

ANNOUNCES HIS ACTION: President Kennedy speaking to the nation last night on radio and television. He told of moves to keep offensive equipment away from Cuba.

Associated Press Wirephoto

Moscow Says U.S. Holds 'Armed Fist' Over Cuba

By SEYMOUR TOPPING

Special to The New York Times

MOSCOW, Tuesday, Oct. 23—In a broadcast before President Kennedy's speech on the missile build-up in Cuba, the Moscow radio said that the unusual activity in Washington indicated that the United States "once again was raising its armed fist" over Cuba." The broadcast said there was "real hysteria" in Washington.

A Soviet reply to the United States note on Cuba that was given last night to Anatoly F. Dobrynin, the Soviet Ambassador to Washington, was expected to be delivered in 24 hours. It was expected that the reply would take the form either of a diplomatic communication or a message to President Kennedy from Premier Khrushchev.

Western observers said it appeared inevitable in view of recent Soviet statements that the reply would be a denial of any offensive Soviet intent and a charge of United States aggression against Cuba.

Veracity Questioned

The veracity of the Soviet Government was directly questioned in President Kennedy's speech, which was given after delivery of the note. The President said evidence had been obtained that Moscow was constructing offensive missile bases on Cuban territory.

The Soviet Government stated only in Berlin and West Germany but all over the world have been placed on emergency tack on Cuba would mean war, but no one could predict on the diplomatic plane

Continued on Page 18, Column 3

Canada Asks Inspection of Cuba; Britain Supporting Quarantine

Diefenbaker Comments

By RAYMOND DANIELL

Special to The New York Times

OTTAWA, Oct. 22 — Prime Minister John Diefenbaker of Canada declared tonight the time had come for an impartial inspection of what is happening in Cuba by eight of the "nonaligned nations."

Interrupting debate of the Canadian economic crisis in the House of Commons, Mr. Diefenbaker described President Kennedy's speech on Cuba as "somber and challenging."

"Naturally," he said, "there has been little time to give consideration to positive action that might be taken. But I suggest that if there is a desire—and I am sure there is—on the part of the U.S.S.R.—to have the facts, if a group of nations, perhaps the eight comprising the unaligned members of the 18-nation disarmament committee, are given the opportunity of making an on-site inspection of Cuba to ascertain what the facts are, a major step forward would be taken."

Meanwhile it was disclosed that Canada has barred the use of her airfields, including that

Continued on Page 21, Column 2

British Note Peril

By DREW MIDDLETON

Special to The New York Times

LONDON, Oct. 22—Qualified sources said today that approval for President Kennedy's military quarantine of Cuba could be expected from the British government.

A Foreign Office spokesman declared, "Revelation of the Soviet build-up in Cuba will come as a shock to the whole civilized world."

Official comment cannot be given until after Prime Minister Macmillan and his Cabinet have discussed the President's statement.

Initial reaction among diplomats was that the President had taken the most reasonable course to frustrate what military circles regard as evident buildup of Soviet nuclear capacity in Cuba.

The danger that war might result from a Soviet attempt to break what amounts to a military blockade of Cuba is accepted. But one experienced airman expressed the general feeling this way: "War can come from any one of a number of causes.

Continued on Page 21, Column 1

PRESIDENT GRAVE

Asserts Russians Lied and Put Hemisphere in Great Danger

Text of the President's address is printed on Page 18.

By ANTHONY LEWIS

Special to The New York Times

WASHINGTON, Oct. 22 — President Kennedy imposed a naval and air "quarantine" tonight on the shipment of offensive military equipment to Cuba.

In a speech of extraordinary gravity, he told the American people that the Soviet Union, contrary to promises, was building offensive missile and bomber bases in Cuba. He said the bases could handle missiles carrying nuclear warheads up to 2,000 miles.

Thus a critical moment in the cold war was at hand tonight. The President had decided on a direct confrontation with—and challenge to—the power of the Soviet Union.

Direct Thrust at Soviet

Two aspects of the speech were notable. One was its direct thrust at the Soviet Union as the party responsible for the crisis. Mr. Kennedy treated Cuba and the Government of Premier Fidel Castro as a mere pawn in Moscow's hands and drew the issue as one with the Soviet Government.

The President, in language of unusual bluntness, accused the Soviet leaders of deliberately "false statements about their intentions in Cuba."

The other aspect of the speech particularly noted by observers here was its flat commitment by the United States to act alone against the missile threat in Cuba.

Nation Ready to Act

The President made it clear that this country would not stop short of military action to end what he called a "clandestine, reckless and provocative threat to world peace."

Mr. Kennedy said the United States was asking for an emergency meeting of the United Nations Security Council to consider a resolution for "dismantling and withdrawal of all offensive weapons in Cuba."

He said the launching of a nuclear missile from Cuba against any nation in the Western Hemisphere would be regarded as an attack by the Soviet Union against the United States. It would be met, he said, by retaliation against the Soviet Union.

He called on Premier Khrushchev to withdraw the missiles from Cuba and so "move the

Continued on Page 18, Column 1

BIG FORCE MASSES TO BLOCKADE CUBA

Armada Is Under Orders to Open Fire if Necessary— All Troops Are Alerted

By JACK RAYMOND

Special to The New York Times

WASHINGTON, Oct. 22 — American ships and planes began preparing tonight to impose a blockade of Cuba. United States forces are under orders to thwart any attempt to deliver offensive weapons to Havana.

A Defense Department spokesman said that a large force of ships and planes concentrating in the Caribbean area had instructions to use force if necessary, including the sinking of ships, to carry out President Kennedy's orders for a "quarantine" of Cuba.

The Pentagon said also that United States military units throughout the world, including the garrison in Berlin and the nuclear-armed Strategic Air Command, had been placed "on alert."

Dependents of servicemen at the Guantanamo Bay Naval Base in Cuba have been evacuated, the department said.

Forces at Base Doubled

It added that the military forces there, which were previously put at 3,300 naval officers and men and several hundred Marines, have been doubled.

Air defense units in the United States, particularly radar warning stations, interceptor aircraft and ground-to-air missiles, "have been redeployed," the department spokesman said.

The orders for additional defense precautions were taken, the spokesman continued, on the basis of aerial photographic evidence of long-range ballistic missile bases and the arrival of Soviet Ilyushin-28 bombers in Cuba.

The spokesman displayed some of the aerial photographs and pointed to some missile sites that, he said, had been established only in the last 10 or 15 days.

He said some of the missile

Continued on Page 20 Column 1

KENNEDY CANCELS CAMPAIGN TALKS

He and Johnson Take Step to Concentrate on Crisis

By CABELL PHILLIPS

Special to The New York Times

WASHINGTON, Oct. 22—The White House announced tonight that President Kennedy and Vice President Johnson would make no further political appearances in the Congressional campaign because of the Cuban crisis.

The move by the Administration was considered evidence not only of the seriousness of the situation but also of the desire of the President to unify the country behind his blockade order and keep the issue out of partisan politics.

In this connection, the White House said the President personally informed several Republican Presidents Dwight D. Eisenhower and Herbert Hoover, as well as former Democratic President Harry S. Truman, of his decision.

And the White House announced that John J. McCloy, former disarmament adviser to the Kennedy Administration and a Republican, had been as-

Continued on Page 18, Column 7

All Military Forces Mobilized by Castro

By The Associated Press

KEY WEST, Tuesday, Oct. 23—All of Cuba's military forces have been mobilized as a result of the news from the United States," the Havana radio said today.

Official comment cannot be given until after Prime Minister Macmillan and his Cabinet statement.

The broadcast said the order was issued by Premier Fidel Castro, who will address the nation later today.

"Our combat units rapidly placed themselves on a fighting basis," said the Havana broadcast.

"Hundreds of thousands of men were mobilized in the course of a few hours," added the broadcast, which followed by some hours President Kennedy's announcement of a naval blockade against Cuba.

During the evening, Havana appeared slow to react to President Kennedy's broadcast and

Continued on Page 20 Column 5

But the President emphasized that discussion in any of these forums would be undertaken "without limiting our freedom of action." This meant that the United States was determined on this course no matter what any international organization—or even the United States' allies—might say.

Support from Congress

Congressional leaders of both parties, who were summoned to Washington today to be advised by the President of the crisis and his decision, gave him unanimous backing.

Mr. Kennedy went into considerable detail in his speech in outlining the nature of the military threat in Cuba, and this country's response.

He said "confirmed" intelligence indicates that the Cuban missile sites are of two types.

One kind, which his words implied were already or nearly completed, would be capable of handling medium-range ballistic missiles. The President said such missiles could carry nuclear weapons more than 1,000 nautical miles—to Washington, the Panama Canal, Cape Canaveral or Mexico City.

The second category of sites would be for intermediate range ballistic missiles, with a range of more than 2,000 miles. The President said they could hit "most of the major cities in the Western hemisphere" from Lima, Peru, to Hudson's Bay in Canada.

Mr. Kennedy Declared:

"This urgent transformation of Cuba into an important strategic base by the presence of these large, long-range and clearly offensive weapons of sudden mass destruction constitutes an explicit threat to the peace and security of all the Americas."

He said the Soviet Union's action was "in flagrant and deliberate defiance" of the Rio (Inter-American) Pact of 1947, the United Nations Charter, Congressional resolution and his own public warnings to the Soviet Union.

Moscow Says U.S. Holds 'Armed Fist' Over Cuba

By SEYMOUR TOPPING

MOSCOW, Tuesday, Oct. 23—In a broadcast before President Kennedy's speech on the missile build-up in Cuba, the Moscow radio said that the unusual activity in Washington indicated that the United States "once again was raising its armed fist over Cuba." The broadcast said there was "real hysteria" in Washington.

A Soviet reply to the United States' note on Cuba that was given last night to Anatoly F. Dobrynin, the Soviet Ambassador to Washington, was expected to be delivered in 24 hours. It was expected that the reply would take the form either of a diplomatic communication or a message to President Kennedy from Premier Khrushchev.

To Western observers it appeared inevitable in view of recent Soviet statements that the reply would be a denial of any offensive Soviet intent and a charge of United States aggression against Cuba.

Veracity Questioned

The veracity of the Soviet Government was directly questioned in President Kennedy's speech, which was given after delivery of the note. The President said evidence had been obtained that Moscow was constructing offensive missile bases on Cuban territory.

The Soviet Government statement of Sept. 11, which warned the United States that an attack on Cuba would mean war, contended that weapons supplied to Cuba were of a defensive nature.

Western observers said the crisis over Cuba would enter a critical phase when and if United States war vessels sought to halt and search a Soviet ship bound for Cuba. A number of Soviet vessels carrying civilian goods and possibly military equipment are now believed to be at sea or ready to depart for the Caribbean.

Western observers said Moscow would as a matter of international prestige regard such a search as intolerable. However, the Soviet Union lacks the naval and air units and bases to support a military operation in the Caribbean to breach the quarantine.

The observers speculated that the Soviet Union would be more likely to withhold its shipping from the Caribbean while attempting in the debate in the Security Council to obtain some breach in the quarantine.

The loophole might take the form of an acceptance of some kind of inspection by a neutral party.

The sudden increase in tension over Cuba appeared to threaten a round of exploratory talks on a Berlin settlement. New talks, after the United States Congressional elections, had been urged by Premier Khrushchev.

It was considered unlikely that the Soviet Union would make any overt move in Berlin unless the conflict over Cuba erupted.

President Kennedy delivered his message at 2 A.M., Moscow time and in the early morning hours there was no apparent official Soviet reaction.

Soviet Challenges U.S. Right to Blockade; Interception of 25 Russian Ships Ordered; Cuba Quarantine Backed by United O.A.S.

Blockade Begins at 10 A. M. Today

Proclamation Is Signed by Kennedy—McNamara Gets Power for Enforcement

---

By E.W. KENWORTHY

WASHINGTON, Oct. 23—The United States blockade against ships delivering offensive weapons to Cuba will go into effect tomorrow at 2 P.M. Greenwich time (10 A. M. Eastern daylight time).

President Kennedy signed a proclamation of the blockade almost 24 hours after he announced to the nation that he intended to order a naval and air quarantine of Cuba because the Soviet Union had established offensive-missile sites there.

The Defense Department decided tonight to make public the photographs of the missile sites after the United States Embassy in London distributed aerial photographs of them at a news briefing hours earlier.

Banned Weapons Listed

The President declared that Secretary of Defense Robert S. McNamara was empowered to use the land, sea and air forces of the United States and those offered by other members of the Organization of American States to enforce the proclamation.

The proclamation declared that the offensive material to be barred from Cuba included the following:

"Surface-to-surface missiles, bomber aircraft, bombs, air-to-surface rock-ets and guided missiles, warheads for any of the above weapons, mechanical or electrical equipment to support or operate the above items, and any other classes of materiel hereafter designated by the Secretary of Defense for the purpose of effectuating this proclamation."

Proclamation Broadcast

As soon as the proclamation was signed, the United States Government immediately sent texts of it in uncoded transmission to the capitals of all nations.

The State Department also began calling in all Ambassadors in Washington to deliver copies to them. The Voice of America also began to broadcast the proclamation on all its channels.

> *". . . the peace of the world and the security of the United States and of all American states are endangered . . ."*

Under usage established in international law, a nation intending to establish a blockade is required to give advance announcement of its intentions and state the time that the blockade will go into effect. The blockading nation must also impose the blockade impartially against the ships of all nations which may be suspected of carrying contaband proclaimed in the blockade.

The President declared that any ship proceeding toward Cuba could be intercepted and directed to identify herself, her cargo, equipment and stores and her ports of call. The ship could also be ordered "to lie to, to submit to visit and search" by a boarding party.

When such a vessel is found to carry any of the proscribed contraband, the President said, she would be directed to proceed to "another destination."

Should the vessel disobey such an order, she will be taken into custody and sent to a United States port "for appropriate disposition."

The President gave notice that ships of the blockade would not use force unless intercepted vessels refused to comply with orders "after reasonable efforts have been made to communicate with them." The blockading ships can also use force if attacked.

"In any case," the President declared, "force shall be used only to the extent necessary."

Signing Was Delayed

The signing of the proclamation was originally planned for 4 P. M. It was delayed because the Organ of Consultation of the Organization of American States had not at that time approved a resolution recommending the use of armed force to prevent the delivery of material to Cuba that might threaten hemisphere peace and security.

Since this resolution was to be cited by the President as contributing authority for the imposition of a blockade, it was necessary to wait for its approval.

The resolution was approved, 19 to 0, with 1 abstention by a delegate who had not received instructions from his Government—Uruguay.

President Kennedy spent much of the day in meeting with his advisers. This morning he conferred for an hour and 20 minutes with a new executive committee of the National Security Council.

The committee is made up of Vice President Johnson, Secretary of State Dean Rusk, Mr. McNamara, Secretary of Treasury Douglas Dillon, Attorney General Robert F. Kennedy, Gen. Maxwell D. Taylor, chairman of the Joint Chiefs of Staff, and John A. McCone, director of the Central Intelligence Agency.

Also, Under Secretary of State George W. Ball, Deputy Secretary of Defense Roswell Gilpatric, Llewellyn E. Thompson Jr., special adviser to the President and Mr. Rusk on Soviet affairs, McGeorge Bundy, the President's assistant on national security affairs, and Theodore C. Sorenson, the President's special counsel.

Advisers to Meet Daily

The Vice President and the Secretaries of State and Defense are statutory members of the National Security Council. However, the other members of the new executive committee often attend its meetings. Mr. Dillon did not attend this morning. He was en route to Washington from Mexico City.

Pierre Salinger, White House press secretary, said that the committee would meet daily with the President at 10 A.M. for the foreseeable future.

Pentagon officials last night said that any Soviet ship refusing to obey orders would be sunk. Thus, it was noteworthy that the President emphasized that force would be used only to the extent necessary.

Officials declined to say what would happen to a ship that was taken into custody. Actually, international practice varies greatly. When nations are at war, such ships are usually confiscated. However, ships of third powers may simply be impounded and later re-

Aerial picture of a Soviet ship taken off the coast of Cuba. (AFP/Getty Images)

turned to their owners without the confiscated contraband.

Officials said tonight that consultations had already begun with some Latin-American governments on contributions by them to the blockading.

In his proclamation the President said that the Secretary of Defense would designate the area and the routes "within a reasonable distance to Cuba" where vessels would be intercepted.

A nation that has proclaimed a blockade may intercept vessels at any time after they have cleared a port of origin until they return to it.

However, officials made clear tonight that United States naval vessels would intercept only those ships bound for Cuba within a relatively short distance of Cuban shores.

In the preamble to the proclamation the President, as he had last night, put responsibility for the crisis—and thus for the blockade—directly on the Soviet Union. But it was significant that he also included Communist China, which also is believed to have sent some military material and technicians to Cuba.

The President said that "the peace of the world and the security of the United States and of all American states are endangered by reason of the establishment by the Sino-Soviet powers of an offensive military capability in Cuba, including bases for ballistic missiles with a potential range covering most of North and South America."

Khrushchev, in Letter to Russell, Suggests Summit Meeting to Avert Nuclear War

---

By SEYMOUR TOPPING

MOSCOW, Oct. 24—Premier Khrushchev suggested today a summit meeting to avert the danger of a thermonuclear war with the United States over the Cuban question.

He urged the United States not to carry out its naval quarantine of Cuba and promised that the Soviet Union "will not take any reckless decisions."

Mr. Khrushchev made his declaration in a letter to Bertrand Russell, the British philosopher and pacifist leader. Lord Russell had written to the Soviet Premier, President Kennedy and other statesmen expressing concern over the Cuban crisis.

Moscow broadcast Mr. Khrushchev's reply to Lord Russell just five hours after the United States naval quarantine went into effect.

Propaganda Overtones

While the Khrushchev letter was viewed by Western observers here as a serious bid for a meeting with President Kennedy, it was also noted that it had strong propaganda overtones. The Premier accused the Kennedy Administration of imposing the quarantine because of hatred for the Cuban people and out of "pre-election considerations."

Denouncing the decision of the Kennedy Administration to bar the movement of ships carrying offensive bombers and missiles to Cuba, Mr. Khrushchev warned:

"If the American Government will be carrying out the program of piratic actions outlined by it, we shall have to defend our rights and international rights which are written down in international agreements and expressed in the United Nations Charter."

"We have no other way out."

Earlier today the Soviet Foreign Ministry formally refused to take cognizance of the naval measures proclaimed by President Kennedy to cut off the shipment of offensive weapons to Cuba. The ministry returned a copy of the Presidential proclamation and a covering note that had been delivered by the United States Embassy here.

Western officials saw the Ministry's action as a warning that Soviet ships bound for Cuba would ignore the regulations stipulated in the proclamation for the halting, searching and diversion of ships transporting offensive arms.

[But the United States Defense Department said in Washington that some of the Soviet-bloc ships had altered their course, thus avoiding immediate contact with American naval forces blockading Cuba.]

Calling upon the United States to "display reserve and stay the execution of its piratical threats which are fraught with most serious consequences," Mr. Khrushchev concluded his message by declaring:

"The question of war and peace is so vital that we should consider useful a top-level meeting in order to discuss all the problems which have arisen, to do everything to remove the danger of unleashing a thermonuclear war. As long as rocket nuclear weapons are not put into action, there is still an opportunity to avert war. But once aggression is unleashed by the Americans such a meeting will already become impossible and useless."

Conference Possible

The threatening situation in the Caribbean made it possible that a summit conference might be arranged soon.

In an interview last April with Gardiner Cowles, a United States publisher, Mr. Khrushchev cited two situations in which he would be amenable to a meeting.

The Premier said he believed that he should meet with Mr. Kennedy after preliminary agreements had been negotiated or "to prevent a spark which might cause a military conflagration."

Mr. Kennedy has also expressed the belief in the past that under these circumstances a summit meeting should be arranged.

It was regarded as likely here that the Soviet Government had instructed its Cuba-bound vessels to avoid an outright clash with United States warships until some action is taken on the suggestion for a summit meeting.

New Hope Raised

The proposal for a summit meeting would be seen by many Russians as a means of avoiding what had been portrayed to them as an imminent danger of war because of the United States quarantine.

In his message to Lord Russell, Mr. Khrushchev said:

"I should like to assure you that the Soviet Government will not take any reckless decisions, will not permit itself to be provoked by the unwarranted actions of the United States of America and will do everything to eliminate the situation fraught with irreparable consequences which has arisen in connection with the aggressive actions of the United States Government."

Mr. Khrushchev continued:

"We shall do everything in our power to prevent war from breaking out. We are fully aware of the fact that if this war is unleashed from the very first hour it will become a thermonuclear and world war. This is perfectly obvious to us, but clearly is not to the Government of the United States which caused this crisis."

Kennedy Agrees To Talks On Thant Plan, Khrushchev Accepts It; Blockade Goes On; Russian Tanker Intercepted And Cleared

---

WASHINGTON FIRM

Insists on Continuing Quarantine Until the Menace Is Ended

By MAX FRANKEL

WASHINGTON, Oct. 25—The United States held firm today to its demand that the Soviet missile threat in Cuba be dispelled before there is any respite for East-West negotiations.

A White House official said it was "self-evident" that as long as Soviet ships continued to sail toward Cuba with unknown cargoes, the blockade by United States naval forces would continue. Other sources said that the East-West challenges set in motion by the blockade could not end until all offensive weapons in Cuba were under international supervision.

White House and intelligence sources agreed today that work on the Soviet bases in Cuba was continuing. For that reason alone, it was said, the idea of easing the pressure on Cuba at this time was unthinkable.

Further Contacts Expected

The apparently uneventful passage of one Soviet tanker through the blockade this morning made no difference in the situation, officials said. Further contact with Soviet vessels, in possibly more difficult situations, is expected within 48 hours.

The turn-around of 12 or more Soviet ships that had been steaming toward Cuba was interpreted as another sign of Moscow's temporary caution while the Soviet leaders consider the United States' challenge.

But the mood here remained grim and Administration leaders saw the nation facing danger for the indefinite future. They felt certain that the direct confrontation with the Soviet Union would soon produce tests of will around the globe.

The pressure for negotiations from the United Nations and other quarters made little change in the basic position outlined Monday evening in the address by President Kennedy. Leading officials said they were always prepared to talk, but without limitations on their freedom of action.

Meeting Appears Remote

There was general agreement here that a meeting between President Kennedy and Premier Khrushchev seemed remote at this stage. The prevailing view was that neither of the two leaders saw much value in a face-to-face encounter now.

The next move, it was stressed, was Moscow's.

All inquiries brought the same essential response: that the objective was the dismantling of Soviet bases in the Western hemisphere and that further measures would be taken if no satisfaction could be obtained. The proposal by U Thant, Acting Secretary General of the United Nations, for a moratorium on the blockade and on Soviet weapons shipments to Cuba was considered an unacceptable arrangement, even if only temporarily. The conditions for any change in policy were plainly stated here.

There must be fool-proof inspection to make certain that offensive bases in Cuba are not in operation or under construction, plus impartial verification that no further weapons were reaching Cuba.

There was no inclination here to rely once more upon the word of the Soviet Union or of Cuba about the nature of the military buildup on the island.

At the same time, neither the Soviet Union nor Cuba was expected to accept the kind of inspection that would satisfy the Administration. Premier Fidel Castro already has declared that inspectors would be met by force.

Russians Expected to Act

That is the reason for the general absence of any relaxation here. The relatively cautious Soviet statements so far are interpreted as temporizing propaganda while the Kremlin shapes its response.

The Russians are expected in the end to counter the blockade move with an initiative of their own to regain a balance of pressures from East and West.

Despite the international appeals for negotiation and the Administration's preference for a peaceful settlement, the commitment by Washington to its objectives is being constantly reinforced with the passage of time.

Congressional leaders, still campaigning for the Nov. 6 elections, diplomats and important figures are moving in and out of Administration offices, seeking information and guidance. They emerge with sober reiterations of the President's tough line.

Need for Firmness

They are told that the failure to respond vigorously to the Soviet buildup in Cuba would mean letting Russian offensive power appear in the Americas and also represent a serious setback for the Western powers in the world struggle with Moscow.

Those visitors who ask whether Washington had not set severe conditions requiring a public change of pos-

President Kennedy prepares to address the nation on the Soviet nuclear weapons build-up in Cuba, October 22, 1962. (Getty Images)

ture and attitude by the Soviet leaders are told that since Moscow upset the status quo, it was Moscow's turn to retreat.

Quarantine Will Go On

Today only one White House source allowed himself to be quoted, though not named. He said:

"It is self-evident that the quarantine will continue. There are still Soviet ships headed toward Cuba and the only way this Government can get precise information on some of those ships or the cargo they are carrying is through the quarantine.

"I might add, as the President stated, in his speech and in his message to the Secretary General, the object of the quarantine was the elimination of the offensive-missile bases from Cuba, and work is continuing on these bases."

The executive committee of the National Security Council, the President's main strategy board for the current crisis, met twice today for more than an hour in the morning and again in the evening. Nothing was disclosed about its deliberations.

★ ★ ★

"My fellow citizens: let no one doubt that this is a difficult and dangerous effort on which we have set out. No one can see precisely what course it will take or what costs or casualties will be incurred. Many months of sacrifice and self-discipline lie ahead—months in which our patience and our will will be tested—months in which many threats and denunciations will keep us aware of our dangers. But the greatest danger of all would be to do nothing."

Stevenson Dares Russian To Deny Missiles Charge

By ARNOLD H. LUBASCH

UNITED NATIONS, N.Y., Oct. 25—Adlai E. Stevenson dramatically challenged Valerian A. Zorin in the Security Council tonight to deny the United States charge that the Russians had installed offensive-missile bases in Cuba.

When the chief Soviet representative did not reply "yes or no" to the question, Mr. Stevenson introduced photographic evidence to support the charge.

He presented a display of enlarged photographs and maps to pinpoint the location of the missile bases.

The chief United States representative issued the challenge and introduced the evidence after Mr. Zorin had indicated that the charge should not be believed.

Data Termed False

Earlier in today's Security Council deliberations Mr. Zorin noted that photographs in the press this week constituted Washington's evidence of Soviet bases on Cuban soil. He said this was "falsified information" put together by the United States Central Intelligence Agency.

"Falsity is what the United States has in its hands, false evidence," he said.

The Soviet spokesman insisted that the United States had no evidence that "a series of offensive-missile sites" was being prepared in Cuba.

One Simple Question

"All right, sir," Mr. Stevenson said later, "let me ask you one simple question:

"Do you, Ambassador Zorin, deny that the U.S.S.R. has placed and is placing medium and intermediate-range missiles and sites in Cuba? Yes or no? Do not wait for the interpretation. Yes or no?"

Mr. Zorin, who was listening to a simultaneous translation of Mr. Stevenson's statement, replied immediately in Russian:

"I am not in an American courtroom, sir, and therefore I do not wish to answer a question that is put to me in the fashion in which a prosecutor puts questions. In due course, sir, you will have your reply."

Pressing for a direct answer, Mr. Stevenson told Mr. Zorin that he was "in the courtroom of world opinion right now."

When Mr. Zorin maintained his refusal to answer, Mr. Stevenson called for a suspension of all Soviet arms shipments to Cuba while the United States suspended its naval quarantine.

The Soviet Premier's brief message of acceptance appeared unconditional. However, President Kennedy's agreement solely to preliminary talks with Mr. Thant implied that the United States would insist on certain conditions to halt the build-up of the offensive-missile bases in Cuba.

If general agreement is reached, the suggestion of Mr. Thant for a period of

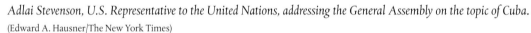

Adlai Stevenson, U.S. Representative to the United Nations, addressing the General Assembly on the topic of Cuba.
(Edward A. Hausner/The New York Times)

Cuban anti-aircraft battery erected during the missile crisis between the Soviet Union and the United States, October 1962. (Reuters)

two to three weeks in which to negotiate a settlement would fit the schedule of Mr. Khrushchev quite nicely.

Soviet sources earlier today asserted that Premier Khrushchev was hopeful that President Kennedy would accept his bid for a meeting.

Publication of the Khrushchev message this morning resulted in an obvious easing of tension in the Soviet capital. A more hopeful mood was evident throughout the day.

The Moscow radio at 10:45 P. M. Moscow time interrupted a concert to broadcast the texts of the messages exchanged by Mr. Khrushchev and Mr. Thant.

The hopeful accent in Soviet newspapers and radio broadcasts on a negotiated settlement of the Cuban controversy, exemplified by the news bulletins of the peace appeal of Pope John XXIII, was balanced with expressions of military firmness.

Krasnaya Zvezda, the paper of the Soviet armed forces, published a speech by Defense Minister Rodion Y. Malinovsky in which he said that the nation's military establishment was in a state of the highest battle readiness.

U.S. Finds Cuba Speeding Build-Up Of Bases, Warns Of Further Action; U.N. Talks Open; Soviet Agrees To Shun Blockade Zone Now

CAPITAL IS STERN

Weighs Direct Steps if Soviet Defiance Is Continued

By E.W. KENWORTHY

WASHINGTON, Oct. 26—The White House made public tonight a new intelligence report showing that construction of Soviet missile bases in Cuba was proceeding at a rapid rate with the apparent intention of "achieving a full operational capability as soon as possible."

High officials said that such work could not be allowed to continue indefinitely.

There was some encouragement here tonight when it became known that Premier Khrushchev had agreed, in response to an appeal by U Thant, Acting Secretary General of the United Nations, to order Soviet ships bound for Cuba to stay away temporarily from the blockade zone.

Missile Sites Crucial

However, officials here have always thought that the real clue to Soviet intentions was not whether the Russians would attempt to challenge the blockade but whether they would continue or discontinue construction work on the offensive-missile sites.

Therefore, President Kennedy, in a message to Mr. Thant assuring him that American ships would do everything possible to avoid a direct confrontation with Soviet ships outside the blockade zone, reiterated United States "require-

ments" that the offensive-weapons systems be withdrawn.

"I must point out to you," he wrote to Mr. Thant, "that present work on these systems is still continuing."

The verified cessation of work on these sites, officials said, was a prime condition for agreements by the United States to enter into with the Soviet Union.

Direct Action Weighed

Officials close to rapidly moving developments indicated that, unless work on the sites came to a halt within a few days, the United States must consider what further action should be taken toward achieving its firm objective of the elimination of the missiles.

These and other developments strengthened the impression in the capital that the Government was looking beyond the effort to settle the Cuban crisis at the United Nations and toward the possibility of further direct action by the United States.

The general expectation here was that the Soviet Union would refuse to meet the American condition that the construction must be brought to a verified halt before talks on the substance of the dispute could begin. These were the elements in the evolving situation that underlined the Government's apparent resolution:

In a meeting this morning of the Executive Committee of the National Security Council, according to informed sources, Adlai E. Stevenson, United States Ambassador to the United Nations, intended to make clear

to Mr. Thant that the United States was immovable in its determination to get the missile bases out of Cuba.

The White House said this afternoon that "the Soviets are rapidly continuing their construction of missile and launch facilities" and gave no evidence of "any intention to dismantle or discontinue work on these missile sites."

The State Department this morning drew attention to a sentence in President Kennedy's speech of Monday night that read:

"Should these offensive military preparations continue, thus increasing the threat of the hemisphere, further action will be justified."

In the Organization of American States, Latin-American Ambassadors agreed with the United States' view that the resolution unanimously approved last Tuesday gave the United States and other members of the O.A.S. the right to dismantle the missile bases by force if necessary.

Although Pierre Salinger, White House press secretary, denied reports that Congressional leaders had been asked by the President to return to Washington next Monday, sources on Capitol Hill said these leaders understood after the second meeting with the President on Wednesday that they would return Monday for a report of the situation.

Activity Found Continuing

In its statement the White House said that as of yesterday, "definite build-ups in these offensive-missile sites continued to be made."

"The activity of these sites," the statement continued, "apparently is directed at achieving a full operational capability as soon as possible."

At the sites being constructed for intermediate-range ballistic missiles, with a reported reach of more than 2,000 miles, the White House said, bulldozers and cranes were observed yesterday "actively clearing new areas

EXCOMM meeting during the Cuban Missile Crisis, October 29, 1962. (Cecil Stoughton/John F. Kennedy Library)

within the sites and improving the approach roads to the launch pads."

"For example," the White House reported, "missiles were observed parked in the open on Oct. 23. Surveillance on Oct. 25 revealed that some of these same missiles have now been moved from their original parked positions. Cabling can be seen running from the missile-ready tents to generators nearby."

Conditions on U.N. Talks

Officials did not expect the climax to be reached in gunfire at sea but in the political arena at the United Nations over the conditions the United States will set on the beginning to talks. Officials said these conditions are three:

First, work on the missile sites shall stop and not be resumed.

Second, the missiles and the sites shall be made and remain totally inoperable.

Third, no more offensive missiles shall be sent to Cuba.

The United States, officials said, will insist that each of these steps must be verified by observers sent by the United Nations.

There was little expectation here tonight that the Soviet Union would agree to these conditions, reinforced by inspection. Consequently the White House may have to decide over the weekend what further actions to take.

Officials said there were several possible actions short of invasion.

The most likely, it is believed, would

be the extension of the blockade to include all goods. Some officials here are dissatisfied with the limitation of contraband to offensive weapons.

They argue that this does not touch the problem since oil, food, machinery and spare parts can be brought in to keep the economy limping along while the missiles are already there in sufficient number to pose a real threat.

Another alternative under consideration is pinpoint bombing of the missile sites.

A third, which would be an accompaniment of either of the first two, would be encouragement of guerrilla warfare.

Officials are quite aware that the Soviet Union might respond to either a total blockade or pinpoint bombing by retaliatory action against the access routes to Berlin.

This is a matter of great concern, because any action against Cuba that presented the West with the alternative of retreating in Berlin or fighting for it would probably arouse concern among our European allies. Some officials fear that in such a situation the support that the President had so far had from the NATO countries might weaken.

However, officials here say, that this was a risk accepted when the Cuban policy was framed. Furthermore, they say that the allies must also recognize that failure to carry through in Cuba would also gravely impair the West's position in Berlin by casting doubt on the credibility of the United States pledge to fight for Berlin.

Pentagon Stresses Threat

If the Soviet Union should agree to the United States conditions, the Administration would be willing to halt the blockade and begin talks aiming at the dismantling of the sites.

But officials said that before United States ships were withdrawn, some way must be established to insure that Soviet vessels do not continue to enter Cuban harbors. They point out that it would be easy for United Nations observers to verify that work on missile sites had stopped.

The Pentagon, apparently for emphasis, distributed copies of the White House statement that the construction of ballistic missile bases in Cuba was proceeding at an accelerated pace.

Also for emphasis apparently, the Pentagon announced an unusual flurry of launchings of the United States' own long-range ballistic missiles for training or scientific purposes. The Pentagon pointed out the following:

Two Thors, the 1,500-mile intermediate-range ballistic missile, were used in scientific booster missions, one in the launching of a nuclear device over Johnston Island in the Pacific last midnight, and the other in the launching of an unidentified satellite from Vandenberg Air Force Base.

Also at Vandenberg, an Atlas intercontinental ballistic missile, with a credited range of 6,000 miles, was launched in a "routine training" test. A Titan II ICBM was launched 5,000 miles in a development test at Patrick Air Force Base, Florida, the Pentagon said.

President Kennedy and his closest adviser, his brother, Attorney General Robert Kennedy, conferring in the West Wing Colonnade. (George Tames/The New York Times)

U.S. To Act If Work On Bases Goes On

Stevenson Tells Allies Air Strike Will Be Launched Unless Build-Up Halts

By THOMAS J. HAMILTON

UNITED NATIONS, N.Y., Oct. 27— Adlai E. Stevenson, chief United States representative at the United Nations, told the Western allies today that the United States intended to take military action to eliminate Soviet missile bases in Cuba "in a brief space of time" unless work on the bases halted.

Reliable sources said Mr. Stevenson made clear that the military action contemplated, if no way is found to stop the development of the bases, would be in the form of an air strike to put the bases out of action, not an invasion of Cuba.

The chief United States delegate at the United Nations told delegates of 13 countries that the development of the Cuban bases was threatening to change the nuclear balance of power in favor of the Soviet Union.

He emphasized that, according to the latest United States' reports, work on the bases was continuing at increased speed.

Mr. Stevenson's meeting with the United States allies came in the midst of a series of conferences between U Thant, the Acting Secretary General, and the parties to the Cuban dispute.

Mr. Stevenson spent half an hour this morning with Mr. Thant discussing Premier Khrushchev's letter to President Kennedy offering to give up Soviet missile bases in Cuba in exchange for the withdrawal of North Atlantic Treaty Organization missile bases in Turkey.

Mr. Stevenson's gloomy appraisal of the Cuban situation was presented at a private meeting in the United States delegation building.

Thant-Zorin Meeting

Later in the day Mr. Thant received Valerian A. Zorin, the Soviet representative, for a talk of an hour and a half. Mr. Zorin handed Mr. Thant a copy of Mr. Khrushchev's letter making the Cuba-Turkey offer.

Mr. Thant's messages to the heads of government of the United States, the Soviet Union and Cuba were sent in response to an appeal by the neutralists, who requested him to urge the three parties to the dispute to refrain from any action that would "exacerbate" the situation.

Reporting the United States' attitude to Mr. Khrushchev's offer of a deal on Cuba and Turkey, Mr. Stevenson told the allied representatives that if the United States agreed to negotiate, only the bases in Cuba would be considered in the first phase.

According to reliable sources, the United States representative emphasized that there must be proof that the Cuban bases had been made "inoperable."

According to these sources, Mr. Stevenson placed great emphasis upon the fact that a letter from Mr. Khrushchev to Mr. Kennedy, which reached the White House last night and has not been made public, was much more encouraging.

The conditions fixed by this letter, Mr. Stevenson said, dealt solely with Cuba, and did not mention a deal regarding Turkey or any other country. He declared that if today's letter offering the Turkey-Cuba deal had not arrived, the Cuban crisis could already have been settled on the basis of the letter of last night.

According to reliable sources, Mr. Stevenson offered no explanation for the stiffening of the Soviet position since yesterday. Neither did he amplify the White House reply to the offer by Mr. Khrushchev regarding the bases in Turkey and Cuba.

Other dependable sources said that in the last 24 hours Mr. Stevenson had held extensive discussions with Latin-American delegates about the arrangements for a United States air strike on the Cuban missile bases under the auspices of the Organization of American States.

The United States contends that a resolution adopted in Washington by the Organization of American States authorized the destruction of the bases by air bombardment, but not by landing United States troops.

Thant Is Bypassed

According to reliable sources, the United States views Mr. Khrushchev's offer regarding Cuba and Turkey as a diversionary move. The letter containing the offer, and the letter last night, were both sent direct to Mr. Kennedy, ignoring Mr. Thant.

The Acting Secretary General served as an intermediary between Washington and Moscow in working out the arrangements yesterday whereby Soviet merchant ships and the United States naval patrol around Cuba will give each other a wide berth.

In the opinion of these sources, the United States believes that the fact that Mr. Thant was bypassed marks an attempt by the Kremlin to reduce the role of the United Nations in bringing about a settlement.

According to reliable sources, Mr. Khrushchev's letter to Mr. Kennedy last night was concerned solely with the arrangements desired by the Soviet Union in Cuba as a preliminary to a two-or-three-week respite suggested by Mr. Thant to provide for negotiations.

Mr. Thant suggested that the United States suspend the "quarantine" during that period and that the Soviet Union suspend all arms shipments.

U.S. AND SOVIET REACH ACCORD ON CUBA; CAPITAL HOPEFUL

Plans to End Blockade as Soon as Moscow Lives Up to Vow

By E.W. KENWORTHY

WASHINGTON, Oct. 28—President Kennedy and Premier Khrushchev reached apparent agreement today on a formula to end the crisis over Cuba and to begin talks on easing tensions in other areas.

Premier Khrushchev pledged the Soviet Union to stop work on its missile sites in Cuba, to dismantle the weapons and to crate them and take them home. All this would be done under verification of United Nations representatives.

President Kennedy, for his part, pledged the lifting of the Cuban arms blockade when the United Nations had taken the "necessary measures," and that, the United States would not invade Cuba.

U. S. Conditions Met

Essentially this formula meets the conditions that President Kennedy set for the beginning of talks. If it is carried out, it would achieve the objective of the President in establishing the blockade last week: the removal of the Soviet missile bases in Cuba.

While officials were gratified at the agreement reached on United States terms, there was no sense either of triumph or jubilation. The agreement, they realized, was only the beginning. The terms of it were not nailed down and Soviet negotiators were expected to arrive at the United Nations with a "bag full of fine print."

Although Mr. Khrushchev mentioned verification of the dismantling by United Nations observers in today's note, sources here do not consider it unlikely that the Russians may suggest that the observers be under the procedures of the Security Council.

This would make their findings subject to a veto by the Soviet Union as one of the 11 members of the Council.

> *The White House said that the "first imperative" was the removal of the threat of Soviet missiles.*

No Big Gains Envisioned

United States officials did not expect a Cuban settlement, if it materialized, to lead any great breakthroughs on such problems as inspection for a nuclear test ban and disarmament.

On the other hand, it was thought possible that a Cuban settlement might set a precedent for limited reciprocal concessions in some areas.

The break in the crisis came dramatically early this morning after a night of steadily mounting fears that events were running ahead of diplomatic efforts to control them.

The break came with the arrival of a letter from Premier Khrushchev in which the Soviet leader again changed his course.

Friday night Mr. Khrushchev had sent a lengthy private letter to the President. Deep in it was the suggestion that the Soviet Union would remove its missiles from Cuba under supervision and not replace them if the United States would lift the blockade and give assurances that United States and other Western Hemisphere nations could not invade Cuba.

The President found this generally acceptable and yesterday morning his aides were preparing a private reply. Then the Moscow radio broadcast the text of another letter that was on its way.

The second letter proposed that the Soviet Union remove its missiles from Cuba in return for the dismantling of United States missiles in Turkey. This was advanced as an equitable exchange.

Fearing that it would be viewed in this light by many neutral nations, the White House immediately postponed a reply to the first letter and issued a statement on the second.

The White House said that the "first imperative" was the removal of the threat of Soviet missiles. The United States would not consider "any proposals" until work was stopped on the Cuban bases, the weapons were "rendered inoperable," and further shipments of them were halted.

Then White House aides turned back to drafting a reply of the first letter. They hoped to persuade Mr. Khrushchev to stand by his first offer.

The President accepted the first Khrushchev proposal as the basis for beginning talks. But he planted in it two warnings which, the White House hoped, would not be lost upon Mr. Khrushchev.

Threat of Action Noted

First, he said the arrangement for putting into effect the Khrushchev plan could be completed in "a couple of days"—a warning that the United States could take action to halt the work on the missile bases if Mr. Khrushchev did not order it stopped.

Second, the President said that if the work continued or if Mr. Khrushchev linked Cuba to the broader questions of European security, the Cuban crisis would be intensified.

Just before 9 o'clock this morning, the Moscow radio said there would be an important announcement on the hour. It turned out to be a reply to Mr. Kennedy's letter of the night before.

Mr. Khrushchev said that in order to "complete with greater speed the liquidation of the conflict dangerous to the cause of peace," the Soviet Government had ordered work stopped on the bases in Cuba, and the dismantling, crating and return of the missiles.

Mr. Khrushchev said he trusted that, in return, "no attack will be made on Cuba—that no invasion will take place—not only by the United States, but also by other countries of the Western Hemisphere."

Kuznetzov to Negotiate

Mr. Khrushchev said that he was sending Vassily V. Kuznetzov, a First Deputy Foreign Minister to the United Nations, to conduct negotiations for the Soviet Union. He arrived in New York tonight.

Without waiting for the formal delivery of the letter, the President issued a statement at noon, saying he welcomed "Chairman Khrushchev's statesman-like decision" and an "important and constructive contribution to peace."

Shortly before the statement was issued, the President flew by helicopter to Glen Ora, his country home in Middleburg, Va., to have lunch, and he spent most of the afternoon with his wife and children.

All the communications this week between the two leaders—and there have been several more than have been made public—have been sent by the usual diplomatic route. First, they have been delivered to the Embassies, there translated, and sent to the State Department or the Soviet Foreign office for delivery to Mr. Kennedy or Mr. Khrushchev.

Process Too Slow

This is a time-consuming process, and late this afternoon, the last section of Mr. Khrushchev's letter had not yet arrived at the White House when it was decided to make the President's reply public and speed it on its way.

The President said that he welcomed Mr. Khrushchev's message because "developments were approaching a point where events could have become unmanageable."

Mr. Kennedy said:

"I think that you and I, with our heavy responsibilities for the maintenance of peace, were aware that developments were approaching a point where events could have become unmanageable. So I welcome this message and consider it an important contribution to peace."

He also stated that he regarded his letter of the night before and the Premier's reply as "firm undertakings" which both governments should carry out "promptly."

The President hoped that the "necessary measures" could be taken "at once" through the United Nations so that the quarantine could be removed on shipping.

All these matters, the President said, would be reported to members of the Organization of American States, who "share a deep interest in a genuine peace in the Caribbean area."

And the President echoed Mr. Khrushchev's hope that the two nations could now turn their attention to disarmament "as it relates to the whole world and also to critical areas."

The President by tonight had not named the negotiator for the United States, but it was reported by authoritative sources that Adlai E. Stevenson, the head of the United States delegation at the United Nations, would get the assignment. The talks are expected to begin soon, probably tomorrow.

A spokesman at the State Department said in reply to questions:

"The quarantine remains in effect but we don't anticipate any problems of interception since there are no ships moving into the quarantine area that appear to be carrying cargoes on the contraband list."

Fears About Castro

There was also some concern that Premier Fidel Castro, out of chagrin, might cause incidents over the United States surveillance flights.

Officials here believed that Dr. Castro was making a major effort to bring in extraneous issues such as the evacuation of the United States base at Guantanamo Bay, to salvage his prestige.

The United States was not prepared to deal over the base, and the feeling here was that no other matters except the President's guarantee not to invade could be discussed until the dismantling of the missiles had been verified.

Officials emphasized today, as they reflected on the events of the week, that at all times the White House was trying to keep things on the track. At no time, they insisted, was any ultimatum delivered to Mr. Khrushchev, although he was made to understand that the missiles would be destroyed unless they were removed in a short time.

Looking Back

The Possibility of Nuclear War

By Roger Cohen

The labeled black-and-white aerial photographs presented on October 16, 1962, to President John F. Kennedy told an unmistakable story: Soviet nuclear missile sites were under construction in Cuba, 90 miles off the Florida coast. So began a crisis that almost gave the Cold War another name. By the time it was over 13 days later, the world had come to the very brink of thermonuclear war. The possibility of Armageddon was real: Miami obliterated, Berlin reduced to rubble once more, humanity devoured by its destructive ingenuity to a point unimaginable and perhaps irreparable. Robert Kennedy, the president's brother, estimated the potential toll as nothing less than "the end of mankind."

Many of the president's aides prepared for the worst, evacuating their families. Supermarket shelves were empty, bunkers prepared. Kennedy himself, eyeball to eyeball with Premier Nikita S. Khrushchev, put the chance of war at close to even. On October 19, Air Force General Curtis LeMay, arguing for direct military action, suggested the president's refusal to order immediate air strikes was "almost as bad as the appeasement at Munich." Even if they did not invoke Chamberlain—always the warmonger's most facile analogy—several other generals agreed: The Communist enemy's tactical nuclear weapons trained on the U.S. eastern seaboard must be hit at once. The pressure on the president was unrelenting. He absorbed it. When LeMay told the commander-in-chief he was in "a pretty bad fix," Kennedy then deadpanned: "You're in there with me."

All humanity was in there. That was the thing. History happens—but only just. Without the two chief protagonists' personal knowledge of the horror of war, and consequent abhorrence of it, events might have tipped in another direction. Fidel Castro, the 35-year-old revolutionary leader of Cuba, was prepared, even eager, for cataclysm: "If they attack Cuba, we should wipe them off the face of the earth!" he shouted at the startled Soviet ambassador in Havana.

To read the transcripts of Kennedy's tense conversations with his divided inner circle, to follow Khrushchev's lurches from confrontation to ultimate conciliation, to know that the stand-off happened without a Washington–Moscow hotline (it was only installed

after the crisis) is to understand that there was nothing inevitable about a peaceful denouement.

It is never pleasant to have no good options. At the same October 19 meeting with the Joint Chiefs of Staff three days into the crisis, Kennedy began by saying: "If we attack Cuban missiles, or Cuba, in any way, it gives them a clear line to take Berlin." The nation "would be regarded as the trigger-happy Americans who lost Berlin" to Moscow. Already the previous year, the city at the apex of a divided Europe had been divided by a Soviet-built wall. But inaction was not an option—"We've got to do something," Kennedy said. Cuba could not in perpetuity point a nuclear warhead at America's heart.

The question was what to do. That, in turn, depended on the true nature of Khrushchev's gamble. He was a "goddamn mystery" to Kennedy. Top Soviet officials had lied throughout 1962, telling the president nuclear missiles would never be installed in Cuba, only to do just that. Perhaps the Soviet leader's calculation was that after the fiasco of the U.S.-orchestrated 1961 Bay of Pigs invasion of Cuba by a band of 1,400 C.I.A.-trained Cuban exiles, Kennedy was a weakened figure who would not go to war. Or did he see the Cuban gambit as quid pro quo for the installation of U.S. Jupiter missiles in Turkey? In any event, Khrushchev wrote later in his memoirs, he was determined "to maintain the independence of the Cuban people." The risk he took to that end was enormous; and Kennedy's calibrated but resolute response seems to have surprised and, in the end, disoriented him.

For six days the crisis was kept under wraps. Such secrecy in the midst of a confrontation of this magnitude seems almost unthinkable in the Twitter age, although the tracking and then killing of Osama bin Laden in 2011 suggests it is not impossible. Kennedy, after seeing the photographs, asked his inner circle—about 15 officials forming the Executive Committee of the National Security Council, or "ExComm"—to review options but ensure word did not get out. His brain trust included Secretary of State Dean Rusk; Secretary of Defense Robert McNamara; Theodore Sorensen, special counsel to the President; and McGeorge Bundy, the national security adviser. They were supplemented at times by diplomatic sages of former administrations, including Dean Acheson.

By October 21, two options had been formulated: the immediate air strikes favored by LeMay or a quarantine of the island—effectively a blockade—to prevent further Soviet materiel from arriving. General Maxwell Taylor, chairman of the Joint Chiefs of Staff, presented the argument for war; McNamara argued for buying time through a blockade. Kennedy, in McNamara's recollection, then asked Air Force General Walter Sweeney if he was confident all Soviet missiles would be destroyed in the planned attack. Sweeney responded: "If we can't do the job, nobody can. But can I say there is no chance that one or two missiles and nuclear warheads might still be operational, and can still be fired, after the attack? No, Mr. President, I can't say that."

The clinching argument for quarantine as a first step had just been made through the scrupulous honesty of a military hawk.

Kennedy made his first public pronouncement the next day, October 22. His message was directed at the Kremlin, not Cuba. Castro, the loose cannon, was to be marginalized. The tone was firm: "It shall be the policy of this Nation to regard any nuclear missile launched from Cuba against any nation in the Western Hemisphere as an attack by the Soviet Union on the United States, requiring a full retaliatory response upon the Soviet Union." If Khrushchev had any doubt about the 45-year-old American president's readiness for all-out war, he could no longer cling to it. Soviet intelligence gathered during the crisis of U.S. plans for an invasion of Cuba only added to the Premier's disquiet. He had misread Kennedy, whose response to "anti-imperialist" braggadocio was to stand firm.

There were many near-fatal misunderstandings. Khrushchev looked like the wild man, Castro's nuclear enabler. In fact he was aghast at how trigger-happy the Cuban leader was. "Castro clearly has no idea what thermonuclear war is," Khrushchev told a visiting Czech leader just after the crisis passed, adding that, "Millions of people would die, in our country too. Can we even contemplate a thing like that?" If the Soviet leader was a bully, he was a bully with a warrior's conscience.

The Kremlin had banked on Kennedy's inexperience. Here the truth was another story: Kennedy had been the skipper of a PT boat in the South Pacific during World War II. He had the bitter wisdom only war can impart. When on October 27—the Black Saturday of a world on the precipice—an American U-2 spy plane strayed into Soviet territory, prompting Soviet MiG fighters to scramble, Kennedy responded with a commander's cool: "There's always some son of a bitch who doesn't get the word." He was similarly unruffled over the shooting down the same day of a U-2 spy plane over Cuba.

Mistakes happen. The critical thing is that during the Cuban crisis they were not compounded. It is sobering to reflect that within two years of the crisis, Kennedy would be dead and Khrushchev gone. With different men the story might well have ended with a bang rather than a whimper.

As it was, a last-minute deal was crafted. On October 27 General Taylor recommended that the air war begin October 29, to be followed by an invasion. No more time could be allowed the Soviets to ready the missiles and warheads (in fact, as would only be discovered later, the weapons were already in place). Kennedy, rather than accept inevitable war, put all his diplomatic ingenuity to work.

His offer had three elements: a public pledge that the United States would not invade Cuba if the Soviet Union withdrew its missiles; a private ultimatum setting the October 29 deadline; and a top-secret offer to withdraw U.S. missiles from Turkey after the resolution of the crisis. This last, critical element was communicated by Kennedy's most trusted man, his brother Bobby, to the Soviet ambassador, Anatoly Dobrynin, on October 27. The president, Bobby said, was willing to withdraw the Jupiters. But this could not be divulged; it had to appear as the fruit of an already adopted NATO decision to replace them with Polaris missile submarines.

The resolution of the Cuban missile crisis was a lesson in diplomatic art, involving concessions, imagination, and resolve. Kennedy had received two letters from Khrushchev on October 26 and 27, the first conciliatory, the second a confrontational demand that the United States "evacuate its analogous weapons from Turkey." He chose to finesse the second and focus on the first, in which the Soviet Premier had written: "If indeed war should break out, then it would not be in our power to stop it, for such is the logic of war. I have participated in two wars and I know that war ends only when it has rolled through cities and villages, everywhere sowing death and destruction."

Khrushchev, then, did not want war, did not want it with a passion. What, given this obsession, would his bottom line be? To be able to say he had stopped a U.S. invasion of Cuba. And so it proved. On October 28—just hours before U.S. air strikes were set to begin—agreement was reached that the missiles would be dismantled and removed.

Who won? Kennedy forced Khrushchev to cave—and the Soviet leader never quite recovered. On the other hand, Khrushchev won a commitment from the United States that Cuba would not be attacked, and its imprisoning revolution, like Castro himself, survives to this day. The real winner, of course, was humanity, whose ultimate nightmare was averted.

Roger Cohen is a columnist for *The New York Times*. He is completing a family memoir.

Vietnam Heartened by Major Victory Over Reds

Many Call It Most Decisive Triumph for Government Since Long War Began

By DAVID HALBERSTAM

SAIGON, Vietnam, Nov. 26—Vietnamese soldiers wrote a song today to celebrate the heroes of the outpost of Phuoc Chia. Some of the heroes were toasted at a luncheon. At the outpost itself, a small garrison fortress in the mountains, Americans incredulously counted the Communist dead.

Phuoc Chia is that rare thing in South Vietnam's war against the Communists: a clear and sharp victory for the Government. Many military observers believe it is the most decisive single victory gained by Government troops for it was fought at a time and place and under conditions chosen by the Communists.

Phuoc Chia is about 70 miles south of Danang. The area around it has been a Communist stronghold for years. Two months ago the Government built the outpost as a first step in establishing its presence in the area. A company of troops uses the outpost as a base for probing missions.

Early yesterday two battalions of Communist, or Vietcong, troops attacked the outpost. It was a familiar Communist pattern against isolated and undermanned outposts: strike at night with a troop advantage of seven to one, kill as many regular troops as you can, make off with Government weapons and let the peasants in the surrounding countryside know who is boss.

Attacks like this have been a Communist trademark. But today in Phuoc Chia there are 124 Communist dead,

including two battalion commanders. There are also three Communist prisoners and one of the most valuable yields of Communist weapons in years plus Communist documents. The figure of dead was revised today. The number given yesterday was 109.

There are no Government dead, and only eight Government wounded.

The attack started at 3 A. M. Intelligence had warned the troops in the outpost that an attack was coming, but did not say just when. An added bit of warning was provided by an approaching Communist who stepped on a mine.

Government troops were ready with machine guns, automatic weapons and barbed wire. In addition, two artillery pieces at an outpost 6,000 yards away were aimed at the approaches to the area. When the Communists attacked, the artillery opened up. According to one observer, it was devastating with its accuracy.

Government troops, knowing that letting Communist troops through meant death, held their ground.

Red Troops Were Regulars

The Communist troops, known as hard helmets, are well-armed and well-equipped regulars belonging to a numbered unit. They have fought together for years and many are believed to have been part of the Vietminh when it campaigned successfully to topple French rule in Indo-China.

On this occasion they climbed up the main ridges to attack. One Ameri-

can military adviser surveying the scene said he believed this was their big mistake. He said they should have come up the little corridors running between the ridges. It was easier for Government troops to defend against the main ridges and concentrate their fire than against the corridors.

The attacks from three points were supposed to be simultaneous. But they were not, perhaps because the exploding mine upset their timing.

The battle lasted three hours. The unusually large commitment of Vietcong troops probably forced them to stay longer than they otherwise would have. Usually in a situation like this, where they are on the defensive and run into heavy Government firepower, they simply blend into the scenery and disappear.

At dawn the Communists withdrew. They had never penetrated the barbed-wire perimeter.

Military sources were particularly pleased by the operation because this was entirely a Vietnamese victory. The Vietnamese fought as they had been trained to fight and they won not because they had helicopters or fighter planes, but because they were well prepared and fought well.

The military sources said that not only was this by far the most successful military battle for the Government in the north where the war is slow and where the terrain makes it particularly difficult to chase communists, but also perhaps in the entire guerrilla war.

They noted that in the Mekong Delta on the few occasions in which as many Communists had been killed it was the results of a giant Government attack supported by United States helicopters against a badly outnumbered enemy. Here it was just the other way around. It was a Communist attack on a badly outnumbered Government battalion.

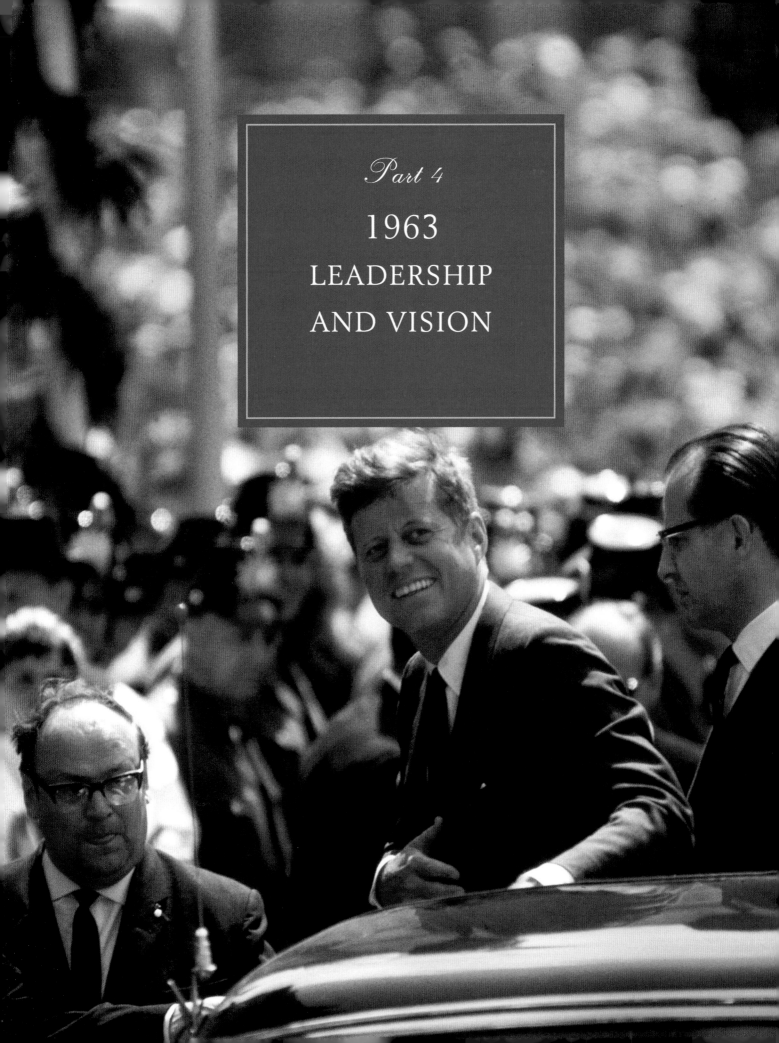

Part 4

1963
LEADERSHIP
AND VISION

Willy Brandt, center, then mayor of West Berlin, President Kennedy, and German Chancellor Konrad Adenauer, right, tour Berlin during Kennedy's visit on June 26, 1963. (Associated Press)

Freedom has many difficulties and democracy is not perfect,

but we have never had to put a wall up to keep our people in,

to prevent them from leaving us. —*President Kennedy in Berlin*

The Final Year

The last year of Kennedy's presidency was dominated by two great struggles—the civil war in Vietnam and the spotty, virtual civil war in the American South over the revolution by African Americans demanding integration of public facilities and in public schools and universities.

The president was nervous about events in Vietnam, according to his brother, Attorney General Robert Kennedy. As the year began, 45 of the more than 15,000 Americans now there had been killed in the Vietnam War (that number would balloon to 58,520 by April 29, 1975, when the U.S. finally gave up and withdrew from the country). But publicly Kennedy was resolute, personally writing a letter to the family of one of those soldiers, James McAndrew, a helicopter gunner. The letter began: "Americans are in Vietnam because we have determined that this country must not fall under Communist domination . . ."

More bad news on the war was in newspapers day after day, most of it in *The New York Times* dispatches from David Halberstam, a young correspondent who, Kennedy said, futilely and foolishly, should be brought home. The president had been told by military intelligence that the war could be won by 1965. Among Halberstam's most important articles was his vivid reporting during the spring and summer on the mass protests of South Vietnam's Buddhists—the vast majority of the population—led by monks against the Catholic Diem regime and its oppressive cadres. And when monks self-immolated on the streets of Saigon, the galvanizing shock of anti-Diem public reaction was felt across the world.

The scene of battle changed in April, when the Reverend Martin Luther King Jr. was arrested in Birmingham, Alabama, while leading a march demanding desegregation in one of the toughest cities in the South. One month after King's arrest, bombs went off at his younger brother's home and at a black-owned motel. Not for the first time, Kennedy was forced to send in troops. Soon enough, though, Americans in the rest of the country were shocked by television coverage showing dogs and fire hoses being used to subdue young demonstrators. In September, Americans were shocked again when a bomb placed at a black church killed four little girls inside, prompting another protest by thousands of people.

In June, Alabama Governor George Wallace, determined to stop two black students from enrolling, appointed himself as provost of the University of Alabama and stood in the doorway of its main building, surrounded by state troopers. Wallace had already closed public schools scheduled to be integrated. When federalized soldiers of the Alabama National Guard appeared by the hundreds, Wallace left the campus.

Not all was grief and hatred. That same month, more than a million West

Berliners emotionally cheered the visiting president as the savior of their freedom. The feeling was mutual as Kennedy saluted them as courageous citizen-soldiers in the world's struggle for freedom.

And in what may be remembered as John F. Kennedy's most notable achievement, a treaty was signed in August with Britain and the Soviet Union that banned all nuclear tests except those underground. Moscow rejoiced and so did the president. He called the first formal treaty of the nuclear age "a victory for mankind," though not the millennium. By then he was thinking about his re-election and, particularly, about changing minds in Texas, where intra-party battles might hurt his chances in 1964. He wanted to go to Houston and Austin, then Fort Worth and Dallas.

—Richard Reeves

VIETCONG DOWNS FIVE U.S. COPTERS, HITS NINE OTHERS

Defeat Worst Since Build-up Began—Three Americans Are Killed in Vietnam

By DAVID HALBERSTAM

SAIGON, Vietnam, Jan. 2—Communist guerrillas armed with automatic weapons inflicted a major defeat today on United States helicopters carrying troops into an operation in the Mekong Delta. Five helicopters were shot down.

Fourteen of the 15 helicopters taking part in the operation were hit by guerrilla gunners. Three Americans were reported killed. One was an infantry captain serving as an adviser to a ground unit, one a crew chief in an armed helicopter and the third a gunner of a transport helicopter. It is believed that six or more Americans were wounded during the long and bloody fight.

It was difficult to estimate the casualties on the ground. One source placed the South Vietnamese casualties at 50, including dead and wounded. An HU-1A pilot, who made several strikes, said he believed that up to 100 Vietcongs were killed.

One Craft Not Hit

This was by far the worst day for American helicopters in Vietnam since the American buildup began here more than a year ago. Up to today there was a widespread feeling that the addition of armed helicopters had made the use of the slower transport safer.

At one point in the action in a rice paddy, about 50 miles southwest of Saigon, three American crews were stranded as other Americans and Vietnamese were unable to get to them. However, eight hours after they were shot down, B-26 fighter-bombers, using bombs and napalm, softened up Communist resistance to permit the evacuation of the crews. There were no Americans stranded in the paddy tonight, although fierce fighting was going on.

When the helicopters came in to drop the troops as the operation began, the Vietcong, using .30-caliber and .50-caliber machine guns, opened up with murderous fire. Of the five heavily armed turbo-prop helicopters sent in as escorts to the mission, four were knocked down by fire, although all but one were able to fly out later.

U.S. military helicopter in Vietnam. (Larry Burrows/Time & Life Pictures/Getty Images)

A U.S. helicopter crew chief watches ground movements of Vietnamese troops during a strike against Vietcong guerrillas in the Mekong Delta area, January 2, 1963. (Associated Press)

Of an estimated total of 10 H-21 transport helicopters used on the mission, one returned to the base without having been hit.

The Vietcong force was estimated to be about 400 men.

Though the guerrilla technique is to avoid a fight and disappear into swamps after initial contact, the Communists were making a strong effort to hold their ground, apparently in an attempt to destroy the helicopters. As a result, the South Vietnamese Government forces were making an all-out effort to push through to the downed craft.

Late in the afternoon the Vietnamese rushed airborne troops to the area and an armed helicopter company sent in another platoon to chew up the area with rockets to help the men in the stranded helicopters and advancing Government troops. Nightfall was expected to stop the air operations. Throughout the afternoon Vietnamese fighter planes and fighter-bombers raked the area.

The fighting started in the morning in the operation that was aimed at a point where a canal intersects the Mekong River. A tree line turns the area

into a rough triangle and the helicopters landed in the middle of the triangle.

Crewmen said there was no firing on the first two lifts, but on the third the Vietcong opened with devastating automatic fire. They apparently hit the helicopters when they are most vulnerable, when they are coming in slowly and stop momentarily to let out the troops.

It was reported that the Vietcong's reaction indicated a trap had been sprung after it had become known Government forces were coming into a set spot.

Vietnamese Reds Win Major Clash

Inflict 100 Casualties in Fighting Larger Force

By DAVID HALBERSTAM

SAIGON, Vietnam, Jan. 3—Communist guerrillas, refusing to play by their own hide-and-seek rules in the face of Government troops, stood their ground and inflicted a major defeat on a larger force of Vietnamese regulars yesterday and today. Then the guerrillas slipped out of the area before reinforced Government troops could encircle them.

In the opinion of observers here the defeat was the worst that the Government troops had suffered. Government casualties in the two-day fight near this Mekong Delta village were "well over 100," one American official said.

When the Government troops entered this little village 24 hours behind schedule today they found only three Vietcong bodies.

Search Goes On

What made this defeat particularly galling to the Americans and the Vietnamese alike was that this was a battle initiated by the Government forces in a place of their own choice, with superior forces and with troops of the Seventh Vietnamese Division, which is generally considered an outstanding one in the country.

Today the Government troops got the sort of battle they wanted and they lost. An estimated total of 300 Communists withstood awesome air attacks and turned back several charges by the Vietnamese armored personnel carriers. The Vietcong simply refused to panic and they fired with deadly accuracy and consistency. The Vietnamese regulars, in contrast, in the eyes of one American observer, lost the initiative from the first moment and never showed much aggressive instinct and consequently suffered heavier casualties than they might have had they tried an all-out assault of the Vietcong positions.

"The Vietcong were brave men," one American officer said. "I think any officer would have been proud to have that unit. My God, we got a fix on one machine gun position and made 15 aerial runs at it, and every time we thought we had him, and every time that gunner came right back up firing."

Vietnam Defeat Shocks U.S. Aides

Saigon's Rejection of Advice Blamed for Setback

By DAVID HALBERSTAM

SAIGON, Vietnam, Jan. 6—The battle of Ap Bac in which attacking South Vietnamese troops were badly beaten by Communist guerillas, has bewildered high United States officials in Saigon.

The defeat at Ap Bac has two major aspects. The first, more dramatic and less significant, was the shooting down of five helicopters. Many Americans view this as virtually inevitable.

The helicopters went into an area protected by deeply entrenched, well-armed, well-trained Communist troops. Since three of five aircraft were downed while trying to rescue other downed crews, this has raised the question of what American pilots should do when a helicopter is down in a field of Communist fire.

A less spectacular and more important aspect of what happened at Ap Bac is defeat on the ground, the failure, once the Communist unit was pinpointed, to overrun it and subsequent mistakes that allowed it to slip out of the area after the battle.

These mistakes, the Americans say, were bound to happen some day in major battle.

"Time after time I have seen the same Vietnamese officers and troops make the same mistakes in virtually the same rice paddy," said one United States adviser. "The only difference was that usually they get away with it without getting hurt because the Commu-

nists simply slip away. This time the Communists fought, and so our people were torn up."

Lack of Interest Cited

Moreover, American officers throughout the Mekong Delta feel that what happened at Ap Bac goes far deeper than one battle and is directly tied to the question—whether the Vietnamese are really interested in having American advisers and listening to them.

These sources note that at several crucial moments during the battle United States advisers pleaded with certain Vietnamese units to attack or to take certain positions, usually in vain. They also note that, with reinforcements on the way and the eastern flank open, the Americans pleaded for reinforcements to come in on the east to close a ring around the Vietcong, but Vietnamese at a high level disregarded this, reinforced on the west and gave the Vietcong an escape route.

PRESIDENT PROPOSES NET TAX CUT OF $10 BILLION OVER THREE YEARS; HE IS HOPEFUL ON WORLD OUTLOOK

Message on State of Union Also Requests Reform of Levies

By TOM WICKER

WASHINGTON, Jan. 14—In a State of the Union Message notable for its tone of confidence in the nation's domestic and foreign prospects, President Kennedy called today for a three-year program of tax reduction totaling $13,500,000,000.

The tax cut would be coupled with unspecified tax reforms beginning in 1964, that would recover $3,500,000,000 of the loss in tax revenues. This would mean a net tax reduction, at the end of the three-year period, of $10,000,000,000.

The President proposed an initial reduction of $6,000,000,000 in the first year, beginning sometime in 1963, but did not indicate how the further reductions would be made in the succeeding two years.

Of the $13,500,000,000 total, the President said, $11,000,000,000 would result from reducing the tax rates of individuals and $2,500,000,000 from reducing the rates on corporations.

Effect on Individual

To the effect on individuals, the Treasury estimated that a taxpayer with a wife and two children and an income of $3,000 a year would get a reduction of $18, or about 30 per cent, on his present tax of $60.

A taxpayer with the same size family earning $10,000 would get a reduction of $304 or 22.5 per cent, on his present $1,375 tax.

Mr. Kennedy told members of the 88th Congress that his tax program was designed to stimulate economic growth and reduce unemployment. The enactment this year of a program of tax reduction and reform "overshadows all other domestic problems," he said.

Note of High Hope

Millions of Americans, watching Mr. Kennedy on the television networks, heard him close on a note of high hope.

"These are proud and memorable days in the cause of peace and freedom," the President said. "The winds of change appear to be blowing more strongly than ever, in the world of communism as well as our own. For 175 years we have sailed with those winds at our back, and with the tides of human freedom in our favor . . .

"Today we still welcome those winds of change—and we have every reason to believe that our tide is running strong."

This outlook was based, Mr. Kennedy said, on reverses and strains within the Communist world and his belief that "through the ages of the atom and outer space, the American people have neither faltered nor has their faith been flagged."

"If at times," he added, "our actions seem to make life difficult for others, it is only because history has made life difficult for us all."

While Mr. Kennedy devoted much of his address to a review of foreign developments and challenges, his primary proposals were centered on domestic affairs. Only in the field of taxes and economic affairs did he offer many details.

The Domestic Program

Among domestic programs he touched upon but did not outline fully were the following:

Increased educational and job opportunities for young people.

A domestic peace corps, serving in mental hospitals, on Indian reservations, in centers for the aged or delinquent, and elsewhere.

Medical help for the aged through their own contributions to the Social Security system.

Strengthening the right to vote: Administration sources said a new bill was being delivered to insure that persons, regardless of color, who wanted to register and vote could do so.

Increase the capacity in medical, dental and nursing schools, and a program of alleviation of mental illness and mental retardation.

Assurance of the right to counsel for all citizens accused of crime in Federal courts.

Improved transportation facilities through "increased competition and decreased regulation," and Federal assistance in the development of urban mass transit.

Further development of parks, recreational areas and natural resources.

Mr. Kennedy devoted almost a fifth of his prepared text to a strong justification of foreign-aid and mutual-assistance programs—a subject regarded coldly in the Congress. Little enthusiasm was shown for this part of the address, although the President was interrupted by applause 17 times, mostly by Democratic members.

The most eagerly awaited part of Mr. Kennedy's speech came soon after its opening when he said:

"If we are to prevail in the long run, we must expand the long-run strength of our economy. We must move along the path to a higher rate of growth and full employment."

To do so, he proposed a reduction in individual and corporate tax liabilities totaling $6,000,000,000 in 1963, with the rest of the aggregate of $13,500,000,000 coming in two subsequent annual stages.

The three-year total would result in a lowering of individual rates from the present range of 20 to 91 per cent to a new spread of 14 to 65 per cent.

The present first bracket of 20 per cent on the lowest levels of individual income would be divided into two brackets, the President said.

The upper level of the corporate tax would be reduced from 52 per cent—which, Mr. Kennedy said, "gives the Government today a majority interest in profits," to the pre-Korean War level of 47 per cent.

These slashes in tax liabilities would be about 25 per cent. They would be offset by what Mr. Kennedy calls "selected structural changes, beginning in 1964, which will broaden the tax base, end unfair or unnecessary preferences, remove or lighten certain hardships." These reforms would recover $3,500,000,000 of the Government's revenues lost by reduction of rates.

General Levels Lower

On foreign aid, the President said:

"It makes little sense for us to spend $50,000,000,000 a year to prevent [communism's] military advance—and then to begrudge spending, largely on American products, less than one-tenth of that amount to help other nations strengthen independence and cure the social chaos in which communism has always thrived."

American aid programs, he said, had contributed "to the fact that not a single one of the nearly fifty United Nation members to gain independence since the Second World War has succumbed to Communist control."

It was largely for that reason, he suggested that "today, having witnessed in recent months a heightened respect for our national purpose and power—having seen the courageous calm of a united people in a perilous hour—and having observed a steady improvement in the opportunities and well-being of our citizens—I can report to you that the state of this old but useful union is good."

Kennedy Offers Revised Program On Medical Care

Name Changed to 'Hospital Insurance'— Plan's Cost Is Nearly $10 Billion

By MARJORIE HUNTER

WASHINGTON, Feb. 21—President Kennedy asked Congress today for a nearly $10,000,000,000 program to provide medical care and other services for the nation's older citizens.

His medical program, defeated by Congress last year, was given a new look and a new name. It will be called "hospital insurance" instead of "medical care" and it provides expanded coverage and several new features. It would go into effect Jan. 1, 1965.

But even before his special message reached Congress, a fight already had shaped up.

An Administration official asserted that Republican liberals had backed off from efforts to reach a bipartisan approach by offering their own medical-care bill earlier this week.

Timetable Revised

However, a White House official said that the Republican move came as no surprise. He said that because the program was a generally popular issue with the voters, both Democrats and Republicans would seek to take credit for passage.

He predicted that it would be late summer before a medical-care program assured of passage would be hammered out in committee.

The Administration's efforts will be centered on passage of tax reform and tax reduction this year.

The Democratic and Republican bills are similar in many respects. But the bills differ on one major point. The Republican measure would allow beneficiaries the option of being insured under private plans, with the Federal Government paying the benefits. The Administration bill would not allow a private-insurance option.

The health insurance program was only a part of the sweeping program for the aged outlined for Congress today by the President. He called for 36 separate programs, ranging from improved housing to employment opportunities.

The total program would cost $9,821,000,000 over a five-year period. More than half—$5,245,000,000— would come from a special Social Security trust fund to finance hospital insurance. Social Security taxes would be increased from the present $3\frac{5}{8}$ per cent paid by both employer and employee to $3\frac{7}{8}$. The wage base on which Social Security taxes are paid would be increased from the present $4,800 to $5,200.

Atomic Submarine With 129 Lost In Depths 220 Miles Off Boston; Oil Slick Seen Near Site of Dive

Thresher Hunted

Rescue Craft Search Area of Last Test in 8,400-Foot Water

By ROBERT F. WHITNEY

WASHINGTON, Apr. 10—The Navy said tonight that its atomic submarine Thresher and 129 men aboard "appeared to be lost" in the Atlantic.

An oil slick was reported to have been sighted in the area where the vessel took a deep test dive at about 9 o'clock this morning in water 8,400 feet deep, 220 miles east of Boston.

"At that depth," said Adm. George W. Anderson, Chief of Naval Opera-tions, "rescue would be absolutely out of the question."

Loss of the Thresher and 129 men would be the Navy's worst peacetime submarine disaster.

However, the navy still clung to the possibility that there had been a communications failure and the $45,000,000 submarine was unable to report by radio or otherwise.

This appeared to be a dim hope after the ship, named for the thresher shark, had not been heard from since early morning.

Radiation Peril Denied

Admiral Anderson announced that the accident would be investigated by a court of inquiry headed by Vice Adm. Bernard Austin, president of the Naval War College.

Admiral Anderson, who was at the Pentagon answering reporters' ques-tions about the disaster, assured them that there was "no chance of nuclear explosion in the submarine" or of "ra-dioactive contamination" dangers to shipping.

The Navy chief said quietly:

"To those of us who have been brought up in the traditions of the sea it is a sad occasion when a ship is reported lost."

The Navy's first announcement that the Thresher was missing came after reports flooded Newport, R. I., that a submarine was "on the bottom and un-able to rise."

Rescue Vessels Sent

With the Thresher missing, the Navy sent destroyers from Newport and aircraft from Quonset, R. I., Air Station. They are probing for possible radio signals and a fix on the subma-rine's position.

Nuclear-powered submarine the USS Thresher *steers through the sea, early 1960s.* (Pictorial Parade/Getty Images)

The 129 men aboard include 96 enlisted men, 16 officers and 17 civilian technicians from the Portsmouth, N. H., Navy Yard.

The Thresher had recently been at Portsmouth for overhaul and had gone out for deep diving tests. With her was the submarine rescue ship Skylark, which lost contact after the Thresher's dive.

The depth at which the Navy thinks the Thresher may be lying would doom the vessel and her crew. Pressures at such a depth would crush the hull, it was said.

The Thresher was launched in 1960 and commissioned in August, 1961. She is a nuclear attack craft, the newest of her class, which are the fastest and deepest operating submarines in the fleet.

The possible crushing of the Thresher's hull immediately raised a question as to whether her nuclear reactor would be torn apart and the area of sea contaminated with radioactivity.

Admiral Anderson said he had checked this with Vice Adm. Hyman G. Rickover, the Navy's nuclear propulsion expert, and received assurances that this was a "negligible possibility."

The Thresher was the first of her class of nuclear attack submarines. Two others, the Permit and the Plunger, are in operation and 22 more are under construction.

An attack submarine like the Thresher is said to be able to operate as deep as 1,000 feet below the surface. It is believed that ships of this class have an underwater speed in excess of 30 knots.

The actual maximum depths at which United States submarines can operate are secret.

Submarine Rescue Vessels

The submarines of the Thresher's class have the so-called albacore hull—resembling the shape of the fish—are sonar geared, and carry torpedoes and other weapons. They were designed for attacking shipping and finding and destroying other submarines.

Dr. King Arrested At Birmingham

He Defies a Court Injunction by Leading Negro March—60 Others Seized

By FOSTER HAILEY

BIRMINGHAM, Ala., April 12—The Rev. Dr. Martin Luther King Jr. was arrested this afternoon when he defied a court injunction and led a march of Negroes toward the downtown section.

The marchers were halted after four and a half blocks—but not before more than a thousand shouting, singing Negroes had joined in the demonstration.

In addition to Dr. King, the Rev. Dr. Ralph D. Abernathy, secretary of the Southern Christian Leadership Conference, and more than 80 others were taken into custody. There was no violence.

[In Clarksdale, Miss., firebombs were thrown at a Negro leader's home where Representative Charles C. Diggs Jr. of Michigan was staying, but no one was hurt. Two young men were arrested and admitted the bombing, but said they were "just having fun."]

White Clergyman Held

For the second time a white man joined the Birmingham Negro demonstrators and was arrested.

Today it was Dr. Robert Fulton, a middle-aged Presbyterian clergyman who is teaching at Miles College, a co-educational Negro school in Birmingham. Several days ago, Carl Keith of Evanston, Ill., was arrested when he joined a group of pickets at a downtown store. He is still in jail.

Dr. King was among the first to be put behind bars. Safety Commissioner T. Eugene Connor, who directed the arrests, said Dr. King would be charged with violation of a city ordinance in parading without a permit and also with defying a state court injunction against demonstrations.

The penalty on conviction of the city charge is 180 days in jail and a fine of $100. Punishment for the injunction violation could be much more severe.

The injunction was issued by Circuit Court Judge W. A. Jenkins Wednesday night. Dr. King announced yesterday his intention to defy it.

Opposition to King

The march was the most spectacular of many demonstrations held since a direct action assault on Birmingham racial barriers was begun 10 days ago under the leadership of the local affiliate of the Southern Christian Leadership Conference.

It was the first in which Dr. King has taken part. His major effort here the last 10 days has been to rally support behind the direct action campaign.

There has been much opposition in the Negro community here of more than 100,000 to pressing the campaign, just as a new and moderate city administration is taking office, and to the participation of Dr. King, even though he has said he was invited to come. There also has been some reported grumbling that Dr. King was letting local people get arrested and staying safely behind the lines himself.

Counting today's arrests, more than 150 persons have been taken into custody.

More than 40 of that number, several of them leaders of the campaign, have been released on cash bail of $300. Twenty four have been tried, convicted and given maximum sentences. Trials of the others were halted when defense attorneys invoked a 95-year-old section of the Federal Criminal Code concerning civil rights and the Federal Court here agreed to rule on its validity. A hearing will be held next week.

Dr. King would be charged with violation of a city ordinance in parading without a permit.

Today's march was the most widely advertised demonstration yet held and was viewed by larger groups of Negroes than any of the others. It was originally scheduled to start at noon from the Sixth Avenue Zion Hill Baptist Church, a small church at 14th Street and Sixth Avenue North, three blocks inside the main Negro section of the city.

It was 2:40 P. M., however, before Dr. King and the others emerged from the church doors and started east up Sixth Avenue. Dr. King and Dr. Abernathy were at the head of a procession of 40 or 50 marchers. They were dressed in blue jeans and blue cotton shirts to dramatize the efforts they have been making to bring about a Negro boycott of Easter buying at downtown white stores.

The march continued up Sixth Avenue to 17th Street, where police had sealed off a whole block, obviously hoping to trap the marchers there and keep onlookers back. It was at that corner that the only violence of the last 10 days occurred last Sunday when police dogs were used to drive back onlookers.

Instead of proceeding up Sixth Avenue toward City Hall, as the police had expected, the marchers turned south at the corner and marched on toward Fifth Avenue and the downtown business section.

'Stop Them There'

At Fifth Avenue they turned east again. The police, meanwhile, had redeployed their forces and were waiting halfway down the block. As the head of the march passed behind some trucks at the entrance to a garage, Commissioner Connor told his forces "stop them there."

Two motorcycle patrolmen and two detectives grabbed Dr. King and Dr. Abernathy and hustled them into a police van a few steps away. The order of the marchers, which had started out two abreast, had been disrupted as eager onlookers joined in behind them and on either side. Thus police had difficulty trying to sort the marchers from spectators.

Most of the marchers, however, including Dr. Fulton, voluntarily stepped forward and lined up to enter other waiting police vans. One of those who did not was the Rev. Fred L. Shuttlesworth, head of the local Christian Movement for Human Rights, which initiated the campaign here. He was arrested last Saturday but was released on bail Monday night.

Mr. Shuttlesworth was arrested later at a motel.

There were shouts of anger from the several hundred Negroes who were in sight of the arrests and who had been singing and clapping hands as they walked or ran alongside the marchers.

When police moved toward them and ordered them back west down Fifth Avenue most of them gave way freely. Three who stopped to argue with policemen were arrested.

The police quickly cleared the streets and sidewalks for two blocks and even moved onlookers out of a small park on 17th Street, but Mr. Connor ordered them to let the people in the park alone.

"Let them stay there and sing all they want to," he said.

When the demonstration started, Mr. Connor asked an onlooker what he thought of the parade, but without pausing for an answer, inquired:

"Was King in that bunch?"

Told that he was, Mr. Connor said:

"That's what he came down here for, to get arrested. Now he's got it."

What effect Dr. King's arrest will have on the campaign is problematical. His father and brother, the latter a clergyman at nearby Ensley, Ala., are still here and all the local leaders are now out of jail.

Mass kneel-ins had been planned at white churches Sunday and those presumably will be attempted. King and the others have rebuffed efforts to get them to halt their direct action campaign until Mayor-elect Arthur Boutwell and the new city council form of government takes office Monday.

Dr. King and the local leaders say that no matter who is arrested others will step forward to take their place. They say that the campaign will be continued until there is at least a beginning made in easing discrimination.

Alabama Burning

VIOLENCE EXPLODES AT RACIAL PROTESTS IN ALABAMA; 10 ON FREEDOM WALK SEIZED AT ALABAMA LINE

Negroes and Whites Arrested by Patrolmen Wielding Electrical Prod Poles

By CLAUDE SITTON

HAMMONDVILLE, Ala., May 3—Alabama highway patrolmen wielding electrical prod poles arrested five white and five Negro "Freedom Walkers" today. A crowd of 1,500 whites shouted their approval.

The 10 men, who set out Wednesday to complete an ambushed postman's march from Chattanooga, Tenn., to Jackson, Miss., were jailed at Fort Payne on charges of breach of the peace.

Five are members of the Congress of Racial Equality, or CORE, and five of the Student Nonviolent Coordinating Committee.

Three demonstrators lay down on the pavement of U.S. Route 11 just inside the Alabama line from Georgia as troopers sought to lead them to waiting patrol cruisers.

Patrol officials brought up three-foot-long prod poles, usually used for forcing cattle into chutes, and jabbed the demonstrators, giving them repeated electrical shocks.

As one of the Negroes flinched and twisted in the grip of four troopers, an elderly, toothless white man shouted from a roadside pasture: "Stick him again! Stick him again!"

Alfred Lingo, State Commissioner of Public Safety, directed the operation, closing the Federal highway to all traffic for ten minutes after the Freedom Walkers crossed.

Although 12 blue-and-gray clad troopers refused to allow reporters to follow the demonstrators, they made no attempt to prevent the crowd from streaming over a fence and across a creek to reach the arrest scene.

Commissioner Lingo first shouted over a public address system to the marchers to disperse. When they held their ground, he called to his men to arrest them.

Later, the commissioner said, "They'll be taken to the DeKalb County Jail and charged with breach of the peace, period."

The arrest came at 3:40 P. M. about three and a half hours and six and a half miles after the marchers resumed their journey on the crest of a forested hill between Lookout and Fox Mountains northeast of Rising Fawn, Ga.

A band of white teen-agers numbering at various times from 20 to 50, followed the demonstrators all the way to the Alabama line.

They were held somewhat in check by Capt. P. C. Peacock and Trooper H.

M. Turner of the Georgia State Patrol. Nevertheless, the whites pelted the ten men occasionally with rocks and eggs.

At a lunch stop southwest of Rising Fawn, a white man struck the neck of Winston Lockett, a 21-year-old CORE member, bruising it severely.

Mr. Lockett fell to the pavement and clasped his hands behind his neck but his assailant moved off.

Reporters were harassed along the line of march and at the roadblock on the Alabama line. A white man driving an automobile with Alabama license plates kicked one reporter outside Rising Fawn.

Another was shoved as he climbed a barbed wire fence at the state line. And a third, a woman, was threatened by men in the pasture at the arrest scene.

The "Moore Memorial Trek" grew out of an attempt by CORE and the Student Committee to carry out the one-man Freedom Walk started by William L. Moore, a white, 35-year-old Baltimore letter carrier and member of CORE.

He was shot to death the night of April 23 on U. S. 11 near Keener, Ala.

Nine other Student Committee members who sought to resume the march at Attalla, Ala., earlier this week

A 17-year-old civil rights activist is attacked by police dogs in Birmingham, Alabama, May 3, 1963. (Bill Hudson/Associated Press)

also were arrested and charged with breach of the peace.

The ten marchers arrested today began their journey Wednesday morning at the Greyhound bus station in Chattanooga. This was the starting point for Mr. Moore, who was bearing a sign with integration slogans and a letter for Gov. Ross R. Barnett of Mississippi urging racial toleration.

Start Was Delayed

They delayed their start today until shortly after noon in the hope that an injunction proceeding would be filed in the Federal District Court at Montgomery. It would have requested that Gov. George C. Wallace and other state officials be prohibited from denying their right to walk peacefully along the state's highways, according to them.

A crowd of 150 whites stood around the departure point, gossiping, exchanging jokes and whittling. "They ain't never gonna make it to the Alabama line," predicted a white youth.

Told that Commissioner Lingo and 20 troopers were waiting at the Alabama line to arrest them, Richard Haley, 46, assistant national director of CORE, replied:

"We have come a pretty good distance. We have much further to go. Our destination is Jackson, Miss. What occurs between here and there, we simply have to meet it as it comes.

"Whatever does arise, we are keeping in mind that our destination is Jackson. We have had much discussion of this among ourselves and we are all of one mind."

Singing their freedom song, "We Shall Overcome," the walkers stepped off rather briskly despite blistered feet behind Sam Shirah, 20, a Student Committee field secretary.

Mr. Shirah, a native white Alabamian, had especially wanted to lead the group, according to Mr. Haley, carrying across his shoulders two cardboard placards with the slogans from the

Moore sandwich board: "Eat at Joe's Both Black and White," and "Equal Rights for All (Mississippi or bust)."

Down the long green valley they tramped, past the meadow where, according to legend, a Cherokee father saw a fawn rising one morning and gave the name to his child, which was later adopted by the hamlet of 500 persons at the foot of Fox Mountain.

As the demonstrators crossed the line, the crowd spilled into the pasture on the right and up the hill. "Get the goddam communists!," shouted a white as the commissioner gave the order to arrest the marchers. "Throw them niggers in the river!," yelled another.

Behind them came a procession of more than 50 cars, trucks and station wagons, slowing traffic along the highway.

"Troopers ain't gonna do you no good down there in Alabama," shouted one white youth of a group of 50 or more clustered in front of a filling station.

"Kill them white men first!" yelled another.

Federal Bureau of Investigation agents rolled past the line in cars, filming the white harassers with movie cameras and jotting down automobile license numbers.

A yellow-and-maroon spotter plane, presumably from Alabama, made frequent passes along the highway. And Sheriff Allison Blevins of Dade County and a deputy cruised up and down the line of march.

One egg and then another sailed through the air, striking William Hansen, 23, and Carver Neblett, 20, Student Committee field secretaries, and Zev Aelony of CORE.

Little Boy Waves

As the walkers passed beneath 11 Confederate battle flags strung across the highway in front of a souvenir shop, a little white boy clutched his mother's skirts with one hand and waved to the demonstrators. The mother quickly pressed the hand down.

An Alabama youth sitting on the fender of his car parked in the wild onions on the shoulder shouted: "You won't make it. Georgia may take it but Alabama won't ever stand for it."

As the marchers stopped for lunch beneath a clump of young redbud trees, a jet knifed across the sky, trailing contrails.

A group of whites raced by in a car shouting obscenities. One yelled: "Come on down to Alabama, you—."

As the band of teenagers edged forward toward the resting marchers, Captain Peacock admonished them with the words: "The first thing those European newspapers would do would be to jump on us. We need friends wherever we can get them."

Minutes later, Mr. Lockett was attacked as he returned from a mobile

"Freedom Canteen" sent out from Chattanooga by the National Association for the Advancement of Colored People.

"He tried to run over me," the white assailant said. Then he disappeared into the crowd.

Shortly before he resumed the hike, Robert Gore, assistant community relations director for CORE, was struck on the left temple by a rock.

Other rocks hit Mr. Hansen and Mr. Aelony as the group approached the Alabama line. Trooper Turner had taken charge of the teenage whites at this point.

Hundreds of cars lined the highway along a hill leading down to the creek that marks the state line. As the marchers passed the cluster of service stations at the top, the crowd began to form at the roadblock.

As the demonstrators crossed the line, the crowd spilled into the pasture on the right and up the hill.

"Get the goddam communists!," shouted a white as the commissioner gave the order to arrest the marchers.

"Throw them niggers in the river!," yelled another.

"Kill him! Kill him! Kill him!," screamed a woman with her hair in plastic curlers.

Eric Weinberger of CORE, Mr. Aelony and John Robert Zellner, another Alabamian and a Student Committee field secretary, fell on the pavement in the posture of nonviolent resistance. Troopers picked them up and an electric prod pole was brought into play.

"Low white man!" yelled a white. "A dog and a fox got better sense than you."

The crowds broke up as the patrol cruisers sped away toward Fort Payne with the demonstrators, and Commissioner Lingo signaled to his men to lift the roadblock.

U.S. Seeking a Truce in Birmingham; Hoses Again Drive Off Demonstrators

---

Two Aides Meeting With Leaders—Negroes Halt Protests Temporarily

---

By FOSTER HAILEY

BIRMINGHAM, Ala., May 4—The Justice Department sent two high officials here today in an apparent attempt to bring about a truce in the tense racial situation, pending official establishment of the new city government.

The two officials are Burke Marshall, assistant attorney general in charge of the department's Civil Rights Division, and Joseph F. Dolan, assistant deputy attorney general.

Demonstrations by Negroes seeking the lowering of racial barriers continued with fierce intensity. Firemen again used fire hoses, turning them on groups of Negro spectators who disregarded police orders to disperse.

When the water was turned on, rocks and broken bottles were thrown at the firemen.

At the height of the disturbance, one of the demonstration leaders, the Rev. James Bevel, borrowed a bull horn from the police and called on the crowds at 17th Street and Fifth Avenue to leave.

"Everybody get off this corner," he said. "If you're not going to demonstrate in a nonviolent way, then leave."

His plea and the high-pressure streams of water drove the crowds from the intersection. The police then moved in and also cleared a block-square park nearby.

Shortly thereafter Mr. Bevel, who is Mississippi field secretary of the Southern Christian Leadership Conference, called off further demonstrations today. He said he had seen several pistols and knives being carried by spectators and was afraid of more serious trouble.

Police turned hoses on a groups of black demonstrators in Birmingham, Alabama, May 4, 1963.

(John Duprey/*New York Daily News* Archive/Getty Images)

The only weekend activity, he said, would be "prayer vigils" at white churches tomorrow. The street demonstrations will be renewed at 9 A.M. Monday, he said.

Mr. Bevel's action in calling off the demonstrations today apparently had no connection with the arrival here of Mr. Marshall and Mr. Dolan.

Mr. Marshall was known to have appointments to meet with Sheriff Melvin Bailey and with the Rev. Dr. Martin Luther King Jr., head of the Southern Christian Leadership Conference and leader of the direct-action anti-segregation campaign here.

Mayor Albert Boutwell, head of the new government whose right to City Hall is being disputed, said, however, that he had not been in contact with Mr. Marshall.

Mr. Marshall did speak to one of Mr. Boutwell's aides, but he did not ask for a meeting with the Mayor.

The office of Police Chief Jamie Moore said that neither the chief nor safety commissioner T. Eugene Connor had seen the Civil Rights Division Chief, nor did either have an appointment to do so.

In late afternoon the Juvenile Court said 111 demonstrators under the age of 18 had been arraigned there and sent to the juvenile detention home. At the city jail it was said that adults taken into custody were still being processed but that their number would exceed 100. This would raise the total of arrests for both adults and juveniles over the last three days to more than 1,100.

The police and sheriff's deputies maintained a close watch on the park and the adjoining Negro areas during late afternoon, but there were no further major disturbances or arrests. Whenever more than five or six persons began to congregate, the police moved in to disperse them.

The demonstrations today centered, as yesterday, at 17th Street and Fifth Avenue, on the edge of the Negro business district.

The city's squad of police dogs was again on the scene, but they were not used.

It was estimated that there were perhaps 2,000 Negroes in the park and the immediate vicinity today.

Several hundred white persons who had gathered to watch the demonstration were moved out of the area by the police. Roadblocks then were set up by the police and sheriff's deputies a block in each direction from the park and from the 16th Street Baptist Church.

Demonstrators All Young

Again the demonstrators were all young people. Some were no older than 10 or 12 years old.

The Negro demonstrations, in their fifth week, obviously are going to be continued until some relaxation of racial barriers is achieved.

Dr. King told a mass meeting last night that there must be no let-up in the drive for equality.

"Today [Friday] was D-day," he said. "Tomorrow will be Double D-day."

The demonstrations today began shortly after noon. Moving in groups of twos and threes, Negroes began to walk toward City Hall. They were not organized in a march, nor did they carry banners.

Just to the north of City Hall, at 19th Street and 8th Avenue North, several of the smaller groups merged into one, and a girl unfurled a banner reading: "Love God and Thy Neighbor."

Mr. Connor, who had just left City Hall, immediately ordered their arrest. Policemen marched them down a ramp into a detention pen in the basement of the big sandstone building.

There were 25 in the group. All but three or four were in their teens, and four boys appeared to be not more than 10 or 12 years old. They smiled at cameramen standing on the wall above them as the police led them away.

They had hardly disappeared into the interior of the building when a young girl and a woman came strolling by and kneeled on the steps of City Hall. They, too, were arrested. Then came two girls in their teens, and they also were marched off to the basement.

The police sergeant in charge then ordered all groups of Negroes turned back if they attempted to approach the hall.

. . . a girl unfurled a banner reading: "Love God and Thy Neighbor."

The strolling groups represented a demonstration tactic not used heretofore. Previously the demonstrators, both adult and younger moved in columns of twos, carrying banners, or have gone by car to an agreed-on place and broken out their banners there.

Several hundred young demonstrators had again been marshaled to walk and perhaps join in jail or the juvenile detention home the almost 1,000 persons arrested Thursday and yesterday.

Two churches were being used today, the 16th Street Baptist and the Greater A. O. H. Church.

When the demonstrations began, the police closed the doors of both churches. A fire truck was stationed outside the second church for use if needed.

The number of persons inside the two churches was not determined, but apparently there were hundreds.

The disturbance at 17th and Fifth Avenue, which had menacing implications for a few minutes, lasted about half an hour. With the area cleared of spectators, vehicular and foot traffic again was permitted through. Yesterday the area was closed for more than two hours, creating a major traffic jam in adjoining streets.

One middle-aged Negro man, sitting atop a parked car near the 16th Street Church today observing the disturbance a block away, said bitterly:

"I've been a citizen until today. Those people should be ashamed, both races. We've got radicals on both sides."

RIOTING NEGROES ROUTED BY POLICE AT BIRMINGHAM

3,000 Demonstrators Crash Lines—Highway Patrol Is Sent Into the City

---

CROWD THROWS STONES

N.A.A.C.P. Calls for Protest by Pickets Across U.S.— Hopes Raised by Talks

By CLAUDE SITTON

BIRMINGHAM, Ala., May 7—The police and firemen drove hundreds of rioting Negroes off the streets today with high-pressure hoses and an armored car.

The riot broke out after 2,500 to 3,000 persons rampaged through the business district in two demonstrations and were driven back.

The Negroes rained rocks, bottles and brickbats on the law-enforcement officials as they were slowly forced backward by the streams of water. The pressure was so high that the water skinned bark off trees in parks and along sidewalks.

Highway Patrol Called

Policemen from surrounding cities and members of the Alabama Highway Patrol rushed to a nine-block area near the main business district to help quell the riot.

An undetermined number of persons were injured in the demonstrations against segregation. They included the Rev. Fred L. Shuttlesworth, a Negro leader, and two city policemen and a Jefferson County deputy sheriff.

[The National Association for the Advancement of Colored People called for peaceful picketing in 100 cities around the country to protest the ac-

tions of the Birmingham officials. In Greenfield Park, N. Y., a group of Conservative rabbis left for Birmingham in a "testimony on behalf of the human rights and dignity" of Negroes.]

Appeals to President

Clarence B. Hanson Jr., publisher of The Birmingham News, the city's afternoon daily, appealed today in a telegram to President Kennedy to persuade Negro leaders to halt the demonstrations. The text of the telegram was carried on the front page of the newspaper.

Burke Marshall, chief of the Justice Department's Civil Rights Division, met privately with white business, professional and civic leaders from Birmingham and Jefferson County. The group was reported to be in telephone contact with Negro leaders. Later, a spokesman said the group had "high hopes" for developments in the next day or two that would ease the tension here.

In the demonstrations today, only 28 persons, including four juveniles, were arrested, as compared with some 1,000 yesterday. The police apparently wanted to avoid further arrests. Sheriff Melvin Bailey conceded that, from the standpoint of prison space, "we've got a problem."

Gov. George C. Wallace ordered 250 highway patrolmen to this Southern steel center, which has been torn by racial strife for five weeks. Some of the patrolmen have been trained in controlling riots.

Brig. Gen. Henry V. Graham of the Alabama National Guard arrived here after the situation was under control. He served as State Adjutant General under former Gov John Patterson and enforced martial law in Montgomery, the state capital, in the Freedom Rider riots of 1961.

It could not be learned immediately whether his presence indicated that Governor Wallace was considering the use of the National Guard here.

In Montgomery, Governor Wallace addressed the opening session of the state legislature. He promised to "take whatever action I am called upon to take" to preserve law and order.

"I am beginning to tire of agitators, integrationists, and others who seek to destroy law and order in Alabama," he said.

The Rev. Dr. Martin Luther King Jr. called the reluctance of the police to arrest Negroes a victory. The Atlanta minister, president of the Southern Christian Leadership Conference, is leading the integration campaign.

Dr. King and his lieutenants appeared to have little control of the demonstrations, which were joined by hundreds of bystanders. One conference official accused leaders of the Nonviolent Coordinating Committee, an Atlanta-based integration group, of "whipping up" the emotions of the many teen-age participants.

The rioting broke out at about 2:45 P. M., Central Standard time, when Negroes jammed along sidewalks on the

Birmingham, May 1963. (John Duprey/*New York Daily News* Archive/Getty Images)

south side of the Kelly Ingram Park began hurling stones at the policemen and firemen.

Orders Use of Hoses

Safety Commissioner Eugene Connor, who is in charge of the Fire and Police Departments, gave the order to turn the hoses on them. For almost an hour a seesaw struggle was waged around the park, and in side streets and alleys.

The rioters were driven back at one point, only to appear again at another point to rain stones on the authorities. A deputy sheriff was struck by a stone opposite the 16th Street Baptist Church, the departure point for the demonstrations. He was carried to a hospital in a police cruiser.

A monitor, an extremely high-pressure fire nozzle fed by two, two-and-a-half-inch hoses, skidded out of control on its tripod mount opposite the church and struck two policemen. One suffered rib fractures and the other a leg injury.

Mr. Shuttlesworth, head of the Alabama Christian Movement for Human Rights, who also serves as pastor of a church in Cincinnati, Ohio, was struck by a stream of water and was hurled against the side of the church. He was carried inside and was later removed in a stretcher to an ambulance, which drove him to the Holy Family Hospital. Doctors said he had suffered chest injuries but was not hurt seriously.

Commissioner Connor arrived after the minister was driven away, said "I waited a week to see Shuttlesworth get hit with a hose. I'm sorry I missed it."

A newsman noted that Mr. Shuttlesworth had been carried away in an ambulance.

"I wish they'd carried him away in a hearse," commented the commissioner.

Mr. Connor pointed out that several policemen had been injured and said, "We've just started to fight, if that's what they want. We were trying to be nice to them but they won't let us be nice."

The armored car, looking much like a tank with six wheels instead of tracks, roared backward and forward on 16th Street, forcing Negroes to the curb. Warnings to disperse were sounded repeatedly from loudspeakers atop the vehicle. There were a number of gun ports in the armor, but no guns were in evidence.

The stream from one fire hose picked a man up and flipped him over, then sent him skittering along the grass in the park. Gutters along the southern edge of the elm-shaded square were overflowing.

Urge Crowd to Leave

Hundreds of whites massed along 18th Street to the east but made no effort to break through the police lines, thrown up at intersections to seal off the area.

> *"I am beginning to tire of agitators, integrationists, and others who seek to destroy law and order in Alabama."*
>
> —*Governor George Wallace*

Shortly after 3 P. M., Mr. Shuttlesworth marched into sight on the southern edge of the park at the head of 300 Negroes, many of them children. As they turned north, a monitor nozzle opened up and drove them all to cover.

Two Negro leaders, accompanied by Capt. George Wall of the police, walked along 16th Street for two blocks urging the crowd to go home. Their efforts had little apparent effect.

A few minutes later, 15 patrolmen armed with nightsticks charged behind a row of tenements opposite the church, confiscated a pile of stones and drove off the rioters who had been throwing them.

Five German shepherds, trained as police dogs, were brought up but were not used. They had been in past disturbances.

Before the demonstrations and the subsequent rioting, Dr. King voiced confidence over recent developments here. He and Mr. Shuttlesworth held a news conference at the Gaston Motel, headquarters for what Negroes call "The Movement."

"Activities which have taken place in Birmingham over the last few days, to my mind, mark the nonviolent movement coming of age," Dr. King said. "This is the first time in the history of our struggle that we have been able, literally, to fill the jails."

"In a very real sense, this is the fulfillment of a dream." Dr. King contended, as he has in the past, that imprisonment of Negroes "will lay the issue before the conscience of the community and the nation."

He said further that there would be no let-up in the demonstrations until the demands of the Negroes are met. He said white leaders seemed to recognize that the demands were just.

"But, at this point, I would not say that negotiations have been satisfactory," he said. "The demonstrations will go on until some progress has been made."

Less than two hours later, the first group of demonstrators, 14 schoolchildren, marched out of the 16th Street Church. Some clutched paper lunch bags, others had books. One child in a later group carried a suitcase.

The first 14 walked by twos east on Sixth Avenue past the Jockey Boy restaurant to 17th Street, where a policeman turned them north. Two other policemen at the next corner took their placards but allowed them to continue.

Juvenile authorities, their detention home and make-shift centers bulging with more than 1,000 demonstrators, began releasing children to their parents today on signed appearance bonds. Previously, cash bonds of $100 were required.

More than 100 juveniles were released, officials said, most of them under 13 years old. One was a 7-year-old girl arrested yesterday.

Dale Oltman, the chief probation officer of Juvenile Court, said authorities had called parents to encourage them to pick up their children. "We were concerned about having these younger children in detention," he said. "We felt they should be home with their parents."

Fund Drive Opens Here

A campaign to enlist financial and moral support for the Birmingham civil rights drive was started here yesterday.

The movement, known as Back Our Brothers, is led by Noel N. Marder of Yonkers, head of an encyclopedia sales company, and Jackie Robinson, former Brooklyn Dodgers baseball player. Mr. Marder told a news conference at Sardi's, 234 West 44th Street, that the movement's first public function would be a $100-a-plate dinner at the Park Sheraton Hotel on June 18.

Mr. Robinson said he had sent a telegram to President Kennedy declaring that "the revolution that is taking place in this country cannot be squelched by police dogs or high power hoses."

A. Philip Randolph, president of the Negro American Council, termed the actions against Negroes in Birmingham "treacherous barbarism." State Attorney General Louis J. Lefkowitz said the events there were "a terrible outrage."

BOMBS TOUCH OFF WIDESPREAD RIOT AT BIRMINGHAM

Negroes Attack Police After Blasts Rip Home of King's Brother and a Motel

STATE PATROL CALLED

Violence Follows Accord on Limited Integration and End to Demonstrations

By HEDRICK SMITH

BIRMINGHAM, Ala., Sunday, May 12—The bombings of a Negro motel and an integration leader's home touched off widespread rioting on the edge of this city's business district early today.

Angered by the attacks, thousands of Negroes poured into the streets and engaged the police, firemen, state highway patrolman and Jefferson County deputy sheriffs in a running battle that raged through four or five blocks.

One policeman was stabbed in the back, at least three struck by missiles and an undetermined number were injured.

As of 3:30 A.M., New York time, the rioting was still going on and growing in intensity.

The first explosion rocked the home of the Rev. A. D. King, a leader in the Birmingham desegregation drive and the younger brother of the Rev. Dr. Martin Luther King Jr., president of the Southern Christian Leadership Conference.

Worst Violence

The second of last night's blasts struck minutes later at the A. G. Gaston Motel, half a block away from Kelly Park, scene of last Tuesday's rioting.

Alabama Highway patrolmen rushed here to reinforce local and Jefferson County authorities. The police used an armored riot car and police dogs in a futile attempt to disperse the mob in the vicinity of the motel and the park.

The bombings and the riot followed by only one day announcement of an agreement between white and Negro leaders on a four-point limited desegregation plan for Birmingham.

The riot grew in intensity as it raged on into the night, becoming without a doubt one of the worst racial explosions seen in the South in years.

First reports said that there were no injuries at the A. D. King home.

The Rev. Wyatt Tee Walker, executive assistant to Dr. King, made repeated futile attempts to disperse the mob in front of the motel and at the park.

"Will you cooperate with him (Dr. King) by going to your homes?" he demanded.

Showers of gravel, bottles, rocks and bricks struck police cruisers and patrol wagons in the area.

"They started it!" the Negroes shouted.

At least two policemen were hit by missiles.

The mob attacked a car parked in front of the 16th Street Baptist Church, departure point for last week's mass demonstrations, overturned it and set it afire. The Negro driver fled.

Dogs Kept Leashed

Some members of the mob tried to restrain others who were attacking the police. The dogs were held in check on their leashes and were used as a show of force.

As the riot car raced down the streets and sidewalks in the area with its siren screaming, an officer inside shouted over the loudspeakers, "Everybody get off the streets now. We cannot get ambulances in here to help your people unless you clear the streets."

A spokesman at the University of Alabama hospital here said four injured persons had been brought in from the motel bombing. He said none was in serious condition. He was unable to identify them.

One Negro asserted, "I said there'd be a race riot and this is it."

At one point, as a shower of rocks struck the advancing policemen, members of the mob shouted "Kill 'em, Kill 'em."

Earlier yesterday, Public Safety Commissioner Eugene Connor urged white citizens to boycott merchants who have agreed to desegregate lunch counters and other store facilities.

"The white people and other people of this city should not go in these stores," Mr. Connor declared. "That's the best way I know to beat down integration in Alabama."

He also called on the merchants to "have backbone enough to come out" and identify themselves.

Assault on Settlement

Commissioner Connor's comments, carried on a newscast by radio station WBRC, were the first public, frontal attack on the settlement that ended

Birmingham's five-week racial crisis.

Desegregation of downtown store facilities within 90 days was one of the terms of agreement announced yesterday by the Rev. Dr. Martin Luther King Jr., the Atlanta integrationist who has spearheaded the civil rights drive here.

However, neither Dr. King nor Sidney W. Smyer, a spokesman for white businessmen who negotiated the agreement, disclosed which stores were involved.

The anonymity was apparently aimed at keeping to a minimum the reaction from strong segregationists.

Most Negroes seemed to take a cautious, wait-and-see attitude toward the desegregation pact.

"It's all right if they do what they say they're going to do," said a Negro porter. "I don't think they will."

A lawyer was slightly more optimistic. He called the agreement an "important step forward, but it's only a start."

Negroes to Ease Boycott

The pact included promises rather than immediate action. In return, Negroes called off their mass demonstrations and promised to "ease" their boycott of downtown Birmingham stores.

Besides store desegregation, the white businessmen also agreed to establishing a biracial committee within two weeks and promoting and hiring Negroes.

About 250 young Negroes attending a mass meeting yesterday were urged to remain vigilant. The Rev. James Bevel, of Cleveland, Miss., an aide to Dr. King, urged the crowd to be prepared to resume demonstrations "if the agreement were not lived up to."

"To some folks, this is a victory," he said. "This was not a victory. This was an indication that victory is possible if we remain nonviolent and if we continue to insist on righteousness.

"If we got anything—I don't know if we got anything yet—we must devise a way of preserving it when we get it."

John J. Drew, a Negro leader who helped negotiate the agreement, said he was convinced it would be carried out. He said:

"We will see tangible gains on all points within 90 days. We may not get all the things we want, but a good move will be made."

Implementation of the agreement rests, in part, on the resolution of Birmingham's governmental crisis.

The election of Mayor Albert Boutwell and nine new City Councilmen has been challenged in the courts by the present City Commission, of which Mr. Connor is a member.

In a case to be heard by the Alabama Supreme Court next Thursday, the Commissioners contend that the city cannot legally change its form of government until their terms expire in 1965.

Supporters of Boutwell

Both administrations have asserted that they were not involved in the arrangements worked out by the merchants. But Mr. Boutwell's administration is expected to take a more tolerant attitude toward the agreement, which is stoutly opposed by Mr. Connor.

Police officers arrest a demonstrator in Birmingham for "failure to move on."
(John Duprey/New York Daily News Archive/ Getty Images)

U.S. SENDS TROOPS INTO ALABAMA AFTER RIOTS SWEEP BIRMINGHAM; KENNEDY ALERTS STATE'S GUARD WARNING ISSUED

President Appeals for Peace and Vows to Keep Order

By ANTHONY LEWIS

WASHINGTON, May 12—President Kennedy tonight dispatched Federal troops to bases near Birmingham, Ala., for use if racial violence breaks out again.

His action followed hours of rioting early this morning in which 50 persons were injured. The rioting erupted after two buildings were bombed.

The President also ordered all "necessary preliminary steps" be taken to call the Alabama National Guard into Federal service. The actual call can then be accomplished in minutes if the President decides it is needed.

[Air Force C-47 transports with troops and equipment began arriving at Maxwell Air Base, about 80 miles south of Birmingham, within an hour after the President announced the move, United Press International reported. It said 10 transports had arrived by 12:45 A. M. Monday, New York time, and other troops were moving into Fort McClellan, 40 miles east of Birmingham.]

Confers With McNamara

The President made known these emergency moves at the White House tonight. He appeared before the press and television cameras at 8:48 P.M. to read a grave statement on the Birmingham crisis. The President declared:

"This Government will do whatever must be done to preserve order, to protect the lives of its citizens and to uphold the law of the land. I am certain that the vast majority of the citizens of Birmingham, both white and Negro—particularly those who labored so hard to achieve the peaceful, constructive settlement of last week—can feel nothing but dismay at the efforts of those who would replace conciliation and good will with violence and hate."

The President's statement made clear the deep concern of the Administration over last night's bombings of Negro residences in Birmingham and the resulting riots and police action.

Concerned Over Police

Government sources said the events of the night gave an entirely new cast to the Birmingham racial crisis. From a protest demonstration, they said, it had become an ugly, violent struggle.

In addition to concern over the bombings and the rioting, officials were disturbed by the police reaction. It was reported that the Birmingham police, behaving efficiently and fairly, had the situation under control when state troopers came in and revived tensions.

The eruption of violence threatened the agreement reached last week, with the help of Federal mediation, to end the Negro protest demonstrations. White business leaders had agreed to gradual desegregation of their facilities.

President Kennedy emphasized tonight the need to preserve that agreement. He said:

"It recognized the fundamental right of all citizens to be accorded equal treatment and opportunity. It was a tribute to the process of peaceful negotiation and to the good faith of both parties.

"The Federal Government will not permit it to be sabotaged by a few extremists on either side who think they can defy both the law and the wishes of responsible citizens by inciting or inviting violence."

He called on all citizens of Birmingham, Negro and white, "to restore the atmosphere in which last week's agreement can be carried out." He added, bluntly and with an implied warning:

"There must be no repetition of last night's incidents by any groups."

The President expressed the hope that Birmingham's citizens would "make outside intervention unnecessary."

New Outbreak Feared

Evidently the Administration was concerned about a fresh outbreak of violence tonight or tomorrow morning. It hoped by a show of determination to avoid the ultimate step of using Federal force.

But the third severe test of Mr. Kennedy's racial policy was plainly at hand. Two years ago Federal marshals protected Freedom Riders and others from violence in Montgomery, Ala. Last fall troops intervened to rescue beleaguered marshals in Oxford, Miss., but two civilians were killed.

Cooper Maneuvers To A Bullseye Landing With Manual Control As Automatic Fails; 'I'm In Fine Shape,' He Says After 22 Orbits

DRAMATIC RETURN

*Astronaut Was Aloft
Over 34 Hours—Aided
by Glenn*

By RICHARD WITKIN

CAPE CANAVERAL, Fla., May 16—Maj. L. Gordon Cooper Jr. landed safely in the Pacific today after a magnificently executed 22-orbit flight.

The closing phase of his flight was highlighted by a dramatic descent from orbit during which the astronaut guided himself to safety by manually controlling his capsule when his automatic controls failed.

The astronaut was picked up in his Faith 7 capsule by the carrier Kearsarge after a bullseye landing about 115 miles east-southeast of Midway Island.

Major Cooper's flight of 34 hours 20 minutes ended at 7:24 P. M., Eastern daylight time. It lasted almost four times as long as the longest previously flown by an American.

Flew 600,000 Miles

In all, Major Cooper flew about 600,000 miles in an orbit that ranged between a low point, or perigee, of 100.2 miles and a high point, or apogee, of 165.8 miles.

Major Cooper, after 29 hours in which he did a highly professional job on a spacecraft that functioned nearly perfectly, demonstrated his talents beyond question when electronic trouble confronted him with a difficult final phase of flight.

The trouble meant that the 36-year-old, Oklahoma-born astronaut had to perform a critical series of jobs usually entrusted to an automatic, computerized system.

Maneuvered Precisely

He had to maneuver his capsule in orbit to precise position for firing the retro (slow down) rockets. He did it so well that, when asked how his position was for retro firing, he radioed: "Right on the old bazoo."

He had to push a retro-firing button at the end of a countdown relayed to him from a ship near Japan by Lieut. Col. John H. Glenn Jr., who was the first American to make an orbital flight.

He had to hold the position as the rockets kicked against the blunt heat shield at his back to slow the capsule enough to get out of orbit.

Major Cooper accomplished it all with such precision that his capsule hit the water a scant 7,000 yards from the Kearsarge.

Walter C. Williams, operations director of Project Mercury, said Major Cooper's performance demonstrated more than ever the importance of man in space flight—as a pilot, not a passenger.

The big question the Cooper flight was intended to help answer was the degree to which a day and a half of weightlessness would affect a human pilot.

In line with the medical aims on the Cooper flight, the astronaut had to submit to a check as soon as his capsule was lifted onto the deck of the carrier.

Before he was allowed to step out onto the red carpet rolled up for the occasion, a space-agency physician reached in the capsule hatch to take his blood pressure and an electrocardiogram.

Schirra's Pattern Recalled

This new procedure was occasioned by the fact that Commander Schirra had experienced low pressure reading and high heart rate when going from prone to standing position over a period lasting 20 hours after his flight.

It was suspected this was a result of his six orbits without the normal downward tug of gravity. The physicians wanted to see if 22 orbits, flown by Major Cooper, produced worse symptoms.

Dr. Charles A. Berry, head of the space-flight medical team, reported to newsmen here that Major Cooper showed minimal changes in blood pressure, though he did show symptoms similar to Commander Schirra's.

Felt a Little Dizzy

Dr. Berry said Major Cooper did feel some dizziness when he first stood up. But he said it lasted only a few seconds and much more severe effects might have been expected.

About 80 minutes before the descent from orbit, Dr. Berry suggested that the astronaut take a Dexedrine stimulant pill, which he did.

During his 34 hours in orbit, Major Cooper was both an active and passive participant in an unending series of medical experiments to test the effects of weightlessness.

He also deployed and tracked a flashing light; took roll upon roll of still and motion pictures; became the first American astronaut televised from space; and managed to sleep, so soundly he insists he did not dream, for about seven and a half hours.

He flew over about 100 countries, including Communist China, which had not been on the track of any previous United States manned space flight. Efforts were made, without success, to find out whether the astronaut had any comments about how China looked from space.

Gordon Cooper made a "textbook" flight in space. Behind him are President Kennedy and fellow astronauts Virgil Grissom, Alan Shepard, Walter Schirra and Scott Carpenter. (Hulton Archive/Getty Images)

James E. Webb, head of the National Aeronautics and Space Administration, said in Hartford yesterday it would be the last if all the information sought on the Cooper mission was obtained.

Perfect at First

Major Cooper's trip was repeatedly referred to as a "textbook flight" until trouble developed without warning midway in the 19th orbit.

What happened first was that a so-called ".05G" light on his dashboard flashed green long before it was supposed to.

The malfunction occurred as the astronaut was operating a switch to dim the main light in the compact cockpit.

The light is supposed to turn on only after the capsule has come out of orbit and is beginning its re-entry into the atmosphere.

It signifies that gravity is once again beginning to exert its force (5/100 of normal gravity as the light's label implies) on the capsule after its whirling through space.

The malfunction did not cause any serious concern among members of the Mercury team at the control center.

Their tracking network showed that the capsule was maintaining more than sufficient velocity to stay in orbit and could not have started a premature, hazardous descent at an unplanned point over the earth.

They also knew that, if there was something wrong with the electronics aboard the capsule, there was a manual system that would permit the astronaut to return safely.

New Trouble Crops Up

The new difficulty was the failure of the inverter supply alternating current to the whole auto-pilot system.

When the reserve inverter also failed to work, it became clear that the pilot would have to control the spacecraft manually all the way down.

Major Cooper took it all with detached calm.

When the time came for firing the slowdown rockets, Colonel Glenn counted from 10 to zero as the count came to him from the control center here.

Major Cooper held perfect position for the firing. He used "gunsight" cross hairs on his window. These matched the horizontal line with the horizon and vertical lines with a line of stars selected before the flight for use on such an occasion.

A Welcome Reaction

After the astronaut had punched the retro-rocket button, he felt the kick behind him and the welcome signals of a proper firing were immediately recorded on the ground.

By the time Major Cooper was beginning to push into the atmosphere, it was evident that he had performed to perfection.

Colonel Glenn knew the worst was over and felt easy enough to radio:

"Okay, Gordo. It's dealer's choice on re-entry. Manual proportional or fly by wire." He meant the astronaut could choose between two control methods for the final descent.

The rest went like clockwork. And it was not long before the youngest and lightest of the original seven astronauts—the last of the six still eligible to take a rocket ride—was safely aboard the Kearsarge. He stepped onto the deck of the ship at 8:11 P. M., Eastern daylight time.

3 IN SIT-IN BEATEN AT JACKSON STORE

Group Set Upon by Whites—Mayor Disputes Negro Leaders on Concessions

---

By JACK LANGGUTH

JACKSON, Miss., May 28—Two Negroes and a white college professor were beaten and kicked today in a sit-in demonstration that marked the start of a drive by Negroes here against discrimination.

Later, at a mass rally, Negro leaders said Mayor Allen Thompson had granted their demands at a closed meeting. Mr. Thompson immediately denied that he had made most of the concessions and accused the leaders of "misrepresenting" his position.

[At Biloxi, Miss., Federal Judge Sidney Mize ordered the University of Mississippi to admit a Negro to its law school for the summer term beginning June 5, The Associated Press reported.]

The violence broke out before noon today in a downtown store when three young Negroes staged a lunch-counter sit-in. One Negro youth was knocked off a stool at the F. W. Woolworth Company and kicked repeatedly in the face by a man who was later identified as a former Jackson policeman.

Uniformed city officers remained outside the store while a crowd of several hundred white persons pushed Negroes to the floor and doused them with ketchup, mustard and sugar.

A white professor at Tougaloo Southern Christian College, John R. Salter, was struck by an unidentified white youth when he joined the Negroes at the Woolworth counter.

Mr. Salter's cheek was cut. Other white youths poured salt and pepper into the wound and emptied ketchup and mustard dispensers over his head.

Benny G. Oliver, 26 years old, a former policeman, pushed through the crowd and knocked Memphis Norman, 21, a Negro, from his stool at the counter. Mr. Oliver also pushed two Negro girls, Annie Moody, 22, and Perlina Lewis, 21, off their seats to the floor.

Kicked in the Face

As Mr. Norman lay on the floor, Mr. Oliver began kicking him in the face until blood spurted from his mouth and nose. City Detective J. L. Black, who watched this assault, came to the scene after a few moments and placed both Mr. Oliver and Mr. Norman under arrest. Mr. Oliver was released on a $225 bond. After treatment at a hospital, Mr. Norman was released on bond.

In addition to today's clash at Woolworth's—which led to the store's being closed by company officials three hours after the sit-ins began—pickets also appeared in front of two Jackson stores. Eight of the pickets were arrested and freed on bonds.

Chief of Detectives M. B. Pierce said the uniformed police remained outside because city attorneys had advised them "not to go onto private property without an invitation."

Mayor Thompson said that the procedure would be changed in the future.

"We're not going to sit back and wait until we're asked in," the Mayor said. "We're going to do what's right."

Closed Meeting Held

The Rev. G. R. Haughton told 500 Negroes at a church meeting tonight that his group of Negro leaders had met at a closed session with the Mayor this afternoon. Thirteen Negroes on Monday had walked out of Mayor Thompson's office when they thought he was refusing to discuss their demands.

According to Mr. Haughton, Mayor Thompson agreed today to hire Negro policemen and school crossing guards, to desegregate city facilities and to upgrade Negro employment in city jobs and had committed himself to several other Negro demands.

City officials promised to begin tomorrow to screen Negroes for police duty, Mr. Haughton said. Negro women would serve as street crossing guards around Negro schools when classes begin again in September, he said.

"The Mayor told us, `We know times have changed. We know this is a new day,'" Mr. Haughton told the cheering audience.

Mayor Thompson confirmed that he had promised to employ Negro policemen for Negro sections of the city and crossing guards for Negro schools. But upon hearing other statements made to the rally, Mayor Thompson said he was withdrawing those concessions for the time being.

"There will be no Negroes hired as police tomorrow," he said.

Statement on Parks

Speaking of parks and libraries, Mr. Haughton quoted the Mayor as having said: "Tell the people I said go on down to the parks, but don't go down there and take over everything."

Mayor Thompson said he had informed the Negroes only that the city would be "quite liberal for a few days" about parks and other facilities, in view of a Supreme Court decision ordering desegregation of parks in Memphis, Tenn.

"I told them if they go down there and run all over the parks, then we'll close every single one of them," the Mayor said. "I'm convinced, though, that after a little while, the Negroes will be back in their parks and the whites in theirs."

Saigon Situation Moving To Crisis

Diem's Sister-in-Law Calls Buddhists Reds' Dupes

By DAVID HALBERSTAM

SAIGON, Vietnam, June 8—Relations between Buddhists and the Government appeared to be deteriorating fast tonight. Some sources felt the situation in this city and the country was becoming increasingly ominous.

A cooling-off period, designed to ease the way for high-level negotiations between the Government and Buddhists leaders appeared to be over.

A powerful women's group headed by Mme. Ngo Dinh Nhu, sister-in-law of President Ngo Dinh Diem, issued a sharp denunciation of Buddhist priests who have been leading demonstrations of religious protest. The group's statement called them Communist dupes.

Acts of Bad Faith Charged

Mme. Ngo Dinh Nhu is one of the most powerful figures in the regime, as is her husband, the President's closest political adviser, thus the statement is considered almost an official pronouncement.

Vice President Nguyen Ngoc Tho, head of the special Government committee appointed to meet with the Buddhists, accused them of committing acts of bad faith that violated the cooling-off agreement.

The Buddhists themselves said they now believed the Government was acting in bad faith. They said they doubted there would be any mutual benefit from further negotiations.

Vice President Nguyen Ngoc Tho's statement said that unless Buddhist leaders carried out what the Government considered to be mutual promises, "the Government will be compelled to take appropriate measures."

The religious split between the Government and large numbers of Buddhist priests began a month ago when troops ended a religious protest demonstration in Hue by firing into a crowd killing nine persons. The troops stopped a student protest in Hue Monday with gas grenades, which sent 67 demonstrators to hospitals.

The Buddhists want the government to assume responsibility for the May 8 deaths. They want to fly their flag without the national flag, and they want what they say is religious equality.

The Government says religious equality already exists, and insists that its flag be flown higher than the Buddhist flag. The government contends that a Communist agitator threw a grenade that killed the nine Buddhists.

Diem Asks Peace In Religion Crisis

But Buddhists Still Protest Dispute Seems Worse

By DAVID HALBERSTAM

SAIGON, Vietnam, June 11—President Ngo Dinh Diem of South Vietnam appealed to the nation to remain calm today after a 73-year-old Buddhist priest committed suicide to dramatize the Buddhists' protest against the Government's policies on religion.

President Ngo Dinh Diem, in a radio speech, said: "The state of affairs was moving forward so smoothly when this morning, acting under extremist and truth-concealing propaganda that sowed doubt about the goodwill of the Government, a number of people got intoxicated and caused an undeserved death that made me very sorry.

"If in the ranks of the Buddhists there are still elements who, listening to propaganda, wrongly think that there is any scheme to unjustly crush Buddhism, I solemnly declare to you that behind the Buddhists in this country there is still the Constitution, that is, I myself."

No Easing in Dispute

The feeling was that the dispute was still as severe as ever and that the Buddhists were now determined to resume an all-out campaign of anti-Government demonstrations.

The Buddhists want the Government to assume responsibility for the deaths and to punish those responsible. The Buddhists also demand what they call equality for their religion. Seventy per cent of the South Vietnamese are Buddhist, but the President and members of his Government are Catholic.

Demonstration Defies Ban

The suicide took place in front of the Cambodian Legation. About 700 Buddhist priests formed a circle around the priest who set fire to himself.

The demonstration was held in defiance of a Government ban on further protests. In another act of defiance, the Buddhists raised their flag by itself during the procession back to their pagoda, and later flew the flag from the roof of the pagoda.

South Vietnamese law forbids the display of any flag but the national one. A major Buddhist demand in the dispute has been for the right to fly Buddhist flags from pagodas and shrines.

'PEACE STRATEGY'

President Asserts East and West Must Alter Their Basic Attitude

___

By TAD SZULC

WASHINGTON, June 10—President Kennedy proposed a "strategy of peace" today to lead the United States and the Soviet Union out of the "vicious and dangerous cycle" of the cold war.

As a first step, the President announced that high-ranking representatives of the United States, Britain and the Soviet Union would meet in Moscow soon in a renewed effort to agree on a treaty banning nuclear weapons tests.

He announced also that the United States, "to make clear our good faith and solemn conviction on the matter," would refrain from tests in the atmosphere so long as others did likewise.

Study of Attitudes Urged

The President's speech at the commencement exercises at American University here was dedicated to the theme that the time had come for a break in the cold war and that both the United States and the Soviet Union should re-examine their basic attitude toward each other.

Mr. Kennedy announced the decisions on nuclear testing after telling his audience of about 10,000 that a test ban was a major subject of East-West negotiations where "the end is in sight" but "where a fresh start is badly needed."

Hope Tempered With Caution

"Chairman Khrushchev, Prime Minister Macmillan and I have agreed that high-level discussions will shortly begin in Moscow, looking toward early agreement on a comprehensive test-ban treaty," he said. "Our hopes must be tempered with the caution of history but with our hopes go the hopes of all mankind."

Promising that the United States "will not be the first to resume" testing in the atmosphere, the President emphasized that "such a declaration is no substitute for a formal binding treaty but I hope it will help us achieve one."

"Nor would such a treaty be a substitute for disarmament," he added, "but I hope it will help us achieve it."

Applause broke out from the crowd at the outdoor exercises when the President announced the Moscow meeting and when he pledged the United States to refrain from atmospheric testing.

Applauded on Civil Rights

The President was also applauded when he said that "this generation of Americans" has had more than enough of war and hate and when he defended the civil rights of all Americans. He received a standing ovation at the end of his 28-minute address.

In dealing with the broader aspects of the cold war, the President found that the United States and the Soviet Union had certain things in common. He said the two countries would be primary targets if total war should break out.

Both, he said "have a mutually deep interest in a just and genuine peace and in halting the arms race."

The White House had in advance described the speech as one of the most important statements by President Kennedy on foreign affairs.

While it repeated the exhortations for peace contained in his inaugural address and in his speech at the United Nations in September 1961, it carried a new tone of conciliation toward the Soviet Union and a call to both nations to take another look at each other.

Mr. Kennedy expressed regret that the Soviet Union makes the "wholly baseless and incredible claims" that the United States is preparing for a war, but he said that this was "a warning to the American people not to fall into the same trap" of seeing only a "distorted and desperate view of the other side."

The President stressed that a "mutual abhorrence of war" was the strongest common trait of the United States and the Soviet Union.

"Almost unique among the major world powers, we have never been at war with each other," Mr. Kennedy said.

Asserts People Can Help

Describing peace as "a way of solving problems," the President asserted that the people of the United States could help the Soviet leaders to adopt "more enlightened attitudes" by "re-examining our own attitude."

"We must conduct our affairs in such a way that it becomes in the Communists' interest to agree on a genuine peace," he said.

"The United States, as the world knows, will never start a war," the President said. "We do not want a war. We do not now expect a war. This generation of Americans has already had enough—more than enough—of war and hate and oppression."

"We shall do our part to build a world of peace where the weak are safe and the strong are just," he said. "We are not helpless before that task or hopeless of its success. Confident and unafraid, we labor on not towards a strategy of annihilation but towards a strategy of peace."

The phrase, "strategy of peace," was used by the President as the title of his book published in 1960.

The speech represented an important foreign policy pronouncement prior to the President's trip to Western Europe, and to the Soviet-Chinese ideological confrontation in Moscow, opening July 5.

President Kennedy's commencement address at American University, Washington D.C., on June 10, 1963, carried a new tone of conciliation with the Soviets. (Cecil Stoughton/ John F. Kennedy Library)

President Kennedy on World Peace, June 10, 1963

𝓘 have . . . chosen this time and this place to discuss a topic on which ignorance too often abounds and the truth is too rarely perceived—yet it is the most important topic on earth: world peace.

What kind of peace do I mean? What kind of peace do we seek? Not a Pax Americana enforced on the world by American weapons of war. Not the peace of the grave or the security of the slave. I am talking about genuine peace, the kind of peace that makes life on earth worth living, the kind that enables men and nations to grow and to hope and to build a better life for their children—not merely peace for Americans but peace for all men and women—not merely peace in our time but peace for all time.

I speak of peace because of the new face of war. Total war makes no sense in an age when great powers can maintain large and relatively invulnerable nuclear forces and refuse to surrender without resort to those forces. It makes no sense in an age when a single nuclear weapon contains almost ten times the explosive force delivered by all the allied air forces in the Second World War. It makes no sense in an age when the deadly poisons produced by a nuclear exchange would be carried by wind and water and soil and seed to the far corners of the globe and to generations yet unborn.

Today the expenditure of billions of dollars every year on weapons acquired for the purpose of making sure we never need to use them is essential to keeping the peace. But surely the acquisition of such idle stockpiles—which can only destroy and never create—is not the only, much less the most efficient, means of assuring peace. . . .

In short, both the United States and its allies, and the Soviet Union and its allies, have a mutually deep interest in a just and genuine peace and in halting the arms race. Agreements to this end are in the interests of the Soviet Union as well as ours—and even the most hostile nations can be relied upon to accept and keep those treaty obligations, and only those treaty obligations, which are in their own interest.

So, let us not be blind to our differences—but let us also direct attention to our common interests and to the means by which those differences can be resolved. And if we cannot end now our differences, at least we can help make the world safe for diversity. For, in the final analysis, our most basic common link is that we all inhabit this small planet. We all breathe the same air. We all cherish our children's future. And we are all mortal. . . .

While we proceed to safeguard our national interests, let us also safeguard human interests. And the elimination of war and arms is clearly in the interest of both. No treaty, however much it may be to the advantage of all, however tightly it may be worded, can provide absolute security against the risks of deception and evasion. But it can—if it is sufficiently effective in its enforcement and if it is sufficiently in the interests of its signers—offer far more security and far fewer risks than an unabated, uncontrolled, unpredictable arms race.

The United States, as the world knows, will never start a war. We do not want a war. We do not now expect a war. This generation of Americans has already had enough—more than enough—of war and hate and oppression. We shall be prepared if others wish it. We shall be alert to try to stop it. But we shall also do our part to build a world of peace where the weak are safe and the strong are just. We are not helpless before that task or hopeless of its success. Confident and unafraid, we labor on—not toward a strategy of annihilation but toward a strategy of peace.

" I am talking about genuine peace, the kind of peace that makes life on earth worth living, the kind that enables men and nations to grow and to hope and to build a better life for their children . . ."

Alabama Redux

ALABAMA ADMITS NEGRO STUDENTS; WALLACE BOWS TO FEDERAL FORCE; KENNEDY SEES 'MORAL CRISIS' IN U.S.

Governor Leaves

But Fulfills Promises to Stand in Door and to Avoid Violence

By CLAUDE SITTON

TUSCALOOSA, Ala., June 11— Gov. George C. Wallace stepped aside today when confronted by federalized National Guard troops and permitted two Negroes to enroll in the University of Alabama. There was no violence.

The Governor, flanked by state troopers, had staged a carefully planned show of defying a Federal Court desegregation order.

Mr. Wallace refused four requests this morning from a Justice Department official that he allow Miss Vivian Malone and James A. Hood, both 20 years old, to enter Foster Auditorium and register.

This was in keeping with a campaign pledge that he would "stand in the schoolhouse door" to prevent a resumption of desegregation.

Students Go to Dormitories

The official, Nicholas deB. Katzenbach, Deputy Attorney General, did not press the issue by bringing the students from a waiting car to face the Governor. Instead, they were taken to their dormitories.

However, the outcome was foreshadowed even then. Mr. Katzenbach told Mr. Wallace :

"From the outset, Governor, all of us have known that the final chapter of this history will be the admission of these students."

Units of the 31st (Dixie) Division, federalized on orders from President Kennedy, arrived on the campus four and a half hours later under the command of Brig. Gen. Henry V. Graham.

'Sad Duty' Emphasized

In a voice that was scarcely audible, General Graham said that it was his "sad duty" to order the Governor to step aside.

Mr. Wallace then read the second of two statements challenging the constitutionality of court-ordered desegregation and left the auditorium with his aides for Montgomery.

This sequence of events, which took place in a circus atmosphere, appeared to have given the Governor the face-saving exit he apparently wanted.

Whether the courts find that he actually defied the order issued last Wednesday by District Judge Seybourn H. Lynne in Birmingham remained to be seen. Significantly, Edwin O. Guthman, special assistant for information to Attorney General Robert F. Kennedy, noted that the students had not presented themselves for admission until Mr. Wallace had left the campus.

It thus appeared that the Kennedy Administration had saved itself the political embarrassment of bringing a contempt-of-court action against a second Southern Governor.

Gov. Ross R. Barnett of Mississippi now faces a trial for contempt as a result of his repeated defiance of orders directing the admission of James H. Meredith, a Negro, to the University of Mississippi last fall.

Tonight Mr. Guthman, in a news conference, said that it would be up to the courts to determine if Mr. Wallace should be prosecuted. He declined repeatedly to say whether the Justice Department would bring charges.

Governor Wallace gave no indication whether he still planned a show of defense Thursday, when another Negro is scheduled to register at the university's Huntsville branch.

He is Dave M. McGlathery, 27, a mathematician for the National Aeronautics and Space Administration at the George C. Marshall Space Flight Center in that northern Alabama city.

However, there was speculation among Wallace aides that the Governor would not seek to interfere with Mr. McGlathery's registration.

Mr. Guthman told newsmen that Federal officials did not now plan to send troops to Huntsville. "The situation will be handled by state and university officials," he said.

Stems From '55 Injunction

Judge Lynne's preliminary injunction against Governor Wallace followed a finding by District Judge H. H. Grooms that the university must admit the three students under a permanent injunction issued by Judge Grooms.

Alabama Governor George Wallace, left, raises his hand to stop Deputy Attorney General Nicholas Katzenbach, who attempted to enroll two black students on the University of Alabama campus in Tuscaloosa, June 11, 1963. (Tuscaloosa News)

"I stand here today, as Governor of this sovereign state, and refuse to willingly submit to illegal usurpation of power by the Central Government."

"Governor, I am not interested in a show," Mr. Katzenbach went on. *"I don't know what the purpose of this show is. I am interested in the orders of these courts being enforced."*

That order brought the registration of Miss Autherine Lucy, the first Negro to attend a formerly white public education institution in this state.

Miss Lucy, now Mrs. H. L. Foster, went to classes for three days in 1956. She withdrew and was later expelled after her lawyers had accused university officials of conspiring with the rioters who opposed her presence.

The injunction against Governor Wallace prohibited him from taking any of the following steps:

Preventing, blocking or interfering with—by physically interposing his person or that of any other person—the Negroes' admission.

Preventing or seeking to prevent by any means the enrollment or attendance at the university of any person entitled to enroll under the Lucy injunction.

The long-awaited confrontation between Governor Wallace and the Federal officials came shortly after 11 o'clock [1 P.M., New York time] on the sunbaked north steps of Foster Auditorium, a three-story building of red brick with six limestone columns.

Approximately 150 of the 825 state troopers, game wardens and revenue agents under the command of Col. Albert J. Lingo, State Director of Public Safety, lined the concrete walkways at the auditorium.

Others in this group, brought here to prevent any outbreak of violence, stood guard at entrances to the campus and patrolled the tree-shaded stretch, which reaches westward to the banks of the Black Warrior River.

Shortly after 9:30 A.M., the Governor's aides and legal advisers arrived at the auditorium accompanied by two of his brothers, Circuit Judge Jack Wallace of Barbour County, and Gerald Wallace, a Montgomery lawyer.

Mr. Wallace was dressed neatly in a light gray suit, a blue shirt, a blue and brown tie with a gold tie clip and black shoes. He joked with the some 150 newsmen waiting in the broiling sun that sent the temperatures near 100 degrees. Then he went inside to an air-conditioned office to await the arrival of the Negro students.

Four Federal officials entered the auditorium a few minutes later. However, the scheduled arrival time of 10:30 A.M. passed with no sign of the students.

At 10:48 A.M., a white sedan followed by two brown sedans pulled up before the auditorium. Mr. Katzenbach emerged and walked to the entrance accompanied by Macon L. Weaver, United States Attorney for the Northern District of Alabama, and Peyton Norville Jr., the Federal marshal for this area.

Governor Wallace stood waiting behind a lectern placed in the doorway by a state trooper. He wore a microphone around his neck that was connected to a public address system.

Mr. Katzenbach said he had a proclamation from President Kennedy directing Governor Wallace to end his defiant stand. He asked the Governor to give way, but Mr. Wallace interrupted him and began reading a lengthy statement.

"The unwelcomed, unwanted, unwarranted and force-induced intrusion upon the campus of the University of Alabama today of the might of the Central Government, offers a frightful example of the oppression of the rights, privileges and sovereignty of this state by officers of the Federal Government," he asserted.

Mr. Wallace cited the provision of the 10th Amendment that provides that powers not delegated to the Federal Government are retained by the states.

"I stand here today, as Governor of this sovereign state, and refuse to willingly submit to illegal usurpation of power by the Central Government," he said.

The Governor implied that there might have been violence were it not for his presence when he said:

"I stand before you today in place of thousands of other Alabamians whose presence would have confronted you had I been derelict and neglected to fulfill the responsibilities of my office."

He concluded by asserting that he did "denounce and forbid this illegal and unwarranted action by the Central Government."

"I take it from that statement that you are going to stand in the door and that you are not going to carry out the orders of the court," said Mr. Katzenbach, "and that you are going to resist us from doing so. Is that correct?"

"I stand according to my statement," replied Mr. Wallace.

"Governor, I am not interested in a show," Mr. Katzenbach went on. "I don't know what the purpose of this show is. I am interested in the orders of these courts being enforced."

The Federal official then told the Governor that the latter had no choice but to comply.

"I would ask you once again to responsibly step aside," said Mr. Katzenbach. "If you do not, I'm going to assure you that the orders of these courts will be enforced."

The Deputy Attorney General then asserted:

"Those students will remain on this campus. They will register today. They will go to school tomorrow."

Lips Are Sealed

After several pleas in a similar vein, including the one in which he forecast the students' admission, Mr. Katzenbach waited for the Governor to reply. Mr. Wallace stood defiantly in the door, his head thrown back, his lips pressed tightly.

The Federal officials returned to the car in which Miss Malone and Mr. Hood had been waiting. Mr. Katzenbach and Miss Malone then walked unmolested to nearby Mary Burke Hall, the dormitory in which she will live.

John Doar, first assistant in the Justice Department's Civil Rights Division, drove with Mr. Hood to Palmer Hall. Several student council members shook hands with Mr. Hood.

Both students ate lunch later in university cafeterias without incident.

President Kennedy's Address to the Nation
on Civil Rights, June 11, 1963

*"We are confronted primarily with a moral issue.
It is as old as the scriptures and is as clear as the American Constitution."*

Today we are committed to a worldwide struggle to promote and protect the rights of all who wish to be free. And when Americans are sent to Viet-Nam or West Berlin, we do not ask for whites only.

It ought to be possible, therefore, for American students of any color to attend any public institution they select without having to be backed up by troops.

It ought to be possible for American consumers of any color to receive equal service in places of public accommodation, such as hotels and restaurants and theaters and retail stores, without being forced to resort to demonstrations in the street, and it ought to be possible for American citizens of any color to register to vote in a free election without interference or fear of reprisal. . . .

We are confronted primarily with a moral issue. It is as old as the scriptures and is as clear as the American Constitution.

The heart of the question is whether all Americans are to be afforded equal rights and equal opportunities, whether we are going to treat our fellow Americans as we want to be treated. If an American, because his skin is dark, cannot eat lunch in a restaurant open to the public, if he cannot send his children to the best public school available, if he cannot vote for the public officials who will represent him, if, in short, he cannot enjoy the full and free life which all of us want, then who among us would be content to have the color of his skin changed and stand in his place? Who among us would then be content with the counsels of patience and delay?

We preach freedom around the world, and we mean it, and we cherish our freedom here at home, but are we to say to the world, and much more importantly, to each other that this is the land of the free except for the Negroes; that we have no second-class citizens except Negroes; that we have no class or caste system, no ghettoes, no master race except with respect to Negroes?

Now the time has come for this Nation to fulfill its promise. The events in Birmingham and elsewhere have so increased the cries for equality that no city or State or legislative body can prudently choose to ignore them.

N.A.A.C.P. LEADER SLAIN IN JACKSON; PROTESTS MOUNT; WHITES ALARMED

Victim Is Shot From Ambush—158 Negro Marchers Seized

By CLAUDE SITTON

JACKSON, Miss., June 12—A sniper lying in ambush shot and fatally wounded a Negro civil rights leader early today. The slaying touched off mass protests by Negroes in which 158 were arrested. It also aroused widespread fear of further racial violence in this state capital.

The victim of the shooting was Medgar W. Evers, 37-year-old Mississippi field secretary of the National Association for the Advancement of Colored People. Struck in the back by a bullet from a high-powered rifle as he walked from his automobile to his home, he died less than an hour later—at 1:14 A.M. (3:14 A. M., New York time)—in University Hospital.

Agents of the Federal Bureau of Investigation joined Jackson, Hinds County and state authorities in the search for the killer.

Suspect Is Released

A 51-year-old white man was picked up, questioned for several hours and released. Investigators discovered a .30-06-caliber rifle with a newly attached sight in a vacant lot near the honeysuckle thicket from which they believed the fatal shot had been fired.

[In New York, the N.A.A.C.P, offered a $10,000 reward for information leading to the arrest and conviction of Mr. Evers's killer. The Rev. Dr. Martin Luther King Jr. mourned Evers as a "pure patriot."]

The first demonstration began today at 11:25 A. M., when 13 ministers left the Pearl Street African Methodist Episcopal Church and walked silently toward the City Hall.

The police, who refused to let them proceed by twos at widely spaced intervals, arrested all 13. The group included many of the Negro leaders who had been working with white officials in efforts to resolve the city's month-old racial crisis.

An hour and a half later approximately 200 Negro teenagers marched out of the Masonic Building on Lynch Street, site of Mr. Evers's office. Some 100 city policemen, Hinds County deputy sheriffs and state highway patrolmen, armed with riot guns and automatic rifles, halted them a block away.

A total of 145 demonstrators, including 74 aged 17 and under, were then arrested. One girl was struck in the face by a club, deputies wrestled a middle-aged woman spectator to the sidewalk and other Negroes were shoved back roughly.

Mrs. Evers spoke tonight to some 500 persons at a mass meeting in the Pearl Street church. Dressed in a pale green dress, she appeared tired but composed. Many women in the audience wept openly.

Referring to her husband's death, she said, "It was his wish that this [Jackson] movement would be one of the most successful that this nation has ever known."

Sought Opportunity

Mrs. Evers, who had requested that she be given the opportunity to speak, said that her husband had spoken of death last Sunday and said that he was ready to go.

"I am left with the strong determination to try to take up where he left off," she said. "I hope that by his death that all here and those who are not here will be able to draw some of his strength, some of his courage and some of his determination to finish this fight."

"Nothing can bring Medgar back, but the cause can live on."

Leaflets distributed at the meeting urged Negroes to return to the church tomorrow "prepared for action."

Other speakers also called on the audience to mourn Mr. Evers's death by wearing a patch on their clothing for at least 30 days and by boycotting downtown white merchants.

A fund designed to provide for the education of the Evers children was started here at the meeting. Speakers called on persons all over the nation to contribute to it.

The slaying, coupled with the arrests, led to sorrow mixed with anger among Negroes. Whites in this strongly segregationist community publicly expressed shock. But privately they showed more concern over the possibility of Negro retaliation.

The sentiment of Negroes seemed to be summed up by a slogan lettered on a white N.A.A.C.P. T-shirt worn by one of the demonstrators. "White Man, You May Kill the Body, but Not the Soul," it declared.

There were well-founded reports that a number of Negroes had armed themselves.

Gov. Ross R. Barnett and other offi-

Attorney General Robert Kennedy and Burke Marshall, head of the Justice Department's Civil Rights Division.

(Walter Bennett/Time & Life Pictures/Getty Images)

cials issued statements deploring Mr. Evers's slaying and offering rewards for the arrest and conviction of the guilty.

Many of them, including Governor Barnett and Mayor Allen C. Thompson, are members of the Citizens Councils, a racist organization with national headquarters here.

The Mississippi Publishers Corporation, publisher of The Clarion-Ledger and Jackson Daily News, offered a $1,000 reward. These newspapers have spearheaded the campaign to maintain 100 per cent segregation throughout the state.

In a statement, Governor Barnett said of the killing:

"Apparently it was a dastardly act and as Governor of the State of Mississippi, I shall cooperate in every way to apprehend the guilty party.

"Too many such incidents are hap-

pening throughout the country, including the race riot last night in Cambridge, Md."

Governor Barnett and other officials here have frequently attacked the N.A.A.C.P. as an organization inspired by Communist aims and dedicated to the subversion of "the Southern way of life."

Mayor Thompson broke off a brief visit to a Florida resort to fly back to Jackson. He and City Commissioners D. L. Luclcey and Tom Marshall announced the city was offering a $5,000 reward.

"Along with all of the citizens of Jackson, the commissioners and I are dreadfully shocked, humiliated and sick at heart that such a terrible tragedy should happen in our city," Mr. Thompson said in a statement.

"We will not stop working night or

day until we find the person or persons who are responsible for such a cowardly act, and we urge the cooperation of everyone in this search," the Mayor said.

Mayor Thompson declined to comment on the mood of white residents of the state capital. He said he had been too busy with the investigation to talk to many of them.

However, one policeman said of the slayer:

"He destroyed in one minute everything we've been trying to do here."

He then asserted, "We're just scared to death. That's the truth."

Jimmy Ward, editor of The Jackson Daily News, expressed concern over the damage that the incident might cause to Jackson's reputation.

He did so in his daily front-page column, which frequently contains jokes aimed at the N.A.A.C.P., other civil rights organizations and their leaders and members.

'Inhuman Behavior'

"Despite numerous, most earnest appeals for law and order at all times and most especially during the current racial friction in Jackson," Mr. Ward wrote, "some conscienceless individual has stooped to violence and has greatly harmed the good relations that have existed in Jackson. All Mississippians and especially this shocked community are saddened by the dastardly act of inhuman behavior last night."

Mr. Evers, a native of Decatur, Miss., and an Army veteran of World War II, had been one of the key leaders in the Negroes' drive here to win a promise from the city to hire some Negro policemen and to appoint a biracial committee.

He left a mass meeting at a church last night, stopped at the residence of a Negro lawyer and then drove to his home on the city's northern edge. Before leaving the church, he remarked to a newsman that "tomorrow will be a big day."

He arrived at his neat, green-paneled and buff-brick ranch-style home on Guynes Street shortly after midnight. The accounts of the authorities, his wife and neighbors showed that the following series of events had taken place:

He parked his 1962 light blue sedan in the driveway, behind his wife's station wagon.

As he turned to walk into a side entrance opening into a carport, the sniper's bullet struck him just below the right shoulder blade.

The slug crashed through a front window of the home, penetrated an interior wall, ricocheted off a refrigerator and struck a coffee pot. The battered bullet was found beneath a watermelon on a kitchen cabinet.

Mr. Evers staggered to the doorway, his keys in his hand, and collapsed near the steps. His wife, Myrlie, and three children rushed to the door.

The screaming of the children, "Daddy! Daddy! Daddy!" awoke a neighbor, Thomas A. Young. Another neighbor, Houston Wells, said he had heard the shot and the screams of Mrs. Evers.

Mr. Wells, according to the police, said he had looked out a bedroom window, saw Mr. Evers's crumpled body in the carport and had rushed out into his yard. He said he had crouched behind a clump of shrubbery, fired a shot into the air and shouted for help.

The police, who arrived a short time later, helped neighbors place Mr. Evers in Mr. Wells's station wagon.

As the station wagon sped to University Hospital, those who accompanied the dying man said he had murmured weakly, "Sit me up," and later, "Turn me loose."

Dr. A. B. Britton, Mr. Evers's physician, a member of the Mississippi Advisory Committee to the Federal Civil Rights Commission, rushed to the hospital. He indicated that the victim had died from loss of blood and internal injuries,

City detectives making the investigation found a newly cleared space in the honeysuckle some 200 feet southwest of Mr. Evers's home. They speculated the killer had hidden there while awaiting the arrival of his victim.

Myrlie Evers and her son Darrell Kenyatta during the funeral of her husband, Medgar Evers, who was murdered in Jackson, Mississippi.

(John Loengard/Time & Life Pictures/Getty Images)

KENNEDY ASKS BROAD RIGHTS BILL AS 'REASONABLE' COURSE IN CRISIS; CALLS FOR RESTRAINT BY NEGROES

MESSAGE SOMBER

Bids Congress Remain in Session to Enact Omnibus Program

By TOM WICKER

WASHINGTON, June 19—President Kennedy called on Congress today to enact extensive civil rights legislation that he said would "go far toward providing reasonable men with reasonable means" for dealing with the national crisis in race relations.

Mr. Kennedy's program asked:

A legal guarantee to all citizens of access to the services and facilities of hotels, restaurants, places of amusement and retail establishments in interstate commerce.

Legislation authorizing the Attorney General to start school desegregation suits when he is requested to do so by someone unable to sue.

Broad Federal action to halt discrimination in Federal jobs and activities financed wholly or in part with Federal funds.

Creation of a Community Relations Service to act as a mediation agency in communities with racial tensions.

Passage of a provision "making it clear that the Federal Government is not required, under any statute, to furnish any kind of financial assistance to any program or activity in which racial discrimination occurs."

Says 'Time Has Come'

The President proposed that Congress remain in session this year until his omnibus bill was passed.

"The time has come," Mr. Kennedy said in a somberly worded 5,500-word

message, "for the Congress of the United States to join with the executive and judicial in making it clear to all that race has no place in American life or law."

His program could strike at discrimination on a broad front. It was concerned not only with the immediate grievances of the Negro but also with the increased economic and educational opportunities that could yield them a greater share of American life.

The most controversial proposals could prohibit discrimination in privately owned establishments like theaters, restaurants and motels, and arm the Attorney General with power to speed school desegregation.

Warns of Alternative

The alternative to such legislation, the President warned, "will be continued, if not increased, racial strife—causing the leadership on both sides to pass from the hands of reasonable and responsible men to the purveyors of hate and violence, endangering domestic tranquility, retarding our nation's economic and social progress and weakening the respect with which the rest of the world regards us."

That warning was coupled with an admonition to Negroes to avoid "demonstrations which can lead to violence" as well as undue pressures and "unruly tactics" in support of the legislation.

"While the Congress is completing its work," the President said, "I urge all community leaders, Negro and white,

to do their utmost to lessen tensions and to exercise self-restraint. The Congress should have an opportunity to freely work its will."

That opportunity may require months, particularly in the Senate, where virtually unlimited debate is possible for Southern Democrats.

"I am proposing," the President said, "that the Congress stay in session this year until it has enacted—preferably as a single omnibus bill—the most responsible, reasonable and urgently needed solutions which should be acceptable to all fair-minded men."

Proposal Is Explained

The proposal to outlaw discrimination in public accomodations would affect theaters, sports arenas, retail stores, gasoline stations, restaurants, lunch counters, and the like, if such establishments met any of four conditions. These are:

That the establishment's goods, services or other offerings to the public are available "to a substantial degree to interstate travelers."

That a "substantial portion" of its goods offered for sale move in interstate commerce.

That its activities or operations otherwise "substantially affect interstate travel or the interstate movement of goods in commerce."

That it is an "integral part" of a parent organization meeting one of the first three conditions.

Thus, the public facilities section of Mr. Kennedy's omnibus bill is based largely on the Federal Government's right to regulate interstate commerce. But the measure also invoked the "equal-protection-of-the-laws" clause of the 14th Amendment to the Constitution.

The extent to which this amendment may affect private commercial activities will have to be determined in the courts.

Burden of Guilt Shifted

One significant effect of this proposal would be to shift the burden of guilt from participants in a lunch-counter sit-in to the proprietor of the establishment. That is, the proprietor would be breaking the law if he refused to serve them, rather than they for requesting the service.

The proposal was coupled with an enforcement provision. The aggrieved person or persons could file civil suit for injunctive relief from the discrimination. Or the Attorney General could do it for them, after receipt of a written complaint and proof that the aggrieved persons were unable to bear the cost of or otherwise carry out the necessary legal proceedings.

Another section of the bill would grant similar authority to the Attorney General in school desegregation.

That is, if a parent or a group of parents complained in writing to the Attorney General that their minor children were being discriminated against by a local school board, or if an individual complained in writing that he was excluded from a public college because of "race, color, religion or national origin," the Attorney General could sue in Federal court for relief.

It was apparent from early Congressional reaction that the hardest opposition would be concentrated on desegregation of public facilities.

Another provision of Mr. Kennedy's program suggested a Congressional declaration giving Federal administrators discretionary authority to withhold funds from any federally financed or assisted program in which persons were being discriminated against because of race, color, religion or national origin.

He also asked that the President's Commission on Equal Employment Opportunities, headed by the Vice President and aimed at ending discrimination by Government contractors, be authorized by statute, rather than by Executive order.

Mr. Kennedy also called for a Community Relations Service to help states and localities resolve racial disputes. The Attorney General, when asked to file suit over discrimination in public accommodations, for instance, would first refer the matter to this service for a possible voluntary solution.

Increased educational and employment opportunities were asked for Negroes, under a number of specific proposals.

These proposals include expansion of the Manpower Development and Training Program to lower the minimum age for training allowances from 19 to 18, to provide literacy training, and to increase efforts to train out-of-school youths for employment.

Mr. Kennedy also asked additional funds for the youth employment bill and for vocational education, funds for a new "work-study" program to train school students, increased adult education facilities, and greater Federal participation in programs to put employable but unemployed welfare recipients to work.

These programs would cost about $400,000,000, Mr. Kennedy said. This sum, he stressed, has been "more than offset" by reductions he has already suggested in the budget for the fiscal year ending June 30, 1964.

In addition to these new proposals, Mr. Kennedy again asked for the passage of bills he proposed earlier this year. One would continue the life of the Civil Rights Commission for four more years, and establish it as a "national clearing house" for information, advice and technical assistance on civil rights.

Another would assist qualified Negroes to register and vote by providing temporary Federal voting referees to serve while civil suits are pending, by prohibiting discriminatory literacy and other tests for voting applicants, and by declaring that a sixth-grade education is presumptive evidence of literacy.

The latter bill has been altered to provide that schools where a sixth-grade education is obtained need not be accredited. This followed testimony in a Congressional hearing last week that only eight of more than 200 Negro schools in Mississippi were accredited by the state.

The third bill proposed earlier would provide Federal technical and financial assistance to aid school districts in desegregating.

Mr. Kennedy also endorsed a bill that would establish Federal standards of fair employment practices. This measure was not proposed by the Administration, although Secretary of Labor W. Willard Wirtz has testified in favor of it.

The bill was approved in a House Labor subcommittee today.

Finally, the President seized the opportunity to make renewed pleas for non-civil rights legislation that would affect the economic and educational opportunities of all Americans, Negro and white.

These included "prompt and substantial tax reduction," which he said was "the key to achieving the full employment we need"; "adequate financing" for the Area Redevlopment Program, denied in a close vote in the House recently; accelerated public works; and general aid to education "at every level from grade school through graduate school."

Kennedy to See Leaders

Meanwhile, President Kennedy invited a group of about 30 civil rights leaders, including the Rev. Dr. Martin Luther King Jr., to the White House Saturday.

Looking Back

A President Declares
for the Minority

By Richard Reeves

One of the Eisenhower men asked to stay on in the Kennedy administration was Father Theodore Hesburgh, the president of the University of Notre Dame, who was serving as chairman of the new Civil Rights Commission. Hesburgh, who didn't much like Kennedy, said "Yes," though he suspected the president wanted to use him to tamp down any civil rights debates in Congress, which in 1961 was controlled by a coalition of Southern Democrats and Republicans.

Civil rights was never Kennedy's strong suit and he hoped to ignore it if he could. He actually saw it as a foreign policy issue: the Communists used racial prejudice and trouble in the U.S. as propaganda, particularly in Africa.

Now he was being questioned by Hesburgh, who was telling him the White House had not had a liaison to the commission since 1958. He said he needed a name and a number to call.

"I already have a special assistant working on that full-time," said Kennedy.

"Who?"

"Harris Wofford."

"Really?" said Hesburgh. Wofford was one of his closest friends and a professor of law at Notre Dame. In fact, they had breakfast that morning and Wofford never mentioned any of this. What Wofford, who was a neighbor of the Kennedys on "N" Street in Georgetown did tell Hesburgh was that Senator Kennedy had picked him up one morning for the trip to the Capitol and Senator Kennedy, then the presidential nominee of his party, had said: "Okay. Tell me the ten things I have to know about this civil rights mess."

As soon as Hesburgh left after his February 6 meeting at the White House, telephone operators there were told to find Wofford immediately. When he arrived he was met by a man he didn't know who was holding a Bible.

"You Wofford?" asked the man, whose name was William Hopkins. "Raise your right hand, please."

"What for?"

"I'm supposed to swear you in."

"For what?"

"I don't know," said Hopkins. "I just got word from the President to swear you in as a Special Assistant."

"But I haven't seen the President. I don't know what this is all about."

I don't know about you," said Hopkins "but I take my orders from the President. Raise your right hand please . . ."

Jack Kennedy voted against the Civil Rights Act of 1957, but he was certainly no bigot. But he had grown up in a world of the rich—exclusive schools and the segregated U.S. Navy—where the black man he had spent the most time with was his valet of 14 years, George Thomas, who was, literally, a gift from his father's great friend, Arthur Krock, the chief of *The New York Times* Washington bureau. During the campaign, Kennedy had led his entourage from a hotel in Paducah, Kentucky, when the management refused to rent a room to Simeon Booker, a black reporter from *Jet* magazine. More famously, at Wofford's suggestion, he had telephoned Mrs. Martin Luther King Jr. and volunteered to do whatever he could when her husband was sentenced to four months of "hard labor" for a traffic violation in Georgia. "What the hell?" said Kennedy. "It's the decent thing to do."

It also turned out be the political thing as well. Kennedy won more than 70 percent of the black vote in 1960, more than twice what Adlai Stevenson got as the Democratic nominee in 1956. That included Martin Luther King Sr., a prominent Republican in Georgia, who said he would vote for Kennedy, even though he was white and Catholic, because of the phone call to his daughter-in-law, Coretta King.

When he heard that bit of news, Kennedy cracked, "So Martin Luther King's father is a bigot." He paused, then said, "Well, we all have fathers, don't we?"

"I guess I have to start meeting with the civil rights people." And he did, calling in white activists, including Joseph Rauh, the general counsel of the United Auto Workers. But Kennedy began listing Negroes—the word of the day—he had appointed to Federal offices. The president was defensive. He resented liberals criticizing him on civil rights and made it clear that he would not be speaking out on the subject anytime soon "Oh shit!" thought Rauh. "Nothing is going to happen."

But things did happen. Events were in the saddle, riding mankind. On May 15, 1961, the president woke when George Thomas knocked on his bedroom door and dropped the morning newspapers on his bed. *The New York Times* front page showed a burning Greyhound bus on Alabama Route 78 outside Anniston, Alabama, a bus chartered by white and black people who called themselves "Freedom Riders" and hoped to provoke the Federal government into enforcing Federal laws barring discrimination in interstate commerce. The bus had been attacked and burned—and the riders beaten—by local folks determined to preserve segre-gation.

Kennedy was preparing for a European trip before a summit meeting with Soviet Premier Nikita Khrushchev. He called in Harris Wofford again, and said: "Can't you get your God-damned people off those buses? Stop them!"

Kennedy was feeling sorry for himself and mad at liberals and black leaders demanding more Federal civil rights action. From his perspective, he was taking real risks of losing the support of Southern Democrats in Congress for other programs, other priorities. The first Gallup Poll on the "Freedom Rides" indicated that 63 percent of Americans were "against the riders." Greyhound and Trailways drivers in Alabama were refusing to drive if activists were on their buses. They agreed to go back to work only after Attorney General Robert Kennedy called the presidents of the bus companies and reminded them of the power of the government under interstate commerce laws. The buses rolled but were blocked by white mobs, who clubbed passengers while local police watched. Among those beaten almost to death was John Seigenthaler, a former reporter for the *Nashville Tennessean* working as an assistant to the Attorney General. One of the organizers of the riders was Diane Nash, a student leader at Fisk University in Nashville, whom Seigenthaler had interviewed in the past.

He asked her, as the president had asked him, where these young riders were getting their ideas. Nash replied: "We're going to show these people in Alabama who think they can ignore the President of the United States."

"You're never going to make it to New Orleans," Seigenthaler told Nash." You're going to get your people killed."

"Then others will follow," said Nash, who was 20 years old. They were ready to bear any burden, she said. The ideas were coming from Kennedy's own words.

And they did. The nation, aroused by television coverage of Southern segregation and police brutality, exploded into something close to a revolution. Hundreds of thousands of Americans, black and white, marched and demonstrated and sat-in at lunch counters and department stores in the segregated cities of the South. Birmingham, Alabama, was called "Bombingham" after three young girls were killed by a bomb planted at the First Baptist church in that city. The Justice Department under Robert Kennedy brought 57 desegregation suits against local officials in the South. Twice President Kennedy federalized the National Guard when the governors of Mississippi and Alabama were using it to pre-

vent black students from entering state universities. One minute governors were the commanders of Guard units in their states. The next minute Kennedy was the commander-in-chief and ordered the guns to turn on local officials, escorting students to their rooms on the campuses.

The administration's struggle with the segregationist governors climaxed in June of 1963, when George Wallace of Alabama appointed himself as chief operating officer of the state university. He stood in the doorway of the Tuscaloosa campus surrounded by state troopers, until one hundred federalized guardsmen, ordered by the White House, marched onto the campus. Deputy Attorney General Nicholas Katzenbach took the two black students, Vivian Malone and James Hood, to their rooms. The officers of the Student Council stepped out of the doorway, held out their hands and said, "Welcome to the University of Alabama." A window on the third floor opened and a student waved an American flag over Malone and Hood as they entered.

Wallace saluted and left the campus with his troopers.

"I want to go on television tonight," the president said after watching the Wallace-Katzenbach confrontation on the networks. "I'm going to the pool"—which he did for 20 minutes—"get something together," he told Theodore Sorensen and others. There was no prepared speech. Perhaps the most influential input was from one of Lyndon Johnson's assistants, a former newsman named George Reedy. Like everyone else in the White House, Reedy had been asked by Kennedy, "How can we stop this?" Reedy gave Johnson a memo, which the vice president passed on to Sorensen. The basic point of the memo was that Kennedy had to choose sides: White Southerners believed the president was secretly on their side, just another Northern politician pandering to Negro voters. And the Negroes believed the opposite, that Kennedy was their man but had to play ball with Southerners.

The troubles, said Reedy, would not stop until the president chose sides. He did that on national television that night.

"If an American, because his skin is dark, cannot eat lunch in a restaurant open to the public, if he cannot send his children to the best public school available, if he cannot vote for the public officials who will represent him . . . then who among us would be content to have the color of his skin changed? Who among us would be content with the counsels of patience and delay?"

The president of the United States had declared for the minority. No small thing in a democracy.

PRESIDENT HAILED BY OVER A MILLION IN VISIT TO BERLIN; HE SALUTES THE DIVIDED CITY AS FRONT LINE IN WORLD'S STRUGGLE FOR FREEDOM

Looks Over The Wall

Says Berliners' Experience Shows Hazard in Trying to Work With Communists

---

By ARTHUR J. OLSEN

BERLIN, June 26—President Kennedy, inspired by a tumultuous welcome from more than a million of the inhabitants of this isolated and divided city, declared today he was proud to be "a Berliner."

He said his claim to being a Berliner was based on the fact that "all free men, wherever they may live, are citizens of Berlin."

In a rousing speech to 150,000 West Berliners crowded before the City Hall, the President said anyone who thought "we can work with the Communists" should come to Berlin.

However, three hours later, in a less emotional setting, he reaffirmed his belief that the great powers must work together "to preserve the human race."

President Kennedy reviewing troops and weaponry during an inspection at Hanau, Germany. (Keystone/Getty Images)

President John F. Kennedy delivers the "Ich bin ein Berliner" speech to a massive crowd, Berlin, June 26, 1963.

(PhotoQuest/Getty Images)

Warning on Communism

The President's City Hall speech was the emotional high point of a spectacular welcome accorded the President by West Berlin. He saluted the city as the front line and shining example of humanity's struggle for freedom.

Those who profess not to understand the great issues between the free world and the Communist world or who think Communism is the wave of the future should come to Berlin. In his later speech, at the Free University of Berlin, President Kennedy returned firmly to the theme of his address at American University in Washington June 10 in which he called for an attempt to end the cold war.

'Wounds to Heal'

"When the possibilities of reconciliation appear, we in the West will make it clear that we are not hostile to any people or system, provided that they choose their own destiny without interfering with the free choice of others," he said.

"There will be wounds to heal and suspicions to be eased on both sides," he added. "The difference in living standards will have to be reduced—by leveling up, not down. Fair and effective agreements to end the arms race must be reached."

The changes might not come tomorrow, but "our efforts for a real settlement must continue," he said.

Then the President introduced an extemporaneous paragraph into his prepared text.

"As I said this morning, I am not impressed by the opportunities open to popular fronts throughout the world," he said. "I do not believe that any dem-ocrat can successfully ride that tiger. But I do believe in the necessity of great powers working together to preserve the human race."

Nuances of policy, however, were not the center of attention today in this city of at least 2,200,000 alert people. For them the only matter of importance was to give a heartfelt and spectacular welcome to the United States President and to see a youthful-looking smiling man obviously respond to their warmth.

Pierre Salinger, the President's press secretary, said the reception here was "the greatest he has had anywhere."

Along the route from Tegel airport to the United States mission headquarters in the southwest corner of Berlin, waving, cheering crowds lined every foot of the way.

Banners Hung at Gate

The crowds must have nearly equaled the population of the city, but many persons waved once and then sped ahead to greet Mr. Kennedy again.

Only once in a jammed eight hours, during which he was almost uninterruptedly on a television screen, did Mr. Kennedy fail to dominate the scene.

Shortly before noon he approached Brandenburg Gate where he caught his first view of the Communist-built wall that partitions Berlin.

The President had been scheduled to gaze over the wall through the gate onto Unter den Linden, once the main avenue of the German capital. However, the five arches of the gate were covered by huge red banners, blocking his view there of East Berlin.

The cloth barrier was put up by East Berlin officials last night.

Just across the wall from the podium where the President's party stood was a neatly lettered yellow sign in English. It cited the Allied pledges at the 1945 Yalta conference to uproot Nazism and militarism from Germany and to see it would never again endanger world peace.

Asserting that the pledges had been fulfilled in East Germany, the sign called on President Kennedy to see that they were fulfilled in West Germany and West Berlin.

The President appeared not to read the words, busying himself with a map indicating key points along the wall.

Rudolph Wilde Platz, West Berlin. (Robert Knudsen/John F. Kennedy Library)

The Brandenburg Gate is sealed off in the Soviet-occupied sector of East Berlin, Germany. Located at the center of the German capital, the gate stands behind part of the Berlin Wall that divides East and West Berlin. (Associated Press)

Sees East Berliners

At Checkpoint Charlie, the United States-controlled crossing point to East Berlin on the Friedrichstrasse, Mr. Kennedy had an unobstructed view several hundred yards into the eastern sector.

About 300 yards away, well beyond the 100-yard forbidden zone decreed by the Communists last week, he glimpsed a small group of East Berliners attracted by his presence. Though he could not hear them, they cheered.

In West Berlin there was no Communist attempt to embarrass the President. The problem for West Berlin's 13,500-man police force and the President's Secret Service guards was to restrain excited crowds from rushing to the President to shake his hand or hand him gifts.

Brandt Gives Reassurance

Mayor Willy Brandt, greeting the President, said West Berliners did not expect constantly renewed assertions of allied guarantees "because we trust our friends."

The President responded by saying: "The legendary morale and spirit of the people of West Berlin has lit a fire throughout the world. I am glad to come to this city. It reassures us."

At the first six stops on the tour— the modernistic Congress Hall where the West German construction workers union was in convention, Mr. Kennedy told the union delegates a free trade union movement was a guarantee and proof of democracy. He urged West German unions to help newly independent countries establish a strong free union movement.

The Presidential motorcade arrived 15 minutes behind schedule at Schoneberger Rathaus, West Berlin's city hall.

Mr. Kennedy's speech was emotional and the West Berliners responded in like manner. Several times they chanted "Kennedy! Kennedy!"

The only break in the day of speech-making and waving to the crowds was a luncheon in the city hall given by Mayor Brandt.

From there, the President drove to the Free University, endowed in 1948 by the Ford Foundation, where Mr. Kennedy was made an honorary citizen of the university. This is a traditional form of honor, dating from the days when European universities enjoyed autonomous political rights.

The motorcade went next to Clay Alley, named after Gen. Lucius D. Clay, defender of West Berlin during the blockade 15 years ago and who, as a member of the Kennedy party, won special cheers today. There, the United States community of 15,000 soldiers and diplomats and members of their families greeted the President.

"No beleaguered garrison serves in comparable conditions under conditions so dangerous and with adversaries so numerous," the President told the soldiers.

President Kennedy's Speech to the People of Berlin, June 26, 1963

I am proud to come to this city as the guest of your distinguished Mayor, who has symbolized throughout the world the fighting spirit of West Berlin. And I am proud to visit the Federal Republic with your distinguished Chancellor who for so many years has committed Germany to democracy and freedom and progress, and to come here in the company of my fellow American, General Clay, who has been in this city during its great moments of crisis and will come again if ever needed.

Two thousand years ago the proudest boast was "civis Romanus sum." Today, in the world of freedom, the proudest boast is "Ich bin ein Berliner."

There are many people in the world who really don't understand, or say they don't, what is the great issue between the free world and the Communist world. Let them come to Berlin. There are some who say that communism is the wave of the future. Let them come to Berlin. And there are some who say in Europe and elsewhere we can work with the Communists. Let them come to Berlin. And there are even a few who say that it is true that communism is an evil system, but it permits us to make economic progress. Lass' sie nach Berlin kommen. Let them come to Berlin.

Freedom has many difficulties and democracy is not perfect, but we have never had to put a wall up to keep our people in, to prevent them from leaving us. I want to say, on behalf of my countrymen, who live many miles away on the other side of the Atlantic, who are far distant from you, that they take the greatest pride that they have been able to share with you, even from a distance, the story of the last 18 years. I know of no town, no city, that has been besieged for 18 years that still lives with the vitality and the force, and the hope and the determination of the city of West Berlin. . . .

Freedom is indivisible, and when one man is enslaved, all are not free. When all are free, then we can look forward to that day when this city will be joined as one and this country and this great Continent of Europe in a peaceful and hopeful globe. When that day finally comes, as it will, the people of West Berlin can take sober satisfaction in the fact that they were in the front lines for almost two decades.

All free men, wherever they may live, are citizens of Berlin, and, therefore, as a free man, I take pride in the words "Ich bin ein Berliner."

> **"All free men, wherever they may live, are citizens of Berlin, and, therefore, as a free man, I take pride in the words "Ich bin ein Berliner."**

County Wexford Greets Its Own Son; Kennedy Sees the Cousins Who Didn't Catch the Boat

By TOM WICKER

DUBLIN, June 27—President Kennedy lifted the spirits of County Wexford today. He lifted them higher than they've been since the Rising of '98.

Irish eyes were glued to television screens "from the Aran Islands to the coal quay in Cork," as one of Mr. Kennedy's happy welcomers said with no more than a touch of the Blarney. But it was in County Wexford on the Irish Sea, where the Kennedy family dates at least to 1654, and from which Patrick J. Kennedy sailed for the New World in the late eighteen-forties, that the President appeared in person and the crowds turned out to cheer.

The "homecoming" brought out a full-throated Irish welcome.

It was Patrick Kennedy who became a cooper in Boston and founded the American branch of the family of which the President is the most noted member.

Greeting to His Kin

"I am glad to see a few cousins who did not catch the boat," said the President to the Kennedy kin among his welcomers.

On the quay at New Ross where his great-grandfather last stood on Irish soil, Mr. Kennedy spoke to a crowd of 10,000. Then he visited Dunganstown, where Patrick probably was born, and where a cousin, Mrs. Mary Ryan, and her two daughters live.

From there, the President went by helicopter to the "Ancient Burrough of Wexford" to become the 13th Freeman of that city, and to tell a crowd of 6,000 that the "Irish experience" had shown the world it was possible for a people despite "a hundred years of foreign domination and religious perse-

cution . . . to maintain their identity and their strong faith."

"Therefore," Mr. Kennedy said, those "who may believe that freedom may be on the run, or that one nation may be permanently subjugated and eventually wiped out, would do well to remember Ireland."

The President had scarcely set foot on Wexford turf, at the Sean O'Kennedy Football Field outside the ancient town of New Ross, when his hosts reminded him that the "rising" against the British in 1798 was one of Wexford's most precious lost causes.

Children from the Christian Brothers School were waiting to sing a rousing marching song, "Boys From Wexford," which ends:

"We are the boys from Wexford who fought with heart and hand to burst in twain the galling chain and free our native land."

Youngsters in white spread out on the green grass of the field to spell out "failte" as a Gaelic "welcome" when the President's helicopter came in from Dublin. He is staying there at Phoenix Park, the Ambassador's house.

It was truly "failte" in nearby New Ross when Mr. Kennedy arrived at the quay. An Irish band played, the crowd cheered and laughed, and a placard was raised that read: "Johnnie, I hardly knew ye!"

It took him 115 years, 6,000 miles and three generations to make the trip, the President said. He praised his "inheritance" from Patrick Kennedy: "A strong religious faith and a strong desire for liberty."

If his great-grandfather had not left Ireland, Mr. Kennedy said, "I would be working over at the Albatros Company, or perhaps for John V. Kelly." The Alba-

tros Company is a fertilizer plant visible across the river from the quay. John V. Kelly is an auctioneer whose old stone building was directly in front of the speaker's stand.

Mr. Kennedy closed with an anecdote about an Irish family that went to the United States, visited Washington, had a picture taken before the White House, and sent it to relatives in Ireland with the message: "This is our summer house. Come and see us."

"Well," the President said, "it is our home also in the winter and I hope you will come and see us."

150 Meet Him On Lane

From New Ross, he drove four miles to the Kennedy homestead at Dunganstown—the remnant of a once-flourishing village where Patrick Kennedy is thought to have grown to manhood before the great Irish famine. He was met on the lane by 150 persons, and got a kiss on the cheek from Mrs. Ryan.

Kennedy did not enter the hut that may have been his great-grandfather's birthplace. Instead, he visited Mrs. Ryan and her daughters in the newer and more substantial farmhouse built a hundred years ago.

At a picnic table in the farmyard—newly covered with concrete—the President ate a sandwich, cut a piece of cake for Mrs. Ryan and drank a cup of tea "to all the Kennedys who went and those who stayed."

By helicopter, Mr. Kennedy flew to Wexford, the county seat, where he laid a wreath at the statue of Commodore John Barry, spoke briefly, and was the center of an Irish political set-to.

Commodore Barry was an Irishman who became a leading figure in the American Navy in the Revolutionary War. A statue of him was given to Wexford by the American Government in 1956.

Speaking from a stand in front of the railroad station, Mr. Kennedy said there was "an impression that there are no Kennedys left in Ireland, that they are all in Washington."

Looking Back

JFK and the Power of the Spoken Word

By Terry Golway

During the darkest days of the Great Depression, President Franklin Roosevelt initiated a series of "fireside chats," informal talks over the radio to the American people designed to assure them that America's greatness would survive the devastating result of the worst financial collapse in our history. Three decades later President John F. Kennedy would engage the nation in a series of televised speeches and news conferences in which he defined American values and objectives in the struggle against communism and in the fight for civil rights for all citizens. From his magnificent Inaugural Address in 1961 to a series of speeches in the spring and summer of 1963, John Kennedy gave us some of the most memorable phrases and word pictures in American political history.

Kennedy's ability to inspire people was entirely unexpected. He was an awkward figure during his first campaign for Congress in 1946. His voice was scratchy, his delivery wooden. He won anyway, of course, but his speaking style remained a weakness as late as 1959, when he was preparing to run for president. One Democratic Party official that year praised the content of JFK's speeches, but complained that the young senator rushed his words, seemingly without pause for a breath. That fall, as the campaign loomed, Kennedy made a conscious effort to improve his delivery, an effort that culminated in the near-perfect delivery of his powerful and instantly famous Inaugural Address.

In another sense, however, Kennedy's success with words should not be so surprising. Until he took up politics, young Jack Kennedy thought of himself as a writer. He was barely out of his teens when his senior thesis at Harvard was published (with the literary assistance of *The New York Times* columnist Arthur Krock) as *Why England Slept* (1940), an account of Britain's appeasement of Adolf Hitler in the 1930s. After the war, Kennedy considered high-end journalism as a career path, and covered the opening of the United Nations for the *Chicago Herald-American* in April 1945. And, of course, Kennedy won the Pulitzer Prize for biography in 1957 for his book *Profiles in Courage*, his account of the courageous stands of several U.S.

senators from the nation's history who put their careers on the line for the sake of principle. The book was written in unacknowledged collaboration with Theodore Sorensen, but Kennedy was most certainly involved in the writing and editing.

So words and language were not foreign concepts to Kennedy. He clearly had a keen appreciation for the power of the right phrases, delivered under the right circumstances, by the right speaker. He demonstrated that in the weeks before his inauguration, when he and Sorensen labored over the words that would become part of presidential lore. He was determined to deliver a speech that would be remembered alongside Lincoln's Gettysburg Address (which he asked Sorensen to study as a model of literary precision).

In the months and years that followed, Kennedy established a new standard of presidential oratory through dozens of nationally televised speeches, not to mention 64 news conferences, most of which were televised. Whether delivering a set-piece speech from the Oval Office or bantering with reporters, Kennedy demonstrated that words still mattered in the new age of television, that speeches still reflected and directed public policy, and that language could still inspire.

During a 16-day span in June 1963, he gave three remarkable speeches. The first was little noticed at the time, but has become part of the Kennedy canon in the half-century since his death. On the afternoon of June 10, a sleepy Sunday in Washington, JFK donned the formal robes of academia to deliver the commencement address to American University's class of 1963. In this speech, JFK the cold warrior became JFK the conciliator, the very antithesis of the man who just over two years earlier spoke of a twilight struggle against communism. Kennedy told the graduates that he was before them to speak about "the most important topic on Earth: world peace." He asked his fellow Americans not to prepare themselves for imminent conflict or to steel themselves for protracted confrontation with the Soviet Union. Instead, he asked that the nation "re-examine our attitude toward the Soviet Union." In fact, he asserted that Americans ought to consider how much they had in common with the Russian people. "We all breathe the same air," he said. "We all cherish our children's future. And we are all mortal."

These were extraordinary sentiments from a man who, just eight months earlier, confronted the Soviets in Cuba, risking a nuclear conflagration. But the Cuban missile crisis was very much part of the process that led Kennedy to announce at American University that the U.S., the British and the Soviets would begin negotiations designed to ban the testing of nuclear weapons in the atmosphere. The Cold War struggle had brought the world to the brink of nuclear war, and Kennedy used his American University speech to implore his fellow citizens to reconsider—as he clearly had—the consequences of Cold War rhetoric and actions.

Two weeks after the speech, Washington and Moscow established the famous hot line, a dedicated telephone line over which the president and Soviet leader Nikita Khrushchev could speak directly. Soon, after years of negotiations, they would sign the Nuclear Test Ban Treaty. The Cold War was by no means over, but Kennedy's speech at American University helped to change the conflict's dynamics and established a measure of trust between its two main antagonists.

Even as Kennedy finished his emotional appeal to influence American public opinion, a conflict of another sort was raging several hundred miles from the American University campus. Alabama Governor George C. Wallace was preparing to resist federal efforts to register two African American students at the all-white University of Alabama, a state institution. Kennedy arrived back at the White House after his American University speech to learn that Wallace was prepared to block the Kennedy Administration's effort to enroll the black students. A violent confrontation seemed very likely.

Speechwriter Theodore Sorensen suggested that Kennedy deliver a nationally televised speech on civil rights and the crisis in Alabama the following evening. Kennedy seemed skeptical, but his brother, Attorney General Robert Kennedy, argued that a presidential speech was critical, especially if the White House wished to build support for a promised civil rights bill. JFK remained undecided. The following morning, hundreds of National Guard troops were prepared to deploy at the University of Alabama in case of violence, but technically they were under the command of Governor Wallace. The governor personally halted the students and federal agents from gaining access to the registrar's office. On live television, Wallace denounced the "illegal" actions of the "central government."

Wallace's theatrics enraged both Kennedys. Although the students were brought to another part of the campus and quietly enrolled after Wallace left the scene, the Kennedy White House immediately federalized the Alabama National Guard, taking command out of Wallace's hands. JFK told his staff that he would deliver a speech on civil rights that very evening.

Addressing himself to the nation's white majority, he asked if they would be content "to have the color of [their] skin changed" and stand in the place of an African American denied access to a lunch counter, to good schools, to the ballot box. Every American, he said, ought to "examine his conscience."

Kennedy had long avoided broad public pronouncements about civil rights. He sometimes seemed to regard civil rights as a distraction, in fact, as a potential embarrassment in the struggle for the world's hearts and minds. He knew perfectly well that Southern Democrats were a formidable bloc on Capitol Hill, particularly in the Senate, and he needed their support to get anything—including the treaty to ban nuclear testing in the atmosphere—accomplished. After the speech of June 11, however, the Kennedy White House was fully committed to civil rights, even though both JFK and his brother, the Attorney General, believed that they would suffer politically in the South.

The day after JFK's speech, civil rights activist Medgar Evers was shot in the back and killed in front of his wife and children in Mississippi. President Kennedy sent a civil rights bill to Congress on June 19.

In late June President Kennedy returned to more familiar turf, when foreign policy once again had his full attention. He traveled to Europe for a four-nation tour which included a stopover in West Berlin, deep behind the Iron Curtain in Communist East Germany. The divided city was a symbol of Cold War tensions ever since the end of the World War II. The construction of a wall through the heart of the city in 1961 added a measure of ugliness and hopelessness to the city's plight. On one side of the wall was West Berlin, allied with the U.S. On the other side was East Berlin, aligned with the Soviets. Kennedy arrived in West Berlin on June 26. He was due to give a speech outside West Berlin's City Hall, in full view of the wall. Journalists and other observers noted that Kennedy's demeanor grew more serious after he climbed a guard tower and caught a glimpse of a nearly lifeless East Berlin.

As he stood before hundreds of thousands of West Berliners gathered in a plaza near City Hall, Kennedy displayed a passion and anger the American public rarely saw. And he told Berliners—residents of a city left in ashes by Allied bombers fewer than 20 years earlier—that they were comrades in arms in the fight for freedom.

"There are many people in the world who really don't understand, or say they don't, what is the great issue between the free world and the Communist world," he said. "Let them come to Berlin." Over and over again, he invited skeptics to come to Berlin. And he famously announced that in the "world of freedom, the proudest boast is 'Ich bin ein Berliner'"—I am a Berliner.

Terry Golway is a professor of History at Kean University and the co-author of *Let Every Nation Know: John F. Kennedy in His Own Words.*

Vietnam Orders Rein On Protests

Policemen in Saigon Club Buddhist Demonstrators—Kennedy Urges Accord

By DAVID HALBERSTAM

SAIGON, Vietnam, July 17—The police were reliably reported tonight to be under orders to use force to break up Buddhist demonstrations. This report followed a police attack on Buddhist demonstrators, who were clubbed into submission.

About 200 persons—Buddhist priests and nuns and women and children—were arrested. The demonstrators were beaten for their part in the protests.

All Buddhist pagodas were sealed off today with barbed wire. No one was allowed to enter, and no one was allowed to leave. The priests who had been arrested were being interrogated by the police about the leadership of their protest movement. Arrests of leaders, it was reported, might follow.

[President Kennedy said at his news conference that Vietnam's religious crisis was impairing the fight against Communist guerrillas there. He urged Saigon to reach an accord with the Buddhists.]

Vietnam's Buddhists have been protesting for 10 weeks against what they consider to be restrictive religious policies of the Government of Ngo Dinh Diem, a Roman Catholic. On May 8 troops in the city of Hue fired on Buddhists who were demonstrating for the right to fly their religious flag.

There were indications tonight that Buddhist demonstrations would continue and that Buddhists might commit suicide in protest, as a priest and a writer have done so far.

This was the second day of demonstrations since the Buddhists announced that they would reopen the campaign. An uneasy month of sparring followed the signing of a joint communiqué a month ago by both sides. The communiqué failed to settle the crisis.

At Giac Minh pagoda, at 8:10 A. M., about 1,000 persons led by 150 priests, massed to march down the street to the Xa Loi pagoda several blocks away. But the police had strung up barbed wire. The Buddhists rushed the barricade, but the police won the struggle.

Secret Police Join Fray

Then Buddhists sat down in the street. The sitdown continued for more than an hour until secret police started a counter-demonstration. They carried banners charging that the Buddhists were being exploited by Communists.

Then uniformed, specially trained riot police drew back the barbed wire, and 100 of them went in after the demonstrators.

The policemen grabbed priests as they knelt and clubbed them. They grabbed seated old women and smashed down with clubs. In one alley, several policemen grabbed an old woman and beat her.

The riot policemen were joined by some of the 100 secret policemen at the scene.

The entire attack took less than 15 minutes. It went on as other policemen, with new submachine guns at the ready, stood by. As the struggle was going on, one police official turned to reporters and said, "That's what happens when there is too much liberty."

President Ngo Dinh Diem. (Keystone/Getty Images)

The Nuclear Test Ban Treaty

Khrushchev Opens Test-Ban Parley In A Jovial Mood

3 1/2-Hour Discussion With Harriman and Hailsham Raises No Bar to Pact

GUARDED HOPE PERSISTS

Premier Silent on Condition That West Opposed— He May Rejoin Sessions

By SEYMOUR TOPPING

MOSCOW, July 15—Premier Khrushchev opened the talks today on a treaty to forbid nuclear testing. Restrained hope about the prospect for agreement persisted.

In a relaxed and jovial mood, Mr. Khrushchev outlined the Soviet views in his Kremlin office. He talked for three and a half hours with W. Averell Harriman and Viscount Hailsham, chief delegates of the United States and Britain.

It was understood that no new serious obstacle to an accord had been raised during the introductory statements of Mr. Khrushchev and the Western delegates.

Negotiations and a detailed exploration of Soviet attitudes will be undertaken tomorrow when the Western delegates resume the talks with a Soviet team under Foreign Minister Andrei A. Gromyko.

Premier May Join Talks

Mr. Khrushchev has reserved the right to join the talks when he wishes.

Western hopes for a partial test ban were raised by Mr. Khrushchev's speech in East Berlin on July 2. The Premier said then that the Soviet Union was ready to outlaw tests of nuclear weapons in the atmosphere, in space and under water.

Previously Moscow insisted on including an uncontrolled moratorium on underground testing. The Western powers have been unwilling to subscribe to such an arrangement, citing as a reason the Soviet abandonment of a similar moratorium on atmospheric testing in August, 1961.

The three countries have entered these negotiations with the understanding that underground testing may be dealt with later. Moscow has resisted Western demands for comprehensive international inspection to guard against concealed underground tests.

Detectors Found Adequate

The three powers agree that detection devices in their own countries are adequate to discern explosions abroad in the atmosphere, in space and under water.

The United States and Britain believe that a partial treaty on testing would significantly ease cold-war tensions. They believe it might encourage other limited East-West agreements.

A joint communiqué issued tonight on the opening of the talks did not disclose their substance. The West has concurred with a Soviet proposal to conduct the talks without the publicity that attended the Geneva negotiations within the framework of the 17-nation disarmament conference. The communiqué, which was broadcast, said views had been exchanged on "questions related to the discontinuance of nuclear tests and other questions of mutual interest."

The subjects discussed with Mr. Khrushchev, it was understood, included his proposal for a nonaggression agreement between the North Atlantic Treaty Organization and its East European counterpart, the Warsaw Pact.

An agreement to withold nuclear weapons from nations that do not already possess them was also touched upon.

Mr. Khrushchev was jovial when he welcomed the Western representatives and their deputies to his office. He had an especially warm greeting for Mr. Harriman, who was Ambassador to Moscow from 1943 to 1946.

'Start Right Away?'

The Premier took the first seat on the side of the table with his back to a window on Red Square. Mr. Harriman sat opposite him, with Lord Hailsham at his side.

"Shall we start off by signing the agreement right away?" Mr. Khrushchev asked.

Mr. Harriman pushed a pad and pencil to the smiling Russian leader. Mr. Gromyko advised the Premier: "Fine. Then leave it to be filled in."

In his remarks, Mr. Khrushchev did not specify that the Soviet Union would make a partial test ban conditional on a NATO nonaggression agreement with the Warsaw Pact countries. The nature of the Soviet link between the questions remains obscure, and the position will not be clear until the substantive negotiations are under way.

U.S., SOVIET AND BRITAIN REACH ATOM ACCORD THAT BARS ALL BUT UNDERGROUND TESTS; SEE MAJOR STEP TOWARD EASING TENSION

TREATY INITIALED

Rusk and Lord Home Will Go to Moscow to Sign Pact

By SEYMOUR TOPPING

MOSCOW, July 25—The United States, the Soviet Union and Britain concluded today a treaty to prohibit nuclear testing in the atmosphere, in space and under water.

The historic document was initialed at 7:15 P. M., Moscow time, by W. Averell Harriman, Under Secretary of State for Political Affairs; Soviet Foreign Minister Andrei A. Gromyko, and Viscount Hailsham, British Minister for Science.

A communiqué on the initialing said:

"The heads of the three delegations agreed that the test ban treaty constituted an important first step toward the reduction of international tension and the strengthening of peace, and they look forward to further progress in this direction."

Austrian Treaty Recalled

It was noted in the diplomatic community here that the treaty represented the first major East-West accord since the conclusion of the Austrian State Treaty on May 15, 1955. That agreement ended the postwar four-power occupation of Austria.

The United States and Britain agreed at the test-ban talks to further discussion on the Soviet proposal relating to a pact of nonaggression between the North Atlantic Treaty Organization and the Soviet-bloc's Warsaw Pact alliance. The communiqué said this would be done in consultation with the NATO allies "with the purpose of achieving agreement satisfactory to all participants."

Mr. Harriman, who appeared tired but happy after 10 days of intensive negotiations, said the test-ban treaty would relieve the fears of people all over the world about nuclear contamination of the atmosphere.

Others Urged to Join

He expressed the hope that other nations would adhere to the test ban treaty, which provides for the accession of other members.

The treaty, after signing, would be subject to parliamentary ratification by the United States Senate, the Supreme Soviet and the British Parliament.

The Western delegates to the three-power talks were unable to persuade Mr. Gromyko to accept international on-site inspection to verify the nature of seismic disturbances. The treaty, therefore, does not cover underground nuclear testing.

The preamble to the treaty pledges the three nations continue negotiations for the discontinuance of all test explosions for all time.

The second article of the five-article treaty binds the signatories to "refrain from causing, encouraging or in any way participating in" any nuclear explosion in the prohibited environments.

The United States and Britain would thereby be barred from assisting France in her contemplated testing program, which is directed at developing an independent nuclear striking force. The Soviet Union similarly would be restricted in extending any assistance to the weapons program of Communist China.

Abrogation Clause In Treaty

The treaty is of unlimited duration, but it contains an abrogation clause that already is the subject of controversy in the gathering battle for ratification in the United States Senate.

The clause states: "Each party shall, in exercising its national sovereignty, have the right to withdraw from the treaty, if it decides that extraordinary events related to the subject matter of this treaty have jeopardized the supreme interests of its country."

Three months advance notice of withdrawal is required.

Treaty Can Be Amended

The treaty can be amended by a majority of its members. The majority, however, must include the votes of the three original signatories.

The three Governments proclaimed in the preamble that their principal aim was "the speediest possible achievement of an agreement on general and complete disarmament under strict international control in accordance with the objectives of the United Nations."

The preamble said that such an agreement "would put an end to the armaments race and eliminate the incentive to the production and testing of all kinds of weapons, including nuclear weapons."

The reaction of Soviet officials and ordinary Muscovites to the outcome of the talks was one of pleasure. There were cautious expressions of hope that it might signify a break in the cold war.

Atmosphere Cheerful

The feeling that perhaps a start had been made in arranging a détente between East and West was reflected in the atmosphere in the conference room of the Foreign Ministry's reception mansion.

Correspondents, upon entering the gilded, high-ceilinged room, found the delegates seated about a round table looking somewhat weary after two hours and 45 minutes of discussion prior to the initialing of the treaty.

Behind the banter that the delegates engaged in for the benefit of photographers, there was an air of solemnity and of historic moment.

The United States and Soviet delegates shouldered their way through the crowd and met at the rim of the conference table. Mr. Harriman grabbed the hand of Mr. Gromyko, whom he has encountered over the years at a series of tension-ridden and fruitless conferences. The tall, 71-year-old diplomat said: "Thank you." Mr. Gromyko replied: "Thank you. Till we meet tomorrow, Good-bye."

The conference, which marks the first notable success in more than five years of negotiations on a test-ban treaty, ended on this note. Mr. Harriman later said: «It was a businesslike talk. There was goodwill throughout.»

The most difficult phase of the negotiations took place during the last four days in defining the link between the conclusion of a test ban treaty and the Soviet-proposed East-West nonaggression pact.

Mr. Harriman, who appeared tired but happy after 10 days of intensive negotiations, said the test-ban treaty would relieve the fears of people all over the world about nuclear contamination of the atmosphere.

The Soviet Government, until the final stage of the negotiations, had insisted on a simultaneous signing of the agreements. The Western delegates resisted on the ground that they were not authorized to negotiate a nonaggression agreement since this would have to be done in consultation with the other North Atlantic allies.

The alliance members, especially West Germany, had opposed the form of the Soviet proposal put forward on Feb. 20, which in effect involved the recognition of East Germany.

The compromise, which was worked out last night, was incorporated in the final paragraph of the communiqué. It said:

"The heads of the three delegations discussed the Soviet proposal relating to a pact of nonaggression between the participants of the North Atlantic Treaty Organization and the participants in the Warsaw Treaty."

"The three Governments have agreed fully to inform their respective allies in the two organizations concerning these talks and to consult with them about discussion on this question the purpose of achieving agreement satisfactory to all participants."

Mr. Harriman and Lord Hailsham avoided any implied recognition of East Germany by insisting on the term "participants" in the Warsaw Pact rather than member nations, which is the phraseology of the Soviet proposal.

Mr. Gromkyo attempted in negotiating the phraseology of the communiqué to bind the United States and Britain as closely as possible to a commitment to negotiate seriously on a nonaggression agreement.

Assurances Given

The Soviet aim in seeking a nonaggression pact has been to obtain Western acceptance of the status quo in Eastern Europe, particularly the division of Germany.

In the exchange of opinions at the three-power talks Mr. Harriman outlined a possible formula for a nonaggression treaty that might be acceptable to the United States and its allies. This would not entail recognition of East Germany.

Such an agreement would bar the use of force in Europe and guarantee the security of West Berlin. It would be realized through parallel declarations by the military groupings rather than through the signature of a common document.

The process of consultation with the allies on a nonaggression agreement is scheduled to go forward after Mr. Harriman's return to Washington.

Secretary of State Rusk is expected to carry on the discussions of a nonaggression treaty and other measures with Foreign Minister Gromyko when he comes here for the signing of the test-ban treaty.

KENNEDY AND KHRUSHCHEV CALL PACT A STEP TO PEACE BUT NOT A WAR PREVENTIVE

PRESIDENT ON TV

Tells Nation Treaty Is 'Victory for Mankind' but Not Millennium

---

By TOM WICKER

WASHINGTON, July 26—President Kennedy, speaking to the nation tonight in a "spirit of hope," described the treaty for a limited nuclear test ban as a "victory for mankind" in its pursuit of peace.

The treaty, initialed in Moscow yesterday by representatives of the United States, the Soviet Union and Britain, would ban nuclear tests in the atmosphere, in space and under water.

Describing the agreement as a "shaft of light cut into the darkness" of cold-war discords and tensions, Mr. Kennedy nonetheless warned that it was "not the millennium."

"It will not resolve all conflicts, or cause the Communists to forego their ambitions, or eliminate the dangers of war," he said. "It will not reduce the need for arms or allies or programs of assistance to others."

'A Step Away from War'

"But it is an important first step—a step toward peace—a step toward reason—a step away from war."

If "this short and simple treaty" could now be made a symbol of "the end of one era and the beginning of another," the President said, it could lead on to further reductions of tensions and broader areas of agreement.

Among them, he suggested, might be "controls on preparations for a sur-

prise attack, or on numbers and types of armaments."

"There could be further limitations on the spread of nuclear weapons," he added.

The important point, Mr. Kennedy said, is that "the effort to seek new agreements will go forward."

The President appeared on all three national television networks and his words also were heard on four radio networks. He spoke from his office in the West Executive Wing of the White House.

Immediately after the speech, he departed for a weekend at Hyannis Port, Mass. There he will confer tomorrow with Under Secretary of State W. Averell Harriman, the United States representative to the successful nuclear test ban talks, which began July 15 in Moscow.

Mr. Kennedy spoke with unaccustomed slowness, as if to emphasize the gravity of the matters he discussed.

One by one, mostly from a prepared text but from notes at the conclusion of his speech, he made his points, the most important of which were as follows:

The treaty did not endanger the national security and the nation would continue both underground testing and its readiness to resume all testing if required.

But the treaty offered a promising

opportunity to negotiate further relaxations of the cold war and to avoid the ultimate horror of nuclear war.

Therefore the Senate should ratify it and the American people should support it, even though it signified no more than a beginning of what remained a hard road to peace.

"There is an old Chinese proverb that says, 'a journey of a thousand miles must begin with a first step,'" the President said in conclusion.

'First Step' Is Urged

Looking up from his notes and gazing directly into the cameras, Mr. Kennedy said slowly and distinctly:

"My fellow Americans—let us take the first step."

With an unusual ring of emotion in his voice, he also painted a grim picture of the possibilities of nuclear war.

"If only one thermonuclear bomb were to be dropped on any American, Russian or other city—whether it was launched by accident or design, by a madman or an enemy, by a large nation or a small, from any corner of the world—that one bomb could release more destructive force on the inhabitants of that one helpless city than all the bombs dropped during the Second World War," he said.

And in a full-scale nuclear exchange "lasting less than 60 minutes," the President added, more than 300,000,000

Americans, Europeans and Russians would perish.

Mr. Kennedy also quoted Premier Khrushchev's warning to the Chinese Communists that, in such an event, survivors in a devastated world "would envy the dead."

Reassurance Is Offered

Looking beyond American shores, the President also sought to reassure the nation's allies in two important respects.

First, he said, in any subsequent negotiations to meet the desire of the Soviet Union for a nonaggression pact or declaration, there would be "full consultation with our allies and full attention to their interests."

To President de Gaulle of France, which now possesses nuclear weapons, there was a special word. Mr. Kennedy linked France with the United States, the Soviet Union and Britain as "the four current nuclear powers."

These powers, he said, "have a great obligation to use whatever time remains to prevent the spread of nuclear weapons, to persuade other countries not to test, transfer, acquire, possess or produce such weapons."

France is not a party to the three-power test ban and has given no indication that she is "ready to become one." Her accession to it would be regarded here as a long step toward prevention of the proliferation of nuclear weapons to still more countries.

"I ask you to stop and think for a moment what it would mean to have nuclear weapons in many hands—in the hands of countries large and small, stable and unstable, responsible and irresponsible, scattered throughout the world," Mr. Kennedy said, perhaps to General de Gaulle.

"There would be no rest for anyone then, no stability, no real security, and no chance of effective disarmament. There would only be increased chances of accidental war, and an increased necessity for the great powers to involve themselves in local conflicts."

A "small but significant" number of nations already had the capability to buy or produce nuclear weapons, the President said, but, on the other hand, "already we have heard from a number of countries who wish to join with us promptly."

Mr. Kennedy dwelt at length on the subject of national security. He conceded the possibility that secret tests might be conducted in outer space, but downgraded the risks inherent in such tests.

Tests Hard to Conceal

If necessary, he said, means of detecting such tests could be constructed. And, in any case, he added, "Tests which might be conducted so far out in space, which cannot be conducted more easily and efficiently and legally underground, would necessarily be of such magnitude that they would be extremely difficult to conceal."

But secret violation or sudden withdrawal from the treaty is possible, he said, and therefore "our own vigilance and strength must be maintained, as we remain ready to withdraw and to resume all forms of testing, if we must."

Underlying this statement was the fact that some United States testing will continue underground and that the remainder of the testing apparatus of the United States will be kept in readiness. Tests of peaceful applications of nuclear energy continue too, leading, it is believed here, to a number of gains in this field within five years.

It is also believed in Washington that Soviet underground testing capability lags behind that of the United States and cannot be brought to parity in less than six months to a year.

The strategic view here is that neither side will be able to make gains in weaponry under the treaty sufficient to alter the balance of power.

Risks Held Convincing

The President stated his belief that "the far greater risks" of unrestricted testing, the nuclear arms race, atmospheric pollution and nuclear war would convince all parties to the treaty that observing it would be "a matter of their own self-interest."

For the United States, he said, the treaty would be "safer by far" than an arms race.

The President also spoke with great feeling about the hazards of radioactive fallout to children yet unborn.

"The loss of even one human life, or the malformation of even one baby, who may be born long after we are gone, should be of concern to us all,'" Mr. Kennedy said.

"Our children and grandchildren are not merely statistics toward which we can be indifferent."

"And children," he added, "have no lobby here in Washington."

The President urged full discussion of all these matters in the Senate and among citizens.

"A document which may mark an historic and constructive opportunity for the world deserves an historic and constructive debate," he said.

★ ★ ★

"So let us try to turn the world away from war.
Let us make the most of this opportunity,
and every opportunity, to reduce tension, to slow
down the perilous nuclear arms race, and to
check the world's slide toward final annihilation."
—President Kennedy

TEST BAN TREATY SIGNED IN MOSCOW; LEADERS REJOICE

Khrushchev and Ministers Join Glittering Reception After Solemn Ceremony

WARM SPIRIT PREVAILS

Thant and 70 U.S., Russian and British Officials Attend—'First Step' Is Theme

By HENRY TANNER

MOSCOW, Aug. 5—The foreign ministers of the United States, Britain and the Soviet Union signed the test ban treaty today at a ceremony that was both solemn and joyous.

Then, led by Premier Khrushchev, they strode into one of the Kremlin's most glittering ballrooms for a reception as a Soviet band played Gershwin's "Love Walked In."

The song summed up the mood of the day. From the start of courtesy calls by the ministers at 9 A.M. to the end of the gala reception just before nightfall it was filled with firm East-West handshakes, warm smiles, friendly jokes and toasts to "peace and friendship" drunk in Soviet champagne.

Premier Poses With Clergy

One diplomat called it a "unique day" in East-West relations, "Peace—it's wonderful," said another, and meant it. Premier Khrushchev, who insists he does not believe in religion, was moved by the spirit of conciliation to the point of posing for pictures with the elders of the Russian Orthodox Church.

The signing of the 1,500-word treaty banning nuclear tests in the atmosphere, in space and under water took only five minutes.

Soviet Premier Nikita S. Khrushchev and British statesman Edward Heath watch Soviet foreign minister Andrei A. Gromyko and Alec Douglas-Home signing the Nuclear Test Ban Treaty in Moscow, August 5, 1963. (Terry Fincher/Express/Getty Images)

It was held in Catherine Hall, a vaulted, white marble chamber in the Kremlin's Great Palace.

Bathed in White Lights

Secretary of State Dean Rusk, Foreign Minister Andrei A. Gromyko and the Earl of Home, Britain's Foreign Secretary, sat in gold-trimmed chairs at an oblong table as they affixed their signatures to the three copies of the document.

"Peace—

it's wonderful."

Above their heads was a huge, glittering chandelier. They were bathed in the brilliance of the klieg lights set up for Soviet and Western television.

Standing behind them and watching the signing were about 70 Soviet, American and British dignitaries led by Premier Khrushchev. U Thant, the United Nations Secretary General, stood next to the Premier.

The Soviet group included Leonid I. Brezhnev, the Soviet chief of state, and almost all the key leaders of the Soviet Government with the exception of Anastas I. Mikoyan, a First Deputy Premier, who is ill.

British Groups Smaller

The large American delegation included Adlai E. Stevenson, Senators J. W. Fulbright, Democrat of Arkansas; George D. Aiken, Republican of Vermont; Leverett Saltonstall, Republican of Massachusetts; John J. Sparkman, Democrat of Alabama; Hubert H. Humphrey, Democrat of Minnesota,

and John O. Pastore, Democrat of Rhode Island, and Ambassador to the Soviet Union.

After the signing, the foreign ministers made short statements.

Each stressed the theme that the treaty, in which the world's three most powerful Governments pledge to refrain from further contaminating the air and the oceans with nuclear tests, was merely a first step.

Each pledged that his government and his nation was intent on taking further steps toward easing world tension and creating the conditions for lasting peace.

After each declaration the assembly raised long-stemmed champagne glasses to drink to "peace and friendship," the toast proposed by Mr. Gromyko and seconded by Mr. Rusk.

Americans and Russians, Britons and Russians, and Americans and Britons in turn clinked glasses, smiled and nodded at each other and took a few sips as the television cameras whirred.

No one smiled more broadly and clinked glasses more eagerly or more often than Premier Khrushchev. He stood in the center of a group, wearing a gray suit and silver tie and a row of three medals hanging from red ribbons.

Although he did not speak, he obviously assumed the role of host and, by implication, of chief architect of the treaty.

The three-power communiqué issued after the signing echoed the declarations of the foreign ministers.

'Important Initial Step'

It said that government regarded the partial ban on testing as an "important

initial step" and hoped that "further progress" toward peace would be achieved.

The communique expressed the hope that other states would join the treaty. It announced that the treaty would be available for signing in London, Moscow and Washington beginning Thursday.

Thirty-three states had served notice by early this afternoon that they wanted to sign the treaty now. Thirty additional governments have said that they plan to do so later.

In spite of the smiles and the champagne, the day was not all celebration.

There were moments when the statesmen showed their old wariness and engaged in some deft diplomatic fencing.

Secretary Rusk made a point in his statement of stressing some of the things the treaty did not do.

"It does not end the threat of nuclear war," he said. "It does not reduce nuclear stockpiles, it does not halt the production of nuclear weapons, it does not restrict their use in time of war."

The American delegation here regards the reference to the possible use of nuclear weapons in time of war as an important one.

There has been some concern among legal experts in the Administration that the language of the treaty is ambiguous on this point and that an attempt may be made later to interpret it as forbidding the use of nuclear weapons in time of war.

The concern prompted a clarifying statement from President Kennedy 10 days ago. Secretary Rusk seized the opportunity of today's formal ceremony to restate the American position.

President Urges Repeal Of Quotas For Immigration

He Asks Congress to Admit Aliens Without Regard to Country of Their Origin

---

BAR TO ASIANS OPPOSED

New System Would Allot Highest Priority to Those With Useful Talents

---

By TOM WICKER

WASHINGTON, July 23—President Kennedy asked Congress today to abolish the quota system of immigration within five years.

The quotas, in effect since 1924 and based upon the Census of 1920, would be reduced by 20 per cent in each of the five years, until they disappeared. With them would go the system by which the United States has sharply limited immigration from southern Europe and Asia.

The country most affected would be Italy. Government officials estimated today that Italian immigration would rise from the present annual quota of 5,500 to an average of more than 16,000 in each of the five years that would follow enactment of Mr. Kennedy's proposals.

Terms of Kennedy Bill

The President's bill would provide for an eventual annual immigration total from all countries of about 165,000 persons. They would be ad-

mitted generally without regard to country of origin but by no means at random.

In addition to this major goal, Mr. Kennedy proposed the abolition of racial-origin restrictions against persons of Asian descent. His bill would also end the requirement that persons seeking immigration on grounds of their special skills or talents first obtain employment in this country.

It would permit the immigration, in addition to the established annual quota and without numerical restriction, of parents of American citizens, and of residents of Western Hemisphere nations that have gained independence since 1952—Jamaica, Trinidad and Tobago.

Cites 'Compelling Need'

Congressional approval of these changes, most of them controversial, is not believed likely this year and promises to be difficult at any time in the House of Representatives.

However, Mr. Kennedy, the author in 1958 of a little-known book called "A Nation of Immigrants," said that there was a "compelling need" for an immigration law "that serves the national interest and reflects in every detail the principles of equality and human dignity to which our nation subscribes."

The system he proposed as a replacement for national quotas would

give first priority to persons of useful skills and attainments—those as Mr. Kennedy said, "with the greatest ability to add to the national welfare." Engineers, doctors, teachers and scientists would probably be high in this category.

Second priority would go to persons whose immigration would reunite a family—to the unmarried, adult daughter, for instance, of parents already living in the United States.

A Government officer estimated that under these priorities relatives of persons already in the United States would provide more than half the annual total immigration.

One Restriction Proposed

After these priorities, admission would be governed by the date of application, still without regard to country of origin.

The only national restriction would be that no country could provide in any one year more than 10 per cent of the total annual immigration.

Thus, the present inflexible assignment of quotas would be eliminated. Under the quota system, 68,000 immigration places went unfilled in 1962 of a potential total of 157,000.

This was because many countries, notably Ireland and the United Kingdom, did not fulfill their large quotas. But the unused places could not be transferred to countries like Italy with small quotas and huge backlogs of would-be immigrants.

It is estimated here that 300,000 persons have registered for emigration to the United States in Italy since World War II, in addition to those who have been admitted.

Vietnam in Turmoil

60,000 Buddhists March In Vietnam

Mourn Monk in 4 Cities—
Regime
Rebuffed Again

By DAVID HALBERSTAM

SAIGON, July 30—Tens of thousands of Buddhists staged protests today in Saigon and four other main cities as South Vietnam's religious crisis ended its 12th week. But the Government made no effort to suppress the demonstrations, and there were apparently no major incidents. About 60,000 demonstrators took part.

The protest services were in memory of the Rev. Quang Duc, a Buddhist priest who burned himself to death as a protest against the religious policies of President Ngo Dinh Diem's Government.

Buddhists massed here and in Dalat, Nha Trang, Quin Nhon and Hue. These cities are in the central and central coastal regions of the country, where the Buddhists command the most popular support.

Buddhist leaders also rejected the Government's latest offer to form a joint commission to investigate religious grievances.

Condition Is Imposed

President Ngo Dinh Diem, a Roman Catholic, is accused by the Buddhists of discrimination. About 70 per cent of Vietnam's population belongs to sects that consider themselves Buddhist.

The Buddhists said they would not join a commission unless the Government accepted responsibility for the incident on May 8 that set off the crisis. Troops fired then on Buddhists demonstrating against a ban on displaying their religious flag. Nine Buddhists were killed. In the face of eyewitness reports and photographs backing the Buddhist accusation, the Government insists that a Vietcong guerrilla threw a grenade into the crowd.

In the new Saigon protest, 15,000 Buddhists attended prayer services at the main pagodas. But there was nothing approaching a general strike, which some Buddhist leaders hoped to achieve.

In Hue, where religious feeling is considered much stronger, more than 15,000 marched to the main pagoda to pray for the dead priest. Most stores in Hue were closed for part of the day in protest.

Government sources said that 10,000 Buddhists attended services in the three other cities. They charged that Buddhist leaders had selected these cities as strongholds where they could make their best showing.

Twelve weeks after the Hue incident, there is neither settlement nor even progress. Both sides appear inflexible.

Another Buddhist Immolates Himself

By DAVID HALBERSTAM

SAIGON, Vietnam, Aug. 13—A 17-year-old Buddhist student priest burned himself to death today. It was the third Buddhist self-immolation since South Vietnam's religious-political dispute began more than three months ago.

The novice was identified as Thich Thanh Thuc. He apparently was alone when he poured kerosene on his body and set himself afire at about 2 A.M. His body was found at 6 A.M. by priests.

By mid-morning more than a thousand people had gathered at Phuc Duyen pagoda near Hue, the scene of the suicide. Thousands of others started out for the pagoda from Hue, three miles away. The Government set up road blocks.

Tension in Hue was reported growing. The city was put under a curfew from 8 P. M. to 6 A. M. Three companies of soldiers and a platoon of armored cars were moved into the city and took up positions at strategic points. The troops wore full battle gear.

The charred body of the novice lay draped in a Buddhist flag while Government and Buddhist officials argued over where the body would be buried.

The suicide came a few hours after an 18-year-old Buddhist girl in Saigon attempted to chop off her left hand in another protest against Government religious policies. Nine days ago a young priest burned himself to death in Phan Thiet. The first protest suicide by a priest took place June 11.

The religious crisis seemed to be gaining force. The suicide today and the girl's self-mutilation caught Buddhist leaders by surprise. Observers believed feeling was now so strong among many Buddhists that their leaders could no longer control individual protests.

The dispute began over a Government ban on the public display of religious flags. On May 8, nine Buddhists were killed when troops broke up a protest demonstration at Hue. The Buddhists accused the regime of President Ngo Dinh Diem, a Roman Catholic, of religious persecution.

Regime Denies Charge

The Government denies persecuting the Buddhists and has wavered between attempting to conciliate them and repressing their protests.

When news of the latest suicide reached Hue, Buddhist followers began to flock to the pagoda. About 1,500 reached the site before the Government blocked the roads and started turning them back.

Buddhist leaders wanted to hold the burial ceremony in Hue, but the Government insisted that the service take place at the pagoda. A Buddhist leader said, "We will bring the body into Hue one way or another."

In Hue, a city of 100,000 where religious feeling is particularly strong, a funeral procession for a monk could be an explosive force.

Observers feel that Hue is already close to religious war. The city is the see of Archbishop Ngo Dinh Thuc, brother of the President, and Roman Catholics are strong and well organized there while the Buddhists, who make up 85 per cent of the city's population, are unusually militant.

In Saigon, Vice President Nguyen Ngoc Tho, a Buddhist, held a news conference at which he attempted to belittle the importance of recent statements criticizing Buddhist leaders by Mrs. Dinh Nhu, sister-in-law of the President. He said Mrs. Nhu had never spoken in an official capacity.

The Vice President said he had received no directive from President Ngo Dinh Diem to change the Government's policy toward the Buddhists from what he said was a conciliatory approach.

Mr. Nguyen Ngoc Tho said discussions were going on between Buddhists and Government officials.

A Buddhist monk burns himself to death on a Saigon street to protest persecution of Buddhists by the South Vietnamese government.

(Malcolm Browne/Associated Press)

Thousands of Buddhists Rally
at Saigon Pagoda

By DAVID HALBERSTAM

SAIGON, Vietnam, Aug. 18—About 15,000 Buddhists, most of them young people, crowded around Xa Loi Pagoda today and for 12 hours sat in sun and rain and pledged themselves to fast in protest against the Government of President Ngo Dinh Diem. Observers were impressed by the confident appearance of the Buddhist leaders, and by the emotional response of the crowd. Some Vietnamese likened the crowd's enthusiasm to that of the early days of the Ngo Dinh Diem regime in 1954, when the Government gave the area its only hope of not being overrun by the Communists of Ho Chi Minh from the north. The crowd became particularly militant when the name of Archbishop Ngo Dinh Thuc of Hue was mentioned.

"Down with Thuc," the youths shouted.

When the rain began, Buddhist leaders asked the crowd to go home. The youths refused and started clapping.

Crowds at Xa Loi, which seemed to be tapering off about six weeks ago, have grown larger and more enthusiastic each week for a month. Today's service, heavy with political overtones and criticism of the Government, the President's brother, Archbishop Ngo Dinh Thuc, and his sister-in-law, Mrs. Ngo Dinh Nhu, followed a week in which there had been three self-immolations by Buddhist clergymen.

Last Thursday a 71-year-old priest, Tieu Dieu, burned himself to death in Hue. The day before Dieu Quang, a nun, killed herself in the same way, and on Monday Thanh Thuc, 17, a novice priest, set himself on fire.

There had been three previous suicides, two by burning, beginning with the self-immolation of Quang Duc, a priest on June 11.

In Hue where 47 professors resigned yesterday in protest against the Government's dismissal of the university rector, students revolted against a leader who had gone on the Hue radio to criticize their demonstrations.

Sources said about 500 students were angered by the radio statements of Trinh Giao Kim, head of the Student Association, who said that protests over the ouster of the Rev. Cao Van Luan, a Roman Catholic, had "dangerous political tones."

Five hundred other students met for two hours, with the university's secretary general serving as moderator, and elected Nguyen Van Thai, a Catholic, as their new president.

It was clear that the Buddhists' leaders were not yet ready to unleash the full force of their followers' devotion. Instead, one high Buddhist source said, the Buddhists of Saigon plan to demonstrate right after the arrival on Aug. 26 of Henry Cabot Lodge, the new United States Ambassador. They also plan demonstrations just before the United Nations General Assembly convenes Sept. 17.

The stress on these dates is an obvious move to increase pressure on the United States, which provides the major base of support for the Ngo Dinh Diem Government. Buddhist officials said they were seeking to have other predominantly Buddhist countries in southeast Asia bring the matter before the General Assembly.

The crowd gathers in front of Xa Loi Pagoda on August 20, 1963, in Saigon.
(J.M. Burfin/AFP/Getty Images)

CRISIS IN SOUTH VIETNAM DEEPENS AS DIEM'S FORCES RAID PAGODAS; U.S. SEES ITS TROOPS ENDANGERED BUDDHISTS SEIZED

Police Hurl Tear Gas and Grenades During Saigon Attacks

By United Press International

SAIGON, Vietnam, Wednesday, Aug. 21—Hundreds of heavily armed policemen and soldiers, firing pistols and using tear-gas bombs and hand grenades, swarmed into the Xa Loi pagoda early today and arrested more than 100 Buddhist monks.

. . . more than 15,000 Buddhists held an all-day sitdown hunger strike in front of the pagoda . . .

The big pagoda has been the scene of frequent clashes between Buddhists, demonstrating against what they call religious persecution by the Government, and Government troops.

Policemen and soldiers also stormed into three other pagodas in Saigon, but the Xa Loi pagoda is the main cathedral of the Buddhists, who have been embroiled in a religious and political crisis with the Government.

Grenade explosions were heard and tear-gas smoke could be seen rising from inside the walls of the main pagoda.

Outspoken Opponent

On Sunday more than 15,000 Buddhists held an all-day sitdown hunger strike in front of the pagoda to protest the policies of President Ngo Dinh Diem and of his sister-in-law, Mrs. Ngo Dinh Nhu, both Roman Catholics.

Mrs. Nhu, one of the most outspoken opponents of the Buddhists, has accused them of treason, murder and communist tactics and has ridiculed the Buddhist suicides by fire.

Violence has also been reported in Hue and other Buddhist centers. Martial law was imposed yesterday in the coastal city of Danang after demonstrators clashed with soldiers during a Buddhist mass march.

Danang, about 380 miles northeast of Saigon, is headquarters for the Vietnamese First Army Corps and is a major military base on the northeast coast.

Regime Cites Protests

The Government press agency said officials imposed martial law after a Vietnamese soldier was wounded and a Government vehicle damaged during protests Sunday by about 1,000 demonstrators.

A Buddhist protest letter to President Ngo Dinh Diem said that 36 demonstrators were injured, 18 seriously, and that 200 Buddhists were arrested in Danang. It said eight priests and nuns were among those seriously injured.

Tinh Khiet, Vietnam's supreme Buddhist priest, charged that Government troops were too harsh in putting down the demonstrations.

Other sources in Saigon reported that the demonstrators in Danang numbered about 3,000. They said the trouble began when a Vietnamese Army captain and two soldiers riding in a jeep became entangled in a long procession of demonstrators.

A dispute broke out between the soldiers and the demonstrators, the sources said, and one of the soldiers fired three shots into the crowd, wounding two demonstrators slightly.

The sources said the crowd turned on the captain, beating him, pummeled the soldier who fired the shots, and burned the jeep.

In Hue, a group of professors who resigned from the University of Hue last week in protest against Government policies called on the nation's intellectuals to support them.

In an open letter, signed by 41 of the 47 who resigned, the professors reaffirmed their determination not to return until the Buddhist crisis was settled.

The resignations were specifically in protest against the dismissal of the university's Roman Catholic rector, the Rev. Cao Van Luan. The reason given for his dismissal was that he had failed to prevent students from joining in Buddhist demonstrations.

TWO VERSIONS OF THE CRISIS IN VIETNAM: ONE LAYS PLOT TO NHU, OTHER TO ARMY

Sources in Saigon Say Military Did Not Order Attacks— Washington's Reports Indicate Diem Yielded to Officers

Plan Said to Be Nhu's

By DAVID HALBERSTAM

SAIGON, South Vietnam, Aug. 22—Highly reliable sources here said today that the decision to attack Buddhist pagodas and declare martial law in South Vietnam was planned and executed by Ngo Dinh Nhu, the President's brother, without the knowledge of the army.

These sources said that the Vietnamese Army had not seized power and that army commanders had been presented with a fait accompli.

Mr. Nhu is the chief adviser of President Ngo Dinh Diem. He is also head of the secret police, or special forces, which were said to have been his military arm in the main moves Wednesday morning.

The secret police were reported to have acted under the guidance of Col. Le Quang Tung, a man personally loyal to Mr. Nhu. The colonel was said to have carried out the raids on the pagodas with secret policemen dressed in the uniforms of various branches of the Vietnamese Army.

Lodge Arrives in Saigon

As mass arrests of Buddhists, opposition leaders and other dissidents continued in Saigon, Henry Cabot Lodge arrived by way of Tokyo to take up his new post as Ambassador to South Vietnam.

Mr. Lodge, who was originally scheduled to arrive next Monday, flew here on orders from the White House. A 9 P. M. to 5 A. M. curfew is in effect and Mr. Lodge landed at a virtually deserted airport aboard a military plane. He was accompanied by his wife and two special assistants, Frederick Flott and James Dunn. He was greeted by American officials and a representative of the Vietnamese protocol office.

"I don't have to tell you I have arrived under very special circumstances and my time to make declarations has not yet arrived," Mr. Lodge said. He refused further comment.

His staff was handed special passes permitting them to move about the city after curfew. It was reported that Mr. Lodge also received such a pass.

Mr. Nhu and his wife are regarded as being somewhat anti-American. Both have favored a hard line against the Buddhists, who have charged the Diem regime with religious persecution. The President and his family are Roman Catholics.

The Nhus have denied a policy of persecution but both were opposed to the President's announced policy of conciliation.

The raids on the pagodas and the declaration of martial law followed recent pledges by President Diem that he would seek to end the rift with the Buddhists. The violence drew a harsh statement yesterday from the United States.

The State Department charged the Diem regime with having violated its pledge and deplored repressive actions against the Buddhists.

There are about 13,000 United States military personnel in Vietnam, many of whom are directly engaged in the war against the Vietcong (Vietnamese Communist) guerrillas. The annual cost of the United States operation exceeds $250,000,000.

The sources in Saigon now feel that the situation is that Mr. Diem remains President but that the Nhus have gained so much power that they may be more important than the President.

These sources said that the Nhus acted to crush the Buddhists, to teach the Americans—who had been urging a conciliatory approach—a lesson, and to warn all dissident elements in the population.

Military Plays Along

It was also suggested that the Nhus may have acted when they did in order to present Mr. Lodge with an accomplished fact on his arrival. Mr. Lodge is replacing Frederick E. Nolting Jr. as Ambassador.

These sources said that the events during the last 36 hours in Saigon represented a "semi-coup" of a Government against itself.

The military, while surprised, was said to have apparently been willing to go along with the situation.

The sources said efforts by the Government to emphasize the role of the military were an attempt to demonstrate unity among the military when in fact none existed.

They were also said to be a move to show evidence of military support for the Government's strike against the Buddhists so as to make it seem there was broad backing for such a move.

It was reported that Maj. Gen. Tran Van Don, who was made chairman of the Vietnamese Chiefs of Staff, did not learn of the events in Saigon until 5 A.M. yesterday. He was called into the palace then and told that he had just been named chairman and that the country was going to be put under martial law.

There was a possibility that martial law might be ended in about a week.

Today, the Government radio made increasingly bitter attacks on Buddhist leaders, calling them Communists and lackeys of colonialists.

The radio, apparently because officials were angered that newsmen had managed to get out word of the attacks on Buddhist pagodas, also attacked foreign correspondents.

The radio said that the Government would release those Buddhists who, in time, could "distinguish between politics and religion."

It said that those who had committed "subversive acts" would be court-martialed.

About thirty top Buddhist leaders were reported to be under heavy guard in a building along the Saigon riverfront. Hundreds of other Buddhists were detained in quarters outside a cemetery in the Phu Lam area.

Government officials said that only one of the leaders, the Rev. Thich Tri Quang, had escaped during the attack on the Xa Loi pagoda. He is considered one of the two top Buddhist leaders.

Defection is Feared

There was fear among some Vietnamese today that he and other Buddhist leaders might defect to the Communists because of the brutal Government attack on the pagodas.

Until now, the Buddhist leadership was widely considered to be both anti-Government and anti-Communist. Now, however, anti-Government feeling is probably even stronger than anti-Communist feeling.

The Government was reported to have issued a call to its troops in one area to rally behind President Diem.

There were reliable reports that there had been mass defections among troops of the Vietnamese Army's Second Corps because of the attacks on the Buddhists.

In Hue, Government sources said that about 500 persons were arrested, including priests, nuns and many students.

There was sharp fighting in Hue between troops who attacked the pagoda there and Buddhists and their followers who fought them off with sticks and stones. Nine Government soldiers were reported to have been injured.

It was in Hue, a city five miles from the coast of the South China Sea, that the dispute between the Buddhists and the Diem regime broke into violence on May 8.

Nine Buddhists participating in a mass demonstration were killed. Their deaths led to further demonstrations, arrests and suicides by Buddhist priests.

It was reported today that in the new violence in Hue the pagoda there was wrecked and a giant statue of Buddha demolished.

Yesterday there was fierce fighting between armed troops and about 5,000 unarmed Buddhists. Many Buddhists were badly beaten and many were arrested.

Forty-seven faculty members at the

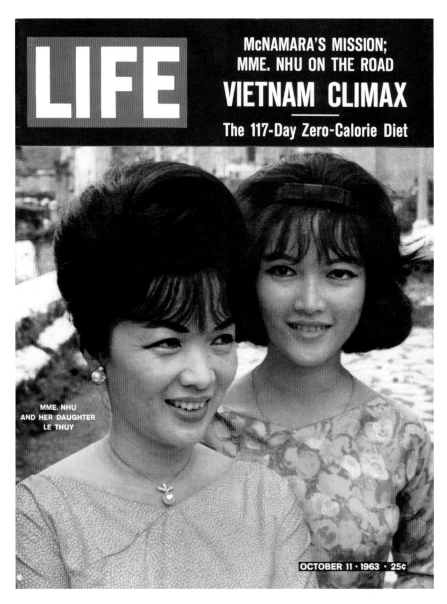

South Vietnam's Madame Nhu, a powerful hardliner against the Buddhists, and her daughter, Le Thuy. (John Loengard/Time & Life Pictures/Getty Images

Henry Cabot Lodge Jr. and family during visit to Vietnam, 1963. (Larry Burrows/Time & Life Pictures/Getty Images)

University of Hue who resigned in protest over the dismissal by the Government of a popular rector were said to have been arrested. About 200 students who signed protest petitions were also reported under arrest.

> *There were reliable reports that there had been mass defections among troops of the Vietnamese Army's Second Corps because of the attacks on the Buddhists.*

It was reported that a total of 1,000 persons might be under arrest in Hue.

Raids and arrests were said to have taken place throughout the country and the Government was reported to have seized every major pagoda in the country by Wednesday morning.

There was no estimate of the total of Buddhists arrested, but the figure may reach into the thousands.

Reliable sources in Saigon said that about 600 university students at the local polytechnic school had failed to show up for classes this morning, despite Government orders that they must attend classes. It was feared that they would be arrested.

Students Are Militant

Student leaders were becoming increasingly militant and the police thought they might try to replace the Buddhists as a spearhead for what is acknowledged to be extremely widespread anti-Government feeling.

The Government press agency in Saigon asserted that life in the capital was normal this morning and that the public had welcomed the troops enforcing the martial law decree.

Despite this contention the populace in Saigon remained both frightened and angry.

Several American officials here were reported to have had their phone lines deliberately cut by the Government.

Two Buddhist priests who took refuge in the headquarters of the United States mission Tuesday were still in the building today, according to sources here.

200,000 MARCH FOR CIVIL RIGHTS IN ORDERLY WASHINGTON RALLY; PRESIDENT SEES GAIN FOR NEGRO ACTION ASKED NOW

10 Leaders of Protest Urge Laws to End Racial Inequity

By E. W. KENWORTHY

WASHINGTON, Aug. 28—More than 200,000 Americans, most of them black but many of them white, demonstrated here today for a full and speedy program of civil rights and equal job opportunities.

It was the greatest assembly for a redress of grievances that this capital has ever seen.

One hundred years and 240 days after Abraham Lincoln enjoined the emancipated slaves to "abstain from all violence" and "labor faithfully for reasonable wages," this vast throng proclaimed in march and song and through the speeches of their leaders that they were still waiting for the freedom and the jobs.

Children Clap and Sing

There was no violence to mar the demonstration. In fact, at times there was an air of hootenanny about it as groups of schoolchildren clapped hands and swung into the familiar freedom songs.

But if the crowd was good-natured, the underlying tone was one of dead seriousness. The emphasis was on "freedom" and "now." At the same time the leaders emphasized, paradoxically but realistically, that the struggle was just beginning.

On Capitol Hill, opinion was divided about the impact of the demonstration in stimulating Congressional action on civil rights legislation. But at the White House, President Kennedy declared that the cause of 20,000,000 Negroes had been advanced by the march.

The march leaders went from the shadows of the Lincoln Memorial to the White House to meet with the President for 75 minutes. Afterward, Mr. Kennedy issued a 400-word statement praising the marchers for the "deep fervor and the quiet dignity" that had characterized the demonstration.

Says Nation Can Be Proud

The nation, the President said, "can properly be proud of the demonstration that has occurred here today."

The main target of the demonstration was Congress, where committees are now considering the Administration's civil rights bill.

At the Lincoln Memorial this afternoon, some speakers, knowing little of the way of Congress, assumed that the passage of a strengthened civil rights bill had been assured by the moving events of the day.

But from statements by Congressional leaders, after they had met with the march committee this morning, this did not seem certain at all. These statements came before the demonstration.

The human tide that swept over the Mall between the shrines of Washington and Lincoln fell back faster than it came on. As soon as the ceremony broke up this afternoon, the exodus began. With astounding speed, the last buses and trains cleared the city by midevening.

At 9 P. M. the city was as calm as the waters of the Reflecting Pool between the two memorials.

At the Lincoln Memorial early in the afternoon, in the midst of a songfest before the addresses, Josephine Baker, the singer, who had flown from her home in Paris, said to the thousands stretching down both sides of the Reflecting Pool:

"You are on the eve of a complete victory. You can't go wrong. The world is behind you."

Miss Baker said, as if she saw a dream coming true before her eyes, that "this is the happiest day of my life."

But of all the 10 leaders of the march on Washington who followed her, only the Rev. Dr. Martin Luther King Jr., president of the Southern Christian Leadership Conference, saw that dream so hopefully.

The other leaders, except for the three clergymen among the 10, concentrated on the struggle ahead and spoke in tough, even harsh, language.

But paradoxically it was King—who had suffered perhaps most of all—who ignited the crowd with words that might have been written by the sad, brooding man enshrined within.

As he arose, a great roar welled up from the crowd. When he started to speak, a hush fell.

"Even though we face the difficulties

Martin Luther King Jr. gave his "I Have a Dream" speech on August 28, 1963. (AFP/Getty Images)

of today and tomorrow, I still have a dream," he said. "It is a dream that one day this nation will rise up and live out the true meaning of its creed: 'We hold these truths to be self-evident, that all men are created equal.'"

Dream of Brotherhood

"I have a dream . . ." The vast throng listening intently to him roared.

". . . that one day on the red hills of Georgia, the sons of former slaves and the sons of former slave-owners will be able to sit together at the table of brotherhood.

"I have a dream . . ." The crowd roared.

". . . that one day even the State of Mississippi, a state sweltering with the heat of injustice, sweltering with the heat of oppression, will be transformed into an oasis of freedom and justice.

"I have a dream . . ." The crowd roared.

". . . that my four little children will one day live in a nation where they will not be judged by the color of their skin but by the content of their character.

"I have a dream . . ." The crowd roared.

". . . that one day every valley shall be exalted, every hill and mountain shall be made low, the rough places will be made plain, and the crooked places will be made straight, and the glory of the Lord shall be revealed and all flesh shall see it together."

As Dr. King concluded with a quotation from a Negro hymn—"Free at last, free at last, thank God almighty"—the crowd, recognizing that he was finishing, roared once again and waved their signs and pennants.

But the civil rights leaders, who knew the strength of the forces arrayed

against them from past battles, knew also that a hard struggle lay ahead. The tone of their speeches was frequently militant.

Roy Wilkins, executive secretary of the National Association for the Advancement of Colored People, made a plan that he and his colleagues thought the President's civil rights bill still did not go nearly far enough. He said:

"The President's proposals represent so moderate an approach that if any one is weakened or eliminated, the remainder will be little more than sugar water. Indeed, the package needs strengthening."

Harshest of all the speakers was John Lewis, chairman of the Student Nonviolent Coordinating Committee.

"My friends," he said, "Let us not forget that we are involved in a serious so-

Civil rights leaders hold hands as they lead a crowd of hundreds of thousands at the March on Washington for Jobs and Freedom, Washington D.C., August 28, 1963. (Hulton Archive/Getty Images)

cial revolution. But by and large American politics is dominated by politicians who build their career on immoral compromising and ally themselves with open forums of political, economic and social exploitation."

He concluded: "They're talking about slowdown and stop. We will not stop.

"If we do not get meaningful legislation out of this Congress, the time will come when we will not confine our marching to Washington. We will march through the South, through the streets of Jackson, through the streets of Danville, through the streets of Birmingham.

"But we will march with the spirit of love and the spirit of dignity that we have shown here today."

The great day really began the night before. As a half moon rose over the lagoon by the Jefferson Memorial and the tall lighted shaft of the Washington Monument gleamed in the reflecting pool, a file of Negroes from out of town began climbing the steps of the Lincoln Memorial.

The day dawned clear and cool. At 7 A.M. the town had a Sunday appearance, except for the shuttle buses drawn up in front of Union Station, waiting.

By 10 A.M. there were 40,000 on the slopes around the Washington Monument. An hour later the police estimated the crowd at 90,000. And still they poured in.

As a result the whole affair at the monument grounds began to take on the spontaneity of a church picnic.

Even before the entertainment was to begin, groups of high school students were singing with wonderful improvisations and hand-clapping all over the monument slope.

Civil rights demonstrators who had been released from jail in Danville, Va., were singing:

"Move on, move on. Till all the world is free."

And members of Local 144 of the Hotel and Allied Service Employes Union from New York City, an integrated local since 1950, were stomping:

"Oh, freedom, we shall not, we shall not be moved. Just like a tree that's planted by the water."

Then the pros took over, starting with the folk singers. The crowd joined in with them.

Joan Baez started things rolling with the song—"We Shall Overcome."

"Oh deep in my heart I do believe, We shall overcome some day."

And Peter, Paul, and Mary sang "How many times must a man look up before he can see the sky."

And Odetta's full-throated voice carried almost to Capitol Hill: "If they ask you who you are, tell them you're a child of God."

Jackie Robinson told the crowd that "we cannot be turned back," and Norman Thomas, the Socialist, said: "I'm glad I lived long enough to see this day."

Apparently forgotten was the intention to make the march to the Lincoln Memorial a solemn tribute to Medgar W. Evers, the N. A. A. C. P. official murdered in Jackson, Miss., last June 12, and others who had died for the cause of civil rights.

The leaders were lost, and they never did get to the head of the parade.

All spoke at the memorial except Mr. Farmer, who is in jail in Louisiana following his arrest as a result of a civil rights demonstration. His speech was read by Floyd B. McKissick, CORE national chairman.

At the close of the ceremonies at the Lincoln Memorial, Bayard Rustin, the organizer of the march, asked Mr. A. Philip Randolph, who conceived it, to lead the vast throng in a pledge.

Repeating after Mr. Randolph, the marchers pledged "complete personal commitment to the struggle for jobs and freedom for Americans" and "to carry the message of the march to my friends and neighbors back home and arouse them to an equal commitment and an equal effort."

More than 200,000 people attended the March on Washington. (PhotoQuest/Getty Images)

'Hot Line' Opened by U.S. and Soviet to Cut Attack Risk

Special to the New York Times

WASHINGTON, Aug. 30—A diplomatic "hot line" between Moscow and Washington went into operation today with the simultaneous clattering of telecommunication machines in the Kremlin and the Pentagon.

The emergency communications channel is designed to reduce the risk of accidental war. The opening was announced in a one-sentence Defense Department statement:

"The direct communications link between Washington and Moscow is now operational."

No ceremony accompanied the implementations of one of the few arms control measures that the United States and the Soviet Union, the two major nuclear powers, have been able to agree upon in years of negotiations.

Text Message Is Sent

There was no exchange of official messages. Instead, from Washington went the message used by Teletype operators to test whether a circuit is operating—"The quick brown fox jumped over the lazy dog's back 1234567890."

Back from Moscow came a similar test message in Russian, which was completely unintelligible to the United States operators but at least showed that all the characters on the Teletype were working correctly.

After a series of exchanges of such messages, the Pentagon said, it was determined that the link was "completely satisfactory" and it was "declared operational and made available for exchange of official messages between the two Governments."

Now that the link has been established, it will be used only "in time of emergency" and then only for exchange of messages between the two heads of Government.

The decision to establish the "hot line" is a direct outgrowth of the serious delays that developed in diplomatic communications between the two capitals during the Cuban crisis last fall. Diplomatic messages are now sent over normal commercial channels to the United States and Soviet Embassies in Moscow and Washington.

With the time consumed by transmission, coding and decoding, translation and delivery, hours are often required before a message reaches its destination.

The direct link, which is available 24 hours a day, will make it possible for the heads of the two Governments to exchange messages in minutes.

A message from President Kennedy to Premier Khrushchev, for example, will be sent to the Washington terminal of the link in the National Military Command Center in the Pentagon. There American Teletype operators will type the message on a teleprinter and a punched tape.

After checking the typed message against the original copy, the Teletype tape will be fed into a Teletype transmitter. As the message goes out, it will be encoded by a "scrambling device" to prevent anyone from reading it at relay points along the 10,000-mile cable circuit.

In Moscow, the message will go through a decoding device and appear on a Teletype machine in the Kremlin near the office of Premier Khrushchev.

Translation Necessary

The plan calls for the United States to transmit messages in English and the Soviet Union in Russian. Thus at each end it will be necessary for the messages to be translated before they can be delivered to the leaders.

The agreement to establish the link was reached in Geneva June 20, about eight months after the Cuban crisis. The idea had been studied for several years.

Since June, Soviet and American technicians have been rushing to install the equipment by a Sept. 1 deadline.

Four American Teletype machines—the 66-word-a-minute Model 28 manufactured by Teletype Corporation of Chicago—were carried to Moscow by plane in July and installed in the Kremlin by Aug. 1.

The decision to establish the "hot line" is a direct outgrowth of the serious delays that developed in diplomatic communications between the two capitals during the Cuban crisis...

Four comparable Soviet machines, built in East Germany, arrived last weekend at the Soviet Embassy here and were delivered to the Pentagon on Monday. On Tuesday, the machines were installed in an office in the section of the Pentagon occupied by the office of the Joint Chiefs of Staff.

American technicians report that the German-built equipment was "very good" and that the installation and the first test transmissions in the last few days had gone "remarkably smoothly." The two countries also exchanged a year's supply of spare parts, special tools, operating instructions and telecommunication tape. In addition, there was an exchange of encoding equipment, which under normal circumstances is treated with the highest secrecy.

Walter Cronkite interviews President Kennedy on a range of topics, including the 1964 election, the nuclear test ban treaty, and the Vietnam War for the CBS Evening News, in Hyannis Port, Massachusetts, September 2, 1963. (Cecil Stoughton/John F. Kennedy Library)

According to officials, the nature of the encoding equipment was a major difficulty in working out the hot line agreement. It was finally decided that what is known as "one time tape system encoding equipment" would be used.

This equipment is employed by commercial as well as military systems, so that no military secrets were divulged in making it available to the Soviet Union.

The one time tape system, regarded as being virtually "breakproof" by cryptographers, works in this fashion:

As the Teletype tape containing a message is fed into one transmitter, an encoding "keying tape" is fed into another transmitter. The result is to scramble up the letters in the outgoing message so that it is unintelligible.

At the receiving end, the same keying tape is fed into the Teletype, and the message comes out decoded. A keying tape is used only once, thus making the coding system impervious to "breaking" by cryptographic analysis.

Under the agreement, the two sides exchange keying tapes. Thus, when the Russian center wants to send a message, for example, it sends along a number identifying the tape to be used in the Pentagon machines.

Circuit's Route Given

The two terminals are linked by cable and radio circuits, with the two sides sharing the cost of leasing the circuits from commercial companies. The cost is expected to range from $80,000 to $90,000 a year.

The principal circuit is a land-line

and ocean cable connection running from Washington to London, Copenhagen, Stockholm, Helsinki and Moscow.

It is a duplex telegraph circuit capable of handling two simultaneous Teletype transmissions.

In addition, there is a duplex radio circuit going from Washington to Tangier in North Africa and from there to Moscow.

The radio circuit will be used for coordinating operations between the two terminals. But it will also be used as a stand-by Teletype connection, in the event that trouble develops on the land-line connection.

Alabama Subdued

Birmingham Shuts Schools Scheduled for Integration

By CLAUDE SITTON

BIRMINGHAM, Ala., Sept. 5—The Birmingham Board of Education today closed three white schools at which Negroes had been scheduled to begin classes this morning.

It acted at the request of Gov. George C. Wallace. In making the announcement, the board cited the bombing of a Negro lawyer's home last night and a resulting riot by Negroes in which one man was killed.

Attorneys for five Negro students who were to attend the three schools filed requests with the Federal Court urging immediate action to reopen the three closed schools—West End High, Ramsay High, and Graymont Elementary.

Federal District Judge Seybourn H. Lynne was asked to issue a temporary restraining order against the school board. It would prohibit the shutdown on the grounds that students of both races were suffering "irreparable harm."

He also was asked to order Governor Wallace to show cause why he should not be made a party to the desegregation case here and be enjoined from further interference. Judge Lynne scheduled a hearing on the matter for 1:30 P. M. Friday.

Troopers Move Out

In a news conference in Montgomery, Governor Wallace scoffed at reports that he had yielded to desegregation by failing to prevent the registration of Negroes to enter previously white classes here and in three other cities.

"I haven't yielded to anything," he asserted. "There hasn't been any public school integration anywhere in Alabama."

Under his orders, state troopers guarded the three Birmingham schools and continued to seal off the Tuskegee public school, which he closed Monday.

All but 50 of 450 troopers here began pulling out of Birmingham before noon. Some went to Mobile, others toward Huntsville. Capitol sources indicated that the troopers mission was to halt the start of desegregated classes tomorrow in those two cities. Tonight, the Huntsville School Board announced that it had turned down a Wallace request to postpone the opening of desegregated schools. A similar action was taken in Mobile. Classes at Huntsville were to have started last Tuesday, but they were delayed voluntarily, at the Governor's bidding, until tomorrow.

Wallace aides conferred with a group of lawyers here in the Redmont Hotel. They reportedly were preparing a series of suits aimed at throwing up new hindrances to desegregation.

Governor Wallace's comments and actions seemed to make it plain that he would not confine himself to postponing desegregation elsewhere in the state until it had begun here, as previously indicated. Instead, he appeared determined to bring a second showdown between himself and the Kennedy Administration by defying the courts.

Mr. Wallace physically barred the admission of two Negroes to the University of Alabama last June until ordered to stand aside by Alabama National Guardsmen acting under instructions from President Kennedy. He is said to feel that another confrontation of this type would aid him politically in his announced desire to cause the President's defeat in the 1964 elections.

A Justice Department source in Washington has said the Administration was aware of the Governor's intentions but would prefer to avoid further use of Federal force. Nevertheless, this source emphasized that court desegregation orders would be enforced, even if the use of troops was necessary.

It seemed yesterday that the Governor had relented from his no-compromise position. This belief was based on what some feel is mounting resentment over his actions regarding the schools here and elsewhere and concern over possible violence for which he might share the blame.

Observers speculated that he subsequently saw sufficient reason to step in because of skirmishes yesterday between the police and segregationist demonstrators here, coupled with last night's bombing and rioting.

The explosion caused about $1,200 damage to the home of Arthur D. Shores, a lawyer who has played a major role over the years in desegregation cases. The low, red brick ranch house is in a middle class Negro neighborhood called "Dynamite Hill" because there has been almost a bombing a year there for the last decade.

The blast threw Mrs. Shores out of a bed and part of a chandelier struck her on the head. At first she was thought to have suffered only a slight shoulder injury. She was taken to Holy Family Hospital this morning. Dr. J. T. Montgomery reported that she was in fair condition with a cerebral concussion.

Scaffolding stood around a carport and a corner family room, where workmen were repairing about $10,000 in

James Armstrong escorting his sons to the all-white Graymont School with the help of Reverend Fred Shuttlesworth (at right).

(Lynn Pelham/Time & Life Pictures/Getty Images)

damage caused by a bombing the night of Aug. 20.

The explosion gouged a hole in the lawn on the undamaged corner of the home, stripped off paneling under the eaves, smashed the glass in a double casement window and other windows, buckled an aluminum front door screen, stripped branches from shrubbery in the yard and blew dirt up to the roof.

Negroes from other homes in the area and a housing project at the foot of the hill streamed into the streets shouting, cursing and sobbing. Scant minutes after the blast, which occurred at 9:40 P. M. central standard time, the crowd had turned into a mob.

Police cruisers roared into the area and the policemen formed a roadblock at the bottom of the hill on Center Street. The Rev. Fred L. Shuttlesworth, president of the Alabama Christian Movement for Human Rights, and James Edward Lay, a Negro civilian defense captain, sought unsuccessfully to calm the mob.

Volleys of bricks, rocks and other missiles were hurled as the policemen shoved the Negroes back out of the streets and onto the sidewalks. At 10:05 P. M., the police began firing pistols, automatic rifles and submachine guns over the heads of the rioters.

John Coley, a 20-year-old Negro, was shot in the back of the neck and through his chest and an arm. He died later at a hospital.

The police said the victim had burst from the front door of a home firing a gun. Two men in a television camera crew and Mr. Shuttlesworth denied that the victim had a gun.

"He turned to run," asserted Mr. Shuttlesworth. "That's why he was shot in the back of the neck." He added, "If he wasn't deliberately murdered he must have been shot accidentally."

Twenty-one other persons, including four policemen, were injured in the melee, which raged for almost two hours.

Some of those hurt were occupants of passing cars, which were showered

with bricks and rocks. The arrival of the police department's armored riot car, which resembles a tank, infuriated the mob. Police officials said some Negroes had returned their gunfire.

Squads of policemen, assisted by Jefferson County sheriff's deputies, gradually cleared the area, moving along one street after another firing over the heads of the rioters.

Administration Chided

Mr. Shuttlesworth and the Rev. Dr. Martin Luther King Jr. led a five-week campaign of mass demonstrations for lunch counter desegregation here last May. Mr. Shuttlesworth argued that the bombing was "part of a plot to enmesh the city in trouble," and provide an opportunity for Governor Wallace to step in.

"I do feel that the national Administration is making a mistake in playing cat and mouse with George Wallace and regarding this as a purely local matter," Mr. Shuttlesworth asserted.

Wallace Closes 4 More Schools Due To Integrate

Troopers Block Huntsville Openings—Judge Orders Birmingham Hearings

By CLAUDE SITTON

BIRMINGHAM, Ala., Sept. 6—Gov. George C. Wallace used state troopers today for the second time this week to prevent the beginning of public school desegregation in Alabama.

Despite objections from local officials, the troopers barred all but a handful of determined white pupils from four Huntsville schools that had registered one Negro each under a Federal court order.

Troopers dispatched to Mobile by Governor Wallace permitted Murphy High School to open. But this was done only after pressure from the state Capitol had brought a promise that two Negroes would not attend.

Monday Opening Seen

The troopers continued to deny admission to the Tuskegee Public School. It sought unsuccessfully to open last Monday after having registered 13 Negroes in compliance with a Federal court decree.

Meanwhile, in Montgomery, Mr. Wallace abandoned a legislative proposal that would have permitted the Governor to succeed himself. He said he did so to assure passage of a bill to finance most state services during the next two years.

Raymond Christian, Huntsville Superintendent of Education, said he had been assured by Wallace aides that classes could begin Monday without interference. Officials in Mobile and Tuskegee also felt that Governor Wallace would end his efforts to keep Negroes out of white schools in their cities on that day.

Appeal to Courts

Attorneys representing five Negro students in Birmingham took their fight for admission to white classes into the Federal courts. The Board of Education shut down the three schools they had been scheduled to attend yesterday at the request of the Governor.

In response to their suit, District Judge Seybourn H. Lynne issued an order directing Mr. Wallace or a representative to appear at a hearing here at noon Thursday. The Governor was told to be prepared to show cause why he should not be enjoined from interfering with desegregation in Birmingham.

Judge Lynne took no action on the lawyers' request for a temporary restraining order against the school board that would have forced it to reopen the schools immediately. Instead, he set a hearing for noon Wednesday.

The lawyers contended that the likelihood of further violence, which was cited by the board, did not constitute legally sufficient ground for the closings. Mrs. Constance Baker Motley, associate counsel of the N.A.A.C.P. Legal Defense and Education Fund, argued the case for the students.

Mrs. Motley also filed a request for a second restraining order prohibiting interference by the Governor in the Huntsville case. Earlier, the Fifth Circuit Court of Appeals handed down a decision in Tuscaloosa denying a request that it delay desegregation in Birmingham indefinitely because of possible violence. It was filed Wednesday night by six parents of children in the three schools. They were joined in the suit by the city school board.

Monday Opening Sought

The board shut down the schools after two skirmishes between the police and segregationist demonstrators during registration at two of the three schools Wednesday and the bombing of a Negro home and resulting riot that night. At a meeting yesterday, some board members indicated they might be willing to reopen the schools Monday.

The Justice Department gave no active support to the legal efforts to end Governor Wallace's defiance of the Federal Courts of the Northern and Middle Districts of Alabama. The department continued its role as observer and counselor, acting through Civil Rights Division attorneys and Federal Bureau of Investigation agents on the scene.

Confusion and resentment mounted throughout the state, especially among the parents of some 5,850 students barred from classes. Estimates of educators indicated that the students affected number 2,675 in Birmingham, more than 2,000 in Huntsville and 600 in Tuskegee.

State capitol observers said the confusion extended even to the Governor's office in Montgomery, which was busily assuring officials in Huntsville and Mobile that their schools would be free to open Monday. If the pledges were fulfilled, it would raise the question of what point Mr. Wallace had made with his actions.

One scathing comment after another was expressed by officials and the press. Some of the criticism came from longtime Wallace supporters.

The Montgomery Advertiser, whose editor, Grover Hall, has been a close confidant of the Governor's commented:

"The Advertiser must sorrowfully conclude that, in this instance, its friend has gone wild. Alabama is not a banana republic. It is in no need of an adventurer to ride down upon local authority."

WALLACE ORDERS GUARD UNITS OUT FOR SCHOOL DUTY

They Replace State Troopers—Negro Students Barred in 3 Alabama Cities

HUNTSVILLE ADMITS 4

Five Federal Judges Enjoin Governor—U.S. Marshals Forced to Quit Capitol

---

By CLAUDE SITTON

BIRMINGHAM, Ala., Sept. 9—Gov. George C. Wallace called out National Guard units tonight after all five Federal District Court judges in Alabama had enjoined him from halting public school desegregation.

[In Montgomery, Governor Wallace ordered three United States marshals from the Capitol grounds early Tuesday and the marshals complied, The Associated Press reported. They had been waiting to serve the Governor with the injunction issued by the Federal judges. Mr. Wallace then left his office, where he had been in consultation with his aides.]

Governor Wallace earlier today had permitted four Negroes to attend previously all-white schools in Huntsville, marking the first desegregation below the college level in Alabama.

However, in deliberate defiance of earlier court orders, state troopers under his orders barred 20 students from schools in Birmingham, Tuskegee and Mobile.

Troopers Withdrawn

Hours later the five District Court judges, acting on a Justice Department request, issued a sweeping order against the Governor and the troopers. It prohibited not only resistance to the segregation but also any failure to maintain "peace and order within and around the schools."

A short time later a spokesman in Mr. Wallace's office said troopers were being withdrawn from the schools because highway patrol officials had been served with the new court order. He contended this would prevent them from preserving the peace at the schools.

The spokesman said the Guardsmen, whose number and units were not disclosed, would protect "the school property and students and personnel and schools from possible disorder."

James A. Simpson, a Birmingham lawyer and adviser to Mr. Wallace on segregation matters, was asked if the Guardsmen would be used to prevent desegregation. He refused to comment.

Judges' Action Rare

These developments cleared the way for the showdown that the Governor had sought with the Kennedy Administration. A highly placed Washington source indicated that further interference by Mr. Wallace would result in the federalizing of National Guard troops and their use to carry out the court orders.

In a rare legal action, the Federal judges of the Northern, Middle and Southern Districts of Alabama signed the temporary restraining order. The order had been requested by Attorney General Robert F. Kennedy and John Doar, deputy chief of the Justice Department's Civil Rights Division.

Judge Frank M. Johnson of the Middle District granted the order in Montgomery. It was then signed in Mobile by Judge Daniel H. Thomas of the Southern District and in Birmingham by Judges Seybourn H. Lynne, H. H. Grooms and Clarence W. Allgood of the Northern District.

Besides Governor Wallace, the order named several officials of the state Public Safety Department and of the state police.

The defendants were ordered to appear in District Court in Montgomery next Monday to show cause why a preliminary injunction should not be issued against them to prevent further defiance of court desegregation orders.

The court directive enjoined them from "harassing or punishing any students, teachers or other authorized persons for having entered" the schools.

The judges said that if the order had not been issued, the Federal Government and the immediate and irreparable injury Negro students would "suffer consisting of impairment of the judicial process of the United States courts, the obstruction of the due administration of justice and the deprivation of rights under the Constitution and laws of the United States."

The complaint submitted to Judge Johnson by Mr. Doar said that "the policy of George C. Wallace has been and is to prevent Negro children from attending the same public schools in Alabama attended by whites."

President Kennedy federalized the Alabama National Guard last June, when Governor Wallace physically blocked the admission of two Negroes to the University of Alabama. The Governor then stepped aside.

The Administration had refrained from taking action against the Governor in the school desegregation controversy until today.

A Washington spokesman said the delay had stemmed from the hope that local resentment over Mr. Wallace's action last week in closing some of the affected schools might cause him to retreat.

These hopes were shattered before dawn. Then, in a series of three executive orders, the Governor gave permission for the desegregated schools to open but he directed troopers to bar the Negroes.

Unlike his orders postponing the start of classes last week, no reference was made to threats of violence. Instead, the orders asserted that "the threat of force and the unwarranted integration of the public schools of this state is detrimental to the public interest."

The orders continued:

"Integration of the public schools will totally disrupt and effectively destroy the educational process and constitutes an abridgment of the civil rights of other children attending the schools, and deprives them of the equal protection of the laws and constitutes and abridgment of their rights, liberty and property without due process of law . . ."

This reasoning was taken from a decision handed down by Federal District Judge Frank Scarlett at Savannah, Ga., last June 28 in an attempt by whites to prevent desegregation of public schools there. The ruling was subsequently reversed by the United States Court of Appeals for the Fifth Circuit.

Following the issuance of the Governor's orders, Col. Albert J. Lingo, state director of public safety, stationed forces of troopers and deputized National Guardsmen, game wardens and sheriff's deputies at the affected schools in Birmingham, Tuskegee and Mobile.

But the troopers did not appear at Huntsville. And at approximately 8:15 A.M. (10:15, New York time) 6-year-old

Sonny V. Hereford 4th entered the Fifth Avenue elementary school with his father.

He began classes in the first grade, becoming the first Negro to attend public school in Alabama. The three other Negro pupils arrived at three other schools later. All had been ordered enrolled by Federal court orders.

Neither the Governor, his aides, nor Huntsville officials offered any explanation for Mr. Wallace's failure to prevent the Negroes from attending classes in that Tennessee Valley city, the site of one of the nation's major space-industry centers.

However, officials, civic leaders and most residents protested strongly last Friday when Mr. Wallace ordered the start of classes in schools put off until today and ringed the schools with troopers, who turned back all students.

The initial defiance of the Federal Court orders took place at Mobile's Murphy High School. Some 175 troopers and deputized law enforcement officers stood guard there under Maj. Joe Smelley, chief of the highway patrol's uniformed division.

Henry Hobdy, 17, and Dorothy Davis, 16, arrived by car at the school's main entrance shortly after 7 A.M. Major Smelley met them, handed them copies of the Governor's executive order and told them they would not be permitted to enter. They left immediately.

Attorneys for the two students appeared before Judge Thomas within an hour and obtained an order restraining Mr. Wallace from further intervention.

The most clear-cut case of defiance came at Birmingham's Graymont elementary schools when James Armstrong Sr., a Negro barber, arrived with two of his sons, Dwight, 11, and Floyd, 9.

They were accompanied by Ernest Jackson and Oscar Adams, their attorneys, and the Rev. Fred L. Shuttlesworth, president of the Alabama Christian Movement for Human Rights, and the Rev. Charles Billups, a

board member of the Alabama Christian Movement.

Colonel Lingo, dressed in a light blue helmet and the navy blue shirt and Confederate gray trousers of the highway patrol, held up his hands for them to halt as they approached a side entrance. He then handed a copy of the Governor's order to one of the lawyers and told them, "you will leave immediately."

Mr. Jackson noted that a Federal Court order directed the admission of the students. Colonel Lingo asked the attorney if he had a copy of that order.

"Would you obey that order if I had it?" asked Mr. Jackson.

"I will not," Colonel Lingo replied.

Earlier, the colonel had denied two Negro girls entry at West End High School. Capt. T. L. Payne of the patrol turned back a third at Ramsay High School.

Mr. Shuttlesworth and Mr. Billups said an automobile driven by a white man had repeatedly bumped the car carrying one of the girls who was being driven away from West End High. They said the police had made no attempt to prevent the bumping.

Thirteen Negroes who arrived at the Tuskegee public school on a school bus were turned back by Capt. Claude S. Prier of the state patrol.

Only 125 white students reported for classes in that Black Belt community in east-central Alabama. They constituted approximately 22 per cent of the normal enrollment. Most of the absentees were students in grades 7 through 12, which the Negroes had been scheduled to enter.

A private school system, known as the Freedom of Choice School, began accepting applications from white students in those grades this morning.

WALLACE ENDS RESISTANCE AS GUARD IS FEDERALIZED; MORE SCHOOLS INTEGRATE; 20 NEGROES ENTER

12 Whites Arrested in Birmingham—Other Cities Are Peaceful

By CLAUDE SITTON

BIRMINGHAM, Ala., Sept. 10—Twenty Negroes attended previously white schools in three Alabama cities today after President Kennedy's federalization of the state's National Guardsmen ended the defiance of Gov. George C. Wallace.

The police here arrested 12 whites in a rowdy, two-hour demonstration over the admission of two Negro girls to West End High School under a Federal court order. This, coupled with already existing racial tension, raised a threat of further disorder.

No major incidents marred the desegregation of two other schools here, four in Huntsville—where classes began yesterday—and one each in Tuskegee and Mobile. The 425 Guardsmen ordered to active duty by Federal officials remained in their armories.

Combined school attendance here at West End and Graymont elementary school, where two Negroes enrolled, dropped by almost 90 per cent. But Ramsay High School, which accepted one Negro, showed a slight increase.

Concedes Defeat

Only some 165 of an expected total of 550 students appeared for classes at the Tuskegee public school, which 13 Negroes are attending. Attendance figures at four Huntsville schools that have one Negro pupil each and at Murphy High School in Mobile, which has two, were near normal.

Governor Wallace conceded at a news conference in the state Capitol in Montgomery that for the second time in three months he had been forced to retreat from a posture of massive resistance to desegregation in education. "I can't fight bayonets with my bare hands," he said.

A legal battle directed by Mrs. Constance Baker Motley of New York, associate counsel of the N.A.A.C.P. Legal Defense and Educational Fund, was largely responsible for the governor's predicament. To preserve the right of admission this effort had won for the 20 students, Justice Department attorneys obtained a sweeping court order against Mr. Wallace last night.

The temporary restraining order, signed by all five of Alabama's Federal District judges, prohibited him and state troopers from any further interference with desegregation.

The Governor then ordered the troopers withdrawn from the schools in Birmingham, Tuskegee and Mobile, where they had denied entry to the Negroes yesterday. He followed this up by ordering National Guardsmen to replace the troopers.

But President Kennedy signed a cease-and-desist order against Mr. Wallace today, federalized the Alabama National Guard and directed Defense Department officials to take all necessary steps to carry out the court order.

These actions, the Governor asserted in a formal statement, brought "the most potent instrument of force in the world, directed by the ruthless hand of the Attorney General, against the people of Alabama."

Wallace Arrest Avoided

The Kennedy Administration had given every indication that it would avoid, if possible, any confrontation with the Governor that might result in his arrest. This was the policy in the dispute over desegregation at the University of Alabama last June. Mr. Wallace staged a show of defiance there by blocking two Negro students, but he retreated in the face of National Guardsmen called out by the President.

Further, a Justice Department spokesman here emphasized that the 300 guardsmen being held in readiness at Birmingham, the 75 at Mobile and the 50 at Tuskegee would be used only if needed by local officials to maintain order.

The effect of the Administration's actions in Alabama was to clear the way for local officials in the four cities to implement plans for compliance, however reluctant, with the desegregation directives.

All these officials had demonstrated their willingness to do so last week after the scheduled beginning of classes. But through a combination of force and persuasion, Governor Wallace prevented this action on the ground that desegregation would bring violence.

The only serious threat of disorder began to develop at West End High School here shortly after two Negro girls arrived by automobile at 7:45 A. M. (9:45, New York time).

Few students saw them enter. But a blond girl standing nearby turned to a boy and began sobbing on his shoulder. Another girl sniffled.

"I hope my momma heard, so she'll come get me," said one girl among the group that began streaming out of the two story, red brick building as the news of the Negroes' arrival became known.

'Go Home!'

Some 75 youths gathered across the driveway in front of the school, near the car that had brought the students.

"Keep the niggers out!" they shouted. "Go home!"

Other students soon swelled their ranks to more than 300 and they began chanting, "Two, four, six, eight, we don't want to integrate."

Some teachers smiled from the windows and students yelled encouragement to those who remained inside to leave the school, calling them "nigger lovers."

Led by a crew-cut youth in a yellow shirt and gray slacks, some 150 boys fell into a loose column. With the girls joining in, they marched around the driveway and lawn between the school and the street. Some waved Confederate battle flags and a student played "Dixie" on a trumpet.

About 150 policemen in the area at the time kept the sidewalks and street clear in front of the school. But whites clustered at the two ends of the grounds. Negroes, many of whom live in houses directly south and west of the school, watched from a distance.

"We hate Kennedy!" chanted the students. "We hate niggers! We want Wallace!"

Police Capt. Glenn Evans, using an electric bullhorn, told the crowd:

"We're going to ask you to either go to your classes or leave the school grounds."

The students shouted "No!" But they moved away.

A scuffle broke out among the milling students and adults on the north end of the campus as the police seized David Stanley, a youthful Canadian who is a member of the National States Rights party. This anti-Semitic and anti-Negro group, whose member-

ship is believed to number fewer than 100 persons, passed out Confederate flags and segregationist placards to the students.

Stanley fought back, but one policeman held his neck in a half-nelson, another twisted his arm behind his back and two others assisted them in handcuffing him and dragging him away. He was charged with inciting to riot.

A girl, knocked down accidentally in the skirmishing, fainted.

The police riot squad, armed with shotguns and carbines, arrived at the scene, and some Jefferson County sheriff's deputies pulled up at the school in squad cars.

The police began driving the crowd up both sides of the street to the north of the school. A man who sought to break through their lines was seized and began struggling. He was clubbed into submission with night sticks. A second white man who attempted to interfere was hurried away to a patrol wagon.

White students jeer as two black girls are integrated at Birmingham's West End High School, September 1963.
(Rolls Press/Popperfoto/Getty Images)

BIRMINGHAM BOMB KILLS 4 NEGRO GIRLS IN CHURCH; RIOTS FLARE; 2 BOYS SLAIN

Guard Summoned

Wallace Acts on City Plea for Help as 20 Are Injured

By CLAUDE SITTON

BIRMINGHAM, Ala., Sept. 15—A bomb severely damaged a Negro church today during Sunday school services, killing four Negro girls and setting off racial rioting and other violence in which two Negro boys were shot to death.

Fourteen Negroes were injured in the explosion. One Negro and five whites were hurt in the disorders that followed.

Some 500 National Guardsmen in battle dress stood by at armories here tonight, on orders of Gov. George C. Wallace. And 300 state troopers joined the Birmingham police, Jefferson County sheriff's deputies and other law-enforcement units in efforts to restore peace.

Governor Wallace sent the guardsmen and the troopers in response to requests from local authorities.

Sporadic gunfire sounded in Negro neighborhoods tonight, and small bands of residents roamed the streets. Aside from the patrols that cruised the city armed with riot guns, carbines and shotguns, few whites were seen.

Fire Bomb Hurled

At one point, three fires burned simultaneously in Negro sections, one at a broom and mop factory, one at a roofing company and a third in another building. An incendiary bomb was tossed into a supermarket, but the flames were extinguished. Fire marshals investigated blazes at two vacant houses to see if arson was involved.

Mayor Albert Boutwell and other city officials and civic leaders appeared on television station WAPI late tonight and urged residents to cooperate in ending "this senseless reign of terror."

Sheriff Melvin Bailey referred to the day as "the most distressing in the history of Birmingham."

The explosion at the 16th Street Baptist Church this morning brought hundreds of angry Negroes pouring into the streets. Some attacked the police with stones. The police dispersed them by firing shotguns over their heads.

Johnny Robinson, a 16-year-old Negro, was shot in the back and killed by a policeman with a shotgun this afternoon. Officers said the victim was among a group that had hurled stones at white youths driving through the area in cars flying Confederate battle flags.

When the police arrived, the youths fled, and one policeman said he had fired low but that some of the shot had struck the Robinson youth in the back.

Virgil Wade, a 13-year-old Negro, was shot and killed just outside Birmingham while riding a bicycle. The Jefferson County sheriff's office said "there apparently was no reason at all" for the killing, but indicated that it was related to the general racial disorders.

Another Negro youth and a white youth were shot but not seriously wounded in separate incidents. Four whites, including a honeymooning couple from Chicago, were injured by stones while driving through the neighborhood of the bombing.

The bombing, the fourth such incident in less than a month, resulted in heavy damage to the church, to a two-story office building across the street and to a home.

Wallace Offers Reward

Governor Wallace, at the request of city officials, offered a $5,000 reward for the arrest and conviction of the bombers.

None of the 50 bombings of Negro property here since World War II have been solved.

Mayor Boutwell and Chief of Police Jamie Moore expressed fear that the bombing, coming on top of tension aroused by desegregation of three schools last week, would bring further violence.

George G. Seibels Jr., chairman of the City Council's police committee, broadcast frequent appeals tonight to white parents, urging them to restrain their children from staging demonstrations tomorrow. He said a repetition of the segregationist motorcades that raced through the streets last Thursday and Friday "could provoke serious trouble, resulting in possible death or injury."

The Rev. Dr. Martin Luther King Jr. arrived tonight by plane from Atlanta. He had led Negroes, in a five-week campaign last spring that brought some lunch-counter desegregation and improved job opportunities. The bombed church had been used as the staging point by Negro demonstrators.

A plaque in Birmingham's 16th Street Baptist Church is dedicated to the four girls who were killed there by a bomb. (Jim Wilson/The New York Times)

Curfew Plan Rejected

Col. Albert J. Lingo, State Director of Public Safety and commander of the troopers, met with Mayor Boutwell and the City Council in emergency session. They discussed imposition of a curfew, but decided against it.

The bombing came five days after the desegregation of three previously all-white schools in Birmingham. The way had been cleared for the desegregation when President Kennedy federalized the Alabama National Guard and the Federal courts issued a sweeping order against Governor Wallace, thus ending his defiance toward the integration step.

The four girls killed in the blast had just heard Mrs. Ella C. Demand, their teacher, complete the Sunday school lesson for the day. The subject was "The Love That Forgives."

During the period between the class and an assembly in the main auditorium, they went to the women's lounge in the basement, at the northeast corner of the church.

The blast occurred at about 10:25 A.M. (12:25 P.M. New York time).

Church members said they found the girls huddled together beneath a pile of masonry debris.

Parents of 3 Are Teachers

Both parents of each of three of the victims teach in the city's schools. The dead were identified by University Hospital officials as:

Cynthia Wesley, 14, the only child of Claude A. Wesley, principal of the Lewis Elementary School, and Mrs. Wesley, a teacher there.

Denise McNair, 11, also an only child, whose parents are teachers.

Carol Robertson, 14, whose parents are teachers and whose grandmother, Mrs. Sallie Anderson, is one of the Negro members of a biracial committee established by Mayor Boutwell to deal with racial problems.

Addie Mae Collins, 14, about whom no information was immediately available.

The blast blew gaping holes through walls in the church basement. Floors of offices in the rear of the sanctuary appeared near collapse. Stairways were blocked by splintered window frames.

Chief Police Inspector W. J. Haley said the impact of the blast indicated that at least 15 sticks of dynamite might have caused it. He said the police had talked to two witnesses who reported having seen a car drive by the church, slow down and then speed away before the blast.

Vietnam Victory By The End Of '65 Envisaged By U.S.

Officials Say War May Be Won if Political Crisis Does Not Hamstring Effort

WARN ON REPRESSION

McNamara and Taylor Tell the President and Security Council of Their Mission

By TAD SZULC

WASHINGTON, Oct. 2—The United States said tonight that the war in South Vietnam might be won by the end of 1965 if the political crisis there did not "significantly" affect the military effort.

A formal statement of United States policy, by President Kennedy after a National Security Council meeting at the White House, warned that while repressive actions by the Saigon regime had not yet "significantly affected" the war effort, "they could do so in the future."

It said that under the present conditions most of the 14,000 United States military personnel could be withdrawn from Vietnam by the end of 1965 and that 1,000 men might be able to leave by the end of this year.

"The political situation in South Vietnam remains deeply serious," the statement said.

Based on Recommendations

The policy statement was approved on the basis of recommendations from Secretary of Defense Robert S. McNamara, Gen. Maxwell D. Taylor, Chairman of the Joint Chiefs of Staff, and Henry Cabot Lodge, Ambassador to South Vietnam.

Mr. McNamara and General Taylor returned here early today from a week-long fact-finding mission in Vietnam on President Kennedy's orders.

The mission was designed to evaluate the military and political situations in the Southeast Asian country, with particular emphasis on whether the political crisis, stemming from the regime's repression of its Buddhist and other opponents, is affecting the eight-year-old war against the Communist Vietcong guerrillas.

Policy May Be Reviewed

It was hoped that the mission's findings would resolve the differences within the Administration over United States policy toward South Vietnam.

The statement, which was read to newsmen by Pierre Salinger, White House press secretary, after the 50-minute meeting of the National Security Council, deliberately avoided committing the United States to a frozen position toward the regime of President Ngo Dinh Diem.

Administration quarters said later that while the present decision was to maintain military and economic aid to South Vietnam at its present levels, this policy would come under review at any time if it became clear that, indeed, the political crisis was seriously damaging the conduct of the war.

In that sense, it was acknowledged, the United States was, in effect, placing the Diem regime on notice that it might have to reconsider its support for South Vietnam if measures were not taken to redress the political situation.

Officials said that although the pol-

icy statement deliberately avoided making a formal judgment that the war could not be won without a meaningful political change in Saigon, the implication was there for President Diem to see.

The statement said that United States policy remained one of "working with the people and Government of South Vietnam to deny this country to communism," but added significantly that "effective performance in this undertaking is the central object of our policy in South Vietnam."

It said that the United States sought to support Vietnamese efforts to defeat "aggression" as well as "to build a peaceful and free society."

"The United States has made clear its continuing opposition to any repressive actions in South Vietnam," it said.

Up to now, the statement said, the McNamara-Taylor mission found that "the military program in South Vietnam has made progress and is sound in principle, though improvements are being energetically sought."

It said that "major United States assistance" was needed only until the Communist insurgency had been suppressed or until Vietnamese forces "are capable of suppressing it."

Mr. McNamara and General Taylor were reported to believe that "the major part" of the United States military task could be completed by the end of 1965, although a limited number of training personnel might still be required.

By the end of this year, the statement said, the training program for the South Vietnamese forces should have progressed to the point where 1,000 United States personnel can be withdrawn from the country, in the opinion of Mr. McNamara and General Taylor.

United States military strength in South Vietnam has risen from 685 men in early 1961 to more than 14,000 men at this time. The build-up began after General Taylor's first mission to Vietnam in 1961.

840 *Vietnamese paratroopers dropping from U.S. Air Force C-123 transport planes over Tay Ninh province in South Vietnam during the Vietnam War. The operation was known as Phi Hoa II.* (Keystone/Getty Images)

Violence in Saigon Renews U.S. Debate On Vietnam Policy

By MAX FRANKEL

WASHINGTON, Oct. 6—Violence in South Vietnam has rekindled the Washington policy debate that President Kennedy tried to dampen last week. It is expected to bring new demands that the United States apply strong pressure to change the policies and personnel of the Saigon Government.

The issues that have long divided the Administration were suddenly reopened by the fiery suicide yesterday of a Buddhist monk in Saigon, the sixth such protest action, and by the beating of three American newsmen by South Vietnamese plainclothesmen.

"We're right back where we started from," one official here remarked today. "The same arguments are going to flare all over town, and this time you have more Congressmen in the act and Mrs. Nhu all over television."

The official meant that Mr. Kennedy would again be bombarded by conflicting advice from Americans handling the war against Communist guerillas in South Vietnam— advice that would have him either ignore the political turmoil in Saigon and press the military campaign, or finally decide that the war cannot be won without political changes.

Mrs. Ngo Dinh Nhu is the wife of the brother and most influential adviser of South Vietnam's President, Ngo Dinh Diem. She is scheduled to arrive in New York tomorrow for a three week tour to defend her family's regime.

Her charges that Americans are sabotaging the war effort and behaving like "spectators" in her country were aired on television this afternoon.

Two Officials Optimistic

The new debate will come less than a week after President Kennedy sought peace among his own advisers by endorsing a cautiously optimistic report on a visit to Vietnam by Robert S. McNamara, Secretary of Defense, and Gen. Maxwell D. Taylor, Chairman of the Joint Chiefs of Staff.

They called the political situation in Vietnam deeply serious, but said it had not yet affected military operations. They expressed hope that the progress of the war effort would enable the United States to withdraw most of its troops and aid to Vietnam by 1965.

With these statements, the President apparently tried to gloss over the differences here over whether the war can ever be won without major political reform. He also avoided a decision on how long he would support the Ngo Dinh Diem regime.

Mrs. Ngo Dinh Nhu, who was interviewed in Paris for the American Broadcasting Company's program "Issues and Answers," denied any need for political reform. She said the "so-called Buddhists" were Communist-led agitators trying to topple her family's Government and using Americans in Vietnam as their "instruments."

Confusion reigned among Americans in Saigon, she said, citing an old Vietnamese proverb that "when there are too many doctors, they will only meet the corpse."

The principal difficulty between officials of the United States and South Vietnam Governments, she said, is that "Americans don't take seriously enough their role as an ally."

"They give the impression that they consider themselves just spectators to a show," she remarked. "We have absolutely the impression that they do not participate."

Mrs. Ngo Dinh Nhu plans to visit Washington on her tour, but so far the administration has no plans to take note of her presence. Although she is regarded as an influential force in her politics, she has no official position.

Defense Secretary Robert McNamara and U.S. Army Chief-of-Staff General Maxwell Taylor meet with President Kennedy prior to their visit to South Vietnam to review military efforts, September 24, 1963. (AFP/Getty Images)

DIEM AND NHU ARE REPORTEDLY SLAIN; ARMY RULING SAIGON AFTER COUP; KENNEDY REVIEWS VIETNAM POLICY

SUICIDES DOUBTED

Deposed Chiefs Fled, Then Were Seized—Throngs Exult

By DAVID HALBERSTAM

SAIGON, South Vietnam, Nov. 2—President Ngo Dinh Diem and his brother, Ngo Dinh Nhu, are dead in the wake of the military uprising that ended their regime.

While the Saigon radio announced that they had committed suicide, reliable private military sources said that they had been assassinated.

With Saigon under military rule, crowds of jubilant youths set fire to the homes of government security officials, of government-controlled newspapers and police stations.

[The military leaders set up a Buddhist-led provisional Government with Nguyen Ngoc Tho, former Vice President, as Premier, The Associated Press reported. The recently elected National Assembly was dissolved.]

Reports on Death Conflict

The military sources that reported that the brothers had been killed said they had escaped from the palace by a tunnel shortly before marines overran it.

Later, Ngo Dinh Diem was seen in a small Roman Catholic church in Cholon, a suburb of Saigon, it was reported. The military leaders sent troops and armored cars and both men were taken prisoner.

They were placed inside an armored personnel carrier and were guarded by several soldiers, according to this account. On the way to military headquarters, an informed source said, an order was given to kill both. When the armored car arrived at headquarters both men were dead.

Military men said that both men shot themselves while in transit.

Captured After Escape

The reports that the President and his brother, considered the most powerful man in his regime, had committed suicide were received skeptically in some quarters since both were Roman Catholics. The President was considered particularly devout.

The military, denouncing what it termed the Diem Government's despotism and corruption, suspended the Constitution and ended the presidential system. Imprisoned Buddhist monks were freed.

The military coup d'etat ended nine years of Ngo Dinh Diem's rule shortly before 7 A.M. when the palace was stormed by marines. Moments before this, both Ngo Dinh Diem and Ngo Dinh Nhu had told the military they were surrendering. But, according to reliable sources, they then escaped.

The new military revolution committee immediately pledged itself to continue the war against the Communist insurgents.

Reliable sources believed the military might try to turn the government over soon to a temporary civilian regime. This, it is believed, would be headed by Nguyen Ngoc Tho, Vice President under Ngo Dinh Diem and a Buddhist, and would include certain political oppositionists, including Dr. Phan Huy Quat.

Nguyen Ngoc Tho would serve as Premier if there was a provisional government, these sources said.

Though Nguyen Ngoc Tho served under Ngo Dinh Diem he is considered acceptable to varying elements in the country and was considered by many sources as a dissident within the Cabinet who was disturbed by the Government's treatment of the Buddhists.

Buddhist leaders who led the religious political protest movement against the Government and had been imprisoned since Aug. 21 when the Government raided pagodas, were freed today by the army. They were acclaimed by a huge, emotional crowd at Xa Loi Pagoda as they returned from prison.

Seven Buddhist monks had burned themselves to death as part of the protest.

Throughout the city, the population acclaimed the troops and food was given to the soldiers by many people. Though the city was under martial law, there was an air of jubilation.

Newspaper Offices Attacked

Youths tried to sack the offices of several pro-Government newspapers. They also burned hundreds of copies of The Times of Vietnam, an English-language paper that was identified with the Nhus.

Youths also set afire and razed the building of the Government-controlled Vietnam Press, which had been strongly pro-Nhu in recent weeks. They also damaged shops allegedly belonging to Archbishop Ngo Dinh Thuc of Hue, brother of Ngo Dinh Diem. He is out of the country.

The homes of the Minister of Interior and the Minister of Civic Action and of several Deputies also were burned. The offices of Mrs. Ngo Dinh Nhu's women's solidarity movement were sacked.

When the youths converged on the National Assembly building, the Government sent in troops to protect the structure. The youths attacked police stations and appeared to concentrate on those aspects of the Ngo Government that had drawn their disfavor.

Ex-Officials Seized

Informed sources said that Col. Le Quang Tung, commander of Special Forces, who was the President's political arm, was under arrest, along with his brother. Also under arrest was Ngo Trong Hieu, Minister of Civic Action, who was considered extremely close to the President. There were reports that all three might be executed.

An important contribution to the coup's success is attributed to Gen. Ton That Dinh, previously loyal to the Government and commander of large numbers of troops in the Saigon area. He is believed to have supplied a regiment of regulars to support the anti-Diem troops.

It is reported that Ngo Dinh Can, overlord of the central region of Vietnam, is among the Diem adherents under arrest.

Authoritative sources said other officers were urging Maj. Gen. Duong Van Minh, apparently the key man in the coup, to take a position in the Government if a new one was formed. But he is said to be unwilling to accept a position, feeling that this would cast aspersions on his role in the coup and make it appear that he had participated for the sake of personal gain.

The coup appeared to have been extremely well planned and to have gone like clockwork. Step by step, various areas of the city were sealed off and anti-Diem troops moved into key positions.

Around noon yesterday, Colonel Le Quang Tung was summoned by generals to a conference at military headquarters. He arrived with his brother and they were immediately arrested.

The Presidential Palace in Saigon, riddled with bullet holes, gutted and ransacked after a military coup that overthrew the Diem government.
(Larry Burrows/Time & Life Pictures/Getty Images)

Moments later, fighting broke out nearby between some of the colonel's Special Forces troops and anti-Diem troops of the headquarters staff. At this point the generals forced the colonel to telephone to his people to stop fighting. That sealed off one of the major units loyal to the President.

Simultaneously, the barracks of the Presidential brigade were sealed off by troops with armor and the area was pounded by anti-Diem mortars.

Thus early in the day the palace was cut off from the main segments of its two special hand-picked units. From then on, according to the sources, it was primarily a matter of applying pressure.

The military, denouncing what it termed the Diem Government's despotism and corruption, supended the Constitution and ended the presidential system.

The anti-Diem forces took the telegraph office, police headquarters and the radio station. Commanders of several units who were considered loyal to the President were arrested and the commander of the navy, Ho Tan Quyen, apparently was killed.

Slowly the palace area was ringed with anti-Diem troops and armored vehicles.

During this period the generals attempted to get Ngo Dinh Diem and his brother to surrender, it is reported. They were said to have been told that if they surrendered immediately they would be permitted to leave the coun-

try, but that if they continued to resist they would be killed.

The negotiations apparently broke down. The President and his brother were stubborn and resilient men. In the past, cornered in situations like this, they had been saved, and this time they evidently hoped for someone to arrive and rescue them.

But this time every general with troops was lending his name and support to the coup. In early morning, after the palace had been ringed with armored vehicles, at almost point-blank range the building was shelled. The fierce barrage continued for hours. Apparently the idea was to use the immense firepower to destroy the will to resist and save lives. Casualties were considered extremely light.

Escape Is Unexplained

Apparently around 6 A.M. there was a cease-fire and the President and his brother agreed to surrender. Then marines stormed into the palace. There was more sharp fighting for brief moments and the palace was captured. But Ngo Dinh Diem and his brother were gone. Military leaders were unsure as to how they got away.

Seven of the President's ministers were said to have joined the military leaders.

The special United Nations fact-finding commission investigating alleged government discrimination against the Buddhists was left without a mission. The government has changed and the Buddhists are free.

The struggle for survival of the Ngo Government has always been a difficult one. Plotters and would-be successors have always been numerous. Yet, in the view of some informed observers here, the Government sealed its own fate this year and turned increasing numbers of nominally loyal military leaders and public servants against it.

Ngo Dinh Diem and his brother had made the climate for a coup unusually ripe. In their very tightening of police controls in recent months to protect

themselves, and the subsequent mass arrests, they increased uneasiness and unrest until the sense of fear and despair was extreme and widespread.

There was no one element that led to this climate but a complex intermingling of factors.

The first was repression against first the Buddhists and then students during the spring and summer unrest. If there is any one factor that began to generate an atmosphere in which the Government would fall, it was the Buddhists' protest, which began in Hue.

By failing to solve the question when it was a relatively minor religious protest, the Government angered a vast section of population, underrated the ability and intensity of the Buddhists and gave the latent opposition a spearhead and form.

Ngo Dinh Diem found it increasingly difficult to meet the demands of the Buddhists as the protest continued and similarly refrained from crushing it until it was almost too late. When he and Ngo Dinh Nhu did crush it, they crushed something very close to the Vietnamese, and with a violence that first frightened and then angered elements of the population.

Similarly, when students, many of them sons and brothers of military officers, sprang up as successors to the Buddhists, the Government again crushed the movement, but again at an extremely high price.

A second factor, in the view of some officers, is that there was fear among many high officers that Ngo Dinh Nhu was talking with Hanoi about the possibility of a neutralist Vietnam. For many officers, deeply committed to years of fighting the Communists, a neutralist solution might mean death for them and their families.

At the Edge of the Quagmire:

The War in Vietnam

By Robert Dallek

During the first two years of John Kennedy's presidency, between January 1961 and the spring of 1963, Vietnam was a relatively minor problem. Although not a week went by during this time without discussions somewhere in the government about a Communist insurgency threatening to topple Ngo Dinh Diem's pro-American government in Saigon, it was never at the center of Kennedy's concerns. Like the administration, *The New York Times* gave Vietnam only limited coverage. There were more compelling problems at home and abroad: Cuba, especially the missile crisis that could have erupted into a Soviet-American war; Berlin; nuclear testing; and sporadic violent demonstrations across the South by African Americans struggling to attain equal rights—all loomed larger as public concerns than dangers of a significant American involvement in a Southeast Asian conflict.

Beginning in the spring of 1963, however, Vietnam began to command more of the administration's attention. It began to compete with domestic tensions over civil rights that compelled Kennedy in June to put a seminal proposal before Congress to outlaw segregation in all places of public accommodation. A trip to Europe in June that took Kennedy to Italy, Germany, Great Britain, and Ireland, where adoring crowds in Berlin and Ireland cheered the young president, temporarily distracted him from growing problems with Saigon. In addition, the election of 1964 began to preoccupy the White House. But the struggle to preserve South Vietnam's autonomy from a Communist takeover had become a day-to-day issue of deepening White House concern.

The problem had been inherited from the Eisenhower administration. In 1954, after the French defeat at Dien Bien Phu and their departure from Vietnam, the country was split between North and South at the 17th parallel. The Eisenhower White House immediately launched an undisclosed policy of assuring South Vietnam's autonomy, as well as that of Laos and Cambodia, from Communist control. Convinced that the defense of Southeast Asia from Sino-Soviet domination was vital to U.S. national security, a "domino theory" justified Eisenhower's investment of money, war materiel, and some 600 military advisers in South Vietnam: If Vietnam fell to the Communists, all the other countries in the region would topple as well.

During the transition from Eisenhower to Kennedy, Ike encouraged the in-coming president to follow his lead in making Vietnam and all of Southeast Asia a priority in the Cold War. Despite his reluctance to become enmeshed in a jungle conflict so far removed from American shores, Kennedy felt compelled to defend South Vietnam. Setbacks at Cuba's Bay of Pigs and the Vienna summit with Nikita Khrushchev in the first six months of his administration convinced Kennedy that he could not afford to "lose" Vietnam. An American withdrawal could encourage guerrilla insurgencies in other Third World countries and undermine his political standing at home.

The decision to defend Vietnam triggered a slow escalation of the U.S. committment, with increases in the number of advisers, the use of air power, including napalm attacks against Viet Cong insurgents, and a dramatic increase of aid dollars exceeding anything going to other developing countries.

Despite these commitments, by the spring of 1963, South Vietnam seemed on the verge of collapse. When confronted by this possible defeat, however, Kennedy was reluctant to become more involved in a civil war that could escalate into an unwanted larger conflict. But the prevailing wisdom in the State and Defense Departments and at the C.I.A.—that losing Vietnam to the Communists would be a serious blow to U.S. national security—forced the crisis to the center of Kennedy's foreign policy discussions.

However eager he was to keep Vietnam and Southeast Asia more generally out of the Communist orbit, Kennedy believed a dominant role for the United States in South Vietnam's civil war would be a questionable use of military and economic resources. Still, the pressures on him from within his administration and from Saigon's increasing disarray compelled him to increase supplies of war materiel and the number of U.S. military advisers to more than sixteen thousand. At the same time, U.S. planners convinced Diem and his brother Ngo Dinh Nhu to expand a Strategic Hamlet program that aimed to defend the countryside and particularly the agriculturally rich Mekong Delta from Vietcong insurgents preying on vulnerable peasant villages. The program was supposed to reduce the Vietcong's capacity to live off the land, and the training of South Vietnamese forces was preparing them to defeat the Communists in pitched battles.

In January 1963, however, at Ap Bac in the Mekong Delta, Saigon's U.S.-trained troops suffered a disturbing defeat. The battle exposed the unwillingness of the South Vietnamese to fight aggressively against the insurgents. ARVN officers, who were principally Diem loyalists rather than skilled commanders, refused to antagonize Diem or their troops by risking significant losses.

As striking as the battlefield defeat, however, was an argument that erupted among Americans in Vietnam and Washington about the battle and the war. American journalists in Saigon, led by Neil Sheehan of UPI, saw the Diem government as corrupt and incapable of defeating the Communists. Most of the U.S. military in Vietnam under General Paul D. Harkins and the Joint Chiefs of Staff in Washington, led by Maxwell Taylor, thought the journalists were hypercritical and an impediment to victory; they were antagonizing Diem by writing critical stories about his government and discouraging Americans from supporting Saigon with money and U.S. military personnel. The correspondents also angered Kennedy officials, who complained that they were undermining the war effort. Some of them, however, shared the journalists' belief that Vietnam needed a more effective leader than Diem if it were to win the war and that Washington needed to encourage a coup by more pliant generals.

The Saigon press corps and the U.S. military specifically disagreed about Ap Bac: with the exception of John Paul Vann, a colonel with extensive first-hand knowledge of ARVN's performance in the field, the U.S. Chiefs in Saigon and Washington put Ap Bac aside as being of small consequence. When Admiral Harry Felt, the commander of all Pacific forces, visited Vietnam, he told Sheehan that he ought to get his facts straight. Ap Bac was a victory. Harkins echoed Felt's assertion. But Sheehan stood his ground, asserting that his reporting rested on daily visits to Mekong, not on armchair speculation by officers remote from the battlefield.

In the spring and summer of 1963, a crisis erupted when Diem and Nhu, both Catholics, launched a campaign of repression against the country's Buddhist majority protesting government restrictions on their religious freedoms. It was a terrible mistake. The repression embarrassed and frustrated the Kennedy administration, especially when Buddhist monks immolated themselves. The Embassy and C.I.A. in Saigon now began discussions with Vietnamese generals about overturning Diem's regime.

A fierce debate erupted among Kennedy's advisers on whether ridding themselves of Diem would advance or retard the government's anticommunist campaign. Frederick Nolting, the retiring Ambassador in Saigon,

joined by Maxwell Taylor, was convinced that a coup would be a grave mistake, believing that no one of comparable national stature could replace Diem and his successor would be pilloried as an American puppet—a new Bao Dai—the last French-appointed governor of Vietnam. Diem's successor would give the Communists a new political advantage in the contest for hearts and minds.

Kennedy also doubted the wisdom of a U.S.-sponsored coup. It seemed certain to deepen American involvement in a conflict he did not believe the United States should fight directly. Memories of the stalemate in Korea and the political demise of Harry Truman's presidency as a consequence partly shaped his concerns.

Averell Harriman, Under Secretary of State for Political Affairs; Roger Hilsman, Assistant Secretary of State for Far Eastern Affairs; and Michael Forrestal, National Security Council expert on Vietnam, argued vigorously for a coup that they considered essential to victory in Vietnam. The refusal of the Vietnamese generals to launch a rebellion in the summer, however, increased doubts about U.S. capacity to control events in so unstable a country. But Henry Cabot Lodge, the new Ambassador to Saigon, saw no way to retreat from a coup: "We are launched on a course from which there is no respectable turning back," he told Kennedy shortly after arriving at his post. Kennedy accepted his conclusion, but wanted to be sure that any uprising would be successful. He insisted on the freedom to change course at the last minute if he believed an uprising would fail. "I know from experience that failure is more destructive than an appearance of indecision," he told Lodge.

During September and October, in a last-ditch effort to save Diem's regime, the Kennedy administration struggled to find some formula to help him advance the war in Vietnam. The debate in Washington was an open secret. *The New York Times* carried several front-page stories from David Halberstam, its bureau chief in Saigon, about the divisions among Kennedy's advisers. Kennedy told aides that he was "disturbed at the tendency both in Washington and Saigon to fight our own battles via the newspapers." What he described as a "zealous spirit of criticism and complaint" particularly bothered him. He worried that it might increase pressure on him to make hasty and unwise decisions on whether to increase or diminish aid to Diem's regime. As a consequence, in October, he tried to mute negative press accounts from Saigon by asking *Times* publisher Arthur Sulzberger to remove Halberstam from Vietnam. Believing this an assault on freedom of the press, Sulzberger refused.

The back-and-forth over what to do lasted only until

November 1, when a U.S.-supported coup toppled Diem and Nhu and cost them their lives. Kennedy had worried that if the coup failed, "We could lose our entire position in Southeast Asia overnight." When the coup succeeded, Kennedy was relieved, but the Diem-Nhu assassinations horrified him. He refused to believe that they had killed themselves, as the coup generals alleged. He said, "Diem had fought for his country for twenty years and that it should not have ended like this."

On November 4, Kennedy privately recorded a statement for future historians to consult. He had private doubts about the wisdom of toppling Diem and laid the blame for the coup on himself. He decried the August cable in which he had given initial sanction to an uprising. "The question now," he said, "is whether the generals can stay together and build a stable government or whether Saigon will begin—whether public opinion in Saigon, the intellectuals, the students, etc.—will turn on this government as repressive and undemocratic in the not too distant future." In short, had the coup opened the way to instability in Saigon that would eventually facilitate a Communist victory or force the United States into using its forces to fight the war?

Sadly, Kennedy's assassination on November 22, 1963, never allowed him to decide on how to proceed in Vietnam or see the disastrous consequences that expanded U.S. involvement in the conflict brought over the next twelve years. No one can say exactly what Kennedy would have done in that star-crossed country if he had lived to serve a second term. But judging from his skepticism about a larger U.S. role in Vietnam and his caution about being overcommitted in an unstable Third World nation, we can speculate that Kennedy would not have increased American involvement in the war as Lyndon Johnson, his successor, did. Indeed, we can imagine that he would have moved ahead with plans already in place for the withdrawal of the 16,000 plus U.S. advisers. Tragically, this can only be conjecture, but it echoes the difficult debate that preceded Kennedy's death and will remain an enduring part of the argument among historians about Vietnam.

Robert Dallek is a presidential historian and the author of *An Unfinished Life* (2003), a biography of John F. Kennedy.

Kennedy Pledges Space Advances; Opens Texas Tour

Dedicates San Antonio Site and Declares Research 'Must and Will Go On'

PARTY SPLIT EVIDENCED

Yarborough Scores Connally and Refuses to Accompany Johnson on Motorcade

By TOM WICKER

HOUSTON, Nov. 21—President Kennedy mixed a strong defense of his space program with some old-fashioned, earthbound politics today as he opened a two-day tour of Texas.

In this space-conscious state, he pledged that the conquest of that "new frontier" would go ahead.

He gave the reassurance despite Congressional reductions in his space budget.

He declared in a speech at Brooks Air Force Base:

"There will be setbacks and frustrations and disappointments. There will be pressures for our country to do less and temptations to do something else. But this research must and will go on. The conquest of space must and will go ahead. That much we know. That much we can say with confidence and conviction."

Cheered by Crowds

The President was welcomed by crowds lining the streets of San Antonio and Houston as he and Mrs. Kennedy drove past in an open car.

His San Antonio motorcade took him from the city's International Airport to the new Aero-Space Medical Health Center at the nearby air base.

After he helped dedicate a new $6 million facility there he flew on to Houston for a dinner honoring Representative Albert Thomas, one of the most influential men in Congress.

Even before his plane landed at San Antonio International Airport, Mr. Kennedy became involved in the volatile passions of the faction-torn state Democratic party.

Texas's senior Senator, Ralph Yarborough, was aboard the Presidential plane and was asked how he felt about not being invited to a reception tomorrow night for the President and Mrs. Kennedy by Gov. John B. Connally Jr.

"I desire that my friends take no offense at this," the Senator replied. "I want everyone to join hands in harmony for the greatest welcome to the President and Mrs. Kennedy in the history of Texas. Besides, Governor Connally is so terribly uneducated governmentally, how could you expect anything else?"

That statement was only a sample of what Mr. Kennedy can expect on the shifting political sands of this state. Liberal elements were sure to search with burning eyes for any slight to their leaders, Senator Yarborough and Don Yarborough of Houston.

Yet, it was Governor Connally who rode in the same car with Mr. Kennedy in the San Antonio and Houston motorcades today.

Senator Yarborough twice refused an invitation from Vice President Johnson to ride with him and Mrs. Johnson. Instead, the Senator occupied another car farther back in the motorcades.

The bitter factional dispute is a major concern for President Kennedy. The White House is said to be pushing a compromise plan that would have all Texas Democrats join in supporting Governor Connally and Senator Yarborough for re-election next year.

The Kennedy-Johnson ticket carried Texas in 1960 but the Democratic factionalism and the rise of a strong Republican party in the state have made their prospects for 1964 somewhat cloudy—particularly if Senator Barry Goldwater of Arizona should be the Republican nominee.

Mr. Thomas, whose testimonial dinner the President attended, was an important figure in House deliberations on the space budget. He was also instrumental in getting a huge new space center, where much of the moon-exploration program will be carried out, for Houston.

Mr. Kennedy delivered a glowing tribute to Mr. Thomas, whom he called "one of the most remarkable members of Congress."

"Albert Thomas has lived with change," he said. "He understands the meaning and importance of growth."

Before attending the Thomas dinner, Mr. and Mrs. Kennedy made an unscheduled stop at a dinner dance of the League of United Latin American Citizens.

That provided Mrs. Kennedy with her only opportunity of the day to speak in public and she met it with a brief, quietly delivered talk in Spanish. She stumbled only slightly.

The Latin-American tradition in Texas, she told the attentive audience of several hundred, "began a hundred years before my husband's state, Massachusetts, was settled, but it is a tradition that is today alive and vigorous."

The San Antonio and Houston appearances were the main events of the President's tour of Texas, which will continue tomorrow with a breakfast speech in Fort Worth, a luncheon address in Dallas and a party fund-raising dinner in Austin.

After the Thomas dinner the President and Mrs. Kennedy flew to Fort Worth, where they spent the night at the Texas Hotel.

Part 5

FOUR DAYS
IN NOVEMBER

President John F. Kennedy's flag-draped casket lies in state in the East Room of the White House.
(Abbie Rowe/National Park Service/John F. Kennedy Library)

> *But he is gone now at 46, younger than when most Presidents have started on the great adventure. In his book, "Profiles in Courage," all his heroes faced the hard choice either of giving in to public opinion or of defying it and becoming martyrs.*
>
> —*James Reston of* The New York Times, *1963*

A Nation of Tears

It is said that almost every American can remember where he or she was at the moment that John Fitzgerald Kennedy died. Strangers sought out each other to grieve and remember. Emotions ranged from tears and anger to bewildered disbelief. He was a great athlete who died young. He will always be young because he and his beautiful wife were more than President and First Lady, a couple at the pinnacle of their powers. They were cultural icons who changed the way millions of Americans thought of themselves and their country: The best was yet to come. So was the myth of Camelot.

I was in Morristown, New Jersey, a reporter for the *Newark Evening News*. "Get local reaction," I was told—and walked across the hall to interview J. Raymond Manahan, the mayor of the town and chairman of the county's Democratic Party. We were both at the edge of tears when a window cleaner in a safety harness tapped on the glass outside the office. He was grinning, saluting us with the squeegee. He didn't know yet.

Mary McGrory, a star reporter at *The Washington Star*, broke into tears and leaned on J. Patrick Moynihan, then an Assistant Secretary of Labor. "We'll never laugh again," she sobbed. "No, Mary, we'll laugh again," he said. "But we'll never be young again."

The New York Times, which assigned all available reporters, editors and photographers to the story, chartered a plane from Washington to Dallas. Advertising was dropped from the first 16 pages of the paper for coverage of the assassination. The presses rolled at 8:40 P. M., printing 864,000 copies, 50 percent more than usual.

Tom Wicker, White House correspondent, dictated the lead story of 4,000 words from the Dallas airport to the tape banks the *Times* used in those days. He was crying as he spoke. Suddenly, we became a nation of tears.

Most of the articles that follow appeared in that 16-page section of the newspaper of November 23, 1963, shock after shock: Robert Semple's vivid memories of the mood in Washington and reactions from places farther off; Gladwin Hill's account, two days later, from the basement of Dallas police headquarters, on the killing of the alleged assassin, Lee Harvey Oswald, shot point-blank by a bereft night-club owner, Jack Ruby, on live national television; Tom Wicker on the funeral of a President, President Johnson's whirlwind early days in office; Anthony Lewis's report on the Warren Commission's investigation; and finally Sam Tanenhaus's look back over the outpouring of conflicting conspiracy theories behind JFK's murder, a few of which are still researched and published today.

—Richard Reeves

The presidential motorcade through Dallas on the morning of President John F. Kennedy's assassination. (Cecil Stoughton/John F. Kennedy Library)

KENNEDY IS KILLED BY SNIPER AS HE RIDES IN CAR IN DALLAS; JOHNSON SWORN IN ON PLANE

Gov. Connally Shot; Mrs. Kennedy Safe

President Is Struck Down by a Rifle Shot From Building on Motorcade Route—Johnson, Riding Behind, Is Unhurt

By TOM WICKER

DALLAS, Nov. 22—President John Fitzgerald Kennedy was shot and killed by an assassin today.

He died of a wound in the brain caused by a rifle bullet that was fired at him as he was riding through downtown Dallas in a motorcade.

Vice President Lyndon Baines Johnson, who was riding in the third car behind Mr. Kennedy's, was sworn in as the 36th President of the United States 99 minutes after Mr. Kennedy's death.

Mr. Johnson is 55 years old; Mr. Kennedy was 46.

Shortly after the assassination, Lee H. Oswald, who once defected to the Soviet Union and who has been active in the Fair Play for Cuba Committee, was arrested by the Dallas police. Tonight he was accused of the killing.

Suspect Captured After Scuffle

Oswald, 24 years old, was also accused of slaying a policeman who had approached him in the street. Oswald was subdued after a scuffle with a second policeman in a nearby theater.

President Kennedy was shot at 12:30 P.M., Central standard time (1:30 P.M., New York time). He was pronounced dead at 1 P.M. and Mr. Johnson was sworn in at 2:39 P.M.

Mr. Johnson, who was uninjured in the shooting, took his oath in the Presidential jet plane as it stood on the runway at Love Field. The body of Mr. Kennedy was aboard. Immediately after the oath-taking, the plane took off for Washington.

Standing beside the new President as Mr. Johnson took the oath of office was Mrs. John F. Kennedy. Her stockings were spattered with her husband's blood.

Gov. John B. Connally Jr. of Texas, who was riding in the same car with Mr. Kennedy, was severely wounded in the chest, ribs and arm. His condition was serious, but not critical.

The killer fired the rifle from a building just off the motorcade route. Mr. Kennedy, Governor Connally and Mr. Johnson had just received an enthusiastic welcome from a large crowd in downtown Dallas.

Mr. Kennedy apparently was hit by the first of what witnesses believed were three shots. He was driven at high speed to Dallas's Parkland Hospital. There, in an emergency operating room, with only physicians and nurses in attendance, he died without regaining consciousness.

Mrs. Kennedy, Mrs. Connally and a Secret Service agent were in the car with Mr. Kennedy and Governor Connally. Two Secret Service agents flanked the car. Other than Mr. Connally, none of this group was injured in the shooting. Mrs. Kennedy cried "Oh no!" immediately after her husband was struck.

Mrs. Kennedy was in the hospital near her husband when he died, but not in the operating room. When the body was taken from the hospital in a bronze coffin about 2 P.M., Mrs. Kennedy walked beside it.

Her face was sorrowful. She looked steadily at the floor. She still wore the raspberry-colored suit in which she had greeted welcoming crowds in Fort Worth and Dallas. But she had taken off the matching pillbox hat she wore earlier in the day, and her dark hair was windblown and tangled. Her hand rested lightly on her husband's coffin as it was taken to a waiting hearse.

Mrs. Kennedy climbed in beside the coffin. Then the ambulance drove to Love Field, and Mr. Kennedy's body was placed aboard the Presidential jet. Mrs. Kennedy then attended the swearing-in ceremony for Mr. Johnson.

As Mr. Kennedy's body left Parkland Hospital, a few stunned persons stood outside. Nurses and doctors, whispering among themselves, looked from the window. A larger crowd that had gathered earlier, before it was known that the President was dead, had been dispersed by Secret Service men and policemen.

Priests Administer Last Rites

Two priests administered last rites to Mr. Kennedy, a Roman Catholic. They were the Very Rev. Oscar Huber, the pastor of Holy Trinity Church in Dallas, and the Rev. James Thompson.

President John F. Kennedy approximately one minute before he was shot in Dallas, Texas, on Nov. 22, 1963. In the car with him are Jacqueline Kennedy, Nellie Connally and her husband, Governor John Connally of Texas. (Associated Press)

Mr. Johnson was sworn in as President by Federal Judge Sarah T. Hughes of the Northern District of Texas. She was appointed to the judgeship by Mr. Kennedy in October, 1961.

The ceremony, delayed about five minutes for Mrs. Kennedy's arrival, took place in the private Presidential cabin in the rear of the plane.

About 25 to 30 persons—members of the late President's staff, members of Congress who had been accompanying the President on a two-day tour of Texas cities and a few reporters—crowded into the little room.

No accurate listing of those present could be obtained. Mrs. Kennedy stood at the left of Mr. Johnson, her eyes and face showing the signs of weeping that had apparently shaken her since she left the hospital not long before.

Mrs. Johnson, wearing a beige dress, stood at her husband's right.

As Judge Hughes read the brief oath of office, her eyes, too, were red from weeping. Mr. Johnson's hands rested on a black, leather-bound Bible as Judge Hughes read and he repeated:

"I do solemnly swear that I will perform the duties of the President of the United States to the best of my ability and defend, protect and preserve the Constitution of the United States."

Those 34 words made Lyndon Baines Johnson, one-time farmboy and schoolteacher of Johnson City, the President.

Johnson Embraces Mrs. Kennedy

Mr. Johnson made no statement. He embraced Mrs. Kennedy and she held his hand for a long moment. He also embraced Mrs. Johnson and Mrs. Evelyn Lincoln, Mr. Kennedy's private secretary.

"O.K.," Mr. Johnson said. "Let's get this plane back to Washington."

At 2:46 P.M., seven minutes after he had become President, 106 minutes after Mr. Kennedy had become the fourth American President to succumb to an assassin's wounds, the white and red jet took off for Washington.

In the cabin when Mr. Johnson took the oath was Cecil Stoughton, an armed forces photographer assigned to the White House.

Mr. Kennedy's staff members appeared stunned and bewildered. Lawrence F. O'Brien, the Congressional liaison officer, and P. Kenneth O'Donnell, the appointment secretary, both long associates of Mr. Kennedy, showed evidence of weeping. None had anything to say.

Other staff members believed to be in the cabin for the swearing-in included David F. Powers, the White House receptionist; Miss Pamela Turnure, Mrs. Kennedy's press secretary, and Malcolm Kilduff, the assistant White House press secretary.

Mr. Kilduff announced the President's death, with choked voice and red-rimmed eyes, at about 1:36 P.M.

"President John F. Kennedy died at approximately 1 o'clock Central standard time today here in Dallas," Mr. Kilduff said at the hospital. "He died of a gunshot wound in the brain. I have no other details regarding the assassination of the President."

Mr. Kilduff also announced that Governor Connally had been hit by a bullet or bullets and that Mr. Johnson, who had not yet been sworn in, was safe in the protective custody of the Secret Service at an unannounced place, presumably the airplane at Love Field.

Mr. Kilduff indicated that the President had been shot once. Later medical reports raised the possibility that there had been two wounds. But the death was caused, as far as could be learned, by a massive wound in the brain.

Later in the afternoon, Dr. Malcolm Perry, an attending surgeon, and Dr. Kemp Clark, chief of neurosurgery at Parkland Hospital, gave more details.

Mr. Kennedy was hit by a bullet in the throat, just below the Adam's apple, they said. This wound had the appearance of a bullet's entry.

Mr. Kennedy also had a massive, gaping wound in the back and one on the right side of the head. However, the doctors said it was impossible to determine immediately whether the wounds had been caused by one bullet or two.

Resuscitation Attempted

Dr. Perry, the first physician to treat the President, said a number of resuscitative measures had been attempted, including oxygen, anesthesia, an indotracheal tube, a tracheotomy, blood and fluids. An electrocardiogram monitor was attached to measure Mr. Kennedy's heart beats.

Dr. Clark was summoned and arrived in a minute or two. By then, Dr. Perry said, Mr. Kennedy was "critically ill and moribund," or near death.

Dr. Clark said that on his first sight of the President, he had concluded immediately that Mr. Kennedy could not live.

"It was apparent that the President had sustained a lethal wound," he said. "A missile had gone in and out of the back of his head causing external lacerations and loss of brain tissue."

Shortly after he arrived, Dr. Clark said, "the President lost his heart action by the electrocardiogram." A closed-chest cardiograph massage was attempted, as were other emergency resuscitation measures.

Dr. Clark said these had produced "palpable pulses" for a short time, but all were "to no avail."

In Operating Room 40 Minutes

The President was on the emergency table at the hospital for about 40 minutes, the doctors said. At the end, perhaps eight physicians were in Operating Room No. 1, where Mr. Kennedy remained until his death. Dr. Clark said it was difficult to determine the exact moment of death, but the doctors said officially that it occurred at 1 P.M.

Later, there were unofficial reports that Mr. Kennedy had been killed instantly. The source of these reports, Dr. Tom Shires, chief surgeon at the hospital and professor of surgery at the University of Texas Southwest Medical School, issued this statement tonight:

"Medically, it was apparent the president was not alive when he was brought in. There was no spontaneous respiration. He had dilated, fixed pupils. It was obvious he had a lethal head wound.

"Technically, however, by using vigorous resuscitation, intravenous tubes and all the usual supportive measures, we were able to raise a semblance of a heartbeat."

Dr. Shires said he was positive it was impossible that President Kennedy could have spoken after being shot. "I am absolutely sure he never knew what hit him," Dr. Shires said.

President Kennedy moments after being shot, with Mrs. Kennedy holding him.

(Three Lions/Hulton Archive/Getty Images)

Mrs. Kennedy stands over the fallen president and a Secret Service agent climbing aboard as the limousine speeds toward Parkland Hospital.
(Bettmann/Corbis/Associated Press)

Dr. Shires was not present when Mr. Kennedy was being treated at Parkland Hospital. He issued his statement, however, after lengthy conferences with the doctors who had attended the President.

Mr. Johnson remained in the hospital about 30 minutes after Mr. Kennedy died.

The details of what happened when shots first rang out, as the President's car moved along at about 25 miles an hour, were sketchy. Secret Service agents, who might have given more details, were unavailable to the press at first, and then returned to Washington with President Johnson.

Kennedys Hailed at Breakfast

Mr. Kennedy had opened his day in Fort Worth, first with a speech in a parking lot and then at a Chamber of Commerce breakfast. The breakfast appearance was a particular triumph for Mrs. Kennedy, who entered late and was given an ovation.

Then the Presidential party, including Governor and Mrs. Connally, flew on to Dallas, an eight-minute flight. Mr. Johnson, as is customary, flew in a separate plane. The President and the Vice President do not travel together, out of fear of a double tragedy.

At Love Field, Mr. and Mrs. Kennedy lingered for 10 minutes, shaking hands with an enthusiastic group lining the fence. The group called itself "Grassroots Democrats."

Mr. Kennedy then entered his open Lincoln convertible at the head of the motorcade. He sat in the rear seat on the right-hand side. Mrs. Kennedy, who appeared to be enjoying one of the first political outings she had ever made with her husband, sat at his left.

In the "jump" seat, directly ahead of Mr. Kennedy, sat Governor Connally, with Mrs. Connally at his left in another "jump" seat. A Secret Service agent was driving and the two others ran alongside.

Behind the President's limousine

was an open sedan carrying a number of Secret Service agents. Behind them, in an open convertible, rode Mr. and Mrs. Johnson and Texas's senior Senator, Ralph W. Yarborough, a Democrat.

The motorcade proceeded uneventfully along a 10-mile route through downtown Dallas, aiming for the Merchandise Mart. Mr. Kennedy was to address a group of the city's leading citizens at a luncheon in his honor.

In downtown Dallas, crowds were thick, enthusiastic and cheering. The turnout was somewhat unusual for this center of conservatism, where only a month ago Adlai E. Stevenson was attacked by a rightist crowd. It was also in Dallas, during the 1960 campaign, that Senator Lyndon B. Johnson and his wife were nearly mobbed in the lobby of the Baker Hotel.

As the motorcade neared its end and the President's car moved out of the thick crowds onto Stennonds Freeway near the Merchandise Mart, Mrs. Connally recalled later, "we were all very pleased with the reception in downtown Dallas."

Approaching 3-Street Underpass

Behind the three leading cars were a string of others carrying Texas and Dallas dignitaries, two buses of reporters, several open cars carrying photographers and other reporters, and a bus for White House staff members.

As Mrs. Connally recalled later, the President's car was almost ready to go underneath a "triple underpass beneath three streets—Elm, Commerce and Main—when the first shot was fired.

That shot apparently struck Mr. Kennedy. Governor Connally turned in his seat at the sound and appeared immediately to be hit in the chest.

Mrs. Mary Norman of Dallas was standing at the curb and at that moment was aiming her camera at the President. She saw him slump forward, then slide down in the seat.

"My God," Mrs. Norman screamed, as she recalled it later, "he's shot!"

Mrs. Connally said that Mrs. Kennedy had reached and "grabbed" her husband. Mrs. Connally put her arms around the Governor. Mrs. Connally said that she and Mrs. Kennedy had then ducked low in the car as it sped off.

Mrs. Connally's recollections were reported by Julian Reade, an aide to the Governor.

Most reporters in the press buses were too far back to see the shootings, but they observed some quick scurrying by motor policemen accompanying the motorcade. It was noted that the President's car had picked up speed and raced away, but reporters were not aware that anything serious had occurred until they reached the Merchandise Mart two or three minutes later.

Rumors Spread at Trade Mart

Rumors of the shooting already were spreading through the luncheon crowd of hundreds, which was having the first course. No White House officials or Secret Service agents were present, but the reporters were taken quickly to Parkland Hospital on the strength of the rumors.

There they encountered Senator Yarborough, white, shaken and horrified.

The shots, he said, seemed to have come from the right and the rear of the car in which he was riding, the third in the motorcade. Another eyewitness, Mel Crouch, a Dallas television reporter, reported that as the shots rang out he saw a rifle extended and then withdrawn from a window on the "fifth or sixth floor" of the Texas Public School Book Depository. This is a leased state building on Elm Street, to the right of the motorcade route.

Senator Yarborough said there had been a slight pause between the first two shots and a longer pause between the second and third. A Secret Service man riding in the Senator's car, the Senator said, immediately ordered Mr. and Mrs. Johnson to get down below the level of the doors. They did so, and Senator Yarborough also got down.

The leading cars of the motorcade then pulled away at high speed toward Parkland Hospital, which was not far away, by the fast highway.

"We knew by the speed that something was terribly wrong," Senator Yarborough reported. When he put his head up, he said, he saw a Secret Service man in the car ahead beating his fists against the trunk deck of the car in which he was riding, apparently in frustration and anguish.

Mrs. Kennedy's Reaction

Only White House staff members spoke with Mrs. Kennedy. A Dallas medical student, David Edwards, saw her in Parkland Hospital while she was waiting for news of her husband. He gave this description:

"The look in her eyes was like an animal that had been trapped, like a little rabbit—brave, but fear was in the eyes."

Dr. Clark was reported to have informed Mrs. Kennedy of her husband's death.

No witnesses reported seeing or hearing any of the Secret Service agents or policemen fire back. One agent was seen to brandish a machine gun as the cars sped away. Mr. Crouch observed a policeman falling to the ground and pulling a weapon. But the events had occurred so quickly that there was apparently nothing for the men to shoot at.

Mr. Crouch said he saw two women, standing at a curb to watch the motorcade pass, fall to the ground when the shots rang out. He also saw a man snatch up his little girl and run along the road. Policemen, he said, immediately chased this man under the impression he had been involved in the shooting, but Mr. Crouch said he had been a fleeing spectator.

Mr. Kennedy's limousine—license No. GG300 under District of Columbia registry—pulled up at the emergency entrance of Parkland Hospital. Senator Yarborough said the President had been carried inside on a stretcher.

Lyndon Johnson being sworn in on Air Force One with Mrs. Kennedy and Mrs. Johnson by his side. (Cecil Stoughton/John F. Kennedy Library)

By the time reporters arrived at the hospital, the police were guarding the Presidential car. They would allow no one to approach it. A bucket of water stood by the car, suggesting that the back seat had been scrubbed out.

Robert Clark of the American Broadcasting Company, who had been riding near the front of the motorcade, said Mr. Kennedy was motionless when he was carried inside. There was a great amount of blood on Mr. Kennedy's suit and shirtfront and the front of his body. Mrs. Kennedy was leaning over her husband when the car stopped, Mr. Clark said, and she walked beside the stretcher into the hospital. Mr. Connally sat with his hands holding his stomach, his head bent over. He, too, was moved into the hospital in a stretcher, with Mrs. Connally at his side.

Robert McNeill of the National Broadcasting Company, who also was in the reporters' pool car, jumped out at the scene of the shooting. He said the police had taken two eyewitnesses into custody—an 8-year-old Negro boy and a white man—for informational purposes.

Many of these reports could not be verified immediately.

Eyewitness Describes Shooting

An unidentified Dallas man, interviewed on television here, said he had been waving at the President when the shots were fired. His belief was that Mr. Kennedy had been struck twice—once, as Mrs. Norman recalled, when he slumped in his seat; again when he slid down in it.

"It seemed to just knock him down," the man said.

Governor Connally's condition was reported as "satisfactory" tonight after four hours in surgery at Parkland Hospital.

Later, Dr. Shaw said Governor Connally had been hit in the back just below the shoulder blade, and that the bullet had gone completely through the Governor's chest, taking out part of the fifth rib.

After leaving the body, he said, the bullet struck the Governor's right wrist, causing a compound fracture. It then lodged in the left thigh.

Dr. Shaw said it would be unwise for Governor Connally to be moved in the next 10 to 14 days. Mrs. Connally was remaining at his side tonight.

Tour by Mrs. Kennedy Unusual

Mrs. Kennedy's presence near her husband's bedside at his death resulted from somewhat unusual circumstances. She had rarely accompanied him on his trips about the country and had almost never made political trips with him.

The tour on which Mr. Kennedy was engaged yesterday and today was only quasi-political; the only open political activity was to have been a speech tonight to a fund-raising dinner at the state capitol in Austin.

In visiting Texas, Mr. Kennedy was seeking to improve his political fortunes in a pivotal state that he barely won in 1960. He was also hoping to patch a bitter internal dispute among Texas's Democrats.

At 8:45 A.M., when Mr. Kennedy left the Texas Hotel in Fort Worth, where he spent his last night, to address the parking lot crowd across the street, Mrs. Kennedy was not with him. There appeared to be some disappointment.

"Mrs. Kennedy is organizing herself," the President said good-naturedly. "It takes longer, but, of course, she looks better than we do when she does it."

Later, Mrs. Kennedy appeared late at the Chamber of Commerce breakfast in Fort Worth.

Again, Mr. Kennedy took note of her presence. "Two years ago," he said, "I introduced myself in Paris by saying that I was the man who had accompanied Mrs. Kennedy to Paris. I am getting somewhat that same sensation as I travel around Texas. Nobody wonders what Lyndon and I wear."

The speech Mr. Kennedy never delivered at the Merchandise Mart luncheon contained a passage commenting on a recent preoccupation of his, and a subject of much interest in this city, where right-wing conservatism is the rule rather than the exception.

Voices are being heard in the land, he said, "voices preaching doctrines wholly unrelated to reality, wholly un-suited to the sixties, doctrines which apparently assume that words will suffice without weapons, that vituperation is as good as victory and that peace is a sign of weakness."

The speech went on: "At a time when the national debt is steadily being reduced in terms of its burden on our economy, they see that debt as the greatest threat to our security. At a time when we are steadily reducing the number of Federal employees serving every thousand citizens, they fear those supposed hordes of civil servants far more than the actual hordes of opposing armies.

"We cannot expect that everyone, to use the phrase of a decade ago, will 'talk sense to the American people.' But we can hope that fewer people will listen to nonsense. And the notion that this nation is headed for defeat through deficit, or that strength is but a matter of slogans, is nothing but just plain nonsense."

Jacqueline Kennedy, her skirt and stockings soaked in blood, arrives at Andrews Air Force Base. (Bettmann/Corbis/Associated Press)

"All the News That's Fit to Print"

The New York Times.

LATE CITY EDITION
U. S. Weather Bureau Report (Page 58) Forecast:
Cloudy, windy, chance of showers
today and tonight. Cold tomorrow.
Temp. Range: 62—54; yesterday: 64—51.

VOL. CXIII. No. 38,654. © 1963 by The New York Times Company. Times Square, New York 36, N. Y.   NEW YORK, SATURDAY, NOVEMBER 23, 1963.   TEN CENTS

KENNEDY IS KILLED BY SNIPER AS HE RIDES IN CAR IN DALLAS; JOHNSON SWORN IN ON PLANE

TEXAN ASKS UNITY

Congressional Chiefs of 2 Parties Give Promise of Aid

By FELIX BELAIR Jr.
Special to The New York Times
WASHINGTON, Nov. 22 — Lyndon B. Johnson returned to a stunned capital this evening to assume the duties of the Presidency.

The new President asked for and received from Congressional leaders of both parties their "united support in the face of the tragedy which has befallen our country." He said it was "more essential than ever before that this country be united."

Partisan differences disappeared in the chorus of assurances with which the Congressional leaders responded.

Mr. Johnson was described by those who talked with him as "stunned and shaken" by the assassination of President Kennedy.

Discusses U.S. Security

But he moved quickly from problems of national security and foreign policy to funeral arrangements for Mr. Kennedy.

Across the street from the West Wing of the White House, the President conferred with officials in his old Vice Presidential offices in the Executive Office Building.

Senator George A. Smathers, Democrat of Florida, a personal friend of the dead President, was one of those who described Mr. Johnson as shaken.

"Everyone is," he added. "But the President is the more so because he was right there when the tragedy occurred."

While flying to Washington aboard the Presidential plane, Mr. Johnson arranged for a meeting with Cabinet members to ask that they remain at their posts. He made the request of staff members in the executive offices.

Meets With Harriman

"Calm and contained" was the way Senator J. W. Fulbright described the President's manner during a discussion of foreign-policy matters with Under Secretary of State W. Averell Harriman. The Arkansas Senator said the President had been working on "what looked like a statement"—presumably an assurance of continuity of the nation's foreign policy.

The new President's first conference was aboard the helicopter that flew him the 15 miles from Andrews Air Force Base

Continued on Page 11, Column 3

Henry Grossman
"This is a sad time for all people. We have suffered a loss that cannot be weighed. For me it is a deep personal tragedy. I know the world shares the sorrow that Mrs. Kennedy and her family bear. I will do my best. That is all I can do. I ask for your help —and God's."—President Lyndon Baines Johnson.

PRESIDENT'S BODY WILL LIE IN STATE

Funeral Mass to Be Monday in Capital After Homage Is Paid by the Public

By JACK RAYMOND
Special to The New York Times
WASHINGTON, Saturday, Nov. 23—The body of John F. Kennedy will lie in state in the rotunda of the Capitol tomorrow and then will be borne to St. Matthew's Roman Catholic Cathedral for a pontifical requiem mass at noon Monday.

The President's body was returned to Washington yesterday in the same Air Force jet that carried him to Texas Thursday. The plane, with Mrs. Kennedy, the new President, Lyndon B. Johnson, and Mrs. Johnson aboard, arrived at Andrews Air Force Base at about 6 P.M.

It was announced later that Mr. Kennedy's body would lie in the East Room of the White House today from 10 A.M. to 6 P.M., during which time Government and diplomatic officials will pay their respects.

The coffin will be taken from the White House to the Capitol rotunda tomorrow morning,

Continued on Page 9, Column 3

PARTIES' OUTLOOK FOR '64 CONFUSED

Republican Prospects Rise —Johnson Faces Possible Fight Against Liberals

By WARREN WEAVER Jr.
Special to The New York Times
WASHINGTON, Nov. 22 — President Kennedy's assassination threw the American political scene into turmoil today.

It removed at a single blow the man who would have been nominated for a second term in the White House by acclamation nine months from now.

It elevated into the Presidency and the leadership of the Democratic party an older, more conservative man still emerging from his Southern heritage.

It increased immeasurably for the leaders of the Republican party the prospects of electing a President next November.

The shock of the President's death stilled the official voices of politics in the capital. But so profound was the potential effect on the Government and leadership that private consideration could not be silenced.

Before, there had been facts and strong probabilities on the

Continued on Page 6, Column 3

LEFTIST ACCUSED

Figure in a Pro-Castro Group Is Charged— Policeman Slain

By GLADWIN HILL
Special to The New York Times
DALLAS, Saturday, Nov. 23 —Lee Harvey Oswald, a 24-year-old warehouse worker who once lived in the Soviet Union, was charged late last night with assassinating President Kennedy.

Oswald was arrested at 2:15 yesterday afternoon, nearly two hours after the assassination of the President, as the suspected killer of a policeman on the street in the Oak Cliff district, three miles from where the President was shot.

Chief of Police Jesse Curry announced that Oswald had been formally arraigned at 1:40 A.M., Central standard time, today on a charge of murder in the President's death. The arraignment was made before a justice of the peace in the homicide bureau at Police Headquarters.

Capt. Will Fritz, head of the homicide bureau, identified Oswald as an adherent of the left-wing "Fair Play for Cuba Committee." But there were also reports that Oswald, apparently politically erratic, had once tried to join anti-Castro forces.

Worked in Warehouse

Oswald was employed in the Texas School Book Depository, the warehouse from which the fatal shots were fired at the President's car.

The police said at least six witnesses placed Oswald in the building at the time of the assassination.

One was quoted as saying that Oswald had stayed behind on an upper floor when other employes went down to the street to see Mr. Kennedy pass by.

The defendant's only comment, shouted at reporters as he was led handcuffed through a police building corridor to be questioned, was "I haven't shot anybody." "He has not con-

Continued on Page 4, Column 1

NEWS INDEX

	Page		Page
Art	24-25	Music	22-23
Books	27	Obituaries	22-23
Bridge	28	Screen	22-23
Business	36, 44	Ships and Air	58
Churches	21	Society	32
Crossword	27	Sports	33-35
Editorial	28	Theaters	22-23
Financial	36-44	U. N. Proceedings	25
Food	20	Wash. Proceedings	30
Letters	28	Weather	58

News Summary and Index, Page 31

John Fitzgerald Kennedy
1917-1963
Henry Grossman

Why America Weeps

Kennedy Victim of Violent Streak He Sought to Curb in the Nation

By JAMES RESTON
WASHINGTON, Nov. 22—America wept tonight, not alone for its dead young President, but for itself. The grief was general, for somehow the worst in the nation had prevailed over the best. The indictment extended beyond the assassin, for something in the nation itself, some strain of madness and violence, had destroyed the highest symbol of law and order.

Speaker John McCormack, now 71 and, by the peculiarities of our politics, next in line of succession after the Vice President, expressed this sense of national dismay and self-criticism:

"My God! My God! What are we coming to?"

The irony of the President's death is that his short Administration was devoted almost entirely to various attempts to curb this very streak of violence in the American character.

When the historians get around to assessing his three years in office, it is very likely that they will be impressed with just this: his efforts to restrain those who wanted to be more violent in the cold war overseas

City Goes Dark

By ROBERT C. DOTY
Shock and sorrow for the murdered President darkened and silenced midtown Manhattan last night.

In early afternoon, when the first radio and television bulletins carried the news, the city began its mourning. By nightfall, the normal quick Friday night pace had slowed as near to a halt as it ever comes.

Many of the city's normal weekend commercial, social and sporting activities were canceled. Decisions for closings by many stores and other businesses were being debated.

Courts closed in the middle of hearings yesterday. Hundreds of public and private social functions and sporting events were interrupted or postponed. Most midtown legitimate and motion picture theaters, night clubs and dance halls locked

Continued on Page 5, Column 2
Continued on Page 7, Column 6

Gov. Connally Shot; Mrs. Kennedy Safe

President Is Struck Down by a Rifle Shot From Building on Motorcade Route— Johnson, Riding Behind, Is Unhurt

By TOM WICKER
Special to The New York Times
DALLAS, Nov. 22—President John Fitzgerald Kennedy was shot and killed by an assassin today.

He died of a wound in the brain caused by a rifle bullet that was fired at him as he was riding through downtown Dallas in a motorcade.

Vice President Lyndon Baines Johnson, who was riding in the third car behind Mr. Kennedy's, was sworn in as the 36th President of the United States 99 minutes after Mr. Kennedy's death.

Mr. Johnson is 55 years old; Mr. Kennedy was 46.

Shortly after the assassination, Lee H. Oswald, who once defected to the Soviet Union and who has been active in the Fair Play for Cuba Committee, was arrested by the Dallas police. Tonight he was accused of the killing.

Suspect Captured After Scuffle

Oswald, 24 years old, was also accused of slaying a policeman who had approached him in the street. Oswald was subdued after a scuffle with a second policeman in a nearby theater.

President Kennedy was shot at 12:30 P.M., Central standard time (1:30 P.M., New York time). He was pronounced dead at 1 P.M. and Mr. Johnson was sworn in at 2:39 P.M.

Mr. Johnson, who was uninjured in the shooting, took his oath in the Presidential jet plane as it stood on the runway at Love Field. The body of Mr. Kennedy was aboard. Immediately after the oath-taking, the plane took off for Washington.

Standing beside the new President as Mr. Johnson took the oath of office was Mrs. John F. Kennedy. Her stockings were spattered with her husband's blood.

Gov. John B. Connally Jr. of Texas, who was riding in the same car with Mr. Kennedy, was severely wounded in the chest, ribs and arm. His condition was serious, but not critical.

The killer fired the rifle from a building just off the motorcade route. Mr. Kennedy,

Continued on Page 2

Capt. Cecil Stoughton via United Press International
THE NEW PRESIDENT: Lyndon B. Johnson takes oath before Judge Sarah T. Hughes in plane at Dallas. Mrs. Kennedy and Representative Jack Brooks are at right. To left are Mrs. Johnson and Representative Albert Thomas.

Associated Press
WHEN THE BULLETS STRUCK: Mrs. Kennedy moving to the aid of the President after he was hit by a sniper yesterday in Dallas. A guard mounts rear bumper. Gov. John B. Connally Jr. of Texas, also in the car, was wounded.

LEFTIST ACCUSED

Figure in a Pro-Castro Group Is Charged—Policeman Slain

By GLADWIN HILL

DALLAS, Saturday, Nov. 23—Lee Harvey Oswald, a 24-year-old warehouse worker who once lived in the Soviet Union, was charged late last night with assassinating President Kennedy.

Oswald was arrested at 2:15 yesterday afternoon, nearly two hours after the assassination of the President, as the suspected killer of a policeman on the street in the Oak Cliff district, three miles from where the President was shot.

Chief of Police Jesse Curry announced that Oswald had been formally arraigned at 1:40 A.M., Central standard time, today on a charge of murder in the President's death. The arraignment was made before a justice of the peace in the homicide bureau at Police Headquarters.

Capt. Will Fritz, head of the homicide bureau, identified Oswald as an adherent of the left-wing "Fair Play for Cuba Committee." But there were also reports that Oswald, apparently politically erratic, had once tried to join anti-Castro forces.

Worked in Warehouse

Oswald was employed in the Texas School Book Depository, the warehouse from which the fatal shots were fired at the President's car.

The police said at least six witnesses placed Oswald in the building at the time of the assassination.

One was quoted as saying that Oswald had stayed behind on an upper floor when other employees went down to the street to see Mr. Kennedy pass by.

The defendant's only comment, shouted at reporters as he was led handcuffed through a police building corridor to be questioned, was "I haven't shot anybody." "He has not confessed," Chief Curry said. "Physical evidence is the main thing we have."

He murmured seeming assent to a suggestion that such evidence included the assassination gun.

Fingerprint experts had been conspicuous in the procession of officers into and out of the homicide bureau during the afternoon and evening. They included agents of the Secret Service and the Federal Bureau of Investigation, who collaborated with city, county and state law enforcement officers in investigating the crime.

Three and a half hours before Chief Curry's announcement, Oswald had been arraigned on a charge of murder in the death of the policeman, J. D. Tippitt.

Dallas County District Attorney Henry Wade said there were "a few loose ends" in the case to be wrapped up, and he expected that the case would not go to the grand jury before next week.

Oswald faces a death sentence if convicted.

Appears in Line-Up

After the arraignment, the suspect, a slight, dark-haired man, was taken downstairs to appear in a line-up, presumably before witnesses of the Kennedy assassination.

The sequence of events leading to his arrest was as follows:

As a citywide manhunt began during the hour following the assassination, an unidentified man notified police headquarters, over a police-car radio, that the car's officer had been shot and killed. The car was in the 400 block of East Jefferson Boulevard in the Oak Cliff section, on the edge of the downtown area.

The car's driver, Patrolman Tippitt, had not made any call that he was going to question anyone.

Eight other officers converged on the spot. They found Patrolman Tippitt lying on the sidewalk, dead from two .38-caliber bullet wounds.

They began a search of nearby buildings for the killer.

Then another call came to police headquarters from Julie Postal, cashier of the Texas Theatre at 231 West Jefferson Boulevard, six blocks from the scene of the policeman's slaying.

She said an usher had told her than a man who had just entered the theater was acting peculiarly.

The investigating police officers were dispatched to theater. They began checking patrons, starting at the front of the house.

One of the officers, Sgt. Jerry Hill, said that when they came to Oswald, sitting in the rear four seats in from the aisle, the suspect jumped up and exclaimed: "This is it!"

The Dallas Police Department appeared to be the nerve center of the overall investigation of the President's death, although the various lines this might be taking were not defined.

State Has Jurisdiction

The Justice of the Peace before whom Oswald was arraigned, David Johnston, said the assassination was a matter of state jurisdiction so far.

Little was known here about Oswald, except reports published locally in 1959 when he went to the Soviet Union after his discharge from the Marine Corps.

He was said to have tried to renounce his United States citizenship by turning in his passport to the United States Embassy in Moscow. The Embassy, it was reported then, advised him to hold on to it until he had some

Lee Harvey Oswald shortly after his arrest just hours after the assassination.
(Associated Press)

assurance of Soviet citizenship. He was reported to have worked in factories in the Soviet and to have married a Russian girl.

At the time of his quasi-defection, his mother and his brother, a milkman in nearby Forth Worth, sent messages vainly trying to dissuade him.

Shortly after he was escorted from his arraignment last night, a tall, slender women with a little girl about 2 years old and baby in her arms left the homicide bureau. An officer said they were the suspect's wife and daughter.

A housekeeper at Oswald's rooming house said the young man entered his room shortly after the shooting of the President, got a coat, and went back out.

The housekeeper, Mrs. Earlene Roberts, said:

"He came in in a hurry in his shirt sleeves and I said, 'Oh, you're in a hurry,' and he didn't say anything. He went on in his room and got a coat and put it on. He went out to the bus stop and that's the last I saw of him."

Mrs. Roberts said Oswald rushed into the rooming house, at 1026 North Beckley Road in suburban Oak Cliff. This was shortly after Mrs. Roberts had learned, in a telephone call from a friend, that the President had been shot. She said she had not connected Oswald's appearance with the shooting.

She described Oswald, who had lived in the house since the end of October, as quiet.

Justice of the Peace Johnston said he was one of four from outlying communities, assembled for the Kennedy visit, who had been recruited to assist law enforcement officers with the inquiry.

Judge Johnston said Judge Theron Ward had been assigned to the President's death and Judge Joe B. Brown Jr. to the death of the policeman. Judge Johnston and Judge Lloyd Russell were assisting in such matters as the issuance of search warrants and handling the arraignment.

The arraignment involved no plea. Oswald was held without bail for grand jury action and was advised of his rights to counsel.

Captain Fritz emerged from the homicide bureau after the arraignment and said: "We've charged this man with the killing of the officer."

Asked whether Oswald had been linked with the assassination, the officer replied: "He doesn't admit it—we have some more work to do on that case."

The revolver carried by Oswald in the theater was not suspected of having figured in President Kennedy's death.

Police ballistics experts were still studying, with apparently no conclusive findings, the rifle found in the book warehouse.

Captain Fritz said it was of obscure foreign origin, possibly Italian, of about 1940 vintage, and of an unusual, undetermined caliber. He displayed a bullet he said fitted the gun. It was about .30 caliber and about two and one-half inches long, with a narrow tapered nose.

Sergeant Hill said Oswald had a .38-caliber revolver under his shirt, and that in a scuffle that ensued, it was fired once, harmlessly. The time was 2:15 P.M. yesterday.

Oswald was subdued, handcuffed, rushed to downtown police headquarters and put in a fifth-floor cell.

At 6:35 P.M. he was taken down to the third-floor homicide bureau. He wore black slacks, black loafer shoes, a white undershirt and an olive plaid sport shirt, unbuttoned.

His left eye was slightly blackened, and there was a contusion on his right cheekbone.

Why America Weeps

Kennedy Victim of Violent Streak He Sought to Curb in the Nation

―――――

By JAMES RESTON

WASHINGTON, Nov. 22—America wept tonight, not alone for its dead young President, but for itself. The grief was general, for somehow the worst in the nation had prevailed over the best. The indictment extended beyond the assassin, for something in the nation itself, some strain of madness and violence, had destroyed the highest symbol of law and order.

Speaker John McCormack, now 71 and, by the peculiarities of our politics, next in line of succession after the Vice President, expressed this sense of national dismay and self-criticism:

"My God! My God! What are we coming to?"

The irony of the President's death is that his short Administration was devoted almost entirely to various attempts to curb this very streak of violence in the American character.

When the historians get around to assessing his three years in office, it is very likely that they will be impressed with just this: his efforts to restrain those who wanted to be more violent in the cold war overseas and those who wanted to be more violent in the racial war at home.

He was in Texas today trying to pacify the violent politics of that state. He was in Florida last week trying to pacify the businessmen and appealing to them to believe that he was not "anti-business." And from the beginning to the end of his Administration, he was trying to damp down the violence of the extremists on the Right.

It was his fate, however, to reach the White House in a period of violent change, when all nations and institutions found themselves uprooted from the past. His central theme was the necessity of adjusting to change and this brought him into conflict with those who opposed change.

Thus, while his personal instinct was to avoid violent conflict, to compromise and mediate and pacify, his programs for taxation, for racial equality, for medical care, for Cuba, all raised sharp divisions with the country. And even where his policies of adjustment had their greatest success—in relations with the Soviet Union—he was bitterly condemned.

The President somehow always seemed to be suspended between two worlds—between his ideal conception of what a President should be, what the office called for, and a kind of despairing realization of the practical limits upon his power.

He came into office convinced of the truth of Theodore Roosevelt's view of the President's duties—"the President is bound to be as big a man as he can."

And his Inaugural—"now the trumpet summons us again"—stirred an echo of Wilson in 1913 when the latter said: "We have made up our minds to square every process of our national life with the standards we so proudly set up at the beginning and have always carried at our hearts."

This is what the President set out to do. And from his reading, from his intellectual approach to the office, it seemed, if not easy, at least possible.

But the young man who came to office with an assurance vicariously imparted from reading Richard Neustadt's "Presidential Power" soon discovered the two truths which all dwellers on that lonely eminence have quickly learned.

The first was that the powers of the President are not only limited but hard to bring to bear. The second was that the decisions—as he himself so often said—"are not easy."

What He Set Out to Do

Since he was never one to hide his feelings, he often betrayed the mood brought on by contemplating the magnitude of the job and its disappointments. He grew fond of quoting Lord Morley's dictum—"Politics is one long second-best, where the choice often lies between two blunders."

Did he have a premonition of tragedy—that he who had set out to temper the contrary violences of our national life would be their victim?

Last June, when the civil rights riots were at their height and passions were flaring, he spoke to a group of representatives of national organizations. He tolled off the problems that beset him on every side and then, to the astonishment of everyone there, concluded his talk by pulling from his pocket a scrap of paper and reading the famous speech of Blanche of Spain in Shakespeare's "King John":

> *The sun's o'ercast with blood:*
> *Fair day, adieu!*
> *Which is the side that I must go withal?*
> *I am with both; each army hath a hand,*
> *And in their rage, I having hold of both,*
> *They whirl asunder and dismember me.*

There is, however, consolation in the fact that while he was not given time to finish anything or even to realize his own potentialities, he has not left the nation in a state of crisis or danger, either in its domestic or foreign affairs.

World More Tolerable

A reasonable balance of power has been established on all continents. The state of truce in Korea, the Taiwan Strait, Vietnam and Berlin is, if anything, more tolerable than when he came to office.

Europe and Latin America were increasingly dubious of his leadership at the end, but their capacity to indulge in independent courses of action outside the alliance was largely due to the fact that he had managed to reach a somewhat better adjustment of relations with the Soviet Union.

Thus, President Johnson is not confronted immediately by having to take any urgent new decisions. The passage of power from one man to another is more difficult in other countries, and Britain, Germany, Italy, India and several other allies are so preoccupied by that task at the moment that drastic new policy initiatives overseas are scarcely possible in the foreseeable future.

At home, his tasks lie in the Congress, where he is widely regarded as the most skillful man of his generation. This city is in a state of shock tonight and everywhere, including Capitol Hill, men are of a mind to compose their differences and do what they can to help the new President.

Accordingly, the assumption that there will be no major agreements on taxes or civil rights this year will probably have to be revived. It is, of course, too early to tell. But it is typical and perhaps significant that the new President's first act was to greet the Congressional leaders of both parties when he arrived in Washington and to meet with them at once in the White House.

Today's events were so tragic and so brutal that even this city, which lives on the brutal diet of politics, could not bear to think much about the political consequences of the assassination.

Yet it is clear that the entire outlook has changed for both parties, and the unexpected death of President Kennedy has forced Washington to meditate a little more on the wild element of chance in our national life.

This was quietly in the back of many minds tonight, mainly because President Johnson has sustained a severe heart attack, and the constitutional line of succession places directly back of him, first Speaker McCormack, and then the president Pro Tempore of the Senate, 86-year-old Senator Carl Hayden of Arizona.

Again a note of self-criticism and conscience has touched the capital. Despite the severe illnesses of President Eisenhower just a few years ago, nothing was done by the Congress to deal with the problem of Presidential disability.

The President somehow always seemed to be suspended between two worlds— between his ideal conception of what a President should be, [and] what the office called for . . .

For an all too brief hour today, it was not clear again what would have happened if the young President, instead of being mortally wounded, had lingered for a long time between life and death, strong enough to survive but too weak to govern.

These, however, were fleeting thoughts, important but irritating for the moment. The center of the mind was on the dead President, on his wife, who has now lost both a son and a husband within a few months, and on his family which, despite all its triumphs, has sustained so many personal tragedies since the last war.

He was, even to his political enemies, a wonderfully attractive human being, and it is significant that, unlike many Presidents in the past, the people who liked and respected him best were those who knew him the best.

He was a rationalist and an intellectual, who proved in the 1960 campaign and in last year's crisis over Cuba that he was at his best when the going was tough. No doubt he would have been re-elected, as most one-term Presidents are, and the subtle dualism of his character would have had a longer chance to realize his dream.

But he is gone now at 46, younger than when most Presidents have started on the great adventure. In his book, "Profiles in Courage," all his heroes faced the hard choice either of giving in to public opinion or of defying it and becoming martyrs.

He had hoped to avoid this bitter dilemma, but he ended as a martyr anyway, and the nation is sad tonight, both about him and about itself.

There is one final tragedy about today: Kennedy had a sense of history, but he also had an administrative technique that made the gathering of history extremely difficult. He hated organized meetings of the Cabinet or the National Security Council, and therefore he chose to decide policy after private meetings, usually with a single person.

The result of this is that the true history of his Administration really cannot be written now that he is gone.

He had a joke about this. When he was asked what he was going to do when he retired, he always replied that he had a problem. It was, he said, that he would have to race two other members of his staff, McGeorge Bundy and Arthur Schlesinger Jr., to the press.

Unfortunately, however, he was the only man in the White House who really knew what went on there during his Administration, and now he is gone.

---

*Opposite page:
Jacqueline Kennedy leaves the
U.S. Capitol building with her children
John and Caroline after attending a
ceremony for John F. Kennedy.*
(National Archive/Newsmakers/Getty Images)

GRIEVING THRONGS VIEW KENNEDY BIER; CROWD IS HUSHED

Mourners at Capitol File Past the Coffin Far Into the Night

By TOM WICKER

WASHINGTON, Nov. 25—Thousands of sorrowing Americans filed past John Fitzgerald Kennedy's bier in the Great Rotunda of the United States Capitol yesterday and early today.

Mr. Kennedy's body lay in state in the center of the vast, stone-floored chamber. Long after midnight the silent procession of mourners continued.

Some wept. All were hushed. As the two lines moved in a large circle around either side of the flag-covered coffin, almost the only sounds were the shuffle of feet and the quiet voices of policemen urging the people to "keep moving, keep moving right along."

By 2:45 A. M. today 115,000 persons had passed the bier.

Yesterday afternoon a crowd estimated at 300,000 lined Pennsylvania and Constitution Avenues to watch the passage of the caisson bearing the body of the 35th President of the United States, slain in the 47th year of his life by an assassin's bullet.

A Riderless Horse

Behind the caisson, following military tradition, came a riderless bay gelding, with a pair of military boots reversed in the silver stirrups.

The horse was Sardar, the thoroughbred that belongs to Mrs. John F. Kennedy.

Mrs. Kennedy, her two children, President and Mrs. Johnson and Mr. Kennedy's brother, Attorney General Robert F. Kennedy, rode in the first car of a 10-car procession that followed the caisson.

The procession moved at a funeral pace, to the sound of muffled drums, from the White House to Pennsylvania Avenue. It was a journey Mr. Kennedy had made formally four times.

At the Capitol, brief ceremonies of eulogy were held in the Rotunda before the admission of the waiting thousands who swarmed over the plaza and stretched in a long line up East Capitol Street.

At the conclusion of the ceremonies, Mrs. Kennedy and her daughter, Caroline, stepped a few feet forward. Each reached out and touched the flag and the coffin it covered.

Mrs. Kennedy knelt, kissed the coffin, then rose and led her daughter away.

President Johnson had already come forward, following a soldier who walked backward carrying a wreath of red and white carnations. As the soldier placed the wreath at the foot of the coffin, the man who had taken Mr. Kennedy's place in office stood with his head bowed, then withdrew.

The wreath was marked "From President Johnson and the Nation." Numbers of other wreaths and sprays, sent despite White House requests that flowers be omitted, were arranged in nearby rooms.

After a short interval, during which workers of the Senate and the House of Representatives and their guests were admitted to the Rotunda from the North and South Wings of the Capitol, the great central doors of the Capitol were thrown open to the people.

Across the East Plaza in long, silent lines, they came—patient, quiet, thousands upon thousands of them. They moved slowly up the towering marble steps, above which, on Jan. 20, 1961, a platform had been built for the Inaugural of John F. Kennedy as President of the United States.

As they entered the Rotunda, they formed two lines, each moving in a great semi-circle around the Rotunda. Only red velvet ropes and 25 feet of stone floor separated them from the catafalque upon which rested Mr. Kennedy's coffin.

Long after midnight the silent procession of mourners continued . . .

Enlisted men from each of the armed services stood motionless at the four corners of the catafalque. As the guard changed every half hour, first an Army officer, then a Marine Corps officer, then an officer of the Navy and the Air Force took up his position at the head of the coffin. They rotated command of the guard through the night.

Behind the commander, a sailor held the flag of the President. To the sailor's right stood an unattended American flag.

Footprints on Catafalque

Yesterday afternoon the dusty footprints of the military men who had placed the coffin upon the catafalque were still visible on the catafalque's black velvet drapings. At each side of the coffin were sprays of chrysanthemums and white lilies.

That simple scene was all the people saw as they filed past—the coffin covered with its flag, the motionless guards, the two listless flags upon their standards, the traditional flowers of death.

The police were nearly overwhelmed by a crowd far beyond their expectations. Within the Rotunda, however, all was order and silence. The lines moved rapidly around the circle—about 35 persons a minute in each line—and were directed out the west door to the wide porch that overlooks the Mall and the Washington Monument.

Outside, virtually the whole Metropolitan police force was on duty. At 4:30 P.M., the lines of those waiting to get in the Capitol stretched across the East Plaza back and six blocks past the Supreme Court building on East Capitol Street.

At 9 P.M. the waiting line stretched for 30 blocks, with four to six persons abreast. And the line was growing, as people joined it faster than it moved through the Rotunda.

Thousands Turn Back

Originally, it had been planned to close the Capitol's doors at 9 P.M., reopening the Rotunda for an hour this morning. When the size of the crowds became apparent, it was decided to keep it open as long as people came.

Thousands were giving up late yesterday, however, under the impression that the doors would be closed by the time they reached the Rotunda. Families from as far away as Baltimore and Richmond left without having gotten near the Capitol.

However, millions throughout the county were watching on television. The brilliant lights needed for the cameras played steadily on the Rotunda and broadcasters spoke constantly in low monotones into their microphones.

President Lyndon Johnson placing a wreath at the coffin of President Kennedy in the Capitol Rotunda. (Abbie Rowe/John F. Kennedy Library)

Across the wide lawns and the paved drives of the Capitol Plaza, the people coming and going swarmed like ants. Most were good-natured. There was little pushing and shoving, and no fighting was observed. But confusion was constant as people tried to find out how to get into line, how long it was and how to get out of the jammed plaza.

Even Mrs. Kennedy was inconvenienced by the crowds in the plaza. When she left the Capitol, in a limousine with her children and Attorney General Kennedy, her planned route along Independence Avenue was impassable. She was rerouted over other streets, led by a motorcycle escort.

Throughout yesterday among the throngs that watched the procession and those that jammed around the Capitol, there were few evidences of open emotionalism. Not many people wept, or cried out. The mood was rather one of sorrow and respect.

Even among teen-agers, of whom thousands and thousands seemed to be present, there was quiet. People passing through the Rotunda were told that no photographs were to be taken; only a few, looking somewhat furtive, broke the restriction.

The police said some persons began lining up at midnight Saturday. Yesterday morning, hours before the procession began, crowds began to form along the streets and in Lafayette Square across Pennsylvania Avenue from the White House.

A half-hour before the procession began, the news reached the White House that Lee H. Oswald, charged with the murder of Mr. Kennedy in Dallas on Friday, had been shot down in that city.

Among the crowds many had transistor radios, and the news from Dallas swept rapidly. It was a constant subject of conversation in the crowd, and one gray-haired woman, seated on a bench in Lafayette Square, told her husband: "I told you last night, Henry, I had a feeling something like this would happen. That man held so many secrets, some one had to kill him."

Another woman exclaimed: "My God, how long will this go on?"

On the lawn before the north portico of the White House, a small crowd of White House employees and workers in the Executive Office Building was permitted to assemble. The circular drive in front of the mansion was lined, shortly after noon, with black limousines. Near the northeast gate, an honor guard and the bearers of flags of all the states were lined up.

At 12:40 P.M., President and Mrs. Johnson arrived at the north portico and entered the black-draped doors of the building that will now be their home. Shortly thereafter, the empty caisson, draped in black and drawn by six gray horses, came up the drive and stopped under the portico.

It was the same caisson upon which the body of Franklin D. Roosevelt was carried from the White House to the Capitol in 1945.

Behind it was Sardar. The horse had been given to Mrs. Kennedy in March, 1962, by President Ayub Khan of Pakistan when she visited that country. The White House said Mrs. Kennedy had requested that the horse be used as the traditional symbol of a fallen warrior. A black-handled sword hung in a silver scabbard from the saddle.

Eight enlisted men of the various armed services carried the coffin out onto the north portico, down the few steps and placed it on the caisson. The military aides moved to the front. The caisson pulled slowly away, followed by the black horse. And a limousine slid into place at the foot of the steps.

Mrs. Kennedy, in black and wearing a black mantilla, came out, holding Caroline and John Jr. by the hand. The children were dressed in identical shades of blue. The three entered the car and 2-year-old John Jr., apparently unaware of the nature of the occasion, bounced up on the seat and peered out the rear window.

Attorney General Kennedy followed them into the car. President and Mrs. Johnson took the jump seats, and the limousine pulled away.

In rapid order, other limousines drove up to the steps and were filled. In the second car were Mr. Kennedy's sisters Patricia and Jean, and their husbands, Peter Lawford and Stephen E. Smith. In the third were Mrs. Kennedy's stepfather and mother; Mr. and Mrs. Hugh D. Auchincloss, and others of the Auchincloss family.

Mrs. Robert Kennedy, several of her children, and Sargent Shriver, the husband of the former Eunice Kennedy, were in the next car. Mrs. Shriver, her mother, Mrs. Rose Kennedy, and Senator Edward M. Kennedy, the youngest brother, were flying to Washington from Hyannis Port, Mass., and were not in the procession.

A number of employees of the Kennedy family and the White House rode in another car.

Other cars with officials, security agents and policemen joined the line. As the procession moved slowly onto Pennsylvania Avenue, turned briefly on 15th Street, and then rounded on to the long straight stretch of Pennsylvania that reaches from the Treasury Building to the Capitol, the line was about two city blocks long.

Joint Chiefs March

In advance of the caisson, on foot, were policemen, the escort commander—Maj. Gen. Philip C. Wehle of the Military District of Washington—five military drummers, a drum major and a company of Navy enlisted men. They walked at funeral pace; 100 paces a minute.

Behind them was a special honor guard composed of the Joint Chiefs of Staff led by their chairman, Gen. Maxwell D. Taylor, and followed by Mr. Kennedy's military aides.

The national colors immediately preceded the caisson. Between it and the car carrying Mrs. Kennedy and President Johnson, there were personal flags, the marching body bearers, and the riderless Sardar. Three clergymen also marched in the procession.

Crowds lined the entire route at least 10 deep, and twice that thick at some places. Others stretched up the side streets, hung from windows of buildings along the street, lined open-tiered parking buildings and mounted the pedestals of the street's numerous statues.

At 25-foot intervals, soldiers with fixed bayonets lined the street on each side, standing at parade rest.

For the first few blocks, the crowds stood silently, almost unmoving, as each element of the procession passed. As at the Capitol later, there were few evidences of emotionalism—very little, for instance, of the weeping, screaming and kneeling in the street that was observed at the last such occasion, the funeral procession for President Franklin Roosevelt 18 years ago.

The caisson and the cars following reached the east steps of the Capitol at 1:50 P.M., 45 minutes after the coffin had been borne from the White House. A 21-gun salute boomed across the crowd and echoed across the vast plaza stretching north to Union Station.

A military band played "Hail to the Chief." As the eight bearers removed the coffin from the caisson and bore it slowly up the marble steps, the band softly played—perhaps in honor of the service during which Mr. Kennedy nearly gave his life in World War II— the Navy hymn, "Eternal Father, Strong to Save."

The various parties from the limousines followed the coffin in the order they had arrived. Inside the Rotunda, members of the Senate, House and Cabinet and other dignitaries stood in a semicircle. Mrs. Kennedy, President and Mrs. Johnson and others who had come in the procession stood in the northeast quadrant of the hushed chamber, near a temporary lectern.

The members of the Kennedy family gathered near them. Caroline and John Jr. stood holding their mother's hands,

Caroline sedately, John occasionally capering about.

Among those in the Rotunda was former President Harry S. Truman. He was accompanied by his daughter, Mrs. E. C. Daniel of New York.

Senator Mike Mansfield of Montana, the Democratic leader of the Senate, was the first eulogist.

Mansfield's Eulogy

As television lights washed the Rotunda in a harsh, artificial glare, Senator Mansfield spoke in tones that grew ever more ringing.

Four times, in praising the man who was dead, and the life he had lived for his country and with his wife, Senator Mansfield repeated:

"In a moment, it was no more. And so she took a ring from her finger and placed it in his hands."

A fifth time he said it and added— "and kissed him, and closed the lid of a coffin."

The Senator referred to Mrs. Kennedy's having put her ring on a finger of the President and having kissed him as the body was about to be taken to the plane for its return to Washington.

At that moment, the Senator said, "a piece of each of us died."

Mr. Kennedy, he said, "gave us of his love that we, too, in turn, might give. He gave that we might give of ourselves, that we might give to one another until there would be no room, no room at all, for the bigotry, the hatred, the prejudice and the arrogance which converged in that moment of horror to strike him down."

Speaker of the House John W. McCormack was more personal.

"As we gather here today, bowed in grief," he said, "the heartfelt sympathy of the members of the Congress and of our people are extended to Mrs. Jacqueline and to Ambassador and Mrs. Joseph P. Kennedy and their loved ones."

"Their deep grief," he went on, "is also self-shared by countless millions of persons throughout the world; considered a personal tragedy, as if one had

lost a loved member of his own immediate family."

Most of these remarks were inaudible to many in the chamber, which was not designed for speeches. Even strong voices are lost in the vast open space that rises above the stone floor to the top of the Capitol Dome.

During the eulogies, Mrs. Kennedy stood with regal bearing, seeming to listen intently. Tears rolled down the face of Robert F. Kennedy. At the moment that Mrs. Kennedy walked forward and knelt by her husband's coffin, all who saw her were profoundly moved.

Then it was over. Mrs. Kennedy and her children walked slowly down the steps of the Capitol. President and Mrs. Johnson followed. At the foot of the steps, in the softer light of the afternoon, they talked for a few moments.

Mrs. Johnson held Mrs. Kennedy's hands as they spoke; once she leaned forward and placed her head near Mrs. Kennedy's. Then the President took Mrs. Kennedy's hand in one of his, patted it with the other. Mrs. Kennedy, her children and Robert Kennedy entered a car and sped away.

Mr. Johnson, headed for one of the important meetings that will constantly occupy him in the coming days, entered another car with Secret Service men and a military aide. After him, alone with her driver and a security guard, rode the new First Lady.

Behind them, in the stillness of the Rotunda, they left the body of John Fitzgerald Kennedy upon the same catafalque on which had rested—98 years ago—the body of Abraham Lincoln, the first American President to be murdered. Gazing on the scene with silent stone eyes from beside the north entrance was a statue of James A. Garfield, the second President to fall before an assassin.

It was time, then, for the doors to be opened to those waiting outside.

PRESIDENT'S ASSASSIN SHOT TO DEATH IN JAIL CORRIDOR BY A DALLAS CITIZEN

One Bullet Fired

Night-Club Man Who Admired Kennedy Is Oswald's Slayer

By GLADWIN HILL

Dallas, Nov. 24—President Kennedy's assassin, Lee Harvey Oswald, was fatally shot by a Dallas night-club operator today as the police started to move him from the city jail to the county jail.

The shooting occurred in the basement of the municipal building at about 11:20 A.M. central standard time (12:20 P.M. New York time).

The assailant, Jack Rubenstein, known as Jack Ruby, lunged from a cluster of newsmen observing the transfer of Oswald from the jail to an armored truck.

Millions of viewers saw the shooting on television.

As the shot rang out, a police detective suddenly recognized Ruby and exclaimed: "Jack, you son of a bitch!"

A murder charge was filed against Ruby by Assistant District Attorney William F. Alexander. Justice of the Peace Pierce McBride ordered him held without bail.

Detectives Flank Him

Oswald was arrested Friday after Mr. Kennedy was shot dead while riding through Dallas in an open car. He was charged with murdering the President and a policeman who was shot a short time later while trying to question Oswald.

As the 24-year-old prisoner, flanked by two detectives, stepped onto a basement garage ramp, Ruby thrust a .38-caliber, snub-nose revolver into Oswald's left side and fired a single shot.

The 52-year-old night-club operator, an ardent admirer of President Kennedy and his family, was described as having been distraught.

> *Millions of viewers saw the shooting on television.*

[District Attorney Henry Wade said he understood that the police were looking into the possibility that Oswald had been slain to prevent him from talking, The Associated Press reported. Mr. Wade said that so far no connection between Oswald and Ruby had been established.]

Oswald slumped to the concrete paving, wordlessly clutching his side and writhing with pain.

Oswald apparently lost consciousness very quickly after the shooting. Whether he was at any point able to speak, if he wanted to, was not known.

The politically eccentric warehouse clerk was taken in a police ambulance to the Parkland Hospital, where President Kennedy died Friday. He died in surgery at 1:07 P.M., less than two hours after the shooting. The exact time Oswald was shot was not definitely established.

Four plainclothes men, from a detail of about 50 police officers carrying out the transfer, pounced on Ruby as he fired the shot and overpowered him.

Ruby, who came to Dallas from Chicago 15 years ago, had a police record here listing six allegations of minor offenses. The disposition of five was not noted. A charge of liquor law violation was dismissed. Two of the entries, in July, 1953, and May, 1954, involved carrying concealed weapons.

The city police, working with the Secret Service and the Federal Bureau of Investigation, said last night that they had the case against Oswald "cinched."

After some 30 hours of intermittent interrogations and confrontations with scores of witnesses, Oswald was ordered transferred to the custody of the Dallas County sheriff.

A Change in Plans

The original plan had been for the sheriff to assume custody of Oswald at the city jail and handle the transfer. Late last night, for unspecified reasons, it was decided that the city police would move the prisoner.

Police Chief Jesse Curry declined to comment on suggestions that he had scheduled the transfer of Oswald at an unpropitious time because of pressure from news media.

Chief Curry announced about 9 o'clock last night that the investigation had reached a point where Oswald's presence was no longer needed. He said that Oswald would be turned over to the county sheriff today.

Asked when this would take place, the chief said: "If you fellows are here by 10 A.M., you'll be early enough."

When newsmen assembled at the police administrative offices at 10 o'clock, Chief Curry commented: "We

Lee Harvey Oswald, under arrest after being charged with the assassination of President John F. Kennedy, is shot at point-blank range by Dallas night-club owner Jack Ruby, as he was being escorted by police. (Popperfoto/Getty Images)

could have done this earlier if I hadn't given you fellows that 10 o'clock time."

Armored Van Used

Chief Curry disclosed this morning that to thwart an attempt against Oswald, the trip was to be made in an armored van of the kind used to transfer money.

"We're not going to take any chances," he said. "Our squad cars are not bullet-proof. If somebody's going to try to do something, they wouldn't stop him."

A ramp dips through the basement garage of the municipal building, running from Main Street to Commerce Street. Patrol wagons drive down this ramp and discharge prisoners at a basement booking office. The garage ceiling was too low for the armored car, so the van was backed up in the Commerce Street portal of the ramp.

The plan was to lead Oswald out the doorway in the center of the basement and about 75 feet up the ramp to the back of the armored car.

Prisoner on Fourth Floor

At about 11 o'clock, Chief Curry left his third-floor office, followed by plain-clothes detectives and newsmen, to go to the basement. Oswald was still in a fourth-floor jail cell.

As the group with the chief walked through a short corridor past the base-ment booking office and out the door onto the guarded ramp, uniformed policemen checked the reporters' credentials. But they passed familiar faces, such as those of policemen and collaborating Secret Service and F.B.I. agents.

Ruby's face was familiar to many policemen who had encountered him at his two night clubs and in his frequent visits to the municipal building.

Inconspicuous in Group

Neatly dressed in a dark suit and wearing a fedora, he was inconspicuous in a group of perhaps 50 men who for the next 20 minutes waited in a 12-foot-wide vestibule and adjacent portions of the ramp.

Television cameras, facing the vestibule, were set up against a metal railing separating the 15- foot-wide ramp from the rest of the garage. Some newsmen clustered along this railing.

Across Commerce Street, in front of a row of bail bonds-men's offices, a crowd of several hundred persons was held back by a police line.

Soon Oswald was taken in an elevator to the basement. He was led through the booking office to the open vestibule between two lines of detectives.

There was a sudden loud noise that sounded like the explosion of a photographer's flashbulb. It was Ruby's revolver firing.

Walks Behind Captain

Captain Fritz, chief of the police homicide division, walked just ahead of him. Oswald was handcuffed, with a detective holding each arm and another following. On Oswald's right, in a light suit, was J. R. Leavelle and on his left, in a dark suit, L. C. Graves.

As they turned right from the vestibule to start up the ramp, Ruby jumped forward from against the railing. There was a sudden loud noise that sounded like the explosion of a photographer's flashbulb. It was Ruby's revolver firing.

A momentary furor set in as Ruby was seized and hustled into the building. Policemen ran up the ramp in both directions to the street, followed by others with orders to seal off the building.

About five minutes elapsed before an ambulance could be rolled down the ramp to Oswald.

The ambulance, its siren sounding, was followed by police and press cars on the four-mile drive to the hospital.

Oswald was moved almost immediately into an operating room, at the other end of the building from the one where President Kennedy was treated.

The bullet had entered Oswald's body just below his heart and had torn into most of the vital organs.

Dr. Tom Shires, the hospital's chief of surgery, who operated on Governor Connally Friday, took over the case. The gamut of emergency procedures—blood transfusion, fluid transfusion, breathing tube and chest drainage tube—was instituted immediately.

But Dr. Shires quickly reported through a hospital official that Oswald was in "extremely critical condition" and that surgery would take several hours.

Family Put in Custody

Oswald's brother, George, a factory worker from Denton, Tex., got to the hospital before the assassin died.

The police took Oswald's mother, wife and two infant daughters into protective custody. They were escorted to the hospital to view the body, then were taken to an undisclosed lodging place in Dallas.

Governor Connally is still a patient at the Parkland Hospital. The excitement of the Oswald case swirled around the temporary office the Governor had set up there.

Back at the jail, Ruby was taken to the same fourth-floor cellblock where his victim had been the focus of attention the last two days.

Reports that filtered out about his preliminary remarks said that he had been impelled to kill President Kennedy's assassin by sympathy for Mrs. Kennedy. It was reported he did not want her to go through the ordeal of returning to Dallas for the trial of Oswald.

A half-dozen lawyers who have worked for Ruby converged on police headquarters in the next hour or two. They said they had been directed there by relatives and friends of Ruby and had not been called by Ruby himself.

One lawyer said that he had arranged for a hearing before a justice of the peace tomorrow morning to ask for Ruby's release on bail.

"He's a respectable citizen who's been here for years and certainly is entitled to bail," the lawyer said. "We'll make any amount of bail."

"He is a great admirer of President Kennedy," the lawyer said, "and police officers."

The last remark was an allusion to the fact that Oswald was accused of fatally shooting the Dallas patrolman after the President's assassination.

Ruby, the lawyer said, "is a very emotional man."

Chief Curry called the second formal news conference of the last three days in the police headquarters basement assembly room at 1:30 P.M.

His face drawn, he said in a husky voice:

"My statement will be very brief. Oswald expired at 1:07 P.M.

"We have arrested the man. He will be charged with murder. The suspect is Jack Rubenstein. He also goes by the name of Jack Ruby. That's all I have to say."

Opposite page
The family of President Kennedy leads mourners leaving the White House for his funeral.
(John F. Kennedy Library)

A HERO'S BURIAL

Million in Capital See Cortege Roll On to Church and Grave

By TOM WICKER

WASHINGTON, Nov. 25—The body of John Fitzgerald Kennedy was returned today to the American earth.

The final resting place of the 35th President of the United States was on an open slope among the dead of the nation's wars in Arlington National Cemetery, within sight of the Lincoln Memorial.

Mr. Kennedy's body was carried from the Capitol to St. Matthew's Catholic Cathedral for a requiem mass. From there, in a cortege, it was taken to the cemetery.

During the day, a million people stood in the streets to watch Mr. Kennedy's last passage.

Across the land, millions more—almost the entire population of the country at one time or another—saw the solemn ceremonies on television.

Cushing Says Mass

At the pontifical low mass said by Richard Cardinal Cushing of Boston, and following the caisson bearing Mr. Kennedy's body to his grave, were notable figures—among them President Johnson, President de Gaulle of France, Emperor Haile Selassie of Ethiopia, King Baudouin of the Belgians, Queen Frederika of the Hellenes, and Prince Philip, husband of Queen Elizabeth II of Britain.

As the caisson reached the graveside below the Custis-Lee Mansion that dominates the Arlington National Cemetery, a flight of 50 jet planes thundered overhead—one representing each state of the Union that Mr. Kennedy often called "the Great Republic." The jets were followed by Air Force 1, the President's personal plane.

Cardinal Cushing repeated the ancient words of the Roman Catholic graveside service, interpolating the phrase "this wonderful man, Jack Kennedy." Cannon boomed a 21-gun salute across the rows upon rows of white stones. A bugler sounded taps.

The eight body bearers who had placed Mr. Kennedy's coffin above his open grave folded the flag that had covered it for three days. It was presented to Mrs. Kennedy, who stood erect and still, her head covered by a long black veil.

Then she and Mr. Kennedy's brothers, Attorney General Robert F. Kennedy and Senator Edward M. Kennedy of Massachusetts, each touched a flaming wand to an "eternal flame" placed at the head of the grave.

That was all. For John F. Kennedy, 46 years of age, three years leader of his nation and the Western world, herald of a new generation of American purpose, the tumult and the shouting died. The captains and the kings departed.

This was a cold clear day in Washington—a day of hushed streets, empty buildings, silent throngs standing in their massed thousands to watch the cortege pass, a day of brilliant sunshine falling like hope upon a people that mourned a fallen leader but had to set their faces to the future.

The casket of President Kennedy leaves the U.S. Capitol, bound for his burial.
(John F. Kennedy Library)

Officially, the day began at 10:41 A.M. when Mrs. John F. Kennedy, with Robert and Edward Kennedy, entered the great, still Rotunda of the United States Capitol, where John Kennedy's body had lain in state since yesterday afternoon.

Hundreds of thousands of Americans had filed silently past the catafalque—the same upon which the murdered Lincoln lay 98 years ago—in a procession that continued through the night and until after 9 A.M. today.

Mrs. Kennedy, Robert and Edward Kennedy knelt by the coffin for a minute, then arose, backed away several steps, turned and went down the central steps of the Capitol to the East Plaza.

Between sentinels of all the armed services, posted in two long lines down the steps, the eight body bearers carried the flag-draped coffin and placed it upon the waiting caisson. Six matched gray horses pulled it away, carrying John Kennedy on his last journey to the White House.

The Kennedy family and others followed in a solemn line of cars along Pennsylvania Avenue. At the White House, the Kennedys left their car and went inside for a few minutes.

Across the street, in Lafayette Square, thousands stood to watch the procession to the church forming in the White House drive.

At 11:25, the foreign dignitaries who had come to pay respects began lining up—President de Gaulle in the uniform and cap of the French army, the diminutive Haile Selassie in gorgeous braid, Prince Philip in the blue of the British Navy, others in top hats, sashes, medals, or simple civilian clothes like those worn by Queen Frederika.

Altogether, State Department officials said, 220 persons representing 92 nations, five international agencies and the papacy came to Washington. Among them were eight heads of state, ten prime ministers, and most of the world's remaining royalty.

In the distance, as they waited, tolled the bells of St. John's Protestant Episcopal church on the other side of Lafayette Square. The flags of the 50 states, displayed along the White House drive, were dipped in the presence of the caisson.

Mrs. Kennedy Takes Place

At 11:35, Mrs. Kennedy came down the steps of the north portico, as a choir of midshipmen sang softly. She took her place behind the caisson, flanked by Robert Kennedy on the right, Edward Kennedy on the left. Only once, as she waited, did she break her stillness to glance around at the world's great standing silently behind her.

Then, to a distant skirl of bagpipes from the Black Watch, flown to Washington to march in the funeral procession, the caisson and its followers moved down the drive, into Pennsylvania Avenue, past Blair House and onto 17th Street.

Five yards behind Mrs. Kennedy walked President Johnson and his wife, discreetly accompanied by numerous security agents.

Next, in a limousine, came Caroline and John Kennedy Jr., the dead President's children.

On foot behind them, in what soon became a straggling confused mass came the visiting delegations—a con-

JFK's funeral procession arrives at Arlington National Cemetery. (Time & Life Pictures/Getty Images)

trast to the precision of the military units and bands that marched ahead of the caisson.

Along 17th Street and Connecticut Avenue, on the eight-block route to St. Matthew's Cathedral, crowds had been gathering since early morning. They massed on the sidewalks and spilled over the curbs, clustered in the buildings that line one of Washington's smartest office and shopping areas, and backed up into the side streets.

Seldom had such personages gathered at once; certainly never had such a gathering been seen walking on foot along one of the busiest streets of the nation. De Valera, Mikoyan, Erhard, Douglas-Home, Ikeda, Thant—the parade of famous figures seemed endless.

Behind them came the Supreme Court Justices and the Cabinet; and after them, in a group of their own, some of Mr. Kennedy's closest associates. Another group of personal friends followed.

At the cathedral, those who were not marching in the procession had been gathering since before 11 A.M. Admission was by invitation only, and the capacity of the green-domed build-

ing limited those invited to somewhat more than 1,100.

These guests were varied: Harold Wilson, leader of the British Labor party; Mrs. Nelson Rockefeller and her husband, the Governor of New York; White House staff members; members of the Senate, among them Barry Goldwater of Arizona and members of the House.

There was Gov. George Romney of Michigan and his wife; Gov. Bert Combs of Kentucky; David L. McDonald, president of the United Steelworkers of America; Mayor Richard J. Daley of Chicago and former Gov. Ernest Hollings of South Carolina; Gov. George C. Wallace of Alabama; Richard M. Nixon and Mrs. Nixon; Gov. and Mrs. William W. Scranton of Pennsylvania and Gov. Edmund G. Brown of California.

Seated near the front of the church were former President Harry S. Truman and his daughter, Mrs. E. C. Daniel of New York. Former President Dwight D. Eisenhower, with his wife on his arm, was seated near Mr. Truman.

The diplomatic corps arrived in a body. Military ushers and several friends of Mr. Kennedy—among them two reporters, Hugh Sidey of Time magazine and Benjamin Bradlee of Newsweek—showed the great and the small to their seats.

The church was silent. Six massive candles, in tall gold holders, stood upon the white marble altar. From the ornate, domed ceiling—designed by Grant LaFarge—paintings, carvings, inscriptions looked down upon the rapidly filling cathedral.

Then came the sound of drums. The Black Watch bagpipes could be heard, faintly at first, rising as they passed the open doors, falling into silence. Shouted military commands sounded clearly through the door.

The choir in the loft above and to the left of the altar began to sing. Cardinal Cushing and a long line of prelates followed a crucifix held aloft by an acolyte as they marched slowly along the aisle to the open porch in front of the cathedral.

The caisson halted before the cathedral at 11:57 A.M. Mrs. Kennedy, walking with a sure and rapid stride, was just behind it with her husband's brothers. Cardinal Cushing in his lofty white mitre came down the steps.

Mrs. Kennedy's children, clad in identical blue and wearing red shoes, were brought to her and she took them by the hand. She bent to kiss the Cardinal's ring, then walked with Caroline and John Jr. into the cathedral.

Members of the Kennedy family and of Mrs. Kennedy's family followed. President and Mrs. Johnson came just behind them and were seated across the aisle.

As the mass of dignitaries and foreign visitors filed in, the coffin waited outside on its caisson. At 12:08, the body bearers lifted it, carried it across the street and to the cathedral porch. Cardinal Cushing sprinkled it with holy water, then bent to kiss it.

At 12:15, the acolyte carrying the crucifix moved slowly back up the aisle, flanked by two others carrying candles. The Cardinal, chanting in Latin, and the prelates followed.

Behind them, at funeral pace, stiffly erect as automatons, came the eight body bearers, wheeling the flag-draped coffin—three at each side, one at its head, another trailing.

The coffin was placed in the front and center of the church, a few feet from where the family sat. The bearers marched stiffly away. The doors of the church closed on the still, waiting crowds outside.

As Cardinal Cushing, in the familiar droning voice that had sounded the invocation at Mr. Kennedy's inauguration on Jan. 20, 1961, said the requiem mass. Luigi Vena sang from the choir loft Gounod's "Ave Maria."

Sang at the Wedding

Mrs. Kennedy had requested that Mr. Vena do so. He had sung the same music at her marriage to John F. Kennedy in Newport, R.I., on Sept. 12, 1953—a ceremony at which Cardinal Cushing had also officiated.

The Cardinal—a tall and imposing figure in the massive church—said the mass entirely in the traditional Latin ("Dominus vobiscum. Et cum spiritu tuo.")

He moved steadily and without hesitation, sometimes in a sing-song voice that sounded more like a steady drone of sound than enunciated words— through the Introit, the Kyrie ("Kyrie eleison—Lord, have mercy. Christe eleison—Christ have mercy"), the con-

secration, through all the other forms of the mass familiar to millions of Roman Catholics the world over, to the communion.

Mrs. Kennedy and Robert Kennedy were the first to receive communion. Edward Kennedy followed. Hundreds of others in the church also received communion and were given the peace of the Lord ("Pax Domini sit semper vobiscum").

When the celebration of the mass ended ("O God, who alone art ever merciful and sparing of punishment, humbly we pray to Thee in behalf of the soul of Thy servant, John Fitzgerald Kennedy, whom Thou hast commanded to go forth today from this World . . ."), the Most Rev. Philip Hannan, Auxiliary Bishop of Washington, ascended to the pulpit and spoke for 11 minutes in English.

Quotes Kennedy Speeches

In a clear, almost uninflected voice, Bishop Hannan spoke of Biblical passages in Mr. Kennedy's speeches, including one from one of the last addresses he ever made, in Houston last Thursday night:

"Your old men shall dream dreams, your young men shall see visions, and where there is no vision the people shall perish."

He concluded with a reading of Mr. Kennedy's Inaugural Address with its famous passage, "Ask not what your country can do for you—ask what you can do for your country."

And once again, in the Bishop's unimpassioned voice—so different from that of the young President who spoke that snowy day in 1961—there rang out a challenge that had stirred a nation:

Opposite page:
*On his third birthday,
the president's son, John, salutes
as his father's coffin passes by.*
(Associated Press)

"Now the trumpet summons again—not as a call to bear arms, though arms we need—not as a call to battle, though embattled we are—but a call to bear the burden of a long twilight struggle, year in and year out, rejoicing in hope, patient in tribulation—a struggle against the common enemies of man: tyranny, poverty, disease and war itself."

The words did not seem less relevant—in the aftermath of Mr. Kennedy's murder they seemed if anything more challenging—than the day, on than crest of hope and belief, when he said them.

At 1:15 P.M., the church doors were opened, the cathedral service concluded. Once again, the procession of prelates followed the crucifix slowly up the aisle. The body bearers moved Mr. Kennedy's coffin behind them. From the street came the stirring sounds of "Hail to the Chief," to which Mr. Kennedy had stepped so often in his brisk stride.

Mrs. Kennedy Waits

Mrs. Kennedy, holding Caroline's hand—John had been taken from the church at the beginning of the mass—followed it. For a long moment, as the coffin was being taken down the steps and mounted for the third time upon the caisson, she had to stand in the aisle waiting.

She was weeping behind her veil. But as she stood unmoving and erect, she took control of herself with an obvious effort, and moved on out of the church. Robert Kennedy followed her with his mother, Mrs. Joseph P. Kennedy, on his arm. Then came the rest of the family mourners.

President Johnson and his family followed. In the jam of persons leaving the church, the foreign dignitaries stood for long moments in the aisle. President de Gaulle whispered something to King Baudouin.

Outside the church, Caroline and

November 24: A flag flutters over a caisson carrying President Kennedy's casket. (George F. Mobley/National Geographic/Getty Images)

John Kennedy entered a limousine with their nurse, Mrs. Maude Shaw, and were driven to the White House.

Cardinal Cushing wiped tears from his eyes with a handkerchief as an Army band played a dirge. Attorney General Kennedy helped Mrs. Kennedy into a limousine. Both General Eisenhower and Mr. Truman leaned into her car and spoke to her briefly. They had been chatting on the cathedral porch as they waited for cars.

Later, the two former Presidents, none too friendly since the 1952 election, rode together in the procession to Arlington National Cemetery.

That procession formed up slowly in front of the cathedral in a jam of waiting limousines, and the dignitaries began to crowd to the curb. Angier Biddle Duke, the State Department's chief of protocol, gave up the effort to escort each of them to a car, but all eventually found their places in the long, solemn parade.

Eight Secret Service men flanked the car in which President and Mrs. Johnson rode. Another large group of agents guarded the car of President de Gaulle.

So large was the Kennedy family group that President and Mrs. Johnson, whose car was immediately behind the group, were 10th in the long cortege.

Once again on its final journey, the caisson rolled down Connecticut Avenue and Seventh Street, then turned right on Constitution Avenue. Behind it, Black Jack, the riderless gelding with the traditional reversed boots in the silver stirrups, pranced and pawed at the pavement.

Untold thousands stood at the curbside along the same route taken by masses of Negroes and whites last Aug. 28 in the March on Washington that Mr. Kennedy had encouraged.

Past the noble white marble of the Lincoln Memorial, over the long stone reach of the Memorial Bridge, across the serene Potomac toward the green slopes of Arlington and the pillared mansion where Robert E. Lee made his tragic choice to leave the Union with his state—onward to the grave rolled the cortege of the great grandson of an Irish immigrant.

Behind him, the leaders of the world—royalty and commoners, generals and revolutionaries—came on endlessly in their mourning-colored cars. The crowds watched silently, sorrowfully, respectfully.

In the cold and waning sunshine, they stood patiently, seeming almost not to move.

More than an hour after it had left the church, the caisson arrived at the graveside. On a nearby slope, masses of flowers were arranged. The metal coffin railings gleamed with polish. Beyond the river, the Lincoln and Jefferson Memorials, the soaring stone of the Washington Monument could be plainly seen.

Mrs. Kennedy, Robert and Edward Kennedy, the Kennedy sisters Patricia, Eunice, and Jean, and their mother, were seated in a single row at the front of the family group. As the limousines arrived one by one, the dignitaries took their places—President de Gaulle and Haile Selassie at the head of the grave.

For the graveside services, Cardinal Cushing spoke mostly in English. The words were familiar ("I am the Resurrection and the Life . . .")

Occasionally, he seemed to be hurrying, as if to end more quickly the anguish of Mrs. Kennedy and her family. But his harsh voice rang plainly across the hillside and the watching crowds and the thousands of graves as he intoned:

"O Lord, we implore Thee to grant this mercy to Thy dead servant, that he who held fast to Thy will by his intentions, may not receive punishment in return for his deeds; so that, as the true faith united him with the throng of the faithful on earth, Thy mercy may unite him with the company of the holy angels in Heaven."

Three cannons, firing by turns, boomed 21 times in the stillness. President de Gaulle and the other military men came to the salute. Then three riflemen fired three sharp volleys into the arching sky. Sgt. Keith Clark, an Army bugler, sounded the clear, melancholy lament of taps across the cemetery.

The flag was removed from the coffin, folded with whiplike precision by the body bearers, passed to Mrs. Kennedy. She and her husband's brothers lit the eternal flame. Cardinal Cushing cast holy water upon the exposed coffin.

Stumbles and Recovers

Robert Kennedy led Mrs. Kennedy away. After a few steps, she stumbled on broken turf, quickly recovered her stride and went steadily on.

The procession had been so long that many dignitaries, far back in the line of cars, were only arriving at the graveside. But if it had taken a long time for the men who followed John Kennedy to arrive at his last resting place, it seemed to take hardly any for the throng of uniforms and morning frock coats and veils and simple dark clothes to disperse and leave the dead for the living.

At 3:34 P.M., the coffin was lowered into the earth. The short life, the long day, was done forever. And none of the pomp and pageantry, none of the ceremony and music, none of the words and grief, none of the faces at the curb, none of the still figures in the limousines, had seemed to say more than the brief prayer printed on the back of a photograph of the dead President that had been distributed at the cathedral:

"Dear God—please take care of your servant—John Fitzgerald Kennedy."

Looking Back

Four Days in November

By Robert B. Semple Jr.

Ray O'Neill, the *Times'* national news editor, usually came to work during the noonday lull. On this Friday, November 22, 1963, he had just settled in at his desk on West 43rd Street when a copy editor handed him a bulletin from the Associated Press, datelined Dallas and timed at 1:39 P.M. EST: "PRESIDENT KENNEDY WAS SHOT TODAY AS HIS MOTORCADE LEFT DOWNTOWN DALLAS." Thus began four of the most tumultuous days in the history of the paper and the life of the nation—the four days encompassing President Kennedy's assassination in Dallas at 12:30 P.M. Dallas time; the arrest and subsequent murder of the shooter, Lee Harvey Oswald; the swearing-in and ascension to power of a new president, Lyndon Johnson; and Kennedy's funeral at Washington's St. Matthew's Cathedral and his burial in Arlington National Cemetery.

I was a newly hired desk editor in the paper's Washington bureau and, like most people of a certain age, I can remember exactly where I was when the news came from Dallas—in a car wash in Northwest Washington, listening to the manager's transistor radio and getting ready to drive to New Haven for the next day's Harvard-Yale game, which of course was cancelled along with just about everything else in a nation stunned by events and rightly fearful of doing anything that might devalue the solemnity of the moment. My job gave me what amounted to a ringside seat to the tragedy, and even now, 50 years on, a memory grown faulty with age can still summon with amazing clarity not just the specific images of those four days—the bloodied limousine, the brave widow, the solemn new president, the Cardinal, the cortege—but also the emotional trajectory I went through at the time, beginning with shock and sadness and confusion, and ending, in remarkably short order, with a sense of hope and renewal. It is a trajectory, I think, that much of the country experienced as well.

First the shock. Before 1963, three American presidents had been assassinated in office, and Franklin D. Roosevelt had the narrowest of escapes. But why now and why, in particular, this president—a buoyant, charming, intelligent, ironic and (except perhaps to Southern racists) ideologically unthreatening young man whose enthusiasm had lifted up a generation of younger voters and indeed the very idea of public service, and whose grace disarmed all but his most virulent political enemies. Why?

Then the sadness—for the president's wife, for his two young children, for the entire Kennedy family, for the slain president himself. Chicago's Mayor Richard Daley, (a tough old buzzard and Kennedy loyalist who was thought by some to have engineered enough creative vote-counting to swing Illinois in the 1960 election) burst into tears upon hearing the news, one among millions of Americans who also cried. The sadness, too, or more nearly the sudden disappointment of an unfinished agenda—a space program triumphantly if barely launched, an ambitious civil rights agenda stalled in Congress, a foreign policy marked by Kennedy's increasing sureness of touch, improved relations (after a disastrous start) with the Soviet Union and unresolved questions about the nature of America's commitment in Vietnam.

Finally, the confusion and among some, fear. Was the murder a product of a right-wing conspiracy—after all, it happened in Texas and in his column the next day, the esteemed *Times* columnist James Reston referred pointedly to "the violent politics of that state." Was it the handiwork of Fidel Castro, whom Kennedy had angered with the Bay of Pigs invasion? Was it, more broadly, a Communist plot? Oswald, it quickly turned out, had spent time in the Soviet Union, studying and admiring Karl Marx. As the Warren Commission determined, Oswald acted alone, but for a day or two the entire nation had a very bad case of the jitters. This was, after all, the nuclear age, and if it was a conspiracy, who knew whether the Soviet Union might seek to take swift advantage of an untried leader?

Slowly, though, while the sadness lingered, the confusion and fear gave way to a gradual but unmistakable settling of the nerves and a realization that the country would in due course right itself; that what Kennedy himself had called "this old but youthful union" in his State of the Union address earlier in the year would endure. As the *Times* editorial on November 23 observed, the nation had already witnessed "grim moments of civil war and world wars, of presidential transfers of power caused by sudden death as well as normal succession [but] our government of law, not men, insures that no assassin's act can overturn the institutions of the United States."

Several factors accounted for the nation's calm, not least the basic good sense of the American people at the time. Here are three more: One was the swift decisiveness of Lyndon Johnson in taking charge. The fourth volume of Robert Caro's masterful history of Johnson's life describes his decision to hold the swearing-in aboard Air Force One before it left Dallas, with the coffin on board and Jackie Kennedy, in blood-stained stockings, by his side—a visual as well as constitutional affirmation of continuity.

A second was the measured pace of the pageantry itself—Sunday's procession to Capitol Hill, with muffled drums, the wooden caisson bearing the coffin, and Black Jack, the riderless horse; and then Monday's equally solemn funeral procession from St. Matthew's to the Arlington Cemetery, the stoic widow and little John-John and his poignant salute, Black Jack again, and, this time, hundreds of dignitaries and heads of state. As much as the assassination itself, these images indelibly imprinted the Kennedy presidency on the public mind, giving it a historical resonance beyond what it had actually achieved in its brief life. Yet no less importantly, the events proceeded in such a way as to transfix and even tranquilize an anxious nation—an unintended result, perhaps, but therapeutic nonetheless.

Which brings me to the third reason why the nation was able to gather itself: television. TV's crucial role was not well understood until later, but both Caro and the late Tom Wicker (in an introduction to an earlier book on the assassination) have argued, correctly in my view, that television was instrumental in holding the nation together. Wicker referred to television—in newsgathering terms, still a relative infant in 1963 with only three networks—as akin to a "national nervous system." Caro describes the nation as having "gathered in one vast living room," there to learn whatever was known and could be told about the President's death, to watch live the moment when Jack Ruby shot and killed Oswald, and to absorb the pageantry and transfer of power.

Walter Cronkite soldiered on for three days without sleep, as did the American people themselves. The average American family, according to surveys, spent 31.6 hours watching television over these four days, or almost 8 hours a day. Arthur Gelb, then the *Times'* deputy metropolitan editor, would later recall that the biggest problem in the paper's newsroom that day was pulling editors and reporters away from the television screens.

Caro argues that this immersion "intensified, sharpened, deepened" the impact of the assassination, and "therefore the concern about whether government would continue to function." This was undoubtedly true for many people, but in my own view the continuous coverage did more to relieve anxieties than to reinforce them. I also believe that this would not be the case today, with multiple online and cable news outlets competing for the next breathless headline, but that is a story for another day.

On November 29, after some hesitation, Johnson established the President's Commission on the Assassination of President Kennedy, known informally as the Warren Commission. Some 10 months later, on September 24, 1964, after examining thousands of documents, interviewing 552 witnesses and entertaining every possible scenario and hypothesis, the commission presented its 888-page final report to the president, who made it public three days later. As Anthony Lewis reported in the *Times* on September 28, its bottom-line conclusion was one of stark simplicity: "The assassination of President Kennedy was the work of one man, Lee Harvey Oswald. There was no conspiracy, foreign or domestic."

As to motive, it concluded that Oswald had no rational purpose other than a desire to be somebody, to find in one blinding moment the recognition denied by what the Commission described as a lifetime of "isolation, frustration and disappointment."

Tom Wicker put his finger on what I think may be the overriding reason why, for many Americans, the single-assassin theory was not enough and never will be enough—the notion that the murder of an American president, their president, this "young American emperor" in particular, deserved a more serious explanation—political, military or international—than the twisted ambitions of a pathetic loser. It seemed such a cruelly pedestrian ending for a glamorous presidency cut cruelly short.

Robert B. Semple Jr., who won a Pulitzer Prize for editorial writing in 1996, has been a reporter and editor at the *Times* since 1963. He is currently associate editor of the editorial page.

Visitors to the Gallery of Modern Art at Columbus Circle in New York City pause before a bust of President Kennedy, one year after his assassination. (Allyn Baum/The New York Times)

Epilogue

JOHNSON NAMES A 7-MAN PANEL TO INVESTIGATE ASSASSINATION; CHIEF JUSTICE WARREN HEADS IT

Texas Offers Aid

President Asks Board for a Public Report After Full Inquiry

By JOHN D. MORRIS

WASHINGTON, Nov. 29—President Johnson created a special commission tonight to investigate the assassination of President Kennedy. He appointed Chief Justice Earl Warren to head the panel.

The White House, in announcing the action, said the Chief Justice would serve as chairman of a seven-member commission that also includes two Senators, two Representatives and two former Administration officials.

It added:

"The President is instructing the special commission to satisfy itself that the truth is known as far as it can be discovered, and to report its findings and conclusions to him, to the American people and to the world."

Will Evaluate Data

Others appointed to the commission were: Senator Richard B. Russell, Democrat of Georgia; Senator John Sherman Cooper, Republican of Kentucky; Representative Hale Boggs, Democrat of Louisiana; Representative Gerald R. Ford, Republican of Michigan; Allen W. Dulles, former director of the Central Intelligence Agency, and John J. McCloy, former disarmament adviser to President Kennedy.

The commission, according to the White House statement, will be instructed "to evaluate available information concerning the subject of the inquiry."

It said that this would include evidence obtained by the Federal Bureau of Investigation in a special inquiry previously ordered by Mr. Johnson. The F.B.I. report on that investigation is expected to be ready next week.

Texas to Cooperate

The Attorney General of Texas, Waggoner Carr, has "offered his cooperation," the White House said. This means, officials explained, that evidence obtained by a state court of inquiry created by the Attorney General will be available to the Presidential commission.

Officials also said that the timing of the inquiry and the procedures—whether public hearings would be held, for example—would be determined by the Chief Justice.

They reported that "necessary powers, including subpoena powers," would be provided.

Congress's Aid Expected

Within the general authority of his office, the President can appoint such commissions to make inquiries as he wishes. An act of Congress, however, will be required to provide the power to subpoena witnesses and documents.

It was taken for granted that Congress would promptly pass a bill providing such power.

The commission will investigate the killing of Lee H. Oswald, President Kennedy's accused slayer, as well as "all facts and circumstances relating to the assassination of the late President," according to the White House announcement.

Besides naming the members of the commission, the announcement said:

"The President today announced that he is appointing a special commission to study and report upon all facts and circumstances relating to the assassination of the late President, John F. Kennedy, and the subsequent violent death of the man charged with the assassination.

"The President stated that the majority and minority leadership of the Senate and the House of Representatives have been consulted with respect to the proposed special commission.

"The President stated that the special commission is to be instructed to evaluate all available information concerning the subject of the inquiry. The Federal Bureau of Investigation,

The Warren Commission meeting over the Kennedy assassination. (Bettmann/Corbis/Associated Press)

pursuant to an earlier directive of the President, is making a complete investigation of the facts. An inquiry is also scheduled by a Texas court of inquiry convened by the Attorney General of Texas under Texas law.

"The special commission will have before it all evidence uncovered by the Federal Bureau of Investigation and all information available to any agency of the Federal Government. The Attorney General of Texas has also offered his cooperation. All Federal agencies and offices are being directed to furnish services and cooperation to the special commission. The commission will also be empowered to conduct any further investigation that it deems desirable.

"The President is instructing the special commission to satisfy itself that the truth is known as far as it can be discovered, and to report its findings and conclusions to him, to the American people, and to the world."

One purpose of the Presidential inquiry is to head off competing investigations by House and Senate committees and give the public a single report that would command the nation's full confidence.

Preparations for an investigation by the Senate Judiciary Committee already were well along when President Johnson decided to create the special commission.

The committee chairman, Senator James O. Eastland, Democrat of Mississippi, reached by The Associated Press at his Mississippi farm, said that the committee would now cancel its plans.

"You couldn't have both a Senate investigation and a Presidential commission at the same time," he said. "I favor what the President is doing."

The Legacy of the 1,000 Days

John F. Kennedy declared that his task would only be begun in his first 1,000 days in office— and he lived little beyond that. But his vision is still there for us to make real.

———

By JAMES MacGREGOR BURNS

Dec. 1—In his long quest for the Presidency John F. Kennedy again and again promised "1,000 days of exacting Presidential leadership." He was killed in action shortly after passing his 1,000th day in the White House.

History has dealt harshly with short-term Presidents. If Lincoln had been struck down in his third year in office rather than in his fifth, historians might still be searching in the mid-Civil War disarray for the grand design of reunion that we now know was there. All our great Presidents needed time to consolidate their successes as well as to conceive them. In their first three years in office Jefferson effected the Louisiana Purchase, Lincoln signed the Emancipation Proclamation, Wilson put through a major legislative program, and Franklin Roosevelt brought off both the "100 days" of crisis action and the "second 100 days" of major social reform.

I believe that Kennedy had the greatness of these men. Yet his place in history will be based less on tangible achievements—though there were important ones—than on the quality of the man, his statecraft in managing foreign affairs, and the clarity and persistence with which he articulated the nation's needs and purposes at home.

He was an utterly simple, natural and engaging man. Never—not even in the Senate and least of all in the White House—did he take on the deliberate speech and ponderous ways of so many young men aiming at university deanships or corporation vice presidencies.

Yet this simplicity as a human being was somehow combined with a Presidential style and versatility that were quite complex and all his own. He was a tough, literal-minded person who, with the help of his wife, brought poetry, art, music and literature to the White House. He disliked sentiment, purple prose and shibboleths, but could himself utter gleaming phrases that verged on the rhetorical. He was bored by run-of-the-mill politics and by hand-pumping politicos, yet himself had become a political professional in the best sense, and like many a professional athlete he had developed a special style that went beyond mere technique.

His humor was natural, too; it was neither contrived nor effusive. It was the wry, self-belittling, mildly joshing humor that thrives under stress. One day, after his election in 1960, I was sitting with him in Palm Beach when he was called to the phone; he came back and said with a grin: "That was one of our Boston friends with an indictable proposition!"

His most impressive quality was a special brand of courage that Hemingway once called "grace under pressure." He stood up under all kinds of pressures and provocations, not only in the agony of personal mortification, as after the Bay of Pigs, but in all the ceaseless frustrations that plague candidates: the amplifying systems that break down, the transportation that fails, the reporter who arrives late (as I saw once in Indiana) and wants the press conference all over again (he got it). This grace under pressure stemmed, I think, mainly from a remarkable detachment about himself.

Behind the humor and the courage was a steely but subtle will. In his own way, Kennedy was a serious, urbane tenacious man, completely committed to the goals he enunciated. He had a passion for the specific, the precise, the detailed. He had an analytical, curious, penetrating mind, rather than a speculative one; he was more skeptical than sanguine, and like most politicians was more effective at seizing on ideas than in creating new ones. He prided himself on being an artist of the politically possible—once he was certain that the possible could be brought about by the vigorous application of pressure.

But behind the humor and the courage and the steel lay—what? I often wondered, as I looked into those friendly but flat and impenetrable eyes, whether there lay in him any ultimate commitment, or even strategic design that led the men he apotheosized in "Profiles in Courage" to go down to defeat in behalf of some cause.

I believe that he did make a complete political and intellectual commitment to his policies and programs. It will never be known whether he ultimately would have made a commitment of the heart. In his 1,000 days he was always the pragmatist, carefully measuring and even hoarding his political influence against future needs, circling around political breastworks instead of breaking lances against them, accepting defeats on Capitol Hill and in foreign capitals with grace and dignity. "He's got the words but not the tunes," an old crusader said; actually Kennedy could sound the trumpet, but he did not believe in gallant stands in behalf of lost causes.

For he saw no quick victory to be won by a single dramatic summons to men; the trumpet, he said "sounded a call to bear the burden of a long twilight struggle year in and year out" —a struggle against "the common enemies of mankind: tyranny, poverty, disease and war itself." He rejected pusillanimity but not patience.

It was in the managing of foreign relations that Kennedy's tough-mindedness served him best. He had *le sens de l'etat*, as the French call it—a feel for the subtly interlaced strands of influence along which action moves or is blocked, a sense of the limitations as well as the possibilities of the state. In foreign relations he had the amplitude of political power that he sorely needed; he possessed both the constitutional authority over foreign policy and the administrative and planning agencies that had been bequeathed him by his predecessors in office.

He inherited also a bipartisan foreign policy based on the strategy of dealing with rival powers in a conciliatory style but from a position of strength, and of trying to make numerous day-to-day adjustments in the ever-shifting balances of world power.

Kennedy conducted this "strategy of peace," as he called it, with at least as much adroitness, decisiveness and patience as any of his predecessors in the White House.

The great exception was the Bay of Pigs—but the first Cuban crisis taught him a lesson. He had found, he told me later during a new crisis—this time in the Congo—that he could not rely completely on subordinates far down the lines, that he simply had to draw the operational details into his own hands, check out all the information and work closely with his staff until the crisis was resolved. In these and later emergencies, the White House was converted into a command post where Kennedy and his gifted assistants directly supervised the field of conflict—whether in Berlin or Vietnam or Mississippi—and marshaled their forces.

The President found, in short, that he must directly administer the details of foreign policy. He was willing to pay the price of endless conferences, staccato telephone calls and all-day vigils. Another price was heavier. Because he wanted the widest arc of power along which he could maneuver, as well as the power *not* to act despite the goading of extremists, he felt that he could deal with unpredictable rivals like Khrush-

chev and uncertain friends like de Gaulle only by massing the people behind him so that he could operate from a basis of wide popular support.

But the more he spoke and acted in terms of national unity and bipartisanship, the more he dulled his image as a leader moving strongly ahead, and in a partisan direction, at home. As in the case of Presidents before him, his role as chief of state had to pre-empt his role as party chief and legislator-in-chief.

Still, the settlements and détentes that the President achieved overseas were doubtless worth this price. It was when he tried to use the same tactics of bargain and barter in Congress that he met his worst setbacks. There he was dealing with seasoned politicians on their own terrain; he was playing with their dice, as John P. Roche observed, and in politics all dice are loaded.

Kennedy was cut down before he could secure the legislative program that has come to be the acid test of the modern President's effectiveness. It is here, I think, that historians will face their hardest test in assessing Kennedy's quality as President. Many observers, including a number of Washington journalists covering White House-Congressional relations, felt that the President failed on Capitol Hill mainly because of lack of firmness and persistence, that he relied too much on techniques that Helen Fuller summarized as "Blarney, bludgeon and boodle."

The judgment of history may not be so harsh. As we take a longer perspective and recall the Congressional counterattacks on Roosevelt during his second term, the legislative difficulties that dogged Harry Truman and Dwight Eisenhower, and the slowdown and stalemates that will doubtless frustrate President Johnson and his successors, it will become clearer, I think, that no Presidential skill, no governmental gimmick, no legislative staff can overcome the deep and structured differences that separate President and Congress today. As long as the committee chairmen speak for small rural

groups steeped in conservatism and negativism, and as long as they stand at the apex of a powerfully entrenched system of legislative slowdown and deadlock, Congress will be at odds with any President trying to respond to the acute social and economic needs of the nation.

It was less the President's legislative tactics than his aplomb in the face of defeat that perplexed observers. Where, they asked, was the fighting Irish blood? The answer probably lay in Kennedy's sense of timing. At the beginning of his Presidency, when he barely won a moderate improvement in the makeup of the Rules Committee, he concluded that he simply lacked the votes for any major change in the organization of Congress. His only hope was the election to Congress of enough new Kennedy supporters in 1964 to reform the national legislature and put through his program during his second term.

Could he have pulled off such a major feat? The late President had not yet laid the groundwork for an appeal to the country against a do-nothing Congress, such as Harry Truman made in 1948. But his open indignation over the battering of his foreign-aid bill and his dismay over the delays in his civil-rights and tax measures indicate that he would have gone to the country on this issue next year. And he would have done so at the moment that a President is at his political peak—when he is appealing to the country for a second term.

Kennedy might have been defeated next year; or he might have won an electoral landslide and a strongly Kennedy Congress. But the most likely outcome, I think, would have been his own reelection along with the return of a Congress about as much opposed to his program as the present one.

If that had indeed been the outcome, Kennedy's second term might have seen the most spectacular display of peacetime executive power in the history of the Presidency. Confronted by racial crises, economic sluggishness and ever-rising urban difficulties, the

President would have had to exploit every precedent in the use of executive power and to innovate others. Like Wilson and both Roosevelts, he would have been forced by circumstances to move in an increasingly liberal direction at home. This was the imperative of both his personality and of the Presidency as he conceived it.

After Kennedy's first year in office I wrote in these pages that there were really four Kennedys—the rhetorical radical of the stirring campaign promises and New Frontier idealism; the policy liberal who showered specific proposals on Congress; the fiscal moderate who sought to balance the budget even while stepping up spending; and the institutional conservative who op-posed major changes in the executive or legislative branches of government.

I also suggested that in the long run these four roles would be incompatible, and that under the pressure of events the last two roles would tend to give way to the first two. This was beginning to happen. The fiscal moderate was yielding to the fiscal imperative of deliberately—and admittedly—unbalancing the budget. The institutional conservative would have had to fortify the embattled Presidency even if he could not have brought about Congressional reform.

All this is speculation, but not idle speculation. For we can never understand the greatness of John F. Kennedy unless we project his aspirations and potentials into the second 1,000 days in office that he was not to have. His hopes, he said on taking office, would not "be finished in the first 1,000 days, nor in the life of this Administration, nor even perhaps in our lifetime on this planet. But let us begin."

John F. Kennedy made a magnificent beginning. Only we who survive can fashion an ending that will be his monument in office and that will secure his place in history.

James MacGregor Burns is a Pulitzer-Prize winning historian. This piece appeared in *The New York Times Magazine* only ten days after the assassination.

Jacqueline Kennedy and her children depart the White House for the last time, December 6, 1963. (John F. Kennedy Library)

WARREN COMMISSION FINDS OSWALD GUILTY AND SAYS ASSASSIN AND RUBY ACTED ALONE

Rebukes Secret Service, Asks Revamping

Panel Unanimous

Theory of Conspiracy by Left or Right Is Rejected

By ANTHONY LEWIS

WASHINGTON, Sept. 27, 1964—The assassination of President Kennedy was the work of one man, Lee Harvey Oswald. There was no conspiracy, foreign or domestic.

That was the central finding in the Warren Commission report, made public this evening. Chief Justice Earl Warren and the six other members of the President's Commission on the Assassination of President John F. Kennedy were unanimous on this and all questions.

The commission found that Jack Ruby was on his own in killing Oswald. It rejected all theories that the two men were in some way connected. It said that neither rightists nor Communists bore responsibility for the murder of the President in Dallas last Nov. 22.

Why did Oswald do it? To this most important and most mysterious question the commission had no certain answer. It suggested that Oswald had no rational purpose, no motive adequate if "judged by the standards of reasonable men."

A Product of His Life

Rather, the commission saw Oswald's terrible act as the product of his entire life—a life "characterized by isolation, frustration and failure." He was just 24 years old at the time of the assassination.

"Oswald was profoundly alienated from the world in which he lived," the report said. "He had very few, if any, close relationships with other people and he appeared to have had great difficulty in finding a meaningful place in the world.

"He was never satisfied with anything.

"When he was in the United States, he resented the capitalist system. When he was in the Soviet Union, he apparently resented the Communist party members, who were accorded special privileges and who he thought were betraying Communism, and he spoke well of the United States."

The commission found that Oswald shot at former Maj. Gen. Edwin A. Walker in Dallas on April 10, 1963, narrowly missing him. It cited this as evidence of his capacity for violence.

It listed as factors that might have led Oswald to the assassination "his deep-rooted resentment of all authority, which was expressed in a hostility toward every society in which he lived," his "urge to try to find a place in history" and his "avowed commitment to Marxism and Communism, as he understood the terms."

The reports' findings on what happened in Dallas contained few surprises. The essential points had leaked out one way or another during the ten months since President Johnson appointed the commission last Nov. 29.

But the commission analyzed every issue in exhaustive, almost archaeological detail. Experts traced the path of the bullets. Every critical event was re-enacted. Witnesses here and abroad testified to the most obscure points.

The question now is whether the report will satisfy those, especially abroad, who have insisted that there must have been a conspiracy in the assassination. The commission attempted to answer, specifically, every such theory and rumor.

The report did have surprises in its appraisal of the protection provided for the President by Federal agencies, and in its recommendations for improved methods of protection.

It was critical of the Secret Service for inadequate preventive measures, and of the Federal Bureau of Investigation for not giving the Secret Service the adverse information it had on Oswald. It called for higher-level Government attention to the problem of protecting the President, and possibly for reorganization.

The commission made public all the information it had bearing on the events in Dallas, whether agreeing with its findings or not. It withheld only a few names of sources, notably sources evidently within communist embassies in Mexico, and each of these omissions was indicated.

All the testimony taken by the commission and its staff—from 552 witnesses—will be published separately. It will fill 15 supplementary volumes, and there will be eight or nine more large volumes of exhibits. They are to be made public soon.

The report itself ran 888 pages, with eight chapters and 18 appendices. The commission's thoroughness is indicated by the fact that it interviewed every known person who met Oswald during a brief trip he made to Mexico. Interviewing continued into this month.

Drafting of the report was done by the commission's legal staff under J. Lee Rankin, general counsel. But all seven members of the commission themselves went over, edited and substantially rewrote the entire work.

'A Group Product'

A staff lawyer remarked that this report was probably unlike any other in the history of commissions—"It really is a group product, the work of the commissioners."

The members, in addition to the chief justice, were Senators Richard B. Russell of Georgia and John Sherman Cooper of Kentucky, Representatives Hale Boggs of Louisiana and Gerald R. Ford of Michigan, Allen W. Dulles and John J. McCloy. All are Republicans save Mr. Russell and Mr. Boggs.

In a foreword, the commission says that it operated not as judge or jury—because Oswald could never have a trial—but as a dispassionate fact-finder. This is borne out by the report, which is neutral in tone and makes every effort to be fair in its discussions of Oswald.

Despite the group authorship and the legal approach, the report often achieves a genuine literary style. The very detail of the narrative is fascinating, and there are many moving passages.

Few who loved John Kennedy, or this country, will be able to read it without emotion.

Cheering Crowds

As the President's motorcade drove through Dallas on Nov. 22, large crowds cheered. Gov. John Connally's wife, who was in the car, said to Mr. Kennedy, "Mr. President, you can't say Dallas doesn't love you." He answered, "That is very obvious."

A moment later the shots were fired.

Mrs. Kennedy, according to the report, "saw the President's skull torn open" by the second bullet that hit him. She testified that she cried out, "Oh, my God! They've shot my husband. I love you, Jack."

A reader of the report is struck again and again by the series of events that had to fall into place to make the assassination possible. Over a period of years, so many men could have done so many things that would have changed history.

On Oct. 31, 1959, Oswald appeared at the United States Embassy in Moscow and stated that he wanted to renounce his citizenship. While he had a right to do so at once, consular officials did not want to let a young man take so final a step precipitously. They told him to come back the following week.

He never came back. If Oswald had been allowed to expatriate himself at once, he would have found it difficult or impossible to return to the United States when he tired of the Soviet Union.

Similarly, American officials helped Oswald and his Russian wife, Marina, when they wanted to come to the United States in 1962 because they thought it better for this country to bring a defector back. The report says "it is only from the vantage of the present that the tragic irony of their conclusion emerges."

When Oswald shot at General Walker, he told Marina. She warned him not to do a thing like that again—but she did not tell the police or anyone else. If she had…

When he returned from Mexico, he applied for a job with a printing company in Dallas. He was not hired be-cause a previous employer told the company he was a "troublemaker." On Oct. 15, 1963, he got a job with the Texas School Book Depository. A month later a Presidential route was chosen that went by that building.

The Federal Bureau of Investigation learned in early November, 1963, that Oswald—whom it knew as a defector and proclaimed friend of Castro—was in Dallas and worked at the depository. The agents neither interviewed Oswald nor reported the fact to the Secret Service when the President's motorcade route was published.

Oswald had an exaggerated sense of his own importance.

At the time of the assassination, Oswald had a room in Dallas while his wife stayed with friends in nearby Irving. The evening of Nov. 21 he asked her to move to Dallas with him. She was angry with him, and she refused.

In the depository the next day, Bonnie Ray Williams ate a lunch of chicken on the sixth floor and then went down to the fifth floor to watch the motorcade with friends. That left Oswald alone on the sixth.

It rained in Dallas that morning, but the rain stopped and so officials took the plastic bubbletop off the President's car. That top was not bullet-proof, but Oswald might not have known that and might in any event have had greater difficulty sighting through it.

Finally, there was the arrangement of the Presidential car.

Mr. and Mrs. Kennedy sat in the rear, Governor and Mrs. Connally on the jump seats. A Secret Service agent drove, and another sat next to him, but they were separated from the passenger compartment by the front seat and a metal bar 15 inches above it. And the

President had asked that no agents ride on small running boards provided at the rear.

The second bullet that hit the President was the fatal one. The commission found that if a Secret Service man had been in a position to reach him quickly, "it is possible" that he could have protected the President from the second shot.

Confusion on Shots

The report clarified what had been considerable confusion about the bullets. Much of this stemmed from the necessarily hasty examination made by doctors at Parkland Memorial Hospital in Dallas in their desperate effort to save the President's life.

The commission found that in all probability three bullets were fired. Three empty cartridges were found inside the sixth floor window of the depository. Also recovered were one nearly whole bullet and fragments of one or two others.

One of the bullets missed, the report said. It was not certain whether this came before, between or after the two that hit.

The first of the two shots that did not miss hit the President in the lower back of the neck and emerged at the lower front. Mr. Kennedy grabbed at his throat and said, "My God, I'm hit."

"President Kennedy could have survived the neck injury," the commission found. But between 4.8 and 5.6 seconds later—the time was calculated from an amateur movie film—the fatal bullet hit the back of the President's head.

Condition Hopeless

The time was 12:30. When he arrived at the hospital five minutes later, the report said Mr. Kennedy was alive "from a medical viewpoint; " there was a heart beat. But "his condition was hopeless." He was pronounced dead at 1 P.M.

Some uncertainty remains about how Governor Connally was hit. But the commission said the probability

was that the first bullet that struck the President went on through the Governor's chest, then his wrist and finally lodged in his thigh.

All of these points were demonstrated by the commission with elaborate re-enactments, expert testimony and experiments on simulated skulls and bodies. The report contains many macabre pages of such detail.

"The cumulative evidence of eyewitnesses, firearms and ballistic experts and medical authorities," the report said, demonstrated that the shots were fired from the sixth floor of the depository building.

Experts said flatly that the nearly whole bullet and two large fragments recovered could only have been fired by the 6.5 millimeter Mannlicher-Carcano rifle found inside the depository window.

> *. . . the report portrayed a man of strange contradictions. He said he was "a Marxist but not a Leninist-Marxist."*

No Bullet From Front

One apparent conflict dismissed by the report was the talk that a mark on the Presidential car's windshield had been made by a bullet coming from in front of it. Experts testified that the glass had been hit by a fragment from behind. The commission found that no shots had come from the front.

In painstaking detail, the report connected Oswald with that rifle and that position at the window.

It traced his purchase of the gun. It showed that he had taken the gun to work in a homemade paper bag that morning.

His fingerprints were on the bag,

and on some cartons on which the rifle apparently rested. A witness saw a man who looked like Oswald at the window with the gun.

And the commission found that he had the ability to hit the target easily at that distance, 177 to 266 feet, with a telescopic sight and the target moving off in a straight line from him.

It found that he killed a Dallas patrolman, J. D. Tippit, 45 minutes later. Numerous eyewitnesses saw him during or after this shooting. And the bullets came from the revolver he carried when he was arrested shortly afterward.

In discussing Oswald's possible motives, the report portrayed a man of strange contradictions. He said he was "a Marxist but not a Leninist-Marxist." One of his favorite books was George Orwell's powerfully antitotalitarian "1984."

He wrote letters to American Communist party leaders volunteering his services. But some of these leaders testified that Oswald was never a member, and the commission so found.

The commission also rejected, after complete access to the files of the F.B.I. and the Central Intelligence Agency, the claim that Oswald may have been some kind of American undercover agent.

After his arrest, he told the police that "My wife and I like the President's family. They are interesting people."

He said, "I am not a malcontent; nothing irritated me about the President."

All the frustrations in Lee Harvey Oswald seemed to come to a climax in the last weeks of his life. The report paints a sad, sensitive picture.

His dream of glory in the Soviet Union had collapsed. He had not been able to go to Cuba. He had a menial job, packing textbooks. His wife, the commission said, ridiculed his political views and complained about his sexual capacity.

Oswald ordinarily went from Dallas to the home of Mrs. Michael Paine,

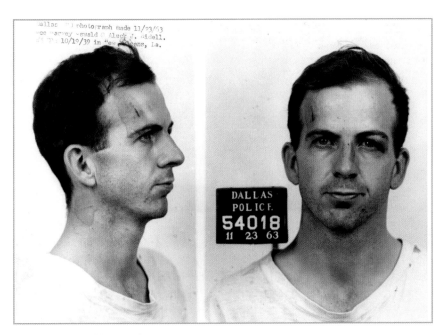

Lee Harvey Oswald's mug shot. (NARA/President John F. Kennedy Assassination Records Collection)

where his family was staying in Irving, Tex., for weekends. Marina asked him not to come the weekend of Nov. 16-17, 1963, because the Paines were having a birthday party.

Then Marina discovered that he was using an alias, O. H. Lee, at his rooming house, in Dallas. When he telephoned on Nov. 18, she was angry with him. When he went to the house on Nov. 21, she at first refused to talk to him and then refused to move the family to Dallas.

"Oswald had an exaggerated sense of his own importance, but he had failed at almost everything he had ever tried to do," the commission concluded.

"It must have appeared to him that he was unable to command even the attention of his family. His family lived with Mrs. Paine, ostensibly because Oswald could not afford to keep an apartment in Dallas, but it was also, at least in part, because his wife did not want to live there with him."

The commission added that it did not believe that "the relations between Oswald and his wife caused him to assassinate the President." It is unlikely that the motivation was that simple.

Discussing the two days of Oswald's detention before his murder, the report rejected claims that he was not allowed counsel or was mistreated by the police. He saw his family and was offered a lawyer, it said.

But the commission was highly critical of the way the press and cameramen were allowed the free run of the Dallas police station, crowding around Oswald and very likely making possible Ruby's entry in the confusion of the final moments.

Police Criticized

During the "confusion and disorder" of those two days, the commission said, the police said much too much— some of it erroneous—about the case. They effectively convicted Oswald before he was tried, and the commission said a fair trial would have been difficult after all the publicity.

All conspiracy theories were flatly rejected in the report.

"The commission found no evidence that the Soviet Union or Cuba were involved in the assassination of President Kennedy," the report said. "Nor did the commission's investigation of Jack Ruby produce any grounds

for believing that Ruby's killing of Oswald was part of a conspiracy."

The report added that these conclusions were also reached independently by Secretary of State Dean Rusk, Secretary of Defense Robert S. McNamara, Secretary of the Treasury Douglas Dillon, the Central Intelligence Agency Director John A. McCone, the Secret Service Chief, James J. Rowley, the Federal Bureau of Investigation Director J. Edgar Hoover, and former Attorney General Robert F. Kennedy, the fallen President's brother.

It said that "because of the difficulty of proving negatives to a certainty, the possibility of others being involved with either Oswald or Ruby cannot be established categorically, but if there is any such evidence it has been beyond the reach of all the investigative agencies and resources of the United States and has not come to the attention of this commission."

The commission reported that many steps had already been taken to tighten F.B.I. and Secret Service measures against potential assailants of the President. It called for further improvements.

On trips, the report said, the President's doctor should always be near him and much greater effort should be made to check buildings along motor routes.

A Cabinet-level committee should review and oversee the whole matter of protecting the President, the commission suggested. It said the question whether the job should remain with the Secret Service might be considered by such a committee.

Congress was urged to enact, at long last, legislation making assassination of the President a Federal crime. The report said such a law would end divided authority and possibly prevent disorder and confusion such as prevailed in Dallas after Nov. 22.

Assassination Panel's Final Report Backs Theory of Plot on Kennedy

By WENDELL RAWLS JR.

WASHINGTON, June 2, 1979—The House Select Committee on Assassinations has gone substantially beyond the findings of the Warren Commission and has concluded that a conspiracy, perhaps involving organized crime figures, led to the assassination of President Kennedy.

After spending two and a half years and $5 million, the committee says in its final report, to be released soon, that the conspirators may have included organized crime figures, Cubans and James R. Hoffa, former president of the International Brotherhood of Teamsters. But a source close to the committee said the investigation did not produce "a smoking gun."

"There is no evidence of a meeting where the murder was planned, there is no account of the details of the plot," the source said. "There is a substantial body of evidence, a web of circumstantial evidence, to connect the death of the President to elements of organized crime. Not to a national crime syndicate, nor to one individual."

G. Robert Blakey, chief counsel and staff director of the committee, said from his home that he would not comment on the details of the committee report. Asked if he had a personal opinion of the committee's findings, Mr. Blakey, now a professor of law at Cornell University, said:

"I think the mob did it."

According to the committee source, the report establishes that "no longer are we able to accept the judgment of the Warren Commission that President Kennedy was killed by a loner who was a lone assassin."

The report will also urge the Department of Justice to renew its efforts to try to determine who worked with Lee Harvey Oswald, named by the Warren Commission as the sole assassin, to plot and carry out the murder of President Kennedy.

About six months ago, the committee presented acoustical evidence that it said showed that two gunmen had fired at the Presidential motorcade as it made its way through Dealey Plaza in Dallas on Nov. 22, 1963. But three members of the committee called the evidence into question and disagreed with its assertion that Oswald was not a lone gunman, as the Warren Commission insisted.

Additional Evidence

The New York Times learned today that the conclusion that the President was murdered as a result of a conspiracy rests on more than acoustical evidence.

According to sources familiar with the committee's investigation and final report, to be made public by the end of this month, extensive electronic surveillance material accumulated by the Federal Bureau of Investigation showed that major organized crime figures were deeply disturbed by prosecutions, investigations, and other actions carried out against them by the Kennedy Justice Department and vowed revenge against both the President and his brother, Robert F. Kennedy, who was Attorney General.

The surveillance was conducted between 1959 and 1965, and thus covered years before and after the Kennedy Administration.

Although the authorities have long contended that the Government's surveillance covered all major rackets figures, the assassinations committee was surprised to find that it was not as comprehensive as generally thought.

Two major underworld figures, Carlos Marcello of New Orleans and Santos Trafficante of Tampa, were not covered by the electronic surveillance.

Oswald and Ruby Connections

According to the committee source, extensive investigation of Marcello and Trafficante lieutenants disclosed they were connected to the two principal figures in Dallas at the time of the shooting—Oswald and Jack Ruby, who shot Oswald to death as millions of Americans watched on live television.

The report will contend that Ruby had stalked his victim from the hours immediately after the assassination until he fired a bullet into Oswald's stomach two days later, and that he had had help gaining access to the assassin, perhaps unwittingly, from Dallas policemen.

The committee report maintains that Ruby also had extensive associations among organized crime figures and discloses that his telephone records indicate a small number of calls, possibly relating to criminal activity, to a variety of people connected with the underworld, including Sam Giancana, who subsequently was murdered in his home in Chicago, and strong-arm men tied to Mr. Trafficante.

The committee discounts Ruby's statement before his own death that he had killed Oswald so that the President's widow would be spared a return to Dallas, where she might be forced to relive the shattering moments of the assassination as a witness at Oswald's trial.

That story was concocted by his lawyer, the committee asserts.

The final report, including some 30 volumes accumulated from public hearings, will also examine a variety of links between Oswald and the Soviet and Cuban Governments, anti-Castro Cuban groups and a small, amorphous left-wing group.

Looking Back

Why Americans Don't Believe the Warren Commission

By Sam Tanenhaus

It was inevitable that the assassination of John F. Kennedy should provoke talk, and fears, of a possible conspiracy. He was the first president murdered—or even fired at—since William T. McKinley in 1901. McKinley's assassin, Leon Czolgosz, was in some respects a forerunner of Lee Harvey Oswald, a self-taught, would-be radical with a history of emotional disturbance. Then too there had been rumors of a worldwide "anarchist" plot to murder world leaders. But since Czolgosz was quickly tried and convicted, and was executed within 45 days of shooting McKinley, the public felt reassured by the verdict.

Of course there could be no trial for Oswald, no prolonged moment when the public might take its measure of him and follow the presentation of evidence and argument. Instead there was the tangle of disquieting facts: the failure of American intelligence agencies to uncover Oswald's plan; his steely accuracy as a marksman; his own murder two days later while in police custody, which prevented a thorough interrogation of Oswald and his murky past, which included travel to the Soviet Union and an attempt to visit Cuba, matters on which the F.B.I. had questioned him as recently as August 1963. While it was true, as a *Times* reporter noted days after the assassination, that in America such acts were usually the work of "a single person, often with little advance planning and often without any real grievance against the person attacked," suspicions took root.

As early as 1966, a Gallup Poll reported that a majority of Americans questioned the "lone gunman" theory. One reason for suspicion was the Warren Commission, which operated outside of public scrutiny and, many thought, with a deficit of accountability. As David Belin, chief counsel to the Warren Commission, later wrote in *The Times Magazine*, Earl Warren erred in bowing to the Kennedy family's private pleas not to hold public hearings because it would cause them unbearable pain to endure the shocking tragedy a second time. "If there had been open hearings," Belin wrote, "people could have watched on television, heard on radio and read in the newspapers what the key witnesses said as the investigation unfolded." Instead there were only the 26 forbidding volumes of the Commission Report, the most telling details buried in a mass of testimony from more than 500 witnesses.

Another reason is that Kennedy, killed so brutally only a 1,000 days into his presidency, was catapulted to the high plane of martyrdom. More than any other modern president, he came to occupy the ambiguous place where "our tradition of anti-governmentalism," as the historian Garry Wills has termed it, collides with an almost cultish fascination with the White House. In death, Kennedy offered the romantic myth of Camelot—of youthful "vigor" and vibrant promise, the handsome, idealistic leader surrounded by a glittering court and married to charming, sophisticated Jacqueline. This later gave way to darker revelations about the Kennedy years: the James Bond–like adventurism, complete with assassination plots, and of Kennedy's own reported liaisons, including at least one with a mob mistress.

Together these threw a freakish glare on his presidency, the suggestion that its bright surface rested on sinister depths. In this sense Kennedy seemed to personify America in the Cold War years—the world's greatest superpower, its footprint felt all over the globe, and yet constantly attuned to perceived danger and threat from the Kremlin.

Add to this the convulsions of the mid- and late 1960s—urban racial strife and the calamitous blunder of the Vietnam War, and the disillusionment they bred. It was in this atmosphere that a busy industry of conspiracy-minded theorists offered up a cast of villains, plausible and far-fetched, including Cuban exiles, the Mafia, the C.I.A., or perhaps some combination of the three. In 1967, when the New Orleans district attorney Jim Garrison, claimed to have unraveled a massive conspiracy, even Robert F. Kennedy, the slain president's brother and former attorney general, "thought Garrison might be onto something," according to his biographer, Arthur Schlesinger Jr. Kennedy also said he had bluntly questioned John A. McCone, the C.I.A. director, if, in Schlesinger's paraphrase, "they had killed my brother, and I asked him in a way that he couldn't lie to me, and they hadn't."

A decade later, the House Select Committee on Assassinations conducted its own investigation, lasting two and a half years and costing $5 million. Its report, issued in 1979, stated that there had indeed been a plot, but identified no actual culprits, though "the conspirators may have included organized crime figures, Cubans and James R. Hoffa, former president of the International Brotherhood of Teamsters," the last a target of investigation by Robert F. Kennedy when he had been chief counsel to the Senate Rackets Committee in 1957. In fact, the committee had initially concluded that Oswald acted alone, but reversed its findings after hearing two "acoustic experts" who said a police microphone had recorded the sound of a second gunman, though this evidence too was repudiated in a later report prepared by scientists.

And in the most thorough account of the alleged plots to murder the president, *Case Closed: Lee Harvey Oswald and the Assassination of JFK* (1994), Gerald Posner painstakingly examined the evidence and assessed—rather, dismantled— every proposed theory. Oswald "was the only assassin at Dealey Plaza on November 22, 1963," Posner wrote. "To say otherwise, in light of the overwhelming evidence, is to absolve a man with blood on his hands, and to mock the President he killed."

Nonetheless the conspiracists, as they have been called, pursued baroque and bizarre explanations. In his movie *JFK*, released in 1991, Oliver Stone cleverly mixed documentary footage with fictional scenes which implied that the vice president, Lyndon B. Johnson, was at the very least a willing accomplice in the assassination, undertaken in part because—in Stone's fabular telling—Kennedy was unwilling to escalate the Vietnam War. The film's credits ended with a portentous dedication "to the young, in whose spirit the search for the truth marches on"—that is, to a new generation with no first-hand memories of the horrific event but now introduced to the staples of the "secret" plots behind the assassination: bullets fired from the "grassy knoll," the Zapruder film, diagrams of bullet shots and angles of entry and exit and much more. As of 1998, according to a CBS poll, only 10 percent of the public believed Oswald had acted alone, while 74 percent were convinced there had been an official cover-up. Five years later, ABC found that 70 percent of Americans believed the president's murder was "the result of a broader plot." The most telling statistic was 77, the percentage of those polled by CBS who said they believed the whole truth of the assassination would never be known.

Uncertainty is the hatchery of conspiratorial thinking. So often equated with delusion and paranoia, it actually rests on something quite different: a passion for order, a liberating explanation. The fevered connecting of dots, the ever-widening nest of conspirators, helps satisfy our hunger to believe that even the most horrific deed is enfolded with the logic of intention and design. For many, Kennedy's death laid a dark curse on the land. It had become the sphinx's riddle. Whoever could solve it might restore innocence to a nation whose faith in its boundless futurity had been profoundly shaken.

Sam Tanenhaus is a writer at large for *The New York Times Book Review*. He is the author of *The Death of Conservatism* (2008).